B E R L I O Z
and the
Romantic Century

VOLUME I

Books by Jacques Barzun

Darwin, Marx, Wagner
Classic, Romantic, and Modern
Berlioz and the Romantic Century
Berlioz and His Century
New Letters of Berlioz
Berlioz' Evenings with the Orchestra *(Translation)*
Music in American Life
Pleasures of Music

Berlioz in 1832, by Signol

"Thus I saw him six years ago for the first time—
and thus I shall see him in my mind forever."
—HEINE (1837)

BERLIOZ

and the

ROMANTIC CENTURY

JACQUES BARZUN

VOLUME I

Third Edition

Columbia University Press
NEW YORK AND LONDON
1969

For permission to quote from Laurence McKinney's *People of Note,* the author acknowledges obligation to E. P. Dutton and Co., Inc. Copyright, 1940, Laurence McKinney; from B. H. Haggin's *Music in the Nation,* to William Sloane Associates, Inc.; from Matthew Josephson's *Victor Hugo* to the Doubleday Company; from Nicolas Slonimsky's *Music Since 1900,* Frederick Dorian's *History of Music in Performance, The Musorgsky Reader,* and from *Harold Bauer: His Book* to W. W. Norton; from Paul Rosenfeld's *Musical Portraits* to Harcourt, Brace and Company; from Thomas Craven's *Men of Art* to Simon and Schuster, Inc.; from Cecil Gray's *History of Music* and André Gide's *Journal* to Alfred A. Knopf; and from John Rewald's *History of Impressionism* to the Museum of Modern Art.

For supplying certain of the illustrations, the author is indebted to Miss Ruth Forbes, Mr. Bernard Van Dieren, Jr., Mr. Cecil Hopkinson, the Joseph Muller Collection of the New York Public Library, the Culver Service Collection, J. M. Dent and Sons, and the Theodore Presser Company, publishers of *The Etude.*

First edition 1950, Little, Brown and Company
Second edition, revised and abridged, 1956, Meridian Books
Third edition, revised from first edition, 1969
Columbia University Press, by
Arrangement with Little, Brown and Company
SBN 231-03135-1
Library of Congress Catalog Card Number: 77-97504
Printed in the United States of America

THIS EDITION IS DEDICATED

TO MY FRIENDS AND FELLOW-STUDENTS OF BERLIOZ

RICHARD MACNUTT DAVID CAIRNS HUGH MACDONALD

AND IN THE SAME SPIRIT

TO THE MEMORY OF

W. ERNEST GILLESPIE

Neither to excuse him nor to revile him,
but to explain, to feel what he is.

— HERDER *on Shakespeare*

Author's Note

THIS BOOK is not a biography in the ordinary sense, and even less strictly a "musical life." The size of the book implies rather the traditional "Life and Times," except that here an effort has been made to organize the materials so as to satisfy most economically the interest of different readers. A glance at Volume Two will show that much of it is taken up with Supplements and Bibliographies for professional users.[1] From the rest, the general reader himself need take only so much as meets his wants. He can, so to speak, carve from these pages several different books: the life of a man who was at once artist, thinker, and doer; a concert or record guide to twelve great works increasingly valued by connoisseurs; an essay on esthetics; an account of nineteenth-century culture; and, I dare say, a tract for our times as well.

In the battle of Berlioz with his age a typical story is dramatized by the events themselves. History spins the plot around the Artist, and the four corners of our society are illumined like a stage. For in a high civilization all social facts and forces become the matrix, and sometimes the subject, of the artist's work; and in the forms and conditions of a collective art like music we find again the elements of familiar history — politics, economics, and other struggles of human groups.

To learn a creator's ways, come to see through his eyes, and discover how past and current achievements affected his gifts in the making of great new work is the business of the historical critic; to generalize and show by a massive instance how in a given age great work gets accomplished, fought over, and slowly assimilated is the business of the cultural historian. It is as an artisan in both kinds that I have tried to present Berlioz in the century of Romanticism.

[1] In the footnotes throughout, the first number refers to the corresponding item in the Bibliography and the second number to the page. For Berlioz' letters and other writings, abbreviations are used in accordance with the key given in the Bibliography. In the text and footnotes, square brackets show additions made in 1969, except that in the Bibliography, where square brackets were already used for another purpose, additions have been explicitly dated.

Preface to the Third Edition

BERLIOZ TWENTY YEARS AFTER

Damn braces; bless relaxes.
—BLAKE

IN A PERIOD when names and faces, subjects and objects flash by with camera speed into instant oblivion, it is cause for surprise that a book of twenty years ago, and one of uncommon bulk, should still be in demand. Five years after its first appearance in 1950, I constrained myself to fashion a single volume of biography from the matter here set out. I then believed my duty fulfilled. So when the present publisher began arguing the need for a new and revised edition of the "life and times," I felt not exactly unmoved, but moved in two contrary directions: gratified, of course, by the thought that these pages were deemed of value still, and appalled at the idea of plunging once more into the sea of facts and sources.

No doubt in twenty years several new generations have grown up, to whom everything is fresh, and their thirst for knowledge deserves quenching. But I had believed that just because the newcomers had matured in this particular span, they would need nothing from me. For in that interval the works of Berlioz have become household furniture: the long-playing disc conveys to the ear all I had said that anyone needs to know. Berlioz has passed from the status of mysterious stranger to that of familiar friend. He has ceased to be the composer of a curious work called *Three Excerpts from The Damnation of Faust* and become the composer of *The Damnation of Faust tout entière*—plus other large works that an interested listener can hope to hear, "live" as well as on discs, more than once in a lifetime.

And he hears this music with ears unconsciously re-trained by the fall of the piano from absolute monarchy in music and the rise in its place of the classical guitar,[1] the vogue of polytonality, of electronic music, *musique concrète*, Theremin sounds, the Partch scale and instruments—and jazz: it is Duke Ellington who is generally credited with discovering the effect of timbre on harmony, a century and a quarter after Berlioz. In a word, the weather has changed, and many a puddle that looked like an inland sea barring access to Berlioz has simply evaporated.

An important part of the altered scene is the new tone of the comments in the press, on the air, in concert programs and post-concert conversations. In the place of conventional, dismissive words, of lofty contempt for "empty rhetoric," of chuckling condescension toward "romantic wildness," there have come the sober and informed comparison of performances, the awareness of passages omitted and liberties taken, the preference for one work over another, and that familiarity with the structure of whole works which permits an audience to understand what it is hearing when given only excerpts—all this, of course, being nothing more than the normal contents of the listener's mind in relation to other great composers.

For Berlioz the new status has been achieved by applying the usual standards of evidence and reasoning to his music and his life and to the century that produced them both. One modern instance will stand for a thousand: in a recent paragraph in *Stereo Review* (July 1969) about a new tape of the Berlioz *Requiem*, the critic notes half a dozen serious faults of performance and sums up the resulting travesty by saying: "The original, in all its glorious and terrifying brilliance, is more impressive." So assured a judgment would have been impossible thirty years ago. Instead, the garbled performance would have been taken as "the original" and been found the reverse of impressive, thus confirming the accepted view.

There is no question, then, that first-hand knowledge of the music was the key to revising the public judgment. But the ability to exercise that judgment had to be set free before the sounds themselves could force an entry. When we speak of prejudice causing a certain blindness in human beings, we are not referring to an abstract passion, but to a mass of strongly held "facts" and "principles" and steadily reinforced

[1] In Berlioz' youth (and not just in his native town), the piano was by no means common. Of the 404 musical instruments taken in Paris from Émigré families between 1790 and 1795, only 61 were forte-pianos, or about 15 percent, though the personages named in the checklist at the Conservatoire are ambassadors, noblemen, or well-to-do bourgeois. (*910*, II, 145-170)

conclusions. This was manifestly the state of mind that kept so many from *hearing* Berlioz when he chanced to be played. The mental set was sustained by the invariable re-appearance of the same anecdotes of his wilfulness, the same "romantic" quotations from his Memoirs, the same *bons-mots* at his expense by other wits. His relations with Wagner, completely inverted as to fact and significance, were always retold to Berlioz' discredit. And since the only large score of his that orchestras occasionally attempted was his first symphony, the *Fantastique*, the program notes, free for once of musical analysis, would rehearse the story of the love affair with Harriet Smithson, and say or imply that the music about to be heard would tell it again. So Berlioz was the program composer par excellence, a strange, undisciplined, ill-trained being, who used a talent for orchestral "effects" to become a scene painter in sounds. In short, all the ways of perceiving Berlioz were false, misleading, or blocked.

To be sure, there had begun to appear after the First World War a number of qualified critics who were convinced that Berlioz was superior to his reputation. This new opinion, scattered in various countries, made converts one at a time and by the 1930s provided an encouraging sign that change was possible. But being critics for the press or musicologists addressing a special public, these writers dealt in conclusions or took up single points. The large body of educated readers and listeners continued to be served as I described above.

In these circumstances what was needed was not merely the correcting of a large number of downright errors, but the re-creation of a context for the life of the man and the work of the artist. Events have justified the enterprise and shown that an imperfect tradition can be revised. Besides serving the reader of biography and history, these volumes of mine could be used as a source of reference for new anecdotes, new quotations, biographical sketches less shopworn than those in stock, and better accounts of many "well-known" incidents and relationships. This is in fact what has occurred. By disposing of a host of clichés and by facilitating the preparation of notes for record jackets and concert programs, my pages fulfilled one of the purposes I had in writing; seeing which, I was ready to see them superseded.

Moreover, the reappearance of Berlioz' music shortly after my publication naturally stirred new waves of scholarship and criticism. Two Berlioz societies were founded, one English, one American, in whose bulletins researchers brought out fresh opinion and findings. Performances of unfamiliar works multiplied, especially in England. Unpublished letters, works, fragments, portraits, and other documents came out of their hiding places in private collections. The culmination of the new activity was the plan to edit in England and publish in Germany the complete musical works, an enterprise generously aided by a grant from the Gulbenkian Foundation.

At that point even the asbestos curtain which France had kept lowered against one of her greatest creators caught fire. A national association was formed and Berlioz' birthplace rehabilitated as a museum. And though in 1953 two French orchestras found a way to celebrate the Berlioz sesquicentennial in concerts containing not one note of his music, by 1969 the editing and publishing by French scholars of all his prose works (including his voluminous correspondence) had begun. In this undertaking the influence of André Malraux, spurred by the urgings of his friend Edgard Varèse, must be noted with gratitude.[2]

This is the position today—satisfactory indeed when one compares past and present. But I can imagine it further improved without being in any way utopian. Take the music first. We have yet to hear and see an adequate performance of one of Berlioz' greatest works, the opera *Benvenuto Cellini.* When Covent Garden attempted it, the effort suffered from the all-too-common impulse that overtakes producers when they venture on the new—"let's make *everything* different!" Berlioz' music was novelty enough; I will not specify the gratuitous handicaps superadded. Clearly, what we need first is an authoritative recording of *Benvenuto*, preferably under Colin Davis, after which the public knowledge of the score will insure somewhere its fit production.

Similarly, we need right recordings of the *Te Deum* (including the Prelude and March), the *Funeral and Triumphal Symphony* (with the full complement of players), the *March for the Last Scene in Hamlet* (with voice obligato), and *Les Troyens* complete. As to the last-named, the whimsical potpourri on two sides of the one disc now on the market may be (as someone called it) a wonderful appetizer, but it is artistically a mutilation and it must be replaced by the work in full.

As I write I learn that Colin Davis has recorded the *Romeo and Juliet Symphony*. We may expect that under his baton the Finale is properly done. No living person has so heard it, not even under Toscanini. When we have singer, chorus, and orchestra in balance and in tune, we shall at last perceive that the conclusion, instead of being the spiritual letdown that some have termed it, is as noble as the music of love and death that comes before.

[2] A further favor would be to make official the use of Berlioz' harmonization and orchestration of the *Marseillaise*. (See below I, 135; 147-8 and *n.*)

With the same view of giving us possession of new music, conductors might think of extracting from *Lélio* a choral-orchestral suite. Nothing of value is lost in omitting the ballad with piano accompaniment and the words of the monodrama; whereas the remaining five pieces are happily characteristic of Berlioz' earliest style—some are in fact his "examination papers" at the Conservatoire, like the *Cléopâtre*, which Mr. Leonard Bernstein has made famous, and the *Mort d'Orphée*, which deserves to be. Finally, we need the complete songs, if only to dispel the idea that *Les nuits d'été* is all that Berlioz wrote in the lyric form. Toward the fulfillment of this program, the new edition of the music will bring the aid of correct and easily accessible scores and parts.

So much for the music. The prose works, as we saw, are being reissued. Remains the illimitable field of biography and criticism. Here one's legitimate demands are doubtless harder to get fulfilled. I set them down nevertheless. To begin with, the public had a right to expect that someone would before now have composed a well-proportioned, exact, and agreeably written life, free of the great load of nonsense which my work had to take up in order to dispose of it. Berlioz' own memoirs, it is true, have just been retranslated and edited by David Cairns. But for reasons that Berlioz was the first to state, the memoirs do not cover "the life." Besides, the many documents that have come to light in the last few years, and the new feeling which surrounds Berlioz' work, alike call for a fresh young view of the whole dramatic tale of his existence.

Recent critical essays do not encourage my hopes, not because they are not astute and scholarly, but because they betray a compulsion to go back to the old absurdities in order to show them up once more. For example, an excellent discussion of Berlioz' "radical harmonic innovations" opens with a paragraph from an ignorant attack in Grove; a student of Berlioz' orchestration quotes a sally of Ravel's out of context; an expounder of the order and consistency of Berlioz' musical thought reminds us of a strongly skeptical view held by Newman in 1905, *which Newman himself recanted in 1925*. All this is worse than a waste of time. What it does, actually, is to prolong the life of hoary prejudices, confuse the public mind by restating error, and, while maintaining an atmosphere of contention, postpone the positive note, the straightforward exposition and criticism that are wanted.

To sum up: new writings on Berlioz should take it for granted that he was great as man and artist and that the secret of his creation has not yet been unriddled. The two propositions can be separately followed, of course, but they have interconnections which we tend to neglect in the study of genius generally and which are worth pursuing. Being a man of honor, as Berlioz was, is considered today a sort of handicap. We are accustomed to the artist scoundrel or specialist in vice, and unaccustomed to the creator in whom passion and reason and moral integrity hold in balance. But greatness of intellect and feeling, of soul and conduct—magnanimity, in short—does occur; it is not a myth for boy scouts, and its reality is important, if only to give us the true range of the term "human," which we so regularly define by its lower reaches.

Especially instructive is the relation of magnanimity to high art, for although the first is not prerequisite to the second, its presence exerts an influence which *is* the puzzling element, notably at the stage of conception: the first vision of the unknown thrill desired comes from the spirit and reveals its quality. As to execution, I have said that Berlioz' method was still to be disclosed. We have had wise words on his harmony foreshadowing the twentieth century and rediscovering the sixteenth, that is, overcoming the relentless grind of the continuo. We have had his melody and counterpoint justly evaluated; lastly we have had studies of his sonic and spatial experiments. The conclusions on these aspects of the art of sound should be amplified and summed up and then completed by the study of one more—rhythm. From the outset Berlioz attached to it great importance, for which reason I have added to this edition a translation of his early essay on the subject.[3]

But separate studies will remain sterile until someone versed in *all* these technical elements (and not just sensitive to one or two, as is frequent among musicians) will undertake to show how Berlioz characteristically shaped his musical substance as one whole. For in a many-faceted art there are internal oppositions and obstacles, material prohibitions against taking advantage of all qualities at once and all the time. Subordination, emphasis, contrast, distortion and compromise are compulsory if form and lucidity are to result; so that until the interaction of his full resources is examined in Berlioz' scores—as the like conditions have been scrutinized and theorized about in Shakespeare—we shall not really know much about Berlioz' art. We shall only be left with the typical mystery embodied in the dialogue between the late Manfred Bukofzer, a first-rate musicologist, and Leon Kirchner, a first-rate contemporary composer. The musicologist pointed out "false relations" in

[3] See Supplement 5.

the counterpoint of the second movement of the *Harold* Symphony, and the composer asked: "All right, but then explain to me why the passage is sublime."

It may well be thought that someone as demanding as I sound should either carry out his own program or stop criticizing the present state of scholarship. Such an ultimatum would be a piece of oblique flattery: I am not competent to do what is required—and, on the other side, perhaps I have earned the right to make the particular criticism I offer. From young manhood to early middle age I sacrificed my pleasure (not to say endangered my reason) by scavenging through the Berlioz "literature," in order that I might rescue from that kitchen midden, not merely the truth of fact, but the wealth of just opinion which accompanied or followed Berlioz' career—from Schumann's to Nietzsche's and beyond to Varèse and Van Dieren. Having done it so that it would not have to be done again, I naturally hate to see the desire for picturesqueness induce a return to the old dungheap. I claim no property rights in it, but I would bid new structures of thought to rise on decontaminated ground.

What have I meanwhile done to make the present two volumes of renewed use to the new times? Much less than I wished to do, for reasons typical of the new times themselves. Technology is so far advanced that its modes and its cost alike preclude resetting the type of such a long work as this. Instead, the old text is photographed, with alterations. But possible alterations are limited to those that can be fitted into the spaces of the original edition. The mosaic workers of Ravenna had a simple task compared to mine. I wanted to remove or condense a paragraph here, a page there, and recast sentences with a free mind: all I might do was tinker. I consoled myself with the thought of Valéry, who once wrote for an Egyptian review an article that had to contain a specified number, not of words, but of letters. It is only fair to add that my publishers were as generous and helpful as they could be in this contingency.

Another hindrance, which no one could alleviate, is the modern fact that time, like matter, comes in small particles. It did not prove possible to squeeze out of the round of duties and demands one uninterrupted week for the kind of attention that might have let me be more adept at making changes. As it is, I have corrected *most* slips and errors of fact and rectified a good many of my own judgments and faulty phrasings. I have removed the "Index of Misconceptions about Berlioz," which caused so much annoyance and derision at first, but served (as the very objections showed) to stimulate a healthy self-consciousness. It is no longer needed, and its room enabled me to insert the essay on Rhythm. To put it among the Supplements, I pushed back to a later place the list of major blunders in the so-called German Edition of Berlioz' Works. The new English edition so far consists of three volumes out of twenty-five, so for some years to come it will be useful for performers to have the *corrigenda* I collected twenty years ago.

Having two pages at my disposal, I have reproduced for the benefit of owners of Berlioz letters the table of his domiciles, which I first compiled for my *New Letters of Berlioz* (1954) and which assists in dating. In the Bibliography and at several other points, I have added citations, remarks, names, and dates. Nowhere did space permit me to be thorough, only indicative. Let this incompleteness spur competition, and produce *the* book by another hand that I desiderate. This one, in the meantime, is rich in quotations from Berlioz and his peers, a feature which, as I look back on it, is enough by itself to justify republication at this or any other time.

J. B.

Contents

VOLUME ONE

Illustrations

VOLUME I

VOLUME II

B E R L I O Z
and the
Romantic Century

Introduction. Berlioz as Man and Artist

We challenge posterity to bear witness: . . . we have maintained from the start that genius burned in this Frenchman. . . . But far be it from us to seek to impose our faith by force.

— Robert Schumann

In the repertory of most modern orchestras, there is a work entitled *Symphonie Fantastique* which was composed well over a century ago by a French youth of twenty-six named Hector Berlioz. A good performance of that work usually leads some thoughtful critic to say that it is still astonishingly modern, or to recall its historic significance at the threshold of a great age of music.[1] This "vivid and dramatic" score has been frequently recorded, and each time the work elicits renewed comments on the brilliancy of its orchestration, the marvel of its originality, or the romanticism of its "program." [2]

So much is common knowledge, and this, with a few biographical facts thrown in, was the standard equipment, so to speak, with which I began some [forty] years ago my acquaintance with Berlioz. Feeling a certain dislike for the "program" of the symphony, I read it no more than once or twice and soon forgot its details. But I kept hearing the music itself, at least semiannually, and I continued to read the notes and reviews about it, though with ever-increasing discomfort: I became convinced that while dwelling on the "program" they scarcely touched the work of art, and while retailing bits of the artist's life they utterly misconceived his character.

By the time that Weingartner's recording — the first electrically transcribed symphonic work to be issued by the Columbia company — came to supplement the live performances, I was familiar with the miniature

[1] *E.g.*, Mr. Olin Downes, *N. Y. Times*, Nov. 2, 1931; June 15, 1941; Mr. Mark Schubart, *Ibid.*, Mar. 17, 1946; [*N.Y. Times Magazine*, Mar. 9, 1969.]

[2] *E.g.*, Philip Hale, Boston Symphony annotator (*635*, *56*) and G. E. Abraham (*692*, 71 and 118). There are at least [twenty] notable sets of records, the latest having appeared in the summer of [1968]. (See *1463*.)

score, Liszt's piano transcription, Robert Schumann's famous essay, and the *Memoirs* of Berlioz himself. I had also looked into the two overtures which formed the remainder of the "repertory," and curiosity had led me to the obvious reference works. I consulted Grove, the Britannica, and some others in an effort to collect from reliable sources the technical and other insights which I felt to be lacking in Berlioz' current interpreters.

I had entered the jungle – for I found that what I read seldom tallied with what I heard. Conversation with musical friends brought out the same discrepancy. Some heard what I heard and were puzzled or untouched by what they read; others adopted this or that view of Berlioz from among the many contradictory ones available in print.

The Bubble Reputation

To me, the conflict seemed to go deeper than tastes and to point to unbridgeable divergencies of assumption and of fact. I read (or was told) that Berlioz had every gift but the melodic, yet listening to him my ear distinctly made out melodies, abundant and remarkable in form as well as varied in kind. Critics moreover assured me that all Berlioz' works, and the *Fantastique* in particular, illustrated events or depicted objects. Yet left to myself I could make out no such storytelling; my mind's eye remained blank, and while having no clear recollection of the "program," I could follow the five movements like any other music.

The same authorities made numerous other assertions that ran counter to the evidence. They declared for example that Berlioz had "a rooted objection to contrapuntal treatment," [3] though a look at half a dozen scores showed a good many passages of *fugato*, canon, and other devices of melodic combination. The *Symphonie Fantastique* itself ended with a double fugue and included several stretches of impressive counterpoint. Similar contradictions, flat, fatal to logic and almost to sanity, rose up in one's path as one went on to explore Berlioz' life, character, and ideas. How was it that a man who had lived so recently, and in the glare of lifelong publicity, could be the object of so much confident misrepresentation?

Being by then committed to the study of cultural history and specializing in the modern period, I began to keep systematic notes, both on this provocative figure and on the nature of the historical myth-making process wherever found. I soon discovered that Berlioz was not the only sub-

[3] M. D. Calvocoressi: 776, 38.

ject of critical error and that I was not alone in my concern about him. Two statements by eminent musicologists confirmed the validity of my inquiry. One was by Romain Rolland, whose great essay on Berlioz has recently been reprinted;[4] the other by Ernest Newman, the biographer of Wagner and the editor of Berlioz' *Memoirs* in English. Both told their readers that no composer was so entirely – they would not say unknown – but "misknown" as Berlioz.[5]

Another English writer, Mr. Cecil Gray, prefaced an enthusiastic chapter in his tough-minded *History of Music*[6] by bringing this failure of criticism home to all concertgoers. For some of them, he said, Berlioz is a "less than second-rate figure, a mere scene painter in sounds, with nothing save a gift for orchestration to commend him"; whereas for others "he is simply one of the very greatest of all composers who have ever lived."[7]

The Protean Berlioz

This head-on collision about an artist is not, as we shall see, so unusual as it seems. But as regards Berlioz, the normal division into two camps was obscured by the very literature that discussed it: there seemed to be as many camps as there were critics. And the reason for this was not hard to fathom: Berlioz, as any reader of his *Memoirs* is aware, was no withdrawn spirit cultivating music in a private shrine. He ranged over its whole domain as critic, theorist, conductor and producer, and for forty years bore the brunt of fighting for the modern art of his epoch. His musical mission was not simply to dethrone Routine in Paris by means of his orchestra and his writings in the press. It was an ecumenical reform carried by him from Moscow to London, and from Vienna to Prague and Berlin. He taught Europe whenever he wielded the pen or baton, supplementing action and publication by an enormous correspondence.

Nor is this all. As a cultured man and observant traveler he thought and wrote about many other things than music; as a dramatic musician and poet he breached the operatic tradition; and as a leader of the musical world he left the impress of his uncommon personality on nearly every important figure in his century. Kings, ministers, and public institutions, no less than poets and musicians, in one way or another came under his spell.

[4] *Essays on Music*, N. Y. 1948. The text of this edition is, however, not complete, nor have omissions been indicated. See *504*.

[5] *504*, 1 and *Sunday Times* (London) June 19, 1921.

[6] In The History of Civilization series, N. Y. 1935.

[7] *719*, 211.

The story of his life's work therefore bears a double character: it is first the epitome of an age; it brings us face to face with every familiar contemporary, raises every intellectual question, and illustrates every practical problem in the life of art. Between Waterloo and Sedan – that is to say from the downfall of one Napoleon to the next – it would be difficult to find any other European whose activity spread over wider territory or engaged the attention of more, and more diverse, minds than that of Berlioz.

In the second place, the story of his life is that of one of the world's very few complete artists. As in a bustling Elizabethan play, the hero moves against a background of historic triumphs, accidents, and revolutions, but he also lives through a private drama of passion, moral conflict, and philosophic doubt. The perfect symmetry of plot and subplot in Berlioz' particular tragedy appears moving and memorable as soon as one enlarges one's view to take in both his public career and his inner life and thus discovers the hidden spring of his actions; in other words, as soon as one looks at the man in history – a Renaissance figure transplanted into the nineteenth century, who by will and genius stamped his effigy upon it.

This view is naturally that of the panorama which one sees all unfolded at the end of the journey. But its scope makes it less surprising that Berlioz' deeds and character should have failed to shine vividly and accurately in the minds of the many who have written about him. My initial assumption that any man who died eighty years ago must have had his measure adequately taken was wholly unjustified. I had overlooked the relation of magnitude to distance which we call perspective. Until recently we were at the foot of the mountain; the foreground of Berlioz' fame was cluttered up with particulars in which his interpreters soon lost themselves, noting at random what they hoped was significant.[8] The clearest disproof of their estimates was the presence of many contradictory views and the persistence of a debate in which everyone shouted and few listened.[9]

Only the Living Invite Violence

One good reason for not listening, that is, for not accumulating bit by bit the results of research and insight, was that Berlioz' music and opin-

[8] The author of a "Berlioz" in a popular musical series ten years ago still declared himself "baffled" at every turn. (*278.*)

[9] The late Sir Donald Tovey, having had occasion to revise an earlier unfavorable judgment, exclaims: "We must be careful! You never know where you are with Berlioz." (*590,* 89 *n.*)

ions kept cropping up in many parts of our culture at a time when a determined reaction to his epoch was under way. He therefore had to be slain over and over again, quite as if he were still alive. Thus his French biographer, Boschot, toiled patiently between 1906 and 1913 to bury him under a monument of denigration. His three volumes (of six hundred pages each) undoubtedly rendered a great service by exhibiting the facts of Berlioz' daily life – where the musician was on a given day and how much he received for a given concert; but by adroitly neglecting Berlioz' artistic existence in favor of the domestic, and by piling up insinuations upon trivia, M. Boschot was also able to create the impression he desired, namely that Berlioz was a wild, "romantic," and largely ineffectual being.

The biographer apparently could not or would not see the paradox he had created for himself: he had (so he said) chosen his man because he was a great genius, yet he had shaped and colored his narrative to show a pantaloon. It was left a mystery how Boschot's Berlioz could have accomplished what the Berlioz of history had actually done, including the twelve great works which his critic analyzed with such flourishes and such ambivalence.

A dozen years after Boschot's acrimonious effort, English-speaking readers were offered the same paradox, applied to other great figures by the skill of Lytton Strachey and his myriad imitators. Few could know that this debunking treatment, which from its beginnings in France had not been reserved for Berlioz alone, was part of a deep-seated anti-Romantic movement with primarily political and religious motives.[10] From France it had spread to this country through adaptation by Irving Babbitt and his disciples – still under the guise of scholarship – so that before and after Strachey, M. Boschot's three dense volumes were taken as a mine of accurate fact.[11] Writers of reviews and concert notes could hardly be blamed for relying on what they found the fullest source, though in

[10] In his excellent *Victor Hugo,* Mr. Matthew Josephson passes judgment on Edmond Biré's four-volume life of the poet in terms that could be transcribed, with nothing changed but the names, to fit Boschot and his *Berlioz:* "Edmond Biré was a pious Royalist and Catholic, . . . his lifelong study . . . making up the testimony of one who was a Boswell-in-reverse, and piling up 1500 pages of denigration and hatred. For a long time this curious performance dominated the Hugolian literature by its weight and accumulated arguments. Biré does not deny the importance of Hugo as a writer and artist, but endeavors to paint him as a fraud and . . . an irresponsible. . . . Even today, Biré's fifty-year-old work is used more than any other writer's by American and English literary scholars, and the most complete existing biography in the English language . . . is a faithful copy of Biré's debunking job and incorporates all of Biré's mistakes as well as his animus." (*1186,* 505–6.)

[11] For Boschot's "mistakes as well as his animus" see below, Supplement 2.

doing so they inevitably absorbed and disseminated some of the critic's errors and venom. This, while lowering Berlioz to the uses of a scapegoat, strengthened the distaste for an epoch that was just then passing through the normal purgatory of the years.

Allowing for this cultural interlude, one can assess M. Boschot's laborious work more justly: it is at once indispensable and untrustworthy – which necessarily brings us back to history as the great corrective, and to the vision of Berlioz as an agent in cultural conflicts still unresolved. Born in 1803, with his roots in revolutionary and Napoleonic France, he was one of the precocious geniuses destined like Delacroix, Victor Hugo, and Stendhal to create a new culture amid the fossil remains of the old regime. Yet the word "revolutionary" does not classify Berlioz, any more than does "Romantic" in its usual acceptation. For he transcended as well as embodied his time, and his greatness for us lies precisely in this, that he gives us text and commentary in one living shape: at all key points his life and art furnish an explicit critique of his age. Hence his lack of immediate usefulness to partisans of every kind. He refuses to fit into any familiar category, which would further explain – if need be – why some observers still see him as through a fog.

Art Criticism and the Musical Fluid

What has so far been said represents half the solution to the supposed "problem of Berlioz": the problem is no more his doing than it is that of Delacroix or Hugo or Stendhal, unless we blame him for a many-sidedness which multiplies the number of facts to be interpreted in an historical light. But the parallel with artists in words or paint suggests the obvious difference that Berlioz worked in a far more volatile medium than they, and one could assert that the relative standing of each today is roughly proportional to the permanence of the impression made respectively by a book, a painting, and a symphony. For many obvious reasons, the value of a printed score in enlightening the critic or amateur is extremely slight; even performance cannot compare with the fullness of effect of a book which may be reread and studied at will; nor with the canvas which, though not always on view, is at least stationary and reproducible.[12] The second half of the Berlioz problem is therefore inherent

[12] It is a challenge to those who consider Berlioz a mere contriver of specious "effects" that the regular and frequent broadcasting of his recorded works within the last dozen years has done more to attract listeners to him than all the previous concert performances at wide intervals.

in the nature of music, and what is worse, in the nature of music criticism.

The unfortunate separation of music from the other arts no doubt comes from the lack of an adequate critical vocabulary, and reflects the indolence and other limitations of those who write about music.[13] Moreover, the belief that painting and literature are closer to the world's concerns because they ostensibly represent objects finds an apparent justification in usage: while the music critic mumbles about dominant sevenths, the art critic can point to the blue sky. But this exclusion of music from the realm of ideas rests also on a thorough-going misconception of all the arts – one that dates back precisely to the anti-Romantics. When we say that we find chairs and tables in a painting or in a novel but not in a symphony, we are falsely assuming that life consists of objects and that some arts copy them. To the artist, life consists of sensations, and these may be reproduced with equivalent effect by widely different physical means. A chord, a shape, or a word are such means. The meaning in the so-called representative arts thus arises from contrasts, rhythms, and evocations which exactly correspond to contrasts, rhythms, and evocations in music. It is an illusion – or better, a convention – that Hamlet is a prince and that we see apples in a Cézanne. Actually, the words and shapes only arouse in us unnamable yet lifelike sensations – as does music; this art is just as representative of human experience, and just as devoid of actual chairs and tables.[14]

The high arts in fact all bear the same relation to life; they are all different from it and expressive of it, else they could not be felt to be equally "significant," "profound," "moving," and "great" in the sense commonly ascribed to them. On this point, the argument put forward by purists who despise subject matter and worship design has not even a ghostly likelihood of being true. We may prize Form as much as they do, share their reverence for the fundamental art of design, and even be ready to grow ecstatic with them about a superb rug, a magnificent rug, a great rug, but we are never tempted to say: "This rug I would place between the *Iliad* and the *Eroica*."

[13] An experienced practitioner, Mr. Mark Schubart, has declared that nothing too harsh can be said against music criticism as we find it. (*N. Y. Times Book Review*, Apr. 14, 1946.) This opinion was confirmed at two recent conferences where music criticism was treated as an element of general culture. (Harvard, 1947; Hartford, 1948, *903* and *902*.)

[14] This question is taken up more fully in the discussion of Program Music (Chapter 7 below).

Berlioz No Program Composer

This view of art – dramatic, presentative, and lifelike though opposed to any confusion between art and life – was properly speaking the Romanticist view; and feeling it to be both congenial and practicable, Berlioz dedicated his genius to exhibiting it in music. His cardinal principle was expressiveness, which does not mean imitation, does not mean formlessness, and does not mean program music. Neither does it mean the destruction or neglect of traditional elements which are rooted in pure sensation and call forth design – from melody and rhythm to harmony and counterpoint. Indeed, to these elements Berlioz was enabled by the technological advances of his age to add the new one of timbre or tone color, which before him had been used for ornament and expression rather than as a part of structure.

Lastly, working as he did after a great social revolution, Berlioz was able to fuse the scattered elements of musical life by combating the prejudices which still tended to keep opera, instrumental music, and church music constrained and separate. In a word, the art of sound was for him a comprehensive social art, recognizing different genres and occasions, but making a clean sweep of the Chinese routines which had previously enfeebled or degraded the uses of music.[15]

Music after the Liberation

So complete was this revolution, based like all the revolutions of mind on a knowledge of the great traditions, that we have almost forgotten it took someone to bring it about. We suppose that music always was what it has been since 1850, because the modern musician, no longer a mere entertainer, has at last taken his place among the great artists as a seer and a thinker. We take it moreover for granted that the public for serious music should be as broad as for any other art instead of remaining a clique of dilettanti.[16] To be sure, Berlioz did not effect this revolu-

[15] Lord Chesterfield in 1749: "Sculpture and painting are very justly called liberal arts; a lively and strong imagination, together with a just observation being absolutely necessary to excel in either, which, in my opinion, is by no means the case of music, though called a liberal art. . . . The former are connected with history and poetry; the latter, with nothing that I know of, but bad company." (*1244*, 220–1.)

[16] Emerson: "How partial, like mutilated eunuchs, the musical artists appear to me in society! Politics, bankruptcy, frost, famine, war – nothing concerns them but a scraping on a catgut, or tooting on a bass French horn." (*Heart of Emerson's Journals*, 294–5.)

tion singlehanded. His model and inspirer Beethoven preceded him in the conception; his other masters, Weber and Gluck, were before him in practical propaganda; and the neglected musicians of the French Revolution had set important precedents. But owing to the incompleteness of these efforts, it was left to Berlioz to create the modern orchestra and its music, and to demonstrate its many possible functions in a modern state.

One has only to read in Berlioz' life about the musical conditions of Paris in 1830, of the Germanies in 1840, of London in the fifties, and by comparing what he found with what he left to obtain the measure of his accomplishment. Though he was alone when he launched his attack against Italian opera and parlor songs and began his crusade in behalf of Beethoven and modern music, he was ultimately seconded by a small army of coadjutors, from Liszt and Wagner in the thirties to Saint-Saëns and the Russians in the sixties, all of whom had their awakening or drew their inspiration from Berlioz.

That this is no mere surmise, any more than it is a denial of others' genius, appears from the testimony of the beneficiaries themselves, with such disclaimers and reservations as one should expect about matters of personal esthetic.[17] Broadly speaking, after the death of Beethoven, Weber, and Schubert (all before 1830) the one seminal mind in music was Berlioz.[18] It was in fact the abundance of the results he begot in others for fifty years after his death which partly cut him off from our view during that time: Wagner emerged in the seventies, the French composers of opera, symphony, and song swarmed in the eighties, with Debussy and the Impressionists treading close behind; while from Russia an astonishing new

[17] Wagner's recollection of what Berlioz meant to him in 1839–1840 may stand as representing this significant relation: "All this [the hearing of Berlioz' first three symphonies] was altogether a new world to me. At first the grandeur and masterly execution of the orchestral part almost overwhelmed me. It was beyond anything I could have conceived. The fantastic daring, the sharp precision with which the boldest combinations – almost tangible in their clearness – impressed me, drove back my own ideas of the poetry of music into the very depths of my soul. I was simply all ears for things of which till then I had never dreamt, and which I felt I must try to realise. [Objections follow] . . . It was however the latest work of this wonderful master, his *Funeral and Triumphal* Symphony . . . [i.e. the fourth] which had at last thoroughly convinced me of the greatness and enterprise of this incomparable artist. . . . It is a fact at that time I felt almost like a little schoolboy by the side of Berlioz." (*My Life*, Part I, "Paris.")

[18] "In those seven years [1827 to 1834] he had not only said things that music had never uttered before, but he, and he alone, had brought French music, at a bound, into line with all the new work that was being donc in poetry, in prose, and in art." (Ernest Newman: *481*, 219.)

school claimed attention, and England, Norway, Finland, and the Germanies added their highly diversified contributions to the stream of music. These successive revelations confused the public by their strangeness and force, which criticism was too hypnotized by minutiae to explain. There could be no history of nineteenth-century art while the nineteenth century lasted.

The New Berlioz Criticism

By 1920 the tide had apparently spent itself and competent observers, fully alive to the variety of genius and tendencies in this great output, began to discern its intimate connections with the work of Berlioz. M. Boschot himself, mellowed by the passage of time and the increase of dissonance, was able to see that much of Berlioz' "madness" had been method, and that his music, "though it resembles no other, has sown germs from which *all* subsequent musicians have profited and continue to profit, even when they do not know it."[19]

Meanwhile students of the Russian school or of French Impressionism, of Wolf or Mahler, and above all of Wagner and his epigoni, traced the same relation, direct or indirect. Berlioz was in fact seen to be the fountainhead of modern music as Delacroix is of modern painting.[20] Put in historical terms, the relation of style, form, and subject matter between the Romanticist founders and their successors is constant. Only, in painting and in music this originating power is virtually concentrated in the work of a single man. This does not preclude real independence and great genius in those who came after, much less imply that music from Berlioz to the present is of one kind: no two artists could differ more than Berlioz and Richard Strauss, yet when Strauss celebrating his eighty-third birthday in London acknowledged his debt to Berlioz[21] he recorded an influence which goes deeper than orchestral effects and is not to be measured by simple borrowings.

The last twenty-five years, in short, have seen the growth of a new Berlioz criticism. It has been especially abundant in Britain and America, and its task has been not so much to bring forward a neglected artist as to place him in his proper niche. The writings of Ernest Newman, Constant Lambert, Cecil Gray, Bernard Van Dieren, W. H. Mellers, Richard Capell, W. J. Turner, Ferruccio Bonavia, Guido Pannain, T. S. Wotton,

[19] 770, 73.

[20] Exception must be made for the domain of the piano, for which Berlioz did not write.

[21] *Musical America*, Nov. 15, 1947, 5.

Paul Rosenfeld, B. H. Haggin, Virgil Thomson, Philip Greeley Clapp, Herbert Weinstock, Peter Hugh Reed, Laurence Powell, James Agate, Sacheverell Sitwell, and others have so to speak taken the mystery and the contradiction out of the old description of Berlioz given in Grove: "A colossus with few friends and no direct followers." [22] The colossus still stands, the friends have grown numerous, and the followers are everywhere.

Berlioz as Artist

Still it is an obviously difficult operation, when the bas-relief of history shows its serried ranks of great figures set as in granite, to reshuffle them and clear a large space in the middle distance for one who has so far been marginal and ill-identified. What is more, the claim to historical importance, though it leads to much that is new and exciting, does not finally captivate our hearts. Rather, in the realm of the spirit we want things-in-themselves and persons-in-themselves: works and men intrinsically admirable. With regard to Berlioz, happily, historical and intrinsic virtues are intimately allied. One cannot reassess his role and substantiate the startling conclusions of modern opinion without at the same time delineating an artist who would deserve our praise and affection even if he had never stirred from his desk, or penned anything but notes.

The only difficulty is to re-create the living Berlioz from the still unsorted mass of fact and testimony. For although the modern critics scoff at the errors enshrined in older authorities, they correct them piecemeal and in a multitude of confusing contexts. Cecil Gray can assert that Berlioz is "a melodist, first, foremost, and all the time"; [23] Weingartner can write that Berlioz was no program composer; [24] Koechlin can show that Berlioz' musical mind was naturally contrapuntal; [25] but these important conclusions remain scattered in a vast sea of books, essays, and newspaper articles, none of which by itself projects a clear image of the man and artist. Even the best modern books, W. J. Turner's and T. S. Wotton's, divide the subject between them, and while one deals with the life and the other with the works, neither aims at fullness and both neglect history.[26] Once again, the "problem of Berlioz" resolves itself into something for

[22] *A Dictionary of Music and Musicians,* London, 1879 (1896), art. "Berlioz."
[23] *719,* 213. [24] *394,* 208. [25] *453,* 193.
[26] W. J. Turner, *Berlioz: the Man and His Work,* London, 1934; T. S. Wotton, *Hector Berlioz,* London and New York, 1935. My debt to Wotton is, however, immense, and I beg to refer the reader to my imperfect acknowledgment below.

which he is scarcely responsible: how to round up the literature in six languages and bring veracity and order into it by scholarly method.

The Swerve of the Atom

Research soon confirms the impression that the printed sources are from one point of view altogether adequate. Everything has been said that needed to be said. Time and again I have found my own unaided reflections upon Berlioz' life or music anticipated by a critic of the present or past century – a corroboration for which, given the nature of my task, I would gladly barter any claim to originality.[27] But this same body of print bears one feature which shows equally clearly that my exploration was not superfluous: the very best of the literature is shot through with error; the most competent judges suffer from sudden and serious lapses. For instance, in the splendid essay by Romain Rolland one finds Berlioz persuasively depicted as a creative artist of the first magnitude; but nearly every remark about his character as a man or an abstract thinker is demonstrably wrong. One turns then to intimate observers of the living man – to Saint-Saëns or to the playwright Legouvé. And here again caution proves indispensable. Legouvé has a real sense of Berlioz' candor, warmth, and greatness of soul, but he tells us that Berlioz was ill-educated, "a man of one book" – although every page that Berlioz wrote shows his wide reading, not only of literature but of history and the sciences in several languages.[28] As for Saint-Saëns, invaluable as are his remarks upon Berlioz' works and personality, he is not to be trusted when it comes to certain aspects of Berlioz' teachings and attitudes.

These examples could be multiplied by the hundred; indeed I have hardly come across any critical document, however brief, which did not contain a grievous error. Like the atom of Lucretius, each writer follows a straight line for a shorter or longer time, then swerves. How is the unprejudiced reader seeking truth and being carried steadily along by a Romain Rolland or a Saint-Saëns to know when he should alight? These considerations necessarily dictated the plan of the present work. Since the Berlioz literature contained all the truth and all the falsehood side by side,

[27] Citing the names of critics once well-known but destined, like most of their kind, to the shadows, is not merely a duty and a pleasure; it is also a guarantee that the many "revised judgments" that I put forward were the original perceptions or conclusions of a great variety of competent minds over a span of 125 years.

[28] Berlioz was perhaps the only Frenchman of his time to whom it would occur naturally to take a motto from Pope's *Essay on Criticism* for one of his own articles (*Grot.*, 169), which served also as the Preface to the score of *La Fuite en Egypte*.

and since the thousands of casual references in other books, in concert notes, in publicity for discs and broadcasts reproduced the same anarchy,[29] what was needed was a canon of correct belief, a *summa* of ascertained truth, a reasoned orthodoxy for the faithful.

To Please Laymen and Professionals

Accordingly, the twenty-five biographical chapters of this book are flanked by twenty-five critical essays that take up the composer's major scores, and, in connection with each, some characteristic feature of his life or art: Berlioz' melody, orchestration, and so on are discussed in close proximity to the work that best exemplifies each, and so is his work as critic, dramatist, and conductor. Likewise treated in concentrated form are the still broader topics raised by his relation to the thought and events of his time. All these "second sections" or subchapters fit into the chronology and present fresh facts that carry the story forward. But they are marked off by a telltale heading coupled with a quotation from Berlioz, so that on a first reading they may be skipped by the impetuous.[30]

For the contemplative, three of the critical portions have been labeled Interchapters, to suggest resting places where in the light of Berlioz' theory and practice one may find reconsiderations of, respectively, Program Music, Romanticism, and the Mind of the Artist. It is important to add that not merely the student of character and lover of music will find here what he may be looking for. Anyone with an interest in history or in art may approach this life of Berlioz, musical matters included, just as one would a book on Leonardo even though one cannot mix paints. And perhaps the working out of this conviction will show that music can enter into the general life of ideas, and that the large number of people who listen to broadcasts, concerts, and discs need not hesitate to reason and argue about their vivid and truthful impressions.

A Handbook for Friends and Detractors

This does not mean that the aim of the present work is to propagandize for either music or Berlioz. No one familiar with the critical *dis*sensus

[29] Mr. Elliot Paul, for example, having been aroused to enthusiasm by a Paris performance of Berlioz' *Requiem* goes on to speak of the other great works that Berlioz was composing "during the late sixties of the last century." (*The Last Time I Saw Paris,* N. Y. 1942, pp. 95 and 173.) The facts are that the *Requiem* was composed in 1837, Berlioz ceased composing by 1862, and died in 1869. Mr. Paul's mistake is not culpable but it is symptomatic.

[30] The reader who wants pure narrative first may begin with Chapters 1 and 2, omit 7, 14, and 20, and read the first sections of all the rest.

which exists about all art and artists [31] would expect to persuade everybody that Berlioz was "simply one of the greatest composers who have ever lived." If any agency can attempt this universal conversion it must be Berlioz' music, which, given a chance, can be safely trusted to exercise its inherent powers. But it is desirable for all concerned that the endless battle of opinions should be as efficient as possible. The proffered "orthodoxy" is therefore an answer to Tovey's plaintive phrase: it is to help Berlioz' admirers "know where they are"; it is also, and in equal degree, a manual which may enable Berlioz' detractors to damn him intelligently.

Consequently, although the size and substance of this work suggest the improbable term "definitive," I should prefer it to be considered a *defining* book which, while telling the story of a complex career, treats the assumptions and the practices of the creative artist as choices which he makes and which no one is bound to endorse. One need only recognize, assess, appreciate the reasons for the choice. "Appreciation," I know, is today a meaningless word. The search for an infallible kind of criticism has discredited the historical method and substituted a number of systems wholly concerned with materials and techniques. This has yielded valuable results, but it has also brought great losses. We have come to forget that the work of art alters with the passage of time and that the observer's mind affects the reality he sees – absolute reckoning is no more possible in art than in astrophysics. And in abandoning the one available and safe way, which is an exacting relativism, we have lost sight of the common goal which the arts aim at. We have denied their common relation to life, which is to say their relation to History.

To set forth this relation no doubt requires a method different from the one condemned as *the* historical method. It must not be reductive: art is no more a "social index" than it is a "neurotic dream" or a set of contrived echoes among pure sensations. Art is art and its study must yield the fullest identification of the unique object. This is but an additional reason for the extent of the work in hand. At the cost of explaining more than some readers will seek – though I trust not more than all

[31] In his little book on *Musical Taste*, the late M. D. Calvocoressi tells of his dismay after sampling opinion: "In due course, I learnt to take nothing on trust, not even praise or blame emanating from the writers whom I considered soundest and most sensitive and thoughtful; for I encountered a bewildering discrepancy of views. Here were two authors who agreed in their appraisement of Beethoven and Wagner but disagreed in their appraisement of Berlioz; another two agreed on Beethoven, Wagner, and Berlioz, but disagreed on Liszt; others, agreeing on Beethoven, Wagner, Liszt, and Berlioz would disagree on Strauss or Hugo Wolf, and so on." (775, 2–3.)

taken collectively will want – this canon of reason and virtue in Berliozian matters should serve the needs of any given reader, who may skip what he will allow to pass unargued.[32]

The Struggle for Truths

For although the unprejudiced reader dislikes argument, preferring the dogmatic tone as more authoritative, it is neither possible nor healthy that he should be indulged in this. The life of ideas thrives on conflict, and good history, as Shaw points out, is mainly recrimination.[33] It is rarely possible to arrive at desired truths without opposition and dispute, and one finds hardly any current biography of the great – were one to go back as far as Euripides – which does not open with fighting words.[34] Given Berlioz' rating in the many works that still indoctrinate young and old, the traditional processes of controversy remain unavoidable and the reader must grow inured to them.

As for Berlioz' detractors, it is idle for them to say that defense of him is special pleading: they are the ones who by their confident misstatements bring on the litigation.[35] Nor can they deprecate full documentation and inquiry into disputed points; they would demand it if it were omitted and claim a kind of victory by default. Lastly, it is simple childishness to complain – as has been done – that favorable views of Berlioz by able critics are prejudiced views, whereas the dwindling band

[32] Despite appearances I did not try to unwind every type of quirk one meets in current criticism. This, for example, is the pattern of many an "objection": a reviewer of the *Fantastic* symphony writes that he finds a simple recitative from Bach's *Saint Matthew Passion* "far more thrilling than all the heroics of Berlioz' March to the Scaffold." How is it the writer does not see that his comparison is null and void? Suppose he was told "For my part I find a simple recitative in Berlioz' *Infant Christ* far more thrilling than all the dramatics of Bach's two choruses shouting 'Barabbas!' " Would the inversion show him that all he has said is: "I prefer quiet recitatives"? If he means to say more, he must either state his preference for Bach dogmatically, or if he wants to argue it, present us with things similar enough to make comparison rational.

[33] *1217*, 40.

[34] *E.g.:* Hadas and McLean's *Euripides*, Wilbur Cross's *Fielding*, Lewes's *Goethe*, Krutch's *Johnson*, Carl Grabo's *Shelley*, Ricardo Quintana's *Swift*, Mark Schorer's *Blake*, Trilling's *Matthew Arnold*, Pulver's *Paganini*, Wright's *Rousseau*, Sassoon's *Meredith* – even Murdock's *Increase Mather:* the list is as extensive as biography itself.

[35] Special pleading, correctly defined, is – or should be – the very principle of biography. It is, says Fowler, "the adaptation to the particular circumstances of the typical formulae or pleadings that may be applicable to them, and that are *ready to be used by either party*." [Italics added.] *Modern English Usage*, 552.

of antagonists are veritable Daniels and Solomons come to judgment.[36]

Happily the newcomer to Berlioz' art may take all this wrangling in his stride, learning from it only how to beware of dogmas that do not disclose their underlying principles, and acquiring the true critical temper which indulges passion without possessiveness. Thus if the sincere amateur finds himself in disagreement with Berlioz' conception of dramatic music, or with his sense of the limits of musical expression, the advantage in having these assumptions explicitly stated is that on hearing the works the listener will discover why he has been puzzled or annoyed and this very knowledge will free his mind for enjoyment. If he should still like to quarrel, the debate will at least be anchored in fact and logic instead of surmises and non sequiturs.[37]

This is a point of capital importance, for in the last analysis what marks off the "Berlioz problem" from any other – the Blake or Brahms or Moussorgsky problem – is the failure of Berlioz' admirers to act with enlightened self-interest as guardians of his fame. I speak of self-interest because it is obvious that the supply of his music available for our enjoyment depends on his reputation at large, and I may add that one of my strongest motives in writing has been the simple desire to hear more of his work and be allowed to talk less about it.[38]

Berlioz' Power of Survival

The extraordinary fact is that without any cult to support him, whether national or snobbish, without any "sample pieces" to carry his name into the musical amateur's home, or any vested interests to nurse his fame for

[36] It is curious testimony to the power of convention that almost every second reference to Berlioz stresses his "overbalance in the direction of volume" – in spite of the better informed view of other observers. Why is this? Because *seeing* the score, or *seeing* the instrumentists on the stage paralyzes the judgment. In 1948 the recordings of the *Requiem* were issued and nearly every critic pointed out how moderate and well-balanced the orchestration was: for the first time, they *heard*. One writer went so far as to say that the large forces were "merely incidental" to the music!

[37] See, for instance, the "refutation" of Berlioz' "system of program music" which is to be found in the third edition of Grove (I, 360) and which consists of the arguments maintained by Berlioz himself in *A Travers Chants*, p. 157.

As for logic, see the inference that because Berlioz wrote chiefly for full orchestra, he must have had a "restricted capacity" for appreciating chamber music. (775, 56.)

[38] [Section 10 of the Bibliography has been kept in this edition to give an idea of what the collector of discs had available before the advent of the long-playing record.]

the sake of royalties, Berlioz has survived. From the beginning he has had the freely given suffrage of the most gifted musicians – composers as well as performers – and in every generation he has found numerous fervent admirers among theorists, academics, and intelligent laymen.[39] It would be still more extraordinary than such proof of the vitality of his music if this spontaneous, unorganized, and unostentatious following had grown out of illusion or frivolous feeling. The reverse being true, it puts a clear obligation on friends and enemies alike. The latter must either drop him entirely (it is mere sadism to keep on writing chapters in which he is loftily patronized) or else they must find a way to express their disapproval in civil words which square with the facts.

As for his admirers they must familiarize themselves with the full range of his achievement so as to be able to turn the tide of misrepresentation.[40] The excellent biographer of Tchaikovsky, Handel, and Chopin, Mr. Herbert Weinstock, justly writes that "the picture of Berlioz, that solemn and many-gifted musician, as an irresponsible and wild-eyed romantic, does little credit to its creators";[41] but the erasing of that picture will not occur by itself. As long as writers on music escape unchallenged when they make the stock references to Berlioz' "sacrificing form to effect"; when they blandly impute to him "love of size," or "inadequate technique"; when they glibly depreciate – as if it were a single entity – "the school of Berlioz, Liszt and Wagner," the conscience of his well-wishers, and even of those who are indifferent to him but who love truth, will carry a burden of guilt.[42]

[39] I may cite at random (besides Schumann, Liszt, Strauss and Wagner) Hugo Wolf, Bizet, Mahler, Bruckner, Gounod, Van Dieren, Busoni, Weingartner, Mottl, Moussorgsky, Sidney Lanier, Paul Dukas, Cornelius, Lalo, Peter Warlock, and G. B. Shaw. Among writers and artists: Gautier, Huysmans, Richard Dehmel, W. E. Henley, James Agate, Odilon Redon, Flaubert, Nietzsche, Van Gogh, and André Gide. And among the professors: Lobe, Ambros, Goetschius, Daussoigne-Méhul, Spalding, Prout, Emmanuel, Otto Luening, Robert Prescott Stewart, Charles Koechlin, William Schuman, and Roger Sessions.

[40] From time to time in these pages, a footnote under the caption "Scholarship" will show – with no sense of pride or any other animus – how wide of the mark a report in good faith may be.

[41] *1308*, art. Berlioz.

[42] Dealing with the comparable ease of The Puritans and Music, Mr. Percy Scholes says "it will need a bonfire of schoolbooks and popular novels" before the new and correct idea will replace the generally accepted one. (*871*, 377.)

The Apperceptive Mass

It may at this point be asked why Berlioz' own *Memoirs* have not long ago dissipated all these mists and why even now the reading of them would not show the man and his work in the best possible light — his own.[43] The answer is simply that although the *Memoirs* faithfully show Berlioz in his fighting trim — or perhaps because they do — the book is by no means a satisfactory portrait; and as an apologia it falls far short of making a sufficiently large claim. This is not the place to examine the *Memoirs'* truthfulness or exaggeration; it will appear later that, as autobiographies go, that of Berlioz is unusually veracious. But addressed as it is by the principal actor to his near-posterity, it takes much of what we need to know for granted; and, Berlioz being at once fundamentally modest and aristocratically reserved, he refrains from marking in a sharp didactic way the significance of his many activities. Hence the reader who comes unprepared to this fluent, humorous, allusive, and closely packed narrative sees only its drama, or feels only the overriding will of its protagonist; he has no means of judging, comparing, and confirming what he is told. He lacks, in short, what the older psychology called an "apperceptive mass" — previous facts and categories with which to take in and organize new knowledge.[44]

The Tone of Time

Such a mass is here, in the pages that follow, and no small part of it consists of the expressions of pleasure, admiration, love, and even worship, which through the years have greeted the revelation of what Mr.

[43] In response to the visibly changing attitude towards Berlioz, Mr. Ernest Newman was asked by his publisher some years ago to write a new life. He declined on the ground that Berlioz had himself done this unsurpassably well, and he contented himself with revising and annotating the English translation. Mr. Newman was right to respect the integrity of the book and I have followed his lead to the extent of quoting from it just as little as possible. [A new and scholarly edition of the *Memoirs*, by David Cairns, appeared in 1969.]

[44] "Were we in perception chiefly passive, could the things of the outer world impress themselves immediately upon our minds and thus stamp their nature upon it, they would necessarily always leave behind the same ideas, so that a variety of apprehension would be impossible and inexplicable. The fact, however, that every observer contributes something to the sensation, and thus alters and enriches it, speaks unmistakably for the activity of the mind, which, upon occasion of sense-excitations, must perform the main office and create the perception. . . . The mind apprehends the things of the outer world with the assistance of what it has already experienced, felt, learned, and digested." Karl Lange, *The Theory of Apperception*, 4.

Bernard Haggin with fine respect calls "the Berlioz mind." For Whitman was right to say that "no really great song can ever attain full purport till it has accrued and incorporated the many passions, many joys and sorrows it has itself aroused." Now, a century and a [half] after Berlioz' first songs, this accrual is impressively large, and of a character no one could infer from that of the more familiar cant. Only by pondering these authentic responses and matching them with the "song" can we become better attuned to the spirit of the man whom Wagner called an "enormous musical intelligence" and "an incomparable artist."

Today, when we are nothing if not social critics, we may find Berlioz most accessible as an avenger of intellect in its struggle with a corrupt society. Certainly, that spectacle is tragically satisfying: to pomposity and pedantry Berlioz opposed wit and irreverence; on easy optimism and the trumpery faith in progress he turned a scornful glance; and against Philistine commercialism he raised a religion of art and nature for which he testified and suffered. Insofar as he stands for the spirit of his age he carries forward the great European tradition of the Gothic artist, of Shakespearean drama, of Renaissance Latinity, and of the Romanticist revolution which revived art by drawing on its native and popular sources. In music considered as an institution, Berlioz was heir to the hopes of Mozart, Beethoven, and Weber, and he lived to fulfill them; for as composer, conductor and organizer of musical celebrations he presided over the establishment of a new spiritual force – the musician as artist.

Berlioz among the Powers

But Berlioz himself towers above this not inconsiderable achievement and he needs but to be known for his metal to be felt as transcending the common stuff of geniuses. "If genius means creative power," writes Romain Rolland, "I hardly see more than four or five of his caliber in the world, and when I have listed Beethoven, Mozart, Bach, Handel, and Wagner, I know of no one in music who is his superior or even his equal." [45]

To describe the natural bent which Berlioz' creation takes we have only the term "originality" or "invention." As Weingartner said, "he does not have to seek, he finds." [46] And this unsought freshness and force, this daemon or magic of the unconscious, was matched in Berlioz by a mind and character of superlative strength and fineness to which his five peers listed above would perhaps not lay claim. It is this which in the

[45] *504*, 25. [46] *394*, 205.

estimation of those who know raises Berlioz to a high and separate pinnacle; and it is this which has so often made him the easy victim of inferior beings. For within the limits of human perfection he had everything, and his offense is not merely that his spiritual riches goad the envious and impotent, but that it deprives even the well-meaning of the chance to pity, condone, or assist.[47] Any lapse of his is at once magnified by contrast and eagerly pilloried by those who would prefer having more to condemn or forgive.[48] Hence his arduous career and hence his kinship with the embattled great, whose biography is bearable only after the passage of time has dulled the pain and dimmed the apparent confusion: one thinks of Dante, Michelangelo, and Swift.

For these reasons it is a portent when we find a critic describing the art of Berlioz' *Faust* as "so inventive, so varied, so cleanly classical."[49] It is fit that this final unexpected term should crown a work whose theme is held to be peculiarly romantic and thus ideally suited to a "fantastic" composer. For if we finally discern the *order* in Berlioz' romantic life and art (which is all that the writer's "classical" means) we have indeed found the clue to all the mazes on our way, and we must be close to the moment in a creator's afterlife when, as for Shakespeare in Berlioz' day, the eyes of all are opened, black turns into white, and every living part – work, intellect, character and artistry – is reborn and transfigured. After which, the world inherits as if by an act of its free will a new and miraculous legacy from an undoubted master of reality.

[47] Compare the many expressions of protective sympathy for César Franck, in whom various incapacities are exhibited, for example by Vincent d'Indy, as real merits. (*945*.)

[48] When T. S. Wotton's book was ready for the press, a publisher's reader was disappointed to find that Berlioz' *Memoirs* were, after all, trustworthy; "he preferred," said he, "to consider Berlioz an outrageous liar." (*154*, 26.)

[49] Richard Capell (*562*).

1. *Time, Place, Persons*

January 1803 to November 1817

> There is a harmony . . . between men's lives and their names: a poetic justice. . . . Hector Berlioz could not have pursued his high-fevered career under the name of Georges Jourdain.
>
> —THOMAS BURKE, 1929

THE YEAR 1803 opened with renewed preparations for war. Europe had been under arms for a decade, but the previous eight months had seen a truce between Bonaparte dictating to France and Great Britain leading the Allies. Now another hundred thousand Frenchmen must join the colors, a new fleet was being built, and the First Consul moved on three continents. Though he was losing India, he held title to Louisiana and had an army in Haiti. President Jefferson was alarmed, and shortly negotiations were begun to buy the future American Middle West from France, whose master was planning the invasion of England with barges and balloons. By the end of the year his army on the Channel had been designated for the Battle of Britain.[1] Yet in retrospect the time would mark its men with other signs than those of war: a new century inheriting the Enlightenment, a new order growing out of the mightiest revolution in history, a new conception of life most vividly embodied in the headlong career of Napoleon.

Just before the year ended and only a few days before Louisiana became American, on Sunday, December 11, at five o'clock in the afternoon, Hector Berlioz was born in the small town of La Côte St. André, thirty-five miles northwest of Grenoble. At that time and place, the date of his birth was set down as the nineteenth Frimaire of the year XII, for France was still nominally a republic and used the emancipated calendar. The child's given names, Louis and Hector, of themselves suggest a period of transition, for Louis is Christian and Hector fulfills the revolutionary behest that parents remember the heroes of antiquity in naming the future heroes of the First French Republic. The revolution, it is true, had at no time been very violent in the southeastern province of Dauphiné.

[1] *L'armée d'Angleterre,* so named on December 2, 1803.

Insurrection had been characteristically prompt and self-controlled. Two years before the nationwide upsurge of the Third Estate, the magistrates of Dauphiné had defied royal encroachment in a fashion resembling England's resistance to "ship money." Again, nearly a year before the outbreak of the revolution, Dauphinois lawyers and notables had held unauthorized assemblies of their own, and in a twelve-hour session at Vizille had "passed" most of the reforms which were later to shed glory on the National Assembly.

Moreover, considering itself a recent acquisition of the French crown – only five centuries old – the Dauphiné still felt stirrings of particularist feeling. Its local heroes were Bayard, the outspoken Knight without fear or reproach, and Lesdiguières, the invincible defender of Protestantism. At La Côte itself Servetus had preached before his exile to near-by Geneva, and from the same village came another Protestant family which was to produce the nineteenth-century economist and historian Sismondi. During the Terror, isolation in mountainous country and moderation in carrying out new laws had spared the region the worst of civil strife; so that by the turn of the century, and in the Berlioz family especially, party feeling had died down. It had not been replaced by enthusiasm for Bonaparte. The household was mildly royalist.

Hector's father, Louis Berlioz, was a physician descended from a long line of residents at La Côte who have been traced back with certainty to 1600. In the attempt to go farther, the name Berlioz (in which you must sound the *z* after the long *o*, all Parisians to the contrary notwithstanding) has been the subject of much profitless speculation on the part of race-thinking critics. The ending in *-oz* is common enough in the southeast, but the root *Berl* has been taken by some to signify Germanic descent. Others, finding the name in Savoy, argue for an Italian origin and so "vindicate" the Latin genius. Finally, there is mention of more than one Berlioz in an ancient roll of noble Crusaders, from which still others deduce a racial superiority of caste.

The simple fact is that three centuries in a narrow corner like La Côte St. André would suffice to acclimatize any alien strain, whether of slave or master race, and turn its representatives into the variable cultural product which you may call at once Dauphinois, Frenchman, and European. The desire to make Hector Berlioz' musical genius come out of either Germany or Italy via the chromosomes of possibly tone-deaf farmers and artisans of La Côte is as childish as it is unhistorical. Where was German music at the time of the Crusades? And why did Berlioz grow up with a particular distaste for Italian music? The effect of time, place, and living persons is a truer aid to understanding the art and temper of the man than all the word-juggling of modern nationalists.[2]

Engaged from the first in the locally important tanning industry, the Berlioz clan had gradually risen in station until by the middle of the eighteenth century its descendants were men of property and education. So much so that Hector's grandfather, the lawyer and tax official, Joseph Berlioz, found himself on a list of suspects during the Terror and suffered the confiscation of his goods. This was the time when the name Côte St. André sounded counterrevolutionary and had to be changed to Côte Bonne-Eau.[3] But Joseph Berlioz gave no further cause for suspicion and he eventually got back his property, both at La Côte and near Grenoble, where at Les Jacques he had a large estate overlooking the great valley and mountain screen of the Grésivaudan.

It was this same Joseph Berlioz who rebuilt at La Côte the house which still stands, and which in 1935 was made into a museum in honor of his grandson. It is a solid, flat-fronted stone house with sloping roof. The spacious rooms are well-proportioned and, except for wainscoting, bare of ornament. From the upper stories one has a superb view of the whole plain, framed within a silver-blue edging of mountains. Behind the house is a courtyard and beyond, a quiet garden with a small stream. When Berlioz was born, the grandfather lived in the house, a widower retired from professional life, but still busy as the largest landowner of the place – virtually a country squire. His physical appearance, as one can judge from a painting, was largely reproduced in his grandson Hector – a thin, high, hooked nose, fine lips with a sardonic curl at the corners, deep-set eyes and a sturdy build.

The son of the suspect, Hector's father Louis, born in 1776, seems by contrast a milder man. For a time, it is true, he was politically at odds with his father. The "noble words Liberty and Equality," the doctor tells

[2] These conjectures have not been confined to fanatics. In the last century men of the stature of Hans von Bülow and Alfred Fouillée gravely discussed Berlioz' "racial" temperament. (*548*, I, 90 ff.; *165*, *passim*.) Today, critics rely on eye- and hair-color (Fr. Baser, *411*, 259), or draw inferences from general impressions of style. Thus the late Paul Rosenfeld thought he saw "in men like Rabelais only the Frank and in men like Berlioz only the atavism to Gallo-Roman times." (*505*, 135.) Contrariwise, Koechlin finds in the art of Rabelais and of Berlioz an exact parallel (*730*, *681*); while P. L. Robert deems the composer "the fine flower of Latin genius" (*668*, 1), and Edouard Schuré is sure he "incarnates the Celtic soul." (*442*, 1.) For the assumed connection between the Frankish race and noble birth, see my monograph, *The French Race: Theories of Its Origins*, N. Y. 1932

[3] This name does not refer to any natural waters of the place, but to its excellent distilled liquors.

us in a diary, had aroused his youthful zeal, which was enhanced by "the success of the citizen armies and the republican evocations of Athens and Rome." He became "quite wild, like many others." [4] But events disillusioned him. He grew very self-contained, although generous feeling and independence of mind were characteristics that remained and influenced Hector, his first-born.

It was in keeping with this quiet but steady unconventionality that Louis Berlioz took to medicine, after giving up the law which his father had chosen for him. The young man taught himself by reading and attending lectures in the metropolis when these were available. Wartime schooling, then as now, is a chancy thing, but finally, two months after Hector's birth, Louis Berlioz went once more to Paris, defended his thesis, and obtained his degree.[5] His age was twenty-seven.

All the while, he had pursued other intellectual interests, notably music, and had learned English and Italian to keep up with contemporary literature and philosophy. The doctor was the first of his family to enjoy moneyed leisure, and he made use of it in the traditional way, for cultivation. Even beyond the small community of five thousand souls which he tended, he would have stood out as an unusual man. A great reader, who also wrote voluminously for his own use, he could combine the meditative life with action, in a manner which we shall find again in his son. The doctor was among the first to practice hydrotherapy and he developed and described other original methods of cure in a prize-winning essay chosen by the Montpellier Faculty in 1810.[6] When rivals used his discoveries without acknowledgment, he remained unruffled and said only, "Let the truth prevail."

Dr. Berlioz soon enjoyed the trust and respect of his neighbors. He overcame their prejudices so quietly that he gained both their affection and the power to help them; and his interest in the welfare of the poor took the practical form of supplying them with housing and hygienic facilities at his own expense. He died a universally beloved public benefactor, a counterpart if not a model of Balzac's famous *Médecin de Campagne*.[7]

[4] *A. R.*, xxxviii.

[5] The essay, a 25-page affair, dealt with the onset of the menstrual cycle; it had been published, or at least dated, the preceding year. (*166.*)

[6] See *167*.

[7] The accredited belief, which there is no reason to dispute, is that Balzac's original was Dr. Amable Rome, a physician practicing at Voreppe, also in the Dauphiné, where Balzac met him while on a walking tour in 1832. (See *1059.*) The social outlooks of the fictional Dr. Bénassis and the actual doctors, Rome and Berlioz, naturally coincide; their personal characteristics also; but there is a further external coincidence that has not been noted. By the time

Hector's mother was cast in a different mold. Whereas her husband was a gently skeptical philosopher, bred on Voltaire and Rousseau, poetry and natural science, Madame Berlioz was a passionate, devout, one-idea'd woman – the daughter of a Grenoble lawyer named Marmion. She was considered a beauty, tall, slim, and remarkable for her fine coloring and glowing health, though in spite of her apparent vitality she suffered from an obscure liver complaint. Friends and family, as is their wont, called it hypochondria, which did not improve the sufferer's irritable temper. Disappointed perhaps at the narrow life afforded to one of her sociable gifts, and driven by the demon of aggressive piety, Marie-Antoinette Berlioz was capable of turning every event of the day into an occasion for outcry – to the point of rousing even the patient doctor to a sudden burst of anger.

The household atmosphere might accordingly be charged with electricity, and although the bolts did not destroy the tight bonds of French family life, the boy Hector undoubtedly sensed the strain. A nightmare he tells of having had in early manhood pictured the attempt of three burglars to kidnap his father: Hector perhaps felt that the doctor had been his guardian angel.[8] Certainly, though the boy was attached to his mother, he never felt for her a completely trusting affection. She lacked moral gentleness, and she was moreover puzzled from the start by her son's character and inclinations.

Besides the young couple with their first child, and Dr. Berlioz' aging father, the house at La Côte came to shelter five more children, of whom two girls, Nanci and Adèle, survived to maturity.[9] The house was also a center for the visits of an extensive *cousinage* scattered among the neighboring hills and reaching as far as Grenoble where both sides of the family had property.[10]

Balzac's novel was published, he had met the rising young composer Hector Berlioz in Paris and was on such friendly terms with him that he dedicated to him his tale "Ferragus," published the same year as the *Médecin.* In this latter work, the nature descriptions and the references to local folk songs suggest the possibility that Berlioz was pumped by the fact-thirsty novelist, and that he furnished useful information about a country doctor's life as well as about its Dauphinois setting.

[8] *A. R.*, 158.

[9] Nanci or Nancy, as she was called, had been baptized Marguerite-Anne-Louise. She was born in 1806; Adèle-Eugénie in 1814. Prosper, the last child, was born in 1820.

[10] Another great Dauphinois, Henri Beyle, known in literature as Stendhal, was in Napoleon's army and stationed at Vienna in 1809. He writes from there to his family: "You must keep this project confidential. Any such thing, mentioned in Grenoble, comes back here: MM. Berlioz, Delaunay . . . Périer, etc. etc. are in the Army or in Vienna. . . ." (*168*, III, 199.)

In this ensemble, an infrequent but distinct note was struck by Mme. Berlioz' younger brother, Félix Marmion. As an officer in training at the Paris Polytechnic School, he was the only Bonapartist of the family, and thereby at odds both with his sister and with her strongly anti-imperialist father-in-law: more wrangling – this time political – for the child Hector to grow resistant to. The young lieutenant nevertheless remained an important link between La Côte and the outer world of great events and distant places. His campaigns took him as far as Prussia and Poland; he fought for four years in Spain; he was shot, enfevered, sabre-cut. Because of his royalist family he did not rise to a captaincy until the Bourbons' first restoration in 1814.

In spite of handicaps, Félix Marmion was gay, gallant and reasonably vain. Sociable like his sister, fond of music and competent on the violin, but even fonder of using his fine voice on a large repertoire of parlor songs and light opera "selections," we can see him as a representative guardsman, in costume and character. Yet the coloring went deeper than the scarlet coat. Like so many of his generation, he was truly enamored of the Napoleonic way of life – that mixture of recklessness, rapid motion, and obsession with glory – which men as different as Balzac, Vigny, and the two Dauphinois, Stendhal and Berlioz, found so gripping and so rich in artistic suggestion.

The young Hector's first acquaintance with imperial institutions was of a different kind. At the age of six, he was sent to the seminary – an agency of mixed monastic and military discipline, designed to form all over France a Napoleonic Youth. There Hector presumably learnt by heart the catechism which told of the Emperor's goodness and divine mission, and he was set to play the drum in uniformed parades with his fellows. Fortunately, a rescript of 1811 abolished this infant prison and Hector was returned to his family, not to leave it again until he went to Paris ten years later.

The doctor took charge of his son's education and made a success of it. Music, mathematics, Latin, history, French literature, astronomy, and geography formed the course of study. Geography occupied a special place, for one of the usual responses to the feeling of mountain fastness is a passion for travel. In Hector it was matched by a thirst for stories of remote parts, and luckily the doctor's library contained many travel books, including the voyages of Bougainville and other explorers, whose daring had enlarged the eighteenth-century horizons. These, with more recent authors – such as Bernardin de St. Pierre and Chateaubriand –

gave Hector glimpses of wild America and the south seas – regions which Diderot and the Encyclopedists had used to prove human diversity and preach tolerance. While still a boy Hector became a cosmopolitan, and he remained true to this vision of earth and mankind.

The great book in the child's curriculum was Virgil's *Aeneid.* It was ideally suited to develop Hector's visible inclinations – the romance of travel, the love of nature, the quick sympathy with varied emotions, and the cultivation of a delicate ear. Indeed the effect of so much art once proved too much for the pupil's peace of mind. In translating for his father the passage that tells of Dido's despair after her desertion by Aeneas, the boy was choked by strong feeling and only saved by his father's adroit overlooking of the trouble and ending of the lesson.[11]

The happy chance of a domestic education helps to explain why Berlioz seems so fully himself so young. Though not a prodigy, he undoubtedly acquired a conscious inner life earlier than most. No one can guess or explain all that goes into the making of an artist, but one element is surely the power to feel intensely and remember past feelings undimmed. It is as if the first impressions of childhood were there forever, fresh and producible, not to be worn away by explanations or worldly maturing. What Berlioz felt about Dido at eleven, he still knew at fifty-five, and the music he then wrote for her death scene echoes these early pangs.[12] For this capacity to experience which, as Wilde said, is an instinct, there is no substitute. Yet it is that instinct which education, and particularly French education, carefully uproots or overlays, so that it takes years of disapprenticeship, or else the sturdy gift of a dunce, for the artistic nature to recover itself.

Berlioz was spared that struggle; he learned without losing sensitiveness. But he paid for the privilege. The home-reared child escapes narcotic schooling but stays too sheltered. Two years older than his oldest sister, with whom he was not especially congenial, Berlioz had too little of that rough-and-tumble with equals and contemporaries which toughens the outer, social skin. Study and solitude were his chief resource, besides

[11] *Mem.*, I, 8.

[12] This is no figure of speech: when Berlioz as a student competed for the Rome Prize and had to set *The Death of Sardanapalus,* he found accents of noble grief and antique grandeur for the king's farewell. Twenty-six years later, he used three of these melodic figures, doubtless unconsciously, for comparable swan songs in *Les Troyens;* and he then wrote to a friend that so far as the musical expression of the feelings in the *Aeneid*, "it was from the outset the easiest part of my task. I have spent my whole life with that tribe of demigods, and I have known them so long that I have come to believe they know me." (*S. W.*, 95.)

the associations — usually with older companions — that music brought him. His relation with his father was close and tender, but even that was hardly free or demonstrative enough. To the end of their days Berlioz never addressed either parent otherwise than as *vous*. One's elders exacted a heavy toll of the staple Respect, and made behavior run ahead of emotions, so that childish impulse had to play hide-and-seek through the forms of a premature *savoir-faire*. In another way, the same was true of religious belief, on which Hector's mother dwelt obsessively.

Lacking a proper guide to the half-reticences and half-spontaneities of social intercourse, Hector had to give himself wholly or not at all, and to be trusted in return before he could feel at ease. Then the pent-up feelings, gay or sad, would overflow, much to everyone's astonishment. Hence his favorite within the family was his second sister Adèle, who was lively and tender and unconventional like her father and himself. But owing to the difference in their ages, Hector could scarcely count on her companionship until his second return from Paris when he was twenty-five and she fourteen.

Despite all this, young Berlioz was not a hothouse plant. On the contrary, his broad shoulders and muscular physique made of him an indefatigable walker and climber, to whom some weathers might seem better than others, though all were good.[13] True, he had what is called the nervous temperament, but his health can be described as robust, for "nerves," until they are overstrained, mean simply energy and responsiveness, not debility. One proof of Hector's health in childhood is that he remained a candid, open, and affectionate character despite the quietism of his father, the tantrums of his mother, and the opportunities of moping afforded by his freedom from school discipline.

As an adolescent, to be sure, he went through a period of melancholy marked by religious fervor and a hopeless love affair. But these manifestations are by no means abnormal. Only their intensity at the time and their aftereffects betray an unusual nature. The story of the boy's infatuation is familiar to the readers of the *Memoirs*. During one of the vacations taken by the Berlioz family at Meylan, the maternal grandfather's house near Grenoble, there was an outdoor party where the military uncle and some neighboring young ladies were brought together. The officer was spirited and duly attentive, but he did not fall in love with either of the prizes submitted to his inspection: as someone has remarked, "he had been in Spain." It was his unhappy nephew Hector who conceived

[13] He and Adèle were fond of going for a walk in the rain, perfectly silent and happy, though the others called them "young fools." (*S. W.*, 149; *91*, 751.)

in secret a violent passion for Estelle Duboeuf, seven years his senior, and naturally disposed to treat Hector as a child.[14] Rather wickedly, however, she teased her helpless and embarrassed admirer in order to amuse the company and possibly to awaken the captain to a sense of opportunity.

What the child saw was a tall, rather determined young woman of nineteen, with black hair and a somewhat provocatively cold glance. That she wore pink slippers – the first he had ever seen – remained indelibly fixed in his memory; which suggests how he kept his eyes shyly lowered. Yet perhaps the dominant fact was her association with the most beautiful landscape he knew: the Saint-Eynard, which one climbs halfway to reach Meylan, and the broad valley of the Grésivaudan, crossed by two rivers and ringed with snow-capped peaks – a majestic panorama. Turning the experience at once into poetry, he christened her his *Stella Montis*, Estelle of the Mountain, an unattainable star, who centered in herself his need to adore, his vague but insistent wish for self-expression, and his religious feeling at the sight of nature. The varied consequences of this early attachment, unfolding through half a century, show it to have been something more than a laughable episode. It was rather the situation of another and equally romantic boy-poet, Dante, with a differently cast Beatrice.

What Berlioz does not tell us about this same formative period is the rapid succession of deaths within the family. Between his sixth and ninth years, three members of the older generation died, including his maternal grandmother and a cousin on his father's side who lost his way and perished in a swamp. In 1815, within two days, his grandfather Joseph Berlioz died and his own eight-year-old sister Louise Virginie; and again, in 1818, his younger brother Louis-Jules-Félix. Then, in Hector's sixteenth year, occurred the presumable suicide of his friend and mentor, the son of his music teacher Imbert. It happened during vacation time, after a solemn and mysterious farewell taken by the older boy. The younger, returning and finding his friend gone, was never able to learn the exact truth.

These were but the beginning of a series of sudden losses that kept shattering his life until the end. If it is true, as Boschot imagines, that in playing about the house the boy sought to harden his feelings by handling the doctor's wired skeleton and staring at anatomical plates, it is even more certain that the succession of deaths, emphasized by the ritual black

[14] *Mem.*, I, 9–11.

drapery, the visits of condolence and the restraint on laughter and games, played a part in the grown man's sense of life's fragility. His whole generation, as Musset and Vigny were to remark, had grown up in the company of death and in the belief that extinction must be redeemed by heroism.[15] Despite young Berlioz' true religious faith – perhaps because of it – this series of shocks, complicated as they were by the conflict between his infidel but loving father and his devout but harsh mother, left him subject to bouts of anxiety during which life seemed remote, outside himself.

Hector moreover seems quite early to have felt at one with the poets, who are traditionally cast by Fate for sorrow. His father's teaching and his own developing gifts made the identification natural enough, but the sentimentalism carried over from late eighteenth-century literature made melancholy worse. Reading the memoirs of Voltaire's protégé, Marmontel (which about the same time were bringing tears to the eyes of the young John Stuart Mill), responding to the gentle wails of the versifiers of the period, or to the grave accents of Chateaubriand's *Genius of Christianity*, strengthened in Hector the link between dark thoughts and artistic feelings.

From Chateaubriand's great work on what may be called the poetry and passion of the Christian religion, the boy copied out in a notebook still extant a revealing passage about André Chénier. This austerely fine poet had been executed by Robespierre in 1794 but his fame waited upon a proper edition of his works in 1820. In that year, the seventeen-year-old Berlioz, writing out the words and music of a song attributed to Chénier, made a note: "The author of these words was a young man who fell a victim to the French Revolution. This unhappy youth" (here Berlioz is quoting Chateaubriand), "on climbing the scaffold could not help exclaiming, as he struck his forehead, 'To die! when I feel something – there!' "[16] The remark is doubtless apocryphal but the Keats-like fear is of the time and mood, and we shall find it again embodied in music. For a youth endowed with imagination, the Red Terror did not seem very far in the past.

Nor was the Napoleonic legend very far in the future. Berlioz was eleven when, after the Emperor's first abdication, La Côte St. André

[15] Musset: "During the Napoleonic Wars . . . our mothers had brought into the world a fiery generation, pale, nervous, . . . reared in seminaries to the sound of drums. . . . Death itself had become so beautiful and great, it looked so much like Hope, that no one believed any longer in old age." (*1266*, 2–3.) Of Vigny, see "The Malacca Cane."

[16] *1243*, I, 279.

La Côte St. André (Isère)

The Alps at Grenoble
(Circle marks Meylan, home of Estelle)

"The country of Berlioz [lies] in the same parallel with Verona, Virgil's Mantua, and Venice . . ."

— CHARLES MACLEAN

was occupied by the Austrians. There was a short resistance to their inroad by partisans of the exiled Emperor; then came the usual resentment against the foreign troops; and shortly Napoleon returned from Elba. The incredible *revenant* passed through Grenoble, where he proclaimed himself a revolutionary soldier – an echo of his first glorious return from Italy in 1797 – and on his journey north he drew near enough to La Côte so that his cannon were heard there. His defeat after one hundred days was like the fifth act of a tragedy. Everything after it was an anticlimax, and most of it proved sordid: a second Austrian occupation, followed by the appalling incidents of the White Terror. In Dauphiné an insurgent named Didier, whose chief crime was incompetence, was turned by popular hysteria into a formidable peril. He and twenty-four others were either slaughtered or guillotined, while the whole province quaked under false alarms.

Dr. Berlioz, never a party man, kept as aloof as he could, though higher authorities looked to him (as chief citizen) to take the lead in a regime of repression. Against his will, he was made Mayor. From then on the events as Hector saw them turned to tragicomedy. His father discovered a falsification in the accounts of his predecessor, who was also a royalist. Notifying his political friends, Dr. Berlioz silently withdrew. He did not foresee the slanders and squabbles which broke out and divided his unhappy town. By a twist of circumstance, the leader of the other faction was a friend of the family's, the father of Hector's closest companion, Charbonnel. The doctor gained nothing but worries from his brief tenure of an office he had not sought, and his son registered one more reason for his contemptuous dislike of politics.

Two years before, Waterloo had seemed to settle some uncertainties, including the survival of Hector's uncle, Captain Marmion; but the Bourbon Restoration, begun in blood and fear like the century, still had the overwhelming past to sort out, to forget, and, if possible, to turn to creative uses.

2. Ce Qu'on Entend sur la Montagne

Circa 1808
to October 1821

I live not in myself, but I become
Portion of that around me; and to me,
High mountains are a feeling. . . .

Then stirs the feeling infinite, so felt
In solitude, where we are least alone;
A truth, which through our being then doth
  melt
And purifies from self: it is a tone,
The soul and source of music. . . .
— BYRON, *Childe Harold's Pilgrimage*

THE BEGINNING of Berlioz' musical vocation was his discovery of an old flageolet in a bureau drawer. His father had played it in his own youth, and he taught Hector the fingering. Berlioz' inclination, it is clear, was marked even before he left for the seminary.[1] Dr. Berlioz went on to teach his boy in a very lucid and logical way — as the pupil looked back on it — how to read notes and sing at sight. Soon the doctor bought Hector a flute, together with the standard method of Devienne. Then, wishing to provide more expert instruction, he arranged to have a local musician, one Imbert, give Hector two lessons a day.

Imbert was a violinist from the Lyon orchestra who had been brought to La Côte in order to lead the players of the National Guard and teach the children of the well-to-do. The revolution had encouraged the use of music — the singing of secular hymns and marching with military bands — as aids to propaganda for republicanism and war.[2] This interest had continued under the Empire and Imbert had been chosen by a committee — a common procedure in Dauphiné — because he was versatile. He was guaranteed twelve pupils. Moreover his son had a gift for playing wind instruments and this would strengthen the chamber ensemble of amateurs. La Côte, without being a musical center, was at least not a tuneless dell.

[1] While there, Hector had found a musical friend in the son of a workman named Favre, with whom he played duets. (*308*, Jan. 10, 1904.)

[2] See Cornwell Rogers: "Songs — Colorful Propaganda of the French Revolution." (*857*, 436–44.)

Under Imbert's tuition the Berlioz boy developed his excellent voice and made rapid progress on the flute. In company with his teacher's son, he also tried his hand at other instruments – his clarinet is still extant. Then in 1819 came the mysterious disappearance of young Imbert. The father then chose to leave and was replaced by one Dorant, an Alsatian. He taught Hector the guitar and attempted to do the same for the elder sister Nanci – but to no avail. In the Berlioz family, as we shall see, musical talent went with the male sex. There can be no doubt that Hector had great natural aptitude: his singing soon gave pleasure at social gatherings, and he entertained with complicated virtuoso pieces on the flute such as Drouet's concertos. At neighboring dances he provided music on the guitar. Dorant shortly had to notify Dr. Berlioz that his lessons might just as well stop – the pupil knew as much as the master.[3]

Still, performing ability is by no means uncommon; creative power is another thing. What is worthy of remark at this stage, is not Berlioz' quickness and facility as an executant, but his spontaneous and persistent desire to compose. His eagerness for new music, not always easy to obtain, led him to improvise variations, supply accompaniments to well-known airs, or transform duets into larger scores. Notebooks have been preserved in which his earliest attempts to achieve variety and expressive force testify to his artistic instinct.[4] He wrote at least two original quintets and one sextet, of which we know nothing except perhaps some of their melodies: two are known with certainty to have survived.

Certain biographers, finding that throughout this period there was no piano at La Côte, have concluded that Hector cannot have been properly initiated into the secrets of music. The fact is that there were very few pianos anywhere in the first two decades of the nineteenth century. The spread of the instrument for domestic use came after 1815, as the result

[3] The instrument that Berlioz mastered, and that he rightly compared to a miniature orchestra, was the classic guitar, equipped with three gut and three silver-wound strings. It is played with the thumb and the first three fingers, not with a plectrum. It does not give the metallic percussive sound of the commonplace guitar, from which it differs in other structural respects, and is in fact a virtuoso instrument which, in Berlioz' day, still rivaled the piano as a means of serious musical study. Weber was another guitarist-composer, and Berlioz' contemporary – later his friend – Paganini at one time thought of giving up the violin in favor of a concert career as guitarist. In our day, Segovia and others have revived the art, and the Spanish school has restored the instrument to its role as a guide to harmony. (See *539* and *827*).

[4] (*308*, Feb. 28, 1904 and *522a*.) These sketches incidentally show Berlioz' mastery of the guitar from the performer's point of view, a fact which, taken with his command of the flute, should modify the statement frequently found in books, that Berlioz "never was a performer on any instrument."

of superior technology and many inventions. The first one in Berlioz' vicinage was bought by General de la Valette in 1818 and by that time Dr. Berlioz, like Pascal's father with the geometry book, withheld from his son the instrument that might too soon fix his career. The deprivation must not be regarded with the eyes of a later period, when music and piano had become almost synonymous terms, and when organized music teaching had induced the belief that the art must be learned learnedly through textbooks and printed classics: where but in a class studying Mozart, Haydn, and Beethoven should a symphonic composer in embryo learn to develop his gifts?

To ask this is to put the cart before the horse. When Berlioz was born, Mozart was still considered a dangerous innovator and was little played in France;[5] Haydn was still alive and very incompletely known; Beethoven was a synonym for cacophony and madness, whom even the younger German composers looked on with distrust. The classical tradition, in short, had not yet crystallized. And with respect to musical studies it is Berlioz, actually, who illustrates the "traditional" way to begin. He began, that is, like Haydn, Lully, Handel, Wagner, Elgar, and the great majority of musicians – with only local help and mother wit. Before the age of standardized, purchasable culture, the rule was to be self-taught or ill-taught, at least at first; young Mozart was an exception.[6] Our institutional minds find it hard to believe that if all textbooks and teachers were annihilated, the art of music could be rediscovered and rebuilt from the simplest folk song or reed pipe, but we should occasionally remember that *in the beginning* there was no G clef, no sonata form, not even an alphabet in which to say A B C D.

Apart from the merits and deficiencies of the musical establishment at La Côte, the place offered other musical resources that young Hector turned to profit, and that could not harm his originality. He himself has recounted with much charm what he called his first "musical impression." He was twelve and a half years old and celebrating his First Communion, on the same day as his sister, at the convent where Nanci was

[5] The leading critic of the Empire period, Geoffroy, found *Don Giovanni* puzzling, complained that the music was frequently undramatic, and asked, "Why tack on a symphony to an opera, where there is always too much music anyway?" (Sept. 24, 1805.) (*1336*, 427.)

[6] Mozart, as everyone knows, learned from his father, virtually from babyhood, but age is not the only consideration in teaching; there is the teacher. It has been said of Leopold Mozart, "you may call him a musician if you like" (*314*) implying that Mozart's technical mastery was due to his genius rather than his training.

being educated. There, amid a cluster of young girls in bridal veils, he stood entranced by their voices, by the beauty of the spring day, and by the liturgy. He did not know that the motet sung on that occasion was based on an air from Dalayrac's opera *Nina, or the Woman Crazed with Love*. It was sweet and sad, and possibly appropriate to an act of wholesouled devotion.[7]

The church certainly afforded him many such "impressions," and long before he reached Paris Berlioz was at home in one ancient musical tradition. One thinks at once of Luther or of Thomas Hardy, reared on the hymns and dance tunes of a pious farming people – the purest source of many an artist's devotion to music. It has yet to be shown that the piano music of houses of ill fame, such as the young Brahms was forced to play and listen to, is a better start for a musical career.[8]

After Sunday mass at La Côte, the string players repaired to the doctor's house where, with the aid of Hector and his friends, the company enjoyed a couple of hours of secular music. They played quartets by Haydn, Pleyel, and Catel, in addition to pieces by Berton, Boieldieu, or Martini, arranged or disarranged to suit the occasion. It was under the inspiration of such models and the demands of this chamber ensemble that by himself Hector composed six-part medleys now lost, and several original works for strings, including a flute quintet. This last proved too difficult for the group, but furnished one melody for a later work.

Apparently no one in the boy's entourage was qualified to help him in his creative efforts. His father, it is true, looked at what he wrote and gave his special approval to that flute melody, but these ambitious attempts to compose chamber music must have presented innumerable problems. The boy persevered. On seeing full-size sheets of score paper, he had exclaimed about the wonderful things one ought to be able to write for so many voices, and in his search for knowledge he had unearthed two treatises on harmony – Rameau's, which proved unintelligible since it was not meant for beginners but for theorists; and Catel's, the official treatise of the period – with the aid of which he exercised his ear. But he did not receive much light of reason, for the book was true to its genre as then understood.[9]

Yet this self-teaching was not valueless. The boy practiced the mental

[7] *Mem.*, I, 3.

[8] *1007*, 37 and 72.

[9] Rousseau, less than a century before: "The difficulty lay in meeting with a good master, for with the aid of my Rameau alone, I despaired of ever being able to accomplish anything, and . . . there was nobody in Savoy that understood the principles of harmony." (*1277*, 241.)

hearing of chords and their inversions on that essentially harmonic instrument, the guitar. Whatever mannerisms this may have left in his later handling of harmony, it gave to his musical idiom a character of unsought originality which is in pleasant contrast to the strainings after freedom of those who have to transcend a more common upbringing.

Limitations, as critical purists often remind us, have great virtues. In young Berlioz' circumstances, the virtue was the tremendous spur given to thinking about music, which presented itself to the boy composer in the form of real problems instead of lessons set. Suddenly, by dint of thinking and hearing, he caught the idea of voice-leading: he was learning from direct struggle with his material.[10] The ultimate advantage of self-training is doubtless proportioned to the student's natural endowment. Without prejudging the result in Berlioz' case, we may note in passing the considered opinion of Bernard Van Dieren, himself a great composer, that Berlioz had, "with the sole exception of Mozart, the most stupendous native gifts of the last few centuries." [11]

In any case, this first phase of Berlioz' initiation into music was only half experimental, for he was not cast by fate on a desert island like Robinson Crusoe; or rather, like Crusoe, he had some aid from civilization. On the one hand, he had ready-made models in the printed music of the day (including some sheets from Gluck's *Orpheus*), and on the other, he worked under the natural restraint of the musical circle for which he wrote. What he produced, though no doubt clumsy and full of technical malpractice, could not be wholly without shape or meaning, or he would have lost the regard of his players, all of whom were older than he and ready to ask that he stop wasting their time. It is a fair guess that the quintet of his composition which the group found too difficult was made so not by its incoherence, but by its originality: at a further guess, it was the rhythm that undid them.

When Berlioz at fifteen finally gathered together some pieces of his own and offered them by letter to the Paris publishers, one may say that his folly was only relative.[12] He was following an impulse which his subse-

[10] This way of beginning musical composition has incidentally received the independent approval of a distinguished American composer, Mr. William Schuman, who has used it in his own teaching. (*873*.)

[11] *526*, 23. This natural endowment accounts for his mastery of orchestration. On the principle of those who base imputations on Berlioz' lack of piano training one should argue that because his birthplace did not boast symphonic concerts he could never learn to write properly for orchestra. We know he did, beginning his study of that difficult art, without teacher or textbook, at the *advanced age* of nineteen.

[12] These letters about music are the first autographs of his that have been preserved. (*A.R.* 1–2; *Corresp.*, 63.)

quent history shows to have been sound: he knew that he was meant for music. This being so, if he managed to get some things published, however few or modest, he would have an argument against the career of medicine which his father was choosing for him.

As for the certainty of his own choice, we have warrant for assuming that like Joan of Arc he heard voices – inner voices. The source of melody was in him and it bubbled up with a force independent of his will. We know this not only from the operation of the gift in later years, but also from a remark he drops concerning his earliest tunes. There must have been a good many, for he says: "My youthful essays in composition were of a melancholy cast; almost all my melodies were in the minor mode. I was aware of the defect but struggled against it in vain." [13]

At the time, no doubt, he was not aware that the character of these melodies was in the highest degree unusual: his musical utterance was completely fresh and underivative. In him the talent that makes a man think in sounds took the form not alone of producing melodies, but of creating a new idiom, a new *melos* – an accomplishment which in the history of music has been reserved to very few. Concertgoers familiar with the *Symphonie Fantastique* will remember the theme of the largo introduction of the first movement.[14] This melody dates from Berlioz' twelfth year, and it is enough to show that even then the turn of his musical mind was perfectly distinct. Composed to fit some contemporary verses, the tune resembles nothing in the fashionable romances of the day. Hector had found in his father's library the works of the poet Florian, who is still read for his charming fables, but whose more ambitious and sugary pastorals were the works in Berlioz' hands.[15] He set several episodes, but one especially appealed to him – "*Estelle et Némorin*." The boy identified the heroine with *his* Estelle, and himself even more easily with the love-sick swain. The melody came with its hesitant pauses and plaintive intervals, rising passionately at the conclusion of the first quatrain:

Je vais donc quitter pour jamais
Mon doux pays, ma douce amie,
Loin d'eux je vais trainer ma vie
Dans les pleurs et dans les regrets!

The other boyhood melody that recurs in Berlioz' mature work is the second subject of his *Francs-Juges* overture. Its family likeness with still

[13] *Mem.*, I, 17.

[14] *Min. sc.*, p. 1 b3 – p. 2 b12.

[15] Jean-Pierre-Claris de Florian was Voltaire's grandnephew, a captain of dragoons, a great lover, and a very popular writer in many genres. The piece chosen by young Berlioz, it is worth noting, deals at length with the kinship between the beauty of nature and the art of music.

another, the *idée fixe* of the *Symphonie Fantastique*, has suggested to T. S. Wotton that the three occurred together, two being variants or accompaniments of one of them.[16] If these three melodies did grow from a common germ, we are confronted with an extraordinary fact: the Estelle melody cited above is *sui generis* in the Berliozian manner; the *idée fixe* is its derivative but has something Beethovenian about it; while the *Franc-Juges* second subject makes one readily think of Weber or Schubert.[17] Now Berlioz' first tune needs nothing to account for it except his genius, but the other two require a miracle to explain how a boy aged perhaps fourteen could, in his rural isolation, chime in with the melodic idiom of two composers of whom he had not heard a single note, nor even yet the name. The historian is tempted to see a traveling *Zeitgeist* at work, with ruled paper in his portmanteau.

Fortunately, it is not necessary to find material causes for the products of art. It suffices to point out the elements, their interaction and coincidences. Church music, we saw, was one of these elements in Berlioz' background and contemporary song writing was another.[18] But music lived outdoors as well in Berlioz' corner of old France. The hunts met frequently and observed the ancient and complex ritual of horn calls – a rich source of melody, echoes of which will be found in later Berlioz scores. Again, shepherds in the mountains could be heard singing or piping to their flocks the traditional *ranz des vaches;* [19] countrywomen – and even Mme. Berlioz – sang folk tunes, as did artisans plying their trade. French folk tunes, it is well known, have long intermingled with church music through their use in the sequences or hymns, which unlike the liturgy have rhythm and marked melodiousness. One of the chants

[16] *533*, 10–11.

[17] For example Weber's *Euryanthe* overture and the last movement of Schubert's Symphony No. 6, dated respectively 1823 and 1818.

[18] The choice of twenty-five songs made by Berlioz in the notebook of his eighteenth year shows a preponderance of arias from good comic operas, rather than the more vulgar "parlor songs" of the period.

[19] The *ranz des vaches* is a type of mountain tune, played on the *cor des Alpes* (Alpine horn) and so charged with feeling for those bred to its cadences that under the old regime it had to be prohibited within the royal precincts because the Swiss guard would desert or commit suicide on hearing it. When Berlioz was sixteen, Samuel Butler's grandfather, traveling from Savoy to Italy, noted in his diary: "About two-thirds of the way down Mont Cenis, I saw a sight that illustrated a passage in Virgil. He makes Discord mount upon the roof of the shepherd's cottage where, he says, '*Pastorale canit signum.*' In the very same situation, on the roof of a chalet, did I see a peasant girl stand blowing the cor des Alpes." (*1150*, I, 203.) The adagio of Berlioz' first symphony begins and ends with just such pastoral pipings.

Berlioz particularly liked, the psalm "When Israel came out of Egypt," is thought to be a folk song as old as Charlemagne. Berlioz' fondness for modal effects in his own music is therefore grounded in a double national tradition. And possibly, on his way through Grenoble at the time of the Peninsular Campaign, the boy also heard the Spanish prisoners singing their native songs in the twilight.

In short, an ancient popular art shaped his early taste. Had Berlioz been born in the same place with the same gifts three centuries before, it is clear that he would have been an anonymous maker of tunes while tanning leather or pruning vines – and no less a musician. For the common assumption that popular art is not created by anybody, and that therefore those who do create it are not artists, is on a par with the technological convention that clings to the piano as the musical box par excellence.

True, the force of early memories and natural influences must not be exaggerated, even in the study of a mind as precociously formed as Berlioz'. But it is worth considering a little further the emotion he felt at his First Communion and in similar circumstances. In speaking of the church ceremony, he himself uses the phrase, "my first musical impression," and this may seem like a slip of the pen; for the child had had musical *impressions* and even musical training before that day. The drum he played at school must have had the power to impress, his flute playing also, and since we are speaking of childish feelings, we should not forget the local brass band, conducted in public in the *halles* of La Côte years before Imbert's time by one Bouchmann.[20]

What Berlioz means about the ceremony is that it was his first experience of a complete musical *occasion* – one might almost say his first musical drama. Its impressiveness lay in the use of appropriate music for an important ceremony in man's life. The memory he kept so vividly as to write of it with emotion thirty-five years later reveals an instinctive choice. From the outset he felt that music was one of the necessities of life, and not a decoration or artificial pleasure. Hence there must be fit occasions, of which church ritual was an obvious kind, when music could be enjoyed for itself, though in a setting. This is, properly speaking, the dramatic view of music. It is equidistant from the two more usual views – the first, that music is to comfort man at any time, a gentle accom-

[20] These *halles*, dating from the twelfth century, are the chief architectural monument in Berlioz' birthplace. They consist of a large-scale tiled roofing over the public market, the wooden pillars and crossbeams being remarkable for their Gothic strength and workmanship.

paniment to sociability; this might be called the courtly or monarchical view. The second is that music exists in a prepared vacuum as an object of contemplation, to which one "subscribes" annually as one of The Arts. This is the modern institutional view. Berlioz' instinct was true to the oldest of the three traditions. Young Hector had every chance to follow the bourgeois version of the courtly idea – music for sociability – and to become just another French composer of parlor songs and light opera. Instead, he found music closer to nature than to the parlor, and he obeyed his temperament in following the muse to her native haunts, where religion had already become her ally.

We know from a second autobiographical description that the rural festival of Rogation Days greatly moved the sixteen-year-old youth. The rite, it so happens, was first established in the very region of Berlioz' birth by the fifth-century bishop of Vienne, Mamertus. Designed to end a local blight, the ceremony may have been a revival of pagan practices. It is a fertility prayer and consists of a procession to invoke the aid of the saints. Three days are devoted to the blessing of all the fields of the parish, which is dotted with improvised outdoor altars embellished with flowers. Green boughs simulate an apse, and bright blossoms surround the images and relics laid on the covered trestles. Women and children follow the priest singing the litany of the saints: it is another occasion for popular art ranging from rustic decoration to song.

In alluding to this scene, the mature Berlioz recalls the musical effect it had upon him once when he experienced a violent attack of his lifelong "homesickness." The adolescent boy was in fact near home, lying in the fields reading a novel. But sudden melancholy seized him, filling his soul with the conviction that "home" was elsewhere. He could see the "slight motion of the grain field under the soft morning breeze"; he heard "the call of the quail to their mates, the bunting singing his joy high up on a poplar; while the mountains, struck by the early sun, flashed back the light in tremendous beams. . . ." The youth surrendered himself to nature only too completely. "Life," he adds curiously, "was evidently outside me, far away, very far." [21]

When the grown man recorded his frequent indebtedness to nature for artistic inspiration, it was in the same contradictory mood of isolation and communion. Paralyzing at the moment, the sight of field and mountain was, when recollected, the source of another and a truer life than his own. "I am but a heavy clod, bound to the earth," said he, but "na-

[21] *Mem.*, I, 245.

ture sings." [22] Like Weber and Beethoven, Berlioz associated certain movements in his music with landscape, possibly with a particular sight of a familiar scene.[23] In the *Symphonie Fantastique*, the pastoral adagio is marked "In the fields"; in the second symphony, *Harold in Italy*, the opening is "In the mountains," and still later, in the *Corsair* overture and *Les Troyens*, it is the sea which is, not indeed depicted, but adumbrated. When such an ideal analogy obtains between nature and the work of an artist, we are bound to ask about the characteristic aspect of his native grounds. In Berlioz the answer to this question is especially instructive.

La Côte St. André, that is the actual ridge named after Saint Andrew, is a steep elevation of eight hundred feet stretching east and west, perpendicular to the Rhone valley. The village clings to its northern slope, sheltered from the sirocco. and overlooks the large plain of Bièvre, where Hannibal is said to have encamped before crossing the Alps. From any point of vantage in good season, the foreground shows the green of field, meadow, and vineyard. In summer the soil is dry, yellow like near-by Provence; contours are clear and sharp. The sky is of a deep blue, thick enough to cut. To the south and west, the horizon is bounded by the purple heights of the Cévennes; to the east by a double screen, of hills first, and then of dimmer peaks in the distance which are the Dauphiné Alps: one is looking towards Grenoble and Savoy.

These shapes and colors are as much a lure to discovery as a barrier to vision. On whatever spot they dwell, high or low, the Dauphinois are perforce climbers; though tillers of the soil, they are not stationary beings rooted in an acre, and for Berlioz among them, excursions began young. The family had its livelihood at La Côte but its pleasance at Les Jacques and at Meylan, both near Grenoble, on opposite sides of the great valley through which flow the majestic Isère and the hurtling Drac.

The sights there are of vasty heights, intersecting valleys, piled-up forests, clouds massed and dispersing, saw-tooth edges, pointed ice caps. Color is always changing, from the gray-green poplars lining the river bank and ruffled by sudden gusts, to the bare rock walls that kaleidoscope the effects of sun and sky. The voices, louder than man's, are of mountain torrents, sudden storms, and shifting winds. All these, with the sharp

[22] *Mem.*, I, 246.

[23] Weber: "How the funeral marches, rondos, furiosos, and pastorales whirl and somersault together when Nature is thus unrolled past my eyes!" (*1017*, 95.) Beethoven: "If you wander through the mysterious fir forests, think that it was there that Beethoven often poetised or, as it is called, composed. . . ." (*165*, I, 364.)

dips of temperature or light, constituted for Berlioz one meaning, the earliest and most impressive, of the word nature.

Form, which is common to nature and the arts, can obviously affect the mind of the budding musician as well as of the graphic artist, particularly forms like those just described, whose relations are in perpetual movement – contrapuntal, if the metaphor may be allowed.[24] There is at any rate, a striking correspondence between Alpine scenery and Berlioz' sense of form: sharpness of definition in his melodic line, as well as the protracted, nonrepeating length of that line; brusque interruptions and changes of mood; balance by asymmetry rather than by identity; sensitiveness to coloring and to the simultaneity of contrasting effects (light in one patch while darkness invades the rest); and above all, perhaps, a sense of scale which achieves the heroic and grandiose without giantism.

These unmistakable features are without doubt among the causes of distaste which Berlioz' music inspires in perfectly sincere listeners. They may not word their objections in the language of geology – since Berlioz is not painting scenes but at most following an ingrained type of design – but it is this underlying pattern that displeases, for it does not appear in the same alluring guise to everyone. Berlioz' biographer, M. Boschot, is quite sure, for example, that the Berlioz country has no beauty; the lines, he thinks, "do not compose musically," there is "no eurhythmic." And he contrasts the landscape with Mozart's Salzburg, where everything seems designed to produce harmony.[25]

[24] From the Goncourts' *Journal:* "Hébert [a painter and a compatriot of Berlioz'] told us that his vocation came to him from the brooks of his countryside, those small streams, the width of a table, swiftly flowing yet seeming quite still, green with the waving of many weeds, upon a gray ground studded with yellow pebbles. . . . This was for him the reflection of his ideal and the inspiration of his career." (*1252*, III, 130–1.)

Compare Sibelius: "Yes, when we see those granite rocks [in a pale blue sea] we know why we are able to treat the orchestra as we do." (*1023*, 97.) On the esthetic import of mountains, one may read with profit what Ruskin has to say in *Modern Painters*, as well as the comments of Louis Arnaud Reid (*1113*, 88).

[25] *267*, 4–5. A very representative Frenchman, Georges Duhamel, has expressed the disquiet caused at large by mountain scenery and hence perhaps by the art it inspires: "I love all things in nature, both Alp and Ocean. But it is here in the Ile de France, chilled beneath this threatening, timid, anxious sky, it is here that I have learned and felt all I know. . . . If I try to meditate in a beautiful amphitheater of mountains, my mind is distracted; it stumbles over the transparent-green ice blocks, it crawls along the rocky summits, it sways dizzily on the topmost peaks. No! No! Let us come down again, I beg you, into my close valley of the Ile de France. It is as narrow as a daily task; everything in it is human and reasonable; the very curve of the hills brings back to their source one's gaze and one's mind." (*1074*, n.p.) It may be noted that Debussy comes from the region Duhamel describes. The modern temper

This is perhaps a roundabout way of saying that one prefers Mozart to Berlioz and Salzburg to the French Alps, but it implies rather too much about the inherent qualities of landscape. What matters in the relation of the young artist to the physical world is what he takes from it and what he makes of it, both being gradual and unconscious operations of the sensibility. At the time of his adolescent *Sehnsucht*, certainly, Hector was not pondering esthetic problems. As far as he knew, he was heading the opposite way – toward a medical career. Dr. Berlioz had both reasoned with him and bribed him. If before going to Paris the boy applied himself, with his cousin Alphonse, to a first course of human anatomy, Hector would be given a flute of the latest model, "with all the keys." The boy, overcome by shyness and fear and temptation, yielded and went off in solitude to purge his soul of conflicting emotions.

Then with Alphonse Robert he bent over the life-size plates spread out under the doctor's finger and handled the driest of "dry preparations." But somehow this new knowledge came hard. It gave Hector creepy feelings to recollect or imagine the last struggles of the dying. Alphonse, who was a good violinist and with whom Hector talked music on their rambles together, was entirely at ease, competent, retentive. He was to become a distinguished Paris physician in whose life music was a diversion. Dr. Berlioz hoped for precisely this as a future for his son.

But before Hector could be admitted by the Paris Faculty he had to have his bachelor's degree, and in March, 1821, he went to Grenoble to pass his examinations. His success there speaks well for the thoroughness of his father's teaching in science and the liberal arts. Shortly thereafter, for the Fête-Dieu, Hector gathered his best instrumentists to accompany the cortege. Later that evening they played at his house for twenty guests. There was dancing and jollification in honor of the eldest son who would soon leave the paternal roof. A second son, Prosper, was not quite one year old and his brief musical role was reserved for a later day.

The remainder of the year passed quietly. On the Fifth of May, a date which soon concerned poets and subsequently Berlioz as composer, Napoleon died at Saint Helena. During the summer months at La Côte Hector finished an interesting guitar accompaniment to the romance "*Fleuve du Tage*," the first "composition" of Berlioz' youth that is still extant. In October he got his passport for inland travel, and with Alphonse took the dusty diligence that was to bring him in about a week to the capital.

---

tends to agree with Duhamel – see for example Gide (*1249*, I, 314); but a man of the Renaissance such as Montaigne felt like the later Romanticists. (*1267*, 107.)

3. *Opera and Conservatoire*

November 1821 to July 1827

And ever as he went he swept a lyre
Of unaccustomed shape. . . .
– SHELLEY

THE MUSIC-HAUNTED youth who arrived in Paris early in November 1821 was still within a few weeks of reaching his eighteenth birthday. Though he was not to grow beyond middle height, he had not yet attained his full stature, and his pale face showed only an adolescent fuzz. His hair, always abundant and overhanging a broad forehead, was of a fiery blond color – not red. His eyes were deep-set and of a clear blue that seemed to darken with changing thoughts; his nose prominent and high-bridged; his mouth wide, thin and even-lipped as befitted a flutist, all these features being mobile and expressive, like the energetic bearing of the whole body.[1]

We can guess at his first impressions of the capital from the feelings that the mingled prospects of medicine and music must have aroused. There may also have been a touch of distaste for the city, such as his compatriot Stendhal had felt two decades before. "The surroundings," said that other self-aware Dauphinois, "seemed to me horribly ugly; there were no mountains at all!" [2] And when he opened his window on an inner court there were not even trees. Yet the Paris of 1800 or 1820 was a city of modest size, from which it was easy to escape into the country. Montrouge was recommended to patients in need of fresh air, and as we shall shortly see, game could be snared within walking distance of the student's lodgings.

The capital had in fact lost something of its animation since the days of the great Emperor. The Triumphal Arch was unfinished and looked in

[1] This description combines the common elements given by (a) Berlioz' passport of 1821, (b) the words of d'Ortigue (*185*, 322) and the portrait by Signol of 1831, (c) a passage in Escudier (*189*, 224), written later but referring to the year 1822; and (d) the account given by Ferdinand Hiller in 1879 of his first acquaintance with Berlioz in 1828. (*352*, 557.) In 1854, Peter Cornelius speaks of "dark-eyed Hector," but *dunkeläugig* doubtless denotes the glance rather than the eye. (*478*, 370.) Indirect confirmation, generally overlooked, is to be found in Berlioz' description of his son. (*A.R.*, 268.)

[2] *1146*, 267.

ruins; the "Marseillaise" and most other warlike symbols were prohibited. Not more than three years had passed since Madame de Staël's book on the revolution had made it possible to speak of that event in favorable terms. The restored Bourbons, while committed to a charter of liberties, lived in fear of all new ideas, whether liberal or Bonapartist, or simply modern and alien. And though Louis XVIII had brought back something of the stability and the elegance of the old regime, France was still feared by Europe as the incurable enemy of peace; even French culture was regarded as subversive. From time to time these fears seemed justified by outbursts of the old violence, as when the Duc de Berry was murdered in February 1820. Oddly enough, this incident had musical consequences: the duke was stabbed in the Opera House; the awkward architecture of the lobby interfered with his being helped, and he bled to death while the show went on and crowds milled around. The archbishop made it a condition of administering the last rites that the theater be torn down; and this led to the building of the new house which was to entice Berlioz away from medicine.

On first arriving, Berlioz and his cousin took up quarters in the rue St. Jacques, on the left bank. Hector's allowance of one hundred and twenty francs a month was for the time a generous budget which enabled him to live like what he was – a son of the landed gentry about to enter a profession. But his first practical taste of medicine was not alluring. The lectures interested him, but when his cousin bought a "subject" and Berlioz had to join him at the dissecting room, "the sight of that human charnel house, those scattered limbs, grinning heads and open skulls; the blood-soaked filth through which we walked, and the revolting odor of the place, with its sparrows fighting over bits of lung, and rats gnawing bones in the corners, so filled me with horror that I leaped out of the nearest window and ran breathless all the way home as if pursued by Death and all her train." [3]

His mind in a whirl, he contemplated "a thousand follies" in order to escape his fate. But twenty-four hours' reflection gave his will a chance to overcome his sensibility. He returned to the task and pursued it faithfully for about a year. To fortify himself, he would turn the most repellent of his duties into occasions for humor, singing grotesquely appropriate words from famous airs as he dissected. The macabre humor

[3] *Mem.*, I, 24–5. "The dissecting-rooms of those days," writes the biographer of G. H. Lewes, "were far from inviting, even to the most enthusiastic student, and Lewes found he could not stand the strain; somewhat reluctantly, therefore, he abandoned physic and anatomy." (*1103*, viii.) Dr. Oliver Wendell Holmes records impressions very similar to Berlioz'. (*1179*, 33.)

of the medical student in fact never deserted him and the vocabulary of the morgue remained a part – not the most attractive – of his literary fantasy. But distaste did not keep him from making friends with one of his teachers, Amussat, to whom he remained attached throughout the years to come.[4] The lectures of Gay-Lussac on experimental electricity also held Berlioz' attention and laid the foundation of his lifelong interest in science. For pleasure, too, Berlioz attended courses in literature and history at the Collège de France.

What he reports to his sister Nanci about the historian Lacretelle does not show the lecturer as profound, but it does show the boy's naive appreciation of drama: "The first day he made upon us all, I may say, a painful impression by recounting the assassination of Henry IV; then, after depicting in lively colors the trouble and disorder of the beginning of Louis XIII's reign, he gave me great pleasure by contrasting with it the composure of the Minister Sully in his retreat . . . Called to the court by Louis XIII, this worthy man brought laughter and ridicule upon himself by appearing in old-fashioned dress; whereupon Sully, approaching the throne and looking with disdain at the wretches, said, 'Sire, when your father the King of blessed memory did me the honor of bidding me to court, he took care beforehand to dismiss the buffoons and mountebanks . . .'

"As for the Opera, now, that's another thing. I don't think I can give you the least notion of it. . . ."[5]

The jump from the history lecture to the Opera is a faithful reflection of the writer's mind: Hector had not let many days elapse before pursuing his Muse; he had become a concert- and operagoer. Nor was he alone in flirting with art while destined for a paying profession. The early 1820's was the time when the geniuses whose works were to fill the first half of the nineteenth century in France were finding themselves and one another. They were fighting their families for the right to be artists, and sitting at the feet of a few pioneering elders. At Chateaubriand's country house or at Nodier's Arsenal Library in Paris, those destined to be – in Henley's phrase – the "glorious boys of 1830" were nursing their talents. Within the next few years Berlioz would meet Victor Hugo, Vigny, Balzac, Delacroix, Gérard de Nerval, Sainte-Beuve, and the brothers Deschamps. Meanwhile, like them, he was fulfilling Stendhal's assertion that

[4] Jean Zulema Amussat (1796–1856) was only seven years older than Berlioz but had already acquired fame as a hero of the Napoleonic wars. Specializing in surgery, he contributed over one hundred memoirs on his subject and proved one of the most daring and successful practitioners of the century.

[5] *A.R.*, 5.

the only hope of art lay in the youths who came to Paris from the provinces in their late teens, with their heads full of antiquated ideas but with their convictions unblunted. This notion was part of Stendhal's witty defense of Shakespeare in the name of energy and realism in drama.[6] But having endured twenty-five years of war the older citizens of France had no use for energy and drama. In 1822 they hissed Shakespeare and pelted the English actors who brought his works to Paris. The gifted, ambitious boys like Berlioz were as yet too young and bewildered to make a stand or even to know exactly where they stood. All they knew was that the postwar world offered them little scope, and those who had energy without special talents, as Balzac observed, could only choose dissipation and intrigue.[7]

In music, as it happened, the "antiquated ideas" that young Berlioz harbored were not wholly out of fashion. After Napoleon's restriction on theaters and the Bourbons' shutting down of the *Conservatoire*, music was enjoying a renaissance. Just as Berlioz was setting foot in Paris a moderately progressive musician, François Habeneck, had been made director of the newly built Opera House. Another, Antoine Choron, had opened a school whose performances of sacred music formed the taste of a whole generation; while the elder Garcia was beginning to train a new group of singers of whom we shall hear further. Instrumental music, it is true, was less favored, caught as it was in the transition between the private patron's orchestra and the establishment of regular public institutions. But chamber music was rather more readily available, and at several smaller theaters – the Odéon, the Gymnase, and the Nouveautés – French comic opera was trying to resist the invasion of the Italians and their precocious maestro, Gioacchino Rossini.

Both because of the brightness and verve of his music, and because of the zeal of many Frenchmen for importations, Rossini soon became a Parisian idol. Literary men took him up and although his lively scores gaily ignored the principles of dramatic truth, he was hailed as the Raphael and Michelangelo of music – that is, as a lyrical and a dramatic genius combined. As always happens in the revolutions of opera, past beauties seemed feeble when compared with the latest "effects." Rossini enchanted the ear with his famous *crescendo*,[8] his sparkling melodies and bubbling

[6] In *Racine et Shakespeare*, which appeared in two parts, 1823 and 1825. (*1054*.)

[7] *1236*, II, 212.

[8] Two measures in the tonic repeated in the dominant, the entire passage done thrice over, louder each time. Apthorp has pointed out that Beethoven did it first in *Leonore No. 1*. Rossini used the effect without stint. (*695*, 100 and *n*.)

violin triplets. The truth was that a new clientele – indeed a new social class – was learning music, and learning it at the best of public schools, the one that relies on visual aid.

This "school" in two senses did not find favor with young Berlioz, whose taste in its broad outlines was already set. All he knew impelled him in the opposite direction, toward an older master – Gluck. For what Berlioz had heard and played and pondered at La Côte came from the French disciples and imitators of Gluck, and Berlioz' background of dramatic thought was classical and religious. To him the Italian plots lacked true musical "occasions," and mishandled those afforded. The few pages of Gluck's *Orpheus* that he had conned at home had not ceased to stir him, nor had he forgotten the article he had read somewhere on the composer's life, on his orchestral effects, on the grandeur of the tragic poems he had composed.

Fortunately the French repertory did not succumb to the new Italian opera until about 1830, so that in these important years for Berlioz he was able to hear and to study at repeated performances, not only Gluck's *Armide, Orphée, Alceste,* and the two *Iphigénies,* but also the works of the Gluckist school – Salieri's *Danaides,* Catel's *Bayadères,* Méhul's *Stratonice,* Sacchini's *Oedipe,* Berton's *Virginie,* Kreutzer's *Abel,* and what is more: Spontini's *Vestale.*

Certain features made these spectacles particularly impressive. The Opera and Opera-Comique numbered a few singers of unusual merit: Mme. Branchu, short and no longer young, but a great artist noted for her dramatic delivery and her mastery of dynamics; the baritone Martin; Dérivis with his powerful bass, and Adolphe Nourrit, a young tenor whom Garcia had trained and whom Berlioz was later to befriend. Staging moreover was improving. Daguerre's diorama, a partly transparent painting for use with special lighting, encouraged the imaginative treatment of scenery, in place of the stiff eighteenth-century sets with their symmetrical balance and fixed vanishing point. About the same time gas lighting replaced the Argand lamps, the house was darkened during the show, and the practice established of lowering the curtain between the acts so as to preserve the unity of mood while shifting scenes.

For Berlioz, of course, the opera meant something more than a show and a pleasant deceit: it meant the revelation of the orchestra as an instrument of dramatic music. This power was first disclosed full strength to him at a performance of *Iphigeneia in Tauris,* probably late in November 1821. Having just told his sister that he could give her no notion of what opera was like, he goes on:

Short of fainting, I could not feel a stronger impression than that of seeing Gluck's masterpiece *Iphigeneia*. Imagine first of all an orchestra of eighty musicians who perform with such perfect ensemble that one would think it was a single instrument. The opera begins. You see a vast plain (I tell you, the illusion is complete) and farther still, the sea. The orchestra presages a storm; black clouds descend on the plain – the theatre is only lighted by flashes, in the most telling and truthful fashion. There is a moment of silence; no actor on the stage; the orchestra is dully murmuring; it seems as if you heard the soughing of the wind (you know how in winter you can hear it speak!). Gradually, the excitement grows, the storm bursts, and you discover Orestes and Pylades in chains, led by the barbarians of Tauris who sing a fearful chorus: "We must have blood to atone for our crimes." It's about the limit of what one can stand: I defy the hardest-hearted being to stay unmoved at the sight of these two wretches longing for death as their greatest hope . . . and when it turns out that it is Orestes' sister Iphigeneia, the priestess of Diana, who must sacrifice her brother, why, don't you see, it is ghastly.

I can't describe to you even approximately the feeling of horror one feels when Orestes, overwhelmed, falls down and says, "Calm is restored to my breast." Half asleep, he sees the shade of his mother whom he has killed; she is hovering about with other shades holding infernal torches above his head. And the orchestra! It's all in the orchestra. If you could only hear how all the situations are depicted in it, especially when Orestes is calm: there is a long hold in the violins suggestive of tranquillity – very *piano;* but below, the basses murmur like the remorse which, despite his calm, throbs in the heart of the parricide.

But I forget myself. Farewell, dear sister; forgive me these digressions and be assured that your brother loves you with all his heart. Give my love to everybody at home.[9]

Dated two days after Berlioz' eighteenth birthday, this letter doubtless conceals from both sender and recipient the inevitable decision to give up medicine for music. At the same time it reveals the intentness with which the aspiring composer spied out the relation between dramatic substance and orchestral effects. Hector soon found out that the library of the Royal Conservatoire was open to the public, and he used it before and after each performance to analyze the scores with his special purpose in view. He copied out passages, compared editions, in short mastered his subject. That is how he came to lead, in behalf of Gluck and his other favorites, a kind of counter-claque actuated by purely artistic motives. As he gained self-confidence he appointed himself the censor of musical morals: the anecdotes are often quoted of his standing up in the pit and shouting, "It's a piccolo, you wretch!" when the part was played on the

[9] *A.R.*, 5–7.

ordinary flute; and again, "Where are the trombones?" when they missed their entrance. His battle against arrangers and perverters of musical truth had begun.

Berlioz thus opened his public career very young, having himself provoked the first skirmishes. Yet however it may look to us, the actions of this barely citified mountaineer were neither unique nor meaningless. Not only his friends – young men of good family – but other artists and even casual strangers responded to these protests against routine or convention.[10] As an aspect of Hector's inner life, the matter is equally clear. He felt a strong daemonic impulse – his genius – which he tried to repress for reasons of conscience: his family trusted him to pursue an established career. But that family had also bred in the boy a shyness which only an effort of will could conquer. Until his personality was formed, the struggle of these elements was doubtless an ungainly sight; and balance was achieved rather slowly because, unlike the ordinary youth, he was not exclusively concerned with himself but with his art. As Bernard Shaw said of his own similar predicament: "I had not then tuned the Shavian note to any sort of harmony, and I have no doubt [others] found me discordant, crudely self-assertive, and insufferable." [11]

None the less the young men whom Berlioz gathered together into a Gluckist party all felt his personal charm and the strength that comes of knowledge allied to conviction. The mild poet Humbert Ferrand became his earliest confidant; the aristocratic Augustin de Pons, the politically influential Albert du Boys, the devout musician d'Ortigue; another poet (who knew English) Thomas Gounet, and another cousin, Auguste Berlioz, soon formed a loyal band. They shared their leisure hours in discussion at one another's rooms or at "choice dinners" when they were in funds. Three of the group remained Hector's friends for life.

Meantime, Berlioz also led the social life of a well-connected youth. Friendly families in Paris – as well as the Marmion uncle who moved freely from his regimental base at Beauvais – saw to it that Hector frequented the fashionable houses and was invited to dances. "You may think," wrote Berlioz to his sister, "that these affairs are very different from ours – not at all. The only difference is that instead of having sixteen people there are sixty, and the floor is so crowded that . . . one must always study where to put down one's feet. Dress is uniformly white for

[10] Berlioz' lively account of forming a friendship with a young engineer on the strength of just such a piece of musical fanaticism (*Mem.*, I, 82) was taken to be an exaggeration, if not worse, until a contemporary letter was found a hundred years after, confirming all the particulars. (*235*, II, 160.)

[11] *1207*, 40–1.

the ladies and black for the men. The orchestra! You probably imagine it superb. Well! it does not begin to compare with ours. Just think: two violins and a flageolet. Isn't it pitiable? two violins and a flageolet, and those three wretches could only play contredanses taken from the ballets I've heard at the opera: you can imagine the contrast. . . .

"The next day we went to hear Martin in *Azémia* and *Les voitures versées*. That was my compensation. I absorbed all that music. I thought of you, sister, and of the pleasure you would have hearing all this . . . I tell you I would have thrown my arms around Dalayrac had I been near his statue when I heard the air – for which one cannot find a fit adjective – 'Thy love, oh sweetest daughter.' I felt nearly the same impression as when at the Opera I heard in *Stratonice* 'Pour your grief into your father's bosom.' But I cannot undertake to describe such music to you." [12]

Just one year after the beginning of his medical studies, politics for the first and last time served Berlioz' interests: the medical school was shut down. For ten months governmental repression had gone on, liberal plots were discovered everywhere, and purges finally reached the seats of learning. Lecturers were dismissed regardless of their subject matter: the brilliant young historian Guizot lost his chair – but the brilliant young musician found his freedom. When anatomy resumed its rights after three months, Berlioz was dissecting chords, not corpses.

At the library of the Conservatoire he had met a student slightly older than himself named Gerono, of whom little is to be said except that he was the go-between who brought together Berlioz and his teacher Lesueur.[13] It is likely that even before the end of his medical studies, Berlioz had begun to set to music a poem by the popular Millevoye, "The Arab Mourning His Steed." When he decided to approach Lesueur, he submitted this work, adding to it – a characteristic touch – another piece in the form of a three-part canon: professors, he doubtless surmised, like to look on technique bare.

Lesueur's report was encouraging and, in retrospect, very farsighted:

[12] *A.R.*, 8–10. *Azémia ou les Sauvages*, by Nicolas Dalayrac (1753–1809) – the same composer whose air had charmed Berlioz at his First Communion – had a libretto vaguely patterned after the plot of Shakespeare's *Tempest*. The other two works are by Boieldieu (1775–1834) and Méhul (1763–1817) respectively.

[13] Hyacinthe Gerono (1797–1868) entered the Conservatoire in 1813 as a student of the flute and had Lesueur as a teacher of composition. The few songs Gerono left were published under his first name only.

"There is a good deal of warmth and dramatic movement in your cantata but you do not yet know how to write, and besides, your harmony is so full of faults that it would be useless to point them out. Gerono will do you the kindness to inform you of our principles of harmony, and as soon as you know them well enough to follow me, you can be one of my pupils." [14] Either Gerono was a genius at teaching or else it was the pupil who had the genius to learn, for in a few weeks Berlioz had sufficiently mastered "our principles" (derived from Rameau) to sit at the professor's feet.

Jean-François Lesueur, then a man of sixty-two, was with Cherubini the most celebrated teacher-composer in France. A grandnephew of Louis XIV's court painter, Lesueur began at sixteen the career of church musician. He rose to the headship of the chapel of Notre Dame before the revolution, and there put into effect his original views about sacred music. The controversy that ensued led him to write two essays, after which he retired from his post to a country retreat, but not for long. During the revolution he returned to active life as a composer of operas, one of which was highly successful and earned him official rewards. He took part in the foundation and direction of the Conservatoire in 1795, became Bonaparte's First Chapel-Master, and achieved further success with his grand opera, *Les Bardes,* in the year of the coronation. His eminence saving him from reprisals by the Bourbons, he was reinstalled as teacher of composition in the Conservatoire from 1818 to his death in 1837.

Lesueur and Berlioz soon found they had much in common and became full of respect and affection for each other. They admired Napoleon and revered Virgil; they shared a natural bent for dramatic music and for religious subjects, as well as a fondness for folk melodies; both had a detailed knowledge of Gluck's scores. Lesueur was an inquiring mind who had studied plain song and developed a theory of ancient Greek music which for a time his pupil adhered to. What is more, in both men a passion for music was not incompatible with an intellectual interest in history, modern literature, and classical scholarship. Lesueur moreover knew at first hand the difficulties of the composer's career in a centralized state, and he was generous enough to want to help the young. Finally, his artistic integrity and firm character also found echoes in the soul of his new pupil.

Of this new connection the Berlioz family at La Côte did not hear for some time. The dutiful son had been sending home books and knick-

[14] *Mem.*, I, 29–30.

knacks as ordered, and in his letters had only once expressed to his father a desire to devote himself entirely to composition. Dr. Berlioz answered with kind but strong arguments about the trials and uncertainties of success in the arts. Hector had therefore kept up his attendance at medical lectures, while working steadily at composition. What time was left, Hector spent at the library reading scores and at various theaters hearing them. And as a by-product, musical partisanship was plunging him into a third career, that of musical journalism.

It was the age of faith in the printed sheet so intimately described in Balzac's *Lost Illusions.* One of those sheets, *Le Corsaire,* was a daily devoted to all the arts, including ladies' fashions, yet with a special interest in music. This was shown in its masthead by an allegorical female head garnished with violins and flutes. Music was then deemed a popular topic for newspapers because it combined personal news and lively feelings. Accordingly in the *Corsaire* for August 12, 1823, Berlioz' first essay appeared. He had been aroused by an anonymous dialogue in which the Italian opera was praised at the expense of the French. The admirer of Gluck in this tendentious conversation was called *Crifort,* which is to say "Loud Noise," whereas the champion of Rossini took pride, as the custom was, in the name of *Dilettante* – so to say: "true connoisseur." Berlioz' anonymous victim had shown his amateurishness by imputing "love of noise" to his opponents – the eternal and unprovable complaint of those who dislike a particular musical idiom. So "Hector B.," as he signed his reply, carried war into the enemy camp by exaggerating Rossini's faults and restating Gluck's methods and intentions.

The readers of the *Corsaire* could not suspect that this confident champion of Gluck was a provincial fellow of nineteen who had been in Paris barely a year and a half, and to whom before that date all opera scores were but a distant mirage. The modern reader is more astonished still. For here is the full-fledged Berlioz, his musical creed already clear in outline: though angered, he is punctilious; he shows concern about the minutest details of performance and the grading of sonorities, even to the placing of instruments in the hall; he discusses style in orchestration; expresses alarm at the rise in concert pitch and its effect on the singers; deplores the instrumental crudities of the Italians, which ruin voice production or obscure the melodic line; finally, he argues the possibility of creating drama in music by treating the orchestra as a collection of independent groups of timbres.

Lesueur's teaching can hardly be credited with so much influence so soon, unless we assume, as we should, a pre-existing harmony of views in the disciple. The article winds up with an aggressive confession of faith, backed up by cool self-assurance: "Rossini's operas taken together can hardly bear comparison with one line of Gluck's recitative, three measures of melody by Mozart or Spontini, or the least chorus by Lesueur . . . I have read the scores and looked into the matter before passing judgment." If in our mind's eye we see the callow youth, this effusion has a flavor of comedy; but Berlioz's already mature prose commands our respect. Precise, witty, and well-paced, the somewhat stilted period style hides the faults of overinsistence and naivete.

Berlioz was aware of inexperience in everything but his feelings. It therefore struck him as logical to gain experience and express those feelings in one operation which would test his creative powers. In short he must find a librettist who would give him something to compose, and afterwards, a chance to hear the result. This empirical attitude was in keeping with his upbringing, his character, and his epoch. There were, it is true, other motives to the search for a libretto. Like his post-Napoleonic contemporaries he believed not only in art but in glory, and all agreed with Milton that love of fame was a noble failing.

Besides, Hector knew he must convince his father that music was his career. The son therefore wrote to the composer Kreutzer a sincere but laughable letter of extravagant praise on first hearing the opera *Abel's Death*.[15] This bid for an interview having remained fruitless, Berlioz next wrote to Andrieux (an academician whose lectures he was attending) asking him point-blank for a libretto. His curiosity aroused, the old gentleman came in person to deliver his answer and found the would-be composer in chambers, cooking his lunch. The conversation, flavored with the odor of fried onion, brought out the fact that Andrieux was a Gluckist, though not so fanatical as Berlioz. The elder teased his host and ultimately confessed that he felt too old to write an operatic love story. At his age he should be thinking rather of a requiem mass. Undaunted, Hector approached Gerono and, recalling his old love for Florian's *Estelle*, persuaded his friend to base a plot on the romance. The thing was done and the music written — "as ridiculous a score," said Berlioz later, "as the text and rimes of Gerono." [16] At the same time or soon after, Berlioz himself fashioned and composed a series of scenes based on a current drama, *Beverley, or the Gambler*.[17]

[15] *Corresp.*, 63. [16] *Mem.*, I, 35.

[17] This was a melodrama by Bernard Saurin (1706–1781), adapted from *The Gamester* by Edward Moore and Garrick, which in 1753 had proved to London that tragedy could be written in prose. The French version (1768) was in free verse and it attracted Berlioz as being true to modern life.

Berlioz finally had recourse to his master – or at least to his master's principles, which suggested a sacred text, presumably from the Vulgate, but chosen with an eye to situations at once dramatic and musical. Berlioz chose *The Crossing of the Red Sea*, wrote his own words, which he then set as effectively as he could.[18] Lesueur looked at the score and thought well enough of it to arrange for its performance. All was made ready for December 28, 1823 – virtually a celebration of Berlioz' twentieth birthday. One hundred players and as many voices were to gather in the Church of St. Roch, and Valentino, of the Opera, would conduct.

Hector at once notified his father, but soon had to admit discomfiture: the performers, unpaid, had not shown up in expected numbers at the first rehearsal, and those that came were discouraged by the mistakes in the parts copied out by amateur hands. Valentino did his best to rally them, but the difficulties proved too great. As the conductor left, he assured the composer of his help at the first opportunity. Berlioz had learned a lesson about the military character of musical leadership: morale and materiel must be in perfect order for effective mass action.

Meantime, Berlioz had published a second article in *Le Corsaire* – again on the dilettanti – in which a new theme emerges: his dislike of imitative music. He inquires why the admirers of Italian opera "can hardly breathe from sheer emotion" at the pathos of Rossini's *Gazza ladra*, and yet are unmoved by Gluck. Berlioz answers with irony: "Because they sing so badly at the Opera, content as they are to be dramatic and sometimes sublime. How ridiculous is Madame Branchu in the role of Clytemnestra! Why, she does not add a single note to her part, not even in the aria of Jove and his thunderbolts, though on the first verse a 12-note roulade would admirably depict lightning and on the second a little *martellato* ['hammered' notes] would prettily stress the crushing of the Greeks. On the words 'burning ships' a chromatic scale of trills would imitate the whirling flames: – those are the things the *dilettanti* expect from singers, and as long as Madame Branchu will confine herself to making her audience shudder and weep, the *dilettanti* will say she howls. . . . As for the orchestra at the opera, it is fashionable to call it noisy, without inquiring whether it is the composer's or the performers'

[18] Delacroix in April 1824: "That would be a fine subject: 'The Crossing of the Red Sea.' " (*182*, I, 90.) It is not quite enough to say that Delacroix, Berlioz, Hugo, Chateaubriand and other artists of the Romantic Period "went in for Orientalism." What must be added is that the reality of Egypt and the Near East was to them a discovery barely twenty years old – since the return of the scientists attached to Bonaparte's Egyptian expedition, the deciphering of the Rosetta Stone, and the use of Egyptian art in the Empire style.

fault. . . . The objectors never read the scores – for a very good reason which is easily surmised . . ." [19]

The day after this blast, Berlioz was reaping the fruit of his continued labors as a medical student: he had passed the preliminary degree of Bachelor in the Physical Sciences, and so informed his father. But his real reward came later that spring, when the Opera revived *Orpheus.*

In June 1824, after two and a half years of music and medicine in Paris, Berlioz went back to La Côte for a summer visit. He undoubtedly hoped to clear up his ambiguous situation, but from the first it was plain that the word music must not be breathed in Mme. Berlioz' presence. She was sure that all players and artists were doomed to perdition. If his father could be brought to give his consent, his mother would have to be disregarded. Strengthened by Lesueur's encouragement, Hector bent his efforts on persuading the doctor, but he seems to have underestimated his parent's perplexity as well as misjudged his replies. For after a month of conversations, Hector wrote to his teacher that Dr. Berlioz was reconciled to the idea of a musical career. He also wrote to his closest friend, Humbert Ferrand, with whom he had planned an opera, that all was going well and "Father entirely sides with me." [20]

The fact is that Dr. Berlioz was still undecided, paternally as well as maritally ill-at-ease. He wanted to preserve his happy relation with an affectionate and so far dutiful child. And Lesueur's uncommon interest in the boy weighed with him no less than his own knowledge of Mme. Berlioz' prejudiced views. Besides, Dr. Berlioz was himself interested in music and when Hector imparted some of Lesueur's theories about ancient Greek harmony, he was captivated: father and son talked about music a great deal of the time.

Nor had Hector given up working. He had brought with him his oratorio on the crossing of the Red Sea and fragments of a mass begun during the last six months. As was to be his lifelong habit, he composed as fast as he could in the flush of inspiration, then revised and put the work aside. After a space, he took it up again and kept on revising.[21] Now in July 1824, in an affectionate letter to Lesueur, he reports that upon rereading the *Credo* and *Kyrie* of his mass, he feels quite frigid about them, so he will turn to the oratorio. Parts of it seem "terribly

[19] *1379*, Jan. 11, 1824.
[20] *L.I.*, 4.
[21] Balzac to his mother in 1832: "I'm either at my writing . . . or thinking about it." (*162*, 86.)

messy" but he goes to work in hopes of getting an improved score performed in the fall.[22]

Hector's long talks with his father at last aroused the curiosity not of Mme. Berlioz, but of her eldest daughter, Nanci, who as the keeper of a diary felt certain obligations to research. Her confiding brother disclosed the great secret, telling her apparently that all was settled to his satisfaction. Knowing her mother and seeing Hector in a new guise, Nanci was alarmed. "He is unshakable." Soon everyone felt it. Hector, who had been so full of verve earlier in the vacation, and told such good stories that "even Mother laughed," was now a center of emotional tension. Adèle, aged ten, and Prosper, the unruly boy of four, would still trail after the big brother from Paris who knew so many tricks to amuse them, but finally the storm burst. By mistake or not, Nanci revealed to her mother the young man's purpose and his belief in the doctor's acquiescence. Mme. Berlioz made a scene but to everyone's surprise, doubtless including his own, Hector remained calm, polite, indifferent. Meals were a trial, though Dr. Berlioz drew on a reserve of gaiety to cover up the rift. Nanci records in her diary: "My brother is a great source of grief to me. . . . If only he would show a little sensibility, if only he would stay with us a little longer. But he is as inflexible as a rock." And the day after his departure, "he has left. . . . We have all been weeping, Mamma especially." [23]

Not yet twenty-one, Hector had been forced into declaring his independence, not without inner strain. "Showing a little sensibility" was what he would have preferred, but he had been given no chance compatible with his convictions. His father was still a bulwark, though understandably not so "unshakable" as himself. His mother now opposed both and counteracted the doctor's good will. Nanci, unmusical and somewhat obtuse, could only utter pleas for family harmony. It was the first skirmish in a protracted struggle.

Despite this sudden hardening, Berlioz' self-confidence was not blind. He had heard enough from Lesueur to guess how steep must be the artist's path in a country where success depends on personal favors, official appointments, and political considerations. Even before, in his letter to Kreutzer, the nineteen-year-old boy had had a glimpse of the nature of public opinion: "And what will happen to me, if some day my music expresses passion: they will not understand me since they do not [honor] . . . you." [24] Moreover, he knew how much hard study lay ahead, which made him all the more impatient to begin.

[22] *Corresp.*, 358–60. [23] *267*, 140–1. [24] *Corresp.*, 64.

Yet he was also conscious of some advantages, and these he shortly had to turn into arguments. For he had no sooner returned to Paris in August than the blow fell: a letter came from La Côte, the result of what would nowadays be condemned as a parental crime: Hector had left with his parents a note addressed to his cousin Alphonse; someone, probably Mme. Berlioz, had opened it and read of Hector's set purpose, with an account of the family discussions. The doctor seems to have felt misrepresented and he now scolded. Hector's reply was a model of respectful wisdom and pointed reasoning; as so often happens in real life, the son sounds old enough to be his father's father.[25] After begging that Dr. Berlioz will take back the "cruel remarks" contained in his letter, and saying that he cannot think the message to Alphonse can be interpreted as unkind or disrespectful to his own parents, Hector meets the issue:

> I am voluntarily driven towards a magnificent career (no other epithet can be applied to the career of an artist) and I am not in the least heading for perdition. For I believe I shall succeed. Yes, I really believe it. There is no longer any point in being modest about this, since I have to prove to you that I am not drifting haphazard. I think, indeed I am convinced, that I will attain distinction in music; everything points that way from outside, and from within the voice of nature is stronger than the most rigorous dictates of reason. I have every conceivable chance in my favor if you will back me. I begin young, and I shan't have to give lessons, like so many others, to support myself. I have some solid knowledge and the rudiments of other branches, enough to be able to go deeper into them. And certainly I have experienced passions sufficiently strong not to mistake their accents whenever it will be necessary for me to depict or give them voice.[26]

After this remarkable declaration, he goes on to calculate the income he may some day expect, so as to pacify at once the well-meaning provincials. It is a heart-rending calculation that Balzac would find worthy of his *Eugénie Grandet*. ". . . Make it but a mere twelve hundred francs; that's enough for me even though music should never bring me anything. In fine, I want to make a name for myself, I want to leave on this earth some trace of my existence, which is by no means an ignoble feeling — and so strongly do I feel it that I would rather be Gluck or Méhul dead than what I am in the bloom of manhood." [27]

Dr. Berlioz had objected, with the speciousness of anger, that Hector was not learned in the "accessory branches" needed for music — the

[25] Compare Mozart's calming down of *his* father after the break with the Archbishop of Salzburg (*219*, 1088–90)

[26] *A.R.*, 16–7.

[27] *A.R.*, 17.

ancient languages and mathematics. This explains the boy's reference to his present stock of knowledge, and he takes pains to make the matter clear: "As M. Lesueur was telling me again yesterday [no doubt in a consultation upon the doctor's tirade] . . . he began by being a great musician before being a learned musician. He acquired his general information at college like everybody else, and only later saw how it bore on music . . . If I haven't gone in for Greek, Hebrew, and mathematics, I assure you it won't lessen my chances as a musician.

"This is the way I think, the way I am, and nothing in the world will change me. You could cut off my allowance or force me to leave Paris, but I do not believe you will want to make me lose the best years of my life . . . Farewell, dear Papa; read my letter over and do not ascribe it to some excited impulse. I have perhaps never been so calm. I kiss you as well as Mamma and my sisters. Your respectful and tender son.—H. Berlioz." [28]

"Voluntarily driven" at the beginning of the letter is a phrase worth noting, not only for its accuracy as regards Berlioz' inner balance of will and reason, but because it is a spontaneous expression of the true Romantic life, which was then the only acceptable course for youths of spirit. Four months before, Delacroix, aged twenty-six, had written in his journal: "Glory is no empty word to me. The sound of praise intoxicates with a true happiness. Nature has put this feeling in all hearts. Those who give up glory, or who cannot obtain it, do well to exhibit for this vapor, this ambrosia of great souls, a disdain which they term philosophic." [29]

That same spring Byron had died at Missolonghi. Later in 1824, the poet-statesman Chateaubriand was dismissed from office, a sacrifice to prudence as against glory. To his young admirers, who resented the indignity, each of these events was a reminder of how life should be spent—in self-dedication to a cause and in the pursuit of glory.[30] Difficulty or even defeat was no deterrent but rather the final test of devotion. Hence Balzac's youthful heroes write treatises on the will and Stendhal's Julien Sorel rises by the deliberative study of passion. The driving impulse

[28] *A.R.*, 18.

[29] *182*, I, 88. In a later explanation of his conduct to his uncle Victor Berlioz, Advocate-General at Grenoble, Hector also shows his sense of the artist's social mission: "It seems to me moreover that through the arts one can pay to society the tribute it expects from us. This branch of human knowledge, and music especially, elevates the soul by giving it greater sensibility and this quality being the source of the generous emotions, the cultivation of the fine arts cannot deprave man." (*81*, 399.)

[30] Victor Hugo expressed the feelings of the new generation in his "Ode to Chateaubriand," written immediately after the event.

must be worthy and sustained, and the acceptance of death (as Berlioz spontaneously said) must go with it.

While Berlioz tried to make his family share these views, other young artists were combating the same stand-pat, play-safe policy of their own parents and governors, thus pursuing the age-old struggle between society and the creative mind. In the process the Philistine was beginning to sit for his portrait: "A philosopher is a citizen who eats four meals a day as agreeably as possible, and for whom glory, virtue, and nobility of feeling are to be regarded only insofar as they interfere neither with these four indispensable functions nor with one's other bodily comforts." [31] The death of Louis XVIII in that same year 1824 recalled, not the life of glory but, as Delacroix said, "philosophy." Politically, after a brief hope, it meant only a change for the worse. Charles X, who succeeded, proved to be reaction incarnate, and his brother in dying had prophesied quite truly that his heir would not end his days in the royal bedstead. The repressive measures that ensued were in fact a signal for everyone with a spark of independence to start struggling for liberation – liberation from pettiness as much as from oppression.

It took six years in politics, but in culture the battle was joined in this year of change of kings. The French Academy had reached the word "Romanticism" while revising the Dictionary, and appointed one Auger to report on it. Primed by a decision taken in high political circles, he declared war on "the new schism, Romanticism," and attacked the "barbaric poetry," which some were trying to establish "in violation of literary orthodoxy." [32] This was aimed at Nodier's coterie of young poets, at Stendhal's praise of Shakespeare, at all those who admired Madame de Stael's book on German literature or the works of Chateaubriand. But as yet the new forces were scattered. By a paradox, the Romanticists were still royalist in politics, while the political liberals championed academic art. Both groups, however, numbered Bonapartists, and Chateaubriand himself could call the Restoration a regime bottomed on tired revolutionaries, whom he himself served for lack of any real alternative.

Though Berlioz had family ties with the "Ultras" who triumphed under Charles X, he was an admirer of the Emperor, and was already as detached from religious orthodoxy as his own father, the Voltairian doctor.[33]

[31] Delacroix (*182*, I, 89).

[32] His speech is largely reproduced in *1124*, 79 ff., and ably discussed in *1054*, I, cx.

[33] M. Boschot's insistence on Berlioz' "family of Ultras" is an oversimplification, designed, no doubt, to make Hector seem excessively "rebellious" and "romantic."

With all generous young men, Hector felt that the poetry of life lay elsewhere than in politics or the church;[34] and if the chance to do great deeds was denied by historical circumstances, art could at least embody the spirit of greatness. This feeling also made him impatient with the amusements of society which he occasionally had to endure. He and his fellow music student, Louis Schloesser, would escort Lesueur's three daughters to balls, would dance the first cotillion (waltzing was still deemed rather immoral) and since there were usually more gentlemen than needed – bless the dowry system! – would retire to a corner out of the noise and confusion. On Friday nights there was a standing invitation to the house of friends who prided themselves on their musical evenings. But when Hector went it was to drink tea, which he had learned to like and which "helped him to swallow their music."[35]

His real business in Paris, his reason for being alive, was to compose. He accordingly was working again at the score of his Mass. Much of what he wrote was in the style of Lesueur, as was natural, since the two men stood in the relation of master and apprentice for long hours every day. But Hector also read scores at the Conservatoire (despite a brush with the Director, Cherubini, over library rules), and by study was strengthening earlier ideas of his own. We know that while still at La Côte, he had read and reread Chateaubriand's *Genius of Christianity*. This book, which modern critics mention all too casually as "a romantic account of religion" was in fact a little treatise on esthetics, and one reason Berlioz understood Lesueur's principles of dramatic and religious music so readily was that he had been prepared for them by a far greater master.

In Chateaubriand, Hector had found a vindication of the arts based on their religious uses, and a vindication of Christianity based on its awareness of human passions. When Chateaubriand compared the great poets from Dante and Virgil to Milton and Voltaire, Berlioz could gain insight into the character of great lovers, from his cherished Dido to his other favorites, Paul and Virginia; he could even find a description of feelings that he may have thought exclusively his own – the vague longings of young manhood.[36]

In a later chapter, moreover, Chateaubriand said pregnant things about music, which confirmed Hector's emotional response to the psalm *When*

[34] *I.e.*, the "Red" and the "Black" of Julien Sorel's dilemma in Stendhal's novel.

[35] *A.R.*, 14.

[36] See below, Chapter 6, the allusion to these feelings in Berlioz' own account of the *Symphonie Fantastique*, first movement.

Israel, and described the requiem mass as a dramatic masterpiece. Citing Pergolesi's *Stabat Mater,* the critic pointed out that the recall of musical themes to suggest man's return to grief was "a perfect imitation of nature." Again, a sentence such as: "The reasoning spirit, by destroying the imagination, undermines the bases of the fine arts" was to a lively mind a complete lesson in Romanticism, for what it implied was the Gothic as against the neo-classic principle in poetry and the other arts. Even Chateaubriand's treatment of bells contained a social philosophy for musicians: "It is, on the face of it, a rather marvellous thing to have found a way, by the single stroke of a hammer, to cause a thousand hearts to feel the same sentiment in a given minute. . . . Besides, considered as harmony, bells indubitably possess a beauty of the first order, which artists call *grandeur.* The noise of thunder is sublime in the same way, by its greatness, and it is thus with the winds, seas, volcanoes, cataracts, and the voice of a whole people." [37]

Read by a future creator of large works for national occasions, these remarks were not lost. One proof that Berlioz' mind was impregnated with Chateaubriand's ideas is that under the pressure of necessity, Hector imagined the sympathy to be mutual. He had never met the noble poet, recently Minister of Foreign Affairs, but he knew a number of young men in his entourage, and through them knew of Chateaubriand's generous attitude toward young artists. Rather than face the master, Berlioz wrote him a letter asking for nothing less than a loan to permit the production of his first finished work, now known as the *Mass of 1825.*

What had led to this bold step was quite simple: Berlioz' well-connected friend, Albert du Boys, had obtained for Hector two audiences with the King's Superintendent of Fine Arts, the Vicomte Sosthènes de la Rochefoucauld. This gentleman was a simon-pure royalist, the largest landowner in France, a celebrated breeder of horses, and the only statesman who ever used his power in a vain effort to extend the area covered by the ballerinas' traditional costume. Though he was a devotee of Rossini, the Superintendent meant to be fair, so he granted Berlioz permission to use the Opera orchestra at his own expense. Its leader, Valentino, was still willing to conduct and Prévost to sing. But Berlioz remembered his first fiasco and was determined that the orchestra should be paid and the parts correctly copied. For all this he needed twelve hundred francs, which his father would certainly not advance. Here was Chateaubriand's role. Would he lend that sum to a vaguely recommended young artist? The year before, Hector had thought of approaching a well-known actor

[37] *1243,* II, 151.

and asking him to launch one of his songs at a benefit, but on the very doorstep the applicant had been overcome with shyness and had run away. Now he addressed Chateaubriand in a dignified way, which elicited the dignified reply quoted in the *Memoirs:* Chateaubriand did not have the required sum at his disposal, nor had he any influence left in the ministry. But his words generously implied that the petitioner was a fellow craftsman with whose predicament he sympathized.[38]

This autograph document was Berlioz' New Year's gift for 1825. Though just turned twenty-one, he was not the sort to take youth as a pretext for doing nothing, but he began to feel that he had already weathered a good many trials: there seemed to be no way to test his ambition. Nonetheless, having revised and polished the Mass until both Lesueur and he were satisfied, he set himself to copying the parts – a drudgery which took three months. He must have spent rather full days and nights, for he had meanwhile received from Humbert Ferrand the text of a cantata on the Greek Revolution, and the music for it was being put on paper. Since this new work had a topical interest (Byron – Missolonghi – the Philhellenic societies) its completion ought not to be delayed. Already life was passing, pressing, dwindling, as he dreamed of its potential uses. To give up now, and by failing to make his mark be forced to resume the medical apron, could not be borne even in thought. He must produce his Mass.

Augustin de Pons, another of Hector's wealthy friends who happened to be musical, came to the rescue and lent the twelve hundred francs. Everything was set in motion, rehearsals were begun, the newspapers notified, critics invited, the family kept posted, and finally on July 10, 1825, the church of St. Roch, which thirty years before had heard Bonaparte's "whiff of grapeshot" (and still bore its marks), heard something equally important and rather more appropriate.

The performance was a success. Dizzy with excitement, Berlioz heard his imaginings come to life and take effect on an appreciative audience. But he kept his ears open to criticism as well as to compliments, and more especially to the faults that only he could detect by comparing the actual sounds with his intentions. His next thought was to escape friends and inquisitive strangers and to learn what his master thought of the work as performed. The old man had hidden behind a pillar and gone straight

[38] "I love art and artists, but the trials to which talent is sometimes subjected cause it to triumph, and the day of success then repays it for all it has suffered." (*Mem.*, I, 39.) The amount involved seems to have been misread by Chateaubriand, who writes "1500" francs. (*235*, II, 155.)

home to await his protégé. "By heaven," he told Berlioz, "you shan't be a doctor or an apothecary or anything but a great musician . . . There are too many notes in your work, but every intention carries, and makes itself felt even through the exuberance of ideas." [39]

Several newspapers spoke of the Mass "by M. Lesueur's pupil," but the composer waited for further notices before despatching news of victory to La Côte. Then he wrote to his mother, telling her of the "rather brilliant reception of the work," and after "laying its success in homage at her feet," added diplomatically: "Despite your wish to see me take up other studies, your affection toward me is too great for a thing that has caused me so much joy to cause you any pain." He also pointed out that although he relished the approval of the amateur public, what he wanted was "the approval of artists, the opinion of those who know, and I was lucky enough to obtain it." [40]

To Du Boys, who had started the ball rolling, he let himself go about M. Sosthènes: "Would you believe it, he gave me permission to have the musicians of the Opera, provided I paid for them. The good man! He permitted me to spend a thousand francs, if I had them, and he gave the musicians full and complete liberty to take the cash!" Nevertheless, Berlioz adds in a jubilant P.S. that the Mass has been requested by another chapel master for a performance in July, no longer at his expense. "The musicians will be fewer, only about sixty, but that will be enough for the size of the church." [41]

Some days later at the Opera, Berlioz, sitting as an habitué next to the head of the claque, was taken to task by this eminent man, usually known as Auguste.[42]

"Why didn't you tell us you made your debut at St. Roch's the other day? We'd have gone in a body."

"I didn't know you liked religious music as much as that."

"We don't like it at all. What an idea! But we would have warmed up your audience to the Queen's taste."

"But how? You can't applaud in a church."

"I know, but you can cough, blow your nose, move your chair, scrape your feet, hum and haw, lift your eyes to heaven – the whole bag of

[39] *A.R.*, 25–6; corroborated by an earlier letter in *81*, 403.
[40] *A.R.*, 20–1.
[41] *A.R.*, 23, 28. This performance did not take place.
[42] That is, the Emperor Augustus, for the claque were collectively called "The Romans" by analogy with the populace in the circus who decided the gladiators' fate. See in Berlioz' *Evenings with the Orchestra* (N.Y., 1956) a full account of this institution, and in Balzac's *Lost Illusions* an analysis of its corrupt financing. See also *1192*.

tricks. We could have done a sweet job for you, and given you a real success, just like a fashionable preacher."[43]

For the next few days Hector tasted the pleasures of notoriety—met Mme. Branchu at her daughter's wedding, and was taken by other artists into the circle of their awareness. But this whiff of fame did not turn his head. He knew how applause and newspaper notices and the mutual admirations of the artistic world come and go. He also knew that the Mass needed retouching. The best thing in it, the vision of the Last Judgment on the words *Et iterum venturus* was a movement of some value and he must go over it. What the public liked best was the *Gloria*, "a show piece in light style. You might have known they'd prefer it."[44]

But music was a pleasant sort of trouble, which Hector now accepted as synonymous with life. He was committed to art in every way and not merely through that disturbingly large debt to De Pons. Hence when that same year the new German music of Carl Maria von Weber broke upon Paris in an adaptation of *Der Freischütz*, its reception became at once part of his concern. From its new orchestral and operatic style Berlioz had much to learn, but he quickly saw that in addition to being badly sung Weber's work had been mutilated. The man responsible for this desecration was the powerful "XXX" of the *Journal des Débats*, Castil-Blaze.[45] Berlioz watched his chance to attack him directly in the pages of the *Corsaire*. The opportunity arose over Gluck's *Armide*, which the great critic had found "lacking in emotion," full of arias that "stopped short of full development," and built throughout on "a system of declamation which one no longer accepts." This dogmatism gave Hector his chance. After a technical refutation of the other's carping about consecutive fifths, Berlioz winds up: "But who is this 'one' who no longer accepts Gluck's system? It is M. XXX. Who is it that finds half the music of *Armide* ridiculous? M. XXX. Who finds the poem inferior, the main role unmusical, the settings tawdry and the ballets stale? Still M. XXX. But who then is this implacable critic, this universal corrector of taste? He must be some great composer, a lyric poet, or at least a

[43] *Soirées* (7th) *Eves.*, 75–6.

[44] *A.R.*, 24.

[45] François Henri-Joseph Blaze, known as Castil-Blaze (1784–1857) to distinguish him from the minor composer who was his father, was a miscellaneous writer and dabbler in many arts and trades. He composed quantities of "romances" (*i.e.*, parlor songs) and acquired a small fortune by rearranging the operatic works of foreign composers. His music criticism is largely anecdotal and without principle. His youngest brother Ange-Henri, who will occur again in these pages, became a music critic of much greater weight and wrote under the name Blaze de Bury as well as other pseudonyms.

member of the Academy? Not at all: he is more than all these. He is M. Castil-Blaze." [46]

This was the first blast against the man who would shortly be called to account by Weber in person for making a musical hash out of *Freischütz* and *Euryanthe*, and by Weber's publishers for appropriating the receipts of these successful manglings. Young Hector had fired the first shot and carried the war against musical misrepresentation from the opera pit to the printed page. When Weber, dying of tuberculosis, passed through Paris on his way to staging *Oberon* in London, Berlioz could feel qualified to bring him a tribute of praise from the new generation. No one in France would understand Weber more thoroughly, or more naturally resemble him as man of action.[47] But by ill luck, Berlioz missed him at every turn – at Lesueur's, at a music shop, at the Opera. A few months later, *Oberon* failed and Weber was dead.

Meanwhile Berlioz continued to write music and to seek performance. He had finished his "Heroic Scene: The Greek Revolution." He and Ferrand published the text and solicited officialdom. On their behalf Lesueur approached his colleague Kreutzer, who was in charge of concerts at the Opera, but was gruffly challenged: "What would happen to us if we helped newcomers?" Undaunted, the poet-librettist and the composer went on to their next project, an opera based on the history of the Vehmic Courts, or secret "vigilantes" of late medieval Germany. It was entitled *Les Francs-Juges*, and an idea of its *Freischütz*-like atmosphere may be gathered from the opening stage directions: "A cavern showing 12 stone seats around a circular table draped in black, covered with daggers and symbolic objects." [48] But an opera is a laborious thing and Ferrand was not so abundant a poet as his friend was a musician. Berlioz therefore composed songs, placed a few in magazines, and published others at his own expense. Finally he entered the preliminary competition for the Rome Prize and was not admitted.

This brought on a family crisis. Though Hector had begun to pay off his debt for the Mass by cutting his expenses and by giving music lessons, he had not been able to keep the facts from his family: Cousin Alphonse had inadvertently given him away. The doctor paid De Pons

[46] *1379*, Dec. 19, 1825. [47] See below, Chapter 15.

[48] Ms. Bibl. Nat. (*12*). Contrary to the usual statement, the historical substance on which the young men drew came not from Walter Scott (whose *Anne of Geierstein* came out five years later) but from a work published the previous year by the Franco-German writer François Loève-Veimars, about whom see below, Chapter 10. (*1196a.*) On the survival of the Vehmic tradition, see Heine (*Germany*, Ch. 14) and reports of twentieth-century German prisoners in the United States. "The Vehmic Court: a Little Nazi Reich in the U. S. A.," *New Leader*, Mar. 4, 1944.

a sum which he thought the full amount, but which was only about a third, Berlioz having prudently minimized the total. At the same time the father set a date for the end of his son's musical studies. Only a notable success could save Hector and now at the official trial he had failed. Dr. Berlioz immediately cut off all funds. The double blow to pride and pocketbook would surely quash musical inclination forever. But at this point Lesueur intervened, writing direct to the doctor that no doubt was possible about his son's divine gift and future success: "Music streams out of him through all his pores." [49] He urged the parable of the buried talent. Dr. Berlioz replied huffily and ordered Hector home, where the prodigal was uncanonically received with studied coolness. No one spoke. An attempt at discussion between father and son ended in deadlock. Hector went numb and could not eat. The father lay awake at night. At last, one morning, the doctor summoned his boy to the office to say he might return to Paris as a music student. Only, he must leave La Côte without telling his mother.

Hector instantly came back to life and burst to poor Nanci, who records that "he talked to her too long for comfort," and that Mme. Berlioz immediately suspected her son's gaiety. Shortly before leaving he tried to avoid his mother, in vain. She forbade him to leave La Côte, but on seeing his stony expression, she turned from fury to entreaties, begging him on her knees not to disgrace himself and them. "*La considération avant tout.*" [50] Those who have to do with theaters, she cried, are "disgraced in this life and damned in the next." [51] Seeing him adamant, she cursed him and fled to a neighboring cottage. As the time for taking the coach drew near, Hector, his father, and the other children, all weeping, sought her out, but she eluded them and Hector had to leave unblessed and heading for perdition.[52]

[49] *Mem.*, I, 47.

[50] Of this wonderful French commodity, Amiel declares in his *Journal* that it is "a matter of supreme importance—the loss of it an irreparable evil, the acquirement of it a pressing necessity. What, then, is this good thing? The esteem of the public. . . . It is not exactly a good conscience . . . it is the witness from without . . . the homage rendered to a life held irreproachable." (*1234*, II, 185–6.)

[51] *Mem.*, I, 50 and 60. Mme. Berlioz seemed to have public opinion on her side. Not many years before, the body of a celebrated actress, Mlle. Raucourt, had been turned away amid jeers from the very church of St. Roch where Hector's Mass had been given. He could, in rebuttal, have argued that he did not intend to be an actor, and that inside the church Corneille and Diderot lay buried with honor.

[52] It is to this scene that the first letter to his uncle Victor (*81*, 399) unquestionably refers. The editor has therefore misdated it by a whole year, and it should appear as the second of the pair.

Little wonder that when the young man thought of these scenes, of his debts, and of the risks and reckoning to come, he found himself subject to violent "inner storms." He analyzed them with a medical student's attention to physiological detail: when an idea seizes him, he tells Nanci, he is consumed by it, he has chills and fever, and his brain reels until his other ideas absorb the new one. Then he seeks to impart his vision, but everyone is cold and uncomprehending, and the discovery paralyzes him. But only for a time. When he recovers aplomb he knows that he has powers and can produce something that shall be "great, passionate, energetic, and true." He also knows that what makes men cold to his insights is that everyone is wrapped up in his own cloud of perceptions and illusions, which few transcend. He notes moreover that "these bouts of mine are always more violent when I am far from the place where the objects of my emotion are to be found, because the impossibility of verifying the facts necessarily creates illusions or exaggerated realities." [53]

This cool self-criticism, which checks but does not destroy passion and spontaneity, was already apparent in Hector's first letter to Lesueur written in his twentieth year, and it remained perhaps Berlioz' most significant trait. Puzzling to some, and even repellent, its recurrent expression in Berlioz' mind, art, and behavior actually defines a kind of temperament. Stendhal and Delacroix occur at once as men identically compounded of fire and reason, but there were many others among the future great men of this creative period: Hazlitt, Shelley, Büchner, Heine, Dumas, Chopin. Indeed, if one looks into the early life of almost any productive mind, one finds a very similar mixture of emotion and melancholy wisdom. Many a self-possessed genius, an Olympian in later life, began as an untamed youth: Goethe, for example, or Wordsworth; and from the classic centuries: Racine, Pope, Voltaire, and Dr. Johnson.

But the roots of reason and order have to be there from the beginning, and it is important to notice their presence in Berlioz at this early date, for his image in the public mind has too often been that of an eccentric and lifelong adolescent.[54] Yet from the first he displayed a rational conservatism, a prudent regard for the significant proprieties, which in any man doubles the offense of his revolutionary acts. For everyone feels that in these he pretends to "know better," which argues intellectual contempt for the common rule. Never a bohemian like Balzac, nor a

[53] *A.R.*, 29–31.

[54] This is again partly due to the prominence accorded the *Symphonie Fantastique* (and even more, its "program") in the symphonic repertory. It is a work of Berlioz' twenty-sixth year; corresponding samples in point of age would be Wagner's *Rienzi* or Mozart's *Idomeneo.*

dandy like Musset, Berlioz more nearly resembles Vigny in aristocratic self-control, but Berlioz had perhaps more to control, and his blend of passion and deliberateness varied in keeping with the claims now of intellectual good breeding, and now of his daemon. The self-taming process was not always comfortable, and the aftermath of each crisis was likely to be a bout of melancholy, "the evil of isolation" – as he termed it – in short *ennui*. Ennui was simply energy quelling itself, waiting for an outlet and not merely an explosive discharge, seeking fulfillment through coherent expression in lasting forms. The chain of impulse is logical: daemon, self-control, impatience, ennui, "rage for order": art.

By August 1826, Berlioz was a student at the Conservatoire, and allowed to take Reicha's class in counterpoint and Lesueur's class in composition concurrently. Lesueur naturally felt that his pupil – indeed his disciple – was far enough advanced to carry the work easily. At home, Berlioz worked at a new opera based by a friend on Scott's *Talisman*, but it proved inadequate. What was absolutely necessary was to win the Rome prize as a certificate of merit, so Berlioz must learn another set of "our principles" with Anton Reicha.

This Czech musician was a conscientious master who had been a childhood friend of Beethoven's in Bonn, had met him (and Haydn) again in Vienna, and had come to Paris in 1808. He had written successful operas and chamber music, and after ten years had taken Méhul's place at the Conservatoire. His subject was fugue and counterpoint, which he taught, wisely enough, in combination with harmony, as the notebooks of his later pupil, César Franck, indicate.[55] Reicha also showed some interest in instrumentation, and had tried out new combinations of strings and winds. Berlioz found him clear, concise, and even critical of the sanctity of rules. He was willing to argue even when reasons were hard to find. It is true, Lesueur and Reicha did not agree in their systems; nor did Cherubini, the head of the Conservatoire, agree with the other two.[56] As for reconciling the rules with the practices of Gluck and Weber, let alone with one's musical instincts, that was an impossibility.

None the less Berlioz did the prescribed exercises, continued to live as an intimate – almost a son – of Lesueur, and on the side kept on composing *Les Francs-Juges*. All this on a very much reduced allowance

[55] *945*, 91–2.

[56] Gounod was later to suffer from the same cause, learning and unlearning these three systems. He reports Cherubini's impatient words and praises Lesueur as an admirable teacher. (*957*, 45 and 47.)

in order to pay off De Pons. With his childhood friend Antoine Charbonnel (the son of Dr. Berlioz' political opponent of 1817), Hector kept cheaper lodgings and developed the virtuosity of the housewife.[57] But this foretaste of poverty was nothing to the destitution which followed. For De Pons grew restless and wrote to Berlioz' father for the remainder of the money due. The doctor, shocked by the true amount, paid, but for the second time stopped Hector's allowance.

Music lessons – solfeggio, flute, guitar – were the only resource,[58] but the young musician could hardly live on less than one franc a day, and lessons did not bring in that much. He tried to get a place as flutist in an orchestra, but all the desks were filled. He was even ready to go abroad, but agents reported no openings. Finally Hector landed a job as chorister in the Théâtre des Nouveautés, after astonishing the manager by his knowledge of the whole opera repertoire. He could sing at sight, so the appalling rehearsals of the nonsense given in that playhouse were pure torture – "it will make me into an idiot and give me cholera morbus" [59] – but the thirty francs a month with his days largely free for his classes meant the difference between victory and defeat.

When Charbonnel, a student of pharmacy, was not running after the girls, he proved handy with snare and shotgun and brought home game from Montrouge, which eked out the cheap staples open to their budget. Hector meanwhile was thinking of the prize competition – "that deadly system," as Balzac calls it "which we owe to the Pompadour's brother." [60] For this, too, Berlioz must save money, since those who enter it are *en loge* (incommunicado) for two weeks and must put up money for their board. Correspondence with La Côte was limited to letters from Adèle and Nanci, to whom Hector gave sardonic glimpses of his plans. The younger girl need not worry about the forwarding of her mail if he should go abroad – whether as prize winner at Rome or flutist in

[57] The account book of those days, together with some kitchenware, is still to be seen in Berlioz' birthplace at La Côte, and it confirms the veracity of the report in the *Memoirs*.

[58] A scholar in matters pertaining to the guitar reports that Berlioz published compositions for the instrument in the form of etudes, but these have never been traced. (*539*.)

[59] *Mem.*, I, 69. The pieces were of the lowest order of musical farce, as the titles – *Grandmother's Fiancé*, etc. – amply suggest.

[60] *Cousin Pons*, Ch. 1. Balzac is referring to official competitions at large. The Rome prize in music had actually been established in the year of Berlioz' birth, 1803. It provided a stipend for five years, of which two must be spent in Italy, in imitation of the reason that had long brought painters and architects to Italy, the "mother of the arts."

Australia — for "the only country to which letters are not forwarded is the country from which no traveller returns." [61]

In June, Berlioz again took the preliminary test for admission to the trial. He wrote his fugue and Cherubini passed it. The subject of the finals was a "lyric scene" or brief cantata, "The Death of Orpheus at the Hands of the Bacchantes." The theme seemed most auspicious and Hector let himself go, hoping by a display of knowledge and imagination to carry the day. But the first prize went to one Guiraud, and Berlioz did not even receive a second prize.[62]

New Instruments: New Style

"Imagine first of all an orchestra . . ."
— Berlioz at eighteen

The score of *The Death of Orpheus,* lost until twenty years ago, was quite fittingly chosen by the national libraries of France after one hundred and three years, as one of the publications commemorating the centenary of Romanticism. *Orpheus* corresponds in Berlioz' career to Victor Hugo's *Cromwell* of the same year, 1827. There is in both that touch of defiance which goes with the first conscious innovation — in Hugo, the famous preface, in Berlioz, on the rejected manuscript, the no less famous note: "This work declared 'unplayable' by the Music Section of the Institute — Played on July 22, 1828." [1]

What had happened at the Institute was that the pianist assigned to perform the competing cantatas for the judges had floundered over Berlioz' score. It was taken for granted that these prize pieces, though required to be written for voice and orchestra, could be easily reproduced on the piano. And most of them, having been first conceived in a keyboard way, lost nothing by reduction to their embryonic state. But on

[61] *A.R.*, 14.

[62] Jean-Baptiste Guiraud later came to the United States and directed the musical institutions of New Orleans. His son Ernest was born there, returned to France while still a youth to make his way as a composer, and was soon assisting Berlioz at the rehearsals of the *Infant Christ.* He lived to fulfill Berlioz' prediction of success (*Corresp.*, 222) and became professor of composition at the Conservatoire. As such he was Debussy's chief teacher.

[1] *21*, title page. The concert did not take place on that day, owing to the singer's illness, but the rehearsals sufficed to vindicate the composer.

this point Berlioz' *Orpheus* – and this is the epoch-making fact – differed completely from all the rest. It had been not only scored but conceived for orchestra – and an original orchestra at that. From the point of view of Berlioz' success, the pianist's failure was ominous. It is true that even had the performer managed his reduction at sight, other aspects of Berlioz' originality would doubtless have alienated the jury. For applying his dramatic instinct to the musical problem, Berlioz had extracted from the rather dull scene a "Monologue and Bacchanale," and he wrote those two words down as the subtitle of his work, adding a motto from Thomas Moore:

> The sunflower turns on her god, when he sets
> The same look which she turn'd when he rose.[2]

In the score itself there were further signs of innovation in musico-dramatic form: a pastoral Introduction presents, first, the theme of the Monologue, and then a two-bar figure which becomes a veritable leitmotif for the Bacchantes.[3] This introduction is in fact a small prologue or thematic index. The next part (Monologue) is Orpheus's address to his lyre; then the Bacchantes appear, signalized by their leitmotif; in a variety of shapes it accompanies their four-part chorus, which finally overwhelms Orpheus's plea to Apollo. Orpheus dies with Eurydice's name on his lips – whence the motto from Moore. After this comes a long decrescendo of which the latter part constitutes a brief instrumental scena: through the dead singer's broken lyre the wind plays fitfully, while a distant shepherd tries to recall the theme of Orpheus's first song. The pastoral mood of the opening is thus recaptured, and it frames, so to speak, a complete drama in which moods are adroitly linked and contrasted. Almost any part of this musical action was enough to disconcert judges who expected nothing more than an air, chorus, and ritornelle as the proper way to accompany a ladylike lynching of Orpheus.

The fact was that Berlioz had produced *en loge* his first characteristic work. His dozen or so of previous essays, from the childhood quintets to the Mass of 1825, undoubtedly contained (as Lesueur saw at once) intimations of his peculiar genius – here a melody, there an orchestral idea or a dramatic intention. But in *Orpheus*, despite inexperience, every feature is marked with the Berliozian touch – melody, harmony, modulation, orchestration, and form. The three preceding scores had already shown his power to build a movement, however rough in spots or clumsy

[2] Last lines of "Believe me, if all those endearing young charms."
[3] *21*, fol. 6b and Sec. 4, *Allegro assai agitato*, fol. 19a and ff.

in detail.[4] Guided by Lesueur, Berlioz had begun to study the properties of his musical material in order to give it an individual form. But in *The Death of Orpheus* the advance made after one year at the Conservatoire is remarkable. Quite apart from the original use of the leitmotif, one is struck by the bold orchestral innovations – such as the first use of the cornet (commonly attributed to Rossini two years later) or of the mutes for the trombones (usually assigned to recent times) – and what is more, by Berlioz' ability to make these new sounds full of meaning. His study of Gluck's scores had not been in vain. What he had found in them was not simply a set of successful effects to repeat, but the principle by which timbre or orchestral color becomes an object of constant musical and expressive interest. Writing of Gluck later, Berlioz ascribed to him supremacy in "the art of dramatizing the orchestra." [5] The phrase precisely fits what Berlioz had learned from him in score and performance, and was applying to his own work in 1827.[6]

The first part of *Orpheus* is scored for the ordinary woodwinds and strings, with harp added; the second calls in addition for two cornets, two trumpets, three trombones, kettledrums, and three pairs of cymbals, while the flutes are replaced by piccolos. These specifications are enough to show how inadequate must be any rendering on the piano, even by an able performer. They also show that in Berlioz' time, despite Gluck's pioneering, there was no such thing as a standard symphonic band. The modern concertgoer tends to take "the orchestra" as a fact of nature and to attach certain ethical qualities to the number and kinds of instruments a composer uses. He is likely to shudder at Berlioz' three pairs of cymbals in *Orpheus*, for to him strings, wood, and brass are as clergy, nobles, and third estate, and percussion is the rabble. He must therefore be reminded that merit lies in the use, not the matter; and that the orchestra he tolerates or admires, just like the instruments and their "effects," is a product of

[4] Rudolf Louis, writing in the early 1900's after a performance of the "Greek Revolution" scene, speaks of its notable "*Linienführung*" and "*Aufbau.*" (*478*, 377.)

[5] *A Trav.*, 171.

[6] For brevity one may say that Berlioz learned this aspect of orchestration from Gluck, but it should be added that Gluck's followers also contributed instrumental ideas that Berlioz could gauge at the opera. In this regard, Mozart and Spontini belong to Gluck's school, as do the lesser French and Italian composers Catel, Méhul, Salieri, and Lesueur. Even Cherubini was not above joining horns and bells for his "symphony" associated with the crossing of the St. Bernard glacier. But Berlioz disliked merely exotic or imitative effects and he was, as we shall see, striving to go still farther than Gluck's dramatizing of timbre.

invention. These inventions, moreover, are quite recent, contemporary for the most part with the steam engine. So that far from subverting an established and classic tradition, the age of Berlioz was on the contrary the age of exploration and settlement in instrumental and orchestral practice.

But what about Mozart, Handel, J. S. Bach? Did they not write for orchestra – and with a classic perfection not to be outdone? Very likely, but not for *the* orchestra, that virtuoso instrument of recent make which we may use for their works but which never played the original *Saint Matthew Passion* and *Jupiter* Symphony. Indeed, if some of Bach's or Handel's scoring were described without mention of their names, the chances are it would be scorned as vulgar by our over-delicate friends – two orchestras, two choruses, and two organs for the *Saint Matthew Passion;* three flutes in Bach generally, combined with relatively few strings; a surfeit of bassoons in Handel, brass parts written high and shrill, relentless insistence on one tone color throughout a movement: the desire for orchestral richness obviously existed, though baffled by practical difficulties.[7] Bach's love of bells, of volume, and of "orchestral" stops on the organs that he admired is a matter of record, contrary though it be to the conventional view of him as an austere intellectualist who would just as soon have had his ears cut off.

The fact is that all the great musicians have loved sound, full and loud as well as soft and low, and they have always been attacked by the genteel as "noisy." Gluck's orchestration, modest to us, was scorned by no less a musician than d'Alembert as "indiscriminate banging"; Mozart's was still louder and Haydn's seemed deafening, for all of them encouraged and exploited the enlargement of instrumental forces. "Ah, if we only had some clarinets," wrote Mozart in 1773, "you cannot imagine what a magnificent effect a symphony makes with flutes and oboes and clarinets." And Haydn at the end of his life bewailed, "I have only just learned in my old age to use the wind instruments, and now that I do understand them, I must leave them." It was these Oh's and Ah's uttered by composers as well as performers that spurred the making of new or improved instruments, that is, implements for making better noises.[8]

[7] Mozart distrusted woodwinds generally for their inability to play in tune – hence the seemingly capricious scoring of his three great symphonies. When Cherubini was asked by a conductor what could sound worse than a flute in an orchestra he replied "Two flutes." (*799*, 133.)

[8] *1026*, 230; *799*, 132. The public's conviction that love of volume is wicked is probably incurable; nevertheless I add one more proof that it is not shared by instrumentists themselves: when they say of a colleague that he has "a small

With few exceptions, the instruments we know were invented or refashioned in the early part of the eighteenth century, were gradually introduced in the latter part, and were perfected in manufacture and use during the first half of the nineteenth. Thus the cello and double basses date from around 1710; the somewhat earlier clarinet and the later English horn came into general use after 1750; the trombone, a medieval instrument, was reintroduced by Gluck or Gossec about the same time.[9] The harp and pianoforte, both eighteenth-century patents, achieved their modern flexibility and force around 1800, and it was still later that all the woodwinds and brass were improved out of recognition by the genius of Boehm and others, who made possible true intonation and finer nuances through the use of keys, pistons, and valves.

To generalize, one might say that originating in the domestic inventiveness of the eighteenth century, modern instruments developed their high possibilities in the century of industry, the nineteenth. Scientific experiment and the use of metal characterize almost every step of the change. This is even true of the improved violin bow, which through Tourte's efforts (1785) revolutionized the technique of playing and virtually made the fiddle a new instrument by increasing its tone and permitting many new effects.[10] In short, the now familiar orchestra of "one hundred and ten" with an organ in the background and a piano to one side, is as clearly a product of the age of machinery as a Diesel engine. The domestic loom has turned into a factory for sound.[11]

Fortunately, improvement in this sort of machinery does not make obsolete the works written for earlier devices. Better intonation is a net gain. As for increased volume, range, and nuances they simply offer opportunities that composers have always longed for – new meanings through new sensations. We may theoretically divorce art from "effects," and pretend that the distance of a hair or the diameter of a tube are gross trivialities, but we should remember, when we yield to the seduction of *Tristan* or tingle with the champagne of the *Figaro* overture, that

---

tone," they intend anything but praise. And a large tone certainly means volume, though it does not mean playing fortissimo throughout. For the musical virtues of a large mass of singers or instrumentists, see below, Subchapter 13.

[9] The common use of the trombone was probably delayed by its associations with church music. This is but one instance of the strong irrational feelings which the makers of modern music in any epoch have to contend with.

[10] *1355*, 127. The Tourte bow was still made of wood, but the tightening device was a lathe-turned metal screw

[11] Though the manufacture of musical instruments still is less accurate and painstaking than that of cameras and bombsights.

our pleasure depends on this material source. We can neglect it only because others have paid attention to it – the performer first, and before him the instrument-maker and the orchestral innovator.

In relation to the orchestra's history, therefore, Berlioz comes at the critical mid-point where diverse traditions could be unified into a classic discipline, and used to develop an independent genre. Berlioz did not take to orchestral pioneering because of a preconceived notion of his own, but because it was the expanding medium of his day, and because his genius, his exquisitely fine ear, and his patience in study fitted him to master its intricacies.

When Berlioz came on the scene, then, the individual instruments were commanding attention by their improvement, but (as we saw) their collective use was arbitrary. The abandonment of the *continuo* had disorganized the older orchestral balance and a new amalgam had not yet been found. Neither instrumentation nor orchestration was taught as such: even the conventions of writing were in flux. To the ordinary student, Gluck's scores were of little use, for he was an impatient and careless writer who had orchestrated as it were from the podium, leaving riddles which only his presence at rehearsals could solve. The variable composition of most orchestras, operatic or private, was not encouraging to method.[12] It was only in 1803, the year of Berlioz' birth, that Cherubini first adopted the modern notation with the woodwinds at the top of the page, the horns, brass, and timpani in the middle, and the voices and strings below.

One reason for the anarchy was that timbre was not yet considered

[12] In the middle of the eighteenth century the composer did not even bother to write out his full score. He set down verbal indications which a regular employee of the opera turned into an instrumented work. (See Rousseau's *Dictionnaire de Musique*.) Towards the end of the same century, we still find a great orchestrator like Mozart writing out certain wind parts on separate leaves, to be sent or not with the heart of the score as suited the local resources. Some of these sheets naturally became lost and we now rely on hearsay for ascertaining Mozart's original intentions.

As for the numbers and proportions involved, it is of interest to note what Johann Quantz, Frederick the Great's court musician, considered ideal (and rare) in 1752: six first violins, six second violins, three violas, four cellos, two double basses, three bassoons, four oboes, four flutes, one harpsichord "or a fortepiano," and one theorbo (bass lute) when needed. In 1768, the most successful Paris theater had an orchestra of twenty-four musicians. Seven years later the Opera listed sixty-two: one time-beater, one harpsichordist, eleven first violins, eleven second violins, five violas, nine cellos, six double basses, three flutes, two oboes, one clarinet, two horns, eight bassoons, one trumpet, one timpanist, and one tambourine player. About the same time Haydn had at his disposal from sixteen to twenty-two players.

an element of musical form. Tone color was thought of as added to music that stood complete without it – an opinion which indeed still prevails in some quarters. The music of, say, an opera was therefore composed primarily for the "quartet" of strings, which might temporarily become a quintet, or a sextet through subdivision. The "little orchestra" of woodwinds had an accessory role. Sometimes a single wind instrument was given a solo, at other times the group sustained the accompaniment of a singer, or supported the harmony. At still other times they acted as definite symbols. Thus a flute meant love or "heavenly voices" (in Bach almost always "tears" or "melancholy"),[13] a trumpet glory, and horns the hunt. The use of percussion was rudimentary, and when Gluck employed more than the customary pair of timpani in an opera that was not Turkish – in Turkey anything goes – the best wits in Paris accused him of bad taste.

With the French Revolution, however, new purposes arose. The leading composers tried to adapt vocal and orchestral writings to the needs of national and popular emotions. They sought large-scale combinations which should be broadly impressive, and for Napoleon's coronation, Lesueur followed suit with a corps of trombones and salvos of musketry.[14] But these were "effects" in the vulgar sense, that is, applied from outside to a musical thought which could not sustain them; and when the quarter century of war and revolution was over, the incentive to explore further seemed to be lacking. Among Berlioz' teachers, with the possible exception of Reicha, no one could help him. French orchestration was simple and clear, but casual picturesqueness did not create a style; its dramatic purpose was unmistakable, especially in comic opera, but it remained lifeless. The Italians' success in the 1820's was due precisely to liveliness, but they achieved it by crude means which, as we saw Berlioz arguing, either obscured the melodic line or fell into childish "illustration."

It was, according to one scholar, this very scarcity of true art, and especially the inadequacy of Lesueur, that stimulated Berlioz' creativeness. "Mastery over the draftsmanship and color values of sound – as produced by twenty, thirty 'lines' or more, and as organized among

[13] On Bach's orchestra, see *891*. For the pathetic scenes of his *Psyche* (1671) Lully used six flutes.

[14] The tradition of discharging firearms at a climax or on the last chord of a piece goes back to Handel, Stamitz, and even Lully. Hence it is absurd to make Tchaikovsky, or the nineteenth century, bear the brunt of this vulgarity, if it is one. Sarti's *Te Deum* in D, for instance, was given in 1789 at Jassy and St. Petersburg to an accompaniment of bells and cannon shots, in celebration of military victories. (See *1340*.)

themselves to concur in a common expressiveness — was the dream he pursued and made into a reality. Served by a superior instinct, he listened score in hand to the concert of strings, woods, brass, and human voices, until . . . he began to think directly in that tongue, skipping the stage of 'translation' and creating an entirely new 'polychrome.' "[15]

Of course it was because he had "skipped the stage of translation" that his *Orpheus* bewildered his judges, and in this event we see the source of a lifelong misunderstanding between Berlioz and his "judges" in the broad sense: whereas to him every step of his development was clear, logical, solidly based on observation and reflection, to them he no less obviously spoke an unknown tongue. Where, for instance, had he picked up the orchestral ideas for the instrumental opening and close of his cantata? He might have countered, Where were you when Weber's *Freischütz* was being played? For the "advance" in a young artist is often his knowledge of the new great masters.

From Weber's orchestra, though it is neither large nor complete, Berlioz had instantly discovered how one could create "atmosphere" — especially that of nocturnal Nature — which the French and Italian composers ignored entirely. More important still, through Weber, Berlioz was unknowingly drawing on the German tradition of instrumental music, whose happy cross with opera was to yield the dominant forms and character of modern music. Eighteenth-century opera contributed the singing melody and the eighteenth-century symphonists gradually individualized the instruments as "singers": Stamitz, Sammartini, and above all, Mozart and Haydn, introduced the ideas of contrast, nuance, and "dialogue." With his picked players at Mannheim, Stamitz had stretched the range of dynamics from *p* and *f* to *pp* and *ff*, developed the extended crescendo, and under the pressure of "general ideas" — notably those of the Enlightenment and of the later *Sturm und Drang* — tone color began to be used for expressive, as against symbolic, purposes, while the habit of regarding timbre as one of the facets of music grew more familiar. From this it was but a step to using and requiring all available tone color. Whereas in Mozart's great symphonies, for practical reasons, either the flute or clarinet or trumpets or timpani are still absent, in Haydn's later ones, flute and clarinet are regularly used, and treated with great melodic independence. This is why Haydn is often called the father of the modern orchestra — though such artistic fatherhoods have to be shared with so many men as scarcely to flatter the fastidious.

After Haydn and Mozart, then, Weber helped Berlioz to marshal

[15] Maurice Emmanuel, *427*, 242–3.

his native powers and prepared him for the final revelation — that of a composer still living in the year of Berlioz' *Orpheus,* though almost wholly unplayed in Paris — Beethoven. It was not merely that Beethoven raised the "standard" orchestra from Mozart and Haydn's two dozen players to sixty, nor that he gave the drums and basses unaccustomed work to do, but that his idiom was unmistakably orchestral.[16] After Berlioz had assimilated the shock and the knowledge, he was ready to be himself a link in the chain of development as well as an originator in what he would soon call the *genre instrumental expressif.* Even before hearing Beethoven, he was a "modern" studying, as all moderns do, the relation of the new means at hand to the preceding tradition. He sensed that melody, harmony, rhythm or dynamics must now adjust to timbre in order that these elements should form a whole. Hence in *The Death of Orpheus,* Berlioz did not write omnibus pieces to be played by any instrumental group ad lib. He conceived appropriate "color schemes" just as he conceived fit melodies, asking himself, at a given point, how two cornets, two trumpets, two horns, and three trombones would sound together, first *ff* and then *f* and muted, as an echo of the Bacchantes' shrill entrance.[17] This orchestral layout could not be considered in the abstract; its fitness, which is part of its beauty, must be judged at a particular spot in a movement, on a particular chord distributed among the instruments in a particular way.

With this concern of Berlioz aged under twenty-four, compare the outlook of Grétry writing a generation earlier: "I have often neglected the part of the *quinte* [violas] which is so necessary to fill in the gap between the violins and the bass, and I hope that some one may be found to supply the want in my scores . . . It would indeed be easy for me to enlarge the task of the violas and bassoons, yet for whatever reason the idea does not tempt me." [18] Berlioz' view of the violas and bassoons is precisely that they do not *fill in,* but that they have a unique role to fill out, a characteristic voice to make heard, and the possibility does tempt him. In the Mass of 1825, he improved on Reicha's use of chords on the timpani,[19] and on Gossec's fanfare for the *Tuba Mirum.* In the overture to his opera *Les Francs-Juges* and in another, *Waverley,* which was also in progress during 1827, Berlioz was trying out fresh combinations — such as the disjunction of the winds from the mass of strings while

[16] Berlioz was later to write that it took seventy years to discover the possibility of having three kettledrums (for a full chord) in an orchestra. (*Tr.,* 254.)

[17] *21,* fol. 18a and b.

[18] *811,* II, 63–4 (1797).

[19] In Reicha's *Harmonie des Sphères,* reprinted in his *Traité d'Harmonie.*

simultaneously playing unrelated themes in opposite nuances. This involves an accurate gauging of the strength of each instrument, and also explains why the size of the orchestra must be increased: all the formerly "accessory" instruments may be needed for important parts, and to insure balance in the *tutti*, the mass of strings must be larger.[20]

Finally, as we can see from almost any page in these earliest works by Berlioz, this revolutionary conception of instruments explains why a work truly conceived for orchestra cannot be understood from a piano reduction: the *Waverley* overture, for example, opens with a sustained note on the oboe, at the end of which the strings break in with a sharply cut figure. In the orchestra that single pulse is a concise but sufficient "curtain raiser" to the drama; on the piano it is merely an F sharp whose function is lost, for the intended contrast between the reedy tone and the string attack is itself a musical element, a part of Form.

In the light of these facts, the absence of a piano or any regular ensemble at La Côte when Berlioz was a child may be deemed a real advantage. It kept him from getting accustomed to any conventional or half abstract sensation of sound, such as familiarity breeds in the child who equates music with a certain keyboard instrument or a "standard" combination of players. His virtuosity on flute and guitar, as well as the changeable groupings of string and wind players, maintained his curiosity about timbre alive and unsatisfied. When he came to Paris, his powers of judgment were fully awakened, while his responsiveness was still fresh and particular. Thus everything conspired to make him think of music as an art for the ear, to dwell on its concrete existence as performed, and consequently to treat orchestral means as a new and ill-explored musical dimension.

But the instrumental genre consists of more than orchestral ideas, even if these ideas are part of a total conception and are not laid on like ornament. The other components of music as Berlioz understood them will concern us one by one, as we study his later works. Yet even at this prentice stage we should note the important feature of Berlioz' urge to dramatize. We saw what the candidate did with the text of the *Orpheus*

[20] The division of each group of strings into two or more parts further adds to the number of "lines" in the new timbre-polyphony, and requires an absolute increase in the number of instruments. It is therefore not quite accurate to say with the modern poet:

> "The violins have been gregarious
> Right from the time of Stradivarius . . ."

(Laurence McKinney, *People of Note.*)

scene. He took a pair of commonplace stanzas and built out of them a triptych with prologue. Each smaller scene had dramatic point as well as musical form, and the whole was unified by the transformation or recall of musical themes. The choice of subject for his oratorio evinces the same care: *The Crossing of the Red Sea* very likely supplied the occasion for a march and an invocation, and certainly for a hymn of thanksgiving, "The Lord is my strength and song." [21] In the text of the Mass, Berlioz used the same principle, and even in the poem that Humbert Ferrand had made to order for celebrating the Greek Revolution, we find that Berlioz stretched or contracted the verses so as to afford him the chance for a Prayer, a Hymn, a Rhapsody, a Battle Song, and a March-Finale. *Music first,* then drama condensed into scenes – into occasions, that is – for an independent art.

To say this is to say that by 1827 Berlioz was ready to understand both his as yet unknown masters, Beethoven and Shakespeare.

[21] Exodus XV. 2.

4. Faustian Man

August 1827
to December 1829

Au son de ton harmonie
Je rafraichis ma chaleur
Ma chaleur, flamme infinie
Naissante d'un beau malheur.
— RONSARD, "To his Guitar" (*c.* 1550)

THE SUMMER of 1827, the prelude to a feverish autumn for Berlioz, began with depressing calm. Charbonnel had gone back to his parents at La Côte and Hector's other friends had scattered too. He meanwhile continued drudging at the Nouveautés, singing the choruses of lyric gems entitled *The Game of Hide and Seek*, *The Widow's Man*, or *The Bride's Engagement Ring*. Relaxed tension brought on illness. Sore throat developed into quinsy, and after a few days' discomfort Berlioz lanced the abscess himself. News of this reached La Côte, presumably through Charbonnel, and Dr. Berlioz with kindly words restored the mercurial allowance.

This temporary disorder was undoubtedly of nervous origin, for anyone less fundamentally healthy than young Berlioz would scarcely have been able to stand the blows of the next half dozen years. The first and heaviest shock occurred in early September 1827, when an English troupe of actors led by Kemble came to Paris and revealed Shakespeare to young France. Five years before, a similar attempt had proved disastrous. So soon after Waterloo, national pride had been offended by the "invasion," and Shakespeare had been scorned as "an aide-de-camp of Wellington." The hissing was followed by rioting; and a young actress was wounded (while curtsying) by coins hurled at her from the pit by the most polite people on earth. When Desdemona appeared lying on a couch, a voice called asking why the usual bedroom appliances were missing. Thus the wittiest nation of Europe in 1822.

Now in 1827 the enthusiasm for Shakespeare and his actors showed the effect of Nodier's influence, of the young Romantics' articles in *Le Globe*, of Villemain's public lectures, and of Stendhal's attacks on the Academy. Political passion, moreover, had shifted from foreign to home affairs.

So everyone in Paris who had a name or hoped to have one went to the Odéon to see *Hamlet* and *Romeo* as well as *Jane Shore, The Rivals,* and *Venice Preserved.* Though the plays were given in English, people read Letourneur's prose Shakespeare, or simply responded to voice and pantomime just as in the twenties of this century the English-speaking world did at the Moscow Art Theater. Kemble, though fifty-two, was "sensational" as the Prince of Denmark; but the great revelation was a young Ophelia of twenty-seven named Harriet Smithson. She was tall and well-proportioned, had a striking face and beautifully modeled arms, and a moving voice. Her deep blue eyes were large and expressive: She was enchanting to hear and to behold.[1] On this point, the most critical witnesses were at one – Delacroix, Hugo, Vigny, Dumas, and Sainte-Beuve as well as ordinary critics on both sides of the Channel.[2]

They agreed also that she had a genius for tragedy, though few who knew her antecedents could have predicted any such triumph for her. Born in 1800 in Ennis, Ireland, the daughter of a theater manager, she had received a very strict religious upbringing and had gone on the stage only from necessity. To save her from the evils of the profession, she was put under the guardianship of her brother, who exacted references from Abbott, her manager; and when she traveled, it was with her mother and a hunchback sister as chaperones. For three years she toured Ireland, then went to London where her native accent seriously damaged her prospects, even in comedy. On the Continent it passed unnoticed and chance opened to her the half-dozen roles ideally suited to her talents: Abbott had coached her in the traditional business of Ophelia merely in order that Kemble, whose leading lady was needed for the Queen, could play Hamlet.

On the opening night (September 11) as Ophelia played the mad scene, she seemed to have forgotten her part. Blind to her surroundings, she walked as in a trance; she stopped, her face vacant, arms hanging. She

[1] In England, her beauty was universally acknowledged; a critic sang:

> "Can all be dark that life supplies
> Whilst earth can boast of Smithson's eyes!" (*234,* 893.)

See also the *Dictionary of National Biography* and a more recent study of contemporary opinion in *396.*

[2] Three years later, Juste Olivier, a young poet fresh from Switzerland, wrote in his diary (May 13, 1830): "At last! I have seen an actress! No, I saw a woman, a wife, a mother. I saw Madame Smithson in *L'Auberge d'Auray.* She is an English actress who does not know any French and who plays a role in this piece, or rather, she is the whole piece herself . . . After her exit, I did not want to see the rest of the show." (I owe this extract from an unpublished manuscript to the great kindness of the late Professor André Delattre.)

paused, and the whole house was gripped by an absolutely new dramatic emotion. Her song, without art or expression, rose amid the silence, her veil fell, she burst into tears and then slowly walked away. At the end of her second scene, the audience also wept; men sobbed or left hurriedly. The remainder of the play insured the success of the English actors; that night *Hamlet* ended to the sounds of an ovation.[3]

Though seven scenes, eight characters, and seventeen hundred lines had been cut, the play cast a new spell on spectators accustomed to the solemnities of French tragedy. Shakespeare's world had, in Dumas's phrase, "the freshness of Adam's first sight of Eden." Berlioz, also present, was overwhelmed: "I had to acknowledge the only dramatic truth. . . . I could at the same time gauge the great absurdity of the ideas Voltaire had spread in France about Shakespeare . . . and the pitiable narrowness of our old poetics, decreed by pedagogues and obscurantist monks. I saw, understood, and felt that I was alive and that I must 'arise and walk.' "[4] Berlioz saw as in a flash that Shakespeare's "open construction" by scenes and glimpses, leaping over time and space to sum up a character or a situation, was precisely what the dramatic musician needed for his purpose. And what made him feel doubly alive was that he had fallen in love, virtually at first sight, with Ophelia.

He later compared this passion for Harriet Smithson to a bolt of lightning that had struck into his heart as into a virgin forest, and there is no reason to suppose that this was other than literal. He had not been so deeply moved since his unhappy childhood love for Estelle. During his student days we do not hear of any casual love-making nor so much as a flirtation. He was too busy, anxious, fastidious. Moreover, he had been so stupidly teased about the Estelle episode by his family, especially by his mother, that he undoubtedly carried his heart in wraps though appearing to wear it on his sleeve. And just as his boyhood love was linked with the sublimities of nature, heightened by the Virgilian tale of Dido, so this first adult passion was linked with the sublimities of drama, couched in Shakespeare's poetry. As the living sign of Shakespeare's power, Harriet brought devastation of spirit along with inspiration.

In less than half a year, two more such electric experiences were to

[3] The eyewitness sources for this account include Sainte-Beuve, Delécluze, and Charles Jarrin, who is quoted in *307*, 53. The widely scattered testimony is ably condensed in *302*, 14–8. See also *1057*, 20 ff., 55, 90–4.

[4] *Mem.*, I, 98. It was sixty years since Shakespeare had been first presented in France. Half a century after Voltaire, another able critic, La Harpe, had declared *King Lear* a "detestable piece of work, containing some beautiful scenes, to be sure, but no work of art." (*Cours de Littérature*, 1784.)

befall Berlioz, the "virgin forest" of whose soul by then resembled a blasted heath. But these were artistic shocks, from which recovery is sure, and they came in the course of a great intellectual battle, crowned by victory. As if heartened by Shakespeare, the artistic youth of France were feeling their gathered strength and setting off explosive charges all around the academic fortress: Victor Hugo published *Cromwell* with a preface-manifesto, Delacroix exhibited his "Death of Sardanapalus," Rude was starting out as an independent sculptor in Paris, and Sainte-Beuve preached Ronsard and sixteenth-century romanticism. In the circle to which Merimée told his tales of Spanish passion and Stendhal his witty anecdotes of Italian character, came Hazlitt who was at work on his Life of Napoleon. All idolized Shakespeare, and Gérard de Nerval brought out that Shakespearean offshoot, his translation of Goethe's *Faust*, Part I.

It was this poem which worked further havoc in Berlioz' mind. Everything about the "marvellous book" struck home — the theme, the form, the realistic variety, and the Nature philosophy. He read it constantly and urged everyone to read it. More than Werther and René, already a generation past, the figure of Faust seemed to embody the will of the moment, for Faust was more complete. Learned, passionate, curious, tender, courageous, bewitched, and desperate, he stood for genius in all its greatness and misery. The "two souls within his breast" showed him at once a sufferer and a doer:

> Unresting action proves the man.

Yet Faust was a critic of himself no less than a critic of life, and his pilgrimage was a perpetual act of choice. To searchers like the young artists of the new era, it was wonderful to find a fable in which Experience and Wisdom were not shown as already bottled and labeled by the old for the use of the obedient young, but were purchasable solely with risk and effort. Without knowing that Goethe had begun the work as a ballad play, Berlioz immediately felt that *Faust* was made for music. Nerval had translated the songs in verse, and already appropriate melodies were spinning in Berlioz' brain.[5]

Besides this whirl of ideas there were practical matters to attend to, notably rehearsals. On November 22, in the midst of a political riot, Berlioz' Mass was given again in the great church of St. Eustache. Conducting for the first time in his life, he had the satisfaction of successfully leading his favorite portion — the fanfare followed by chorus for the

[5] Berlioz was also unaware that Beethoven had projected music for *Faust.*

Last Judgment — which at the earlier performance had been spoiled. He was so excited at the end of the movement that he had to sit down and literally shake it off. The performance convinced him that only this one section had any merit, the rest being a "clumsy imitation of Lesueur's style" which he might as well destroy.[6]

He knew moreover that the English players were about to leave: Could he bring himself to Miss Smithson's attention? More and more distracted by his all-too-distant love (which so affected him that his friends noticed a Romeo-like jaundice and peakedness in his looks) Hector had resolved on a bold plan: he too would brave the public; he would give a concert of his own works. For this he must use only the best and latest of his compositions, as well as the ablest musicians in Paris. The *Francs-Juges* overture was just finished and Berlioz had another, unplayed, with a title and motto drawn from Scott, *Waverley*. With the "Greek Revolution" and the *Resurrexit* from the Mass, his concert would show enough quantity, quality, and variety.

In the midst of this projected one-man show or "festival" — a thing as yet unattempted by any musician in France [7] — a ministerial decree established the *Société des Concerts du Conservatoire*. Its purpose was to give regular seasons of classical music by drawing on the best players in both the Opera and the Conservatoire. Habeneck was put in charge, and it was stipulated that the repertory should include works by new or neglected composers — those that neither Kreutzer's routine programs at the Opera nor Choron's oratorio society normally took up. In March 1828 Habeneck opened his series with the Third, Fifth, and Seventh symphonies of Beethoven.[8] The result was an artistic furore almost as great as had followed the advent of Shakespeare. On Berlioz the effect was exactly comparable. He saw in a flash what had been missing from his background and his teaching. Lesueur never really swallowed Beethoven, and Cherubini never acknowledged the virtue of symphonic form: "I've tried it and it doesn't strike me as being good." [9] Berlioz on the contrary soon

[6] *Mem.*, I, 36. The portion he kept may be heard, somewhat altered, in the *Tuba mirum* of the *Requiem* which has recently been recorded. (*1448.*)

[7] It had been done in Germany by Beethoven and Weber.

[8] François Habeneck (1781–1849), one of the last "violinist conductors," had been trying to introduce the works of Beethoven for two years. His first rehearsals, attended only by a few friends and colleagues, had sent most of them away disappointed, or — like Kreutzer — shutting their ears with their hands. (*853*, 60–1.) Even under Habeneck, Beethoven's harmony was "corrected" here and there, and the movements of distinct symphonies mixed or reshuffled. He was not played "as written" until Berlioz and Liszt campaigned for it in the newspapers.

[9] *307*, 257.

convinced himself by a study of the scores that Beethoven was the transcendent modern who could not be transcended.[10]

Berlioz' state of mind when this last thunderbolt fell and supercharged him is impossible to describe. He himself tried to give an idea of it, first in intimate letters to friends, and later in the *Memoirs*, where he ushers in the Shakespeare-Goethe-Beethoven sequence with the remark that here was "the great drama" of his life – as we might say, his moment of storm and stress. He tells what he did and how he felt, and from this retrospect biographers have tried to reconstruct the drama and judge it. One writer thinks Berlioz was close to madness; another argues that because Berlioz accomplished a good deal of practical work in that same half year, the report of his excitement must be exaggerated, or must at the time have been a pose. This is the old dispute about Hamlet feigning or being mad. Maybe Hamlet could feign because at times he was. As to Berlioz, who was not only in love but also in a state deserving the name of Prophetic Revelation, we may be sure that he suffered, by turns, wild hopes, doubts and fears. It is true that he kept working but there is nothing unlikely in his saying that his burden often plunged him into depression and despair.

What vitiates any judgment upon him is that verbal descriptions of such states automatically falsify the facts while simultaneously irritating the reader. This is in a degree true also of normal behavior: a host of things said, seen, or done every day without offense cannot be written down without freezing them into an image they never show in life. It is all the more impossible to make readable the antics of love combined with the torments of emotional and artistic maturing. When Berlioz tells us that he suffered insomnia for long periods, that he walked for hours to tire out his ennui, after which he would drop into a stupor, now in a field covered with snow and again at the table of a cafe where he slept so long that he was thought dead, all we can say is that however unprecedented the detail, these are the sorts of things that passionate men have been known to do.[11]

These odd actions of Hector's came in bouts. The salient trait of his temperament, which we find reflected in his music as well as in his calmest

[10] He had read the scores of two before any performances were available. These began with the *Eroica* on March 9, 1828, the first concert of the new *Société;* thereafter and until 1830, the *Eroica* was played three times, the Fifth seven times, the Seventh four, the Pastoral three, the Fourth two and the first two once each. It was not until 1831 and 1832 respectively that the Ninth and Eighth were given, during Berlioz' absence.

[11] Compare Goethe's distracted youth or Hazlitt's unhappy pursuit of Sarah Walker.

letters and most tightly knit articles, is swiftness in associating ideas. Under stress this speed became a headlong rush which on paper seems sheer vibratory sensation. For example, on June 28, 1828, Berlioz wrote a perfectly sensible letter to Ferrand about the music of the *Francs-Juges,* as well as about another theatrical project. But before sending the letter, some thought evidently swamped the writer in despair and he set off on a walk at the double quick to a suburb ten miles away. On coming back exhausted he pulls out his letter and blurts out his thought: "How alone I feel. My muscles are palsied as in those about to die. O my friend send me something to work on, a bone to gnaw. How beautiful the country was today. So much light. All the living beings I met coming back seemed happy. The trees were gently astir and I was alone in the vast plain. Space, absence, forgetfulness, pain, and rage assailed me. Despite all my efforts, life escapes me, I only catch shreds of it." [12]

He intersperses a report of fresh troubles with his family, which doubtless intensified his feeling of isolation. The doctor had once again snipped the lifeline and Hector exclaims, "Money, money, always money. . . . I might be all right if I had a great deal of it." Then after considering death which, he sagely observes, is far from equivalent to happiness, he winds up: "Yet my blood flows through my veins as before; my heart beats as if full of joy. Come to think of it, I am in excellent form. Let us cheer up, by gad, cheer up!" The next day, he soberly closes the incident while reassuring his friend: "Do not worry about these unfortunate aberrations of my heart; the fit is passed." [13]

Perhaps Berlioz should have destroyed these chaotic confessions instead of sending them to his bosom friend, but the nineteenth century in general and Berlioz in particular held to the belief that friendship is graced by openness, and he acted on it.

Yet this naïveté did not preclude his adroit overcoming of the very crass obstacles put in the way of his projected concert. To secure the use of the hall at the Conservatoire, Berlioz needed Cherubini's permission. Now Luigi Cherubini, a Florentine who had settled in France before the revolution, was in 1828 a somewhat embittered man of sixty-eight. He had been disappointed as an opera composer and his affections were concentrated on a very few friends (including Ingres). His musical passion had been replaced by a great love of botany and by artistic conservatism generally. Co-founder and now Director of the Conservatoire, he proved to be an able administrator verging on the martinet. All rules were sacrosanct: he considered Bach a German, bar-

[12] *L.I.*, 15–22. [13] *L.I.*, 20–1.

barian because of his harmonic freedom, just as he considered Berlioz a criminal for entering the building through the wrong door.[14] And the new Concert Society seemed equally subversive. To play Beethoven and encourage young students to have their own works performed would endanger all authority. He told Berlioz he would have the seats and music desks removed from the stage and the flooring *demolished*.[15] But Berlioz was not to be intimidated [16] and he had friends at court. Cherubini therefore promised him the use of the hall if – if the Superintendent of Fine Arts also agreed. Berlioz had a successful audience with the Vicomte, whereupon Cherubini declared that he had never consented, since Berlioz' concert would interfere with the scholastic schedule.[17] This was to underestimate Berlioz' resourcefulness. He penned three letters to officialdom, each text a model of persuasion and tact, and thereby checkmated Cherubini. Later, in a separate note, of a diction exquisitely relaxed to mark the change of mood, Hector topped his victory by asking the Vicomte, as a private patron of the arts, to attend his concert.[18] The same Berlioz who was a mad lover and explosively confessional friend could also handle worldly weapons – it was a question of what he was giving his mind to.

To make the concert a Parisian event so that it might reach the ears of Miss Smithson, Berlioz had to make sure of the newspapers. This was all the more necessary that to take such a step while still a student at the Conservatoire was unprecedented. The last century did not feel as we do about youth and made no effort to bring out new composers, the

[14] *Mem.*, I, 45–6.

[15] *853*, 123 *n.*

[16] Ill-mannered brusqueness was normal with Cherubini: Adolphe Adam tells of being, as a young boy, presented to him by his father who had long known the Director. The only greeting was "My! What an ugly child!" (*924*, 86–7.) Liszt and César Franck had similar experiences with him. At the death of a colleague, a violinist, Cherubini's one remark was: "Small tone, small tone!" But as often happens, this flint-fronted, gallows-faced personage was something of a sentimentalist who had, like the boy Berlioz, composed the *Estelle* romance. It was widely popular, and later formed the subject of a commemorative ballet in which the two composers were imagined as reconciled through the joint use of their music. (*Le Roman d'Estelle*, Paris Opera, Mar. 23, 1916.)

[17] Again an allusion to the trouble caused by playing Beethoven: "These concerts," wrote Cherubini, "together with the rehearsals required, have relaxed student discipline by reason of the absences enforced upon the instructors and part of the classes. It is therefore high time that I should restore the scheduled exercises. If concerts were to continue to be given in the Royal School, I could not undertake to insure this regularity as fully as I could wish." (*853*, 123 *n.*)

[18] *A.R.*, 39–46.

only avenue to success being through a government commission or through the Opera.[19] In announcing his concert, Berlioz drew attention to these conditions and pointed out the risk he was taking: "For four years I have knocked at every door, to no avail. I cannot obtain a libretto to set, nor secure the production of the one I have on hand. I have tried in vain all the usual means of gaining a hearing, except one, which I am now resorting to. Perhaps I should take as my motto Virgil's line, 'To the vanquished, the only salvation is to hope for none' . . . My concert, I know, will have all the disadvantages of musical programs that are made up of only one man's work, but at least good judges will be enabled to decide whether that work shows any promise." [20]

The concert on May 26, 1828 was a triumph. Commenting on it, the *Figaro* took up Berlioz' motto from Virgil and capped it with another, "Fortune favors the brave." The *Waverley* overture, said the critic, had deserved the three salvos of applause that greeted it, and the second part of the "Greek Revolution" was equally admirable. What mattered even more to Berlioz was the impression he had produced on his performers. From the first rehearsal they had been enthusiastic, and their comments established him in the world of professionals – his first conquest in a long series. And already in 1828 the electric quality resulting from the Berlioz pace was evident to all, though diversely judged. The *Figaro* spoke of "a superabundance of verve which at first excites enthusiasm and then tires attention," and the influential theorist and composer, F. J. Fétis in the *Revue Musicale* concluded, "M. Berlioz has genius. His style is energetic and sinewy. His inspirations are often graceful. But still more often he spends himself in combinations of an original and passionate cast, which border on the wild and bizarre and are only saved by the fact that they come off." [21]

The critics generally preferred the Greek scene to the *Resurrexit* and the *Waverley* overture to the *Francs-Juges* – a fair index of what Berlioz was adding to tradition, for the *Resurrexit* contained the core of great movements in later works, and the *Francs-Juges* overture (which has recently come back into the repertory through an excellent English recording),[22] represents the native Berlioz at twenty-four. "One marvels," says a critic looking back after a century, "at the daring and ingenuity

[19] Even the official guarantee to produce the first opera composed by a Rome Prize winner after his return was a dead letter

[20] Four identical letters to the press, the one to Fétis being reprinted in *Corresp.*, 65–6.

[21] *267*, 290.

[22] *1434*. [This remark and its supporting reference date back to 1948.]

of the young musician . . . who could handle such a broad canvas. In it you can find twenty original ideas — enough to make all his confrères green with envy. You may say 'Obvious effects!' True, but they were not obvious before Berlioz invented them and set the pattern." [23]

In the 1820's the first hearing of this overture was understandably called volcanic and terrifying. As always happens with unfamiliar art, listeners ascribed the shocks experienced in one or two places to the whole. They forgot the quiet introduction in F minor (much admired by Bernard Shaw) [24] which is based on a theme derived from the second subject. This in turn was the flute melody of the boyhood quintet, treated here as a march of knightly character. The striking novelties were the recitative for trombones and ophicleides in octaves below the mass of strings, the simultaneous use of contrary nuances, and the scale passage for strings in whole tones. Best of all, from a technical standpoint, was the masterly reintroduction of the second theme in the long crescendo near the close: all in all, a real tour de force for a young dramatic musician working without knowledge of Beethoven.

The concert gave Berlioz the reassurance he required but it brought him little else. He had had to go into debt again and to explain himself at home, where the object of his struggles was still a mystery. Dr. Berlioz understood neither the conditions of music in Paris nor the special difficulties of genius. He evidently thought that if everything Lesueur said of Hector was true, the boy should by now be self-supporting. Why did medicine and agriculture still have to pay the piper? Hector tried to show in one hurtling epistle that innovation was at a discount and natural enmity to talent at a premium, while the public was no reliable arbiter. Berlioz knew even then how much opinion is swayed by habit, and how far his unwillingness to make concessions was a handicap: "I avoid like the plague those commonplaces which all composers (Weber and Beethoven excepted) serve up at the end of their pieces. They strike me as a kind of charlatanism which says, 'This thing is about over: get ready to applaud' . . . Those wretched conventional phrases make every piece resemble every other." [25]

[23] Maurice Emmanuel: *427*, 243–4. Berlioz had to explain in a note what otherwise might seem a copyist's mistake: "Here the orchestra takes on a double character; the strings must, without drowning out the flutes, continue to play in stark accents; the flutes and clarinets, on the contrary, with a soft and melancholy expression." (*Ger. ed.*, IV, 52.)

[24] *880*, 48.

[25] *A.R.*, 49.

It was many years before the doctor finally understood. At the moment he could only give another puzzled yank to the pursestrings. Lesueur had to advance the money for Hector's entry in the approaching Rome Prize, and this determined the young man to compromise so as to win: he would for once compose like *ces messieurs* of the Institute. At the same time he would try other means to secure his independence. The favorable review of his concert in the new daily, *Le Figaro*, gave him an opening to its editor, Victor Bohain, who was also a dramatist and theatrical manager.[26] He had written a *Faust* ballet, which Berlioz agreed to set in a manner that the Opera might accept.

Meanwhile the English players pursued their conquest of France, playing with continued success for Miss Smithson in the large provincial towns. They then returned to Paris, were joined by Charles Kean, and gave *Richard III* and the *Merchant of Venice*. Berlioz saw his idol again, and ventured backstage but was not admitted. He sent messages which were not delivered; he only managed to find out that neither his name nor his recent success had penetrated as far as the insulated world of the foreign company.

Gloomy but undaunted, Berlioz went *en loge* in July, after the usual elimination contest and its obligato fugue. The cantata subject, *Herminie*, by the symbolically named poetaster, Vieillard, retold a scene from Tasso's *Jerusalem Delivered*. It depicted the love of Erminia, an infidel, for the Christian warrior Tancred, who is wounded while storming the gates of her city. Berlioz may well have seen something appropriate to his own situation in a subject by Tasso, the poet driven mad by love and thwarted ambition. At any rate, in musical matters Berlioz was always thoroughly master of himself, and bent as he now was on getting his prize, he produced a perfectly ordered and acceptable piece. He subdued his ideas to others' implied specifications, writing for what he termed "a modest middle-class orchestra," which would sound "interchangeable with its own piano reduction." [27] He even kept the strings going steadily, so that his judges could understand what he was doing at all points. For Erminia's song he used the Estelle theme of his boyhood (later the *idée*

[26] Alexandre-Victor Bohain (1805–1856) had bought *Le Figaro* in 1827 in order to campaign for constitutional liberties against Charles X, and to support the new literature. To the Romantic seizure of the Paris stage he contributed a *Mirabeau* which undeservedly failed in 1831. Thereafter he edited a number of magazines full of talent but short-lived. Heine gives a sketch of Bohain which shows him as an intelligent and generous patron, limping happily on his wooden leg among the literary lights whom he was fond of treating at champagne dinners. (*Confessions: 1261*, V, 91–3.)

[27] *L.I.*, 9.

fixe of the *Symphonie Fantastique*) developing it to a considerable extent but being careful to introduce into its accompaniment phrases in the comic opera style of the day. He again employed a leitmotif, but made sure that its form remained simple and visible. The air of Erminia donning armor, the prayer (which Berlioz liked enough to save it for later use), and the finale brilliantly returning to the initial allegro, were all equally plain and competent. At the very end, however, his decision to be conventional wavered. Instead of ending his piece with a cadence twice repeated, holding the high note and adding an eight-bar ritornello, he conceived a dramatically and musically more interesting close – an instrumental coda which as it were takes Erminia into battle. The gentle decrescendo lets us hear once again the theme of her prayer sung by flute, clarinet, and horns; then the horns drop out while the strings and bassoon continue the march theme to a final *pppp-quasi niente*.[28]

This inspiration was his undoing. After mixed counsels, he was given a second prize. Cherubini apparently spoke for him, and others – outside any of the musical cliques – wondered why a young composer who had won some acclaim in the City was not worthy of a first prize in the Grove. For according to custom the artists of the Institute met first in professional "sections," then as a committee of the whole for the final vote: painters and architects judged scores on the same footing as musicians judged canvases and busts.[29]

The second prize being purely honorific, Berlioz was still in debt, to Lesueur among others, and without word from his father. After consulting with his teacher, he took the not unusual step of writing to the Minister of Fine Arts, Comte de Martignac, asking for a grant-in-aid. Lesueur added a covering note which said that the request was founded on the most brilliant promise; Berlioz – was "born for music" and would in ten years be a great composer and the leader of a school.[30] Without waiting for the reply, Hector decided to go home and plead with his parents again.

He left late in August 1828 hoping to stay less than a month. To his amazement, his second prize had done more to justify him than anything he had said, or done singlehanded. There is indeed no place like home for such touches of subtle flattery. Their "prize-winning boy," "not twenty-five years old," "chosen by the Institute," was feted from house to house

[28] *Ger. ed.*, XV, 58–60.

[29] This rule harked back to the revolutionary fear of tyranny: the mixed votes were counted on to prevent any interference by the executive.

[30] *A.R.*, 51–3.

as far as Grenoble and back; but though he acted his role with affability and showed the native humor and gaiety which, as he once said, "sweeps away all cobwebs," Hector's mind was elsewhere. The songs of *Faust* were in his mind's ear, and on September 14, while riding in a carriage not far from where Estelle used to live, he composed the haunting melody for Gretchen's song of the King of Thule. Two days later he writes to Ferrand to come soon and bring with him a copy of *Faust* if he has one, so that together they can read Shakespeare and Goethe – those "mute confidants of my life." [31] Except for tramping in the rain with his little sister, Hector felt alienated from the family and its concerns; it was the family, rather, who sought a *rapprochement.* Like a magician (now you see it, now you don't) the doctor restored Hector's allowance – luckily, as it turned out, for the Minister of Fine Arts "did not see his way clear to, etc. . . ."

Back in Paris by early October 1828, Berlioz resumed the struggle to establish himself. This crucial prize-giving had denied him the reward he had earned by seven years of hard work. According to any reasonable standard, his cantata should have won the prize – he had unquestionably learned all that the Conservatoire had to teach. With his immense capacity for work, to by-pass the prize and go his own way would at this stage have been of incalculable benefit to his health, morale, and artistic output. But the state of music in Paris made this impossible. Outside the subsidized musical theatres, there was no livelihood for a serious composer, and these monopolistic positions were hard to breach. Hence the *Faust* ballet was Berlioz' first care. Bohain's three-act scenario having been "accepted" by the Opera and partly set by the composer, the latter requested the inevitable Sosthènes to commission the score: "If you wish to know my qualifications, here they are: I have set to music the greater part of Goethe's poems [in *Faust*]. My head is full of the theme and if nature has endowed me with any imagination, I doubt whether I can find a subject more congenial to it." [32] *Faust* being as much in vogue as Shakespeare and more so than Beethoven, its musical prospects were good. Indeed the Opera had accepted not one but three librettos.

[31] *L.I.*, 24.

[32] *A.R.*, 68–9. The modern reader, reared as a democratic man, may need to be reminded that these begging letters are *de rigueur* in a centralized state, and are no index to character; Berlioz wrote them as modern youth fills out application blanks for fellowship awards. But the whole system of state-supported art as we shall see it at work in Berlioz' life should give pause to advocates of its establishment in the United States.

Harriet Smithson in 1827, by Deveria

"A celestial face, like Smithson's . . ."
— SAINTE-BEUVE TO VIGNY (1828)

The Théâtre des Nouveautés had successfully launched an opera based on the poem, and adaptations without music were numerous. Scribe, Boieldieu, and Meyerbeer all tackled the drama, but made no headway with it.

Though Bohain's likewise never saw the light of day, what Berlioz had written to the Vicomte was the truth. While in his native mountains he had begun composing a sequence of eight scenes (comprising nine songs) to the verse portions of Gérard de Nerval's translation of the drama. All other means failing, Berlioz would publish the score at his own expense, dedicating it, in memory of past favors, to the Superintendent of Fine Arts. Finished by February 1829, the work was issued two months later and despatched to Goethe with a modest but fervent letter on April 10. Goethe was charmed by the missive, which he deemed most gentlemanly, and also by the attention, which matched Delacroix's sending of his lithographs. These, Goethe felt, "shed a new light on his own poem." [33] He might have found a similar enlightenment in Berlioz' music had he been able to hear it, but he consulted his old friend Zelter – Mendelssohn's teacher – who replied damning the work as a series of grunts, snorts, and expectorations.[34] This must rank as the first important instance of the unwisdom of judging Berlioz unheard, for whatever may be thought of the rest, Gretchen's two songs, the Concert of Sylphs, and Mephisto's serenade are melodies of the most lyrical character, treated with great simplicity.[35]

Berlioz sent out other copies of his work, which elicited considerable interest. Fétis termed the score highly original, too much so for his taste, but full of talent and ease. He then served notice on the theater managers that they must make use of the composer, who was "destined to the highest success" provided he received encouragement.

As none of these calls brought down the walls of Jericho, Berlioz could only keep on trying all things. He had never been so busy: composing, attending the statutory number of classes at the Conservatoire; finding and teaching pupils – among them a Spanish heiress who paid regularly and well; and finally, for ends of his own which may be guessed, learning English. ("It takes a whole evening in a public course to learn

[33] *1076*, I, 187.

[34] *194*, 362. For the other documents, see *170*.

[35] Anyone who has access to recordings from *The Damnation of Faust*, into which all these songs were later embedded, can assure himself of Zelter's mistake. Berlioz soon learned that another German musician, Adolph Marx, had favorably reviewed the score, calling the author "a disciple of Beethoven." Marx then invited Berlioz to contribute to the Berlin *Musikalische Zeitung*. (See *359a*.)

what a private tutor could tell you in fifteen minutes.") [36] Since the libretto of *Les Francs-Juges* had been definitely turned down, he was recasting parts of the music into a single scene entitled "The Warriors of the Breisgau." And fresh inspiration to compose came from reading translations by his friend Gounet from Thomas Moore's *Irish Melodies*.[37] Soon, Berlioz had nine new songs, of which one, the *Elégie*, in honor of the Irish patriot, Robert Emmet, was perhaps the first modern composition written to a prose text. Berlioz entitled the collection *Mélodies Irlandaises,* thus naturalizing in France the term *mélodie* to denote a song.

Despite much activity, this second half of 1829 brought little change in Berlioz' state of mind. He was feverish and depressed by turns. At one point he secured the post of musical director in a new theater, only to lose it when the backer-manager withdrew. His debts to several friends preyed on his mind, and he took on additional hack work, such as the proofreading of *William Tell*, for which he received two hundred francs. There was compensating pleasure in proofreading the Beethoven symphonies and preserving them from Fétis's numerous "corrections," at the cost of antagonizing the critic.[38] Berlioz' *Faust* score meanwhile earned him very flattering comments by established composers, such as Onslow and Meyerbeer, but the publisher was postponing payment of the slim royalties. To add to Berlioz' distress, his friend Ferrand was ill, and dilatory in his replies as always: more than once Berlioz had had to supply his own lines for the libretto of the *Francs-Juges*. Now for divers reasons, Ferrand was being urged by his parents to drop Hector's acquaintance, and knowledge of this having got back to Berlioz hurt and disquieted him.

In addition, he had perforce taken to regular journalism, as a source of income and a means to power. Although the pressure for copy was great and the pay nonexistent, he was Paris correspondent for Marx's Berlin paper, as well as frequent contributor to a new French weekly, *Le Correspondant*. Despite its strongly royalist and religious bias, this periodical accepted Berlioz' unorthodox views on music. In the issue for April 11, 1829, for instance, he expounded his lifelong tenets regarding the proper treatment of fugal style and the compatibility of dramatic ideas with religious music.[39] In the same place not long after, Berlioz began a

[36] *A.R.*, 60.

[37] Moore's poems represented a tendency with which Berlioz strongly sympathized, namely the attempt to restore folk ballads and folk tunes to favor. For some of the preliminary steps leading to Moore's publication, see the article on Beethoven and George Thomson (*758*).

[38] *853*, 346–7 *n.*

[39] "*Considérations sur la Musique Religieuse,*" reprinted in *595*, 287 ff.

short serial biography of Beethoven, who had died two years before. It is a careful piece of work, giving details which Berlioz had in part gathered from living acquaintances of the master – Reicha, Fétis, Cherubini, and even the gruff Kreutzer.[40] After a century of Beethoven scholarship, this sketch and these recollections have dwindled in value, but one passage has kept its significance about both Berlioz and Beethoven. The writer is speaking of a recent concert at which the C-sharp Minor Quartet was given by Baillot's ensemble:

> About two hundred persons were in the hall listening religiously. After a few minutes, the audience grew restless; people began to talk, each telling his neighbor of his increasing discomfort and boredom. Finally, unable to stand such weariness of spirit, nine tenths of the audience got up and left, complaining aloud that the music was unbearable, incomprehensible, ridiculous – the work of a madman defying common sense.
>
> Silence was at last restored at the request of a few, and the quartet was concluded. Thereupon the voice of condemnation broke out again. M. Baillot was accused of making fools of the public by presenting extravagant nonsense. A few Beethoven devotees apologized, pleading the composer's mental derangement. "What a pity that such a great man should have produced deformities after all his masterpieces!"
>
> Yet in one corner of the room there was a small group – and I must confess, whatever one may say, that I was among them – whose thoughts and feelings were altogether different. This tiny fraction of the audience, suspecting what was going to happen, had huddled together so as not to be bothered in their contemplation. After a few bars in the first movement, I did indeed fear I might be bored, though I kept listening. Shortly the chaos seemed to unwind, and just when the public's patience gave out mine revived, and I fell under the spell of the composer's genius. . . . Here is music, then, which repels almost all those who hear it and which, among a few, produces sensations wholly out of the ordinary. Whence this enormous discrepancy?[41]

Berlioz is sure that musical ignorance is not the answer. He knew that the most distinguished theorist-composers in his entourage were against Beethoven, but while he derived from *Freischütz* and Opus 131 "new sensations," they only wondered what the world was coming to.[42] Each generation, says Berlioz answering his own question, fears change; and the envious oppose what is new, knowing their own incapacity to create.

[40] *1377*, Aug. 4 and 11, Oct. 8, 1829, 179 ff.

[41] *1377*, 251–2. See also the letter written by Berlioz after the concert. (*A.R.*, 71.)

[42] Rossini, though himself a "modern," abused other innovators, saying that *Freischütz* gave him the colic. Because of this remark, when someone offered Berlioz an introduction to him, the younger man declined the favor. (*L.I.*, 40.)

Berlioz' sketch of Beethoven, fortunately published *after* his third prize attempt, amounted in fact to a declaration of war upon his elders. In the last installment, he calmly asserted that the Ninth Symphony, which he had read but which no one in Paris had heard, so far from showing a great man struggling with dementia, was on the contrary a starting point for the music of the present.

To this declaration the standard rebuttal, the eternal rejoinder, was that Beethoven's predecessors Haydn and Mozart had done all that could be done, and had thus left to Beethoven only the bizarre, the contorted, the "rocky ways" of music. Everyone forgot, everyone always forgets, that earlier still it was Mozart who was accused of treading the rocky ways. This historical view is here in point, for Berlioz was perfectly aware even then that he belonged in the sequence. Critics would in time come around to Beethoven, but only to say that he had accomplished all that music can do "along that line," which of course explains why Berlioz had to follow the rocky ways.[43]

Between his return to Paris in October 1828 and the publication of his Beethoven biography in the summer following, Berlioz' imaginings of love had gone through several stages dimly discernible in the record. Having managed to communicate with Harriet Smithson early in 1829, Hector had been led to suppose, or had deceived himself into supposing, that the actress took note of his suit and would test its sincerity by a few months' delay. Two months later, Berlioz, who by coincidence lodged in a house opposite that in which she came to live, discovered that she had left, this time not for the provinces but for Holland, perhaps never to return. For several weeks he put her out of his mind; then in June

[43] On Mozart in 1787: "He carries his effort at originality too far. . . . What a gulf between a Mozart and a Boccherini! The former leads us over rugged rocks on to a waste sparsely strewn with flowers. . . ." (*968*, III, 3 and 6.)

On Beethoven in 1811: "His two illustrious predecessors [Haydn and Mozart] had long since occupied all the main avenues, and had left him only a few steep and rocky paths, in which good taste and the purity of tradition can easily come to grief. . . . Beethoven who is often bizarre and baroque, occasionally dazzles us with passages of extraordinary beauty. Sometimes he soars majestically like an eagle, sometimes he crawls along the rocky ways." (*853*, 121 and 61.)

On Berlioz in 1875: "We have been occupied with Berlioz; Rubinstein had to play us the *Symphonie Fantastique*. . . . There is a great wealth of ideas and melody in it, but they are like the good seed cast upon rocky ground. . . ." (Cosima Wagner: *947*, 655.)

the sight of English newspapers praising her dramatic genius rekindled his flame and made him a prey to new self-torture.

All the while, he had been revolving in his mind a large-scale symphonic work on the theme of *Faust*.[44] For during these eight months Berlioz had perfected himself in the art of living on two different planes. His personal existence, divided between love-longings and the struggle for position, had the breathless, incoherent, obsessive character which the usual accounts of his life like to stress. His artistic inner life, on the contrary, was as steady, coherent, and progressively successful as if he had been a recognized genius in mid-flight. The schemes, hopes, and disappointments suggest a desperate gambler, which is what, for the time being, Dr. Berlioz and the Institute made of him. But the music, the penmanship of letters and scores, the style of musical articles, the work at the Conservatoire – not to speak of the course in English – imply a very different being, whose characteristics are deliberate care, self-control, judgment, method, and an almost academic love of minutiae.

This craftsman's delight in the thing well done was nothing new. When in the throes of adolescence at La Côte, Berlioz had managed to make his notebook of romances as neat and systematic as a legal document. Throughout life his manuscripts were clear and even handsome,[45] for where music was concerned patience never deserted him, not even in the most trying circumstances of the battle still ahead of him. Hence in Berlioz it is more than usually misleading to read the outward event into the work of art. If the two are connected it is deep down, invisibly, and not in the direct way of an offprint which the casual onlooker may read.

Berlioz' love for his unattainable Harriet undoubtedly dwelt with him, influencing his musical inspiration just as Estelle earlier had moved his childish heart and spurred his melodic invention. But other children and other youths have had unhappy loves and composed nothing at all, hence the relation of life to art is not one of simple cause and effect. Again, Hector's love for Miss Smithson seems clearly theatrical in both senses of the word. It is as if Berlioz had *wanted*, rather than had been brought, to love her. In this he was following the very respectable French tradition of the *amour de tête*, which is a form of idealism or true Platonic striving after an imagined perfection. The composer's fancy lighted on a woman who was charming to behold, possessed of talent, praised by others, living the life of art, and intimately associated with the thought

[44] *L.I.*, 30 and 62; *A.R.*, 87

[45] See Moscheles's comment about scanning the "exquisitely penned score" of the *Romeo and Juliet* symphony on Berlioz' desk in 1839. (*979*, II, 54.)

of Shakespeare. It is even possible to conjecture that Berlioz was spiting his family by choosing an actress — or again, that Mme. Berlioz had unwittingly given him a taste for tragic scenes.[46]

This heady passion, in a young man who had as yet had little or no personal attention from women, clearly drew on the emotional resources he had mentioned to his father the first time he spoke of his choice of career; so that far from ascribing the music of these years to the love affair, it would be more plausible to explain the love by artistic passion. At the moment their joint effect was only to stiffen his ambition and sharpen his sense of loneliness. Yet even while he believed that his infatuation would kill him, Berlioz recognized that contrary to all maxims he could apparently love without hope.[47] He has not a shred of hope left, he says as he gets ready for his third try at the Rome Prize in July 1829, but all the same he is copying the orchestra parts of his *Faust* scenes and of his remodeled *Francs-Juges*. The words of this operatic scene are to be translated into German for a possible production by Spohr in Kassel. Berlioz may have already sensed that Germany rather than Paris was his proper battleground, and after Rome (where the prize would compel him to go) he would spend a year in the land of Weber and Beethoven. Meantime he is trying to assure a good reception for the *Irish Melodies* which are in the press, and there is the usual tension preparatory to going *en loge*.

The subject for the 1829 competition was *The Death of Cleopatra*, the words being from the same Vieillard as the year before — feeble but malleable.[48] From his knowledge of Shakespeare Berlioz could of course conjure up a greater Cleopatra, worthier of his music, but quite apart from the musical problem, the politics of the award was ticklish for both sides. It was impossible for the candidate to write a cantata more unlike himself than that of the previous year; it would be a parody.[49] On the judges' side it was understood that a Second Prize normally matured into a First, yet they resented their "pupil's" growing reputation as well as the divided counsels he brought into their midst. The worst of it was that Lesueur was too ill to attend, and at the meeting the performer once

[46] He wrote to his family early in 1829, imparting his intention to marry the actress if she would have him; this did not seem to surprise them, chastened as they were by his independent attitude and musical success. (*L.I.*, 28.)

[47] *L.I.*, 40.

[48] For the type of verses, see *V.M.*, II, chs. 1–3. The themes hardly change: in 1900 Florent Schmitt was still setting a *Semiramis* for his prize.

[49] Ravel lost the prize by making just that mistake, and earned only a severe rebuke: "M. Ravel may take us for stuffed shirts [*pompiers*] but not for imbeciles." (*877*, 346.)

again failed to do Berlioz justice: this time it was the singer who was called to a rehearsal of *William Tell* and sent her neophyte sister. Without proper rehearsal, she freshly murdered Cleopatra, and despite the protests of Ingres and Pradier at this accidental unfairness to the candidate, the jury decided to give no awards, reserving the right to give two the following year.

The music of Berlioz' *Cleopatra* is as interesting as that of his *Orpheus*, freer and still more assured than that of *Herminie*. Rich in melodies – some were too good to waste and Berlioz used them again – the three arias range from antique declamation in Gluck's style to the Shakespearean vision of Cleopatra dreaming that her shade greets those of all the Ptolemies. This section bears a motto from *Romeo and Juliet*, "How if, when I am laid into the tomb . . ." written in English – which probably strengthened the judges' belief that young Berlioz positively declined to be understood. The last section is a subtly scored death scene, here and there suggestive of the love-philter music in *Tristan*, thirty years ahead.[50]

The day after the announcement of the blank result, Berlioz met Boieldieu, the amiable composer of the opera *Dame Blanche*, who had sided with the majority and now tried to explain himself: "My dear fellow, why did you do it? We *wanted* to give you the prize, thinking you would be a better boy than last year. . . . I don't say your work isn't good. But how can I pass judgment on what I do not understand? There are so many things I've had to hear over and over again before I liked them. I couldn't help saying to my colleagues yesterday that with your way of writing you must despise us from the bottom of your heart. You refuse to write like everybody else. Even your rhythms are new. You would invent new modulations if such a thing were possible!"[51]

As for Auber, who like Cherubini had voted for Berlioz, he warned Hector in a fatherly way that if he persisted "the public will not like it and the music sellers will not buy." Berlioz nodded sagely but discharged his retort into the friendly bosom of Ferrand: "If we are supposed to write music for pastrycooks and dressmakers, why do they give us a

[50] Note in passing that Berlioz' dramatic, or poetic, ideas are not single and specific but multiple and general: he is thinking not only of his text but also of Shakespeare's *Antony and Cleopatra* and *Romeo and Juliet*. Later, without changing a note, this same Meditation becomes the "Chorus of Shades" in *Lélio*, introduced by a reference to Hamlet's brooding. Compare the connections between the *Sardanapalus* (of 1830), the *Romeo* (of 1839) and the Dido of 1855.

[51] *A.R.*, 78–9; see also *L.I.*, 45–6 and *Mem.*, I, 142–3.

text involving the passions of the Queen of Egypt and her solemn meditations upon death?" [52]

For the fifth and last time Dr. Berlioz used financial pressure to draw Hector home. This meant three weeks wasted to rehash the old story, not to mention the expense and weariness of the trip: those idle hours in a stagecoach, with one's nerves in knots, and under compulsion to exchange small talk with passengers for whom the few miles of their journey is the most exciting event of the decade.[53] In spite of everything, Berlioz' first symphony was taking shape, and with or without an allowance, he was sure he could last another year. He now had a steady job teaching guitar in an "orthopedic" institution for young ladies, and though not prosperous he was no longer an unknown. All the more reason to act.

He could sense that the cultural movement of which he was a part was about to make its victorious assault on the academic Bastille. The theaters had already surrendered to the new playwrights – to Dumas's *Henry III* and to Victor Hugo's *Hernani*, scheduled for the following season. New names and new genres were gaining currency in pleasant profusion: among novelists, Balzac's *Les Chouans*, Vigny's *Cinq Mars*, and Merimée's *Charles IX*. Sainte-Beuve's *Poetry of the 16th Century* was out in book form. The political historians, Thiers, Guizot, Sismondi, Barante, and Thierry were crowding the market with readable and revolutionary works, Michelet was translating Vico and reinterpreting the whole of Europe's past as a struggle for freedom. And the Salon was being invaded by the colorful enormities of Decamps, Huet, and Delacroix.

Nor did music lag behind: Rossini's new opera, *William Tell*, was a richer and more serious work than his usual "string of romances and cavatinas." Auber had just written his *Muette de Portici*, which would soon cause political riots, not by its form but by its subject – the struggle against tyrants.[54] Outside the operatic stage and the virtuoso platform, Berlioz stood alone, preaching the modern art of Beethoven. But neither

[52] *L.I.*, 47.

[53] *Soirées* (11th) *Eves.*, 139–40.

[54] Known in English as *Masaniello*, the opera is based on the seventeenth-century uprising led by the fisherman, Tommaso Aniello, against Spanish rule in Naples. The music, much admired by Wagner, is indeed revolutionary for a member of the French school, especially in its instrumentation. Various conjectures have been advanced to account for this single burst of daring on the part of a delicate but tame composer, the best being that he caught the ambient fever.

Beethoven nor his prophet would be heard unless Berlioz gave a second concert at his own risk. This time Cherubini gave the hall, the players readily accepted, and Habeneck conducted. To his two overtures and the *Resurrexit* of the Mass (retouched again) Berlioz added the "Concert of Sylphs" from the *Eight Scenes of Faust.* He also induced his new friend Ferdinand Hiller, a young German who taught at the same girls' school, to play Beethoven's piano concerto in E flat – for the first time in Paris. As window dressing, an Italian coloratura and two virtuoso instrumentists were added to the program. Despite the dangerous proximity of Beethoven's masterpiece, the musicians once again acclaimed Berlioz' overtures, and what is more, the box office netted a profit of one hundred and fifty francs. At this the government took notice and awarded Berlioz a bonus of one hundred francs, to offset the "nominal" charge made for the hall.

But the next day Hector was ill and deep in depression. He gave all these news to his father, deploring the absence of any member of the family, and adding: "Since yesterday I am depressed unto death; I should like to weep forever; . . . I wish I could die . . . I cannot connect one idea with another . . . I think I ought to sleep a great deal." [55] The newspapers cordially acknowledged the success of the concert but scarcely analyzed the new music. Only Fétis in his austere *Revue* kept track of "the feverish young man, whose fever is not that of an ordinary being." In Berlioz' music, exclaimed the writer, "What accents from another world! What effects, varied in a thousand ways, sometimes felicitous, sometimes repellent, but almost always new and well found: they have shaken the souls of all the listeners." [56]

One of the works, the Faustian "Concert of Sylphs," which was later rescored and transferred to the *Damnation of Faust,* had missed fire. In a passing reference to this fact, Berlioz who knew its worth, explains that he "had not had time to teach it to the performers nor to the public" [57] – a remark of greater significance to his subsequent career and posthumous fame than he could possibly surmise.

[55] *A.R.*, 83.
[56] *1400*, 1829, 348–52.
[57] *L.I.*, 54.

Berlioz the Melodist

"I'll sing you something new."
—Motto from *Faust* in one of Berlioz' *Eight Scenes*

ALTHOUGH it has been called "the most astounding Opus 1" in musical history,[1] Berlioz' *Faust* of 1828 is entitled to this numbering only in the sense that it was the first work the author deemed fit to publish. He soon had qualms even about this, withdrew the score after a very few copies had been distributed, and made every effort to recall the rest.[2] The impulse which he regretted was contrary to his habit of keeping works for revision after hearing. Still, the date of issue marks a phase in Berlioz' life: seven years of assiduous composing in Paris and more than a decade of melodic creation, now in full swing. For despite his present dissatisfaction with certain details, the *Eight Scenes* were rich enough to become the heart of his mature *Damnation of Faust* in 1845.

The years 1828 to 1830 were indeed for Berlioz a period of tremendous lyric effusion. Under the impact of his "love" for Miss Smithson and of his discoveries in the world of art, he produced not only the nine songs comprised in the *Eight Scenes*, but the nine others which he called *Irish Melodies* and soon published as Opus 2. Half a dozen more found different destinations, from the opera still in progress and the projected First Symphony to the pair of prize cantatas yet to come. The plainest fact about Berlioz is that melodies came to him unbidden, self-sustaining, and fitted to a mood rather than to a particular set of words. When he competed for the prize, the subject of the cantata might reawaken ideas he had already consigned to his notebooks; when a given project fell through he readapted his full-formed melodies to other occasions of a comparable kind. The successive transfers of some of these tunes from an early score to a cantata and then to a later work proves that Berlioz considered his melodies as things-in-themselves,[3] and that like most musicians he attached to them only a broad or generic significance.

[1] Ernest Newman, *577*.

[2] A sign of change in Berlioz scholarship may be seen in this contrast: twenty years ago, Berlioz' presentation copy of this score to his classmate Louis Schloesser was offered for sale in the United States. A distinguished librarian declined to purchase it, on the ground that it was neither rare nor important. (*154* and *155*.) Today, the Goethe collection at Yale University owns another of the few extant copies. [This note refers to 1948.]

[3] Constant Lambert: "A melody . . . is a complete work of art in itself. . . . To a composer gifted with melodic genius there may be problems of technique, but there can be no problem of style." (*732*, 98.)

This is not incompatible with the fact that Berlioz was often inspired by what he read. As an educated man living in a great age of literature he had no reason to conceal his literary tastes, nor did he, like some moderns, feel it necessary to dwell on his technical knowledge. Rather, he said of his musical ideas that they were the product of an "inexplicable mechanism" operating within him, and that composing (as against writing words) was to him "a natural function."[4] Now a mechanism that is inexplicable is no mechanism at all, and it had better be called the Socratic daemon or the Freudian unconscious expressing itself in sound. But what Berlioz meant is clear: under favoring conditions, what he strongly felt or imagined came out as music.[5] As Bach and Handel were moved by the contemporary literature of religion, so Berlioz was moved by that of his own secular day. Late in 1827 he was reading Goethe and the newly found Shakespeare. In 1828, he was rereading Moore's *Irish Melodies* (including the touching account of Robert Emmet's execution after an Irish revolt). Later, Berlioz was struck by the imaginative freedom of Jean-Paul and De Quincey, and by the colorfulness of Hugo's *Orientales*. From these last he composed a Pirate Song, and shortly his friend Du Boys translated a fragment from Herder which Berlioz set as a "Ballet of Shades." Finally, in the last days of 1829, Berlioz came upon Hoffmann's *Tales* which, being written by a composer and music critic as well as a poet-novelist, impressed him deeply. The new literature was in fact full of musical imagery. From Florian's *Estelle*, in which one of the characters comes from Berlioz' countryside and describes a shepherd singing the beauties of nature, to the works just enumerated, storytelling was married to music by authors who knew the art at first hand.[6]

Pre-eminent in this work of reuniting sister arts was Goethe. Not only the songs in *Faust* but the *Walpurgisnacht* (which includes the will o' the wisp later set by Berlioz) was conceived for music. And throughout the rest of the drama the music of nature or of man is brought in as commentary upon thought or action. In 1790 Goethe had appropriately published his first version of the work with two *Singspiele*, and when

[4] *Corresp.*, 240; *Mem.* I, 117.

[5] Mozart: "When I feel well and in good humor . . . ideas come to me in droves and most easily. Whence and how do they come to me? I don't know and it's not my doing." (*968*, III, 423.)

[6] Wagner was also aroused musically by Hoffmann's *Tales*, of which he says in his autobiography that they proved a better music teacher than his own instructor. (*245*, 19, 38.) On Hoffmann in France down to Baudelaire and Offenbach, see *1175*, 382–4

after a study of ballads he expanded the fragment, he called the result a "rhapsodic drama." [7] All this, which Berlioz did not know in the way of scholarship but discerned by reading with an artist's eye, brought him into spiritual correspondence with his author; both men evidently understood music as "music-in-life." Berlioz was not simply composing isolated verses from a book but seeking to recreate a dramatic whole: what he fashioned was not "Nine Songs by Goethe," but "Eight Scenes" from *Faust*.[8] The numerical discrepancy means simply that Berlioz made one dramatic scene out of two lyrical moments, adding the note: "Although in Goethe's *Faust* the soldiers' chorus occurs at quite a distance from Gretchen's song, I have joined the two, thinking that the contrast resulting from the opposition of two such different moods [*caractères*] might heighten the force of each."

This is an important clue to the nature of Berlioz' melody: he started from or hit upon the characteristic, and hence felt free to take liberties with written texts. He ignored Goethe's hint that Gretchen spins while singing and he gave her instead a dramatic *Lied* which sums up her passion and forsaking. This turns the soldiers' roistering outside into a sharp commentary—the external world indifferent to our inner life. Farther on, defying plot, Berlioz gave Mephisto the final word, or rather the final exclamation, sung to a diabolic guitar.

To make clear the *caractère* of every scene, Berlioz sandwiched each song between pairs of poetic quotations—either from Goethe and Shakespeare, or from Goethe and Thomas Moore—with occasional bits of prose dialogue added from *Faust*. These were for the spectator-listener; for the singer and instrumentalists, he supplied brief subtitles in lieu of expression marks.[9] Thus "bitter raillery" characterizes the Song of the Flea, and "simple and ingenuous" the ballad of the King of Thule. Each piece is thus enclosed as in a frame and likewise linked to its next neighbor. Berlioz the budding dramatist was fashioning his own *Singspiel* in

[7] *1250*, xlviii and ff. Other poets and critics—Ludwig Tieck, Gérard de Nerval, Otto Runge, Wilhelm Wackenroder, Christian Körner—specified the nature of the new music as dramatic, popular, and independent of church and stage. These notions had a common origin in the rediscovery of folk art, specifically the ballad, which is at once poetry, music, and drama.

[8] Berlioz had previously set Goethe's ballad *Der Fischer* (*Le Pêcheur*) and thus could have had ten "numbers" for a volume had he conceived the *Faust* lyrics as separate pieces.

[9] Rousseau had done very much the same thing in his *Devin de Village* (1752) by writing in the character of his *récitatifs obligés:* "irony," "tender sorrow," and so on. Gluck was quick to praise the device of using the recitative for psychological differentiation, and Mozart learned it from Gluck.

the ancestral manner of *Aucassin et Nicolette: "ici on chante."* [10] Berlioz' way is extremely concise, his mottoes forming a sort of stage directions which evoke our knowledge of the drama and so establish the occasion for the music. One ought accordingly to invert the usual phrase and say of Berlioz that he does not provide music as a setting of the text but rather uses the text as a setting for his music. The fact that Shakespeare and Thomas Moore contribute lines for a score based on *Faust* proves how unliteral was the composer's view of musical speech. What Berlioz could not know with respect to the form of his score as a whole – since the evidence was first published some ten years after his death – was that he was closely paralleling Goethe's original plan. The Göchhausen manuscript of the *Faust* of 1775 is a Shakespearean mixture of prose and verse in which *Act* and *Scene* are replaced by headings indicating the situation, the whole comprising twenty discontinuous scenes, exactly like the *Faust* that Berlioz was to complete seventy years later.

This relation of music to other arts remained absolutely fixed throughout Berlioz' creative life, and the reason why it should be kept in mind is that his melody occasionally presents *musical* difficulties, which the hasty critic ascribes to a literary intention. Nothing could be more mistaken or misleading. One may or may not like a given Berlioz tune, but its possible failure to please is not due to any programmatic desire on the composer's part.

What is a melody? As Pascal remarked of poetry, "Nobody knows." It has been defined as something that can be easily remembered and whistled, and again – by Mr. Stravinsky – as "the musical chant of a cadenced phrase." [11] While theorists mumble, the public knows what it likes, and there have always been honest men who say that Berlioz is unmelodic, that his themes are but incoherent successions of notes or "effects" accumulated at random. Others point out that on the contrary it is because Berlioz' tunes are long, sinuous, and highly original that the detractors find them wanting: they simply do not hear them. The admirers can at least show that in every generation since Berlioz' time it

[10] Compare the verses that Turner quoted or composed for the canvases of his middle period, and the remarks that Goya inscribed on his war etchings.

[11] *889*, 28. A survey of English opinion brought out the fact that the public's favorite tune was "Onward, Christian Soldiers," which is rather a rhythmical than a melodic idea. And various hypotheses with scientific pretensions (Schenker, Birkhoff) find melodies reducible to numerical formulas. To all of which, one may say with Mr. Constant Lambert that "when melodic line has life dissection becomes impossible." (*732*, 96.)

is the highly accomplished musicians, usually the leading composers, who have praised his melody. If it takes but the judgment of twelve peers to decide when a man has committed a crime, it should take no more to prove whether a man has committed a melody, and in that case Berlioz is vindicated.[12]

But it is scarcely helpful to leave the question unanalyzed, even though the majority vote now favors the composer. The experience that Felix Weingartner recounts of "discovering" Berlioz' melodic powers [13] is open equally to those who are not like him conductors and composers. The

[12] The *locus classicus* for the collision of the two points of view is Felix Weingartner's autobiographical account of his "discovering" Berlioz:

"The first of his scores that I got hold of was the Overture to *Benvenuto Cellini,* and I opened it with the usual prejudice. Yet the first phrase in G Major struck me as fresh and joyful. Well, thought I, this much at least is a theme. On the third page I came to a pause followed by a change of time and tempo. Haha! said I, he has reached the end of his tether; the orchestral effects will now begin. The first *pizzicato* of the basses did not look good to me: I could not see what could come out of it. Six more bars, then the woodwinds began a melodic statement, but this too failed to reassure me. The general opinion must be right, I concluded, invention is not his forte.

"But what do I see? I can hardly believe my eyes. For immediately after these six bars a wonderful broad melody begins, played by all the strings; it rises and falls in the most songful phrasing. I read on to the end of this magnificent theme, fully twenty-three bars long. Going on, I discover also that the *pizzicato* of the basses, which at first had seemed unintelligible, was but the preparation for a new theme, given out by the clarinets and bassoons in their lower register – a complete melody of twelve bars, which one could use for splendid variations. Moreover, the melodic statement in the wood was a bridge which now recurred and led to the main part of the overture *allegro deciso con impeto.*

"Though I had only covered the Introduction, I had already found three great and expressive themes, among them a melody of impeccably classic beauty. The man was not completely uninventive after all, thought I to myself, and I grew ashamed at having stupidly run him down instead of going straight to his works.

"In the Allegro, I met again – though with a different accompaniment – the theme with which the Overture begins. Soon it combined with an entirely new figured motif, which again developed into a complete utterance of twenty-one bars. But even this was still not the second theme proper. We meet it shortly thereafter, in the quite regular key of D major – once more a new, enchanting, and richly patterned melody.

"At this point I began to laugh aloud, half from joy at my new-found treasure, half from fury at the shortsightedness of human judgments. Five themes, each plastic, sharply characterized, wonderfully chiselled, varied, developed, climaxed and concluded – there you have the composer who is 'uninventive' in the eyes of many critics and listeners. . . . Look at the rest of Berlioz' works and you will have the same experience as with the *Cellini* Overture." (*911*, 171–3.)

[13] Given in footnote immediately preceding.

first step to take is implicit in what the Austrian musician points out: Berlioz' melodies are long and often asymmetrical: 16, 23, 12, 21 bars;[14] they are apt to be presented in combinations of two or more, and connecting passages are likely to anticipate the full-blown tune by presenting fragments. The ordinary "first listener" is all too likely to remain bewildered unless he takes pains to hear the movement several times at frequent intervals. Even the student of Berlioz when confronted with a new work is a first listener until he has mastered its melodic organization. For no one more than Berlioz, perhaps, has followed so closely the principle of artistic unity which states that decorative parts must be derived from structural. But in order to maintain variety as well, Berlioz makes these derived ornaments seem independent inventions. Hence the warning that one must be "saturated in the music" before one can fully understand and enjoy it.[15]

A typical example occurs in the first movement of the *Symphonie Fantastique*, where several melodies, seemingly distinct, are in reality variants of the same idea.[16] Nor is it by intellectual note-spinning that this repeated budding comes about: Berlioz *heard* it, and the kinship is easily audible to others as soon as they are intimate with the parent melody. The impression of unmelodic piling up of effects is therefore a paradoxical result of melodic abundance. If the term "continuous melody," first popularized by Wagnerians, has any meaning left, it can never be better used than to describe Berlioz' musical thought. For he not only, as he said, "allowed himself the luxury of lavishness as regards melody," but he also made his fertility serve the ends of development and structure.[17]

Berlioz was the first to add: "Although one ought not to deny the

[14] Charles Maclean: "As to his having no melody, each school makes its own definition of what that is . . . but what for instance is '*Les pèlerins étant venus*' from *The Infant Christ* but a melody, and a beautiful one, forty-five bars long?" (*394*, 157.)

Romain Rolland: "How beautiful . . . is the song-recitative of Berlioz, with its long sinuous lines. . . . With Berlioz phrases are most frequently twelve, sixteen, eighteen or twenty bars long. . . ." (*504*, 49 and *n.*)

[15] T. S. Wotton: *533*, 10 ff.

[16] *533*, 10–5. The need for this steeping in the music is borne out by the frequency with which concert analysts say "at this point Berlioz introduces fresh material." Almost invariably it can be shown that the new figure stems from what has been heard before: e.g., the otherwise excellent notes by Percy Pitt and A. Kalisch for the Centenary Concert (Queen's Hall, Dec. 11, 1903), p. 26, ex. 8.

[17] *533*, 35–7. G. Fink exaggerates only slightly when he says: "His structure is wholly melodic. . . . Unlike Wagner he eschews appogiatura; every passing note carries its own harmony, whence passing notes cease to exist as such." (*280*, 39.)

presence of these melodies, one is at liberty to dispute their worth."[18] Here one comes upon a critical occasion par excellence, namely a point of conflict over which the critic must help admirers and opponents alike to find justification for their respective views in the same features of the work of art: the competent judges who find Berlioz' themes harsh, tortuous, or cold must be given a reason.[19] Obviously, in these critics' mental ear there exists a melodic *beau idéal* which Berlioz fails to meet, and he fails all the more often that as a dramatic musician he naturally aims at diversity of character, and so deviates in a dozen ways from the single standard which it is sought to impose upon him.

This standard applies – or fails to apply – in two respects: form and quality. In form, Berlioz disappoints those who require regularity. Schumann was perhaps the first to draw attention upon Berlioz' easy mixing of even with uneven phrases, adding "I side with those who deny Berlioz melody, but only if it is understood that you mean Italian melody, which one knows before hearing it."[20] He might have included German melody as well, for that idiom is as traditionally foursquare as the Italian and the French. Since to many people music still means German music, the expectation of evenness makes Berlioz' tunes seem like blank verse to a lover of ballad meter. The truth is that after Beethoven Berlioz was the great liberator of melody and rhythm. His "line" seldom repeats within its span; its highly original rhythm acts like a spring imparting energy throughout the great length; while its uncommon intervals and strayings from tonality charge it with "character." He *intends* every step and does not merely pass from one harmonic implication to the next. It is these things that bewilder at first, and that account for the derogatory adjectives.[21] But it is undeniable that in doing as he did, Berlioz was recapturing a tradition as well as foreshadowing the future. Just a hundred years after Berlioz' appearance as melodist *sui generis*, Alban Berg would accept the same challenge: "You probably miss in our [atonal] music

[18] *Mem.*, II, 361.

[19] It has even been said that the singing melody of the Pilgrims in the *Harold* symphony is unsatisfactory. (*1374*, Apr. 1945.) Compare W. J. Turner: "To create such a melody as . . . the theme of the Pilgrims' March in *Harold* is not given to every famous composer." (*309*, 190.)

[20] *508*, 176. This asymmetry bothers professional score-readers even more than listeners. *Looking* at Berlioz' *La Captive* one finds two phrases of five bars set off by one of eight. Yet the tune was catchy enough for people to whistle it all over Rome in 1831. (See below, ch. 8.)

[21] In the *Irish Melodies*, for example, one can find the frequent syncopations annoying or delightful according as one is or is not ready for a subtle irritation of the artistic nerve, for an apparent disorder which leads to equilibrium under greater tension.

the two- and four-bar periodicity as we know it in the Viennese classicists and all the romantics, including Wagner. . . . But even in the Viennese classics, and especially in Mozart and Schubert, we observe again and again, efforts to break away from the restraints of this square symmetry." [22]

Unaccustomed angles and turns in melody are bound to create difficulties in execution – difficulties that are not inherent in the written notes or the construction of musical throats and instruments, but rather in the routine habits of performers matching the routine habits of listeners.[23] The consequence is that even with faith in the account just given one cannot be sure of hearing a Berlioz melody aright. It can be subtly dismembered, as Mr. Ernest Newman has shown, whether by player or hearer. Alter the phrasing and the music is stricken dumb. The critic demonstrates this by taking five bars of the English horn theme from the Roman Carnival overture; [24] but he could generalize about the whole of that melody and say that when it sounds as if fashioned in dreariness for a hurdy-gurdy it is because the phrasing, timing, and mental projection of the notes by the player are false. The performer who does not forehear what Berlioz heard chops it up somehow and kills the tune's ideal motion.

So much for form. Other tunes of Berlioz are not such obvious Cinderellas, whom we can restore to high estate by giving a second glance at their native merits. Some have "a nerve so purely Berliozian that they will always seem dull to people who have no ear for any but German or Italian tunes." [25] With regard to these, Schumann long ago made a practical suggestion: sing out the notes "*mit voller Brust*" and the melody's beauty will be borne in upon you together with its inner "character." [26] It is as if in the rhythms, pauses, leaps, or repeated notes lay hidden some bodily truth which Berlioz discovered and enshrined. The opening theme of the *Benvenuto Cellini* overture can serve as example: its pace, length, punctuation, and ornaments render almost unnecessary the expression mark: *Allegro deciso con impeto*. Translated, this means: joyful, decided, energetic; the theme does not describe, it *is* Benvenuto.

[22] Vienna *Rundfunk*, Apr. 23, 1930; quoted in *1360*, 568.

[23] Ring Lardner, speaking of musical comedy singers: "And the tunes is generally always altered in just one or two spots where the original composer had slipped in a couple strains which the audience might not recognize." From "Why Authors?"

[24] "Eye and Ear in Music" – a remarkable essay which begins with a discussion of phrasing in Schubert and concludes with a philosophy of listening. (*486*.)

[25] *642*.

[26] *508*, 177.

Characterization through melodic line brings us to the second aspect of Berlioz' melodic "difficulty" by reminding us that his ideas came to him "in situation," like chunks of drama – and the *Eight Scenes* show the manner of his reconstructing the whole by the contrast or independence of the parts. Each melody being a self-sufficient object, it follows that the listener must take in and think upon what he hears, rather than expect to be wooed into an indiscriminate reverie. Usually it is the reverie which induces the enjoyer to call a piece of music beautiful, but this will not hold for the true dramatic musician. His standard of beauty is fitness, or to use a more general term, expressiveness; which implies that a melody could be detached from a set of words and retain its character.[27] The reader who has heard the *Symphonie Fantastique* will remember that its leitmotif or *idée fixe* came from an early work after having passed through the *Herminie* prize cantata: throughout, it has a somewhat haughty, almost warlike character, and hence has been found wanting as a love tune. The criticism has only an apparent relevance. We are not to compare the theme with what *we* should like as a melody for the Belovèd, but to consider, in addition to its utility as a binding motif, whether it possesses a clear individual outline. It is unmistakably strong and insistent, like an *idée fixe*, and its "beauty" is so to speak functional.

Nor must we expect that the non-beautiful will be ugly in an interesting manner: it may be simply trivial, like the witches' words in *Macbeth*, from which alone no one would infer that Shakespeare was a great poet. Similarly, if Berlioz had written only the main theme of the *Corsair* overture, it would be hard to classify his melodic genius, for the tune is trivial, even vulgar. What is remarkable about it is that its vulgarity is made significant, is commented on, by the surrounding material; it is not vulgar by accident, nor ordinary in its vulgarity; and it arouses our admiration when we recognize that while it properly belongs where it is, this sea chantey is fashioned from the material forming the preceding "nocturne," which is nothing less than lovely. Add the interest of the delayed cadence, the subtle orchestral harmonies, and the delicacy of the accidentals in the repeated scales for strings, and you have the vulgar tune set "dramatically," as are the witches' rimes in *Macbeth*.

There is thus in Berlioz not one melodic idiom – whether harsh or sweet – but a collection of idioms covering a broad range of expression and deserving more careful classification than they have so far received.

[27] Berlioz' "Estelle" melody, for instance, which fitted so closely the verses of Florian, conveys just as much when it recurs without words in the Introduction of the *Symphonie Fantastique*.

One can distinguish from the outset three types of utterance: the recitative, the song, and the intermediate form, known as *chant-récitatif*, which Berlioz made peculiarly his own. He uses it wherever declamation or "prose" – to speak by analogy – reaches an intensity which will soon burst into full-blown song, but which the transitional or preparatory situation must keep in check. Thus Mephisto evokes the gnomes and sylphs who will lull Faust in a *chant-récitatif* that introduces their lilting chorus; the theme is the same in both parts but treated in these distinct ways.

The songs proper could be subdivided under many heads: lilt, cantilena, *Lied*, dirge, monotone, or simple "call." These are not merely suggestive attributes of a uniform element but separate species of melody. Any of them may have a verselike or a proselike quality, that is, tend more towards decoration than discursiveness, while expressing any imaginable mood. For in Berlioz dramatic variety resides as much in the contrast of forms as in the juxtaposition of atmospheres. Thus in the *Eight Scenes of Faust*, Mephisto's serenade is diabolical through no external means, but only because Berlioz has cast in the regular, obvious serenade form a hurtling, jagged, electrical melody such as only he could find. The singer need not add any sarcasm of voice: the notes do the work.

Sometimes the means are even more simple and virtually defy analysis. For the March to the Scaffold of the *Symphonie Fantastique* Berlioz uses merely a descending scale in G. The variety he extracts from such themes has been remarked upon, for the device is frequent with him.[28] In the *Requiem* (Kyrie), we have another example, very different in effect, and another, again different, in the *Beatrice and Benedict* overture, where he uses a chromatic scale to introduce a singing theme. This last instance, representing what might be called "melodic delay," is so typical of Berlioz that it calls for a word of comment. When one writer complains in Berlioz' music of a "half-stimulating, half-irritating restlessness, a kind of deliberate indecision," he is giving at least a recognizable description of what occasionally takes place.[29] In the adagio of the *Corsair* overture just described, in one of the variations of the Benvenuto theme, and in many other places, Berlioz uses melodic matter in teasing fashion. He does this at times for expressive purposes – giving us a "psychological variation" through the melody's "going to pieces"; at other times, the interest is that of the play of mind with an idea. Berlioz trusts that the

[28] Max Puttmann: *601*, 646.
[29] Martin Cooper: *565*, 628.

listener will find satisfaction in hearing a theme grow, or in recognizing the germ in the unfolded bloom.[30] Absolutely at ease in uttering and handling melody, Berlioz undoubtedly puts the rigidly trained musician at a disadvantage: Weingartner himself could not foresee that the six bars of pizzicato would grow into a grand, even a pompous theme, yet it is from such errors that the legend has grown of a Berlioz who pads with instrumental effects. Others fail to follow when the Benvenuto melody, shorn of its triplets, is reduced at one point to five notes: the original was sixteen bars.[31]

Though it alienates certain hearers, this flexing of the melodic line has compensations. For one thing, it produces, of necessity, a unique texture, orchestral and harmonic. For another, as Professor Ballantine once said, the "music wears like iron";[32] it charms less on first acquaintance, but holds pleasurable secrets for a long while. As for the artistic logic, it is that Berlioz' long and strongly characterized melodies would not bear exact repetition at short intervals. The refrain of a ballad may be repeated over and over again because it is short and because its meaning is vague and applies differently to each stanza. But no one could bear a refrain consisting of the entire fourteen lines of "The world is too much with us." Similarly, Berlioz' melodies are too particular and too complete for any treatment but that which he uses. He shows his awareness of this musical property in two ways: his development proceeds by restatement in altered form, and not by expansion from a short germ;[33] again, when he composes a protracted "monotony"[34] he employs a very short motif, tirelessly repeated against a constantly changing contrapuntal background. That he knew as well as Wagner or any other German technician how to develop a scene from a brief musical motto is shown by "Herod's Dream" from the *Infant Christ*.

Berlioz' own manner, indeed his invention, Weingartner called "dra-

[30] The "play of mind" can also correspond to deep feeling. In the sublime tenor melody of the *Te Deum* ("Therefore we beseech thee") the hesitations and wanderings are so far from playful that after hearing it one can no longer doubt Berlioz' intimate knowledge of the religious experience.

[31] *Min. sc.*, p. 36 bars 4 and 5.

[32] Remark made to the writer.

[33] Brahms took the other road, cutting his long lyric lines into "thematic" lengths for ordinary development.

[34] That is, the use of a single phrase repeated unchanged through the greater part of a movement. Examples of this form are: the Funeral March in the *Romeo and Juliet* symphony, the Offertory of the *Requiem*, the Judex Crederis of the *Te Deum*, and the *Hamlet Funeral March*. Berlioz associated this device with the expression of grief or inevitability.

matic-psychological variation."[35] It rests on melody, and satisfies Berlioz' desire to make musical forms as compact as possible. He assumes that you can skip intermediaries as swiftly as himself, and in fact when he takes pains to insert connecting links, he tends to spoil his work.[36] Conversely, the listeners who come to unfamiliar Berlioz without the power to follow wherever he leads tend to hear only the transitional passages – as it were the prepositions and conjunctions in his poetry – and to put him down as a technician who sought to dispense with melody altogether.[37] The opposite is the case. Berlioz always takes it for granted that music is a substance in which melodies live, grow, and combine. He thinks in lines – one result of his upbringing in an unsophisticated region and away from keyboard instruments. One could even say that his best melodies are essentially vocal, without denying the important fact that many of them are conceived for a given instrument; for each instrument is treated as a voice in more than the usual sense.[38] Usually marked *solo* or *canto* in the score, the instrumental part is supposed to stand out like a singer; at times the line is unaccompanied, or accompanied very lightly, so that its minutest inflection will remain distinct. Thus a movement like the middle one of the *Funeral and Triumphal* symphony justifies its subtitle of *oraison* because the trombone solo delivers a melodic recitation which is phrased like speech or gesture, hesitant at first, then gradually building up an unmistakable lament of twenty-two bars.[39]

These numerous considerations bring us to the final problem. "One does not expect," said Bernard Van Dieren of Berlioz' melody, "that anyone should reveal the secret of its unique power."[40] But one has yet to account for the common and hopeful experience that Berlioz' melodies, "uninviting at first," ultimately reveal their "signal beauty."[41] Why should this be so? An astute answer is given by another compatriot of Van

[35] *754*, 59 and *394*, 200. The unfavorable view of this mode of construction is expressed by Jean Marnold. (*460*, 205–20 and 362–78.)

[36] *E.g.*, the *Dies irae* in doppio movimento in the *Symphonie Fantastique* (last movement) or the repetition of the last bars of the theme in the *King Lear* overture, *Min. sc.*, p. 16 bars 2–3.

[37] The master who attempted this is not Berlioz but Mozart, the great melodist, in the overtures of his later operas. When Mozart was prodigal in his use of melody, Dittersdorf complained that it gave the hearer no time to breathe; yet another contemporary critic could say that there was only one real air in all of *Don Giovanni*. (*968*, II, 457 and III, 185.)

[38] See below, Chapter 16.

[39] See the piano score of the movement, edited by Roger Smith, Mercury Music Corporation, 1947, Andantino, pp. 3–4.

[40] *901*, 232–3.

[41] Dr. Percy Goetschius: *436*, 297

Dieren's: "The truth is that for many people they are too directly *on* the mark. If they had been aimed at sentimentality, just aside of the purity and richness of emotions, they would have had a much better chance of popular success." [42]

At every point, therefore, some aspect of dramatic truth is our proper guide. The critic has merely restated for us the objective character of Berlioz' melody, which we grow to like in proportion as its astonishing vividness ceases to shock us. Whereas most people accept very general renderings – loveliness for love, brightness for joy, weightiness for pomp – Berlioz, like Mozart, means to discriminate further. He does so by instinct and it is *after* the creation that the melody is found to correspond to some psychological reality, independently of this or that musical detail.[43] When Berlioz took up the *Eight Scenes* again for his *Damnation of Faust*, he made the ballad of the King of Thule begin on the second beat of the bar, docked a clarinet part, and suppressed some instructions to the singer. But the melodic character remained what it had been, "simple and ingenuous." It suits Gretchen as it would any other country lass: Goethe's drama was only the catalyst that brought the tune into being, the occasion for its use being a matter of later choice – a choice guided by the very simple idea that a Gretchen differs more from a Cleopatra or a Dido than do these two queens from each other.

At the time of the *Eight Scenes* Berlioz, aged twenty-four, was master of his style and intention, but he was still seeking the larger genre which would make the fullest use of his power as dramatist in melody.

[42] *491*, 339.

[43] Thus Berlioz looking back on his scores of *Romeo* and *Faust* points out differences in the spiritual quality of the two lovers – the first shows a more whole-souled love. (*93*, VIII.)

5. *Revolution in July*

January 1 to July 29, 1830

Composed it on the spot — Mars by day, Apollo by night — bang the fieldpiece, twang the lyre.

— *Pickwick Papers*

EIGHTEEN-THIRTY, the year of revolutions, brought as much inner as outer upheaval in Berlioz' existence. In the career of one who began life so young, this twelvemonth seems in retrospect like the last act of a Shakespearean history in many parts: triumphs and reversals, endings and fresh beginnings crowd the short period to an accompaniment of cannon and trumpets. Not guessing its perfect symmetry, Berlioz opened the year with the musical subject that marked its close: "My working plans," he wrote to Humbert Ferrand on January 2, "are laid down for a good while ahead; I must compose for my concert a great instrumental work. . . ."[1] Berlioz therefore declined a poem dealing with Faust's last night on earth which Ferrand had apparently begun. "If I had it in my hands," the musician argued, "I could not resist composing it." His own ideas about *Faust* were taking another form — that of a grand symphony whose outlines had "long been worked out."[2]

The concert would have to take place before the Prize Competition in July, Berlioz' purpose being, as before — as always — to force the judges' hands or the Opera's doors by conquering the public. This necessity was both individual and cultural. In *The Red and the Black*, "a chronicle of 1830," Stendhal says that life must begin with a duel, and in Balzac's projection of himself, Rastignac looks down from the hills on Paris, saying "It's between you and me." Fiction mercifully reduces to one decisive battle what in many artists' lives is a Thirty Years' War. And besides challenges and victories, war is made up of labors which are

[1] *L.I.*, 62.

[2] *A.R.*, 87–8. Note that the nineteenth-century use of the word "Grand" preceding the title Symphony or Overture is a technical term denoting the length and instrumental richness of the work, and not a mere advertisement. Modern usage reverses the practice by drawing attention to smallness: sinfonietta, little overture for strings.

often sordid: Berlioz was still plagued by money troubles. He was again in debt to several of his friends, and although his father sent him cash from time to time, remittance was usually followed by shopping orders, payable at once and likely to "disturb my whole economy."[3] Two private pupils brought in forty-four francs a month in addition to the salary from Mme. Daubrée's school for young ladies. But the life of art, and particularly of music, is expensive. "I am as hard up as a painter," he reports, using the traditional comparison. Fortunately, as a musician and critic Berlioz had his entrees at all the theaters and he need not disburse for this essential pleasure. Fortunately also, he managed to go on doing his own work in the mysterious oases of a calmed spirit and doing the world's work at the feverish pace that the world exacts.

Having enlisted the good will of the managers at the Nouveautés, the same theater where he had sung for a living not long before, Berlioz felt that his next concert had a fair chance of success. Though the chorus at his disposal was of only average quality, the orchestra was superior, and it was led by a devoted admirer named Bloc. With the addition of some of his other supporters in the Conservatoire and Opera orchestras, he would have a first-class instrument. A date toward the end of May would best fit in with the public's habits and with his own arrangements. Considering the amount of copying, correcting, and rehearsing to do for a work not yet written out, even this schedule would call for rapid composition. Hence the advantage of having ideas in one's head for a good while before committing them to paper.

Berlioz was also occupied during these same months in securing the acceptance of a libretto at the Opera, not to mention keeping up his work as critic and as student at the Conservatoire. But these duties he could easily take in stride. Life was difficult rather on account of the unsatisfactory and unsatisfied state of his feelings. Harriet Smithson continued to come and go, and Berlioz' infatuation with her did likewise, though more fitfully. A promise she had apparently made through go-betweens, of putting her lover on probation, turned out to be an expedient on their part to get rid of him. When he discovered this, his ardor cooled. He enjoyed stretches of peace and freedom, whether she was in London or Paris. Then he suddenly fell again into "the anguish of endless and inextinguishable passion, without motive, without object. . . ." His pain was "useless, terrible."[4]

To heartache was added a persistent toothache, which before the days of the dental drill Berlioz tried to cure by himself. As a student of medi-

[3] *L.I.*, 61. [4] *L.I.*, 64–5.

cine he was almost as patiently experimental as when he composed music, and he finally found a specific, which he communicated to Ferrand suffering from the same cause. The sort of remedy suggested the proper treatment for his own heart: "It can only be cured by a specific against life." [5] He noticed that straining in so many directions paralyzed the will: "I was on the point of beginning my symphony . . . it was all in my head, but I cannot write a thing. We must wait." [6]

This mixture of philosophy and irony was the sign of an inner revolution, indeed a revulsion of feeling. It astonished and upset him that on returning one day from a long walk calculated to wear out his anguish and finding in Moore's poems the text of a Farewell Elegy to the Beloved, Berlioz had been able to compose the music on the spot. The experience shook him so that ever afterwards he declined to have the song performed, but as he himself noted, this was the only instance when he had been "able to render a feeling while still under its immediate and active influence." [7] One may wonder whether this was not the exception that proves to be the rule in disguise; one suspects that the feeling was dead or dying.

Another letter, this time to Ferdinand Hiller, the friendly young German who taught piano at Mme. Daubrée's, and who was further distinguished as having visited Beethoven thrice at his deathbed,[8] marks the change in Berlioz' attachment to his inaccessible Ophelia: "Can you tell me what this power to feel, this faculty for suffering is, which is killing me? Ask your angel, the seraph who has opened to you the gates of heaven. . . . Still, let us not repine. . . ." For when he is tempted to this weakness, Berlioz imagines that "Beethoven looks upon me with severity; Spontini, who is far above ills like mine, regards me with an air of indulgent pity; and Weber, speaking in my ear like a familiar spirit, awaits me in a blessed country to console me. . . . All this is crazy," he adds, "utterly crazy, from the point of view of a domino player at the Café de la Regence or a member of the Institute. No! I mean to live yet awhile. Music is a heavenly art; nothing is above it save true love. The one may make me as unhappy as the other, but I shall at any rate have lived. . . .

"It is today exactly one year since I saw her for the last time. Unhappy woman, how I loved you! I write with a shudder that I do love you. . . . In fact, I am a very miserable man . . . an animal burdened with an exhausting imagination, eaten up with a boundless passion. . . . Yes!

[5] *L.I.*, 63.
[6] *L.I.*, 64.
[7] *Mem.*, I, 99.
[8] Hiller's account of those visits is in *1021*, III, 301–3.

But I have known a few musical geniuses, I have been gladdened by their visions, and I grind my teeth only from unhappy memories." [9]

Berlioz himself will soon be telling us more about this very earthly seraph of Hiller's. The tug of war in Hector's heart was finally decided by mid-April 1830. A kind friend told Berlioz either gossip or fabrications casting doubts on the nature of Harriet's relations with her manager. It was a blow in spite of the lover's natural return to reason. "My vessel," he told Ferrand, "strained at every seam but finally righted itself." He is on the way to a complete cure, or "as complete as my natural tenacity will allow." [10]

Berlioz' natural tenacity had at any rate allowed him to finish his symphony, of which he unfolded the dramatic plan to his friend. The title records the ending of the emotional strain in Berlioz far more than it describes the music itself:

" 'Episode in an Artist's Life' (grand fantastic symphony in five parts) *First Movement:* double, composed of a short adagio immediately followed by a developed allegro . . . *Second Movement:* Scenes in the Country (adagio . . .) *Third Movement:* A Ball (brilliant, headlong music) *Fourth Movement:* March to Execution (fierce, *pomposo*) *Fifth Movement:* Dream of a Witches' Sabbath.[11]

"And now, dear friend, here is how I've fashioned my novel, or rather my story, whose hero you will recognize . . ."

Then follows the first version of the famous "program" of the symphony. It was as secondary in the composer's mind as the place it occupies in this letter, or as its ostensible cause – the hero's love for Miss Smithson. The musical plan, described in musical terms, came first. The letter closed with thoughts of performance and friendship:

"I have just written the last note and I am afraid I shan't be able to have the parts copied in time [that is, by May 30]. For the moment, I feel stupid; the frightful stretch of thought to produce my piece has tired my imagination and I'd like to be able to sleep and rest continuously.

[9] *Corresp.*, 67–8. The contents suggest March 1830 as the time of its writing, though the editor dates it a year earlier. What is more, he does not accurately reproduce the arrangement of Berlioz' lines, which form a kind of modern "plastic poem" such as E. E. Cummings or Mallarmé might have composed. The original is in Hiller (*352*, 559).

[10] *L.I.*, 65.

[11] Notice the order of the second and third movements, inverted in the final version: originally the waltz took the place of a minuet or scherzo third movement. Also, the "adagio" introduction of the first movement is now marked largo.

But though my brain is drugged, my heart is awake and I feel most strongly that I miss you. When, dear friend, *shall* I see you?" [12]

Humbert replied with such delicate sympathy to Hector's news about Harriet, and about the completion of the symphony, that the composer, who sometimes thought of himself as "almost isolated" and struggling amid universal indifference, was deeply moved. Berlioz replied in words that not only testify to his affectionate and remembering nature – his tenacity in feeling as well as in effort – but also confirm the impression that friendship in the Romantic period was a species of love affair: "It is so rare, my dear Humbert, to find a complete man, with a soul, a heart, and an imagination; so rare for characters as ardent and impatient as ours to meet and be matched together, that I hardly know how to tell you the happiness it gives me to know you." [13] Berlioz values Humbert's "solicitude, anxiety, and advice" with regard to the Smithson "episode," and wishes it clearly understood that the symphony is not a deed of revenge. "It is certainly not in that spirit that I wrote the Witches' Sabbath. I pity and despise her. She is an ordinary woman, gifted with an instinctive genius for reproducing the wrackings of the human soul without ever having felt them, and incapable of conceiving a mighty and noble attachment such as that with which I honored her." [14]

It is traditional for the unrequited lover to welcome like a reprieve the news that his idol is unworthy of him, so here again Berlioz is following tradition. Yet his judgment was not far from the truth in estimating the emotional make-up of the Shakespearean actress. Had he only been able to remember his own words when Harriet once more came within his ken, he might have spared himself much anguish. But she was now part of him and his "natural tenacity" would not let her memory go. The suffering and introspection undergone about her had certainly served him, for although his symphony was not in any literal sense about her, any more than his future works were about the accidents of his life, the power which creates music and the power which creates a beloved person are related if not identical.[15] As Yeats says somewhere, "True love is a discipline. . . . Each divines the secret self of the other, and refusing to believe in the mere daily self, creates a mirror where the lover or the beloved sees an image to copy in daily life." Stendhal calls the process "crystallization," comparing the beloved to an ordinary twig

[12] *L.I.*, 66–9.
[13] *L.I.*, 69.
[14] *L.I.*, 70.
[15] Berlioz was himself convinced of this (*L.I.*, 82) and other artists have agreed with him. See below, Chapter 18.

which one dips into a saline spring and which comes out sparkling with a thousand jewels.[16] It is begging the question to say that the lover's view is a deliberate illusion which worldly judgment should help to cure; one should rather note, in the lives of artists especially, the meaning and the successful results of "crystallization." [17]

Whether Berlioz' next essay in loving has or has not artistic significance, it shows at any rate a pleasing variation from his first. At the institution where he and Hiller taught music to the crippled daughters of the rich, they had a third colleague, a pianist like Hiller, named Marie Moke, commonly called Camille. She was the daughter of an unpractical professor from Ghent, whose wife had left him in order to support herself and promote their child's musical career by keeping a linen shop in Paris.[18] The shop had been given up when Camille – a pupil of Kalkbrenner's – had herself become a teacher.[19] She shone by virtue of natural abilities and acquired graces. She was small and of a lively beauty – an oval face, dark hair and blue eyes, a bewitching figure and a light step, which led Berlioz to nickname her Ariel. But though gay and teasing she passed for a proper young lady, ostensibly chaperoned by her mother or a suitable substitute. Gifted and self-assured, she was determined to succeed.

She also liked masculine attentions, and as Hiller tells us in his long-subsequent memoirs, he and Camille found a way to exchange greetings first, then unsupervised visits, which were made possible by Mlle. Moke's having pupils at various points in the city. For some reason Hiller came to use Berlioz as his messenger, with predictable results. Berlioz' reserved manner, the story of his hopeless love for the illustrious actress, his maturer mien – he was twenty-six and Hiller hardly nineteen – aroused Camille's curiosity and she set about to break down his defenses. As Hiller is the first to admit, she finally told Berlioz outright that she loved him and that his reticence was foolish.[20] Hers was the gift that makes artfulness assist and not replace nature: she was a siren as well as an extraordinarily good musician and vivacious companion. It was not long before she achieved her new conquest. By the end of April, Berlioz had

[16] Yeats: (*1285*, 88); Stendhal: (*1242, passim*).

[17] This has of course been done in fiction, from Plato's *Symposium* to Hardy's *The Well Beloved.*

[18] The father, Jean-Jacques Moke, a linguist of some note, was a friend of Fétis's. Camille's brother Henri made a name as lecturer and writer on racialist history.

[19] Her pianistic education was begun by Jacques Herz and Ignaz Moscheles; then she studied with Kalkbrenner and finally achieved her mature style with the aid of Thalberg.

[20] *352, 561–2.*

done with Harriet. By the middle of May, he was completing his arrangements for the concert on the thirtieth; he was in touch with Haitzinger, the leading tenor of the German theater in Paris, for a production of his *Francs-Juges* opera at Carlsruhe, and hoping to go there himself in a few months. He was also pushing the same opera in the lesser Paris houses. By the beginning of July 1830, that is to say before the time set for the Rome Prize competition, Berlioz and Camille were thoroughly in love.

The letters which convey to Humbert Ferrand the progress of this affair doubtless sound foolish, like the earlier rhapsodies about Harriet, but the later ones display a superior brand of foolishness. "All that love offers that is most tender and delicate, I have from her. My enchanting sylph, my Ariel, my life, seems to love me more than ever. Her mother keeps saying that if she read about us in a novel, she would not credit it . . . I'm now locked up in the Institute *for the last time;* I must have that prize, on which our happiness so largely depends. Like Don Carlos in *Hernani,* I say: '*I will* have it.' *She* is anxious about it too, and to reassure me in my prison, Mme. Moke sends me her maid every other day to give me news of them and take back news of me. God! How I shall reel when I see her again in ten or twelve days! We'll have many obstacles to overcome, perhaps, but *we will.* What do you think of all this? Is it conceivable? An angel like her, the finest talent in Europe . . . Oh, my dear fellow, if you heard her *think aloud* the sublime thoughts of Weber and Beethoven, you would lose your wits!" [21]

This is love chatter of the sort that Molière approved when he said that the only reasonable way to love was to love madly. For the first time Berlioz' senses were awakened, and not merely his imagination primed by Shakespeare's art; he was actually loved and kissed and doted over by an intelligent and beautiful creature. Camille must have been equally caught by his great capacity for passionate expression. "Delicate and tender" denote soothing qualities that are too readily ascribed by men to women in general, but that the son of Mme. Berlioz would probably not mistake, even though Camille had been the aggressor. She was so obviously a woman with whom conversation was possible, *the* woman fated by talent and inclination to be Berlioz' partner, comforter, lover — and wife, for Mme. Moke's privity to these love passages meant that Berlioz had made honorable proposals. A M. de Noailles, a friend of the Moke family, had spoken in Hector's favor as a match worth risking from the practical point of view. But this was not decisive. The rival without whom no comedy is complete was a man of fifty-eight, M. Pleyel, successor to the

[21] *L.I.*, 73–4.

firm which Hector had approached about his first compositions when a boy of sixteen. Of course M. Pleyel's solid advantages outweighed those of the impetuous and impecunious young artist, and Mme. Moke's consent to the engagement between Camille and Hector may have been secretly provisional.

As for "Ariel," her coquetry and premeditation at the beginning, together with her greater experience of love-making, led to recurrences of that private double-intention which usually precedes faithlessness. The attentions of her devoted genius no doubt flattered her, his personal magnetism, which so many people were to feel and speak of, moved her, and his obvious innocence touched her. But his musical powers and artistic opinions made her feel an inferiority she sometimes rebelled against. To tease her fiancé and reassert her mastery, she would play him some trivial air, or some Italian cavatina with improvised embroideries that set his teeth on edge. When she declared that those fireworks were at any rate "prettier" and "more amusing" than his favorite Beethoven adagios, Berlioz would storm and preach and remonstrate, unwilling to hide from himself or from her that such a preference cut them asunder. He was head over heels in love, but music was his religion and just criticism a necessity of his nature. And at this she would laugh a shrill laugh.[22] Not that she lacked a soulful side. She could play Beethoven magnificently and even feel or pretend that such playing sapped her strength, so that Hector would beg her to refrain from such musical indulgence. Clearly Camille was a two-sided creature, half Ariel, half coquette, and Berlioz' efforts to keep her at spiritual concert pitch may have sown doubts into her mind whether this orphic lover should enlarge into a husband.

The torments of the artist in love with a woman who by training and taste is conventional and worldly wise have given rise to the maxim that any man with work to do should forego what is called romantic love. Compared with Berlioz, was not the good Hiller, who took his pleasures so placidly, the truly wise man? He had enjoyed his flirtation while it lasted and escaped without scars. To our knowing age, which has discovered that love is a wholly endocrine event, and which believes that romantic passion is what the movies portray, the question may seem settled. But we are perhaps deceived by both the scientific and the theatrical make-believe. The Romanticists themselves knew better than to be either

[22] A legitimate inference from her "portrait" in *Soirées* (12th) *Eves.*, 137. See also the (25th) *Eves.*, 256.

clinical or "romantic" about love. If they had to be given a label, they would have to be called "comprehensive realists," men who instinctively knew that there is more than one layer to experience and many mysteries encountered in exploring it. They took this so much for granted that they seldom bothered to stress their own versatility. Hence we miss the point and value of their multiple perceptions when we tag them all with the one name "romantic."

Consider for example that "romantic" drama and historic event, Victor Hugo's play, *Hernani.* Berlioz was one of the squad of Hugo's defenders who on February 25, 1830, helped make the first night a success, but neither he nor a number of other partisans mistook Hugo's drama for a report on their own view of life, love, or historical truth. Although the play dealt with love in relation to social class, the rallying of an artistic generation to its support is not to be explained by "romantic" interest in this ordinary sense. Why the occasion should be remembered and cited is in fact anything but clear from the usual accounts, which overlook the host of implications that belong to the term Romantic when fully charged. In the first place, the point of the battle was not philosophic but strategic. The victory meant a public recognition of certain technical liberties which had already been wrested in print, and supporting the play meant the public affirmation of freedom for all the arts.

This was something more than defiance and eccentricity, and in stressing the "revolt" we forget the high spirits. We hear of Théophile Gautier, aged eighteen, and of Gérard de Nerval – the translator of *Faust* – each leading his shock troops, whom Hugo had provided with a red card bearing the Spanish password *Hierro* (iron), but we must not miss the tone of self-mocking. We hear of Gautier's red waistcoat, which was in fact pink (on the reversed principle of the English hunting coat which is called pink and is in fact red), but we should recall his intense application as a student of poetry and painting. And at the same time we should think of the Gargantuan picnic held in the deserted theatre hours before the performance, the Rabelaisian traces being left, in the exuberance of youth, to discomfit later comers.[23] Clearly the battle of Hernani was in part a collegiate "rag," in part a public demonstration of bright youth against bourgeois old age. The rebels wore their hair long and left their beards untrimmed in order to be conspicuous and because the academicians in the parterre were baldpates – whence their designation as *perruques* (wigs). There was a hint of flaunted sexual supe-

[23] As the biographer of Gautier has said: "Laughter, the laughter of common sense, was as truly romantic as suffering." (Quoted, in italics, *1182*, 168.)

riority in the manifestation, and its seriousness lay precisely in its refusal to be solemn.

To the playwright and his fellow romanticists, the virtue of this open cabal was that it was not bought support but testimony to principle. It was an artists' claque like the smaller one that Berlioz had himself organized for Gluck at the Opera. Hugo having passed the official barrier of the subsidized *Comédie Française* by getting *Hernani* accepted, it was essential for him and his friends to keep it from being hissed off the stage. But the *perruques* were as determined as the innovators; for them the encounter was not only a defense of taste and tradition but of cash royalties. If the new school won, the old clichés would no longer be marketable. To preserve the sanctity of verse and dramatic seemliness, the *perruques* must shout down this "formless" work in which the scenes were laid in different places, in which the lines did not pause exactly in the middle, in which the meaning overran the riming edge of each verse, and in which such intolerable bluntness was reveled in as saying aloud 'It is midnight.' [24]

Hugo's defenders won. The play ran on for an unusual stretch of forty-five nights, enriching its author though exhausting his friends, for each night a new batch of Parisian bourgeois had to be outfought with lung power. What was finally vindicated, however, was not a new school of drama. Had *Hernani* been too unlike the older plays it would never have been accepted and produced by a company of actors brought up in the old tradition. What was won was the freedom to make verse varied and flexible, and the right of the artist to create reality by using the concrete, particular detail, and even the commonplace. The one scene that hushed both friends and enemies, the love scene between the brigand Hernani and the patrician Doña Sol, implied another lesson based on a natural fact – that love does not consult the Almanach de Gotha; but of equal importance was that it reintroduced lyric utterance into tragedy. These liberties, snatched in public before the habit-ridden Parisians had, for all the arts, the value of a successful revolution.

The new freedom did not of course commit every Romanticist to a complete acceptance of *Hernani*. Berlioz, in giving his sisters an account of the play, made reservations: "I find in it certain things, especially ideas, that are sublime, and other things and ideas that are ridiculous . . . as

[24] To gauge the strength of the academic resistance one should read in Dumas' *Memoirs* (Vol. V) the account of the rehearsals, in which Mlle. Mars kept nagging Hugo about his lines, hoping to make him lose his temper and thus create a pretext for throwing up the part. The exchange of words has been excellently translated by Mr. Biancolli in his *Great Conversations*, 315 ff.

Camille Moke in 1830, by Alophe

"The celestial pianofortist . . ."
— DE QUINCEY

for the verse, which I dislike anyway in the theatre, these run-over lines and broken half-lines which enrage the classicists leave me quite indifferent. When spoken it all sounds like prose and for that reason alone I could prefer it.[25] But since *Hernani* was meant to be in verse and since Hugo knows how to write regular verse when he wants, it would have been simpler to follow the taste of the crowd – it would have saved the breath of all the jackdaws of the pit. The innovation is one that leads nowhere. Still, Hugo has destroyed the unities of time and place and for that I take an interest in him as a daredevil who risks death to set a mine under an old barrier." [26]

With the knowledge of what Shakespearean form could do for his own work, Berlioz supported Hugo on the unities, but curiously failed to see why the poet attacked the rigid, foursquare line and the stopping of sense with rime. Yet it was the same Berlioz whose melody and rhythm broke with rigidity and squareness, and who had written a little earlier: "When I think of this realm of chords which scholastic prejudice has kept untouched to this day, and which since my emancipation [from the Conservatoire] I regard as my own domain, I rush forward in a kind of frenzy to explore it." [27] In effect, Berlioz was accomplishing reforms parallel to Hugo's; and so were Balzac and Stendhal, who sat apart from the rest on the famous night and later voiced strong dissent from Hugo's supposed principles.[28] Delacroix, also present, soon grew to hate the label Romantic, and while indulging his distrust of both Hugo and Berlioz, dissociated himself from the movement which he none the less incarnates in the art of painting.[29]

Thus in the aftermath of *Hernani* Berlioz and four of his peers, working in parallel ways for comparable ends, were kept by the fog of contemporariness from recognizing their intimate kinship. At best they sensed the common resistance and conceded one another a certain esteem. For a time they used, or they redefined for special use, the term "Romanticist." Berlioz, in an article of this very year 1830, discussed "classic and

[25] Berlioz, it will be remembered, liked the realism in free verse of Saurin's *Beverley, or the Gambler.*

[26] *A.R.*, 92.

[27] *A.R.*, 88.

[28] Balzac's review (*1235, Oeuvres Diverses*, II, 115 ff.) attacked Hugo's construction and lack of plausibility; Stendhal disliked the "tirades" reminiscent of classical tragedy and shared Berlioz' preference for the use of prose.

[29] Delacroix (*Journal, passim*) deemed Hugo and Berlioz violent in their effects and loose in their form, not seeing that they might be technicians as fully conscious as himself, against whom the same charge was leveled by the ignorant.

romantic music," but he was not attached to the word, and generally the new artists found the name embarrassing. In truth, all historic names are unsatisfactory — Renaissance, Gothic, Baroque, and Puritan, no less than Romantic. If the historian heeded individual disclaimers, every movement would be entirely emptied of participants. The names remain, for convenience and as a reminder of the stylistic unity which is apparent to later comers and defines for them the time and tone of a period.

Just as this definition calls for a careful sifting of doctrine and polemic in the light of the works themselves, so a knowledge of the Romantic temperament requires that we examine the lives of its representatives in the light of the facts and feelings we actually find. Enough of Berlioz' life has been shown so far to suggest that his "romantic nature" was very complex, and not to be defined as simply "wild" or "rebellious," or as a predominance of heart over intellect. In his first love affair the very opposite was true. His genuinely romantic love was precisely unlike what we think of as a storybook romance: it is the modern, fiction-fed public that boils down *Romeo and Juliet* to the balcony scene, whereas to render the fullness of his conception the Romantic-realist Shakespeare required the feud and the murders, the coarse chitchat of the Nurse, the union of spirits and bodies, and even the preparation of Romeo by an earlier unrequited love.[30]

Berlioz' love for Camille Moke, or Victor Hugo's for Juliette Drouet, each following an attachment (like Romeo's) to a cool or distant goddess, fulfills this condition of completeness, of versatility, of eager exchange of selves, at the price of possible tragedy. The difference between this sort of romance and the ordinary sort is that the first is properly a piece of work, an energetic fusion of mind, sense, and knowledge into passion truly so called. Most people are as incapable, or as unwilling, to make this effort as they are to write a poem or compose a quartet. Convention sustains them in their laziness and so "romance" becomes a byword for trifling. Critics of manners can only conclude that in society a great emotion is as rare as a great idea, and thus on every point the man of thought is bound to conflict with the man of common experience.[31] To the artist,

[30] Often cut from modern productions by actor-managers who know how sentimental ("romantic"!) their audience is.

[31] As Coleridge pointed out, this is what makes Polonius seem so foolish in Hamlet's presence. But this in turn does not mean that the romantic lover must be highfalutin, on the contrary. The Romantic Chateaubriand, speaking of an eighteenth-century translation of Dante, quotes the climax of the Paolo and Francesca episode — "We let fall the book through which was revealed to us the mystery of love" — and dryly adds: "Perhaps this elegant turn of phrase does not quite render the simplicity of the line [in Italian]: 'We read no more that day.' " (*1243*, I, 336.)

idea and emotion are one, and love and art have a common root in the dedication of the person to a self-justifying activity. Hence Berlioz says that great music is only inferior to great love, and conversely that a passion for music is as complete a dedication of one's whole being as love or religious vows.[32] On one side stands flirting or sensual sport; on the other, marriage for convenience, social or personal; and beyond both, romantic love in the tradition of the troubadours, Dante, Heloïse, or Tristram.

Being simply affectionate as well as romantically passionate, Berlioz felt great misery in being at odds with his family over the very reason for his existence as he saw it – art. Until now he was still in their eyes a wayward son. Happily, in the midst of his preparations for the concert of May 1830, Hector received from his father a letter which made the son reply at once: "My excellent Father: How I thank you for your letter! What good it did me! So you are beginning to have a little confidence in me? I hope I may live to justify it. It is the first time you have written to me in this way, and I thank you a thousand times. It is such bliss to be able to bring honor and pleasure to those who are dear to us. Of course I should be delighted to have you hear me – *of course*. But for you to take a trip to Paris there must be more positive assurance of the concert, which in fact can be put off at the slightest whim of those in authority." [33]

This prudent thought proved correct. The concert had to be postponed, each of the several parties to the arrangements waiting upon the others' authorization – the manager of the hall and of the orchestra, the Prefect of Police ("whose subordinates try to make an affair of state out of a mere formality"), and the Superintendent, "who could stop everything if he wishes, for in this free country the musicians are numbered among the slaves."

Other plans included a trip to Carlsruhe for launching the *Francs-Juges* and the winning of the prize – "If I can make myself small enough *to pass through the gates of the kingdom of heaven*." [34] These two objects would not be incompatible, provided the compulsory stay in Italy which went with the prize could be shortened, and the optional sojourn in Germany lengthened. Failing Carlsruhe, there was Kassel, where Berlioz heard that Spohr "unlike the Paris composers" was favorable to new music.

About the same time a libretto based on Chateaubriand's novel *Atala*

[32] *Mem.*, II, 340; *Soirées* (11th) *Eves.*, 128; *L.I.*, 82. Compare Balzac's purpose, at the age of 33, to "consecrate himself to the happiness of a woman." (*163*, 56.)
[33] *A.R.*, 93 ff. [34] *A.R.*, 96.

had been unanimously accepted by the Opera and orally promised to Berlioz for setting. The management had been strongly pressed by the influential composer Onslow, who had read the score of *Les Francs-Juges* and become an enthusiastic supporter of Berlioz. But the inevitable two-party system was developing around the newcomer. The opposition included some who had never heard his music (the Know-Nothings) but who had exercised a preventive caution by circulating the rumor that Berlioz was insane. The libretto moreover alarmed M. Lubbert, the Opera director. *Atala* was in a new genre – romantic, he thought – which "he did not want to introduce." He felt that "Auber and Rossini were enough novelty" and that "even if Beethoven and Weber came back to life, he would have nothing to do with them." [35] The truth was that the director, being responsible to both the government and his financial backers, was looking for a sure draw. Rossini having broken the monopoly of the Gluckist school, the Opera had nothing left. Weber was too great a risk; Mozart always had to be patched up and failed anyhow. A new, adaptable, and money-making composer must be found; it was not likely that a revolutionary like Berlioz would turn into a darling of the public.

Berlioz could see through the director's irrelevant excuses; and writing of the general situation, the composer gives us the mood of 1830 – the sense of a general apathy no longer bearable, especially after the victory of *Hernani*. There is a whiff of apprehension at the government's stubbornness and a hint of disaster, foreshadowing the barricades of July: "The Feydeau house is in the last stages of musical degradation . . . That odious monopoly must fall, and it will fall if the petition is presented to the Chamber of Deputies. Benjamin Constant [a famous liberal member] and two others would have sponsored it if the Chamber had not been dissolved. Would anyone believe that any foreign troupe can set up an opera in Paris, while the French alone must submit to being skinned alive at Feydeau? . . . Apparently nothing must be done to give umbrage to that conservatory of routines and clichés; everything must be done to increase the prosperity of the rondo, the romance, and the duet. And despite the great power of these musical forms we must give subsidies out of the taxes (paid by provincials who never see a comic opera) in order to enable a new director to go bankrupt every other year." [36] Through the voice of the exasperated Berlioz speaks the Liberal of 1830: "Why for heaven's sake not let them all play what they like – operas grand or little – give subsidies to none, and allow bankruptcy to take its course? It

[35] *A.R.*, 97. [36] *A.R.*, 97–8.

will cost the taxpayer less in the end, and some theatres will find a way to thrive."

Unrest was in the air and Berlioz was right to doubt whether his "instrumental drama would inspire sufficient interest to bring back to Paris" the public summering outside the capital. By the end of May, his concert was definitely postponed until autumn. But he had heard his new symphony at the first two rehearsals and he was fully reassured. "I apparently did not fool myself when I was writing it. Everything is as I conceived it. Only the March to Execution is fifty times more terrifying than I expected." [37] The rehearsals were trying, because the orchestra had to "blaze a trail through a virgin forest. Besides many things that are new to them, the greatest difficulty is that of expression, in the first movement especially. . . . It will take angelic patience on the part of the conductor to teach them all the nuances." [38] In spite of contretemps, then, Berlioz' score – a revolutionary work if only in this elaboration of expressive nuances [39] – actually resounded in Parisian air before the Rome Award and before the political revolution.[40]

It came into being also before a new piece by Berlioz – an overture-fantasia on Shakespeare's *Tempest* – whose public presentation happened to precede that of the symphony. The *Tempest* piece owes its double inspiration to Shakespeare and to Berlioz' feminine "Ariel," so it must have been taking shape in his mind in the late spring of 1830. These middle months of the year were in truth dramatically full. Berlioz' revulsion of feeling against Harriet Smithson coincided with her descent to a mute role in an inferior work, under the pressure of financial need.[41] As the play opened, the *Figaro*, still counting on the performance of Berlioz' symphony, published the famous (or infamous) program which is supposed to retrace the development of the composer's love for the actress. The document attracted considerable attention in artistic circles at the time, though as is now clear its biographical worth is slight. Finally, during the early summer, Hector and Camille were making plans to be married as soon as he had won the prize.

[37] *A.R.*, 101. [38] *A.R.*, 94–5.

[39] Wm. Wallace: "Modern orchestration may be said to date from the '*Symphonie Fantastique*' of Berlioz. In the sixty-three bars of the opening Largo there are more expression marks and indicated nuances than in a Mozart symphony. This shows that he attached the utmost importance to tone. . . ." (*1315*, III, 729.)

[40] The work is thus Opus 4a in point of time, and 14a (as usually given) in order of publication.

[41] *234*. Even in the mute role, however, she greatly impressed the spectators. (See above, Chapter 4.)

He went *en loge* for the fourth time on July 15.[42] Like other things, the cantata subject showed the influence of the stirrings of change: the poem on "The Death of Sardanapalus" was an almost prophetic choice. Harking back to Byron, it depicted a king refusing to abdicate and perishing in the fire set by his own hand – a drama which gained in vividness from the recollection of Delacroix's provocative masterpiece, exhibited at a previous Salon. Shut up in his little cell, Berlioz thought he had at last mastered the art of avoiding the evil consequences of his genius. He put all his skill into making a "regular" work, reserving his inspirations for a kind of appendix, which he would tack on afterwards, when the prize was safe in his pocket. For at the public performance in the autumn, he could not afford to appear in the artistic undress of a routine score.

Things fell out as he had planned – or nearly. He won the First Prize by a unanimous vote, which was unheard of, and doubly remarkable because of the unusually large number of candidates. He was moreover the "first first," for the Institute having a prize left over from the previous year, was obliged to choose two firsts. Finally, at the public audition, after Berlioz' *Sardanapale,* that of his running mate, Montfort, suffered the indignity of a polite hissing. As "appendix" Berlioz had composed a "conflagration" in which the king with his treasures, slaves, women, and horses, dies amid the flaming ruins of his palace. All the melodies heard earlier in the scene – from the song of the bayaderes to the declamation of the stubborn despot, return together in altered form to create an expressive confusion.[43] At the public rehearsal of the entire piece on October 29, the audience was uncommonly large and the numerous musicians present gave Berlioz' piece an extremely warm reception.

But the next day – Prize Day – Berlioz suffered a double disappointment. He had to attend alone, for Camille's mother had grown huffy at the failure of his parents to recognize the engagement and would not allow her daughter to appear with him at an official function; nor was Lesueur, ill in bed, able to applaud the public vindication of his pupil and of his own teaching. Worst of all, by accident or design, the performers missed their cue and the "conflagration" finale did not explode. The piece ended in a most *in*expressive confusion. And Spontini had come on purpose! Friends assured Berlioz that his entire work had been "deeply

[42] The caretaker Pingard was by then one of his oldest friends: Berlioz, whose knowledge of geography was extensive and accurate, loved to make him talk about his seafaring adventures, and later retold a few. (*V.M.*, II, 17–28.)

[43] The full score has never been found; a first draft exists in manuscript, from which a piano transcription was published in 1908. (*22* and *20;* see also *606.*)

felt and appreciated," but his sense of reality denied him any comfort — "one can't feel and appreciate what one has never heard." [44]

Meanwhile *The Death of Sardanapalus* had not been Paris's only excitement. Just as Berlioz was finishing his score *in camera*, the bullets and cannon balls of the July insurrection were crashing into the doors of the Institute. On Thursday July 29, after two days of fighting outside, Berlioz left — the earliest of the contestants — and spent hours seeking arms and ammunition in order to take part in the battle for liberty. He had first run to the Moke household to make sure the two women were safe, then accosted a patrol of National Guards, who sent him to the City Hall — in vain. Finally, strangers supplied him with a musket, a knife, powder, and balls, but by then the fighting had died down, and all Hector could do was to lead a street-corner crowd in the singing of the "Marseillaise."

The next day Berlioz went to St. Cloud with a great mob, then back to the gates of Paris at the Etoile. Nothing happened. The revolution was over. Even the guards posted in the Bois de Boulogne were returning to Paris. "The idea that so many good men have paid with their life for the conquest of our liberties," wrote Berlioz to his father, "and that meanwhile I have been useless, upsets me a great deal. It's another anguishing thought added to the rest." [45]

Surprising as it is to hear the unpolitical Berlioz utter such feelings and speak to the doctor about "our liberties," the reasons for the anomaly are not hard to find. The thirst for liberation, and especially for free expression, had come to affect all ranks. The King's ordinances seeking to muzzle the press, the Chamber, and the electorate had set off the riots that destroyed the dynasty. Though violent, the outbreak deserved even an artist's admiration: "The splendid order that reigned during these magical three days," writes Berlioz, "is maintained and confirmed; no looting, no lawlessness of any kind. The people have been sublime." He regretted only "the dead who cannot be brought back to life . . . nor the poor trees on the boulevards, which are cut down too." [46]

By its revolution the nation settled a quarrel of thirteen years' standing. The events that had made so vivid an impression on the boy Berlioz when his father became mayor in 1817 had been part of the royalist reaction seeking to annul the revolution of '89 and bring back the old regime. For ten years the "Ultras" made headway, exercising repression on the press and the schools, on beliefs and manners, and on the arts. They split their own party and angered the country by preventing

[44] *A.R.*, 115. [45] *A.R.*. 104. [46] *A.R.*, 104–5.

Chateaubriand from carrying out a strong foreign policy. Then in 1827 the tide turned; Chateaubriand's group made common cause with liberals of every shade, their bond of union being the resolve to win individual and national self-expression. The young journalists – Guizot, Rémusat, Mignet, Carrel, Thiers – wanted intellectual scope and political careers. The artists wanted the *perruques* retired and the field opened to talent. During nine months of political imprisonment in 1828, Béranger wrote ballads that stirred the people, and when the moderate *Journal des Débats* attacked the Ministry and was prosecuted in August 1829, the alarm became general. Soon an organized refusal of taxes was under way, and too late Charles X planned a campaign in North Africa to secure prestige and divert men's minds. A liberal petition only roused him to issue the July Ordinances, and in three days all was over.

More than most revolutions, that of 1830 concerned the intellect. Precisely what is now felt to be its weakness – the precarious union of extremes that brought it about, its management by bankers and prompt neglect of the masses – shows it to have been mainly permissive: every group wanted the Open Door, feeling that if only it were let alone it could do great things. It could, in Chateaubriand's words, "achieve reality by the path of dreams" – including the dream of high dividends. What the men of 1830 sought and accomplished was change under control, and the revolutionary leaders' appeal made much of their devotion to Order. But the more generous spirits among the young were moved by reforming zeal as well. The need for a more equitable society was preached by many (notably by the followers of Saint-Simon) and one of the most thoughtful among them, Charles Duveyrier, persuaded Berlioz that "the social question" was paramount. About the time that Carlyle and Mill across the Channel were feeling the same influence, we find Berlioz writing that after much reading and reflection, he is eager to add his effort to the rest: "Tell me what I can do and I shall give you my ideas on the ways in which I can be musically useful to the great work when I return to Paris." [47]

For the nation at large, the issue had been Old regime versus New, and the new order should have meant, in Berlioz' words, "the betterment of the most numerous and poorest class, the natural ranking of talent, and the abolition of privileges of every kind." [48] The hope was to carry forward the early work of the Great Revolution, which implied, besides social justice, the individualism of the educated and the articulate. It was

[47] *128* (written from Rome). Liszt was even more deeply involved in Saint-Simonian doctrine. See *210*.
[48] *128*.

precisely this double goal that nullified the Three Days' work: the workmen who had held the barricades were cheated out of their claims by the businessmen and lawyers. While the aged Lafayette played to the gallery and a bourgeois king was handed a scepter in the shape of a green umbrella, the common people were hoodwinked.

They showed that they knew it in the further outbreaks of 1831–1832 and succeeding years. But they were put down because the demand for "the natural ranking of talents" conflicted with ameliorating the lot of the poor. Those who had engineered the revolution knew what they wanted and they wanted it for themselves. Like the young artists, the young journalists and politicians had knowledge behind them and purposes ahead. They seized the facilities they needed with the least show of force because they knew that "perpetual revolution" can be an ideal only for people who have nothing to do. This is what imparts to this historic year the character of a skillful, conscious, and high emancipation, even though the postponement of the social question prepared the next revolution: to stay in power the statesmen of 1830 were driven to destroy the hopes they had aroused. And yet, for a brief time the workaday world seemed to welcome liberty and to emulate the artist in his love of ordered freedom. Great things might indeed be about to begin.

Berlioz' Training and Tradition

> If you really wish to hear . . . my cantata [*Sardanapale*], I must warn you that it is a very mediocre piece which by no means represents my inner musical thought. . . . The score is not in keeping with the state of modern music; it is full of commonplaces and of instrumental vulgarities, which I was forced to write in order to win the prize. Since you are good enough to take an interest in my work, I would rather that you came to hear . . . my overture to Shakespeare's *Tempest* at the Opera. At least there I shall be speaking my own tongue.
>
> — BERLIOZ to Adolphe Adam, Oct. 25, 1830

The men of 1830 rightly felt that their tutelage under sleepy elders was over, but Berlioz' note to Adolphe Adam underlines the piquancy of the recent prize winner's part in that situation. Berlioz is inviting his colleague to a concert at the Opera which would include a mature

Berliozian work,[1] and at the same time answering the other's request for a ticket to what might be called Berlioz' graduation exercises. The young master was a pupil just finishing school; he was supposed to ripen in Rome, but he was already a composer with a symphony in rehearsal which was to prove a landmark in the history of art. This telescoping of chronology has misled many a reader of Berlioz' life. We are used to the undergraduate poet who publishes a masterpiece while still at Oxford, and to the infant prodigy, like Mozart, who fulfills early promise. But Berlioz' is a different case, with few parallels; and because of the technicalities that surround music, the extent and solidity of Berlioz' powers at the age of twenty-six are easy to mistake. Had Berlioz in fact earned the right to "speak in his own tongue," as he intimated to Adam, or was the phrase mere brashness? Was Berlioz as a musician well- or ill-trained? Do his works after 1827 show the vagaries of a tyro, or do they boldly extend a tradition?

These alternatives are often encountered, singly, in the Berlioz literature, the writer's choice depending largely on whether he likes Berlioz' music in general or approves the principles which he thinks it exemplifies. Some, for instance, have found the "explanation" that they wished in Lesueur's long-winded theories. Others blindly accept, as regards Berlioz' technical training, young Mendelssohn's hasty condemnation. In truth one is offered more solutions than there are difficulties to solve. The resulting contradictions put one in mind of Shelley, long considered gifted but brainless simply because his intellectual aims were comprehensive and his preparation remarkably broad.

Certainly Berlioz' technique in 1830 was the product of extensive schooling and a wide tradition, modified by independent thought. After a year's private study with Lesueur, he worked for four years under this same master and his colleague Reicha within the walls of the best school in Europe, the Paris Conservatoire. Founded in 1795, under the leadership of Bernard Sarrette, and enlarged two years later with some of the best musicians of the National Guard, the institution meant to conserve the gains made by the art of music during the French Revolution. It established the first thorough and systematic curriculum for the study of all branches of secular music anywhere in Europe. By 1810, its teaching body numbered 115, and by 1820 it attracted students and instructors

[1] It might have been numbered Opus 13 had Berlioz preserved all his early works, comprising one opera, two overtures, a symphony, a mass, several lyric scenes, the *Faust* suite and a book of melodies. For further details about the *Tempest* fantasia, see below, Chapter 7.

from all countries; the textbooks written by its specialists were standard. By 1830 Cherubini's discipline made it inevitable that any student on its rolls should do at least two things: work extremely hard and master the system. Today this system may well seem antiquated and deficient but at least it enforced industry and imparted a technique.

As for Berlioz' particular teachers, it is worth remembering that Reicha taught César Franck as well as Berlioz, and Lesueur taught Gounod as well as Berlioz. Indeed, of Lesueur's pupils, fourteen took the Rome Prize and became respected professionals. Are we to assume that the master's lessons "took" on them but not on the one whom Lesueur himself singled out as the most gifted and the most likely to honor his country as a composer? Two academic tests prove the frivolity of such an assumption. One is that Cherubini, despite personal animus, passed Berlioz four times in Fugue as a preliminary to competing for the Rome Prize, and finally awarded him that prize in a unanimous vote of the Institute's music section. The other, more conclusive still, is that Berlioz' music criticism, which was technical to a degree no longer current in journalism, demonstrates his thorough knowledge of "the rules." The works that he heard followed these rules, and he judged them accordingly, in detail and by ear. He himself, though departing more and more from the scholasticism that was taught him, retained to the end a respect for the conventions wherever they aided expression instead of shackling it.[2]

So much for Berlioz' relation to the academy. His subsequent history tells us that he went far beyond any of his classmates, however high they rose in the professional world's esteem. Therefore he brought other things to bear on music than Conservatory rules. And here the fact that he began his formal studies at nineteen must be accounted an advantage. The myth that he was by then "too old to learn" rests on a total misconception of what art and teaching really are. For one thing, the parallel with the musical performer is false. To play an instrument calls for a muscular co-ordination which is best acquired in infancy, but composing by no means requires precocious facility.[3] In the second place, it must not be forgotten that Berlioz arrived in Paris with a training which even

[2] It is high comedy to read Berlioz' reservations about Wagner's harmony and Wagner's suggestion that Berlioz should have submitted his symphonies to Cherubini: each speaks of the other like a professor, doubtless for the same reason, that their esthetic purposes were incommensurable. The only common measure they could think of was pedagogic.

[3] Wagner, Albert Roussel, Duparc, Tchaikovsky, and most of the Russians began their studies later than Berlioz and under far less favorable conditions. The dour Fétis himself learned harmony on his own and by composing pieces until he satisfied his ear. (*1398*, Feb. 17, 1944.)

our most enlightened modern schools seldom obtain from their students: competence on two instruments and the ability to sing at sight and realize chords mentally. In short, it was not Berlioz' musical education which began at the Conservatoire, but his academic apprenticeship — a very different thing.

This circumstance was, again, most fortunate. Any good teacher would prefer his most gifted pupil to come to him possessed of a good grounding in the rudiments and nothing more — no premature "style" to unlearn before going on. The reason is that every real education differs from every other, and that the valid discipline of any art is not something that can be taught. On this point our modern faith in ubiquitous "education" is touching but mistaken. In art one can teach only those who already know — those who instinctively feel — how words or paint or sounds can be handled. What makes them pupils is clumsiness, not ignorance. By trial and error (called exercises) an artist teaches himself, though not necessarily *by* himself. Schooling provides useful but limited aid — textbook rules and teacher's tricks; contact with the work of the masters; criticism and encouragement. The true teachers give goals, not rules, and even these goals are but the intermediate steps between what the student can do and what his ultimate wholly individual intention is. Besides, if he is ever to "speak in his own tongue," it is important that he do not show too ready a hand at using his teacher's tricks. Better remain clumsy than turn slick. Berlioz at a later date could very justly speak of young Saint-Saëns's "regrettable lack of inexperience." [4]

Good teachers take these truths as self-evident and recognize that far from conveying the essentials of an art, the rules and problems set down for academic use are but a temporary scaffolding which every genuine creator must sooner or later discard. The reason is that any textbook or system based on past practice necessarily rests on a kind of average of that practice.[5] Fux's *Gradus*, drawn from Palestrina, may be excellent, but it forbids to others much that Palestrina allowed himself, and it destroys the context — musical, emotional and historical — from which Palestrina's art arose. Gédalge, long after Bach, informs you about *the* fugue, but no two of Bach's fugues are alike — and none bears any true likeness to those Gédalge himself has written. The public may like to

[4] *730*, 682.

[5] Hamerton on a sister art: "No drawing-master could earn his living by teaching art seriously, and the chief anxiety of every drawing-master is to invent the prettiest and easiest substitute for real art that he can . . . But the worst of all such systems is that, once their fixed point reached, they arrest the education of the eye." (*1085*, 15.)

think of the "laws of music" as sacrosanct, but these laws are no more fixed than those of writing or painting. Indeed they are possibly less fixed. As Koechlin has pointed out: "There is no rule of harmony without exceptions. . . . The grammar of language is far more fixed, more general, less subject to exceptions than the so-called grammar of music. Most of the 'errors' and 'prohibitions' have never had currency outside the textbooks. Chords are always written *first* by the empirical instinct of creative musicians; but what musical instinct is remains a great mystery. . . . Besides, musicians can use not one, but several distinct vocabularies, idioms, or styles. . . ."[6]

This does not mean "Burn the textbooks," but rather: "Bear in mind the difference between the world of art and the stuff of the handbook." The variety of art and the roughness of its actual texture are at the opposite pole from the artificial neatness of the manual. But only a lively historical sense will keep the busy teacher from equating his convenient sketch map with the reality. In the Paris Conservatoire this awareness was and has remained entirely lacking.[7]

Reicha enforced rules that he could not justify, though he sought mathematical "proofs"; Lesueur deemed Beethoven a dangerous model; Cherubini corrected Bach's "barbarisms." It is perhaps inevitable that instruction in the arts should be narrow and bigoted. Even the student who learns one kind of harmonic analysis from a master-composer finds that another calls it "inaccurate and incomplete"; and this does but express the artistic need to feel things in a definite, exclusive way. This being so, it follows that genuine talents will revolt against masters who cannot see that limited validity is the price of a teaching system.

In Berlioz' day, musical dogma was deceptively "rational," resolutely consonant, foursquare, and timorous to the detriment of musical expression. Formulas took precedence over form, and custom (such as that of writing rapid vocal fugues on the word *Amen*) was the final answer to

[6] *729*, 631–4 and *453*, 176–7. As Shaw long ago pointed out, with only just enough exaggeration to be emphatic: "People would compose music skilfully enough if only there were no professors in the world. Literature is six times as difficult an art technically as composition: yet who ever dreams of going to a professor to learn how to write?" (*879*, II, 40.)

[7] Looking back on his student days, Harold Bauer wrote in 1948: "I have often wondered what the net effects of the Conservatoire method of education were on French musical culture. It was very thorough. It was tremendously serious. It exacted from the students a terrific amount of application and industry. . . . But, says the captious critic, is this enough? Where is the aesthetic thrill, the life substance, the irresistible creative urge? Perhaps we have to look elsewhere for the reply." (*927*, 118.)

all objections grounded on dramatic fitness. It was this body of rules, attitudes, and routines that Berlioz had to pretend to absorb in order to please his teachers and win the prize. The chief virtue of this subjection is that it enables the biographer to refute the charge of "scant schooling." Too many people will judge a canvas only after they have been assured that the artist went to drawing school: well, Berlioz spent five years "learning to draw" and thus ranks among the longest-taught musicians in the history of the art.

In addition to the Rome Prize, Berlioz undoubtedly derived from the Conservatoire further lessons in tenacity and self-discipline. For his success came only by repeated efforts, each of which was a new challenge to compose against the grain of his musical instinct. He thus had to formulate and decide for himself every stylistic question. Although by 1830 his own technique was not fully worked out, his style was set. Its most remarkable feature was balance: the narrowness of his teaching did not beget a compensating wildness, nor did the praise of routine make him seek the false originality which consists in doing everything by opposites. He worked hard for his results. Just as he had to study orchestration by himself because the Conservatoire had no course in this art, so he studied classic and contemporary scores to supply the lack of historical teaching. He "prepared" for every concert and opera he attended, and read Beethoven, down to the last mad, unplayed works. Beethoven was his link with the great traditions that the Conservatoire ignored: German, English, and Italian.

From conversations with Reicha and Lesueur, and reading in the works of their youth, Berlioz was familiar with the conception of revolutionary music, that is to say, music for the public occasions of a sovereign people. At the same time, he neglected neither the tragic style of Gluck and Spontini nor the light, expressive, transparent forms of eighteenth-century French comic opera. Both these schools were in decline, but they still held a message for the synthetic mind who could also assimilate the meaning of Weber's romantic works and remember the moving idiom of folk song and liturgy. In a word, Berlioz took all that the Conservatoire had to offer, and by an eager catholicity filled in most of the deficiencies with which we would now charge the curriculum.

By sifting this broad heritage through a temperament that the academy could hardly weaken, Berlioz had no trouble avoiding the trap of eclecticism. Rather, he rediscovered, or recaptured, the living tradition. This is no mere figure of speech. One has only to compare the music of his teachers with his own early works to see that his kinship is not with them but with great men whom he did not know – Bach, Purcell, or Scarlatti. "It is a miracle," says Koechlin, "that he should have rediscovered so many things virtually unaided. . . . He resuscitated Harmony; finding it feeble and monotonous, he had to re-create it altogether, through the use of significant (and subversive) chords, diminished sevenths with exceptional resolutions, and unexpected progressions of common chords." [8]

Orchestration was in the same anemic condition. "Considering the feebleness of his models," says Emmanuel, "one can only wonder at the ease with which Berlioz found his way in the maze [of orchestral possibilities]." His grouping of timbres and their use for structural purposes was "a new conception of the orchestra, of which he was thoroughly conscious. . . . One can deduce from the *Symphonie Fantastique* all the lessons in instrumentation which his successors have followed with credit and glory." [9]

In melody, as we saw, Berlioz took naturally to the ancient modes. Lesueur, who admired them in the abstract, thought them dead beyond recall, but Berlioz revived their use with the utmost naturalness, and – as Debussy was later to observe – prepared the way for a broadened conception of tonality.[10] Once again a comparison between Berlioz' songs and the airs of the period shows the conscious creator at work. Finally, from this earliest period also, Berlioz' rhythm was varied, vigorous, and free, which was enough to cause his judges the deepest alarm.[11] "Berlioz," says Hadow, "was one of the greatest masters of rhythm and modulation that the world has ever seen. Modulation is a lesser gift, for anyone can learn how to modulate, but only a genius of the highest order could have devised a metrical system of such variety and extent." [12]

Rhythm, melody, harmony, sense of key, orchestration – these comprise the elements of music. What of Berlioz' power to combine them in intelligible forms, in the strict sense, to compose? The question must necessarily recur in connection with each of his major works. Here one can say categorically that form was his preoccupation from the beginning, spurred as he was (once again) by the inadequacies he felt in his teachers and by the stimulus he found in Beethoven. In his daring essay on the master, written at twenty-five, Berlioz declares the Ninth Symphony the starting point of any living music, and he analyzes the work

[8] *453*, 176.

[9] *427*, 243, 246. This is true even though Berlioz' orchestra has never been imitated. See below, Subchapter 16.

[10] *975*, 44.

[11] See in the preceding chapter Boieldieu's friendly tip to Berlioz in 1828.

[12] *443*, 137–8.

not as a source of emotion but as a structure. Despite the superior ignorance of certain analysts, who have created a kind of presumption that Berlioz' music lacks form, it remains a fact that Berlioz invented more than his share of structural devices and established them in modern music.[13] These inventions, which go back as far as the first cantata – that is to say to his school days – were fully under control by the time of his certification as a prize winner; he had then finished the *Symphonie Fantastique*, of which a modern composer has said that "formally speaking, it is among the finest of 19th-century symphonies."[14]

This symphony is of course listed everywhere as program music, a doubtful classification which will be examined later, but which raises here the question of Berlioz' relation to the theories of Lesueur. Berlioz' teacher had written voluminous essays on "a new kind of music," he had exemplified it in his works and been blamed as an innovator, and he certainly imparted his ideas to his pupils. From this it has been inferred that Berlioz' views on music were taken over bodily from the older musician, though carried out with the greater success due to greater gifts.[15] What Lesueur preached was a homogeneous "imitative" style for dramatic use. By "imitative" music he meant music closely molded on stage action, as he believed Greek music to have been when it was used to accompany the so-called "hypocritic pantomime" – or, as we should say, the actor's "business."

No doubt Lesueur's insistence on dramatic meaning chimed in with Berlioz' convictions, derived from the study of Gluck which antedated his lessons with Lesueur. But the main reason for this parallelism was that Lesueur was himself a disciple of the French Encyclopedists who had, in the words of a modern scholar, "firmly established the salient principles of music drama for Gluck, Berlioz, and Wagner."[16] Lesueur then was one link in the chain from Rousseau to Berlioz, and his real influence was

[13] For example the form of Chopin's G-minor ballade, which follows the pattern of the *Fantastique*, first movement.

[14] Constant Lambert: *732*, 162.

[15] This thesis is put forth in its extremest form by Octave Fouque in *Les révolutionnaires de la musique* (Paris, 1882). Boschot in the first volume of his biography takes a middle position, saying that given Berlioz' own inclinations, Lesueur was "the only possible teacher for him." (*267*, 188 and 533.) These two views contradict Boschot's other belief that Berlioz was rebellious to any teaching, and would imply that he was on the contrary a too faithful disciple. The best study of this question remains that of G. Allix (*265*) who concludes that "things are not so simple" as they have been made out by those who call Lesueur a "Berlioz manqué." (Pp. 39–40.) Alfred Einstein confirms this judgment in a passing word of his *Italian Madrigal* (1949) Vol. III, p. 718.

[16] *848*, 168.

to stress the seriousness and the problems of dramatic music. But Berlioz soon discarded Lesueur's solutions together with his secondary theories regarding Greek music. Berlioz did not of course abandon the principle of fitness which in greater or less degree rules all opera since Monteverdi, but he worked more and more away from the eighteenth-century notion of using music to underline dramatic feeling. He sought on the contrary to abolish this duplication and emancipate music from the role of accompanist. It is precisely this divergence from Gluck and Lesueur's "imitative" conception which separates Berlioz' art from Wagner's. From the outset, Berlioz' deviation from Lesueur (temporarily masked though it was by the use of a "program") [17] implied a new standard of perception and judgment. It was Berlioz' own sense of this difference that spurred him on to elaborate new forms.

One may well ask why a young composer should be thinking of new forms, before giving proof that he had mastered the existing ones – fugue, symphony, aria, overture, recitative. It is all too likely that a student's invention will show the prentice hand, or what is worse, that his successes will seem failures for lack of a yardstick to measure them by: the first movement of Berlioz' first symphony is a case in point. Berlioz had of course shown what he could do with a regular form when he composed the *Waverley* overture; but already in that of the *Francs-Juges* his material dictated alterations in the pattern. A real sense of form therefore does the opposite of what is generally assumed; it will not allow formula to take precedence over fitness, and in young Berlioz the recognition that a new melos and new instrumental means called for changed patterns was a sign of natural constructive power. When we speak of the healthful discipline of strict form, we take for granted the suitability of that form, and we think of the desirable pressure which makes the artist squeeze all the significance out of his ideas. Rime, for example, compels the fledgling poet to try a dozen permutations instead of being satisfied with his first line, and leads him to pack his couplets with sense while enhancing their felicity and force. But this only proves that a set form makes it easier, not harder, to achieve merit. Rime is a parapet which

[17] This alludes not only to the explicit program of the *Symphonie Fantastique* which is dealt with in the following chapter, but also to such "Lesueurisms" as the note in the Greek Revolution scene (1826): "The features and voice of the hero, which so far have expressed wrath and indignation, must in these bars [three bars' rest] resume an expression of intense sadness and pity." (*Ger. ed.*, X, 8.) Berlioz obviously wants the singer to act his part as if the cantata were an opera, yet it is noteworthy that even here Berlioz supplies an interval for the change of mien to occur *between* sharply characterized movements.

keeps the versifier from going over the edge into feeble nonsense, whereas blank verse lets him and his ideas slide. The stiff outlines of the form moreover give a decent starched look to the final product, even if it is internally weak. In the ode or in free verse, on the contrary, all the pressure has had to come from the idea within, and nothing but its own strength props the structure.

A sound instinct tells most beginners to follow the models supplied by their teachers. Berlioz did this himself in his first lyric scenes and oratorios. But his quick intelligence saw the weaknesses of Lesueur's music and the futility of trying to charge it with his own high-powered thought. He must forge his own technique out of the diversified tradition at his disposal: tragic eloquence from Gluck, expressive detail from the light operas, popular grandeur from the revolutionary musicians, even a kind of academic rigor from his conservatory training – this was the French heritage. From Germany and his own time, he drew the lessons needed to express his inborn love of nature and dramatic realism. The rest was from himself: orchestral invention called into play his extraordinary ear and melody depended on the secret work of his sensibility. The sum was more than the parts: it was a new musical substance, and Berlioz could not but seek to shape it according to its requirements. Form must change with substance in order that in the finished work the two shall be inseparable. The so-called evolution of the arts is nothing else than this periodic change to fit new matter with a new formal skin. When Berlioz began to compose the *Symphonie Fantastique*, the forms of the past half century needed renovation. Gluck's drama was dead and Beethoven had begun to distend the symphonic-sonata form. No anarchist but a thoughtful architect, Berlioz, like the men of 1830, was going to reconstruct in the spirit of revolution but with the aim of order.

6. *Reveries and Passions:* Symphonie Fantastique

August to December 1830

Is not this something more than fantasy?
—SHAKESPEARE

THOUGH PARIS and Berlioz were impressed by the moderation of the people in their uprising, the rest of Europe, beginning with the French provinces, continued apprehensive. Insurrections of varying success filled the remaining months of 1830. Belgium shook herself free from Holland, and music signalized the event: the singing by the young Frenchman, Adolphe Nourrit, of Auber's *Masaniello* at Brussels in August 1830 precipitated a riot.[1] Elsewhere — in Spain, Italy, Poland, the Rhineland, and Prussia — students and professional men joined with the bourgeoisie and common people in attempts to secure charters granting constitutional government.

But several of Berlioz' friends, having no artistic stake in the revolution, were aghast at the turn of events and at his sympathy with their outcome. Du Boys, the part-time versifier who had composed the words of Berlioz' "Ballet of Shades," gave up his judgeship so as not to take the oath of allegiance to Louis Philippe. As for Hector's bosom friend, Ferrand, religious fervor made him a fanatical enemy of the liberal regime and Berlioz had to beg: "Let us not talk politics." [2] Meanwhile at La Côte, Mme. Berlioz was made ill by the July Days and her son's exultation thereat.

Even from the composer's point of view, a time of revolution had its drawbacks. Although the people had quickly accepted as their Citizen-King the cousin of the deposed monarch, they had had a second spasm of fury. The hungry paraded and broke windows; shops closed down and the new government, run by bankers behind the scenes, had to strengthen as quickly as they could their National Guard of solid citizens. Berlioz did not join it at this time, but later, when membership became compulsory. He contented himself with orchestrating the revo-

[1] See above, p. 104, the note on this opera.

[2] *L.I.*, 78.

lutionary "Marseillaise," for music seemed to be imperiled by the upsurge of the masses. Not only were concerts suspended and theaters empty, but the new patriotic songs were abject. The mediocre poet Casimir Delavigne had written a "Parisienne," which the sublime people "bellowed to an ignoble tune." [3] Meantime nothing was being done for art by the new Minister of Interior. "He has other things to think of: so much agitation everywhere means that politics is the only business." [4]

The recovery of the "Marseillaise" was a clear gain, for music and for the public good. Berlioz arranged it for double chorus and orchestra, assigning the vocal part to "all who have voices, a heart, and blood in their veins." The orchestration was – as one might expect from Berlioz – a dramatization: the first four stanzas are sung in unison, with the band supplying a fanfare. The fifth stanza offers the contrast of softness to underline the words "magnanimous warriors of France" and the final stanza, opening for three unaccompanied voices leads to a tremendous crescendo for the call "To arms, O citizens!" followed by a magnificent chromatic scale beneath the descending fanfare of the *Marchons!* [5]

The young lieutenant of the first revolution, Rouget de Lisle, who had composed the tune in a state of slight inebriation in 1792, was now an old man, obscure and nearly destitute. The revival of his most inspired work drew attention to him. A benefit was held in his honor, and the government which adopted his song as a national anthem gave him a pension. The proceeds of the benefit he gave to aid the victims of the July Days. As for Berlioz' orchestration of his masterpiece, it had the effect of reawakening Rouget's dormant ambitions. In thanking the young composer, he proposed collaboration in a letter of which one sentence is often quoted by itself, with somewhat misleading effect: "Your brain seems to be a volcano in constant eruption. Mine never harbored anything but a straw fire which is petering out with only a bit of smoke to show for it. But perhaps if we combined the resources of your volcano with the remains of my bonfire. . . ." [6] Rouget had two opera librettos to contribute. But by this time, the last months of 1830, Berlioz had to excuse himself. Much was happening to him that engaged all his attention, and moreover he had to leave for Rome.

[3] A soldiers' ditty, said to be of Prussian or Hanoverian origin.

[4] *A.R.*, 109.

[5] On the repetition of this word, Berlioz retains Rouget's original melody – the two middle notes being the same and not a tone apart. Needless to say, Berlioz' orchestration has never become official, and it is even a question whether a French army band would have the legal right to play it.

[6] *Mem.*, I, 158.

The prize had finally removed all paternal objections to Berlioz' career. In a letter to Lesueur, the doctor had made amends for his earlier brusqueness: "If my son is already on the threshold of the Temple of Fame and Fortune, it is to your affectionate counsels, to your learned lessons, to you as friend and master, that he owes the fact." [7] This eighteenth-century *billet* is touchingly sanguine as to Fortune, though one effect of this optimism was the willingness of the Berlioz family to consider Hector engaged to Camille Moke. She was a "player," but not in the same sense as the dreadful Harriet Smithson.

About Harriet, at this time, Hector entertained curious feelings. Believing what he had heard, he "despised and pitied her" and occasionally alluded to her as "the Smithson wench." But other references, colored by Shakespearean associations, show that his "tenacious nature" clung to the idea, if not of Harriet, at least of the Ophelia she had incarnated – a sad beloved, remote but poetic. The thought plunged him into Hamlet-like reveries mingled with tempestuous passion. He was, to be sure, genuinely in love with Camille, whose person, endearments, coquetries, and musicianship set him on fire. Yet he could not sustain the image of her as a poetic heroine. Ariel was an elusive sprite who would not pledge herself wholly and who used her mother's preference for M. Pleyel as son-in-law to keep Hector on tenterhooks. Camille teased him too much about his musical convictions and his one-sided romance with Harriet, and thereby showed a hardness which boded ill for domestic life with the sensitive but energetic Hector.[8]

"Ophelia" was in truth more than ever a proper object of pity. The troupe of which she was leading lady had gone bankrupt in England, and in order to support her mother and sister she was reduced to walk-on parts at the Opéra-Comique. Instead of the former adulation she now evoked only brief sarcasm in notes "of local origin." Berlioz, who could always endure his own misery better than the sight or the imagining of another's, brooded over these reverses. He had had no claim upon her and could certainly not gloat; on the contrary, her misfortunes as an artist established a claim on him simply because he witnessed and understood.

Glimpses of his state of mind show through his account of musical affairs during the last months of 1830: between October 20 and December 5 – six weeks – Berlioz had three concerts to attend to. The first

[7] *A.R.*, 118.

[8] Spontini, who took a lively interest in his junior, apparently urged him to give up the match. (*129*.)

was the public audition of his prize piece *Sardanapalus*, with its added conflagration designed to show the difference between the official and the Berlioz manner. We know how effective it was at the dress rehearsal and how it failed the following day, when Berlioz had "neither father nor mother nor master nor mistress" to comfort him.[9] Perhaps he could recoup himself at the Opera where his overture-fantasia to *The Tempest* would be performed in early November. It was the "newest thing" he had done, and he meant it as a sort of betrothal celebration of and for Camille, who had never heard any of his works. She had obtained her mother's permission to go. In addition, the concert was in the nature of a musical manifesto, the date having been originally set to come immediately after the publication of Berlioz' article on "Classical and Romantic Music."[10] In short, the event was to combine all the meanings, public and private, that it could stand for: the composer, theorist, prizeman, and affianced lover should triumph within the walls of the Opera where nine years earlier he had recognized his vocation. Politics interfered: on the chosen day, the new regime scheduled a parade of National Guards, and Berlioz himself, as a self-manager of increasing experience, preferred to postpone the concert. No one would go to the Opera after a weary day of cheering brass bands. The second date, November 7, was no luckier. This time the elements played Berlioz false. Fire had failed him in *Sardanapalus*, now the heavens opened for his *Tempest* and deluged Paris. The streets ran ankle-deep with muddy water and the house was practically empty.

It is doubtful whether even a dry night would have brought out the aristocratic connoisseurs so soon after the political upheavals. They kept out of sight and sought to undermine the new government by provoking disturbances and boycotting the fashionable places: nothing was quite safe or settled. Berlioz' *Tempest*, for chorus, orchestra, and two pianos – a tone poem in four parts rather than an overture – nevertheless echoed within the vaults of the rue Le Pelletier and impressed its author as worth saving. He kept it for a work that still bore a kind of connection with Camille Moke and from which modern conductors might profitably extract it.[11]

December 5, the date of Berlioz' third and last concert of 1830, marks the official appearance of the *Symphonie Fantastique* and a milestone in

[9] *A.R.*, 112.
[10] "*Aperçu sur la musique classique et la musique romantique*" (*1377*, Oct. 22, 1830).
[11] For a brief analysis, see Chapter 7.

the composer's career. Berlioz was closing one epoch in his life – the years of apprenticeship – and opening to others a new era in music. It is through that work that he first became known, and from it one can date his unremitting influence on nineteenth-century composers. A capital fact emphasizes the relation: Franz Liszt was in the audience.

The concert public, less fashionable and more professional than that of the Opera, turned out in large numbers and responded with as much enthusiasm as Liszt himself. Protracted applause greeted the end of the symphony, and the next days' reviews expressed the shock and pleasure it had given. In his novelistic "program" Berlioz had accurately struck the mood of the moment. People liked the story that filled the gaps between the five highly diversified movements, and they accepted the strangeness of the music more readily when aided by the description of a setting. The character of the last two movements – the only ones to justify the title "fantastic" – was unmistakable, and it was praise when the *Figaro* termed the entire work "bizarre" and "monstrous," for these were qualities in demand after a long course of pallid operatic conventions. If to this day, the Witches' Dance finale still seems modern and aptly monstrous, one can gauge its effect in 1830, on eardrums unaccustomed to dissonance, clashing rhythms, and polytonality.[12] Fétis, as usual, tempered praise with good advice. He found the second and fourth movements ("A Ball" and "March to Execution") "indicative of a vast imagination." Everywhere else he discerned "a strong individual character expressing itself outside the usual forms of art," and yearned for a greater dose of sensuous pleasure. He urged Berlioz to "charm the ear." [13] Spontini, on the contrary, was moved to wholehearted admiration, in token of which he presented Hector with one of his own scores autographed. In a letter of introduction to his brother (who was a monk in Rome) he wrote of Berlioz as "a French composer of the most unmistakable merit." [14]

By a coincidence that Berlioz must have found ironic, the night of the concert (set, as usual, for two in the afternoon) a benefit was held at the Opera for Harriet Smithson. Knowing no French and lacking a singing voice, she was hard to cast, but good will had secured for her the role of Fenella, the deaf-mute in the now ubiquitous *Masaniello*. The critics, however, did not find her pantomime equal to her predecessor's and the success was slight, both financially and artistically. Berlioz of

[12] Usually attributed to Stravinsky's *Petrouschka* (1911), as is also the use of the piano as an orchestral instrument: both the *Tempest* of Berlioz and the *Fantastique* use it as such, though in the latter a set of bells is to be preferred.

[13] *267*, 474.

[14] ". . . *del piu distinto merito.*" (*235*, II, 167.)

course stayed away. Even had he wished to go, his presence would have given rise to malicious gossip after the rumors connecting the "beloved" of the *Symphonie Fantastique* with Miss Smithson. He did not even rejoin Camille at her mother's but gave in to Liszt's passionate entreaties that they dine together and cement their musical friendship in tête-à-tête.

A few days later Mme. Moke once again gave her formal consent to the engagement of her daughter to Hector. But the prudent lady insisted on his going at once to Rome so as not to forfeit his stipend, and she cheerfully named the wedding time as Easter 1832 – eighteen months away. But Hector had other reasons besides the impatience of love for not wishing to go into "an exile enforced by the despotism of custom." [15] He would have preferred a trip to Germany, where new music was thriving, and he felt that the antiquities and plastic arts of Rome had nothing to teach him. He gave his gold medal to Camille in exchange for a plain ring which was the pledge of their betrothal, and set out for his Italian journey, planning a few days' stopover at La Côte.

Berlioz' First Symphony and Its Program

> The particular kind of music which we shall call *genre instrumental expressif* is most closely related to romanticism; . . . in the works of Beethoven and Weber, a poetic idea is everywhere manifest, but music is wholly in command, with no help from words to give it precise expression: we feel no longer as in the theatre; rather a new world opens before us.
>
> – BERLIOZ on Classic and Romantic Music, 1830

Expounding to Fétis his artistic outlook, Berlioz is reported to have said: "I took up music where Beethoven left it." [1] The remark neither utters nor implies a boast: we know from too many other statements that Berlioz put Beethoven at the summit of his musical Olympus, and that he never thought of himself as equalling, superseding, or improving upon

[15] *A.R.*, 121.

[1] *Corresp.*, 37. This would be no recommendation to Fétis who thought half of the Seventh "more bizarre than original." (*853*, 325–6.)

him. Berlioz simply meant what he said, and what we must interpret is not Berlioz' opinion of himself but his understanding of Beethoven. This in turn is made clear through the conscious discipleship which began with Berlioz' first great score, the *Symphonie Fantastique.*

Since it is the most often played of his works, and is moreover the traditional peg on which to hang discussions of program music, this first symphony has gathered around it all of the most conventional ideas about Berlioz. Reading the usual notes about the work makes one feel that the last thing critics are interested in is music, and that they conceive their function to be the purveying of gossip. If they could only clear their minds of cant, all they need give as an introduction to the score would consist of a musical analysis such as Schumann wrote,[2] or more recently T. S. Wotton.[3] But there is the "program" to dispose of, and Harriet Smithson, the opium dream, the Red Terror and the Fantastic – in short the apparent confusion of music, literature, and biography. To unravel this calls for a grasp of the relevant facts in their historical order.

In ranging himself behind Beethoven's leadership, Berlioz aimed at three things: to produce a large-scale piece which should be *une oeuvre* – One Work – not a suite or *divertissement;* to produce a work of dramatic and lyrical significance (we shall later see more precisely what this means); lastly to adapt musical forms to these requirements. To Berlioz the difference between "a work" and a numbered opus was that between music "designed solely to please the ear and interest the mind" and music such as Beethoven's, which was pervaded by a poetic idea addressed to the imagination.[4] So long as music was considered simply an agreeable pastime, the idea of symphonic wholes hardly existed – as is shown by the fact that symphonies were often played in separate movements with solos in between. As late as 1839, Schubert's C Major was submitted to this treatment,[5] and the reason we seldom know the date of the first performance of an eighteenth-century symphony is that the programs carry only the mention "Sinfonie von Mozart," "Sinfonia di Haydn." Anything

[2] *874,* I, 118–51. This essay, Schumann's longest, was written in his first year as critic (1835). When five years later he desired (and obtained) a doctorate, he submitted the piece as a thesis. It is also remarkable as a review of Liszt's first great piano transcription, which in turn was the first of its kind, that is, a full and faithful rendering of the original, with the orchestration indicated. A final "first" to be noted in connection with the Symphony is that of its electrical transcription under Weingartner, whose initial success as a conductor thirty years before was associated with the work. (See *1459.*)

[3] *533.*

[4] From the same essay on Classic and Romantic music. (*1377,* 1830, 111–2.)

[5] Hanslick, quoted in *1294* (1921–2), 1360.

written for strings, or for strings and woodwind, in three or more movements, might be called a symphony. Music came by the yard – in the public's mind if not in the composer's. From Swift to Chesterfield and from La Bruyère to the philosophes, the prevailing opinion was that music gives pleasure amid other occupations or during idle reverie – always, that is, at the expense of the understanding. Such a view hardly encouraged discrimination between one work or composer and the next, and persons who made such distinctions were considered precious or faddish.[6]

The genius of Beethoven, coming at a time of political revolution, changed this courtier view to the modern one that a great symphony is a work of the same spiritual weight as a great poem, painting, or drama. Its parts belong together and no conductor today would dare act like Habeneck who, in the first performance of Beethoven that Berlioz ever heard, substituted the Allegretto of the Seventh for the Scherzo of the Fifth. Imposing our new attitude upon the past we now respect the integrity of Bach's, Haydn's, and Mozart's instrumental music, and ascribe to it significance beyond pleasant sensation and technical skill.

As to the nature of this significance disagreement begins as soon as listeners try to report on what most of them admit they feel. It is generally believed that in the program written by Berlioz for the first audition of the *Symphonie Fantastique* he gave one kind of answer to the problem, namely that music conveys "literary" ideas. His writing a program ought to prove the very opposite, since here is literature *added* to music. His very first words, moreover, are enough to dispel any doubts: "The composer," he says, "has aimed at developing from certain scenes what they contain that is musical." This is not to duplicate literature, nor to imitate real life, but to develop in sounds certain elements which life and music mysteriously hold in common. If we perceive reality once again in music, it is not as in a copy but as in a translation. For like any part of human experience, music suggests other parts by association or by analogy. Beethoven was simply fixing certain associations more firmly when he called a symphony "Napoleon Bonaparte," later "the Eroica." His desire to be known as *Tondichter* rather than *Musiker* (Weber preferred *Tonkünstler*) was consequently not an infringement on the poet's trade but the establishing of a parallel.

It is of course one thing to know all this intuitively as an artist fluent in the medium of his art, and another to convey it to an unprepared and

[6] Chesterfield tells his son that although called a liberal art, music ranks below all the others and its supremacy in Italy is "a proof of the decline of that country." (*1244*, 220.)

inattentive public. Beethoven had to protest against a literal reading of events into his symphonies. Yet he supplied a program for the five movements of the Pastoral and thereby shocked that same public.[7] Berlioz faced the identical problem with added handicaps – the necessity to advertise himself and supply the public with a "story." For by Berlioz' day program writing had become a custom – undoubtedly educational at a time when instrumental music was on the increase. Certainly the eighteenth century found programs natural, and in writing his Berlioz was obeying tradition: Lesueur, Knecht, Schubart, Spohr, Weber and Beethoven had preceded him.[8] Since Berlioz never wrote another, he ranks among the first to break with this practice, which he was far from having originated.[9]

His chief purpose in writing the program, as he tells us in the document itself, was to "furnish an occasion for characteristic pieces of music." He therefore made up a text, suited to the contemporary taste, in which the attentive modern reader can easily separate the musical intent from the verbiage. Berlioz "supposes a young musician in love," who never thinks of the beloved except "as associated with a musical thought," the two forming "a *double* idée fixe" [*italics added*]. His anguish at one point leads him to take opium and dream dreams. The rest of the program takes the artist-hero to a ball, to country scenes, to execution, and to a posthumous revel of witches. In this scenario, action and musical ideas are interwoven quite carelessly, and we find, for example, under the heading "A Ball" a reference to Nature. Further on, the phrase about the shepherds' making dialogue out of a *ranz des vaches*[10] clearly states that no representation is intended. The music *is* the dialogue, just as for the last movement the text draws attention, with no hint of programmatic significance, to the superposition of the witches' dance and *Dies Irae*.

If Berlioz thus mixed two modes of expression that were always distinct in his mind, the public can be forgiven for not disentangling them – at least at first. Unfortunately, his "Episode in an Artist's Life" succeeded all too well as a piece of sensational literature and proved an

[7] Beethoven seems in fact to have been spurred on to composing the work by Heinrich Knecht's feeble *Musical Portrait of Nature* (1784?) of which Beethoven took over the "program" verbatim.

[8] And Spohr continued after, giving programmatic titles to four symphonies and a sonata. Wagner wrote six programs, to works of his own or of Beethoven's.

[9] To this day symphonic societies continue to furnish their patrons with reading matter which supplies every piece with a setting – critical, narrative, or biographical.

[10] Here again, the influence of Beethoven's Pastoral, which also uses a *ranz des vaches*, is evident.

encumbrance to his own freedom as a musician. People discussed what they read and not what they heard, and the ultimate effect on Berlioz' reputation was disastrous. In common opinion he ranks as the program musician par excellence. All subsequent masters, whose works would hardly be what they are without Berlioz' musical pioneering, are assumed to be purists in comparison with him; and while he is talked of as if every bar of his scores inventoried the physical world, he is in fact the least literal or descriptive of dramatic musicians. He does not depict but transmutes, and he is difficult precisely because of this, which throws the listener back upon an explanation – a program to help him over a style.

A second motive besides the traditional one of helping the public may well have influenced Berlioz in the preparation of his text. He speaks of it as "an unspoken libretto," and again as "the words that an antique chorus might sing." These loose synonyms suggest that he was groping toward the formulation of a *raison d'être* for the new form of dramatic music which he found in Beethoven's work and his own. Church music had its *raison d'être* and its setting in the liturgy. French revolutionary music had its pretext and setting in a political situation imparted through oratory and journalism. Their audiences knew ahead of time what all the blowing and banging was for. The opera was equally accessible through convention: it was a stage play with music. What setting could secular, nonpolitical music – assuming it was to be taken seriously and not as a household noise – claim as its own? Wagner later wrote volumes on this central question of nineteenth-century music, trying to prove that legend and the forms of Greek drama supplied the correct answer. But the public knew few legends and less music, and Greek drama was dead, so Wagner wound up at the opera house with a printed libretto, a stage production, and a chart of labeled leitmotives.

Not so Berlioz. Though he did not give perfect theoretical expression to his view of music drama until 1847, when he published his *Romeo and Juliet* symphony, the form itself had been developing steadily since his cantata days: it was, in a word, the organization of musical moments around a single subject, at once musical and dramatic.[11] The idea of a unifying device in the music itself was of that same early date.[12] By 1830, in the *Symphonie Fantastique*, he named this device *idée fixe* and made

[11] Of Beethoven's C Minor, Hoffmann had written – in the second serious analysis of the work: "Beethoven has kept the ordinary sequence of movements; they seem fantastically linked each to the other and the whole reverberates like the rhapsody of a genius . . . but the sensitive hearer will be gripped by *one* lasting impression." (July 1810, quoted in *853*, 209.)

[12] The bacchantes' leitmotif in *La Mort d'Orphée* (1827).

up a set of incidents to fit. The musico-dramatic fusion is automatic: just as the relation of subject and "answer" in a fugue suggests the "chase" which gives the form its name, so the recurrent leitmotif suggests an enduring being or thought, which may then be labeled at the whim of the composer or public, and pass "dramatically" through varied contexts.[13]

It should now be clear how Berlioz, interpreting Beethoven, achieved "one work" and in accordance with Romanticist principles combined within it both lyrical and dramatic significance.[14] This leaves the final question: is the drama of the *Fantastique* autobiographical? Now or never is the time to be literal in order to judge the common belief that Berlioz wrote the symphony about himself and Harriet Smithson. The striking thing is the total lack of connection between Berlioz' relations with the actress and the scenes he chose for his story: he had never taken her to a ball, never been with her in the country – much less at a public execution: he hardly knew her except across the footlights. Even the "revenge" of introducing the love theme into the witches' revel answered far more to the need of using the *idée fixe* in different contexts than to any symbolic significance: this part of the program suggests *Faust* and, as will appear, De Quincey, rather than life.

Knowing Berlioz' mixture of shyness and audacity, one may readily understand how he associated his disappointed love with this *ad hoc* concoction in five parts; but one can say that the "Episode" came from his life only in the generalized sense that all works of the mind distill the experience of the creator.[15] What the story corresponds to structurally is the symphonic plan: allegro, adagio, scherzo, and (here double) finale.[16] The composer's letter quoted above confirms the fact that organization

[13] This is the germ of the symphonic poem, on which see below, Chapter 24.

[14] From Hugo's Preface to *Cromwell* (1827): "Drama is the most complete form of poetry. . . . Our epoch is above all dramatic and by this very fact lyrical also. . . . For lyric poetry finds its best setting in drama: it never interferes with it but on the contrary molds itself to all its whims." (*1262*, 30–1.) Note in passing that the long incubation of Wagner's ideas on Greek drama is not unrelated to this and other ideas of Victor Hugo's. The subject may be further studied in *1101*, *1044;* and *1401*, 1923, 278–9.

[15] Beethoven's *An die ferne Geliebte* could be considered far more exact to the facts of his lost love than Berlioz' scenario, were it not that the song cycle is once again merely *apposite*. New works always seem charged with ego. A Berlin critic of the Ninth Symphony remarked that Beethoven had "made a subject for a work of art out of his own artistic individuality." (*853*, 453.)

[16] It will be remembered that Berlioz first put the ball scene (= Scherzo) third in order, but probably noting Beethoven's using the scherzo as the second movement of the Ninth, followed his example. In the *Fantastique* it had the advantage of separating the waltz from the march and of "centering" the superb adagio, which is also the longest movement.

took precedence over story and that he "did not write the witches' sabbath with Harriet in mind." [17] So little did the facts concern Berlioz that he tinkered his program very freely through five successive drafts [18] — lengthening the opium dream to include more than the last two movements — and this of course without altering the score, since he never for a moment supposed that music can *denote* opium, even though some compositions may induce its physiological effects.

Finally, Berlioz left express instructions that when the *Symphonie Fantastique* is to be played by itself (that is without its sequel for the stage, *Lélio*) the program must not be given out, but only the titles of the five movements.[19] Nowadays these titles could easily be further shortened, reducing them to familiar musical categories as follows:

1. Appassionata
2. Waltz
3. Pastoral
4. Death March
5. Witches' Dance

Given these and a brief musical analysis, there is not an audience in the world that would fail to grasp whatever drama is implicit in the sounds; the *idée fixe* would obtrude itself without bearing that name — all the more without bearing Miss Smithson's.

So much for the "program" written by a would-be dramatist still floundering in literary composition. His mastery of musical form and of his own idiom at the same age is another thing, to which one can turn without regret or apologies. That this artistic competence was ever doubted only matters now as another witness to the fallibility of critics; but that the myth should continue to be repeated argues a really culpable conservatism: Schumann's definitive essay has been out for [135] years.[20]

That Schumann could as early as 1835 characterize Berlioz' genius so exactly, from a piano score and without a hearing, is almost as marvelous a feat as the writing of the symphony itself. What he grasped at a glance

[17] *L.I.*, 70.

[18] The final one is quite short — some two hundred words long — the fullest comment being on the third movement, where "action" is certainly least.

[19] Hence the notes given out at nearly every concert that presents the symphony go against the composer's wishes.

[20] Now available in English by Paul Rosenfeld among the Pantheon books, N. Y., 1947. The quotations in my text are taken from the German but may be found in somewhat different words in the version just cited, pp. 169–82.

was the Shakespearean principle of Berlioz' art: "Though Berlioz absolutely neglects certain details, sacrificing them to the whole, he knows very well how to deal with the fine points which need to be worked at with an artist's hand. . . . All the melodies have the same character of originality and naturalism, but in their development they lose this purely 'characteristic' aspect and rise to that of a more universal beauty." The critic then lists special features worth noting: "Modern music has certainly never produced a work in which even measures and rhythms alternate more freely with uneven. . . . But with what dash does he carry it off! It would be absolutely impossible to add or subtract anything without robbing the idea of its trenchant energy. . . . Side by side with violence and eccentricity, however, one must also draw attention to details of exquisite delicacy and refreshing beauty. Thus I may mention the whole harmonic structure of the largo introduction. . . . Berlioz' harmonies, despite the diversity of combinations he obtains with but few elements, are distinguished by a kind of simplicity and even by a solidity and concision that one finds only in Beethoven. . . . The harmonic richness of the third part is remarkable and will bear comparison with the great works of any master. In the fourth movement [March to the Scaffold] the main theme has a superb counterpoint. . . . As for the double fugue [in the Witches' Dance], though Berlioz modestly calls it *fugato* and it cannot be likened to those of Bach, it is written according to the rules and in a very limpid style."

With regard to form, Schumann sagely remarks that "nothing is more bewildering and provocative of discussion than a new form under an old name," and he cites the late Beethoven quartets. Then returning to Berlioz' symphony he assures his readers that "despite its apparent formlessness, the structure possesses order and regularity, even apart from its intrinsic unity." And since the first movement has been impugned as incomprehensible, he makes a diagram of it, compares it with the conventional pattern and concludes: "We cannot see any advantage that this latter could show over the former with regard either to variety or to the balance of its parts."

Berlioz abandoned the German symphonic plan, says Ernest Newman, "not because he had not the craftsmanship for it," but because his aim was the "sweating all the old superfluous tissue out of the symphony and making it compact and meaningful throughout." [21]

[21] *1407*, Nov. 19, 1933. Gerald Abraham concurs: ". . . for the first movement, the most important of every symphony, Berlioz cast his 'reveries and passions' in the shape of a perfectly comprehensible modification of classical

This is not to say that Berlioz' Opus 4 is flawless. Schumann saw and enumerated some of its faults — clumsy transitions, neglected opportunities, excess of ingenuity — and he even went out of his way to criticize the program, severely but justly: "This sort of prospectus is always somewhat unworthy; it smacks too much of the charlatan . . . But Berlioz was addressing himself to the French public, with whom reserve is not the way to succeed."[22] Schumann does not, unfortunately, deal with the larger question of musical and dramatic unity that Berlioz aimed at. Had he done so he might have remarked that the use of the *idée fixe* is not equally satisfactory throughout. In the second and fourth movements (waltz and march) the binding theme seems tacked on from without — further proof that Berlioz began with the musical ideas for a waltz and a march and not with his scenario. As is true of other composers, ideas for movements came to Berlioz independently — the lyric and the dramatic might belong to different creative spells — so that the problem of uniting them had to be solved more consciously. The waltz and march may have been thought of first as suiting earlier projects[23] and when later, in the *Symphonie Fantastique*, he tried to "bind the parts firmly together" he found that his leading theme could be added moderately well to the waltz but merely as an insertion to the march. It did provide there

---

'first movement form.' The slow introduction is Beethovian and the exposition . . . perfectly normal; moreover, the theme of the *largo* is woven into the *allegro*, which Beethoven had never thought of doing. It is only the development that could puzzle the blindest of school analysts. All that happens, however, is that the recapitulation is an organic continuation of the development, with the second group of themes *not* in the tonic and placed before the first subject instead of after it. In other words, Berlioz like Beethoven conceived form as an organic thing, not as a mechanical affair of rule of thumb." (*692*, 33.)

[22] At the same time, Schumann took pains to vindicate the "Beethovenian idea" of music written on a subject — such as the death of a hero. He goes even farther than Berlioz in associating facts or images with music, and speaks of the actual or fancied flitting of a butterfly over the composer's score paper as the inspiration of one work that he knows of — alluding to his own *Papillons*, Op. 2.

[23] The march is said by Boschot to have originally belonged to the *Francs-Juges* opera, an assertion which aroused the most violent controversy in the whole history of Berlioz scholarship. (See *308*, May 20 to Aug. 5, 1906.) It is unlikely that Berlioz would deplete his finished opera score when he still had hopes of seeing it performed, and it is still more unlikely that the march in its present form would have fitted into an operatic scheme. The evidence from the torn manuscript of a part of *Les Francs-Juges* (Bibl. Nationale) is inconclusive, and so is that of the manuscript of the *Symphonie Fantastique*.

As for Boschot's further assertion that the march cannot have been composed, as Berlioz says, in one night, it rests on the absurd argument that the original destination of a piece is a clue to the time it took to compose.

an opportunity for the brusque cutting off of the melody in a manner suggestive of decapitation, and this has been called "the most dramatic moment in modern music," [24] but it does not show Berlioz at his best in the fusion of dramatic and musical ideas.

The first, third, and last movements, whatever their origin, do provide the double satisfaction he aimed at, and they do it in part by means of the technical resource which was discussed earlier under Melody, namely, Berlioz' seemingly endless power to make a musical idea generate others. The common term "development" hardly describes what is rather a species of procreation. Thus in the first movement—the least pleasing at first, but once it is familiar the most marvelous of all—the theme of the introduction is not only varied in its recurrences, but it supplies decorative phrases for the horns after its initial treatment, and it later yields two separate accessory themes attached to the *idée fixe*, all of which produce intermediate phrases and contrapuntal subjects until the whole is one organic mass and not merely a formal concatenation. With such flexible elements interlinked, dramatic intention is easily served, though the hearer must know the music well before he recognizes that these phrases and echoes are not used for random effects. "Berlioz often gives but a brief sketch," says Schumann, "but it is a sketch of genius, in the manner of Beethoven. He seldom repeats his most beautiful inspirations, or does it as if in passing . . . Then with a delicate hand he completes at a later time an idea which seemed utterly forgotten." [25] When Berlioz was able to do this with an unfailing hand throughout an entire work, as in the *Damnation of Faust*, he had achieved at once his goal and his technique—a technique peculiarly his own in that it did not rely on a system, whether of leitmotives, like Wagner's, or of a single thematic root for all movements, as in Liszt's symphonic poems. The *Symphonie Fantastique* gives a hint of both these subsequent inventions, but it avoids their somewhat mechanical principle, unsuited to Berlioz' conception of fitness through flexibility.

The same symphony which won Berlioz Liszt's friendship contains abundant merits in still other departments of music: orchestral delicacy and power throughout; the full employment of expressive nuances; new atmosphere in passages like the opening of the waltz movement (remembered by Johann Strauss when he wrote the "Blue Danube") or like

[24] Strauss evidently thought so when he paraphrased it (twice) in *Till Eulenspiegel.*

[25] Pp. 173–4 and 174–5.

that of the pastoral adagio (remembered by Wagner in *Tristan* Act III). These and numerous other ideas must rank as major contributions to the stream of music. Indeed from Wagner ("Thought" motif) to Paul Dukas (*Sorcerer's Apprentice*) composers seem to have found these five movements a storehouse of musical material, while – as someone has said – the Witches' Sabbath, with its Stravinskyesque sonorities and the orchestra playing in two keys, is the first piece of Russian music. If Berlioz' score is epoch-making it is entirely for these artistic and musical reasons, first perceived by Schumann and briefly summarized here, and not because Berlioz helped publicize the work by bits of verbal narrative to which he himself attached the label "Fantastic."

Having relegated the program to the role of promotional aid, and found the symphony intelligible as music and enjoyable in spite of certain defects, one may take up the third and last element implied in Berlioz' aim to fulfill the Beethovenian ideal: the message of the tone poet, the spiritual import of his music. To be sure, the message is *in* the music, but there are many listeners to whom that indication may seem oracular or evasive. It would be easy to set them on a plausible track by saying that Berlioz' five movements represent respectively: the hero searching his heart, the hero in society, the hero on the bosom of nature, the hero confronting his fate, and the hero at grips with the supernatural – *Ein Heldenleben* and a half. But it is not like Berlioz to think in this pseudo-philosophical, post-Wagnerian way. His manner of gathering and expressing spiritual truth was much more direct and quite unlike the headings of a dissertation. What imposed itself upon him by repeated experience or reflective reading ultimately came out as music. This is what he meant by saying that the *genre instrumental expressif* embodied the "melodic reflex" of life. In this way, and only in this way the *Symphonie Fantastique* sums up Berlioz' experience from his twelfth to his twenty-sixth year just as, and precisely because, it sums up his musical ideas and artistic powers during the same span.

The key to his "message" therefore lies in the numerous associations that can be traced between his mind and the musical elements of the work. The list begins with the largo introduction of the first movement, based on the "Estelle" melody of his boyhood. The title of the movement, "Reveries and Passions," states a natural contrast, corresponding both to his impulsive-orderly temperament and to his Faustian "double-mindedness." The allusion in the program is a borrowing from Chateaubriand, whom Berlioz read during adolescence. In his chapter on "*le vague des passions*" (intimations of passion) [26] Chateaubriand defines his subject as "a state of the soul which . . . has not yet been adequately studied, namely, that which precedes the development of our passions when our faculties are young, active, and whole, but closed in and exercised only on themselves, without aim or object. . . . One is knowing without experience . . . One's imagination is rich, abundant, full of wonders; life is dry and disenchanted; one lives with a full heart in an empty world." Pondering these words before his fifteenth year, Hector would surely recognize his own unhappy state. Nor is this all. The passage occurs after a section dealing with the interrelations of poetry, religion, and love, in which Chateaubriand argues that the melancholy of the isolated soul is a product of Christianity: it results from the hope of an otherworldly perfection unknown to the Pagans. His illustrations are strikingly apposite to Berlioz' interests. Christianity, he says, augments the play of passion in drama and epic poetry, which reminds us at once of Hector's "first musical impression" in church.[27] But Chateaubriand also speaks of the great passions depicted in ancient literature – of Dido (whose plight disconcerted Berlioz as a child); of Phaedra's love obsession (*idée fixe*); of the tradition of pastoral love (shepherds in the midst of nature); and of the musicality of the Greek words used in idylls (fusion of poetry and music).

On top of this comes the remark on Chénier's execution, which Berlioz had long ago copied into his notebook. He must have brooded over it, as did so many of his contemporaries,[28] and there can be little doubt that the march in the *Symphonie Fantastique* commemorates the young poet going to his death, or – since Berlioz is never literal – the doom of

[26] *1243*, Part III, Ch. IX.

[27] The first movement of the *Fantastique* as we now have it closes with a restatement of the love theme in whole notes, marked *religioso*, and an amended program speaks of *consolations religieuses*. This should be a further warning against literalism in discussing the relation between art and life, and specifically a warning against *programmatizing* Berlioz' music. For we know that Berlioz was in full reaction against his mother's piety and considered himself an atheist. Yet he remained a man of religious feeling with a lifelong penchant for composing on sacred themes. See below, Chapter 8 and Subchapter 22.

[28] Berlioz' generation was as much haunted by the guillotine as we are by the death-camps. Besides Chateaubriand and Berlioz, see the references to Chénier in Hugo's *Misérables* and Vigny's *Stello*. Sainte-Beuve remarks that the historic fact endowed even a dull mind like that of Delécluze with imagination: this second-rate critic, seeing Madame de Noailles in David's atelier, shuddered to think of her handsome neck under the executioner's knife. (*1212*, III, 88.) As late as 1834, Harriet Smithson acted in a melodrama about a worthy noble awaiting decapitation. See below, Chapter 10.

any youth, any creative promise, combined with the terror of extinction.[29] Finally, Chateaubriand refers to *Paul et Virginie,* a tale which remained a favorite of Berlioz', and whose merit is that it states the Romantic theme of close observation of nature in conjunction with love considered as a pure passion.[30] In Berlioz' copy of the book, the title and the closing pages are marked by him with a harmonized phrase, first major then minor, traversed at its close by a new "line" (oboe or English horn) which pathetically rends the sequence of chords[31] – in short, the theme of the book spoke to him in music and thus belongs also to the "sources" of his first symphony.

Harriet's role in the genesis of the work was thus limited to reinforcing the double contrast Reveries: Passions, Living Nature: Death and the Supernatural. She was a duplicate of Estelle, an arbitrarily chosen "aim or object" for passions yet unexercised, which none the less gave intimations of other experiences besides love. The character of the melody chosen for the *idée fixe* is a psychological triumph which confirms this interpretation: it rings proudly and nobly but remains somewhat cold. When Berlioz used it in a prize cantata, it stood for the female warrior Erminia. A symbol for the women he loved from a distance, it marks his awareness of their remoteness and independence, and like an obsession it seems foreign to the true, intimate self.[32] In contrast, the other musical ideas in the first and third movements possess that warmth, urgency, or tenderness we require of love themes. Hence we may safely generalize and say that taken together, these themes make concrete through sounds Berlioz' experience of passion to date: we may merge Estelle and Harriet, Emmet and Chénier, Dido, Paul and Virginie, into the fund of young Berlioz' fears and longings.

All this forms one group of inspirations, the earlier. The later draw on intellectual experiences of the Paris period: Shakespeare, Goethe, Hoff-

[29] This is confirmed by the note which he attached to his *Elégie* written on a text of Moore, about Robert Emmet's execution as an Irish rebel in 1803: Berlioz quotes Emmet's last words to the judge (a classic speech that had moved thousands such as young Abe Lincoln) and by way of introduction tells in moving terms the story of Emmet's love for Sarah Curran. Simultaneously, the Elegy meant to Berlioz his permanent separation from Miss Smithson.

[30] Hazlitt: "I remember how I sat up all night to read *Paul and Virginia.* Sweet were . . . the drops of pity that fell then upon the books I read." *First Acquaintance with Poets.* (*1254,* 13.)

[31] Reproduced in facsimile in Jullien's *Berlioz,* 324–5, and in *Musica,* Mar. 1908, 45.

[32] Note in passing Berlioz' use of the medical term *idée fixe,* drawn from the new psychiatry.

mann, Weber, and Beethoven. Musically, the third movement of the *Symphonie Fantastique* is indebted to the adagios of Beethoven's fourth and sixth symphonies. Complementing Beethoven's ideal of life-inspired music was the Shakespearean pattern of play construction in sharply characterized and contrasting scenes. From this came the idea of a dramatic Episode in an Artist's Life, condensed into five characteristic moments which – to borrow Schubert's bad French – were naturally "moments musicals."

As for the horrendous Witches' Sabbath, which after the Pastoral represents the Terrible or dark side of nature, its inspiration comes from one of the great rediscoveries of Berlioz' period. Through introspection and historical studies, a whole cluster of psychological and cultural truths reemerge with Romanticism; most notably sympathy with the Middle Ages. The eighteenth century, neglecting what it called Superstition, has been justly called the most terrified of all epochs, and until almost the end it hid its own terror from itself.[33] The next generation, inured to war and revolution, attempted to face life's horrors and even to love them. This marks the relevance of De Quincey's report on opium eating: here was a psychologically informative diet. Again, what the Romantic individualists found by their misnamed Egotism or Subjectivism was the Unconscious. It was this nameless irrational thing that primitive minds had objectified into powers of evil. Consequently, "superstition" enshrined truths about life, and hence the literature, the religion, and even the buildings of the superstitious ages must be looked at with fresh eyes. There ensued the rehabilitation of Shakespeare and Dante, of folklore, of gargoyles and witchcraft and Notre Dame. After seeing the black magic in *Freischütz* and reading Goethe's variations on the demonic, it was quite natural for Berlioz to include the Fantastic in his scheme. Specifically, the transmogrified appearance of the beloved in the finale of the *Symphonie Fantastique* is a precipitate of several suggestions: in Goethe's *Faust,* the Brocken scene includes a ghostly appearance of the heroine, and later when she recognizes her guilt in church, the *Dies Irae* resounds, as in Berlioz' symphony. Before Berlioz began this piece, Hugo had published a volume of verse in which a *Ronde du Sabbat* is described in detail with its specters, beasts, and witches reveling in a mockery

[33] Forerunners and sharers in the *Sturm und Drang,* both Gluck (in his Tauris scene) and Mozart (in Don Giovanni's damnation) had given musical expression to the Terrible. In the Renaissance Michelangelo's *terribiltà* expressed itself in works of overwhelming size and strength. Then Raphael came into favor, and the genre was not cultivated again until Salvator Rosa, whom Hoffmann and Berlioz felt kinship with.

of religion: in Berlioz the *Dies Irae* is parodied.[34] Finally, in the early months of 1830, Berlioz may have read De Quincey's *Opium Eater* in Musset's translation and adapted one of its ideas. For the translator took the liberty of inventing a new close, by which the heroine makes a loveless match and is seen by her true lover at a ball, bejeweled but degraded.

As a realm of experience, then, the fantastic meant more in Berlioz' day than it does now: it extended from the dream world to the sinister aspects of nature, taking in religious and subreligious entities on the way. Betokening also a return to one of the oldest elements in European culture, it did not carry its modern connotation of vagrant fancy or unreality.[35] Its vogue in France, personified by Hoffmann, lasted until the 1850's [36] and its essence reaches us through Baudelaire (in his versions of Poe) as well as through Symbolism and Freud.[37] As a title for Berlioz' symphony it is patently an overextension. Only the last movement and possibly the fourth justify it.[38] At any rate, the symphony is not an adventure into the bizarre. What it reflects, what the music may legitimately be associated with, is young love in dramatic contrast with nature, with the presence of death, and the forces of darkness. The caption "Episode in an Artist's Life" merely reminds us that the Romanticists regarded the artist as a culture hero, a representative man. But since Berlioz always seeks to objectify, to dramatize his data, we dare not infer that he was all these things; we dare not even say he felt them; we must content ourselves with saying he "knew" all the emotional and spiritual components of his finished musical drama. The substance and the skill that went into the making of the *Symphonie Fantastique* represent the sum of Berlioz' inward and outward experience during the first twenty-five years of his life. As for the vitality which has carried the work unstaled across the intervening century and a [half], it may be ascribed to causes of

[34] Hugo's *Odes et Ballades*, Ballade XIV. It is quite possible, of course, that the first form and destination of Berlioz' Witch Dance had to do with Bohain's *Faust* ballet of 1827. At any rate, Berlioz seems to have shaped the musical molds for these elements for a long time to come: compare with his episodic finale the first and third movements of Liszt's *Faust* symphony, Dukas' *Sorcerer's Apprentice* and Moussorgsky's *Night on Bald Mountain*.

[35] In Goethe's view of Nature, Alchemy, and Magic, the element he calls *Wahn* is not illusion or delusion but a record of experience and suffering. For a revaluation by a modern critic, see *1040*.

[36] *1175*, 382–4.

[37] After a hundred years' abuse of De Quincey, Coleridge, and other Romantics as "pipe-dream artists," our century discovered through Jean Cocteau that opium may have important esthetic results. (*1077*, 76.)

[38] It may incidentally be noted that the heavy brass stay silent for the first three movements in order to lend their force and color to these closing sections.

divers kinds, but the main reason may be that its spiritual or poetic idea truly answers to the description a modern critic once gave of the symphony: "The only musical work which can compare in sincerity and truth of expression with the literary masterpieces portraying . . . the awakening of the mind under the spell of passion – Shakespeare's *Sonnets* and Dante's *Vita Nuova*." [39]

[39] Ferruccio Bonavia: *630*, 231.

INTERCHAPTER

7. *Program Music and the Unicorn*

Musical and dramatic imagery must maintain an equipoise – as in Berlioz and more than in Liszt.

– Guido Pannain, 1934

Berlioz' determination to "take up music where Beethoven had left it" [1] settled with a finality to which every concert now testifies the right of the composer to be an artist; that is, to do in his own way what we must call "express," "portray," "depict," or "render" human experience. These analogies have to be broadly interpreted since they cover an artistic mystery. But as there remains in some minds – especially after the nonsense uttered on the subject by many a modern composer – the feeling that music is by nature a "pure" art, and that any reference to its meaning degrades it to the lesser art of illustration, not to say the vulgarity of glass eyes in sculptured heads, it is necessary, at the cost of digressing, to discuss farther the relation of music to life, and the traditional ways in which the musician "renders" life without ceasing to be a musician. Those who have already jumped this pons asinorum of musical understanding may skip the present chapter.

The obvious place to begin is with the bugbear known as imitative effects. It has in fact become current usage to call "programmatic" in the sense of "impure" any piece of music which contains, or is said to contain, imitations of natural sounds by means of voices or instruments or both. Little thought is given to the great frequency of these effects in the history of music, but snobbery fills the void left by ignorance and prevents further consideration of what is after all a rather complicated artistic question.

The nineteenth century marks a clear shift in outlook from what went before, and here again Berlioz was among the first to put the new principles into unmistakable language. As early as 1823 he had written iron-

[1] See previous chapter.

ically of the Italian vocalists' illustrative effects.[2] Seven years later, in an expanded version of his program for the *Fantastique*, he defended himself against the charge of having "attempted to depict mountains" in his symphony.[3] Finally, in 1837 he published an article dealing with the subject of imitation in all its phases.[4] In this essay, Berlioz begins with a discussion of Carpani's "Letters on Haydn," both because Carpani held a characteristic theory of imitation, and because Haydn's *Seasons* and *Creation* represented for Berlioz the eighteenth-century descriptive style par excellence. Carpani maintained that the imitation of natural sounds by musical instruments was a tour de force worthy of admiration on a par with a painter's successful imitation of a battle scene. Berlioz replies: "M. Carpani seems to us here to step outside the subject by means of a false analogy. Painting is an art which can and ought to have no other object than to reproduce or imitate Nature more or less closely, whereas music in a very large proportion of cases, is an art *sui generis*, self-sufficing, and able to exert its spell without recourse to any kind of imitation whatsoever." [5]

Berlioz however does not exclude imitation entirely. For one thing he could make his point only by discriminating within the tradition. He therefore sets conditions under which he finds the practice of "direct, physical imitation" legitimate: first, it must never be an end in itself, but a means; second, it must relate to things worthy of attention, not to trivialities; third, it must be simple and plain; and lastly, it must never take the place of *indirect* imitation, which Carpani had called "emotional" (*sentimentale*).[6] The alert reader can guess in what direction Berlioz is leading the argument, namely toward the contrast between Beethoven and the Italians. The storm in the *Pastoral* symphony, says Berlioz, appears to violate his first condition; it seems an end in itself dictating the musical form of a whole movement. But this is not so: "It falls within the category of *contrast, of dramatic effects* motivated by the plan of the work, in that this movement is preceded and followed

[2] See above, Ch. 3, p. 57; and below, *passim*, Berlioz' complaint of the verbal usage by which notes are called "high" or "low." Even teachers of composition recommended as a subtlety the use of ascending or descending scales to accompany the mention of rising suns, etc. (*A Trav.*, 226.) Berlioz found to his regret an instance of this practice in one of Gluck's masterpieces, *Alceste*. (*Ibid.* 227.)

[3] See end of this chapter for the context.

[4] *De l'Imitation Musicale* (*1398*, Jan. 1 and 8, 1837) trans. by Julius Kapp in *Die Musik*, XII, 86 ff. and excerpted (under the misleading caption of "Unknown Essay") in the same periodical (Vol. XXV, p. 29).

[5] *1398* (1837) 9.

[6] *1398* (1837) 10.

by gentle and smiling scenes to which it serves as a foil. This is so true that transplanted into another composition where it would lack a *raison d'être*, the movement would surely lose a great part of its effect." [7]

This positive example calls for a negative, which Berlioz astutely draws also from Beethoven. In the Tomb scene of *Fidelio*, he finds "a piece of childishness" which "one is equally grieved and surprised to have to complain of in the work of a great artist." Berlioz is referring to the short rumbling phrase of the double basses at the moment when the gravediggers roll a stone to the edge of the pit. ("Not to be confused with the *ostinato* figure of the basses which recurs throughout the piece." [8]) To Berlioz this imitation is unacceptable because it is "in no wise necessary, neither to the drama, nor to the music, and hence it is really an end itself: the composer imitates in order to imitate." [9] In short, Berlioz' test is intellectual: neither intention nor execution must offend our reason.

Towards Haydn he is lenient but not approving: he regrets the choice of subjects that led the composer to frequent imitation, even though carried out with restraint and judgment.[10] Berlioz also reproves the passage in Handel's *Israel in Egypt* where, "if it is true, as commonly thought," all the voices imitate the rhythm of jumping locusts.[11] These names, by the way, are enough to show in what good company imitative musicians stand. Condemning as beyond the pale all imitators in the history of music would leave very few if any "serious" composers. From the madrigalists with their cuckoo songs, the contrapuntists' battle scenes and vocal carillons [12] and the virginals players with their storm pieces, through Bach's cantatas and oratorios, to Handel, Haydn, Rossini, Beethoven, Weber, and Berlioz himself, and down further to Wagner, Strauss, and Stravinsky, there is hardly a composer who has not been tempted. We may conclude that musicians are as a class childish – which is quite tenable – or that the temptation is a thoroughly musical one.

In his essay, Berlioz goes on to discuss the far more subtle indirect imitation of life, but before following him into that realm, a preparatory word is needed about the kinds of direct rendering and their psychological bases. One class of effects comprises imitations of music itself – hunting horns, trumpet calls, drum marches, dance orchestras (as in

[7] *1398* (1837) 10.
[8] *Ibid.*
[9] *Ibid.*
[10] *1398* (1837) 16.
[11] *1398* (1837) 10.
[12] *E.g.*, Jannequin's *Battle of Marignan* (1529); Senfl's *Kling-Klang* (*c.* 1550).

Mozart's *Don Giovanni*) and so on. In his *Capriccio on his Brother's Departure*, Bach imitates the postboy's horn. In the *Leonore* overture Beethoven heralds the governor's approach with a flourish of trumpets. All opera is full of such "realism," and the practice can scarcely be objected to as "unmusical," since it is nothing more than the transfer, as it were within quotation marks, of music from life back into a work of musical art.

Next comes the imitation of birds, and less frequently of what Artemus Ward aptly called "zoological animals." Beethoven put three distinct birds into the Pastoral;[13] Haydn gave voice to roosters, lions, flies and others in *The Seasons* and *The Creation*. Here the rendering of life by music, being more approximative – more far-fetched – runs a great risk of artistic discomfiture. Success often depends on the particular performance, on the degree to which the effect is stylized when repeated or developed, and also on the predispositions of the listener. At a first hearing, provided one has not read the program, Strauss's *Don Quixote* can easily pass as a Theme and Variations for Cello and Orchestra; one hardly notices the brief "representative" passage of the battle with the sheep. After reading and looking for it, however, it is equally easy to be irritated by the composer's attempt to make one see. Still later, both experiences being forgotten, one may well recover the sense of a unified musical texture.

When this occurs it yields a clue to much of the hard feeling about imitation. The true listener does not want to see images nor think in words; he wants to follow music and, as we say rather enigmatically, thinks in sounds. The intrusion of other symbols necessarily breaks the "suspension of disbelief," just as would the King in *Hamlet* if having nothing to say on the stage he engaged in an interim chat with a spectator: he would still be using words but out of relation to the context.

It follows of course that "thinking in sounds" also precludes thinking in technical terms while the music is playing. The man who is counting full closes or changes of key is not thinking in sounds either; he may be doing his duty preparing a critical article but he is not listening, he is

[13] The only performance in America of the work Beethoven used as a programmatic pattern – Knecht's *Portrait Musical de la Nature* (by the Philharmonic Chamber orchestra under Hans Lange, Feb. 3, 1936) showed the vast gulf that stretches between intention and execution: Knecht's imitations generally failed under Berlioz' third rule calling for simplicity and plainness. It is only fair to add that on the same principle Berlioz seems to question the merit of Beethoven's nightingale: the bird does not sing on pitch, nor yet in a fixed call. (*1398* (1837) 10.)

construing. But this in turn does not mean that the musically trained may not record in their hinder brain the cadences and modulations as they pass. Just so in the favorable conditions enumerated by Berlioz, certain effects may be recognized as imitative without breaking the musical thread. In the foreground of consciousness is music pure and simple; in the background are faint associations, some originally ours — we cannot help it; others thrust in from outside — we cannot help that either: both legitimate. Indeed it may be that what we feel as the direct sway of music comes from the stirred up depths of this background. For one kind of association merges altogether naturally with musical sensation itself — the associations of rhythms — and it is not surprising that by far the greatest number of imitative effects in music depend solely on rhythm. The device is in fact the most powerful and the least imitative in the copycat sense. Listen to Wagner's "Forest Murmurs" in cold blood and you will find that what you hear is nothing like nature's noises, neither in pitch, timbre, nor design. The persistent rhythm achieves the effect, not through accuracy, since the seesawing on two notes is quite untrue to life, but rather in the way that medieval artists copied leaves in stone — *un*faithfully but with an eye to reproducing the character of the beauty they saw. Beethoven's brook is in the same case: running water does not sound like harmonically ordered sixteenth notes in the lower strings. Yet we are satisfied — as again in Berlioz' "Royal Hunt and Storm" from *Les Troyens* — with a rhythmical design which has an affinity with nature.

It is this affinity which explains Berlioz' second category of effects, termed by him Expressiveness. Its aim he defines as that of "arousing in us the idea of the various affections of the soul and awakening through the ear alone sensations which in nature human beings can perceive only through other senses." [14] In making it clear that "tone-painting" and "descriptive music" are metaphorical terms, he adds that he doubts whether poetry and the art of drawing have anything like the same expressive power as music.[15] In other words human behavior can show the same correspondence with rhythm as brooks or birds, while pitch, timbre, and other elements of music can add their precise vividness.[16] This is all that Strauss meant when he said that music could express anything, even a soup spoon. This unlucky exaggeration has given rise to much needless

[14] *1398* (1837) 16.
[15] *Ibid.*
[16] One is reminded of Locke's blind man restored to sight, for whom the color scarlet was like the sound of trumpets.

groaning, as might be expected from the critics' bad habit of warning us against horrors that cannot in fact be committed and that no one is thinking of committing. No one can say what the rhythm of a soup spoon ought to be, but Bach knew what the rhythm of rending the veil of the temple must be, and he has given it to us twice, in the *Saint John* and in the *Saint Matthew* Passions.[17] Those beautiful arabesques are certainly not imitation in any vulgar sense. We are not meant to see anything, nor to "hear" the tearing of cloth, nor yet to feel any simple emotion. We are only meant to respond to an aptly placed rhythmical pattern which is expressive in and of itself. To this function of music – most strongly shown in rhythm, but not limited to it – we shall shortly return and will then develop the meaning of "expressive in itself."

Whatever program music may be, then, it is not merely music that is pock-marked with imitative effects. These – to sum up – are but touches, usually decorative, though sometimes rhythmically determining a whole section, which like all other decorations or patterns must be judged for their fitness. The best proof that the principle of these effects is genuinely musical is that the overwhelming majority of composers since the thirteenth century have used them or added to the traditional stock.

It is not hard to guess why the same term is used to denote the occasional use of an imitative toot or rumble in a score and the large-scale works stigmatized as "program music." The common element is the elusive relation of sounds to things. But whereas the purist may be able to dismiss a simple imitative effect as an error of taste affecting but a small part, or may even overlook it altogether,[18] the programmatic intention is supposed to infect the entire work. Every bar is accused of pointing to something outside itself, and the whole is held to be "unintelligible" until the listener has memorized a tale. Program music is only to be enjoyed in guilt because in order to render life it violates in us the organ that thinks in sounds.

No one, to be sure, can prove that certain notes are in themselves more musical than other notes, but one can and does say that putting these and

[17] It is worth remembering that for the Passion music many organs possessed a *terremoto* or earthquake stop.

[18] One would of course expect that a given composer might strongly dislike another's mode of imitation – Weber, for example, condemning Beethoven as too literal (*1314*, IV, 395). And since there are also period styles in this regard, the mutual objections of actual creators can be readily understood without damage to the principle itself. But critics should be more judicial and not be seduced by the quaintness of Jannequin's *Battle of Marignan* into an acceptance which they would refuse, *on the ground of imitation*, to Honegger's *Pacific 231*.

these together fails to create musical coherence. "Why," we ask, "does the composer suddenly do *this?*" And we are not appeased when told in a program note that the scrambling harmonies depict the evils of capitalism. We resent being interrupted by extraneous, and what is worse, literal business. Up to that point communication was going on; at the break, it is as if the author abruptly dropped into an unknown tongue – perhaps unknowable, since music, as everybody has been repeating for a hundred years with the air of imparting a great discovery, "cannot tell a story." Yet in this use the phrase is really ambiguous. We should say rather that music cannot give out information. This is the real reason why incoherence in music is fatal, for it cannot be repaired by the experience we have of *things* and their connections: musical sounds do not call up particular objects and any program notes stand outside the work of art. From this truth, some people infer that any piece of music which bears a title, or about which the composer admits that it was inspired by the sea, or by pictures at an exhibition, or by a football game, must necessarily be a fact-giving piece, impure and unintelligible without – without what? Without the facts which the piece was accused of conveying. With this paradox goes the belief that any other work called Suite in G or Opus 51 is *ipso facto* intelligible, coherent, and free of factual inspiration.

These inferences are fallacious. Pieces have to be distinguished from one another somehow, by a name or number or tag, and the degree of explicitness of the name – Academic Overture or *Aus Meinem Leben,* or *Nuages* – tells us nothing about the quality of the music. Conversely the chastity implied by "Movement for Strings" proves nothing, since that caption may be a fruit of fashion like any other. Hearing the music itself and analyzing its structure are essential to settling the musical question – though it may be rash to let the decision rest with those who boast of their strictness, for it often turns out that these musical prudes are actually men of loose critical habits, who have never been strict with their own thoughts and words.

Such imperfect criticism has in the first place ruined the word Expression by making it a correlative term. "This music," we may be told, "expresses the proud consciousness of the Russian people." To which the musical absolutist justly retorts: "Nonsense!" or less irritably, "How do you know?" If the first speaker then brings forward the composer's statement that this is so, the discussion once again goes round and round the old vicious circle. The proper question is to ask how it is that many intelligent persons allow themselves and others to associate music with stories, events, or abstract ideas. The answer is the one reached by a different route a moment ago, that music is expressive in itself. It is expressive apart from the objects of its imitation; and hence can be dramatic in itself apart from the subjects of storytelling. Without reading any tale of adventure into Bach's chaconne for violin, we perceive in the succession of sounds an involvement of parts, a plot, akin to that of a drama. Many of Bach's preludes and fugues, most of Mozart's piano concertos and late symphonies, all of Beethoven's quartets and sonatas, and much of Brahms' chamber music – none of it titled – possess this quality. Any attentive enjoyer could point to passages that are especially significant, that is, expressive. Of what? – of nothing, and at the same time of things which our minds tell us are momentous.[19]

Similarly, an expressive face, an expressive gesture is one which conveys meaning without detailing its cause: an angry face expresses the person and his anger, not the accident, nor the words searing his brain. Any given gesture may occur in different situations and add to each something enlightening; yet it cannot be exactly described or defined, for then the words could satisfactorily replace it. But we know what the orator's gestures add or amplify. We likewise follow pantomime with great immediacy though we do not know the names of the persons nor the cause of their agitation. Pantomime is built up of *expressive* elements we cannot name, but can inwardly reproduce. In this silent drama there is a blend of the general and the particular which approximates what is meant by the expressive character of music. The best single statement about the nature of music implies this very analogy: "There is, in any specific sense, neither love nor tragedy in the music. . . ." The music merely "reproduces for us certain gestures of the spirit." [20]

In a context of its own kind a musical gesture is very exact, unmistakable for any other, hence so rich in significance that it is able to fit

[19] Witness the vast literature about the "philosophic" and "ethical" significance of Bach's and Beethoven's great works, *e.g.*, Dannreuther: "While listening . . . we feel that we are in the presence of something far wider and higher than the mere development of musical themes. . . . The mental and moral horizon of the music grows upon us with each renewed hearing. The different movements . . . have as close a connexion . . . as the acts of a tragedy . . . each work is in the full sense of the word a revelation. . . . The warmth and depth of [Beethoven's] ethical sentiment is now felt the world over . . . he has . . . widened the sphere of men's emotions in the manner . . . of great philosophers and poets." *Macmillan's*, July 1876, quoted in Grove, rev. ed., I, 309–10.

[20] Roger Sessions: "The Message of the Composer" (*878*, 123). Edmund Gurney, in his neglected classic *The Power of Sound* (L. 1880), calls the same inner function of music Ideal Motion. See especially pp. 168–9 and 350–3 of his work.

or correspond to a great many moments in human experience.[21] It has been said that the great argument against descriptive music was that almost any sample of it can be used for a ballet, and intelligent detractors of Berlioz have shrewdly dismissed his symphonic movements as "glorified ballet."[22] Though adversely meant, these two remarks corroborate the reality and set the limits of musical expressiveness: first, music and drama bear to each other the kind of affinity we find in ballet between sound and gesture; but, second, a more literal point by point correspondence between life and sound is impossible.[23] It follows that the crime of the program composer is nonexistent for the simple reason that it cannot be committed. His opponents are in the position of those who prove a man illiterate and then accuse him of forging a check.

The noteworthy fact about Berlioz' view of musical expressiveness is that he dwelt upon its limitations in order that its rights might appear the more plainly. In this he was again amending the eighteenth century, whose theories on the subject he was very familiar with: "Lacépède[24] states . . . that 'music having no means at its disposal but sounds can only act through sound. Therefore, in order to retrace the signs of our affections and perceptions, these signs must also be sounds.' But how," asks Berlioz, "can this be done when music would express that which produces neither sound nor commotion – such as the thickness of a woods, the coolness of a field, the appearance of the moon? Lacépède answers

[21] The German psychologist of music, Ernst Jentsch, has demonstrated this in his study of "Music and Nerves": "If music since Berlioz has employed certain well-characterized tone structures for the special description of definite things, events, and objects and has done this to a higher degree than had been true before, it cannot mean that the structures in question are appropriate only to this office and otherwise have no significance. The overtures of many a master since Berlioz remain the very same works of art even when the hearer does not know the corresponding operatic tale, and it is possible to . . . find correspondences which fit more here and less there when matched with the events of the opera, but about which no explanation seems to be necessary." (*819*, 44.)

[22] Massine's choreography for the *Symphonie Fantastique* (1937) showed how danceable the music was, and at the same time how little the physical motions added to the musical "gestures."

[23] For a complete theory of expressiveness as the source of beauty in all the arts, see L. A. Reid's *A Study in Aesthetics* (*1113*), which is incidentally the best discussion of art yet produced in our century.

[24] Bernard, Comte de Lacépède (1756–1825), was a famous naturalist whose original bent had been toward music and who did not cease to compose and write upon the art during his very industrious career. Gluck had welcomed him from the start and in the musical circles that he continued to frequent he was considered not only an important composer but an exact interpreter of the most advanced views upon the art of music. (See his *Poétique de la Musique*, 1781–5, 2 vols., and Michaud, art. Lacépède.)

'by drawing the feelings these things inspire,' and our Italian critic, M. Carpani finds this kind of imitation noble, beautiful, and entrancing. He deems it the sublime in music. I am far from agreeing with him, for I think he has deceived himself like many others, by a play on words, or rather by lack of precision. . . . Do we in truth find ourselves affected in a uniform, invariable manner by the sight of woods, field or moon? Certainly not . . . [Persons and circumstances differ.] Therefore music may well express love, jealousy, careless gaiety, frightened modesty, strong threats, suffering, or fear, but that these emotions are caused by the sight of a forest or by any other cause music will never tell us. The pretension that would extend the prerogatives of musical expression beyond these already generous boundaries seems to me absolutely untenable. This is why few composers of any merit have ever wasted their time in the pursuit of this chimaera . . . which would be to abandon music for the sake of something that is neither music nor painting." [25]

Within its natural limits, says Berlioz, music achieves expressive results through the use of parallels (*images ou comparaisons*). Here again he is arguing against a tradition which took musical painting for granted and assumed that Handel had actually rendered the falling of snow.[26] "Admitting that there are indeed admirable examples of musical painting which we must take account of, at least as exceptions, we shall find on examination that they do not actually go beyond the vast circle circumscribed by the nature of the art. These imitations are in the first place not presented as portraits of objects, but . . . merely serve to awaken by sensations that are musical the analogues of the original; and even so the hearer must be indirectly notified of the composer's intent. . . . Thus Rossini is held to have painted in *William Tell* the motion of oars, whereas all he has done is to put in his orchestra a rinforzando accented at regular intervals: this is but an image of the rowers' straining in cadence; their arrival has to be announced by the other characters.

"Again, Weber is said to have depicted moonlight in the accompaniment to Agatha's air in the second act of *Freischütz.* This is because the veiled color of his harmonies, which are calm and melancholy, taken together with the chiaroscuro effect of the instrumental timbres, are a

[25] *1398* (1837) 16.

[26] *1398* (1837) 17. Körner was writing about the same time: "Not passion but character is the object of musical imitation; that is to say, music represents the inner world, the expression of the soul." What he called Character Representation is equivalent to Mr. Sessions' "gesture of the spirit," and he specified the ways in which rhythm and melody supply respectively constancy and change in a simultaneous equivalence to the flow of life. (*1097*, 100.)

faithful image of pale light, and moreover express admirably the reverie of lovers beneath the moon which Agatha at that moment invokes. It can be said of other compositions that they represent a broad prospect, the illimitable, and so on because the composer has known how to suggest by broad melodic forms, by the grandeur and lucidity of the harmony and the majesty of a rhythm suitably contrasted with its opposite, the aspect of immensity. . . . But here again, the truth of the parallel will be recognized only by those who know ahead of time the subject treated by the composer." [27]

In short, the critic must once for all separate in his mind information from meaning, denotation from connotation, or to use Berlioz' terms, *image* from *expression.* Critics who assert that music has no meaning may ponder the excellent anecdote which they misuse, of the pianist who was asked the meaning of the piece he had just played: he sat down to play it over again. He did not say, "This piece has no meaning"; he implied, rather, "The meaning is in the piece." It is in fact extremely difficult for music to be undramatic and wholly decorative. Music *ex*presses because it is made by and for humans who, being alive, are necessarily alive to whatever *im*presses. All marked changes – of tempo, register, timbre, loudness, or tonality; all interruptions, and returns to former ideas; all climaxes, falls and silences, yield expression; and it follows that if these expressions are suitably ordered they will create dramatic meaning. In art, the opposite of "expressive" is not "absolute" or "pure" but "perfunctory."

To sum up, we are played upon first by rhythm, then by combinations of all other musical elements in their given form, and from the whole we derive, if we like, a generalized drama. But precision within music can go one step further, owing to the natural or acquired power of melody. The least attentive ear manages to differentiate a dead march from a lilt or a lullaby. The more exercised the organ of inner hearing the more highly characterized does a tune become. We speak confidently of melodies as vulgar or noble, majestic or gay; we compare them to statements, answers, perorations, and dirges; and we logically end by referring to a composer's idiom: melody is a species of utterance.

The musician who deliberately shapes his work to accompany or express a given drama will consequently attend particularly to melodic expression, using it as a means to psychological truth. He can disregard this opportunity only at his peril. His audience will not be made up of technicians, but whatever he proposes to the ear as the "speech" of Faust or Romeo will stamp him as a subtle, commonplace, sublime or

[27] *1398* (1837) 17.

merely ingenious mind. Mozart is called a great psychologist in music because he gives us melodies that fit equally the situation, the dramatis personae, and the chosen musical form.[28] What is more, he endows his characters with melodic thoughts that bear a family likeness each to each, just as the playwright makes his people speak each consistently and all unlike one another. This is genius, dramatic genius, and it is genius-in-music.

In Mozart's day, and down into Berlioz' time, the term "characteristic" was in fact commonly used to denote music of dramatic import, which had the advantage of preventing the ambiguity connected with the term "dramatic music." For this may mean music composed for an opera, or instrumental music standing by itself, the "characteristic overture" being the link between the two and leading to the *genre instrumental expressif* which Berlioz found in Beethoven.[29] The disciple bears witness to the transition from opera to purely musical drama: "In Beethoven's predecessors the feeling for expression seemed to lie dormant and to come to life only when they composed to words. . . . Beethoven began by copying the model of the Mozartian symphony. Then in his second symphony (in D) the style broadens without changing the form; one can already see the emergence of the expressive instrumental style, passionate, chequered [*accidenté*], and dramatic. Next comes the *Eroica* and the *Pastoral*, where the musician imposes a subject on his composition; finally, the great Choral Symphony. There the old mold is broken entirely, which allows the symphony, proud to enlist the aid of voices, to go forth freely and encompass all of time and space." [30]

[28] What Leporello sings in the opening scene of *Don Giovanni* has been criticized as banal. So it is, hence perfectly in keeping, which establishes Mozart's high artistry no less than does "*Il mio tesoro*."

[29] *E.g.*, Beethoven calls his Sixth Symphony a "*Sinfonia caracteristica*, or Recollections of Country Life." Berlioz' *Roman Carnival* overture has the subtitle, "*Ouverture caractéristique pour grand orchestre*."

[30] *M.M.*, 226, 229. Beethoven's own views are unmistakable, though they lack explicitness and seem on the surface illogical. He believed the *Pastoral* intelligible without program notes or headings, yet he provided these. Nottebohm adds with regret: "That is all he tells us." Again, Beethoven told Schindler hopefully that "any competent musician" could understand the character of a piece, yet he annotated his own scores, especially the later ones. Beethoven, in short, sensed the truth that though the music needs no explanation the public needs it – a paradox which can be resolved by distinguishing between the first hearing of complex works and later hearings after years of public commentary. Much like Beethoven, Weber uttered a detailed "story" explaining his *Concertstück* to his pupil Benedict, but was reluctant to have it printed. Berlioz wrote his own commentary on *The Tempest* and the *Fantastique*, but almost immediately discarded everything but the titles for the five movements of the symphony.

These last words show that Berlioz includes voices in the *genre instrumental* and that he finds the distinguishing marks of the genre in its independence from stage action and its kinship with the symphony. This brings us to the last and most contentious matters in dispute. For there is a respectable body of musicians who are willing to admit the inherent expressiveness of music, to take imitative effects in their stride, and even to recognize opera as an art, but who balk at following drama entirely with their ears instead of half and half – half an eye, half an ear. It is they who stigmatize "program music" as a hybrid, an indefensible mixing of music with the written word and the pictorial imagination; and it is they who deplore this modern development as Berlioz' handiwork, indeed as his specialty. We have already seen how different were his views from those attributed to him; it remains to see how muddled and inaccurate is the conventional account of so-called program music in the history of art.

What is confusing is that within the same two hundred years, 1750–1950, the instrumental form known as the symphony was established, and no sooner established than "emancipated," expanded, and crossed with other forms. At the same time, expressive means were enlarged through harmonic and orchestral invention, while the social uses of music were radically altered by the change from courtly to democratic patronage. On top of this a great age of literature and painting poured its treasures in a cataract of associative and suggestive ideas upon contemporary composers. Music ostensibly became multiform, dramatic, pictorial, philosophic, even political – if we count Mozart's Freemasonry and Wagner's Utopias as relevant. In the welter of ideas and suggestions, the one thing that public and critic managed to hang on to was the thing handed them at the door by the usher – the program.

At the opera, the printed words and comments lost importance under the impact of things seen. But in the concert hall the scrap of paper retained its treacherous significance – as Berlioz' mistaken reputation demonstrates. When any new work was difficult to follow and it carried a title or a program, the path of least resistance was to say "literary music."[31] In concertgoers' talk, whatever is not protected by its century (Haydn, Mozart) or by an austere reputation (Brahms) is loosely referred to as

[31] Ernest Newman long ago pointed out that one cause of prejudice against so-called program music was that it compels the listener to follow instead of daydreaming to the sounds. (*374*, 105–6.) But following does not imply feeling or seeing; rather it implies understanding, conceiving, imagining. One need not be angry in order to understand another man's anger, nor does one need to visualize him in order to imagine his passion.

programmatic and probably felt as inferior. But in spite of its professed disdain, the new post-Wagnerian audience for concerts, which was formed in large part by attendance at the opera, remained addicted to explanatory notes in lieu of libretto, and expected them from the critic when the composer failed to supply them. The upshot is that what the public generally knows about the instrumental genre is a mass of biographical scraps interlarded with "explanations" of a poetic or philosophic cast.

In reaction against this superficial education, twentieth-century listeners tend to demand absolute music from composers and relative silence from commentators: they fail to see that if they can now follow a late Beethoven quartet without the "story" that Wagner felt obliged to concoct, it is because a century of dramatic music — the forms and sounds, not the printed leaflet — has taught them. Tradition has achieved what Beethoven himself could not hope to effect without the aid of words. His symphonies having become familiar, the programmatic taint has rubbed off altogether.[32] This has likewise happened for a good many later works in the repertoire, so that there is actually a discrepancy between what is conventionally said about — or against — program music, and what is actually felt while hearing the notes.

In these circumstances, a composer as inadequately known as Berlioz was bound to be made a convenient scapegoat: he was the progenitor of every new title-bearing piece, but when this or that one had been assimilated he was left in isolation as the great and sole enemy of "pure music." The repertory being at no time very extensive, the earlier composers who had written music to subjects were ignored, and critics confidently asserted that the genre Berlioz had "created" was a kind of deviation from the straight path of art.

This massive illusion is in fact wilder than any Witches' Sabbath, for even busy men like newspaper critics can, by picking up any serious treatment of the genre,[33] assure themselves that music implying or using a program had existed long before 1830. No need to read, even: laying a ruler across the thickness of the book would show that five eighths of an inch of the history elapses before one gets to Berlioz. He was working in an ancient, perhaps in the central tradition of music, not in a bypath, nor — as is often absurdly said — in a characteristically French fashion

[32] For Sir George Grove in the sixties and seventies Beethoven was a composer of "program symphonies," of which the *Eroica* was the most obscure and the *Pastoral* the most obvious. In the revision of Sir George's great Dictionary, this aspect of the music is considered negligible. (*1315*, I, 309, n. 5.)

[33] *E.g.*, Frederick Niecks's *Four Centuries of Program Music*, N. Y., 1907.

which amounts to a national failing.[34] Among the older musicians of all nations we find the names of such program composers as Matthias Werrekoren, Josquin des Prés, Nicolas Gombert, Tommaso Cimelli, John Munday, William Byrd, Andrea Gabrieli, Froberger, Vivaldi, Kuhnau, Buxtehude, Dittersdorf, and many others. Their "subjects" range from battle pieces to renderings of city noises, depictions of character (*L'umore grave, gentile, sincero,* etc.), genealogies of Jesus, portraits of kings or gods, and meteorological fantasias (Faire weather, Lightning, Thunder, A Cleare Day).

It is accordingly impossible to escape the conclusion that program music in some form or other has been as congenial to composers of all periods and climes as the use of imitative effects. In Berlioz' time, Spohr, Mendelssohn, Schumann and many of the virtuosos on single instruments composed tons of program pieces; after Berlioz, Liszt, Wagner, Tchaikovsky, Strauss, Mahler, César Franck, Delius, Ravel, Dvořák, Debussy, and d'Indy produced vast quantities too; and in our century, despite many verbal disclaimers the practice continues: Schoenberg, Stravinsky, Elgar, Milhaud, Alban Berg, Honegger, Holst, Ruggles, Shostakovitch, Varèse, Prokoviev and others too numerous to mention have followed suit. It seems therefore a little late in the day to cry "Fie!" and attempt to load all the mischief upon the "revolutionary school of Berlioz, Liszt, and Wagner." [35]

If anything sets them apart from the rest, it is rather their steady soberness in choosing subjects and titles. Berlioz would certainly not have called any piece of music *Clouds, Footsteps on the Snow* or *Enigma Variations;* he would scarcely have composed portraits or pictures at an exhibition, domestic symphonies or memories of a child's Sunday. On the sufficient ground of linguistic fitness it would have seemed to him inartistic to entitle "seven symphonic expressions" *Pauses of Silence,* or

[34] Read Sir Hubert Parry's fantasies about Celtic and Teutonic ideas of music in the article "Symphony" in Grove's Dictionary, rev. ed., as well as Hadow and Wallace, *ibid.*, I, 358–60. Again in the same work, the article "Program Music" by Mr. Percy Buck is more moderate but quite unphilosophic in thought and expression.

[35] A German student of the history of free orchestral forms states: "There have been periods in which Program-music reached much sharper expression, in which composers were much more consciously program-composers, and in which the coloristic element was much more widely used than is true of these three masters." (700, 196.) Corroboration may be found in most of the German reference works that deal with the subject, *e.g.*, Paul Frank's *Tonkünstler Lexicon*, 12th ed.: "Berlioz is not the inventor of program music, which is as old as independent instrumental music itself." (P. 37.)

even to be as specific as Beethoven in his Op. 81a, *Les Adieux, l'absence, et le retour,* which has aptly been called "the round-trip sonata." As for going back to seventeenth- and eighteenth-century "classical" practice and either pretending to describe in music a surgical operation or the attributes of the planets, or seeking to arouse vague reveries by "impressionist" titles such as *Barricades Mystérieuses,* the Romanticists were far too reasonable to favor such a confusion of genres and possibilities.[36]

The devotee of the old masters may reply that whereas these ancients and our moderns content themselves with attaching fanciful names to works in regular form, this "school of Berlioz" tampered with form itself and destroyed it. This is pure assumption, contrary to fact and likely to obscure the real problem of establishing a difference between Beethoven or Berlioz and their predecessors. As to form, judgment must be exact and comparative, that is, based on more than exceptions and accidents. Hence it is wise to consult an historian of music such as Otto Klauwell, who declares himself an opponent of programs, and who has examined the literature of the genre and classified it with regard to form. He distinguishes three varieties:

1. Music in which the program is without influence on the established forms.

2. Music in which the program leads to new forms, not to be measured by old ones, yet intelligible apart from the program.

3. Music which is an insoluble riddle without a program. And he adds the very important observation that the number of works in the third category is relatively small as compared to the total quantity spoken of as program music.[37]

The very possibility of this classification shows that something is wrong with our common division of music into absolute and programmatic, and it strongly suggests a truer one which, if adhered to, might put an end to the tedious wrangle about the whole subject. The suggestion is that we speak of Klauwell's first two varieties as *dramatic* music, and enlarge the term "scene music" to include the third. We should altogether drop "program music" as tainted with bad emotions, and likewise the adjectives "absolute" and "pure" as equally invidious and false.[38] Instead of

[36] These works are, respectively, by Marais (1717), Buxtehude, and Couperin.
[37] *728,* vi-vii.
[38] W. H. Mellers: "There never was a more imbecile notion than the twentieth-century cult of Pure Music, for the simple reason that although in one sense all music must be program music, since it is concerned with human emotions, in another sense music, insofar as it *is* music, can never be anything but pure." (*838,* 480.)

these, we might say decorative or "pattern music." The main contrast would then be between "pattern music" and "dramatic music," as the twin heights of musical art, while "scene music" would properly designate all discontinuous musical effects, whether in the concert room, the opera, the movie house, or the broadcasting studio. Disagreements would continue as to which particular works belonged to each category, but there would be an end of the old-maidish sniffing at works of unexceptionable musical form which happen to bear a title or be linked with a story.

Klauwell goes on to make other comments worth pondering: "In general it is not among the most inventive musicians, but among the great technicians that the representatives of program music are found." [39] Hence even the program is not a crutch to the incompetent. As for literary habits in composers, Klauwell ascribes to Schumann the first use of poetical mottoes in musical scores for the guidance of interpreters; and he calls Berlioz the father of *modern* program (preferably dramatic) music, pointing out how his use of the leitmotif in "pure instrumental music" strengthened the form.[40] For the symphonic movements by Berlioz which he analyzes – the adagio of the *Fantastique;* the march from *Harold in Italy;* the adagio and scherzo of *Romeo and Juliet* – Klauwell has only superlatives.[41] If an opponent of program riddles can say this of Berlioz even when the form is unorthodox, perhaps it will be granted that the dramatic genre possesses independent life – independent both of the story printed in the program and of the goings-on of the opera stage.

Far from being a destroyer of form, dramatic purpose has been an aid to its development; indeed its effect is identical in every art: by seeking lifelikeness at the expense of symmetry and smoothness of surface, drama increases tension and makes the artist more fastidious. A dramatic poet, for example, makes his characters speak not invariably in the most exquisite but in the most appropriate words: every speech must fulfill a double purpose – poetic and dramatic. We might therefore say that in the stage play we have a "program literature" in exactly the same sense as we have so-called "program music." Still in this sense, dramatic purpose has steadily influenced painting, sculpture and architecture, especially in

[39] *728*, 5.

[40] Dyson: "In the earlier symphonic poems [Strauss] obeyed, like Berlioz and Liszt, the normal outlines of symphonic architecture. His themes were broad generalizations of symphonic states and he used them broadly." (*794*, 139.)

[41] "A masterpiece . . . as new as it is great . . . a work of genius . . . full of melodic invention. . . . He . . . brought fresh new blood to the pure instrumental form." (*728*, 105.)

their religious uses. The artist chooses to obey two sets of limitations which are close enough together so that he can conquer both, yet far enough apart so that the task of shaping his material spurs his invention. In a successful work of this sort there is no weak compromise or low cunning, but a product equally satisfying to the musical and to the dramatic sense. As Berlioz wrote to a friend while composing one section of his music drama *Les Troyens:* "I am at this moment seeking for the musical form, without which music does not exist, or else remains only the humbled slave of words."[42]

Whether for the listener or the composer, the points at which drama impinges on a piece of music may be few or many, close or remote. For example, in his first overture, *Waverley*, Berlioz chose a simple contrast, suggested by two lines of verse early in the novel:

. . . dreams of love and lady's charms
Give place to honour and to arms.[43]

In form the overture is absolutely regular, and its drama consists in the opposition of a martial theme and a gentler one, each developed in a traditional manner. The work therefore hangs by the very thinnest thread to its "literary" origin. Other pieces show a more influential connection. It is said that in the *Magic Flute* overture Mozart opens with three solemn chords in the brass in order to suggest the Masonic symbolism of the number three. But the dramatic force of that opening does not depend on familiarity with a ritual which most hearers know nothing about. Again, in the *King Lear* overture, Berlioz begins with three repetitions of a theme in the basses, joined to three "answers," a plan which *may* have been suggested by the King's questions to his daughters; although for the sake of form the third "answer" comes ahead of any "question," and thereafter the substance of the play is untraceable except in the general character of the headlong allegro.[44] The demands of "drama" in these two overtures, as we can see, were slight, or rather, were general. The role of three's is, in any case, well-established in all forms of art: it makes

[42] *S.W.*, 30.

[43] End of "Mirkwood Mere," in Chapter 5.

[44] The belief that the triplets toward the end represent a "demented character" rests on a mistranslation of Berlioz' words to Liszt: "*le caractère échevelé*" refers to the "headlong nature" of the *passage;* the French word for "character" in the sense alleged would be *personnage*. This mistake shows at once how Berlioz understood the embodiment of drama, and how easy it is to misinterpret an artist when some fixed idea of his method has taken root.

repetition emphatic without tediousness. We can hardly imagine Lear with *nine* daughters, and we may be sure that no composer would have stood for it, even if Shakespeare had failed to purge the clan for art's sake. In short, musical and dramatic form show parallelisms that permit a perfectly intelligible double game.

Consider finally an example which at first sight seems to present the most damning traces of the programmatic heresy – Berlioz' treatment of Shakespeare's *Tempest.* Here is a well-known play which the composer thinks capable of translation into music; he is bound to give us imitative effects; and he moreover feels compelled to send the newspaper an explanatory notice, which if he had not discarded it would have become a program: literature fore and aft. Let us read it: "This overture," wrote Berlioz, "is divided into four parts, yet so connected as to form but one piece: the Prologue, the Storm, the Action, and the Denouement." [45] In short, it is an episodic or fantasia overture, reducible to four general terms.[46] The word Prologue, it may be added, is used solely in order to keep to the nomenclature of the playwright: the manuscript score bears instead the musical term Introduction.

The first section is precisely that: an atmospheric piece which sets the mood of the enchanted isle by the delicate orchestration and development of fragments of a forthcoming melody.[47] This melody then becomes a song for high voices which tells in a few words the situation of Ferdinand and Miranda. The delightful spell is broken by figures in the graver strings, reinforced by the horns, trombones, timpani, and shrill flutes in rhythmic counterpoint. Scale passages and a chromatic progression rising to a mighty crescendo simultaneously suggest and conclude the "storm." There is a return to the opening mood of fairyland, interrupted a second time by a heavy rhythmical stomping, given out by the bassoons and violas. The graceful song theme suffers mangling and distortion while the cellos intone an anxious plaint – a double contrast quite independent of any program, and yet truly an "action." The next and last episode ("denouement") gives us the restored "Miranda" theme, followed by a

[45] *Courrier des Théâtres,* Nov. 6, 1830; *Revue Musicale* (1830) 367–9; and elsewhere.

[46] The title of the printed score is: *Grande fantaisie dramatique sur "La Tempête," drame de Shakespeare* (*Ger. ed.*, XIII, 64).

[47] The "delicate orchestration" (first and second violins divided into four groups led by two sets of four *soli*) is famous through Wagner's borrowing of it for his *Lohengrin* Prelude. The effect, says Wagner in his program, represents the soul floating through the ether. (*241*, V, 180.)

return to the musical serenity of the island charm, and it concludes with a march-like *tutti* expressive of gaiety.

We recognize Berlioz' characteristic conception of music-drama: from Shakespeare's play he has taken just four things – the mood of enchantment, the storm, the threatening monster, and the happy ending. By means of appropriate musical ideas – "expressive" through melody, rhythm, timbre, and harmony – he establishes the first mood and sketches the second and third in the most general way.[48] His commentary on the score, written for publicity, names Miranda, Prospero, the King of Naples, and so on, as a reminder of the salient points of the plot. But the music makes no more pretense to *show* Caliban than it pretends to discuss Italian government. In fact, this verbal program is not in any true sense the same as the inherent dramatic program which the composer followed and which we have retraced; for one could conceivably rename the piece "Robinson Crusoe" making the episode labeled "Action" suggest Crusoe's encounter with the cannibals instead of Caliban: the written program would then be different while the music and its intrinsic drama would remain unchanged.[49]

If dramatic and musical patterns are so easily congruent and adjustable, why – it may be asked – bring in Shakespeare? Why not write simply a fantasia overture for chorus and orchestra? One answer is that the play, however distantly followed, helps the composer to plot his tonal and thematic course. For with all due respect to the familiar esthetic pose, music does not write itself from its own inner necessity. The art of sounds, like every other, requires a set of specifications to follow. The composer may spontaneously think of a four-bar theme, but if he merely sets it down it will not rise overnight like a bowl of dough and shape itself into a fugue or sonata. The melodic contour or implicit harmonies may suggest the fugue or sonata as the best form in which to develop the inherent properties of the theme, but these properties are many and their exploitation by no means inevitable. The composer deliberately

[48] Forty-three years later Tchaikovsky's *Fantaisie pour orchestre, La Tempête,* followed much the same plan, which the composer expanded into a little prose poem prefixed to the Hamburg edition of the piano score (n.d., pp. 2–3). His friend Stassov wrote a still longer program, reprinted in *744*, 431–3.

[49] Is it necessary to point out that *The Tempest,* with a large or a small T, has been a traditional subject for musicians from Purcell to Honegger? In fact, various kinds of notable events are associated with the theme, from Filippo Ruggi's "Storm followed by Calm" (1757) to Beethoven's D Minor Piano Sonata about which he said: "Read Shakespeare's *Tempest.*" The half dozen English musicians who had to do with the many revisions of this play are discussed by W. B. Squire in *886*.

builds, like the architect, to a *partie*, that is, a set of demands limiting his fancy.[50]

One is therefore entitled to turn the table on the purists and say — using a word just outlawed — that all music without exception requires a *program*, a "pure" form like the fugue being ruled by the most tyrannical program of all. The composer has learned the outlines of fugue form and knows at what point such and such features are expected, and at what other points he may be free and episodic. It is these *conventional* limits which many musicians call *musical*, as if they were ingrained in music like gravity in matter — whence the false contrast between "musical reasons" and "literary reasons" when both are simply *artistic* reasons to be weighed, at any given point, solely in relation to Form in the broadest sense.[51]

The only quarrel then between "pattern" composers and dramatic musicians is whether the latter may apply two programs of different origin, but both formal, to the raw materials of music. The composers who, like Purcell, Mozart, Beethoven, and Berlioz, live in a great age of literature, may also be tempted to become psychologists and moralists. They are then working at the focus of three converging purposes, three programs: the overture or rondo or sonata or any other form is the musical (or better, tonal and thematic) program; the few well-chosen features of any plot supply the dramatic program; while insight and experience dictate psychological truths affecting the choice of "expressive" or "characteristic" melodies.

It might seem as if every corner of this intellectual thicket had now been probed, yet two tangles remain. One is the supposed difference in intellectual quality between dramatic music and pattern music; the other the real difference between dramatic music in modern and in former times. It has been argued that "the whole character of program music was misconceived by the masters of the first half of the eighteenth century, including the great Sebastian."[52] They failed, it is said, because in

[50] At both extremes of its history, musical forms arose in obedience to external demands, the earliest being those of dancing and religion. In his last and freest period, Beethoven went so far as to say: "I always have a picture in my mind when composing and follow its lines." (To Neate in 1815, *928*, 24.)

[51] In music this broad sense coincides with the basic form of oratory: Exposition, Development, and Recapitulation. This is also to some extent a dramatic pattern, though the distinctions between a speech, a play and a sonata remain important and obvious. See below, Supplement 6.

[52] W. J. Henderson in "Schumann and the Programme Symphony." (*814*, 215.)

their music the "emotional states" did not correspond to their titles. According to this view the program supplies "an emotional schedule" which is as a key to the musical treasure; without this key "the hearer is as helpless as he would be in the presence of a Bayreuth leitmotif divorced from its text." [53] The critic, writing seventy years ago, clinches his point by asking: "Who has solved the riddles of Beethoven's last Quartets and Sonatas?" [54] We have by now the advantage of him, as was said earlier, and have solved these riddles without the aid of any emotional schedule couched in words, simply by becoming steeped in the music of the whole period. This in turn explains the difference we feel between Couperin's elaborate *Fastes de la Ménestrandise* in five detailed acts, and the Beethoven sonatas: in the nineteenth century the expressive means of every instrument, except possibly the human voice, were greatly increased. Consequently, drama, which depends on nuance and contrast, was facilitated, at the very same time as the hopes of being literal and descriptive were decreased. Dramatic music therefore reached a degree of precision hitherto unattainable, expressiveness could now be premeditated and carried out, while form achieved organic instead of mechanical validity. This is the merit of the post-Beethovenian school to which Berlioz gave so much impetus in both theory and practice; for the first time "dramatic and musical imagery stood in equipoise." [55]

This true amalgam of age-old tendencies takes us into the second issue just mentioned, whether the intellectual perfection of which music is capable is not in effect marred by the addition of drama, our interest being divided and the double purpose being equivalent to duplicity. Up to a point, this is a matter for personal choice, or for an alternation of choices. No one need be exclusive on principle and it is a fact that after a great sweep of dramatic works it is a pleasure — even a relief — to hear music that is free of second intentions and that presents its symmetries in single strictness. But if the question means that the arguments of the absolutists have any validity, the candid critic must differ; music does not present us with "pure forms"; the art of music has no essential connection with mathematics; and the Hegelian definition of absolute music

[53] *814*, 216.

[54] *814*, 217.

[55] *746*, 24–5. For a concrete example of what this means, take the close of Berlioz' adagio in the *Fantastique:* the English horn melody of the opening returns, but instead of the expected answer on the oboe, we hear soft chords on the kettledrums. This is indeed a dramatic suggestion of storm, but it is just as much a musical inspiration — a harmonic variation implicit in a part previously heard.

as that "which would survive the destruction of the world" is simply hokum.

These and other intimations of a disinfected, disembodied art belong to the unhappy Puritanism and snobbery of our time.[56] They have never had much currency among creative artists and they are disproved not only by the merest analysis of words but also by a mass of evidence regarding the actual response to music. The classic summary of this evidence is that of Mr. P. E. Vernon, himself a musician, who studied under carefully controlled conditions what happened at concerts in a variously representative group such as inhabits Cambridge University. He sorted out persons according to training and exposed them to performances of every kind, genuine and supposititious, named and unnamed, and concluded that "the extraneous and irrelevant factors [in musical appreciation] are many, and so important that music without them is an impossibility. . . . Completely abstract (that is, purely auditory), music is unattainable." [57]

Anyone who professes to speak about the nature of music would profit from reading the details of Mr. Vernon's results, which incidentally confirm the pioneer work of C. S. Myers.[58] But the most casual observation of what most concertgoers do with music and take for granted about it would lead toward the same conclusions. In the first place, all but a very few listeners, trained or untrained, pure or impure, try to programmatize on their own account. This is a disease: Brahms wrote four untitled symphonies: what do reputable critics tell us the day after a performance? Why, that this or that beautiful passage is the first flush of dawn on their native hills, or the gates of heaven opening, or the feelings of convalescence, or the thrill of reunion with the beloved. Berlioz wrote a characteristic overture which he named *King Lear*. But the late Sir Donald Tovey — professedly an absolutist — insists that the work would be better called Othello.[59] In one of the Bach fugues, that eminent purist, Sir Hubert Parry, discovered the river Lethe.[60] Give these same purists the caption "Tragic Overture" and they vie with one another to guess which tragedy Brahms had in mind.[61] It is a game of won't-you?-then-I-will, and

[56] The absolutists who pride themselves on the classic origins of their theories should turn to Aristotle who in the *Politics* says that music gives us *omoiomata* of the feelings of love, hatred, and so on, and that these act as a moral force whenever men take pleasure in the *mimeseis* or expressions of these feelings. (Bk. VIII, Ch. 5.)

[57] *905*, 123 and 227. [58] *840*. [59] *590*, 84.

[60] Quoted in *892*, 226.

[61] See Mr. John Burk's comment on the commentators, *1295*.

most inspiring to research. Paul Bekker, studying Beethoven's so-called "Ghost Trio" – "because of its mystical, dark-hued second movement" – finds it no mere chance that sketches for this piece occur on the same page as the notes for a projected opera on *Macbeth*.[62]

The lesson is, first, that music is not in itself programmatic or absolute, but rather what the listener makes of it; and second, that people will talk, even if music is hard to talk about. In baffled excitement they grope for analogies which, silly as they are, do not contradict one another so much as they seem to. The gates of heaven and the sight of the beloved and the convalescent's joy doubtless refer to a single perception for which there is no name. Things are alike in this world and music strikes where the likeness dwells. At the same time, artistic experience is quicksilverish, and comparisons are proportional rather than exact: Othello is apparently to Tovey as King Lear was to Berlioz; but later Tovey changed his mind to say that the overture is simply tragic – "the tragedy of the basses" which speak out the opening theme. In short it is language and imagery that are at sixes and sevens, and not music that is flying in all directions.[63]

No doubt this programmatizing is often degrading to the music, for some of the similitudes are "poetic" and "emotional" in a bad sense. Critics lacking in literary gifts borrow from the nineteenth-century tradition, which happened to be poetical, and fall into bathos. In the hands of the makers – Hoffmann, Weber, Schumann or Berlioz – the poeticizing is tolerable, for these men were themselves poets and bred on the poets. In later comers, who do not even read Schumann or Berlioz but their imitators, the style becomes unendurable, and one understands why it has led to the other extreme of dryness and pedantry. Yet there is a sound reason for the habit of discussing music in the vocabulary of action and emotion. The two are in fact one thing – an overt manifestation of our own bodies linked to a motion or gesture of the human spirit. Technical terminology itself records that relation. Music, we say, is walking (*andante*) or at ease (*adagio*) or dying (*morendo*) or growing (*crescendo*) or trembling (*tremolo*) or joyful (*allegro*) or peaceable

[62] *929*, 302.

[63] Hence the experiments which professors occasionally make to test the dramatic or emotional contents of music are beside the point. The diversity they find is in the associations and verbal powers of the listeners and perhaps also in the quality of their ear. For good listeners the music is probably as clearly one and the same as would be any speech or poem or story read aloud. If the discrepant answers about the music were reflected upon instead of just tabulated, it would be seen how little difference exists between one student's "sweep of overwhelming love" and another's "vision of glory."

(*placabile*) or loving (*amoroso*) or joking (*giocoso*) or fleeing (*fugato*), and so on ad infinitum. Any musical rehearsal calls forth still other physical-emotional terms improvised by the leader to convey what he hears mentally and wants executed. However calm before the public, a Kleiber or Toscanini drilling his men goes through a virtual pantomime and exhausts his stock of metaphors. This is true whether the work played is labeled dramatic or not. A Haydn symphony or Bach concerto calls for it as much as a modern tone poem, possibly more, for lack of expression marks in the text.

Since common use makes these expressive words lose their literal meaning without robbing them of their truth, we have here another hint of the right attitude to take toward the fuller poetic or emotional descriptions – toward all programs whatever. There is never any need to track down a series of events or feelings from bar to bar, no need for anxious listening with the memory clutching at wisps of program. The faculty of thinking in sounds is the only one called on for activity during listening, and what it does is to grasp the contours of a mass of sounds. The title or commentary acts there not as a spur but as a brake upon the listener's imagination. Hence the passage that is "dying," the melody that is moaning (*lamento*) may evoke death or sorrow but without the factuality of an obituary. The wailing and extinction of the musical pulse are facts in themselves. Only respond, and it will not seem arbitrary for Beethoven to have marked in the score of *Egmont:* "This [*tutti* of strings] is to represent the death of Egmont"; and elsewhere, above the trumpet part, "Liberty reconquered for the fatherland." [64]

As for the critic who has to guide listeners, he will avoid equating music and life even while relating them by analogy.[65] He will say, "the

[64] Mozart also wrote comments upon instrumental parts; Schumann and Brahms inserted poetic tags and Debussy psychological injunctions – Classics, Romantics, and Impressionists do not differ in this; they differ in their choice of words, which is a matter of temperament and time.

[65] The belief that there are "correspondences" in man's experience is supported not only by the scientific proof that energy is convertible – for example that sound may be transformed into an image, as in the phonodeik – but also by the tendencies of man's sensory apparatus. Persons with hypersensitive hearing simultaneously experience sensations of color when their auditory nerves are stimulated. This so-called "acoustic-optical synesthesia" is abnormal – *i.e.*, unusual – but not degenerate; Scriabin was a synesthetic for whom odors as well as colors accompanied sounds. The older psychology which postulated a *common* sense, that is, a single receiver and converter of the data brought in by the five separate senses, dealt with something that is valid at least for purposes of criticism in the arts. See below the question of Time- and Space-arts, Subchapter 16.

movement suggests," "this passage is like," "one may imagine," and he will thereby keep clear of absurdity.[66] The allegro of the Fifth Symphony is not a record of Fate going about her business; even in literature her knock is only figurative: all the more reason why in music it should remain so. In Berlioz' essays on Beethoven's Nine Symphonies, this distinction is preserved. He does not say the scherzo of the *Eroica* depicts funeral games but that its role and placing suggest this Homeric idea, which fits a work of epic intention: don't go looking for javelins, Beethoven never thought of them. He had other fancies and more pressing cares. His artistic reason for making a "light" movement follow a somber adagio was dramatic variety; his musical reason was that he liked to write scherzos rather than minuets; his psychological reason was that he was celebrating the memory of a hero.

It is the psychological reason, of course, which leads a Beethoven to name his hero, for convenience, Egmont or Bonaparte. But this linking of music and life also establishes the power of the music to comment on the text;[67] we can invert the composing process and reason backward from music to life.[68] From almost all of Mozart's operatic music, for example, we can learn unnamable things about virtue, vice, and love. Listen, in Leporello's enumeration of Don Juan's conquests, for the contrast between the seductive softness of the strings playing thirds, the mocking arpeggios of the bassoons, and the punctuation of the recital by solitary chords in the horns and other woodwinds — all this beneath the coarse bonhomie of the servant's voice. One dare not say that this ensemble constitutes a treatise on morals, but it adds to treatises on morals a concreteness which they conspicuously lack. This addition, for him who takes it in, is music's wisdom, not to say a species of precise reasoning.

[66] It is a characteristic of meaning that it does not bear paraphrase or explanation: the point of a joke, an honorable deed, or a work of art is partly destroyed in the act of being expounded to the slow-witted.

[67] See Jules Combarieu, *Les rapports de la musique et de la poésie considerées au point de vue de l'expression* (779), especially his analysis of the opening movement of Berlioz' *Damnation de Faust*, pp. 283–305.

[68] That is why we can criticize performance and say "The tempo was too fast, which turned a desolate plaint into a dance tune"; or "The choir takes every chorale as if it were a fortified place." The more we know about and around a piece of music, the more faithfully we can perform it and judge its minutest details: this is what sense of style means: *e.g.*, Mr. Noel Straus on Brahms's C minor quartet: "Those who have maligned the work have failed to grasp its extraordinary tragic implications, and more especially in its corner movements. These . . . though played with great finesse, were not delivered with sufficient tragic emphasis to make their intentions clear. . . ." *N. Y. Times*, Jan. 7, 1946

Hence it is by no means an invariable sign of the composer's failure to have to ask "Why does he do *this?*" The critic who cannot answer often condemns the piece, as he thinks, on musical grounds; yet it may be he is in reality trying to impose a dramatic or psychological program of his own. This has happened more than once to works by Berlioz that have overstimulated the creative urge in others. Thus Otto Jahn objected to the *Roman Carnival* overture because it did not remind him of the carnival *he* had attended; Griepenkerl conceived, for Berlioz' *Faust*, a different Gretchen; Hugo Wolf did not think the *Corsair* overture fitting for Byron's poem – which is not surprising since the overture has no connection with a given poem or story.[69] Whatever the merits of any particular instance, the musical-dramatic tension spoken of earlier as a spur to invention in the composer is also a spur to reflection in the listener. When the listener is competent, cultivated, and curious instead of willful, when he does not yield to literalism (which is a form of laziness) he can derive from the contemplation of music a pleasure which is in the highest degree intellectual. And in doing so he justifies the conviction of the great musicians from Bach to Beethoven and Berlioz that through their combining of sounds they were not merely tickling the ear or the wits but speaking their minds.

The discussion of what is implied by their faith has carried us far from the childishness of imitative effects and the vulgarity of programs. To those who would persist in using these opprobrious terms, it can be said: "If the names mean what you suppose, then the thing doesn't exist; if it means something else, then its character being different must be spoken of differently. As a genre, program music is more dinned against than dinning; as an intellectual monster, it's a unicorn." Nothing could better summarize the steps leading to this conclusion than Berlioz' comment on his only program, in the revised handbill of the concert at which he first presented the *Symphonie Fantastique*, on December 5, 1830:

> The following program should be taken as the spoken text of an opera, designed to introduce certain pieces of music, of which it motivates the character and expressiveness.
>
> The purpose of the program is not, as some have affected to believe, to give a detailed account of what the composer has tried to do by means of the orchestra. It is precisely the opposite: the program is to fill the gaps inevitably left in the development of the dramatic plan by the limi-

[69] See below, Chapter 21, vol. II, pp. 49–50.

tations of musical utterance. This is the only reason the composer has for resorting to written prose in explaining and justifying the plan of his symphony. The composer knows quite well that music is a substitute neither for speech nor for the art of drawing. He has never had the absurd pretension of reproducing abstract ideas or moral qualities, but only passions and impressions; nor has he ever entertained the even stranger notion of depicting mountains: he has only wished to reproduce the melodic style and forms of singing common among certain mountain populations, while at the same time imparting the emotion felt by the soul in certain circumstances at the sight of those imposing heights.

If the few lines of this program had been suitable for reciting or singing between the successive movements of the symphony, like the choruses in Greek tragedy, no one could have mistaken their intention. As it is, instead of being heard they must be read; and the objectors to the practice here defended should remember that if the composer held the ridiculous and exaggerated views about the expressive powers of music which are imputed to him, he would certainly not have supplied a program; for on those views he would necessarily consider the program a useless duplication of the music.

As for the imitation of natural sounds, Beethoven, Gluck, Meyerbeer, Rossini, and Weber have shown by famous examples that it falls within the realm of musical art. Nevertheless, being convinced that the abuse of this device is very dangerous, that its applicability is very limited, and that its happiest effects are always close to parody, the composer of this symphony has never considered this branch of his art as an end but as a means. When, for example, in the scene "In the Country," he has tried to render the rolling of distant thunder in the midst of calm, it was not for the childish pleasure of aping the majestic natural sound, but rather to make silence more notable, and thus enhance the impression of anxious sadness and isolation which he wished to create at the close of that movement.[70]

[70] *308*, July 3, 1904.

8. *Roman Holiday:* Lélio

December 1830 to October 28, 1832

The perfection of life is to carry out in maturity the dreams of one's youth.
— Vigny

On December 29, 1830, Berlioz had written to the author of the "Marseillaise," "I am leaving Paris in a few hours" (to comply with the rules of the Institute) "at a time when my presence here would be most advantageous." [1] An acclaimed musician at twenty-seven, a leader, as we should say now, of the *avant-garde*, Berlioz was reluctant to leave the Parisian battlefield. Being moreover betrothed to a volatile pianist, Hector could hardly act the gay prize winner eager for freedom and adventure.

On his way to Rome he stopped at La Côte, where his parents gave him an affectionate welcome intended to wipe out the memory of ten years' misunderstanding. He responded but was not distracted from his anxiety over a separation of eighteen months from Camille. His sisters were sympathetic, young Prosper, aged ten, was entertaining, and the neighbors were full of compliments for the doctor's son who was making a name in the capital; still, to Hector the little village now charged with grim memories was oppressive. Reduced to inactivity, his will fed riotous visions to his mind. Current political news encouraged the thought of a European struggle between the liberal revolution and its enemies. From this uninviting prospect Hector could only hope to snatch the bliss of dying with *her* in his arms.[2] But music held an equal place with love: "Is there still no music in Paris? Have you finished your trios, and is Meyerbeer's new opera in rehearsal? Please greet him for me when you see him." [3]

[1] *A.R.*, 121. Berlioz had requested the Ministry to waive the rule and let him make a longer visit to Germany later on. He had submitted in support a medical certificate stating that his nervous temperament was unsuited to hot climates, and his musical argument had been backed by Fétis, Lesueur, Spontini, and Meyerbeer. (*769*, 131–2.)

[2] *Corresp.*, 70. "We are going to have war! Wreckage everywhere. Men *who think they are free* will hurl themselves against men who are certainly slaves; maybe the free will be exterminated and the slaves will be masters."

[3] *Corresp.*, 70. Meyerbeer's new opera was *Robert le Diable.*

Meantime, though Berlioz reproved himself ("a truce to this gnashing teeth"), he was alarmed at receiving no word from his fiancée. Instead, he received malicious hints from Hiller, Berlioz' predecessor in Camille's favor. Hiller had taken his superseding in good part knowing perfectly well who had engineered the change. Now Ferdinand enjoyed a mild revenge by intimating that Camille did not miss her lover in the least, and that the absent one ought to find consolation wherever he was: "No one was in despair on his account, nor felt any gratitude for *his* despair." [4] Hiller described the physical charms of some other nymph, to which Hector replied testily that he wanted no Epicurean counsels. In an energetic play on words, he repudiated the proffered means for reaching a minor happiness [*arriver au petit bonheur* – "getting there somehow"], and declared for major happiness or death. He was in fact ill. The weather was extremely cold, he had been taken on visits that reminded him of his Estelle, and he felt he was deceiving himself about Camille.[5] He had to take to his bed, while his sister Nanci wrote to Camille and privately pitied her for being involved with a man of persistent ideas and so moody besides. When Camille's reply came Hector had left and his sister's sympathies shifted: in Camille's letter "not a word was written from the heart." [6]

Hector had also had to give up hope of seeing Humbert Ferrand, who was incapable of acting or writing promptly, and he had pushed on to Marseille. There he found several friends from the Conservatoire, went with them to the theater, and was treated by other musicians as a man of rising fame. "The town is superb, and were it not for the turmoil in my thoughts I would have enjoyed it." [7] More important than the town was Berlioz' first sight of the sea. The one available vessel for Leghorn would sail when the skipper chose, so Hector went out for a trial trip in a fishing smack. "Your sea is a sublime monster," he wrote Adèle, "I liked to see it swishing around my feet on the beach, covering them with foam and roaring like an angry beast. It should be magnificent out in the open sea." [8]

He finally embarked for the five-day crossing, which took eleven. While becalmed, one of the old sea dogs related tales from the time when he was skipper to Lord Byron. Then contrary winds came up. Near the Gulf of Genoa the ship struck a gale, which besides being icy

[4] *Corresp.*, 71–2.

[5] Spontini, it will be recalled, had tried to dissuade Berlioz from engaging himself to marry.

[6] From Nanci's diary, *267*, 483.

[7] *A.R.*, 127. [8] *A.R.*, 127.

cold threatened to capsize them. The captain would not or could not shorten sail and for two days tacked and wore in stormy waters. A young Venetian corsair on board predicted disaster. The waves broke on the pitching deck, the passengers staggered about in agonies of fear and seasickness, even the sailors were losing hope, when the corsair, encouraged by some of the passengers, undertook to give orders and take in reefs. The pumps meanwhile had to be manned and a fire, set by the vessel's rolling, had to be put out: activity helped to curb the growing panic. Berlioz, though not seasick, had gone through all the stages of apprehension from the fear of drowning to the fear of not drowning fast enough. To keep himself from swimming he planned to pinion his arms in his own greatcoat, ready to welcome "the white spumed waves . . . that would rock him to sleep without pain." [9]

On land, other troubles awaited him. Although the new French government had decided on peace, revolution was still active on Italian soil, and so were the police. Two of Berlioz' shipmates were arrested while the rest fled to join "the brave and unfortunate Menotti." [10] Berlioz' baggage was repeatedly searched; all foreigners were suspect. "There are fifty formalities to go through before one can stop in a city." Berlioz might have thought himself in the blissful twentieth century except that the inefficient police were more of a nuisance than a threat. Still the Papal Nuncio would not grant him a visa to Rome. At Florence, Berlioz received his first remittance from the Director of the Academy toward which he was bound, and at the same time heard the news that revolution was driving the foreign residents from Rome. "And I must go into that hornet's nest because forty old dotards, high priests of Routine, have decided that I shall be competent only after a stay in that musical sink." [11]

Berlioz' obviously bad mood was not soothed by Italian music. He went to the first night of Bellini's *Romeo and Juliet* and exploded to his father: "Disgusting, ridiculous, impotent. That little fool has apparently not been afraid that Shakespeare's shade might come and haunt him in his sleep. . . . I ran here into a young Danish architect whom I knew in Paris. Danish! That also brings up Shakespeare. We spoke of Elsinore and *Hamlet*. . . . I may be in Italy but my sky is overcast. My life is in Paris and what I suffer cannot be put into words. . . . No letter from Camille. . . . I regret the watery grave." [12]

It was mid-March, almost three months after the arrival of his fellow-pensioners, when Berlioz reached Rome. As a visible presence, the "musi-

[9] *A.R.*, 128–131.

[10] Cino Menotti led an unsuccessful movement to free Italy from the Austrians and was executed in March 1831. [11] *A.R.*, 132. [12] *A.R.*, 133.

cal sink" made a great impression on him: its situation in the flat Romagna, its austerity, the majesty of the Piazza del Popolo, aroused in him a host of esthetic feelings whose roots went back to the words of Virgil and Chateaubriand. The spacious elegance of the Villa Medici — the seat of the French Academy in Rome — completed his conversion. He entered the place just in time for drama. The French, being suspected of revolutionary leanings, were attacked on the streets by partisans of the Pope. They broke into the Academy grounds at night and sent threatening letters by day. Horace Vernet, the director, having made futile representations to the Vatican, decided to arm his young artists. He himself put to flight an Italian whom Mme. Vernet found "armed with a knife and hiding in the shrubbery." [13] If these fanatics, scoffed Berlioz, "had only set fire to the Academy, who knows? — I might have helped them!"[14]

Apart from the risk of murder, the atmosphere of the Villa was anything but solemn. Horace Vernet, then aged forty-two, an historical painter descended from a long line of painters,[15] was a charming, sociable, lighthearted character, for whom noise, masquerades, and parties of all kinds were a tonic rather than an interference. The small, thin, gray-haired artist had come to Rome in 1828 after a rise to eminence packed with incidents: decorated for his early work by Napoleon himself, he had fought on the barricades in 1814 for the Emperor's return, side by side with Géricault; five years later the two had come out in the same Salon, which included Géricault's epoch-making "Raft of the Medusa" and the "Odalisque" of Ingres. Befriended by Guizot and the Duke of Orleans, Vernet had striven for liberty in a Bonapartist spirit and hailed the victory of July 1830. "Now," he had said, "I can paint anything . . . any part of our glory, in any color, without fear of censorship. . . ." [16] Nor did he harden into an administrator: though he had to act as ambassador to the Vatican during the French interregnum, he remained boyish and buoyant, unafraid to give Thiers or the Paris Academy a piece of his mind when they tried to dictate.[17] And for all his ebullience, visible in the disorder of his studio, which was a litter of books, guns, musical instruments, dogs, and official dispatches, he was a great worker.

It was both good and bad luck that Berlioz came into such a household,

[13] *Corresp.*, 79; confirmed by Mendelssohn (*216*, 115).

[14] *L.I.*, 93.

[15] And, according to Conan Doyle, putative ancestor of Sherlock Holmes.

[16] *238*, 81.

[17] *Ibid.*, 88–93. Among other things, Vernet refused to have an "arrangement" painted of Michelangelo's "Last Judgment" — an auspicious point of similarity with Berlioz.

where everyone was or acted young — the director, his charges, his young wife and daughter, and his father also, Carle Vernet, who was mad about music and went dancing in spite of his eighty years. It was unfortunate because Berlioz' black mood of lovesickness was intensified by the attention it received. Whether laughed at or taken to heart, his Werther-like sorrows tended for a time to become institutionalized, as they would not have been in a more sober or preoccupied milieu. The instant camaraderie and general Bohemianism of the place only heightened Berlioz' sense of isolation. Yet it was a piece of good luck that Vernet was a *bon vivant* who had married for love, thrown away his chance of a Rome Prize, and made his way by being jovially unbusinesslike. Another man, more impressed with his own official dignity, might have made Hector suffer in the days of his folly just at hand.

Since leaving France two months before, Berlioz had not heard from Camille or her entourage. Waiting was intolerable, uncertainty was a torture.[18] Being a man of strong and explicit feelings, he could not stoop to assuage his pain with cynicism or foolish hope. He had not left Paris with vague promises: Mme. Moke had publicly acknowledged him as "my son-in-law" and Camille had not withdrawn her plighted word.[19] Hence some plot must be brewing. Vernet had to hold him back from making a flying trip to Paris in order to learn the true state of his marital prospects: if he left the Villa Medici, he would lose the very status upon which his engagement to Camille had been ratified by her mother. After a week of conflict, on April 1, Berlioz left none the less. He went as far as Florence, where fever and sore throat held him in bed. He wrote to a friend in Paris asking for news, and in a few days recovered, but the internal debate continued. The countryside being tempting, he tramped into the hills and there read *King Lear* for the first time. Artistic excitement acted as a safety valve for overwrought feelings as he seized on the proper expression of his troubles: "As flies to wanton boys are we to the gods; they kill us for their sport." [20]

Having brought his manuscripts with him, Berlioz resumed work. He corrected the score of the *Symphonie Fantastique*, and jotted down ideas

[18] A trait he shared with his father: *A.R.*, 32

[19] Hiller, who believed that the girl and her mother were playing a double game, testifies to the fact that they kept up their deliberate deception until Berlioz had left. (*235*, II, 204.)

[20] *Zeitgeist:* It has never been noted how unerringly Berlioz picked out, with no knowledge of English tradition or scholarship, the passages from Shakespeare which the English romantic critics had popularized a decade or so earlier.

for several new works, including in all probability the *King Lear* overture. But there were also long idle hours waiting for an answer from Paris. Going one night to the cathedral, he witnessed the services for a young woman dead in childbirth, with her infant in her arms. The sight of death aroused his sense of life and even reawakened dormant medical knowledge. For lack of anything better to do, he followed the funeral procession and at the cemetery, seeing the corpse nearer to, hazarded a diagnosis, while revolving morbid thoughts.[21]

Still waiting, twelve days after leaving Rome, Berlioz could not help seeing and brooding over another funeral. Young Napoleon-Louis Bonaparte, son of the great Napoleon's brother Louis, was dead at twenty-six. Though succumbing ingloriously to measles, the heir to the name had been leading insurrection in the Romagna; his death left at the head of the clan his younger brother, Louis-Napoleon, with whom Berlioz was later to have dealings. Already in 1831 Berlioz noted with bitterness the music chosen to celebrate these great and unhappy memories: "The organist pulled the piccolo stop and disported himself in the treble, playing gay little tunes akin to the warbling of wrens. . . ." [22]

Staying in Florence was a compromise between giving up his stipend and wearing out his patience under the eyes of the whole Academy, but the protracted silence of the Moke family and of his Paris friends was daily increasing his helpless indignation. His thoughts swung from the desire to join the Calabrian banditti to the planning of an oratorio on the Day of Judgment.[23] Since music was life transmuted, and he was unable to lay violent hands on the Moke family in the style of Gil Blas or Rob Roy, he could at least blow up the world musically in the name of Jehovah. For a start, there was the *Resurrexit* of the Mass of 1825, not to speak of local inspiration from the hand of a kindred world-builder and world-destroyer, Michelangelo.

Finally, on the fourteenth day, the Paris letter came. Camille, said Mme. Moke, was about to marry M. Pleyel, the piano manufacturer. Hector's blood instantly reached the boiling point. At last he could act,

[21] *Corresp.*, 81–2. The thesis put forward by Mr. J. A. H. Ogdon (*491*, 323–66) that Berlioz was another Edgar Allan Poe whose imagination was stimulated *only* by death is contrary to fact – about both artists. Death, like love or nature, was but one starting point for Berlioz' art, as it may be in others for philosophy or religion.

[22] *Corresp.*, 83.

[23] In talking to the sailors who brought him from Marseille and sympathizing with their hard life, he was told that brigandage was the only alternative open to them in Italy.

but his passion was modified as always by amazing (in this case ludicrous) forethought. Mme. Moke's letter was "a model of impudence," in which she "strongly urged me not to kill myself – the good soul!" [24] He decided to exterminate the two faithless women first. But reflecting that if he turned up in Paris the old lady would not receive him, he bought a chambermaid's outfit as a disguise. In addition to loaded pistols, he took vials of laudanum and strychnine for his own quietus, and in a final act of foresight he dispatched his clothes to his father and his scores to Habeneck with directions for carrying out changes recently made in the Symphony.

On the first leg of the trip home, the suitcase containing the disguise was lost. Berlioz bought duplicates at Genoa, but failed to obtain a visa for Turin. His impulse momentarily deflected, it turned on himself and he clumsily attempted suicide by jumping into the sea. Rescued, he returned to his original idea and headed for Nice. On the long road which unrolls the superb panorama of the Riviera, Berlioz came to his senses and in the dusk gave up the whole plan. The sea to his left and mountains to his right dwarfed the importance of the unworthy pair who had injured him. With a sigh of relief he turned his mind to the question of reinstating himself at the Academy.[25] He gave Vernet a straightforward account: "A shameful misdeed, an abuse of confidence of which I have been the victim, has put me in a delirium of rage ever since I left Florence, I was flying back to France to exact a just and dreadful revenge when at Genoa, in a moment of giddiness I gave in to childish despair. An inconceivable weakness got the better of my will. But my sole punishment was to swallow a lot of salt water and be yanked out like a fish . . . People thought I had fallen in by accident while walking along the ramparts . . . Now I'm alive; I *must* live – for my two sisters whose lives would have been broken by my death, and also for my art . . . I am therefore returning to pledge on my honor not to leave Italy. . . ." [26]

Berlioz came to regard this series of events as "an offprint of a Byronic tale," which is only to say that Byron's tales of love, jealousy, and re-

[24] *Corresp.*, 84.

[25] In his first volume, M. Boschot both sneers at this episode and calls the story of the attempted suicide false. Later in his book, he accepts the suicide but without drawing attention to the fact that he has retracted his charge. (*268*, 320). In other essays, he says again: "Berlioz nearly committed suicide." (*270*, 159 and *769*, 115.) Going over the evidence thirty years later, M. Guy de Pourtalès rebukes the earlier biographer: "No one must make fun of Berlioz, for the original, the naïve Berlioz was really dead." (*298*, 109.)

[26] *A.R.*, 135. Nice being then part of Sardinia, Berlioz had technically not left Italy.

venge so popular in Berlioz' day, furnished words and attitudes to fit the eternal flux of human passions. Berlioz would have agreed with Henry James that "art is our flounderings shown," and that "passion can mean only one thing — the enemy to behavior." [27] Having purged his soul in verbal outbursts and calmed his body by exertion while Vernet was taking thought, Hector enjoyed three weeks of springtime convalescence at Nice. As he looked back on them they were the "twenty happiest days of my existence" [28] — in part because pleasure unanticipated is doubled, in part because it was a relief to accept the truth about Camille and her mercenary mother. He wrote very fully to his family, who responded with affectionate consolations, and he told the tale to his Paris friends, asking for musical news in return.[29]

He also composed. The *King Lear* overture was all but orchestrated, and the other overture, "The Tower of Nice" — so called from the ruins of an old tower in which Berlioz sat and worked facing the sea — was well under way. Hearing, moreover, that his old collaborator Victor Bohain was adapting Scott's *Rob Roy* for the stage, Berlioz sketched a third overture, to be named after the novel. In between bouts of composition, he soaked in the myriad impressions of the sounding sea (still a novelty to the mountaineer) under its sky of immeasurable blue.

At last a letter came from "M. Horace" as Vernet was familiarly known, saying that no official notice had been taken of Berlioz' escapade. Hector was still on the list of state pensioners and could return to the Academy without further apologia. The whole Vernet family sent sympathy, and Berlioz himself felt that he was "being born again, a better man than before." [30] He might well have said that the Sappho who cast herself into the sea and the Sappho who wrote poems were not the same person. On the slow journey to Rome he was full of musical ideas and he plotted a sequence of "occasions" which might unite earlier pieces that he wanted to work over. A note in Thomas Moore's poems gave him the idea of a

[27] "The Story in It."

[28] *Mem.*, I, 194.

[29] One of these friends, or else a classmate at the Villa, must have reported the episode to Stendhal, for in the margin of his author's copy of *The Red and the Black*, which he annotated soon after, he wrote a substantially correct account of the events. The novelist's feelings being at one with those of his young compatriot, Stendhal puts as a caption: "Support *for me*" — these last two words being in English — and he adds "The notion of killing Mme. . . ." This obviously refers in the novel to his hero's attempt on the life of his mistress, the entire marginalia being opposite the final paragraphs of Chapter 65, which tell of Julien's purchase of the pistols. (*169*, 140.)

[30] *Corresp.*, 75.

"melologue" which he christened *The Return to Life*, and thought of as a sequel to the *Symphonie Fantastique*.[31] "I hardly know what it's worth," he wrote to Gounet, the translator of Moore, "but I'll tell you this anyhow: my run to Nice cost me a thousand and fifty francs. I'm so glad not to have carried out my original plan that I don't regret the money." [32]

The Villa Medici was no longer besieged but its atmosphere was rather stifling nevertheless — like the narrow, ill-furnished rooms upstairs, or the contents of the library, which had scarcely any new books. The twenty-two pensioners representing five of the fine arts were for the most part "good students" with an assured future in official art. "Two or three," thought Hector, "are mildly exceptional, but no more." [33] It is true, they made up in boisterousness for what they lacked in genius, and for all their frequently low spirits, a good many would sing and play music. After a dinner in town they would make the climb back to the Monte Pincio while singing in chorus as many different tunes in as many different keys as possible. All the dogs of Rome joined in this "English concert," as the band called it, knowing that the tradesmen on their doorsills were sure it was *musica francese*.[34] Among this inner group — Montfort the musician, Dantan and Etex the sculptors, Garrez and Duc the architects — the last-named alone formed a real friendship with Berlioz: he had both music and sensibility in him.

Fortunately for Berlioz, Felix Mendelssohn was at this time in Rome, and despite angularities of character in both the young musicians, their talents and common love of music brought them together. Mendelssohn was prim, pious, and a former infant prodigy to boot. Berlioz, as he was the first to admit, was often intolerant and intolerable. He teased the German about his devout Lutheranism, he played the trick of putting an Italian aria of Gluck's on the piano, so that Mendelssohn ridiculed it before discovering it was by a master they both admired. In short, Berlioz worked off a good deal of ill humor on the person he had most affection for, all the while expressing an unmixed admiration which lasted through life. Writing to Paris in May 1831, Berlioz says of his new friend:

"He is a wonderful fellow. His performing talent is as great as his musical genius, which is saying a great deal. Everything I have heard by him has always delighted me. I am convinced he is one of the highest musical talents of the age. He has been my cicerone. Every morning I would go to his house. He would play me a Beethoven sonata; we would

[31] For the meaning of *Mélologue*, its source and form, see below, pp. 220 ff.
[32] *83*, 13; *A.R.*, 142. [33] *A.R.*, 143. [34] *V.M.*, II, 103.

sing from Gluck's *Armide;* then he would take me to see all the famous ruins which, I confess, did not move me very much."[35] Toward the end of the year, Berlioz tells Hiller by way of introduction: "He has an enormous talent, extraordinary, superb, prodigious. And I can't be suspected of comradely partiality in speaking like this, since he has frankly told me that he understood nothing of my music."[36]

On his side, Mendelssohn was just as confident in writing to his mother about Berlioz: "Without a spark of talent, he gropes in the dark while he thinks he is the creator of a new world. He writes detestable things and thinks only of Beethoven, Goethe and Schiller . . . Full of vanity besides, he lords it over Mozart and Haydn, so that his enthusiasm seems to me suspect . . ."[37] Mendelssohn's mother apparently tried to moderate her son's judgment of Berlioz, for Felix having written that he would "be only too glad to strangle Berlioz – until he chances to praise Gluck," he goes on to concede that his two French friends are "most agreeable and charming . . ." but . . . "you say, dear Mother, that Berlioz must have some real artistic purpose and there I don't agree with you. I think what he wants is to get married, and I think him the most affected of the lot, because I cannot stand this wholly external enthusiasm, this affectation of despair . . . and genius; and if they were not French, that is, people with whom one always has pleasant relations, and who always have something interesting to say, it would be unbearable."[38]

Poor Felix, in short, did not know what to think: the relationship was pleasant, but if it hadn't been it would have been unbearable. Cultural differences account in part for his dislike: it is a conventional vanity that he takes for affectation, for he found it again in Mickiewicz and again imputed it to character.[39] The tradition of boasting which one finds in the real Anglo-Saxons of *Beowulf* has somehow passed to the intellectual classes of the Continent, and only a provincial mind would have taken

[35] *Corresp.*, 79–80.

[36] *Corresp.*, 88.

[37] *215*, 120. Mendelssohn esteemed Montfort, who "has been working for three months at a little rondo on a Portuguese theme. He puts things together with much care, brilliancy, and correctness. He would then like to compose half a dozen waltzes." (*Ibid.*)

[38] *215*, 121. It seems to have escaped notice that Mendelssohn entered into this friendship with a certain prejudice against Berlioz the musician, a prejudice inspired perhaps by his own teacher Zelter. The evidence for this is that in August of the previous year, Mendelssohn's father had met Berlioz in Paris and had written home that "the composer of *Faust*" seemed "agreeable, interesting, and far more reasonable than his music." (*962*, I, 291.) Neither of the Mendelssohns, any more than Zelter, had *heard* the works they condemned.

[39] *215*, 125.

its occasional manifestations seriously. Reared in a different musical tradition, Mendelssohn never lived to see what Berlioz' scores signified. He did like some of his friend's melodies, but could not understand his dramatic structure or unpianistic orchestration. History supplies few such instances, of the mutual liking of two geniuses, of whom the narrower cannot take in the broader, but who despite this sufficient cause for misunderstanding remain actively devoted friends.

Apart from Mendelssohn, Rome afforded little or nothing satisfying to Berlioz' musical passion. Gounet had asked if Berlioz had found some new beloved, he himself having broken off an irksome liaison. Berlioz replied "No . . . but what is worse is that I cannot live without music. I cannot get used to it, it's impossible." [40] During the winter months the *Café Greco* was the meeting place of foreign artists. There Berlioz met Michael Glinka, later to become "the father of Russian music," and now studying under Basili. Despite this connection with the Italian opera, he and Berlioz quickly established sympathetic relations. But it was all talk, not music. At the same *café* Berlioz met two French poets, followers of the English "Lake" school, Auguste Barbier and Auguste Brizeux, and a Paris acquaintance, the singer Duprez, all of whom were to have important dealings with Berlioz in the sequel.

Italian antiquities, Italian religion, Italian music – none of these things fed Berlioz' spirit. He was impressed by the scale of Saint Peter's and the Coliseum, but the best use he could find for the amphitheater was to read Byron there. Church processions, unlike the rural ones he knew, struck him as cheap and mesquin, and the Carnival as gross without gaiety. As for music, "My hatred for what they have the impudence to adorn with that name in Italy is stronger than ever. Their music is a whore: from a distance its appearance spells shamelessness: from nearby, its dull speech proves it a silly fool." [41]

But one prejudice that he had brought with him he quickly overcame: "I find the Italians just as good fellows as anybody else, especially those in the mountains whom I know best of all." [42] This remark alludes to a use of his pensioned time which supplied Berlioz with the most vivid as well as fruitful impressions of his Italian journey – his excursions into the countryside. Here was his real reward for ten years of arduous career-building, the real holiday during which the two halves of the youth's character joined to make the balanced man. In communings with nature, with simple souls, and with himself, Berlioz experienced his "Italian Journey" in the Goethean sense. During the twelvemonth from May 1831 to

[40] *A.R.*, 177. [41] *A.R.*, 178. [42] *A.R.*, 178.

May 1832, he stored up impressions or felt renewed inspiration from sources congenial to his temper and lasting in their effect. One thinks not only of Goethe but of Scott's great tour of Scotland at the age of twenty-three. Without premeditation he was living out the maxims of Schiller, Wordsworth, and Vigny about dreaming dreams in youth for the mature man to turn into realities.

Berlioz of course thought of himself as idle, waiting and wasting his time. Too often he suffered from the malady then known as spleen – boredom – and it was this which drove him to the mountains. "As soon as I find myself more tormented than usual, I put on my hunting coat, I take my gun, and I make tracks for Subiaco, no matter what the weather. A week ago I went from Tivoli to Subiaco under a driving rain which lasted all day. Last month I made my way from Naples on foot, through hills and woods and high pastures, having to take a guide only once. You have no idea how delightful such a trip can be. Fatigue, discomfort, the possibilities of danger – I was enchanted with everything. I spent nine days that I shall long remember. As for my innumerable impressions, I have no room to detail them – only, I still think nothing equals the sea." [43]

While there were rumors of a fresh revolution in France and Horace Vernet rushed to Paris to gauge the political situation, Berlioz was making friends with the peasants and bandits of the Abruzzi. If he took his gun he shot indifferently at a few wildfowl – a bloodless pastime he soon abandoned altogether.[44] When he came to know the villagers he left the gun at home and took his guitar. At nightfall the girls would come out and dance to Berlioz' improvised accompaniments while the old folks watched. Having been content with a meager tambourine, they gave the welcome of a virtuoso (which he was) to the player of the *chitarra francese*. From them, in return, he received hospitality, warmth of feeling, and the delight of real folk music. He jotted down a few of their tunes but remembered even more vividly their mood and pathos, which he would recapture in his own works-to-be. Listening one night to a lover's serenade he found himself transported out of his self-preoccupation. But the singer stopped abruptly; "It then seemed to me that all of a sudden I was deprived of something essential . . . I spent the rest of the night without sleep, without dreams, without thoughts." [45]

Sometimes Berlioz set out with a companion from the academy, usually

[43] *A.R.*, 178.

[44] To Liszt in 1839: "Take your gun, but it is only a pretext. . . ." (*A.R.*, 398).

[45] *V.M.*, II, 143.

a painter in search of scenery. Hector would sing in his natural tenor voice appropriate woodland songs – Lesueur's "Bardic Hunt" or his own "Irish" melody "Hélène." [46] Antoine Etex, now known for his bas-reliefs of the Arc de Triomphe, was one of the walking companions who long remembered these expeditions. "Berlioz . . ., who was as sad and discouraged as I, went with me to the Dominican Fathers with a view to a retreat, but a thousand circumstances plunged us back into our low spirits. One day . . . after walking in the hot sun to Tivoli, and ordering our dinner at the inn, . . . we could not resist the temptation of swimming in the limpid blue waters of the lake. This we did, and as we swam we sang the famous duet from *William Tell*, 'O Mathilda whom my soul adores.' But in those icy waters we suddenly turned blue, our teeth chattering and our gaiety all spent. We got out as quickly as we could . . . and went to our dinner. An hour later we were both asleep. The next day at five, we set out for the mountains in hopes of meeting brigands and taking up our abode with them, but we had no luck." [47]

The intoxication of the senses by nature, the absence of social restraints, and the thronging reminiscences of the historic past repeatedly brought Berlioz in touch with his true inner self. He felt the tragic commingle with a furious *joie de vivre*, and as he tells us, the bout might end in a flood of tears. The thought of death was no longer morbid or sought after as in Florence: when his Italian friends' boy Tonio languished and died, Berlioz was shaken. Another time, having drunk more than usual and lost his way, he found that a canto of the *Aeneid*, forgotten since childhood, came back entire to his memory. This led him to improvise "a wild recitative to still wilder harmonies, on the death of Pallas, the despair of good Evander, the youth's funeral – at which his own horse wept – the dread of King Latinus, the siege of Latium – whose soil I was treading – the sad death of Amata and the cruel death of Lavinia's betrothed. Under the combined influence of memory, poetry and music I reached the highest pitch of exaltation . . . ending in convulsive sobs. What is most singular is that I could pass judgment on my own weeping." [48]

In contrast with natural life, there was the duty of attending some of

[46] *164*, 232; *A.R.*, 162, 164, 167, 176, 184; *Corresp.*, 87, 92. Though Berlioz was no professional singer, his Caruso-like range apparently enabled him to sing bass parts in choruses, and even to substitute for a missing cello in an emergency: see *Mem.*, II, 32.

[47] *190*, 120–1.

[48] *Mem.*, I, 218. Saint Augustine: "I wept for Dido's Death . . ." (*Confessions*, Bk. I, Sec. 13.)

Mme. Vernet's weekly soirees. "It's always the same story: there is dancing, talking about nothing, looking at engravings . . . you drink weak tea and saunter to the balcony overlooking Rome. In the moonlight you can make some well-worn remarks, quite academic and stupid. You refer to cholera morbus, the Paris riots, the Poles' defeat, the defeat of the French in Algiers, the illumination of St. Peter's and the way Mlle. Horace dances. . . ." [49] At one of these evenings, however, he saw Countess Guiccioli, Byron's great love, with her sad face and rich golden hair.[50]

Nor could he get used to the abundance of clerics in the Church's capital: "These abbes, monks, priests are everywhere, right and left, above, below, within, without, with the poor and the rich in church, at dances and cafes, in the theatres, with the ladies in cabriolets, on foot with the men, at M. Horace's evenings, in his studio, in our gardens – Everywhere." [51]

This anticlericalism was not antireligious; on the contrary, Hector's mind was full of musical ideas for sacred subjects. He sketched or composed half a dozen first drafts and finished a "Religious Meditation" on a text from Moore, "This world is all a fleeting show." In the untended gardens of the Villa Borghese not far from the Academy (where Goethe had worked at *Faust* forty years before) Berlioz hid away to revise the pastoral movement of the *Fantastique*. He also added to the first movement the twenty-four bars of the present *religioso* ending; and being obliged to send the Institute a sample of work done at Rome, he dispatched a Chorus and Quartet of Magi, based on an earlier (Paris) draft, and joined to it the *Resurrexit* of his early Mass, once again revised. The artist was more than ever a worshiper, but on seeing a peasant kiss the toe of a statue of Saint Peter, Berlioz envied the "happy biped" who had "faith and hope," for to the educated mind historical criticism stood in the way of literal belief: "This bronze that you worship and whose right hand holds the keys of heaven was once a *Jupiter tonans* holding lightning. But you know it not, lucky biped!" [52]

News from Paris was not encouraging. Plots and riots succeeded each other rapidly. The European cholera (of which Hegel had just died) was carrying off its hundreds, among them the ablest statesman of the

[49] *A.R.*, 167. Mlle. Vernet set the pace by dancing the energetic *Saltarello* of the Romans with her father or grandfather. (*238*, 93.)

[50] *V.M.*, II, 107 *n.* The modern edition of the *Memoirs* (I, 209 *n.*) says "white hair," which is an absurd misreading of Berlioz' original text (p. 135 *n.*). The Countess remained a Titian blond until quite late in life. See *Belgravia*, Feb. 1869, 491.

[51] *A.R.*, 167.

[52] *A.R.*, 184; *V.M.*, II, 108; *Mem.*, I, 210.

new regime as well as a compatriot of Berlioz, Casimir-Périer. And Berlioz' circle of musical friends – Hiller, Richard, Du Boys, Prévost, Turbry, De Pons, Girard, Desmarest, and Stephen de la Madelaine – were dilatory correspondents.[53] Only Gounet, to whom Berlioz felt very close, took pains to keep him posted. Everyone, it seemed, was getting married: Humbert Ferrand, in his province, had obtained the hand of his great love, but in his usual indolence had not written. Berlioz' cousin Auguste was planning to marry, and so was Hector's sister Nanci: Berlioz knew that he would find marked changes in the world of his contemporaries. This made him all the more impatient to leave his "barracks," possibly extending by some months his third statutory year in Germany.

Trouble was still brewing there, as well as in England, where the struggle to pass a Reform Bill brought the realm to the verge of revolution. Sir Walter Scott, dying and in despair, was by doctor's advice taking a Mediterranean cruise. He did not know how near it brought him to his admiring fellow artists, Stendhal and Berlioz – the one in Rome, the other Acting Consul in Civita Vecchia. Stendhal came to Rome and the Villa from time to time, but we do not know whether he and Berlioz met. We know only that during the carnival of 1832 Berlioz caught a glimpse of the elder Dauphinois driving through the streets with "a mischievous look that he vainly sought to render solemn." [54] Hector knew that the novelist had also written about music, in particular an admiring and provocative *Life of Rossini*. This would not endear him to Berlioz, although in reality the two shared many opinions about the state and the purpose of the arts, felt the same way about the average culture of their own country, and even expressed themselves in the same tone of intelligent mockery. But as often happens, none of this was evident to them as it is to us. The musician was irritated by a manner and dismissed the other as a littérateur,[55] and there is no reason to believe that Stendhal would

[53] Hiller, Du Boys and De Pons are already identified; some of the others we shall meet again: Girard became an orchestra leader who conducted Berlioz' early works. Desmarest, a virtuoso cellist, remained a devoted admirer, as did Stephen de la Madelaine, a member of Choron's Choir School, who later became a theater manager, music critic, and office holder in the Ministry of Fine Arts. Richard was poet, musician and linguist, a translator of Hoffmann and of the Ode to Joy in Beethoven's Ninth Symphony. Prévost was a fellow pupil of Lesueur's class, who made his career in New Orleans; and Turbry, perhaps the most gifted of all, was a composer whose will power did not equal his musical talents. He also wrote a *Symphonie Fantastique*, but did not persevere and ultimately died destitute.

[54] *V.M.*, II, 114.

[55] *Mem.*, I, 215 *n.* Imagine Berlioz being told by Stendhal that if Beethoven with his science had had Rossini's ideas he would have been a colossus!

have enjoyed Berlioz' music had he heard any. And yet they stand to each other as prophet and messiah, for Stendhal long before 1830 had predicted, or rather demanded, the Romanticist revolution in music, painting, and drama.[56]

Toward the end of 1831, it seemed as if the cultural renovation desired by Stendhal had been carried to a point far beyond Rossini: the newspapers were full of a great new work which was said to combine music, painting, and drama, and to express to perfection the modern spirit through its *Faust*-like subject matter. Impressive scenic effects employing new machinery, a fresh style of directing and dramatic composition, and above all an expanded use of the orchestra, made Meyerbeer's *Robert le Diable* the model of a new genre – French grand opera.[57] Berlioz read the comments and could hardly sleep. To "rot in Rome" while a renovated dramatic art was making headway in Paris against the old Italian monopoly; to miss the first performance of Beethoven's Ninth – even though given in two halves – was maddening. The critics' references to Weber, Beethoven, and modern instrumentation might mean that the mood of Paris was changing; the title of Houssaye's new periodical, *L'Artiste*, was significant: it implied that the political revolution had vindicated the earlier, cultural reform – in a word, that Berlioz being no longer alone might find his hour about to strike. He asked Hiller to present his sincere compliments to Meyerbeer, who had always shown kindly interest in him and his works.[58]

Having meantime read Victor Hugo's extraordinary new book, *Notre Dame de Paris*, Berlioz indited a rhapsodic letter to relieve his feelings and cheat impatience by taking a sideswipe at Rossini: "It is said that you have made a libretto out of your *Notre Dame* and that the 'gay fat man' is doing the music. He is *such* a gay fat man – naturally, Weber being dead. . . . There, my broadside is discharged. I feel better. . . . *Viva l'ingenio tuo!*"[59] Sensing progress in the French capital Berlioz, whose last published article had dealt with a possible revitalizing of lyric

[56] Respectively in his *Vie de Rossini* (1824), *Histoire de la Peinture en Italie* (1817), and *Racine et Shakespeare* (1823–1825).

[57] See W. L. Crosten's able monograph, *782*.

[58] *Corresp.*, 89. It is more than likely that Meyerbeer's orchestration in *Robert* owed much to Berlioz' inventions; competent judges of the period believed it, and the contrary argument by Niecks (*488*) rests on the erroneous premise that the *Fantastique* was not played until December 1830, *Robert* being virtually finished in July. But the rehearsals of the Symphony took place in May, and the opera was not produced till the next year.

[59] "Long live your genius." *A.R.*, 180–1. The letter seems not to have been sent.

drama by means of the Beethovenian orchestra, was now moved to write a "Letter on Italian music, by an Enthusiast" – an ironic name for himself. In it he points out that the belief in Italy's supremacy in every art is no longer justified. The orchestras are beneath notice; people do not listen but talk,[60] the overtures are strings of platitudes which the organ grinders themselves disdain, and church services consist of operatic airs badly played on the organ or poorly sung by minuscule choirs. In substance, Italian music aims only at "sensory effect and external form," it is "perpetually laughing" – hence Berlioz' nickname for Rossini – and its undeniable melodic exuberance is rendered monotonous by habitual garnishing with *fioriture*.[61]

Real music exists only among the folk – the serenade of a mountaineer to his *ragazza*, or the plaints of the *pifferari* to the Madonna. Berlioz admits that being out of Rome he did not hear the special music of Holy Week, but he wonders with what musicians, hidden for the remainder of the year, it could have been adequately performed. Saint Peter's was a challenge and an opportunity: "It is huge, sublime, overwhelming . . . These paintings, statues, and columns, this grand architecture are the body of the monument; music is its soul, but where is it? Where is the organ?" On searching, Berlioz found a harmonium on wheels, "a kind of accordion behind a pillar." As for the choristers, who should number thousands in order to sound in scale, they were eighteen on ordinary days and thirty-two on special occasions.[62] "Rome," concludes Berlioz, "is no longer in Rome. It is in Paris, Berlin, Vienna, London even . . . , so that the Institute is quite right, its aim being to make young composers waste time, to halt the first steps of their career, and extinguish their fire by keeping them from the great centers of art . . . Theirs is the motto of Molière's doctors – though the patient die, 'we shall not depart one iota from the prescription of the ancients.' "[63]

Berlioz screwed up his courage and asked Vernet for permission to

[60] Respectful silence during music was a recent innovation even in Germany, where Spohr and Weber took the lead in enforcing the demand, at the cost of personal unpopularity.

[61] *V.M.*, II, 218.

[62] *Mem.*, I, 232. Boschot adds a self-incriminating footnote: "Before seeing the Vatican myself, I thought Berlioz had exaggerated. But I must confess that going in on a Sunday during the singing of the Mass, I could only hear a vague, almost indistinct murmur of music . . . I found an inadequate organ and a choir of fifteen to twenty." (*268*, 80.)

[63] *1399*, 53. The "Letter," reproduced in Berlioz' *Voyage Musical* and *Memoirs*, appeared originally in March 1832 in the *Revue Européenne*, which was the conservative *Correspondant* under a new title.

leave early. With a view to giving a concert as soon as possible, he copied out parts of the revised *Fantastique*, of its sequel, *The Return to Life*, of the two new overtures, and of the *Religious Meditation*. Reading Hugo's *Orientales* had moreover put into his head a new song which, yielding to the demands of sociability, he arranged for Mlle. Vernet. *La Captive* was a catchy melody, and soon the whole Villa was humming it. It spread throughout artistic circles in Rome and was whistled wherever Berlioz went. "They want to make me rue it." He deemed it a trifle, but happily the trifle proved to be the germ of one of his finest orchestral songs, which he himself grew fond of.[64]

On Palm Sunday of 1832, Berlioz climbed for the last time the sugar-loaf hill around which spreads Subiaco. He went to church with the village population, sang with them, and on leaving felt a pang of home-sickness. Vernet had consented to Berlioz' leaving on May first, thus reducing the required two years in Italy to fourteen months. Berlioz spent the remainder of April at the Villa, making himself agreeable to the ladies, his fellows, and their guests. When he put his mind to it he could be most entertaining, and though only twenty-eight could act the accomplished man of the world.[65] He told stories and historical anecdotes, he made up musical extravaganzas or sang Gluck in the moonlit gardens so that old Carle Vernet, who had known both Gluck and Piccinni, wept with emotion.[66] Nor did Berlioz unbend only to show off: he asked others to play and sing, and he would inconvenience himself in order to facilitate the amours of a comrade.[67] Near the time of leaving, Berlioz had to sit for his portrait. His housemate Signol did the half-caricature which is reproduced above and which may still be seen in the Director's office at the Villa. One sees, in the becoming costume of a Jeune-France (tight coat, high pointed collar and neckband) a pale face under a glowing mass of hair and deep-sunken eyes of a soft blue, which look out with the candor and inward thoughtfulness of a child.[68]

[64] For its highly original form, see below, Chapter 24.

[65] It was not long after that Ernest Legouvé arrived in Rome and heard Berlioz' name for the first time, hearing also from Vernet and the ladies what a charming conversationalist Berlioz could be. (*362*, 103.)

[66] *A.R.*, 147; *238*, 48.

[67] *M.E.*, 210.

[68] This is most likely the first portrait we have of Hector. That which is labeled Berlioz at the Conservatoire and which was done by the fashionable Dubufe in 1830, seems, despite circumstantial evidence, to be apocryphal. It may be a likeness of a Berlioz cousin, but coloring, shape of face, and expression have nothing in common with Hector's. Moreover, in the busy year 1830 he hardly had time for sittings. We hear nothing of them in any case; nor, since he would not take his own portrait to Italy, do we hear of his

As if reluctant despite his eagerness, Berlioz took the whole month of May for the trip home. He drove by way of Spoleto, Foligno, Perugia, and Lake Trasimene — the scene of Hannibal's victory — reaching Florence for his fourth stay, each time "with a more loving love." He read Dante and Shakespeare and filled notebooks; then pushed on to Milan by way of Lodi which, acting on childhood memories, made him dream of Napoleon's glory, "fled like a mirage." [69] It was already more than a year since young Napoleon-Louis had died on this same spot. Music had not improved. He heard Bellini's *La Sonnambula* which he found pitiful, and in Milan tried to overhear Donizetti's *L'Elisir d'amore* but could make out nothing: "The people talk, gamble, sup, and manage to drown out the orchestra. It's impossible to follow anything but the bass drum." [70]

From Milan to Turin the impressions gathered on the Bridge of Lodi began to take shape as music, and he sketched the plan of a choral symphony, for which he thought that a Napoleonic Ode of Victor Hugo's might furnish the text. But having recently worked on the words of his "melologue," and knowing that the meters of French verse are ill-suited to melody, he began jotting down words of his own — cadenced prose would do as well as rime. The "occasions" for two movements of this symphony suggested themselves as Berlioz followed the conqueror's footsteps: "Farewell to the Fallen Heroes from the Crest of the Alps" and "Entrance of the Victorious Army into Paris." Never composed in this form, the work quite naturally evolved into the Funeral and Triumphal Symphony of 1840.

Coming down into his valley by the Mont Cenis pass and the Isère, Hector felt the shock of familiar beauty and reawakened emotions. He gazed at the St. Eynard and went up it to Meylan for a visit to his maternal grandfather, old Marmion. Here was Hector's chief link with prerevolutionary France; here was Estelle's home; here too, by a contrast suddenly felt, the imagined roar of Paris.[71] The thought was like a stab of pain, quickly forgotten in festivities: Nanci had just been married to a Grenoble judge, Camille Pal, and the family reunion was full of excitement.[72] At La Côte, the house seemed empty without her. Nanci had had

---

leaving it with Camille among the other keepsakes which he recovered. (*Corresp.*, 87.)

[69] *Corresp.*, 97; *A.R.*, 199–200; *L.I.*, 116.

[70] *V.M.*, II, 216–7.

[71] *V.M.*, II, 225.

[72] Berlioz had thoughtfully brought the ladies Italian straw hats, which at every customs barrier cost him additional cash; the musical notebook gives us Berlioz' itinerary by its listing of these places and adding "Straw hats — 30 baiocchi; Milan: straw hats — 2 francs . . ." *A.R.*, 198.

a soothing effect on her mother whose ill temper, now chronic, was aggravated by the behavior of young Prosper. The boy, it is clear, was also endowed with unusual musical talent. Though never taught, he could remember and reproduce on the piano anything he heard. But he had other traits which we can easily recognize as the result of his unhappy upbringing. Besides tantrums and obstinacy, he had compulsions to arrange his clothes in a certain order, only to pretend the next day that he had forgotten how to dress himself. Hector was much concerned. He could relax only with Adèle and with his kindly father who, under the pressure of domestic and political turmoil, was becoming philosophical to the point of solipsism. The doctor nonetheless took pains to bring his son up to date on what was actually happening in France, for in Rome the newspapers ignored French affairs as seditious, and the police, as Stendhal loved to prove, would censor the most trifling remarks in letters as politically sinister.[73]

Hector heard for the first time of the riots in Lyon and Grenoble and the dubious colonial enterprises in North Africa. But his readiness to fight tyranny as in the July days did not make him believe in the "principles" of subsequent French politics. His indifferentism returned when he noticed that there were in fact no principles. He had written to Gounet from Rome: "What are you up to in the midst of all these plots, conspiracies, and factions, which are the desolation of common sense, of the arts, and of peaceable folk? . . . I wish for the sake of your peace of mind that you were no more concerned with them than I." [74] Now he could see how "the traitors of yesterday become the heroes of tomorrow" and how force "blurs right and wrong under the name of legality." [75]

He did not want in any case to argue politics with the neighbors, nor with his new brother-in-law, Judge Pal, whose loquacity thereupon switched to matters of high art in a fashion that "wrecked" Berlioz.[76] Even less did he want people to discuss music. He was willing enough to talk of his travels and to learn of local marriages and deaths,[77] but he

[73] Berlioz had himself experienced this when they examined the words of his Chorus of Shades and read treason in the mysterious tongue invented by the composer.

[74] *A.R.*, 188.

[75] *L.I.*, 107. A causeless riot at Grenoble during the carnival of 1832 only strengthened Berlioz' conviction that people in crowds were little better than foolish children. (*A.R.*, 197.)

[76] He began to regret the life at the Villa Medici, as he told Mme. Vernet in a charming letter of gratitude for her hospitable care. (*Corresp.*, 99–103.)

[77] It was at this time that Mme. Berlioz played a malicious trick on her son,

found the old circle of acquaintances more bourgeois than ever. So many of his friends were now leading the dull existence of married provincials: Charbonnel, Edouard Rocher, Albert Du Boys, Auguste Berlioz, as well as the timid and ill-favored Humbert Ferrand, whom Berlioz went to visit after an absence of more than six years.

A certain constraint at first spoiled the reunion, even though Mme. Ferrand was away, because Ferrand had quite sunk his youthful ideals in domestic comfort and routine. Poetry, heroism, and love seemed far away, but Hector managed to galvanize him a last time. Giving Humbert a glimpse of his own freedom on the Italian hills, Berlioz urged him to write the verses for his projected oratorio on the Day of Judgment. He sketched an outline, a "carcass," on which his friend was to put "muscles." He begged him to follow inspiration freely, "to do without rime whenever it seems needless – which is often the case" and to drop whatever "dusty conventions" belong to "the infancy of art." [78] Ferrand promised to do his best. Later at Aix les Bains, Hector met his friend's wife, whom he found charming, though he still could not conceive how she had weaned Ferrand from artistic ambition. In the end, Ferrand did no writing. When fall came, the return visit to La Côte which they had planned did not take place.

Meanwhile Berlioz was marking time. That is, he corrected scores and copied parts. In his father's library he also reread his old medical books, studied Gall and Cabanis and found them philosophically empty, for they furnish "technical details, terminology, and minor facts of experience," but "refuse to draw the consequences of their principles, from fear of public opinion." [79]

---

sending him to deliver a note to a Mme. Fornier, who turned out to be his first love, Estelle. The mother doubtless thought that two subsequent loves had effaced the memory of the first, a mistake which shows how little she knew her son. (*Mem.*, I, 12.)

[78] *L.I.*, 110. These remarks which may be thought characteristic of the "romantic revolt" were but the shorthand form of ripe considerations. These Berlioz expounded to Ferrand two months later (*L.I.*, 113), giving the musical and literary reasons for using blank verse or rhythmical prose in song, and arguing from the traditions of Latin, German, and English poetry.

[79] *Corresp.*, 105; the conclusion would have been to deny a personal God. Georges Cabanis, the founder of the late eighteenth-century school of *Idéologues*, was a physician and philosopher who did pioneer work in abnormal psychology and was suspected of materialism. The Revolution and Empire obscured his efforts by their censorship, which led to the caution that Berlioz deplores. Stendhal, however, was a close student of *Idéologue* teachings and based his novelistic style and psychological method upon their principles. (See *1208*.)

In the round of dinners and *politesses,* where, to please him, acquaintances broached musical subjects "as if they were talking of wine, women, riots, or other filthiness," Hector found time to make friends with young Prosper. They went on walks, played bowls, or hunted birds' eggs; Hector gave the child the understanding and companionship of an affectionate equal. But Berlioz must think of Paris. If he was to catch up with the current of artistic life and give a concert before his trip to Germany (scheduled for the beginning of the New Year), he dare not linger at La Côte. With ripened mind and heart, he felt his mission more clearly than ever. "You see how patient I am," he wrote at this juncture; "one needs patience not solely in order to bear evils with doggedness, but in order to act." [80] Accordingly, on October 28, 1832, aged not quite twenty-nine, Berlioz set out for his second conquest of Paris.

Melologue No Madness

> The presence of music is justified in mine [the *Melologue*], and I have treated its subject in dramatic form.
>
> — BERLIOZ to Gounet, June 1831

The *Return to Life,* which Berlioz had put together in Rome and copied out at La Côte for a Paris concert, is the work that established him — much more than his first symphony — with the novelty-seeking public of the capital. Berlioz was now by official title an accredited composer, and the score that he brought back from Italy was cast in a form that seemed at once original, entertaining, and easily understood. None of the music was new, it had merely been revised; but virtually no one had heard it in its earlier forms. Of the six parts, the ballad on Goethe's "Fisherman" dated from 1827, the next three numbers came from the prize cantatas of 1827 and 1829, and the Brigand's Song had probably been composed in 1828.[1] As for the finale, it was none other than the *Tempest* fantasia which had been played to a scattering of courageous operagoers during the political and other storms of November 1830.

Here was music too good to discard, and inventions too new to rely

[80] *Corresp.,* 105.

[1] If, as seems likely, it was originally the Pirate Song after Victor Hugo. See above Chapter 4.

on without testing by ear through rehearsal and good performance: Berlioz' musical motives were clear enough. But also having notions about dramatic form, he was loath to present six disconnected numbers. The plan of his *Faust* scenes as well as the setting into which he had inserted the *Symphonie Fantastique* suggested one more step along the road to the dramatic symphony. What he called a "melologue," borrowing the term from Thomas Moore, was a prose scenario to be spoken by an actor, each of whose soliloquies would bring about – would occasion – the playing of the successive pieces.[2]

Today the result seems quite unsatisfactory; the discontinuity of mood is too frequent and the device by which the author tried to palliate it too roundabout. In short, *The Return to Life* is far less "one work" than either the *Faust* scenes or the symphony, and it is the only score of Berlioz' which is improved by excerpting. At the same time its would-be dramatic form has historical interest and historical precedent, and only a flustered critic could say that it shows the composer in a state bordering on madness.[3] In the first place the music, composed from two to five years earlier, is obviously sane, and much of it still sounds fresh and vigorous even to our jaded ears. In the second place, the audience that first heard the work produced accepted it as perfectly rational. Lastly, the best minds in Paris found the significance that the composer attached to his "sequel" so much in keeping with the needs of the day that it established him as a leader in thought and action as well as in music. "The name of Hector Berlioz became famous."[4] So far from having to posit Berlioz' near madness, the historian must record here the single instance in which Berlioz' aim happened to coincide with the contemporary taste. He was understood and the work was enjoyed without effort, partly

[2] For a benefit at the Dublin Theatre, Moore wrote a *Melologue Upon National Music* consisting of verses interspersed with music representing the folk airs of several countries. In a note to the published work he added the remarks that furnished Berlioz with his hint: "With respect to the title which I have invented for this poem, I feel even more than the scruples of the Emperor Tiberius when . . . using the outlandish term 'monopoly.' But the truth is, . . . I thought an unintelligible word would not be without its attraction for the multitude. . . . To some of my readers, however, it may not be superfluous to say that by 'Melologue' I mean that mixture of recitation and music, which is frequently adopted in the performance of Collins' Ode on the Passions. . . ." (*1269*, 536.) One may add, in answer to the common French complaint of Berlioz' dependence upon foreign ideas, that Moore had found the "most striking example" of Melologue he could think of in Racine's *Athalie*.

[3] Mr. J. H. Elliot (*278*, 140). He is not the only one who has been put off by reading the *words* and imputed his bewilderment to the composer of the *notes*.

[4] *185*, 296.

because of the sentiments that "The Artist" expresses in the monologues,[5] partly because the "dramatic" arrangement employing the wings, curtain, and stage were in line with the custom of hearing concerts in the theater. Berlioz knew exactly what he was about and it is perhaps because he made his scheme fit current usage that it seems awkward now.[6]

Written some three weeks after the break with Camille, the text carries forward the sequence of episodes in an imaginary musician's life. In the *Fantastique* the love obsession ends at a Witches' Sabbath. Now Berlioz brings his hero out of his opium dream and gives him a voice: he recites and acts in front of the curtain, behind which are concealed an orchestra, chorus, and soloists. From the wings, at the opening, one hears the hero's friend, Horatio, playing at the piano a song that Lélio had composed for him earlier, on the words of Goethe's Ballad, "The Fisherman." The pleasant barcarolle – interrupted between two of the stanzas by a return of the *idée fixe* – is followed by a soliloquy on religion and art, on Hamlet's doubts about death, and on the possibility of finding a musical subject in the Ghost's revelation of the murder. This is the cue for chorus and orchestra to play the second number, "Chorus of Shades." The piece is a striking, indeed a "modern" tone poem, remarkable for its use of divided strings, the beat of the bass drum covered with a cloth, and the clarinet tied up in a sack. Its bold rhythms and harmonies, plus a characteristic melody too good to lose, justify Berlioz' salvaging the piece from the 1829 cantata on the death of Cleopatra.

The process of its readaptation shows how Berlioz produced *Lélio:* to replace the cantata words by Vieillard, Berlioz made up mysterious syllables which he ascribed to the "unknown tongue" that Swedenborg speaks of as that of the damned;[7] in the music he made but few alterations. Then in Lélio's soliloquy, while the orchestra plays the opening chords,

[5] The artist hero was shortly to be given a name, *Lélio,* and in the revised edition the whole work is so called. (See below.)

[6] Until nearly the end of the nineteenth century music of every kind was usually performed in theaters. Hence the frequent placing of players in the wings, behind the curtain, etc. Wagner's design of the Bayreuth orchestra pit is related to this habit of using effects of distance and muting, which the modern concert hall cannot reproduce: *e.g.*, at Carnegie Hall in New York it is almost impossible to give Berlioz' *Romeo and Juliet* symphony as he intended, for there is no suitable place from which the small chorus of Capulets can be heard *lontano.* [The new Philharmonic Hall is no better.]

[7] In the later version of the melologue, Berlioz substituted French verses of his own in order to keep for the *Damnation of Faust* the tongue he had invented. Hasty readers have thought that these vocables were given in Swedenborg's works but this is not so, nor does Berlioz imply it. (*690* and see below, Subchapter 17.)

he describes the character of the piece: it embodies the mood of the ghost in Hamlet – "a muffled instrumentation, broad sinister harmonies, a lugubrious melody, a chorus in unisons and octaves." In *Cleopatra* he had called the piece "Chorus of Angry Shades" and the details of Vieillard's verses came from Egypt's classical period; here, with the same music, we are to associate medieval and Danish legend – which really means that we are free to associate any appropriate occasion that will not jar with the music.[8]

And so it goes: the transparent device of Lélio's being a musician who reads and reflects on life brings us a Brigand Scene for baritone and chorus, which was first a Pirate Song, and of which a modern listener can say that "the leading theme, with its drop of a fourth on the strings and wind, answered immediately a semitone lower by the brass, has an innate savagery . . . which removes the music far from the conventional stage chorus." [9] The point is: "innate savagery," regardless of text.

After the scene of violence, we hear a Song of Bliss, derived from the *Orpheus* cantata, then The Aeolian Harp – an impressionist reminiscence of the previous song – and to conclude, the Fantasia on Shakespeare's *Tempest*. In the spoken interludes, Berlioz' mind ranges over the questions that preoccupied him in Italy: the delights of a life of freedom, the evanescence of happiness, the magical effect of the sounds of Nature, the genius of Shakespeare, and the sins of critics who damn or who rearrange masterpieces. In a later version Berlioz added a paraphrase of Hamlet's address to the players, giving technical advice about musicianship such as Lélio, who is about to conduct the *Tempest*, might well utter to *his* players at such a moment.

Although these ideas are in themselves acceptable, the prose is overemphatic and it dates in the sense of using images that have lost their force, *e.g.*, the brigand as free man. This is what gives to the whole a tinge of absurdity which is heightened by the peculiar style of translation used in polyglot scores.[10] The feelings uttered are, moreover, such as to tax the powers of the greatest dramatists. For Berlioz' identification of his artist with Hamlet is just: *Lélio* is also an attempt to mingle violence and self-pity with lyricism and protest. We find the mood again in a far greater monodrama of similar pattern, Tennyson's *Maud*, and it may indeed have been from this that Berlioz, being then in England, drew

[8] It will be remembered that the "Meditation" in *Cleopatra* had led Berlioz to attach a motto from Shakespeare's Juliet.
[9] W. G. Whittaker: *639*, 815.
[10] *E.g.*, the English in the *Ger. ed.*

for his second version the title "monodrama" to replace melologue.[11] Tennyson combines in one work the elements that Berlioz divided between the two parts of his Episode in an Artist's Life: the *Symphonie Fantastique* dwelt on the tortures of early passion, *Lélio* expresses personal, social, and religious doubts. But whereas in the *Symphonie Fantastique* the plot was thoroughly objectified with the aid of allusions to current fiction, in *Lélio* Berlioz speaks to us himself of his fears, hopes, and dislikes. It is in the music that both parts are "objective" – as is proved by its frequent readaptation from earlier uses. In other words, the music reveals its author in the legitimate way of art, by giving us a self-sustaining object; the scenario fails by falling short of this crystallization.

This is not to say that Berlioz failed in designing the *structure* of the melologue, nor was it intrinsically ill-chosen for his purpose. He meant the two parts of the "Episode," symphonic and vocal, to be performed at one concert and he adroitly contrasted his effects. After the macabre close of the instrumental first part, the second explores different realms: the opening ballad brings us back to earth and introduces voice and piano, whose sounds we shall hear again in the final number.[12] We next go, via the choral "Shades," to an underworld which is no longer heathen and diabolical but Christian and outraged. The Brigand's Song provides a second solo, in a different register from the opening ballad; after which the Song of Bliss and its echo on the harp lift us to spheres where music is native and where the ethereal atmosphere of the *Tempest* fantasy strikes us as a natural continuation. The progression in scale and in dynamics is steady from the first number to the last, and the gay finale is a happy ending which leaves us in no doubt that the brooding Lélio, who has been twice through the dark regions, has indeed effected a Return to Life.

By the standards of 1830, then, Berlioz' melologue was a complete concert, uniting every usual kind of music.[13] But it was also in a dramatic

[11] Tennyson: *Maud* is "a little *Hamlet;* a hero raised by love, degraded by loss . . . and purified into devotion to mankind." Substitute: devotion to art. (*1220*, I, 396.)

[12] We *may* have heard the piano in the Witches' Sabbath if it is used instead of bells. Compare Wagner's *Parsifal,* for the bells of which a special piano-like instrument was built.

[13] Berlioz is almost always traditional in the constructive sense: he extracts the principle of a convention and retains it under a new guise to introduce his new contents. We can guess that having studied Beethoven's Ninth and proved to himself that he could compose a purely instrumental work of magnitude, Berlioz was eager to try out the vocal-symphonic combination. Adding the

tradition which has by no means died out. Interspersing speech and action with music was so little a piece of Berliozian eccentricity that it may on the contrary be said to be the aboriginal dramatic form: Greek tragedy, the ancient carol,[14] the *Singspiel*, and the Roman liturgy itself. Berlioz' audience did not even need to go back to origins. Méhul's *Joseph* and Weber's *Der erste Ton* [15] were contemporary examples of the form which a little earlier had so greatly excited Mozart under the name of duodrama: "I have always wished to write a drama of this kind . . . the music is like an obbligato recitative. Speaking is sometimes introduced with striking effect . . . One should have mostly recitatives of this kind in opera and only occasionally, when the words are suitable for musical expression, have the recitatives sung." [16] In the note by Thomas Moore which gave Berlioz his hint, he was reminded that Racine's *Athalie* and Collins's Odes employed the same combination of song and speech, and another of his favorite authors, Molière, had adapted the same form to the needs of comedy. What was still more to the point, the second act of Beethoven's *Fidelio* enshrined a small "melodrama," and his *Egmont* was an extended essay in the genre.[17] These numerous models, though differing in particulars, reinforced Berlioz' desire to create a form that would employ all the resources of voice and instruments upon a dramatic theme, and achieve greater variety than oratorio without falling into the rut of opera. *Lélio* is therefore a variant of one consistent purpose, but the genre could not long satisfy a composer who thought that music should predominate over words, and Berlioz went on to invent other, tighter patterns.

The mixed form none the less continued to attract composers after

---

piano to the ensemble was, he thought, an innovation for he did not know Beethoven's Fantasia for chorus, orchestra, and piano. (Op. 80.) The scoring in *Lélio* (two pianos, four hands) was in any case different, for Berlioz wanted not only the crystalline and silvery sonorities of the instrument for the *Tempest* fairyland, but also the percussive quality; and these not in contrast with orchestral tone as in a piano concerto, but in combination.

[14] In French "carole," or dance in ring formation with singing intermingled; later the lyric based on this "form." See Chaucer, *passim.*

[15] Respectively, a sacred opera without action, and a cantata with declamation describing, through the verses of Rochlitz, the origin of music. Weber counted on producing a great effect with it at Munich, but the actor-declaimer spoiled it. (*1017*, 88.)

[16] *1026*, 288–9. Before Mozart, Rousseau and Benda had produced duodramas – also called monodramas, according as one thought of the actor as being alone or of speech and music as forming a pair.

[17] Others of Beethoven's works, notably the Victory Symphony, were "dramatized" in the same way. In London, veterans of Waterloo were hired to take part in such a staging.

Berlioz. Modern critics who have never seen nor hoped to see a melologue are wrong in supposing that cock-and-bull recitations interrupted by good music belong exclusively to the 1830's. Beginning with Mendelssohn's posthumous *Athalie*, which was cast and performed in the same fashion, as the composer wished, an impressive list of similar works could be drawn up.[18] The sober Englishman Sterndale Bennett followed suit in his version of the *Paradise and the Peri*, as another musician who admired *Lélio* — Sidney Lanier — long ago reminded the critics.[19] In our own day Janaček has composed a song cycle *The Diary of One Who Vanished* in the same "original" form,[20] and in fact twentieth-century composers seem uncommonly drawn to the form and its Hamlet-like *Weltschmerz:* Stravinsky's *Histoire du Soldat* is surely as strange dramatically and as valid musically as *Lélio*, and Schoenberg's two monodramas, *Erwartung* and *Die glückliche Hand*, directly meet Berlioz' problem and reproduce part of his effect. The first of these Schoenberg scores is "an original attempt [again!] to make one person bear the burden of the whole dramatic development . . . and to represent dramatically what may happen to a man in a moment of the highest tension and intensity of feeling." [21]

Honegger in *Nicolas de Flue* treats with the same device a more realistic story, but the clinching instance which proves that Berlioz' unsuccessful attempt was none the less aimed in the right direction is that of Stravinsky's opera-oratorio *Oedipus*, which also mingles recitation, singing, two languages, and the functions of action and comment.[22] This of

[18] For *Athalie*, the singer Eduard Devrient wrote and recited lines to link the scenes. Mendelssohn's brother Paul approved, knowing how Felix dramatized the score at the piano. See Moscheles: *980*, 353.

[19] In Bennett's work "words are recited along with or between detached passages of the instrumental music." (*1100*, 8.)

[20] "A psychological drama unfolded in twenty-two lyrics for tenor voice interrupted by a duet for the lovers, a few phrases for female trio offstage representing the voice of conscience, and a pianoforte interlude." (*1315*, II, 758.)

[21] *1036*, 126. The commentator is "certain that nothing approaching this for daring and novelty has ever been written for the stage." As for *Die glückliche Hand*, the man "who sustains the whole of the action . . . is involved in ever-varying circumstances and events, the action being reduced to the most compact form." The drama is "fantastic," the sequences purposely anti-logical and incomprehensible — "A highly personal form of expression through the means of the drama." (*1036*, 130 and 139.)

[22] The reciter, speaking in the vernacular, says toward the end that we are about to hear "the famous monologue." In his *Persephone* the composer likewise follows Berlioz in the use of the orchestral players as members of the cast, and in the ballet *Petrouschka* the orchestral use of the piano.

course creates difficulties of production, though they are less in *Oedipus* than in *Lélio,* where the actor (or his double) must also be an orchestra conductor.[23] In any case, the persistence of the monodramatic idea — notably in Browning [24] — tells us something about the galling inflexibility of theatrical and operatic conventions in the last century and in ours. As will appear, the whole Berlioz-Wagner debate arises from the need to remedy this state of things.

Music being Berlioz' *raison d'être,* both before and after his ill-starred engagement to Camille Moke, one may feel surprised that an experience as upheaving as his return to life yielded only the Melologue, that is to say old material cast in a transitory form. Berlioz could, it is true, point to three new overtures in various stages of completion, the song *La Captive,* a few religious pieces, and the revision of the *Symphonie Fantastique,* but as he himself said, in Italy he could not compose; he was taking in too much to be able to give out. Knowing the future as the artist could not know it, the reader, eager to imagine a steady progress for his hero and seeking relief from having to groan over the artist's vicissitudes, will find himself wishing that great accomplishments might take place outside the conditions of life. He wishes that Beethoven had not been a rude man burdened with disease and a scapegrace nephew; that Swift had not been dependent on ministerial favors or died insane; that Lincoln had not appointed incompetent drunkards to the Federal bench and been on poor terms with his wife; that Berlioz had trod his way from one musical work to another in the peace of some impossible mountain Eden.

This is the naïve, pedestal view of history, though the wish is indirectly a measure of the accomplishments themselves. For the merit of great works lies not merely in their conception but in the power to grip and fix disparate experiences. It is because the work of art has hemmed in and overcome the chaos of existence that it lives and is called great. "Art is our flounderings shown." The raging flux of life need not even mean the visible storms of Berlioz' early years. The monk in his cell can undergo cataclysms of the soul and master feelings akin to those that wreck the world. Only, he must really experience them and not merely play with their abstract names. This difference is no doubt the one which divided Berlioz from the little band of enthusiasts, soon turned into bourgeois, whom he had gathered around him in Paris. There was but

[23] See Sternfeld, "Ist der *Lélio* aufführbar?" (*478,* 372 ff.) In a Berlin performance at the turn of the century, the actor wore a mask. (*343,* 8 *n.*)

[24] *Pippa Passes* is the best example of this discontinuous dramatic form.

one Berlioz among the two dozen residents of the Villa Medici – only one master of reality who used the same common experience, in spite of his own distaste for the time and place, as artistic material.

What Berlioz acquired in these fourteen months of idleness abroad was incalculably great. If childhood at La Côte and youth in Paris supplied two sources of vision and power, manhood in Italy furnished the third and last set of formative impressions. The unimaginable sea and the clear landscape made perhaps the most durable mark, and their musical equivalent recurs in the later works from the *Corsair* overture, begun at Nice, to the septet on the Carthaginian shore in *Les Troyens.* In fact, the atmosphere of five great works comes out of Berlioz' Italian journey: *Harold in Italy*, *Benvenuto Cellini*, *Romeo and Juliet*,[25] *Les Troyens*, and *Beatrice and Benedict.* Berlioz "did not know why" Rome failed to inspire him. Writing to Wagner twenty years later, and without thinking of Italy, he remarked that he could never create while enjoying the spectacle of nature. But he could conceive, and before he crossed Mont Cenis homeward bound, he had noted down these several dramatic subjects. Bellini's version of *Romeo* had spurred him to think of it again as a musical problem: he even gave away to Mendelssohn the idea of writing a "Queen Mab" scherzo. Geographical and historical associations had recalled memories of Virgil to whose verses Berlioz improvised recitatives on the very spot. In the Coliseum he had read Byron, and more important still for the future *Harold in Italy*, the composer had steeped himself in the folk tunes and rural litanies of the Abruzzi. He had not yet, it is true, come across the memoirs of Benvenuto Cellini, but popular dances and songs of Florence and the Campagna stayed in his mind in preparation for the Roman Carnival and other parts of *Cellini.*

In addition, Dante and Michelangelo's Florence combined with the insufficiency of music in Saint Peter's to stimulate his imagination about religious works in scale with great architecture (the later *Requiem*), while the Napoleonic saga (symbolized by a funeral, the Bridge of Lodi and the Alps) brought forth the several plans that finally produced the Funeral Symphony, the *Te Deum*, and two other choral works. Finally, the Religious Meditation and the negligible Christmas songs (including a Chorus of Magi) look forward to the mature oratorio, *The Infant Christ.*

This summary review leads to the astonishing conclusion that by the

[25] The first idea came in 1828, when he saw the play and discussed it with Deschamps, whose manuscript translation circulated among the Romantic group (*1248*, V, 6); but something very like the plan of the symphony was embodied in Berlioz' "Letter on Italian Music." (*1399*, Mar.-May 1832, p. 48.)

time Berlioz returned to Paris in the fall of 1832 he had sketched or conceived or been drawn to the subject of everyone of his major works.[26] To be sure, he had by then little more than glimpses of their form and contents. The raw substance he had stored up was still to be shifted and pulled about several times according to his free way with dramatic material; but his daemon, if not he himself, knew where he was going. Berlioz' mature output was thus the fulfillment of youthful thoughts. When he had written the last note of his last music drama, *Beatrice and Benedict*, he stopped; he had finished what first dawned on his imagination thirty years before.[27]

The catch phrase which seeks to describe Berlioz as "a monument of incompleteness" [28] is therefore so inapplicable that we should absolutely invert it and call him a veritable "monument of completeness." This entails no approval of the work he did; it does entail recognition of a steadily unfolding purpose through the series of herculean obstacles that later chapters will relate. From the "Estelle" melodies of his twelfth year to the nocturne-duet of Hero and Ursula in his sixtieth, Berlioz unweariedly kept recording, embodying, revising and uniting his musical inspirations, until he had put the best of himself in twelve major scores. All of them had roots in fundamental experiences undergone before his thirtieth year; all of them still occupy the most serious attention one hundred years after the composer's death. If this does not exemplify the very essence of artistic fulfillment through self-discipline, then words have no meaning.

Doubtless the taste for gossipy biography has obscured the undeviating continuity of Berlioz' work. Our minds seem to stray even more than Hector's toward Harriet Smithson and Camille Moke, while the diverse origins of the Melologue make us forget that it played a historic role in the development of the dramatic symphony and opera-oratorio. All the same, the opinion that *Lélio* is "the craziest work ever sketched out by a composer not actually insane" [29] must be set aside as exemplifying the truly alarming madness that weak conventional minds love to harbor, and in its stead we must put the fact of Berlioz' relentless sanity of purpose.

After *Lélio* (whose music does not even belong to the Roman period)

[26] The *Damnation of Faust* of course had its inception earlier in the *Eight Scenes* of 1828.

[27] Quickly planned in 1833, then laid aside until 1860, *Beatrice and Benedict* certainly harks back for its Sicilian inspiration to Berlioz' sight of Naples in 1831.

[28] *1365*, art. "Berlioz."

[29] *278*, 140.

it took two years of meditation for a work bearing the name of Italy to come from Berlioz' pen. Had he really been a "scene painter in sounds," he would certainly have been eager and able to work more immediately from life. The Italian notebook bears only eight and sixteen measures respectively of two themes used in the as yet unnamed work next in order. Berlioz had hardly begun to distill his experience, and he was far from thinking of Byron's hero in connection with his Second Symphony. He was intent on testing the Paris public by offering them the madness of *Lélio.*

9. Recollected in Tranquillity: Harold in Italy

November 1832 to June 22, 1834

. . . and thus subdue
Imperious passion in a heart set free.
– WORDSWORTH, *Tour in Italy* (1831–1837)

"I HAVE BEEN in Paris only since yesterday," wrote Berlioz to his sister on November 8, 1832, "and already my musical affairs are under way . . . Everyone here received me with the warmest affection. I dined with M. Lesueur. I am going to see Alphonse,[1] but it's quite a trip because I lodge miles away from him, at No. 1 rue Neuve-St.-Marc."[2] This address, and in fact the rooms that Berlioz occupied, were those formerly inhabited by Harriet Smithson. There is no evidence to show that anything but convenience – with a dash of curiosity – dictated the choice. He was in his old quarter – near the Opera and the *Café Feydeau*, near Lesueur and his own publisher – a central position from which to carry on his work.

Berlioz' first object was his concert. His strategy, the same as before, the same for the rest of his life, was dictated by the facts of Parisian life: concerts created a public, public pressure would force one of the official houses to commission an opera, and if it succeeded an opera brought income and further commissions. No other career was open to a musician except as a virtuoso. Pending this single salvation, the composer had to support himself by journalism and pay his way. So it was and so it remained until the end of the century, after which things did not improve but grew worse.[3] Fortunately, in December 1832 Berlioz could not foresee his long life of quasi-unrewarded artistic work. His energy was at its peak; he had grown in self-assurance in the two years since the *Fantastique*, and he meant to win a place for himself in spite of the competition of the prolific Auber, the adroit and complacent Adolphe Adam,

[1] Berlioz' cousin, the physician.
[2] *A.R.*, 209.
[3] In an essay written in 1920, M. Boschot shows that Berlioz' making himself heard and living comfortably after clearing off his early debts would be a wholly impossible tour de force in the twentieth century. (770, 267.)

and the man who was skillfully adapting to the stage a secondhand romanticism together with the showy side of symphonic music — Giacomo Meyerbeer. The Opera was run by a new director, a Dr. Véron, whose wealth came from patent medicine and the periodical press, and who therefore had an instinct for what the public wanted. He dabbled in the arts with a master hand, founding reviews and attaching to himself the purchasable talents of a certain kind. His reign of five years at the Opera was the only profitable one in its history since Lully's.[4]

It goes without saying that Berlioz' proposal of an opera on the Day of Judgment met with no favor. The last months of 1832 were disturbed by political violence — the arrest of the Duchess of Berry in connection with plots against Louis Philippe, and universal recrimination about these events. The Day of Judgment seemed near enough without paying for a preview at the Opera. None the less, Berlioz prepared his concert. He obtained the hall at the Conservatoire (seating twelve hundred) for the afternoon of December 9, and secured the aid of the popular actor, Bocage, as "melologuist." Then he started rehearsing his orchestra. The cohorts of Romanticism were with him, ardent, curious, sympathetic, and outspoken. For despite dark omens, it still seemed possible to accomplish the great things to which July 1830 had been a prelude. At the concert and also before, at rehearsals, could be found Liszt, Chopin and Hiller; Hugo and the brothers Deschamps, Heine (who had recently settled as an exile in Paris), Eugène Sue, George Sand, Legouvé, Vigny, Dumas, Gautier, and scores of journalists headed by Jules Janin and Joseph d'Ortigue. They prepared the wider public who thronged the hall on the day of performance. The program handed to them consisted of a revised text for the *Symphonie Fantastique*, together with the new libretto of the melologue. Rumor had it that the second part of the musical drama contained things both touching and satirical, and that the satire was aimed at the well-known music critic, F. J. Fétis, representing the clan who "improve" masterpieces and who, "like the vulgar birds that people our public gardens . . . , when they have stained the brow of Jupiter or the breast of Venus, preen themselves as if they had laid a golden egg." [5]

[4] Altogether, 20 years out of 166. Lully ruled the house like a private monopoly from 1672 to his death in 1687. In 1830, the establishment had outstanding debts amounting to 1,200,000 francs. (*738*, ch. 2 ff.)

[5] *Ger. ed.*, Vol. XII, and Tiersot, *308*, Nov. 13 to Dec. 25, 1904. Boschot implies that Fétis as a friend of the Moke family had had a hand in breaking up Berlioz' engagement, and that this was Berlioz' revenge, but there is no evidence that Berlioz knew of Fétis's interference: the artistic grounds were enough.

Fétis, who was in the hall, heard his manner of speech being mimicked by the actor, and naturally wrote an unforgiving review, but Paris had relished on that day one of the many "artistic manifestations" (as they are traditionally called) which enliven its history. "A charming epoch!" exclaims M. Boschot, but he adds: "These swaggerings were far less wounding than the contemptuous knifing in the back of our moderns." [6] True: aristocratic honor was still in vogue and blows were dealt in front of witnesses. The survival of the fittest, which requires the "dirty fighting" taught in the democratic army, had not been invented.

Nor was the declamation purely an aggressive act. Like Hugo's *Hernani*, Dumas's *Antony* (playing at that very time), or Vigny's *Chatterton*, the melologue of Berlioz was in part didactic. The Romantic artist had to explain himself or, as De Quincey put it about Wordsworth, had to create the taste by which he is to be appreciated. We, having learned the lesson, are inclined to be impatient with the textbook, but in 1832 it was by no means pointless for Berlioz to expound the quality of his emotion, the character of his successive pieces, and the attitude he took towards his art. That he was right is shown by the delight of his fellow artists and the public's response. There was a spontaneous demand for a repeat performance of the whole *Episode from an Artist's Life*.

At the *première* of *Lélio* one undesigned dramatic scene had been witnessed and, thanks to gossip, understood by the public: in a box, not ten feet from Berlioz, sat Harriet Smithson, the other supposed protagonist in the "plot" that occupied the stage. Berlioz had certainly not invited her, but the next day he was introduced and they spoke face to face for the first time. No record exists of their conversation; in his letter home after the concert, Berlioz speaks only of its success, of the congratulations of Paganini, Victor Hugo, and Adolphe Nourrit, as well as of the snobbish curiosity of *Tout-Paris*. Newspaper reviews bore out this report. In the *Journal des Débats*, more than ever powerful owing to its association with the reigning house of Orleans, Janin wrote: "This young man has from this day forward an audience at his feet." [7]

Since Berlioz had to leave for Germany by January first, he planned to consolidate his position — and possibly recoup his expenses — at a second performance on December 30. It netted no profit but spread his name still farther: he and Liszt were the twin wonders of the season. The musically reliable d'Ortigue pointed out that Berlioz was the first French composer to "produce in the symphonic genre those picturesque effects,

[6] *769*, 117. [7] *1386*, Dec. 15, 1832.

those lively and strong colors, that elegiac and mystical utterance which the great works of Weber and Beethoven first made known to us. What distinguishes Berlioz is vigor, brilliance, daring, and an almost exuberant power of dramatic expression."[8] The critic warned the authorities: "Do not let this burning gift cool down. . . . Spare him the disgust and mortification which arrest talents on the verge of creation. Take him in his vigorous youth, in the strength of his noble self-confidence."[9]

This advice might well have been heeded by others than musical officials – by Harriet Smithson, for instance. For Berlioz' interview with her had had its sequel too. The actress was in difficult circumstances: the vogue of English plays was declining; her manager was in America, and she lacked business ability. Whether this predicament rekindled warmth of feeling in Berlioz, whether she made an appeal to him in her distress, mistaking one sentiment for another, the fact remains that by mid-December the pair were deeply involved. She had declared herself to Berlioz, who was soon writing to Franz Liszt: "Yes, I love her. I love her and am loved in return."[10] And to another friend: "What an improbable romance life is!"[11] He and Harriet corresponded, each in his own language, and Berlioz, always able to observe himself, could but be amused by the pace of the affair: "What love, . . . what idolatry, *quanti palpiti!*"[12]

Complications soon arose. Harriet having a mother and sister to support was beset by money worries, and the sister, being a jealous and censorious cripple, made as much trouble as she could. It would have been difficult enough without this for both the lovers to overcome their previous qualms about each other. Harriet had been represented to Hector as a woman of easy virtue and he to her as irresponsible and even epileptic. Berlioz, moreover, was a man of quick decision, whom others' delay and shifting thoughts rendered impatient. Insight did not lessen his torture: "She has a true and deep sensibility which I did not suspect. I love her as upon the first day and I think I am sure of being loved by her. But she is timid, hesitant and cannot come to a resolve: how will it all end?"[13]

He naturally gave up all thought of going to Germany. Leaving a *second* beloved a prey to alien influences would have been idiocy. The success of *Lélio* taught a similar lesson. A year's absence abroad would require still another effort to reproduce the present favorable conditions.

[8] *1399*, Dec. 1832.
[9] *1395*, Jan. 4, 1833.
[10] *A.R.*, 215.
[11] *A.R.*, 217.
[12] *A.R.*, 218.
[13] *104*, 218.

To entrench himself with the new authorities and help put Romanticism in power, he must stay active and on the spot. In the midst of a bad moment with Harriet, the Italian Theater asked him for a comic opera. Berlioz chose *Much Ado about Nothing* and sketched the libretto with a speed which argues previous thought. But musical politics are treacherous: thirty years elapsed before he was enabled to carry out this project.[14]

By the next month, February 1833, Hector had decided to end Harriet's vacillations and risk alienating his family by offering her immediate marriage. She accepted his reckless proposal; given her plight and his situation, his offer could only mean absolute devotion. His "tenacity" – loyalty to an idea, rather – was his undoing, for he was conscious of the nature of his passion: "It is no love of the senses; the heart alone and the head are impregnated with this sublime sentiment." [15] Still it was not resignation but fated choice; as before towards music, now towards her he was voluntarily driven: "I shall never leave her; she is my star; she understood me. If this be error, I must be left in the grip of it." [16] And again: "I am immensely happy – until further notice." [17] This refers to the "persecutions" which both their families had begun in order to break the engagement. Dr. Berlioz had uttered an uncompromising "No," but Hector was sure of his own fortitude and "she promises that she will be courageous and firm . . . we shall soon, I hope, overcome these difficulties." [18]

"Soon" turned out to be eight months, during which impediments were aggravated by catastrophes and led to misery in common. By refusing his consent, Dr. Berlioz forced Hector to take laborious legal steps – the so-called *sommations respectueuses* – by which under the Code a son enjoins his father not to cut him off despite the action he is about to take. On Harriet's side, the preparations for two benefit performances were nipped in the bud by her breaking her leg as she stepped from a cab. Financial preoccupations would be enough to explain her misstep, but it is clear that her anxiety was increased by a sense of inadequacy. Under the badgering of her family she grew apathetic, and then distraught by her lover's demands for certitude and action: "A trifle frightens her; she

[14] See below, Chapter 25 on *Beatrice and Benedict.*

[15] *A.R.*, 218.

[16] *A.R.*, 215. This Nietzschean love of fate by no means implies an abdication of the will, nor an acceptance of determinism; it springs rather from the tragic sense of life and expresses a self-reliance which our modern "progressive" liberal minds have no inkling of.

[17] *A.R.*, 226.

[18] *A.R.*, 226.

is afraid of my exasperation . . . we mutually torment each other. . . . But the worse her position becomes, the more devoted I shall be. . . ." [19]

In the interstices of this deplorable drama, there were articles to write and musical proofs to correct. Schlesinger was bringing out three pieces from the Melologue and Berlioz saw to it that they were circulated. By the end of May, Harriet was beginning to walk on crutches, but her sister still hoped to discourage the devoted Hector. The "devilish little hunchback" told him to his face that if she were strong enough she would pitch him out of the window. He kept his temper but agonized over the effect of this nagging on Harriet. His own family, except the faithful Adèle, "treated him like a pariah," and he had to inquire of Paris friends in order to find out how Nanci had fared through her first childbirth.

By mid-June the strain had nearly worn him down. He was anesthetized by the effort toward a seemingly unattainable object. He broke with Harriet, which had the effect of rousing her, but he withstood her entreaties. He ended by giving in: had she not done as much earlier for him? Still his practical sense was revolted. Refusing to accept money from him, she had struggled to obtain from the Ministry of Fine Arts a "gratuity" of a thousand francs, whereas she should have been ready to marry him and help him start rebuilding their finances. But she was still "timid, irresolute, incapable of making a decision." [20] He finally persuaded her to take the step. Her sister tore up the preliminary license. Caught between two strong wills, Harriet reproached Hector with not loving her. Whereupon by way of enraged testimony he swallowed in front of her an overdose of laudanum. Her tears and supplications induced him to take an emetic — a second return to life. Even then the tragic farce was not over. She wanted to "wait a few months." Berlioz determined to leave her, to leave the country and settle in Germany — if need be with a waif of eighteen, whom some friends had rescued from bondage to an exploiter and were trying to distract him with. He no longer cared about his own happiness, and was ready to accept anything as part of his "absurd story." [21]

Four days later, Harriet came to plead with him again, and in return for an ultimate change of his plans, consented to have their banns put up. The waif was taken care of by a collection among friends, and Janin

[19] *L.I.*, 125–6.
[20] *L.I.*, 131.
[21] *L.I.*, 134. His father meanwhile had written him a "dreadful letter." *A.R.*, 239.

undertook to see her out of harm's way.[22] On October 3, 1833, the marriage of Harriet and Hector was solemnized at the British Embassy with Franz Liszt as principal witness.[23]

Aided by Liszt, d'Ortigue, Berlioz, and other musical friends, the Romantics in the several arts had meanwhile joined hands to promote their views and fulfill designs long matured. They enlisted the aid of men high in government places and founded a magazine, *L'Europe Littéraire*, which was to publish their views and, by a foreign as well as native catholicity, help modern art to overcome the usual obstacles of ignorance, Philistinism, and national prejudice. "Art," said the prospectus, "has always been a social and general concern . . . This concern is reflected and made visible through journalism. But hitherto . . . this mirror of the times has only cast back the image of past epochs, and contemporaries have perforce ignored one another." The new organ meant to "focus the rays of all living genius" and raise a "temple to the universality of all the arts." Under Victor Bohain's editorship, men of letters formed the majority of the contributors, but the magazine undertook to sponsor concerts, and this naturally meant featuring the work of the outstanding modern musician, Hector Berlioz.

At the first of these concerts, on May 2, 1833, six of the eight works were by Berlioz – two overtures, three movements from the *Symphonie Fantastique*, and the fisherman's song from *Lélio*. It was a successful as well as fashionable occasion. One could count peers of the realm, great ladies, artists, and critics. Berlioz' friend Girard led the orchestra, even though at another concert two months before he had made a hash of the *Francs-Juges* overture. Habeneck and the Conservatoire Society likewise vied in willingness to tackle the unfamiliar difficulties of Berlioz' scores. On April 14, 1833 they gave his new overture *Rob Roy*, but the work had no success, for the sufficient reason, Berlioz felt, that it was "long and

[22] Boschot thinks, with some plausibility, that "the waif" was a hoax engineered by Janin and others, to turn the current of Berlioz' thoughts. He was certainly in no condition to verify the facts represented to him. (*268*, 195.)

[23] In the printed versions of the official marriage record (*502*, 406; *A.R.*, 237), the signature of another witness shown as "Jacques Henry" should appear as "Jacques Herz," the Anglo-French pianist and impresario (1794–1880). It should be added that Liszt's presence had the double motive of expressing friendship and wiping out the evil gossip about Harriet which he had helped to spread. Berlioz' later word to him about his bride's innocence corroborates what the British press had always said about the purity of her morals and the circumspection of her behavior. It was in fact this habit of prudence which had made Hector's first advances seem to her so suspect.

diffuse." He destroyed it, though keeping in mind some of its melodic material.[24]

Although the Conservatoire was soon to turn against Berlioz by a natural conspiracy which made use of this lack of success,[25] other official bodies seemed at this time fairly well disposed toward the new generation. The Institute, according to its custom, publicly reported on the works sent by its Rome pensioners. Montfort's little pieces received vague compliments but Berlioz was assured with some warmth that he had greatly improved. He had profited from experience and was now "original without eccentricity." This opinion unknowingly bore on music that Berlioz had written before winning the prize, and he enjoyed the irony while noting the Institute's kindly frame of mind. At the same time, the Ministry refused his request for a grant-in-aid and reminded him of his obligation to go to Germany. Subsequently this requirement was waived and Berlioz received fitfully but in full the stipend to which the award entitled him. The sincere patrons of American art who have been trying to obtain governmental support for it might well ponder this and future items in Berlioz' history: State involvement in art means politics, it works by favor and exception, and responds only to the pull of power. This being known to all Parisian artists — Delacroix was at that moment being pushed by Thiers who fancied himself as a connoisseur, and Rude had finally made his mark with his "Neopolitan Fisher-Boy" — Berlioz could "arrive" and be given the leisure to write music only if he forced his way by an alliance with some faction or other. He must also acquire a public personality and become one of those whom the government dare not turn down. In short, he must coerce and cajole like any skillful politician, whatever the risk to the artist in this struggle for power.

This compulsion was the inevitable counterpart of the process by which art had become public and social instead of private and domestic — a change which gives the clue to understanding the fate that overtook Berlioz and his generation: it was the first to struggle under the modern system. So far from being "divorced from society" they were violently thrown into society to sink or swim in competition with other manufacturers and promoters. As individuals, their sole defense was the power of the press. Now the newspaper closest to the government in the 30's was the *Journal des Débats*, where Jules Janin — the Lousteau of Balzac's *Illusions Perdues* — favored Berlioz, originally because the musician was "good

[24] Berlioz destroyed the parts, as he states, but the full score, which he had sent as a Rome Essay, survived and is reproduced in *Ger. ed.*, IV, 143 ff.

[25] The deliberate exclusion of Berlioz as a competitive threat is attested by the historian of the Society. (Deldevez, quoted in *386*, 10–1.)

copy." In a column of literary gossip he could be represented as an uncommon specimen. Soon Janin put him forward as the only living composer likely to bring world renown to the French School. This was sound prophecy, but the need persisted to turn Berlioz' life and character into reading matter, and from this grew the Berlioz legend, itself part of the Romanticist legend.

Because Berlioz himself contributed to this publicity – giving notes to d'Ortigue or Gautier – it has been inferred that he was unusually avid of newspaper notice. In reality he had but little choice. If experts in public relations had been available in 1833, and if he had been able to pay them, he would undoubtedly have hired someone to relieve him of the job. Meyerbeer was soon to assemble a corps of secretaries for just this purpose. But Berlioz, like Weber before him and Hugo and others in his own time, had to create his legend singlehanded. Unlike Hugo, however, he did not play up to it in private life: he was never the maestro, and was in fact repelled by the poet's pose.[26] Of Berlioz' ways among friends at this time, we have an account by d'Ortigue: "His conversation is . . . uneven, abrupt, interrupted . . . sometimes also expansive, but more often reserved and formal, always frank and worthy of respect." [27] "Sometimes expansive, but more often reserved" is the real Berlioz, and one regrets that the legend had to exhibit a creature always flamboyant, volcanic, and indifferent to privacy. Propaganda has to fit the minds of the recipients, and the artist's new patron – at once snob and mob – required its heroes to be patently demonic and self-assertive. In the smaller Paris of those days, of course, legends found their own corrective; they were reinterpreted in the light of common knowledge. Looking back in the 1860's, Sainte-Beuve tells us how incredible it seemed that thirty years before one used to carry on one's life through the columns of the newspapers: "A sheet with five thousand subscribers was practically a family of intimates." [28]

Style in these matters changes quickly, and the biographical "puffs" which an adept journalist like Gautier produced in quantity would scarcely seem to him reliable sources to consult in future. In Berlioz' own reviews and autobiographical fragments one can follow the shifts in tone and substance which each decade brought about from 1830 to

[26] "*Il trône trop.*" (*L.I.*, 152.)

[27] *185*, 323. Confirmed by Liszt: *202*, 289.

[28] *1212*, III, 21. A little later – rather too late – Dickens made ill-advised revelations of his private affairs in the pages of his magazine; which does not prevent Shaw – still another example of the genuinely reserved self-exhibitor – from calling Dickens a deeply reserved man. (*1126*, 29.)

1870; the series amounts to a miniature history of journalism and of class emancipation through widened literacy. In these middle thirties the music criticism he was publishing shows his clear intention of establishing himself as a Personality. Around a musical subject – sometimes with the addition of a short-story plot – he wove fantasies based on his Italian experiences. He had the storyteller's gift and could imbue, for example, an account of the way the Rome Prizes are awarded, with a humorous lifelikeness which secured for him and for music criticism readers hitherto untouched.[29] But here again power created resistance. To take the public as witnesses of musical affairs was to declare war on the Institute and bring on reprisals. In a solemn sitting on October 12, 1833 the secretary read a report in which Berlioz was admonished like a schoolboy. His views on modern music were indirectly assailed and a malicious reference was made to the unapplauded *Rob Roy* overture. Reversing themselves like a supreme court, the judges discovered that Montfort's work was "clear, lively, spirited throughout," in fact remarkable for "elegant melodies and brilliant orchestration."

Except for these skirmishes, his marriage to Harriet, and the concerts previously mentioned, the second half of 1833 brought Berlioz nothing but dull disappointment. He continued to be on distant terms with his family – all but the loving Adèle, to whom he poured out his hopes and his gratitude. With Harriet's debts weighing on him, he had little time or strength to compose. Instead, he struggled to arrange for November a benefit recital for her and himself together. By midsummer he had worked himself to exhaustion in the preliminaries, meanwhile revising and rehearsing his "Heroic Scene" for another ceremony. Napoleon's statue was to be put back on the column, Place Vendôme, and Berlioz' choral work, though first associated with the Greek Revolution, was perfectly suitable.

For the first time since the July Days a popular celebration was to include music on the large scale. Huge stands were built opposite the Tuileries for the three hundred singers and two hundred and fifty instrumentists who were to follow the solemn beating of three or four hundred drums. The official program comprised Rossini's *William Tell* and *Gazza Ladra* overtures, Auber's *Masaniello* overture, a battle piece by the choral composer and conductor Schneitzhöffer, and four other choruses. It was only at the last minute that Berlioz had managed to have his own work

[29] These particular articles appeared in *L'Europe Littéraire*, I, 123–4, 182–3, and 246; reprinted in *V.M.*, II, 5–13. Shaw in 1935, harking back to 1888: "I believed I could make musical criticism readable even by the deaf." (*880, 6.*)

added, certainly the most fitting item on the program. The rehearsals (indoors) under Habeneck created a stir. That hardened conductor wept at the mere richness of sound, and Berlioz, alert to his opportunity, was able for the first time to study the properties of large ensembles.[30] But by the appointed day, Berlioz' piece had been surreptitiously worked off the program. Then the musical part of the festival was drowned out by incessant political demonstrations. The troops were armed and the mob angry. They did not return their King's greeting but shouted *vivas* when the Emperor's statue was raised. The Opera announced that the concert would be given again on its stage. More work for Berlioz to reinstate his "Scene": the concert was canceled.

As for the joint "benefit" for Hector and his wife, it was a fiasco of another sort. It began late and Marie Dorval (Vigny's great love) stole the show. Coming after her, Harriet Smithson found little favor with her pantomime from the fourth act of *Hamlet*. Berlioz and his music did not get under way until 11:30 in front of a politically excited audience. They listened to Liszt, who played superbly; but in conducting his *Sardanapalus* cantata Berlioz miscued his orchestra and the crowd began to demand the *Symphonie Fantastique*. At this point the orchestra had had enough and started to leave. Berlioz had to make a speech of apology to the audience, despite the fact that it was long past midnight and they kept demanding the March from the *Fantastique*. The humiliation of Berlioz and his wife was complete.

This failure, however, netted two thousand francs, which were swallowed up by Harriet's debts and the support of her family. No help was forthcoming from his; so he accepted the post of music critic on *Le Rénovateur* — an offshoot of the *Correspondant*, that is to say ultra-royalist, ultra-religious in tone. But as Berlioz wrote to Adèle: "Since I have no use for politics, their shade of opinion does not bother me in the least." [31] In short order, Berlioz wrote two excellent articles — a diplomatic one on the dancer Taglioni and the new Opera management (Dr. Vèron and Ciceri) which featured her work, and a delicate and penetrating study of Chopin as pianist and composer.

Berlioz did not consider this enough to fill the remainder of the year. A whole month was left in which to turn the defeat of his last concert into a victory. Aware that he lacked experience as a conductor, he did

[30] His conclusion was: "Music is not made for the street nor for the open air." (*L.I.*, 131.) Berlioz' friend, Georges Kastner, records the same conclusion in his manual on military bands published some years later. (*825*, 317–8.)

[31] *A.R.*, 250.

not dare risk a fresh disaster. Only one man in Paris could really give Berlioz' music properly, François Habeneck, but he brusquely refused. Girard was once again called on, the lesser of two risks. Liszt readily agreed to play some Weber, and Paganini's protégé, Haumann, offered a piece of his own composition. The rest was all by Berlioz: two new songs – "*La Romance de Mary Tudor*" and "*Le Jeune Pâtre Breton*," the *King Lear* overture, and the *Symphonie Fantastique*. The effort was worth it; expenses were met, and both public and critical acclaim were considerable. Only Fétis's *Revue Musicale* complained that M. Berlioz did not produce many new works.

Berlioz was by now just turned thirty. He was married, had begun to pay off some fifteen thousand francs on his wife's account, was supplying money to her mother, and was about to become a father. His sole means of support being his pen (plus the uncertain remainder of his prize) he could not afford the time to compose, even though he had a new symphony in his head. Two occurrences came to his aid. His publisher and friend, Maurice Schlesinger, sensing that the new young men would turn out to be the great men of tomorrow, founded a periodical, *La Gazette Musicale*, which was to unite French and German musical thought against the frivolity of the Italians. Since the Paris Schlesinger was the brother and partner of the Berlin Schlesinger, and their firms published music on both sides of the Rhine, the new periodical would aid their business as well as promote the works of a very productive group of performers and composers. Berlioz was at once among the leaders of this enterprise, to which he contributed articles, editorial advice and practical toil.[32]

The second piece of luck was a request from Paganini for a composition in which he might play his newly acquired Stradivarius viola – a concerto for viola and orchestra. To utilize the publicity, the *Gazette* announced a new work by Berlioz for viola, chorus, and orchestra, with the improvised title, *The Last Moments of Mary Stuart*.[33] Within the next

[32] Owing to the vagaries of copyright practice, Schlesinger's arrangement gave him the German rights to any piece of music he bought in France, provided he issued it also in Germany. Hence he stood to gain large sums for an indefinite period, the sale of these works being outright and not on a royalty basis. At the same time he could say in his own defense that without the potential German market he could not have afforded to publish work as "advanced" as that of Berlioz.

[33] The English and Scottish Marys were enjoying a run, due to Hugo's play *Mary Tudor* (1833) and to Béranger's poem "Mary Stuart's Farewell," on which Wagner composed a song as late as 1840. The form "The Last Day of —" was much in vogue.

six months Berlioz finished the work – not a concerto, not for voices, and never again called "Mary Stuart," but during its gestation simply called "the symphony" or "my symphony with viola." It grew from two movements to three, then to four, until on May 31, he wrote to d'Ortigue: "It is nearly finished and will soon be born and baptized." [34] The nameless symphony was associated by the author with some of the musical experiences he had brought back from Italy, so that after casting about for the proper allusive tag he finally hit upon *Harold in Italy*.[35]

The speed and joy with which he composed this sizable score show how ripe it was in Berlioz mind. His "inexplicable mechanism" worked just as soon as he could enjoy a little of the "time and tranquillity" which he said were his sole requirements.[36] Though there were still duns, and some apprehension, both medical and financial, at the forthcoming addition to the family, Hector was in love and happy with Harriet. His need to give and receive affection was satisfied for the first time in his adult life. As Harriet's time approached, the pair moved to a quiet cottage and garden on the hill Montmartre, overlooking a plain as yet free of all industry, whose greenery reminded Berlioz of home and Italy.[37] His good friends Liszt, Chopin, Hiller and others came out to the countrified suburb for the day. At other times there were quartets and piano sonatas at Schlesinger's, readings at Victor Hugo's, dinners where one met other young celebrities such as the ardent Liberal Catholic Lamennais ("What a man! Genius burns him, eats him away, dessicates him. He made me tingle with admiration.") [38] Lamennais was an excellent pianist, he held congenial views about the social role of art, and in fact Berlioz' two closest friends, Liszt and d'Ortigue, were the Abbé's disciples. Of the salons, that of Marie, Comtesse d'Agoult, was at once the least showy and the most lively. It was intellectual and cosmopolitan. Sainte-Beuve, Heine, Mickiewicz, the Princess Belgiojoso, Balzac, George Sand and Berlioz could be found there. Berlioz took Liszt, with the famous result

[34] *Corresp.*, 112.

[35] The viola, he felt, sounded throughout the piece "like a kind of melancholy dreamer in the manner of Byron's *Childe Harold*." (*Mem.*, I, 302.) Not long before this date, J. M. W. Turner had similarly turned his Italian experiences to use. His "Pifferari" and "Childe Harold's Pilgrimage" (1832) are not so much visual records as summaries of diversified impressions.

[36] *A.R.*, 245.

[37] Berlioz' cottage at Montmartre has been sketched and painted several times, once – it is said – by Van Gogh, though confirmation of this fact has eluded research; and in our century, on several occasions, by Utrillo, who seems to have lived in it. See Bibliography, sec. 2D: Iconography.

[38] *A.R.*, 257.

that the pianist and the countess fell in love and eloped. But until this event, there was music, brilliant talk, and friendship among men who could love and admire one another without envy or reserve.

Unfortunately, there was also "an avalanche, a cataract of concerts" to be reviewed. Between *Le Rénovateur*, and *La Gazette Musicale*, Berlioz had to sweat out copy on all conceivable subjects, good and bad, real and imaginary. And the most real were by no means those which induced him to put himself in the limelight as artist-hero of significant adventures. For he had taken on the mission of enlightener to the French in musical matters — an enterprise requiring equal parts of knowledge, tact, firmness, and ability to entertain. Berlioz preached Beethoven, analyzed his symphonies (beginning with the Third, Sixth and Ninth) and dissected the prejudices of those who, in any age, use famous names to damn the moderns without caring about the works of either. By dramatic parallels and allusions designed to rouse the imagination of his readers, and technical arguments designed to quiet their scruples, Berlioz acted as mediator between the academic or fashionable conservatism and the boldness of the late symphonies and quartets. "Art being always a social and general concern," as the romanticists had said, these half-technical, half-poetic sermons wound up with a broadside against the impercipience of the public. "The Greeks made of Homer a god. So long as Beethoven has not a temple in our midst we shall deserve the name of barbarian." [39]

Berlioz also took the opportunity offered by a feeble revival of Mozart's *Don Giovanni* to demonstrate the difference between musical drama and commonplace opera. To the poet Deschamps he wrote in confidence: "I'd like to talk to you about Mozart. We must absolutely lather up the masterpiece in such a way as to bring a fever on the lovers of the big bass drum," [40] *i.e.*, the Italians.

In a society which freely admitted that musicales were held in order to start conversation, and which required tunes (as Berlioz put it) "so written that the ladies and gentlemen who sell ribbon can remember them easily the next morning," the standards that Berlioz tried to establish were exacting but would not seem to us impossibly high. Since it was agreed that "music-desk music" is boring and always too long, Berlioz affirms without mincing words that a nation which is sunk in such Philistinism cannot lay claim to high culture. By witty asides, calculated effrontery, or adroit storytelling he compels the reader to go on and be indoctrinated against his will; he communicates his contempt, his enthusi-

[39] *A.R.*, 254. [40] *L.I.*, 142 and *285*, 88 *n.*

asm, and even his subtlety. Of course, no mere writing makes a musical out of a sow's ear, but something always sticks, which explains why after thirty-five years of Berlioz' propaganda the French public – though possibly still Philistine at heart – could laud Beethoven by rote.[41]

This effort, however, took its toll. In a man of artistic faith, the continual dissent of mankind engenders at last a spiritual weariness. Though not strengthened, faith is made at least cheerful by agreement. In early May 1834, within a month of completing his symphony, Berlioz shared some of his spleen with Liszt, urging him to come out, with Chopin and others, to Montmartre:

> I cannot tell you how much this springtime scene moves and saddens me. Besides, yesterday I suffered several *wounds in my artistic affections*, which make me miserable to the point of tears, and which all my reason (for I have a good deal more reason than you might think) or that of my poor Harriet [42] cannot make me forget or overcome.
>
> Is Vigny coming with you? There is something gentle and affectionate about his mind which always charms me and which today I find I almost need. Why aren't you both here now? Perhaps tomorrow I shall feel differently. Are we really playthings of the air? . . . And is Moore right when he says: "And false the light on glory's plume, As fading hues of even; . . . There's nothing bright but Heaven!" [43]
>
> But I do not believe in heaven. It is horrible to confess it. My heaven is the poetic world and there is a slug on each blossom. Look here, come and bring Vigny with you. I need you both. Why can I not keep myself from admiring with tenacious passion certain works which are, after all, so fragile – like ourselves, like everything that is?

Berlioz then quotes from memory (that is, with some inaccuracy) fourteen bars from Spontini evocative of anxious longing.[44]

The visitors did come and Berlioz could report to Adèle: "We discussed art, poetry, philosophy, music and drama – in a word all that constitutes life – in the presence of this beauty of nature and Italian sunshine which has favored us these few days past." Then in an upsurge of anguish: "My father is well, I gather from the Rocher ladies. Is everyone else well? They tell me you are losing weight. Why? What is wrong? You are so alone, so sad. We shall meet again, I tell you, sooner or later. It is impossible otherwise. Farewell, these thoughts sadden me. Farewell,

[41] From 1835 to 1839, Berlioz' efforts on behalf of Beethoven were seconded by Liszt (see *210*).

[42] To Berlioz always "Henriette" but restored to its original form in this text.

[43] These words are from the second of Moore's Sacred Songs, the one Berlioz had set in Rome as a *Méditation Religieuse*

[44] *A.R.*, 260–1.

I embrace you with my whole affection and that which my good and sweet Harriet bears you." [45]

By the middle of May 1834, three parts of *Harold in Italy* were finished and the composer was offering his old friend Humbert Ferrand the dedication of the work. Practical affairs were once more crowding the desk where only score paper should have been seen. "I am dead tired and bored from scribbling at so much a column for those rascally papers. My opera plans are in the hands of the Bertin family" – owners of the *Journal des Débats* and influential at court. The scheme – most appropriate to Berlioz – was to offer him "a superior libretto" on Hamlet. "Meantime," he adds – for he was inured to delays and never waited for a hare to be caught before starting another – "I have chosen as subject for a two-act comic opera, *Benvenuto Cellini*." This was equally apt, as will appear. By May 31, Berlioz, working day and night, was in sight of the end as regards the symphony: it was soon finished, and "baptized" not long after. The autograph bears the date June 22, 1834.

The Second Symphony and Its "Orgy"

I ask only for time and tranquillity.
– BERLIOZ to Adèle, November, 1833

In the work that he finally christened *Harold in Italy*, Berlioz composed a score which, apart from its power to move us, shows his power to work under the discipline of diverse requirements. He had in the first place to write for viola and orchestra, and being unwilling to produce a mere seesawing of effects between these two instruments, he had to solve the problems of sustained form as well as of contrast and balance in sonority. Dramatizing this problem, he gave to the viola the role of a lyric declaimer, in the mood of melancholy. As he said later, the viola "sticks to its sentimental garrulousness . . . and is present during the action but not mixed up in it." [1] This is but a figurative way of stating what amounts technically to the *canto fermo* or fixed song around which other musical ideas are to group themselves. In the second place Berlioz wished to use a number of melodies which he had already jotted down

[45] *A.R.*, 263–4.

[1] *M.C.*, 8.

and even worked out, notably in the discarded overture to *Rob Roy.* Thirdly, he meant to pursue the goal he had set himself in the *Symphonie Fantastique*, to make "one work."

It seems likely that he also thought of carrying forward his attempt to combine musical means by adjoining voices to the solo instrument and orchestra, as he had begun to do in *Lélio* and the *Tempest* fantasia. This intention he gave up, the only trace of it in *Harold in Italy* being the device of "reminiscences" in the finale – clearly a borrowing from Beethoven's Choral Symphony. Berlioz translated his vocal plan into instrumental expression throughout, very likely because of the nature of his material, which amounted to a series of cantos: in the first movement the viola *sings* its melancholy; when we hear it in the second, the pilgrims are *singing* their evening hymn; in the third the viola returns while a mountaineer *sings* a serenade to his love; and in the fourth, all these lyrics are re-presented against a bacchanalian background. The return in each movement of the viola voice in its original form is both a fresh use of the leitmotif principle and a lavish opportunity for free contrapuntal writing.[2] The whole work is thus more completely pulled together than the *Symphonie Fantastique*, at the same time as the vocal role of the viola and other instrumental groups represents a further step towards the fulfillment of Berlioz' persistent aim: the dramatic symphony.

As for the source and purport of the musical inspiration, the facts are equally plain: Berlioz was re-embodying some of the musical and natural impressions he had received in Italy. Two movements of the symphony were composed very rapidly, then a third and fourth, which is enough to show that he did not work from any scenario based on Byron but simply delved deeper and deeper into emotions which time had caused to settle.

In all these aspects of the symphony, Beethoven was obviously very much in Berlioz' mind. The first movement of *Harold* begins with a *fugato* in the basses, the somberness of which spells Berlioz but the design of which is Beethovenian; in the third movement one hears fleeting echoes of the *Pastoral;* and in the fourth occur the "reminiscences." Apart from this, Berlioz was treading new ground. To make the symphonic form "compact and meaningful throughout," and yet allow the viola to stand out with just enough floweriness of speech, was no mean task. Yet the composer kept the elements so much in equipoise, esthetically as well as audibly, that when Paganini saw the score, he told Berlioz he would not

[2] See the quotation of a passage from the Allegretto in Mr. Walter Piston's brilliant book on *Counterpoint* (*1347*, 80).

care to play the work: "I am not given enough to do." [3] Here was one "program," namely the virtuoso's demand for a chance to show off fingerwork, that Berlioz declined to follow. The two musicians continued to be friends none the less, and it is probable that Paganini gave Berlioz the benefit of his knowledge of viola technique. Certainly the scoring as a whole is what one authority calls it, "a veritable tour de force of concertizing between the soloist and orchestra . . . Any monotony that might result from the viola sound is avoided by adding to it unisons of horns, clarinets, bassoons, or cellos." [4]

The conception of the whole, then, is musically sound, the only evidence needed to prove it being a good performance with a violist possessed of a good tone and willing to play the dynamics as marked. When Lionel Tertis last played the work in London,[5] the critics were astonished at the magical effect of the chords (*sul ponticello*) in the middle section of the March: they had never "come off" under other hands. It is a generality about Berlioz that you have not heard the work until it is played right. This is of course true of all music, but it applies with peculiar force to Berlioz because his limpid scoring never covers up defects of performance. At the same time his genuinely melodic counterpoint requires that each line be given the weight inversely proportional to the strength of the playing instrument. *Harold in Italy* calls for the playing style of the chamber orchestra (notice how many passages use a small though ever-varied ensemble), Berlioz having perfected its adaptation to this work by repeated hearings: six years elapsed before he let the score be published.

The work opens with a melancholy but majestic adagio above which we shortly hear (in the minor) a foretaste of the "Harold" theme for woodwinds, then full orchestra, which ushers in its restatement on the viola above arpeggios on the harp. This was the melody, rescued from *Rob Roy*, which Berlioz had temporarily associated with the *Last Moments of Mary Stuart*. It undoubtedly dates from the time Berlioz spent in Nice after his break with Camille Moke, and it is simply a tuneful plaint which he was loath to discard. A melody, being a pearl fished up from mysterious depths, must not be thrown back but set and reset until it finds its perfect place. In the overture it was contrasted with a more energetic figure which is here used again as second subject, and which

[3] *Mem.*, I, 302.
[4] Pierné: *1503*, 2546.
[5] Under Sir Hamilton Harty, Apr. 8, 1935

distantly evokes the mood of the final movement. The title of this first one is "Harold in the Mountains: scenes of melancholy, happiness and joy," but the music written before the description develops quite classically and concludes with the characteristic Berliozian device of a simultaneous treatment of the opening and closing themes.[6]

Dramatically the movement contrasts three moods; melancholy prevails in the introduction and adagio, happiness and joy dominate the allegro. It is worth noticing the distinction Berlioz always makes between happiness and joy: the latter is always a more turbulent, more physical emotion. As for "the mountains" they are of course nowhere to be seen. Music, like poetry, moves against an invisible *décor*, and although the atmosphere of this first "scene" in the saga of Harold the Wanderer is as vivid as Liszt says, its setting remains distinct from its essence: we end by associating the two, but echoes in later composers show us how easily they can be dissociated.[7]

The second movement is a march which Berlioz tells us he composed while sitting quietly by his fireside with his bride. He rightly predicted that it would "soon have a reputation."[8] It is built on a pattern which has since become familiar through its use by Wagner in his preludes, and which consists of a phrase brought by development to a high point of intensity and then gradually diminished to its first elements – in a word, crescendo-decrescendo. Berlioz seems to have been the first to use and denote the structure by the symbol: < >.[9] The descriptive title of this second movement is "March of Pilgrims Singing the Evening Hymn," and its germ is the musical sensation of a juxtaposed B and C, as of two bells sounding together. Berlioz gives the two notes to woodwinds and strings respectively, after the choral phrase which provides the march theme has run through each "stanza" and before a contrasting rhythm has served as a refrain or litany. Thus the march is at once "sung" and

[6] Liszt remarks in his study of the symphony that "this Allegro builds against a magnificent background of nature a complex of repressed despair and exuberant joy, and the broken rhythms and harmonies of the polyphonic figures – which no one knows how to organize and unify . . . better than Berlioz – serve here to express . . . the alternation of fancy, splendor, and sadness." (587, 390.)

[7] Compare Siegfried's "Rhine Journey," Charpentier's *Impressions d'Italie*, and Strauss's *Aus Italien*.

[8] *L.I.*, 148.

[9] *A Trav.*, 309. In his review, precisely, of the *Lohengrin* prelude which he thought a masterpiece, Berlioz defined his own innovation, though without laying claim to it nor even mentioning himself. Liszt's *Orpheus* and Glazunow's *The Sea and the Woods* are other examples of the form.

"walked" and punctuated by the bell-like harmony. The litany resembles those Berlioz heard in his Italian excursions, so that the whole forms an evocative pattern without being at any point an imitation.

The choral phrase is repeated in rich variation, "like a luxuriant vine," says Liszt.[10] Soon the viola theme joins the canto in a passage of breathtaking counterpoint. An ordinary composer might well have been content with these three elements. But Berlioz wanted an additional contrast, for which he had a further musical idea, also of Italian origin – the quiet psalmody in sustained chords accompanied below by a pizzicato sketching the march, and above by eery viola arpeggios played near the bridge.[11] After this, the choral begins again in lessened volume and dies away as the two notes of the bells, divided among flutes, horns, and harp repeat the "seemingly dissonant but remarkably harmonised seventh, C–B . . . and dwindle away to a final pianissimo." [12]

The manuscript of the score shows, incidentally, with what untiring care Berlioz worked over the composition of his chords and the instrumentation of all the delicate moments. The effect of this search is what made Emmanuel say that in Berlioz "melodic line and balance of forms – whose purity is essential – have as auxiliaries and may even use as substitutes pure motionless sounds considered as a rare and precious substance . . . Listen to *Harold in Italy*, an unequaled treasury of 'durations' and 'accents,' which . . . entitle one to call Berlioz the first of the Impressionists." [13]

After the march and occupying the place of minuet or scherzo is a short "Serenade of an Abbruzzi Mountaineer to his Mistress." It opens with a lively refrain in country style, such as was played by the Italian *pifferari* whom Berlioz heard at Subiaco.[14] This piece of musical folklore is given interest by its instrumentation and unexpected rhythmic turns.

[10] *587*, 391.

[11] Some performers make these arpeggios sound like a vaudeville performer on the "musical saw," and give the impression that Berlioz so intended it. In the Victor recording (*1436*) and in the flesh, Mr. Primrose plays this passage admirably well. [Note of 1948 upon the first recording.]

[12] *587*, 392. Fétis complained that the two notes did not belong to the harmony and to this day musicians who approve the effect (having heard it again in Strauss's *Also Sprach Zarathustra*) carelessly refer to the presence of "the wrong note."

[13] *427*, 255. Those to whom these sensations that have no "motion" – but only recall motion – give no pleasure are bound to find whole stretches of the work "monumentally dull." (Cecil Forsyth: *1310*, 396.)

[14] The *piffero* is a rustic oboe. Berlioz suggested that it might be the instrument mentioned by Virgil: *ite per alta Dindyma, ubi assuetis* BIFOREM *dat tibia cantum.* (*53*, 7.)

Then comes the serenade on the English horn, which the viola theme (in augmentation) soon joins and raises to passionate intensity. The brief variations on these intertwined melodies are a good example of the way in which Berlioz swiftly passes from the picturesque to the sublime. If one lends an inattentive ear, or rather if one judges the movement merely from a general impression of its simple material, it stays in the mind as ordinary folk-pipings, as Romantic local color. But in Berlioz' dramatic style, the sublime arises unexpectedly from the ordinary and the simple, the perpetual sublime being a contradiction in terms. To seek it is to fail, or else to cloy by substituting the pretty. Berlioz accordingly closes his serenade with the *pifferi* again, followed by the briefest echo of the serenade, this time on the viola.[15]

The finale, it is interesting to note on the manuscript, is written in a firm clear hand, like the rest of the score; it shows few corrections and no false starts. Labeled "Orgy of Brigands" it is, as a famous theorist has said, "an orgy, but a genuinely *musical* one, set forth in perfectly clear form."[16] Still, many think this the least satisfactory of the four movements.[17] The rhythmical interest of the piece no one can deny, any more than the art with which the fragments of earlier melodies are introduced and as it were vanquished by the irrepressible "orgy" theme. This finale may well be less enticing because less "beautiful," less soothing than the earlier movements. But the symphony is conceived as a drama, where, as in life, we must not expect sweetness throughout; and the composer has taken pains to prepare us, at the close of the first movement and in moments of the third, for a descent from the elegiac.

But this is not all. The musical form of the orgy involves a conflict between Berlioz and tradition. His natural pace is rapid, his musical mood readily changes into its opposite, but symmetry and expediency alike dictated an elaborate repeat of over a hundred bars in the middle section.

[15] Technically, as Liszt points out, "the crossing rhythms and entwined melodies are balanced with extraordinary ingenuity and finesse and tenderness of feeling – an artistry which is still more evident on reading than on hearing, because in reading one is not too absorbed by the shimmering color and lulling sounds of this *morendo*." (*587*, 394.)

[16] Dr. Percy Goetschius, known as the teacher of several American composers. (*436*, 299.)

[17] For quite a while, despite Liszt's stressing "the greatness of its musical conception," I agreed with its detractors. It was not until a Toscanini performance that I saw its true proportions and lost the feeling that it was episodic. I should add that I was helped to understand by the enthusiasm and insight of the late Robert Pitney, who, before the existence of the recorded version, tirelessly illustrated his views with the aid of Liszt's piano transcription: Berlioz takes study, even and especially when he seems to hold no particular secret.

The dramatic truth is that we should hear this bacchanal, with its superb brass fanfare, only once; the very shape of the component phrases forbids reiteration. And yet, as Berlioz knew, on a single hearing the very vividness would work against proper appreciation. How many listeners would notice the Mozartian passages when the "orgy" theme seems lightly parodied? How many would enjoy the subtle, fragmentary re-entries of the earlier themes? Rather, most listeners would be left thinking of the menacing phrases for trombones, the brusque pauses, and the mad whirl of the concluding bars – "a stretta of incomparable power and color," though it "goes against certain habitual tastes." [18] Berlioz therefore tries to unstiffen our taste by giving us a second hearing soon after the first. This suggests a convenient procedure for the modern student: play this finale two or three times in succession on the gramophone, and each time more melodies, more light and shade, more art will emerge from a movement which at first seemed all brass and noise. With familiarity the central repeat will no longer affect one as a stumbling over rocky ground. All elements being in proper place, the work as a whole will seem "strong and great"; [19] and the finale itself will give the irresistible sense of "freedom under the discipline of a powerful will." [20]

When familiar to ear and mind, Berlioz' Second Symphony resolves itself into the sufficiently explicit series:

1. Adagio and Allegro (*Malinconico e giocoso*)
2. Allegretto (March)
3. Scherzo (Serenade)
4. Finale (*Giocoso e furioso*)

And its biographical or poetic reference can be summed up – if we insist on a verbal link with Byron's *Childe Harold* – in the lines

For I have been accustomed to entwine
My thoughts with Nature rather in the fields
Than Art in galleries.[21]

Such was the spirit of Berlioz' Italian journey, and such the mood indicated earlier by the phrase "Harold the Wanderer." After the "awakening to passion" that informs the *Symphonie Fantastique*, the Italian symphony enshrines the more concentrated, self-propelling emotion of a *Wanderjahr*. The theme for the viola (the French name, *alto*, fits better its grave masculine tone) sustains its character (person or psychological

[18] *587*, 397.
[19] *289*, 145.
[20] *427*, 255.
[21] Canto IV, stanza lxi.

state) in the twilit region between introspection and self-pity. More "objective" drama keeps sentimentality in check, just as it did in the persons of the poets here associated, Byron and Berlioz.[22]

It only remains to ask why Berlioz winds up his wanderings, like his dreams of love, to the tune of a lawless revelry – in a Witches' Sabbath and in a Brigands' Orgy. The latter especially seems to bother certain critics, who find the very notion of brigands and orgies ridiculous and – comic opera excepted – beyond the pale of music. The reason for the musical impulse is obvious: Berlioz felt within himself all the fury and excitement of both those finales and he enjoyed giving them a musical shape, just as Beethoven did in the riotous last movement of the Seventh.[23] This is what art is for. The complete dramatist, whether in music, poetry, or painting, sees life whole and steadies his vision through art by discovering the means for transfixing his aroused emotions: we saw with what a cool hand Berlioz organized both his bacchanals. The one in *Harold* he liked especially to conduct "in my fashion," that is to say, as a great rhythmic display, by turns tender and violent, singing and percussive.[24]

It is the names Berlioz attached to these musical routs that are outmoded, and this simply because they are historical. If age dignifies, then the tradition of witchcraft is surely respectable – what more elemental and productive of music than a *ronde de sabbat?* The notion of brigandage is, if one may say so, no less a part of the European tradition. In Berlioz' Italy, it was of course contemporary history. The sailors on his ship were only sailors because they were not brigands; Berlioz attended the wedding of one such outlaw; the population among whom he lived during his long rambles were subject to the raids of banditti, and the countryside was dotted with graves of brigands or their victims.[25] A brigand, in short, was a gangster – Berlioz did not invent the profession nor learn about it from comic opera: it reached the opera stage because it first

[22] Compare, as to the quality of intentional sentiment, a work patterned after Berlioz' *Harold*, Strauss's *Don Quixote* for cello and orchestra.

[23] "The great combination," as Arthur Machen says of literature, "is the combination of murder with mirth . . . the gross vulgarities of the Drunken Porter and the Gravediggers . . . in the tragedies of *Hamlet* and *Macbeth*." (Foreword to Edwin Greenwood's *Skin and Bone*, London, 1934.)

[24] *Mem.*, II, 81–2. Looking back on those two finales and one or two later ones from the same hand shows how much subsequent musicians derived technically from Berlioz for their own saturnalias. Even the surrealist ballet music of the 1920's, in seeking to render the neglected elements of the vulgar and cruel, did not go much beyond Berlioz' rhythms and instrumentation of a hundred years before.

[25] *A.R.*, 168.

existed in daily life, and although the *term* brigand now sounds ludicrous, the reality of the racketeer is not yet to be gainsaid. For "orgy" – also a piece of period vocabulary – substitute "wild party" and quaintness disappears. The label is indicative merely, as in the titles of twentieth-century works such as "*Bagarre*" and "*El Salón Mexico.*" [26]

The point would not be worth laboring, if certain critics were not so easily diverted from music by what they read in print.[27] Being themselves deeply programmatic, as was shown earlier, they sincerely believe that Berlioz was busy copying scenes in sounds, and are no less sincerely upset when musical material treated for Rob Roy is recast as evocative of Mary Stuart and finally of Childe Harold.[28] No doubt the unimaginative fail to grasp how associations *cluster*. To them the very word association has no plural. To the artist, on the contrary, the task of creation is in part the discovery of symbols at once sharp and ambiguous enough for infinite reference. Berlioz' first sea voyage had brought him into contact with a young Venetian corsair – *i.e.*, a pirate or sea brigand – and with an old sailor who had shipped with Lord Byron. Afterwards in the Coliseum Berlioz read Byron as modern youth might read T. S. Eliot in Canterbury Cathedral; he read *Rob Roy* as one might read the *Saga of Billy the Kid*.[29] The transition from literature to life could not have been easier than in the Abruzzi mountains where Salvator Rosa loved to sketch amid an earlier generation of banditti, and where under cover of great beech and chestnut forests, semisavage primitivism continued until the very end of the nineteenth century.[30] In short, Berlioz was drawing

[26] By Bohuslav Martinů and Aaron Copland, respectively.

[27] In a useful book on *The Concerto*, it is said – with no awareness of self-stultification: "While Weber, Berlioz, Liszt, and Tschaikowsky protested that their music was intended to make sense as music, they were relieved, nevertheless, to have a program on hand, a set of ordered and unambiguous ideas on which to hang their sense of musical coherence." (*904*, 171.)

[28] "It is a wasted effort, trying to find in *Childe Harold* anything that corresponds to Berlioz' program." (*Sic: 904*, 178.) See also Sir Donald Tovey (*490*), who concludes his analysis of "gloriously nonsensical facts" about the score with two misstatements – one, that Paganini played the viola at its *première;* the other, that Byron's line "there let him lay" is a grammatical solecism: it is good eighteenth-century usage, such as Byron heard in his childhood, and the lesson of Sir Donald's mistimed reproof is that critics should first be tolerable historians.

[29] Rob Roy MacGregor was a distinguished agrarian gangster who "guaranteed the future security of herds against, not his own followers merely, but all freebooters whatever," and who at an advanced age died highly respected by the community. (Sir Walter Scott: *1196*, I, 182 and *1279*, 455.)

[30] George Meredith who was war correspondent to the *Morning Post* in 1866 frequently speaks of brigandage; and forty years later Benedetto Croce lodged

on contemporary art *and* contemporary life regardless of place, costuming, or terminology.

The justification for ascribing the orgy to brigands has a further cause. It was in Berlioz' day a common wish to withdraw from society and join a bandit gang. This expressed the period's immense longing for individual liberties. It is no accident that the first Italian emancipators called themselves *carbonari* and at times actually merged with lawless bands.[31] Here again we meet an ancestral custom of preindustrial society: to join the freebooter was to enact revenge against social injustice, real or fancied – the Robin Hood motif. Shakespeare records it in *Two Gentlemen of Verona,* when Valentine, crossed in love, exclaims:

> This shadowy desert, unfrequented woods
> I better brook than flourishing peopled towns.

Similarly, Molière's *Alceste* vows to leave the city for "the rocks." We thus return, via banditry, to the love of nature as healing the wounds of social man. Berlioz had already given vent to the feeling in one of the extravagant soliloquies of *Lélio,* that which introduces the brigands' song and chorus. In *Harold* he purged himself more thoroughly in an instrumental allegro whose therapeutic value may be greater than we think, the release of violence and vulgarity acting as a needful antidote to the repressions of conventional life.

In any event, flirting with the idea of brigandage hinted of the nascent democracy already undermining the bourgeois monarchy of Louis Philippe. By 1834, the King's green cotton umbrella had figuratively extinguished the first high hopes of the culture-makers. What in England would later be known as the Victorian Compromise was beginning to solidify in France. Moralism invaded daily life; masculine clothes lost their superfluities and grew darker until they reached the uniform "decent black" of the mid-century. With moralism came its twin, literalism: at the new "nautical theater" where Harriet Smithson had hoped to be engaged, the great lure was an actual, positive lake, made of water, on which genuine boats could be seen to float.

The so-called practical intellect was in the ascendant. Among the newly emancipated men of affairs, the men of art were looked at askance and forced into the opposition; when King Louis Philippe's son-in-law

a complaint with the University of Naples because "a brigand" had obtained a doctor's degree from it "by blackmail" – obviously an early form of correspondence course.

[31] Byron's forces in Greece were of course outlaws on two counts. See also *A.R.,* 165 and 168.

tried to gather around him a salon of the best talents in France, his efforts were vetoed by "Papa." In order to survive, genius could only pursue a relentlessly anti-bourgeois policy. In a year when young Gautier was being prosecuted for the boldness of *Mademoiselle de Maupin* and was retorting in a pyrotechnic preface; when Rabelais and Villon were denounced in the public prints as being "in exceedingly bad taste," when Berlioz was attacking the Institute and defending Chopin,[32] he privately cheered himself by reading the newly translated *Memoirs* of Benvenuto Cellini, discovering in this "bandit of genius" a perfect subject for another dramatic parable on genius itself. Being, as artist, dedicated to order; and as creator, to freedom, Berlioz' banditry had to be vicarious and, so to speak, reasoned. But society resists reason, and the Romanticists were to find that they could impose their thought but not their will on a commercial and more than ever massive society.

[32] *1398* (1834) 35–8 and 229–39. The second article, in the form of a tale entitled "A Suicide from Artistic Zeal," was reproduced in the *Soirées*(12th) *Eves.*, 128–45. The story depicts a situation akin to his own during the crisis at Genoa, which tends to confirm its historicity.

Berlioz' *Requiem*, by Fantin-Latour

"Your overwhelming music . . ."
— SPONTINI

10. The Gothic Tradition: Requiem Mass

June 23, 1834 to December 5, 1837

> With all his faults, and with all the irregularity of his drama, one may look upon his works as upon an ancient majestic piece of Gothic architecture, compared with a neat modern building. The latter is more elegant and glaring, but the former is more strong and more solemn.
>
> — POPE on Shakespeare, 1728

THE *Harold* symphony once finished, it had to be played – if only because Berlioz wanted to hear and revise it. He must accordingly give one or more concerts at his own risk in the coming winter season. The preparation went on amid expected chores and fresh difficulties. On August 14, 1834, Harriet Berlioz gave birth, after a painful labor of forty hours, to a son, Louis.[1] A few days later, the Opera-Comique turned down the libretto that Berlioz and Auguste Barbier (the well-known poet met in Italy) had fashioned around the figure of Benvenuto Cellini. Meanwhile, Paganini had found the viola part in Berlioz' new work too slight for him, and Urhan, a classmate of Berlioz' at the Conservatoire and a pious Beethovenian, was entrusted with it.

As Harriet slowly recovered, Berlioz breathed easier – on two counts: relief about Harriet and the fact that his family relented, sending congratulations and gifts. Possessed of strong family feeling, the young husband felt as if reunited after a gnawing separation. By further good fortune, the *Journal des Débats,* seeking a new music critic, tried out Berlioz on its readers by reprinting one of his *feuilletons.*[2] Early in November a first concert, still lacking the symphony, brought forth two new choral works – both slight but charming idylls – that Berlioz had somehow found the tranquillity to compose: *La Belle Voyageuse* and *Sara la Baigneuse.* Even this modest program had cost much effort. For a musician without power

[1] Within a month, Berlioz wrote to his sister: "Do not worry; the boy is baptized. He is not named Hercules, John-Baptist, Caesar, Alexander, or Martial [Magloire] but quite simply Louis." *A.R.*, 267.

[2] *1386*, Oct. 10, 1834.

in the regular theaters "nothing is scarcer than passable singers. I cannot find any for my concerts, and twice I have had to postpone a trio to which I attach some importance, for lack of a moderately decent bass. The managers refuse to lend their people." [3]

On the twenty-second, Harriet made her debut at the Théâtre Nautique in an appalling pantomime entitled "The Last Hour of the Condemned." She acted well enough but the piece failed, together with the manager. The theater shut its doors without paying its debts. But the next day, *Harold in Italy* was played with resounding success before a picked audience. Fashion, journalism, and art were represented by Jules Janin, Liszt, d'Ortigue, Heine, Eugène Sue, Legouvé, Barbier, Léon de Wailly, Victor Hugo, Gounet, Sainte-Beuve, Lesueur, Chopin, the brothers Deschamps, Vigny, Gérard de Nerval, Dumas, plus the publishers and patrons of art, Schlesinger and Renduel. Berlioz' prediction came true: the second movement (Pilgrims' March) was wildly applauded and called for twice, but Girard mixed up his cues and ruined the encore. From this moment Berlioz determined to master the art of conducting and lead his own works.

A second performance three weeks later, with Chopin playing one movement of his new concerto in F Minor, brought little into the box office, but the third performance on December 28 netted Berlioz two thousand francs. The toil, the excitement, and the indecisiveness of such artistic victories left Berlioz exhausted. To his previous obligations and the expenses for the newborn child, he found he must add the cost of moving the family back within city limits; his goings and comings were otherwise too tiring. So the year 1835 opened in an atmosphere of worry and strain. He cautioned d'Ortigue: "Please don't stress in your articles my position in regard to money. It's useless to dwell on it." The band of Berlioz' admirers was bent on rousing the nineteenth-century goddess Public Opinion so as to "force the doors of the Opera." They wanted a great public success not only for him but for the satisfaction of their faith. Berlioz must naturally live up to the view they entertained of him as a potential master in the opera, and on the strength of the esteem shown him by the brothers Bertin and the staff of the *Débats,* Berlioz made new overtures to Dr. Véron. Perhaps a revision of the Cellini libretto into a grand opera might suit. Nothing came of it. Instead, for its customary New Year's masked ball, the Opera produced on January 10 a skit parodying Berlioz and his friends.

[3] *A.R.,* 272. The trio was undoubtedly the first piece completed of the *Benvenuto Cellini* score.

It was a sign of celebrity and the parody (greatly enjoyed by the audience) testified to the impact made by the composer's works and ideas upon the public. Berlioz' colleague and rather envious rival, Adolphe Adam, had had a hand in the skit, and the actor Arnal – who later apologized very contritely – played the speaking role. This aped both Berlioz and his projection of himself, Lélio.[4] The mimic told his audience: "You will hear a grand Symphony . . . 'An Episode in a Gambler's Life.' To make my dramatic thoughts understood I have no need of words, singers, or scenery. All this, gentlemen, is in my orchestra. You will hear my hero speak. You will see him portrayed from head to foot, and at the second reprise of the first allegro, I will show you how he puts on his necktie. Ah, the wonders of instrumental music!"[5]

Berlioz was present and laughed good-naturedly. "I sincerely hope," he wrote, "that before next year I can write and perform another *similar* composition to add to the gaiety of the Opera's buffooneries."[6] A touch of bitterness may be supposed to enter here, for on second thoughts, what would be the effect on the unthinking public of the ridicule heaped upon a new and serious esthetic creed – that of drama through music alone? And was it not a bitter thought in itself that the Opera should be

[4] The name Lélio, assigned in place of "the artist" who first figured in his melologue, was explicitly given in the revision of the score in 1855, but it probably dates from 1832 or 1833, for we find the association of ideas mentioned by d'Ortigue in these years (*185*, 304), and much of what he says can only have come from Berlioz himself. D'Ortigue compares "the artist's" feeling for his beloved to "the singular passion of the Marquise of R . . . for the actor Lélio which has lately been recounted with so much skill by a gifted writer . . ." The writer was George Sand, whose tale *La Marquise* describes her artist-hero as a transcendent genius who was grudgingly admired by everyone but the loving Marquise. "He never achieved reputation, whether at court or in the city . . . But later on, his fiery genius and artistic striving were taken into account. . . . In art he was not a man of his century." (*1278*, 196.)

It may incidentally be noted that a common source for the name Lélio in Berlioz and George Sand may have been Hoffmann's tale of "The Empty House" (*Nachtstücke*, II, 1817) in which the especially intuitive character is so named. A French scholar of our century insists that "This name Lélio . . . was probably borrowed by Berlioz from George Sand's *Lélia* and turned into a masculine. . . . It seems to us unquestionable that Berlioz read the novel and drew from it this name Lélio, so well adapted to his symphony." (*298*, 129 *n.*) The trouble with this notion is that the novel *Lélia* came out nearly a year after d'Ortigue's remark establishing the parallel with the earlier tale, *La Marquise*. It was George Sand who borrowed the name from her own work and turned it into a feminine. There is moreover no parallel between the heroine of the novel and Berlioz' artist.

[5] *268*, 288.

[6] *1398*, Jan. 17, 1835.

so easy of access for "buffoons" and so tightly shut against serious composers?

What Berlioz and his friends did not take into account was that to ingratiate himself with the Opera management he would have had to be not merely a different kind of artist but a different kind of man. Under Véron, the house was more than ever a fashionable resort for those bent on self-indulgence: part night club, part house of assignation.[7] The pageantry which Meyerbeer knew how to provide, and which he reinforced with substantial favors and flattery, made that composer *persona grata* on the business side, while setting at rest the susceptibilities of the lubricious Doctor and his ostentatious protégé Loève-Veimars.[8] A man of aristocratic reserve and probity like Berlioz was on the contrary a living reproach to their ways and outlook on life. He was, to be sure, courteously treated by Véron, who would even "lend" him Mademoiselle Falcon for a concert appearance, but he would have been more popular with that crowd had he wished to borrow a ballerina for another purpose.

The Duke of Orleans, with his flair for men of artistic integrity, aided the Bertins to decide on retaining Berlioz for the *Débats*. The latter began his well-paid duties on January 25, 1835, and left the paper only on his resignation twenty-eight years later. Were it not for debts and concerts, his financial situation was now assured.[9] But the expense of furnishing his apartment in town, and providing servants for Harriet and the baby, was aggravated by her want of management and kept him financially harassed. In his student days he had acquired the habit of keeping accounts, preferring to live within his means. His debts then were only for musical purposes – playing or publishing his works – and he could feel personally solvent while using credit as a capital investment in his career. Now the steadily increasing arrears added to the strain of journalism and *non*-composition. Though he complained merely of excess of work, Hector's letters to Ferrand and Adèle show that his mind spent itself in writing several reviews a month for each of three papers, expanding earlier articles

[7] *1142*, 29 and 49 ff.

[8] François-Adolphe Loève-Veimars (1801–54), of mixed French and German parentage, was one of the translators of Hoffmann as well as the author of the history of the *Vehmgericht* on which Berlioz had based his first opera, *Les Francs-Juges*. (*1196a* and *1264*.)

[9] Boschot computes that for the year 1835 at least, by combining work on two newspapers with the remainder of the government stipend, Berlioz must have had an income of 7000 francs. This would probably equal 7000 *dollars* today [1948], free of any but poll taxes.

for serial republication, and keeping in touch with the authorities in hopes of some musical commission — state festival or grand opera.[10]

Family life, it is true, had its rewards. He was passionately devoted to his wife and child. "Our little boy," he confided to Adèle, "continues charming; you have no idea how beautiful he is. He never cries but laughs aloud as soon as one is willing to play with him. Harriet grows prouder of him every day. . . . Incidentally, you miscalculated the size of the kid's head: your bonnet just fits, but a little more width wouldn't have hurt." Then in the margin: "*Important note:* it's not the bonnet, it's the tape that isn't long enough. You are vindicated and I am an ignoramus." [11]

Being concert critic for the most influential newspaper in Paris, Berlioz could choose what to review, which usually meant the programs of the Société des Concerts du Conservatoire. This gave him the chance to expound the principles of modern instrumental music to a wider public. The fifteen to twenty thousand subscribers of the *Journal des Débats* were treated to a virtual course, an orthodoxy, in the principles of Gluck, Weber, and Beethoven.[12] Berlioz repeatedly analyzed the nine symphonies, which he regarded as the fountainhead of the expressive genre. It was his own stake in creation that Berlioz was one-sidedly defending, sometimes at the expense of the eighteenth-century masters — just as Shaw later defended Ibsen at the expense of Shakespeare. The Parisians, then brought up on the early works of Haydn and Mozart, were still one step behind: they could not even keep *Don Giovanni* in the operatic repertoire. Berlioz' defense of that score shows perhaps the exact line separating the eighteenth from the nineteenth century in music, as well as that marking off the public taste of 1835 from "modern" art.[13] What the paying public meant by dramatic music was opera, and opera meant

[10] Jan. to Dec. 1835: *A.R.*, 275–302; *L.I.*, 156–68. One of the periodicals for which Berlioz wrote at this time was Gérard de Nerval's new *Monde Dramatique* (1835–7). Berlioz contributed four articles the first year.

[11] *A.R.*, 276–7.

[12] The music reviews of those days were sizable affairs, six to nine columns long, of a format resembling that of the London *Times*.

[13] *L.I.*, 162. By all accounts the classics were performed in an exceedingly dull manner and with a poorly balanced orchestra. (On this point read Berlioz himself: *L.I.*, 142.) At the Opera, Mozart was ruined by frigidity and other forms of bad musicianship, due to the idea that his music was wholly "formal" and "elegant." It is only within the memory of the present generation that his passionate and tragic grandeur has been recognized in performance; and yet a New York critic had to say in 1945: "Although Mozart's *Magic Flute* is one of the greatest of German operas, the performance granted it yesterday afternoon at the Metropolitan made a dull affair of it." (Noel Straus, *N.Y. Times*, Dec. 2, 1945.)

Rossini, Adam, Auber, and Meyerbeer. Beethoven was still caviar, except to a small band of intellectuals.[14]

A curious record of Berlioz' impact on one avid reader is found in Balzac's short story "Gambara." Written in all probability between January and June 1837, it could not carry so much musical freight unless written by a man quite conversant with Berlioz' life and mind. For example, almost the first reference to music alludes to "the stupendous requiem" of the fictional composer: Berlioz was completing his own just as Balzac wrote these words. The novelist then ascribes some advanced artistic doctrine to the two main characters – Gambara the composer and his quasi-patron, the Count. The latter's harangue on Beethoven and against the Italians is pure Berlioz; Gambara's description of his new opera – a sequel to one that failed – expounds the leitmotif, the new flexible melody patterned on "the voices of nature," the philosophy of tone color, and the joining of symphonic and vocal resources in musical drama.[15] Finally, the discussion of Meyerbeer's *Robert le Diable* echoes or parallels the feeling of Berlioz about eclecticism, which no other critic yet shared. The tale ends tragically, with the last word given to an aristocrat in praise of the artist "faithful to the ideal which *we* have killed."

This view of the social forces shaping the artist's fate had in turn been dramatized a little earlier by another member of the vanguard, Alfred de Vigny, in his play *Chatterton.* As he sent off the work to press, he defined in a preface the situation of the nineteenth-century artist. His words are as it were a transcript of the conversations held at Berlioz' Montmartre cottage or elsewhere, in which Vigny, Liszt, Chopin, d'Ortigue, Gautier, Balzac, Deschamps and others would agree that the "cause" for which they strove was to secure for art a recognized status and function. "That is the question," wrote Vigny, "the perpetual martyrdom and immolation of the poet. Our concern is the right he is entitled to, of staying alive . . . the bread that is denied him, the suicide he is compelled to commit." [16]

[14] There was the usual diversity of temperamental likes and dislikes even among the artist group. As late as the 1850's, Delacroix, who adored Mozart and Chopin, thought Beethoven lengthy and too violent. (*182*, III, 16 and 449.)

[15] It is conceivable that the "program" of the imaginary opera was worked out with Berlioz' help in a spirit of comic hoaxing, for Balzac's tale is partly satirical. But we may be sure that the subject of the opera – Mohammed – was not Berlioz' choice, for he thought religious fanaticism and politics unsuited to music. Moreover Berlioz alluded later on to Balzac's pitiable attempts at technical analysis in this very story. (*Grot.*, 19.)

[16] *Chatterton*, Preface, 1 (written June 1834). In parallel see Liszt's essay on "The Condition of the Artist and his Place in Society," which appeared in the

So far the complaint is familiar, though Vigny was above the need to make it on his own behalf. The unusual part is the description of what results from a general neglect of art:

> Three kinds of men, who must not be mistaken one for the other, act on society through the workings of their minds . . . The man with an aptitude for savoir faire, and who is therefore much valued, is everywhere to be seen. Void of real emotions, he writes of business as if it were literature and of literature as if it were business . . . He is a Man of Letters. Above him is a man of stronger and finer nature. His genius consists of attention brought to its highest pitch. He seeks especially order and clarity, having always in his eye the people whom he addresses. He is the true Great Writer. He is fought, but with courteous weapons. He needs no compassion.
>
> But there is another kind of being, more passionate, purer and rarer. He who belongs to that kind is incompetent for whatever is not the work of divinity. Emotion with him is so deep, so intimate that it has plunged him from childhood in involuntary ecstasies, in endless reveries, in infinite discoveries. Imagination possesses him exclusively. His powerful soul judges and retains everything with a sure instinct and a strong memory. Disgust, vexations and the resistance of human society throw him into deep depression and black indignation. Still, on the day when he bursts forth one would say that he observes as a stranger what takes place within him. He should do nothing useful or workaday so that he may have the time to listen to the chords slowing shaping in his soul. He is the Poet. . . .
>
> It is in his first youth that he feels his strength and foresees the future of his genius, that with love he embraces life and nature, that he arouses mistrust and suffers rebuff. He cries to the people: "It is to you that I speak" and the multitude answer justly enough: "We do not understand." He cries to the state: "Heed me and help me live." But the state replies that it is set up to protect positive interests. "Of what use are you?" Everybody against him is in the right. Is he then in the wrong? What can he do?
>
> If he has bodily strength, he can become a soldier . . . Physical activity will deaden the spiritual. He can become a Man of Letters or even a Great Writer . . . Judgment will kill Imagination . . . but in any case he will kill a part of himself . . . as Chatterton killed himself altogether.[17]

Though the language is strained, the psychological and sociological report is accurate; and though the biography of Chatterton may not sup-

---

Gazette Musicale from May 3 to Oct. 11, 1835. (Reprinted in *210*, 1–83.) Some of Liszt's ideas reflect his earlier attachment to the socialism of Saint-Simon and the more recent religious liberalism of Lamennais and d'Ortigue, but the main arguments are those independently found in Balzac, Vigny and Berlioz.

[17] *1283*, 2–7 (condensed and reparagraphed).

port Vigny's case, the interpretation will still serve to explain what happens to our Van Goghs and Hart Cranes, as well as to understand what stronger natures—like Vigny and Berlioz—felt they were up against. Vigny's bitterness was partly congenital, but in this document it fits a contemporary mood. The observant now knew that the honeymoon between Liberty and the Orleans regime was over. This was the trough of the first wave of disillusion after the liberal revolution. The buoyant and irresistible Hugo himself underwent a period of black depression; he spoke of Darkness advancing, and entitled the poems of this period *Chants du Crépuscule* (Songs at Twilight).

Meanwhile social critics brooded upon the seemingly unquenchable unrest. The merciless shooting of strikers at Lyon in April 1834 was the bloodiest yet of Louis Philippe's efforts to establish himself.[18] Repression was failing, and its opposite no one dared conceive. In a word, 1830 had not closed the era of revolutions, and by 1835 it was evident that the compromise had created no order: from the culture-makers to the textile workers every interest must not merely plead but fight for the recognition of what seemed to each its elementary rights.

For Berlioz, we gather from a note, the *première* of Vigny's play on February 12, 1835 was a doubly poignant spectacle: "My wife did for a moment think of accepting your gracious offer [of a box] but all things considered, the thought of the eclipse in which her talents stand for the time being is too painful to permit her to attend a notable occasion such as that to which you have kindly invited us. I shall therefore go alone to applaud *Chatterton* with all the warmth of affection and enthusiasm which I feel for its author, and for the cause he pleads so well." [19] On her side Harriet, who had become passionately devoted to her husband, was full of self-reproach at seeing him carrying his heavy burden alone. She, who had supported her whole family since her adolescence, was now helpless. She wanted to act again, but her imperfect knowledge of French prevented. Hugo was approached for a play in which this drawback could fit, but all the plots involving mutes and foreigners seemed to have been used up. He none the less promised to try.[20]

[18] Apropos of the riots which had recurred in this industrial center since 1832, Berlioz had written that "the only difference between the fighting there and in Paris is that between a greater and a lesser power . . . Lyon cannot withstand Paris, and is therefore wrong to rouse it to anger." (*L.I.*, 108.) The outbreak of 1834, he called a "wasteful mess" [*gâchis*]. (*L.I.*, 143.)

[19] *A.R.*, 278.

[20] *A.R.*, 281.

Not stopping to consider whether he was a musical Poet or merely a Great Artist, Berlioz had begun composing *Benvenuto Cellini.* Obviously, he still believed in the power of example and the force of integrity. If the Opera would once let him in, he could make its frivolous, overfed, finical and convention-ridden habitués swallow serious music. "I may have to compose for a few years more outside the theatre before I can step on the neck of these stupid manufacturers . . . What wretchedness to see the best years of my life lost for dramatic music simply because three rascals have the misfortune of being idiots as well. Véron, for example, whom Meyerbeer had to compel by law to produce *Robert le Diable* and thus to make his fortune in spite of himself, has since then staged only platitudes of which *La Juive* is the culmination . . . Patience is in order. Everything will come in its time." [21] Ideas for scores kept bubbling up, although Berlioz' conception of dramatic music, which required the musical personnel of the Opera, actually went beyond stage work. As he had written to Ferrand when *Benvenuto* first came into being, he was dreaming of other and greater things than operas: "Music has wings that the walls of a theatre will not allow to unfold." [22] Dramatic music was a generic term under which opera was but a subclass, so in January 1835 he writes again: "If I had time, I would be making progress on the work I am mulling over . . ." – a symphony – "on a new and enlarged plan." [23]

Outwardly Berlioz seemed to prosper. In April, Liszt played a *Fantasia on two themes by Berlioz* ("The Fisherman" and "Brigand's Song" from *Lélio*), and added to the pianistic program "The Pilgrims' March" from *Harold in Italy*. The press hailed the "Paganini of the piano," and Berlioz, writing very discreetly of his own share in the concert, was happy to declare that "our views on music, [Liszt's] and mine, are exactly the same . . ." that is to say in accord "with the exigencies of the times." [24]

The next month, Berlioz gave another concert, consisting of the *Fantastique* and *Lélio*, no doubt as a reply to the New Year parody. Though the box-office receipts were fair and the royal family were present, Berlioz regretted the "detestable performance": for economy's sake, he had scheduled only one rehearsal. Moreover, on that bright day of May the fountains of Versailles were also playing, which somewhat

[21] *A.R.*, 282–3. Véron had put on *Don Giovanni* and Spontini's *La Vestale*, both of which had failed. He therefore sought works which would be sure to entertain.

[22] *L.I.*, 153.

[23] *L.I.*, 159 and 172.

[24] *1386*, Apr. 25, 1835.

reduced attendance at the concert. Shortly thereafter, on May 28, 1835, the Gymnase Musical opened its doors and offered Berlioz another chance to draw the crowd. Unfortunately its musical resources were feeble, and when the Berlioz program took place on June 4 (the *King Lear* overture, *Harold in Italy*, and songs by Gluck and Berlioz), the playing and acoustics were a disgrace. To indemnify Berlioz the management weeded out the poorest performers and a second concert was announced. But the fact that it was to take place at night put it under the jurisdiction of the prefect of police.[25] This official, acting from political prudence and also to safeguard the monopoly of the Opera-Comique, forbade singing. So the program was whittled down to overtures and solos on violin and piano – no vocal numbers "which the public must have." Berlioz wondered how a motet by Palestrina would "compete" with the ariettas enjoyed by "our clever French" at the Opera-Comique. But a rule was a rule, especially when politics and money interests backed it against a mere artist.

The summer did not see the writing of the projected third symphony. There was little time and less tranquillity. The plan nevertheless haunted Berlioz. First conceived in Italy, this Heroic and Funeral Symphony would celebrate the great men of France (in contrast, one supposes, with the "clever French") and it would consist of seven movements. Popular in character, like the finale of Beethoven's Ninth, it would be scored for a large body of players and singers, like the festivals of the revolution. The idea did not die; its elements found a place in several later works, notably the *Te Deum*, *Les Troyens*, and especially the *Funeral and Triumphal* symphony of 1840.[26]

Meantime, with an obsessed spirit bent on not giving up its obsession, Berlioz finished the setting of Béranger's mediocre Ode on the Death of Napoleon, "The Fifth of May."[27] Berlioz' score is not a great work, though genius and craft are visible on every page. The something lacking might be called by a scientific metaphor the "heat of fusion of art," and its absence suggests that in classifying the works of any artist we should perhaps distinguish three kinds – the successes, the failures and the *characteristic* failures. That is, we find in Berlioz: good Berlioz, bad Berlioz, and bad *music;* just as there is good Beethoven, bad Beethoven and bad

[25] Symphonic concerts began usually at 2 P.M.

[26] Criticizing the critics, M. Henri Peyre says: "Berlioz might have created more works like his Symphonie Funèbre et Triomphale if he had not been forced to fight jealousy and inertia." (*1111*, 143.)

[27] The score was in due course dedicated to Horace Vernet, the Bonapartist painter and kindly patron of Roman days.

music which happens to have been written by Beethoven. Only from the first two categories can one learn anything about the spontaneous intentions that fail or succeed in an artist's mind. From the evidence of *Le Cinq Mai,* Berlioz' technique at thirty-two had reached the fullness of a "second manner," but the inner fire was temporarily banked, smothered under too much irrelevant work. Those who have been hacks as well as conscious craftsmen will here salute a brother in sorrow.

Berlioz' next preoccupation had to do with influencing the choice of a new director of the Opera. For after five years of prevailing success Véron judged that his luck could not last and withdrew before it was too late. The Bertin brothers, the politicians, and Berlioz' friends now engaged in the usual intrigues and parleys. Véron wanted his friend Loève-Veimars, to succeed him. His scheme failed, and the unedifying architect Duponchel, who was already in league with Meyerbeer and who had dabbled in several trades, was chosen as a compromise candidate.[28] He would be committed to the *Débats* party, which meant his accepting not only the works of Berlioz, but also those of Mlle. Louise Bertin (the crippled sister of Edouard), whose moderately successful *Faust* gave color to her pretensions as a composer.[29] For his disappointed hopes and wounded feelings, Loève-Veimars received 100,000 francs, besides the Legion of Honor, a baronetcy, and a mission to Russia: in Vigny's classification he should rank as the Man of Letters par excellence.

All was settled when, on the anniversary of the July Days, as the King was reviewing troops, a barrage laid down by one Fieschi felled forty persons. Louis-Philippe miraculously escaped, but Duponchel's appointment was delayed a month. This enabled him to shift alliances and once in office he tried to repudiate his campaign pledges. Further battle led to an agreement that Mlle. Bertin's *Esmeralda* (based on Victor Hugo's own adaptation of *Notre Dame*) [30] would be accepted and that *Benvenuto Cellini* would be "submitted to a committee." Matters stood thus by the fall of 1835. To keep public interest in him alive, Berlioz gave a concert on November 22, in which he presented *Le Cinq Mai* together with a

[28] Charles-Edmond Duponchel (1795?–1863), whom Berlioz was later to satirize as "the celebrated inventor of the canopy, the man who introduced the canopy into opera as the chief ingredient of success; the author of the canopy in *La Juive*, *La Reine de Chypre*, and *Le Prophète*, the creator of the floating canopy, the wondrous canopy, the canopy of canopies." (*Soirées*, 4th.)

[29] On her work and career, see 787.

[30] Hugo wrote several poems of friendship which are inscribed to her in *Les Voix Intérieures* and *Les Rayons et les Ombres*.

song by Meyerbeer – the great power behind the scenes. At a second concert on December 13, Berlioz conducted, not indeed for the first time, but for the first time by deliberate preference: he was adding a weapon to his armory of defenses.

Throughout this period Berlioz could hardly feel that his family, immediate or remote, was giving him much comfort. Since their son's birth, Harriet had insensibly grown restless, vaguely resentful, unhappy at the ending of her career. It was slight comfort, or none at all, to read in the papers that Hector's former fiancée, Camille Moke, had just been repudiated by her husband Pleyel, on grounds of repeated adultery and disorderly conduct. As for Berlioz' relations with La Côte, carried on mainly through Adèle, one senses that the father and mother were again waiting for their son to make a success that they could understand – after the Rome Prize, an opera at the Opera. They had recognized their daughter-in-law and sent gifts for the baby, but they had not supplied what every young couple needs – money. When Adèle, with kind intent, tried to explain the local "prejudices that time would efface" Hector had had to keep the letter from his wife to forestall one of her long bouts of weeping. The elder sister Nanci and her husband were still holding aloof, Berlioz ironically sending his compliments through Adèle to "Their Royal Highnesses." At the same time he was worried about his father's health, about which he was not given enough news. His own constitution was just then suffering from the strain he put upon it. Nervous tension brought on sore throats and headaches. He felt that he wanted to sleep, sleep long restorative hours, as in youth, when he had passed a crisis or a concert; now the very need made for insomnia.

The beginning of 1836 brought reconciliation with Nanci, one word from her being enough to elicit from Hector a quick and warm response. But the New Year also brought the news that the Ministry had canceled Duponchel's private agreement, and that Berlioz' opera was as uncommissioned as on the first day of negotiations. The composer determined to finish it nevertheless. He was in love with the subject and his inner mind worked at it regardless of his will. Besides, the chatter of the press over the whole affair had led someone to announce another "Benvenuto" for one of the lesser theaters. To keep his priority Berlioz made a counter-announcement that he was "just completing the score." This exaggeration (psychological warfare) was soon dangerously tested by the merger of *Le Rénovateur* with another periodical. This cut into Berlioz' income and all other posts being occupied, his situation was extremely difficult. If he tried to make up his loss by free-lance writing, what would happen to the score of *Benvenuto?* In this quandary Berlioz applied to his friend Legouvé who readily advanced two thousand francs.[31]

Meantime Berlioz had a debt of another kind to pay. Mlle. Bertin's *Esmeralda* needed revising and it was as natural that she should apply to him as that he should show his gratitude to her family by giving help. Being half-paralyzed from birth, she also needed a trusted deputy to run the errands incidental to rehearsing an opera in manuscript. Berlioz was this deputy and three quarters of each day for more than a month went into *La Esmeralda* – as many hours taken away from *Benvenuto*. Nevertheless, by sheer application, the writing of his own score was progressing: "I have done about half. It's a long job to write out, but I must say that compared with the problems of symphonic composition it's relatively easy." [32]

The success of *La Esmeralda* would have been of considerable indirect advantage to Berlioz: it could not seriously compete with his work, it would have set a perceptible value on his help – for this fact was generally known – and it would have further heightened the prestige of the Bertin family or at least neutralized the opposition. As it was, the opera reached the stage on November 14 and was hissed off it without reprieve. During the rehearsals Berlioz had written to his sister: "There are charming choruses which rumor does me the honor of attributing to me, though I have had no hand in them. Unfortunately, the single roles are by no means so good, not by a long shot, and the actors make some awful faces." [33]

At the first performance, political feeling burst in a rhythmic chant of "Down with the Bertins, down with the *Débats!*" and the curtain had to be lowered to enable the actors to regain composure. When Quasimodo's aria on the bells of Notre Dame rang out and won applause, Alexandre Dumas, who disliked the Bertins, shouted in his stevedore's voice: "That's Berlioz . . . that's Berlioz!" It was not by Berlioz: "If I had anything to do with its success," he wrote to Adèle, "it's in a trifling way. The air is really by Mlle. Bertin, but (between ourselves) it ended lamely. . . . My help was limited to suggesting a peroration more worthy of the exordium. That's all. . . . As for my own opera, here is how it stands. I have finished it. I have only to write out the denouement and orchestrate the score. According to my arrangement with Duponchel, I am fourth on the list . . . They are now putting on Niedermeyer's *Stradella* . . . Then

[31] It is worth recalling here how Loève-Veimars "earned" his 100,000.
[32] *A.R.*, 314.
[33] *A.R.*, 314.

I should go on next, if nothing else is ready; but Halévy . . . is straining every nerve and writing his new score at a gallop so as not to lose his turn . . . Anyhow, I'm ready to go into rehearsal, and I'd have been ready with all the music long before if, like my hero Cellini, I had had *the metal* with which to cast my statue." [34]

Just lately, "metal" had not been wanting. Besides Legouvé's loan of two thousand francs, Berlioz had received increased honorariums from the Bertins – a tactful acknowledgment of his services to Mlle. Louise – and he had had the pleasant surprise of a gift from his father. He was deeply moved: "I am afraid my excellent father inconvenienced himself to send me this sum, which I was far from expecting, and this thought bothers me more than I can say. Kiss him and Mamma for me." [35]

Moreover, in a cabinet reorganization of September 1836, a new Minister of Fine Arts had taken office whose influence was altogether favorable to Berlioz. Devotees of music should keep a place in their memory for the Comte de Gasparin, who besides becoming Minister became the efficient cause of Berlioz' great *Requiem*. The political basis of this double merit is again quite clear: M. de Gasparin had been prefect in Berlioz' county and doubtless knew the excellent standing of the composer's family. In addition, Gasparin's son acted as his private secretary and had a close friend in common with Berlioz. Politically allied with the *Débats* and personally interested in music, the count was an ideal patron for one in Berlioz' position. His utility was shortly to be seen.

Berlioz' reputation was in fact just on the point of passing from a fighting opinion to an accepted truth.[36] Throughout 1836 he received requests from abroad for copies of his scores – Vienna, Milan, and New Orleans wanted to play him; Schumann had him performed in Leipzig. Local societies at Douai and Dijon gave him a try – all, of course, without royalties. The idea of a trip to the United States even crossed Berlioz' mind, for the artistic exodus in search of American dollars had begun, and the new world seemed to offer opportunities for Harriet's comeback. "All the English actors fly to America. Politics, Puritanism [*Méthodisme*], and the senility of our civilization have killed the

[34] *A.R.*, 323–4. The allusion is to the last scene of the opera, in which Benvenuto runs short of metal in the casting of his masterpiece, the bronze Perseus.

[35] *A.R.*, 312.

[36] George Sand had dubbed him a "Promethean genius" in the musically conservative *Revue des Deux Mondes*. (June 15, 1835, 723; and later, Nov. 15, 1836, 462. *1188*, II, 33 and *passim*.) An amateur herself, she sometimes sang Berlioz' songs and spoke admiringly of his energy and pride.

drama." [37] London, too, had tried Berlioz, but the performers had been unable to get through a rehearsal of the *Francs-Juges*. That same overture had been "arranged" for piano in Germany and published as wholly his own work, but it was so "monstrously mutilated" that Berlioz wrote a protest and decided never to let copies out of his hands nor to sanction any performances until he had gone to Germany and established his tradition in person.[38]

This resolve shows to what extent music was still considered in 1836 a commodity to be sliced and sold at will. Copyright did not protect the author, only the publisher, and musical customs outside a few centers – as Berlioz' long letter of thanks to Schumann shows – were extremely primitive. On a similar occasion, he summed up the state of things: "Music . . . is now flooding in everywhere; but it is like the fury of a child, who lunges at everything that shines, without any idea of its use." [39] In six or seven years, he thought, there might be a public in France for serious instrumental music. This was too sanguine. Had there been such a public, Berlioz would certainly have been its singlehanded creator, for even when his friends showed their enthusiasm for his works, they always thought of him as a champion who would be crowned by acceptance at the Opera. The post-Beethovenian symphony did not exist.[40] "It is at the theatre," exclaimed d'Ortigue, "that we must give Berlioz a rendez-vous." Liszt publicly railed at the Opera directors for excluding Berlioz.[41] And the circumspect Guéroult in *Le Temps* in reproaching officialdom made the same assumption: "No one gives promise of a more brilliant future than Berlioz. It would be at once cruel and ridiculous to affect any further hesitation about him." [42]

The seal of celebrity was put on him by Dantan the younger – the Max Beerbohm of the period – whose series of caricatured busts formed a representative hall of fame: Paganini, Balzac, Victor Hugo, Alexandre

[37] *A.R.*, 290. By "Puritanism" Berlioz means the moralistic tone, later known as Victorian, which was gaining ground even before the Queen's accession, and gripping the Continent as well as England.

[38] *13*. Berlioz' protest is in *Corresp.* 113. "I am threatened also," he tells Liszt, "with an arrangement for four hands of my first symphony, to be done from your piano version." (*A.R.*, 310.) With Chopin's help, Berlioz had just done the piano version of the *Francs-Juges* for four hands.

[39] This partly explains the diehards' resistance. They stood up for the Italians' vocal style and were still fighting Weber as overloaded with instruments. (*1397*, Jan.–Feb. 1836, *678* ff.)

[40] Neither Liszt nor Schumann was yet planning symphonic works. Schubert was dead, and Wagner only twenty-three years old.

[41] *210*, *26* ff.

[42] *300*, 94.

Dumas, Adolphe Adam, and Berlioz among the moderns were adjoined to Horace Vernet and others of the older generation. Reproduced in lithograph, Berlioz with his mop of hair was described as a "musical O'Connell," [43] a pioneer who would reform and galvanize French opera. But Duponchel, with his haughty manners and his monocle, was still dissembling about *Benvenuto Cellini*, for operas are a heavy investment, and like all managerial powers he could form no judgment of his own. "He fancies he likes my music, though he knows as much about it as did M. Véron." [44] Still, in October 1836, he had given Berlioz a written understanding.

Since August Berlioz had been editing the *Gazette Musicale* as temporary substitute.[45] Two concerts, one with Urhan, the other with Liszt, both directed by Berlioz, closed a busy year. Besides his Fantasia on themes by Berlioz, Liszt played his own transcription of the Waltz and the March from the *Symphonie Fantastique:* the effect was extraordinary, pyrotechnic. No one could approach such dexterity and force, and the lady who later complained that it was a shame to put such a fine-looking man at a keyboard would have been answered.[46] As for Berlioz' conducting, it gave him increasing satisfaction: "Apropos of artistic success, I have never had one to equal it, by reason of the superior performance due to my conducting the orchestra." [47] The net return of the two concerts was sixteen hundred francs.

During December also, Harriet Smithson appeared on the boards for the last time. She gave her Ophelia scene, in the midst of a benefit for the great comedian, Frédérick Lemaitre, and the conjunction of genres was disastrous. No one wanted to see the mad scene sandwiched in between farcical skits. Berlioz' friend and colleague Janin counseled her, for Shakespeare's sake, not to appear in anything but a full-length play enabling her to create a distinct atmosphere.

The turn of the New Year was marked by three important events: Niedermeyer's opera failed, *Benvenuto Cellini* was officially announced, and the new Minister of Fine Arts definitely commissioned from Berlioz a Requiem Mass. The intention was to celebrate on its seventh anni-

[43] The Irish revolutionist.

[44] *A.R.*, 292.

[45] Berlioz' editorship lasted from August 1836 to May 1837. (*A.R.*, 318 and 340.) The previous year, seeing him at work, Liszt had described Berlioz in print as a "tireless athlete." (*1398*, July 26, 1835.)

[46] Lady Blessington in 1840 (*203*, 433).

[47] *A.R.*, 321. "The tempi used to be invariably wrong." (*A.R.*, 305.)

versary the death of the heroes of July 28, 1830. This project was of course hedged in by bureaucratic rules: the commission must go to a prize winner of the Institute who had not yet written for the official theaters. Could Berlioz, with his *Benvenuto Cellini* accepted but not staged, be considered eligible? Such a plum could not be handed to anyone without a struggle, several struggles, part of the great struggle for power. The Minister must wrangle for an appropriation, underlings must assert their authority, rival composers must fight for their prestige. Cherubini held office and must be reckoned with. He disliked Berlioz intensely though with less cause than Berlioz had to dislike him in return;[48] and more important, Cherubini had a new *Requiem* of his own just asking to be played. Delaying tactics would be to everyone's interest except Berlioz', for Ministries fall, and in statecraft delay is always the simplest thing to achieve. The comings and goings of all the actors in this veritable Florentine history form an inextricable melee, in which certitude as to the order of events is illusory. What seems clear is that by the end of March 1837, Berlioz had in his pocket the signed ministerial decree. The sum allotted was fourteen thousand francs and the time a little over three months.

In accepting these terms Berlioz was taking a great risk – his position was exactly that of Michelangelo when forced by his enemies to undertake the Sistine Ceiling – but his was a philosophy of risk and unlike Michelangelo, Berlioz had in fact long been preparing for precisely this chance. From his Mass of 1825 he had saved and worked over the *Resurrexit;* in Italy, under the impact of Saint Peter's, he had gathered ideas for a Judgment Day oratorio; more recently, the ceremonies for the victims of Fieschi's attempt on the King's life had reawakened these same thoughts and had inwardly advanced the project of a Funeral Symphony. For the great crowd scene of the *Cellini* opera he had adapted another section from his early mass. Although all but one of these ideas were pre-empted and therefore useless for the *Requiem*, they had a spiritual kinship which was a stimulant. He felt in the mood for "architectural" constructions and mass effects.

So much so that when the signed commission came Berlioz felt no qualms. The sublimity of the subject intoxicated him. "At first my brains boiled over," he writes to Adèle,[49] "I was dizzy. Today the eruption has been regulated. The lava has made its bed and God willing everything

[48] Berlioz' reviews of the master's works were invariably courteous, appreciative, and even occasionally enthusiastic.

[49] *A.R.*, 339.

will go well." It went so well that he had to devise a musical shorthand for fear of losing the thronging ideas. Once before, in composing the *Harold* symphony, he had had to capture fleeting inspiration in a kind of shorthand still visible in the manuscript. He then worked up the bare datum by expansion and embellishment.[50] For the *Requiem* all this had to be done at breakneck speed, since in the twelve weeks at his disposal time must also be found for reviewing concerts and writing an encyclopedia article he had contracted to do.[51] This is the definition of music which now heads *A Travers Chants*, and although the statement was not a new one with him, its reassertion at a time when his oldest musical project — the Mass of 1825 — was being similarly reworked is a symbol of his consistency: "Music is at once a science and a sentiment . . . It must not solely satisfy the ear by correct and artistic combinations of sounds, but must also speak to the heart and the imagination . . . Many persons are not made for music and consequently music is not made for them . . . The musical sense can be trained and exercised, but the motions of the spirit, which are very active in certain people are but slight in others. . . . As for the perceptions that the writer himself owes to the hearing of music, nothing can convey their exact character to one who has never experienced them." [52]

This sense of being apart yet in the melee was not Berlioz' portion alone. An incident with a tragic sequel occurred just then which discloses as in a fictional plot the emotional temperature of musical Paris in the spring of 1837. A new tenor named Gilbert Duprez made his debut in grand opera on April 17. Berlioz knew him since the days of Choron's concerts of sacred music; they met later in Rome; and now the critic praised the newcomer, with only a few reservations: Duprez had a magnificent voice but was a poor actor. He gesticulated too much and overused the *notes sombrées* (veiled tones) for which he had a knack. But the Paris public went wild and with no reservations worshiped a new idol.

The immediate result was that Adolphe Nourrit, after fifteen years of superior craftsmanship, felt cast out overnight.[53] Being short and stout, he was not a theatrically commanding figure, but he was a greater and

[50] *588*, 269.

[51] For the *Dictionnaire de Conversation*, ed. W. Duckett, P. 1833–51, 68 vols. This brought the total of his writing commitments to nine, though he drew on earlier essays for parts of the encyclopedia article. (See *1377*, 110 ff.; *1398*, 405–9.)

[52] *1398*, 405; *A Trav.*, 3.

[53] It is worth noting that whereas Duprez was one of the twenty-two children of a perfumer, Nourrit was the son of a musician and had been trained by Garcia.

finer artist, both as singer and composer. It was he who in his very first role had moved the young Berlioz at *his* first hearing of Gluck; it was he who had roused the Belgians to revolt with his Masaniello in 1830; it was he who had fashioned the librettos of *La Sylphide* and other ballets danced by the airy Romantic dancers, Taglioni and Fanny Elssler. It may even be conjectured that it was Nourrit's uncommon gifts that inspired Berlioz when he wrote the role of the actor-singer in *Lélio*.[54] Nourrit was a musical institution, suddenly overthrown by Duprez' powerful organ.

Very soon after the latter's debut, being momentarily voiceless, Nourrit had what we should now call a nervous breakdown. It was not artistic egotism but artistic sensibility that was wounded. He felt not only dethroned but outraged. Berlioz could readily sympathize, and with his friend the Irishman George Osborne they walked Nourrit up and down the boulevards until a late hour, reassuring him and dispelling a hundred rash resolutions.[55]

Nourrit gave up his first violent projects, but felt he could not stay in Paris nor continue in opera.[56] He applied to Berlioz' other friend, the dramatic poet Legouvé, for a "monodrama" precisely of the type that Berlioz had produced in *Lélio*. When Legouvé had cast in this form the woes of the Italian liberal Silvio Pellico, Lesueur's last pupil, Ambroise Thomas, set the text, and with this work Nourrit toured Italy successfully for two years. But his self-confidence was irreparably shattered, and after an admirable concert at Naples in 1839, he ended the struggle by leaping out of a window, aged thirty-seven.[57]

By the end of May 1837, portions of Berlioz' *Requiem* were in the copyist's hands, but the Ministry, which had not scrupled to delay for its own red tape, was now worried about rehearsals and begging for speed. By dint of exertion, Berlioz finished the last page on June 29.[58] This

[54] Berlioz always believed in composing for particular singers as a dramatist writes for actors. See *Tr.*, 243.

[55] *1016*, 68. Osborne was one of many foreign musicians making their names in Paris, and one of the vanguard. Not long since he had given a piano recital with Julius Benedict, Weber's pupil and biographer, which Berlioz had praised.

[56] He was weary of intrigues, as Liszt's letter to him about Berlioz' struggle implies. (*993*, III, 384.)

[57] For an exhaustive biography of the artist by his son-in-law, see *993*, and in Grove another account by Gustave Chuquet, also a contemporary.

[58] A month before, Harriet had made her last stage appearance, semi-privately, in the last act of *Jane Shore*. (*285*, 87 *n.*) Meanwhile, Hector's maternal grandfather had died, and the harried composer felt guilty at not having written to various members of the family.

left him less than a month in which to have the parts completed and proofread, and to rehearse a chorus and orchestra of four hundred.

The voices were going smoothly when without warning and indeed without notifying Berlioz, the "bureaus" countermanded the entire ceremony. "Ten thousand plagues on their heads!" he wrote to his intimates. "The devil must be in it . . . The scoundrels choose to stop me *now*. It's outrageous!" [59]

Still, as he himself remarked, the work was *there*. "The *Requiem* exists and I swear to you, Father, that it is a piece which will count; sooner or later I'll get it performed." [60] And to his friend, the Librarian of the Conservatoire, Bottée de Toulmon: "I defy them to wear me down." ("*Je les défie à la patience.*") [61] The musical injury was bad enough; there was, besides, the question of who would pay, not the piper merely, but the copyist, singers, and so on – some five thousand francs Berlioz had already spent, exclusive of his own fee. The government not being a person, its morality is often dubious and its memory frail. "M. de Montalivet, Minister of the Interior, asked me how I could be indemnified for this contretemps, which he says has been caused by politics alone; I replied that no indemnity was possible except the performance of the work." [62]

The affair was not calculated to make Berlioz take a more lenient view of politics; rather it reminded him of the very different treatment which Lesueur spoke of receiving from a responsible "tyrant." Berlioz drew hasty inferences. "Oh these representative governments – and cheap ones at that – what a stupid farce! . . . Under the Empire a minister would not have dared act in this manner . . . Napoleon would have attended to him; for I say again, the thing is a swindle. . . ." [63] The minister hinted that Berlioz would at the next opportunity be given the Legion of Honor – that emergency coinage for settling bad debts. He might even be appointed Inspector General of Music for primary schools – an anticipation of Matthew Arnold. In response to all this Berlioz deliberately acted the monomaniac. He had one idea in mind – performance – and he dinned it into the head of every bureaucrat he could reach in the offices of three ministries – Fine Arts, Interior, and War.

It was war, actual war, that finally brought him victory after three

[59] *A.R.*, 345, 346. But compare the cool letter to his choral conductor Dietsch (*A.R.*, 345–6). All this was only six days before the ceremony.

[60] *A.R.*, 351.

[61] *A.R.*, 345.

[62] *A.R.*, 349.

[63] *A.R.*, 350–1.

months of relentless hounding. On October 23, 1837 the news of the taking of Constantine, in Algeria, was relayed by (visual) telegraph from the south of France, and with it the intelligence that General Damrémont, commanding, had been killed in the assault. The government would specially honor his memory, since the feat of arms lent needful prestige to the regime.

At once the unpolitical but not impolitic Berlioz asked Dumas to put in a word in his favor with the Duke of Orleans, to whom Dumas was secretary. The ceremony was soon set for December; a few more letters were exchanged, Berlioz had a cordial interview with General Bernard, the Minister of War, and he finally received the second commission for his one *Requiem.* The terms again provided 14,000 francs for all expenses, plus a bonus of 1500.[64] Berlioz was moreover accorded a sort of public accolade by the Comte de Montalivet who spoke at the Conservatoire graduation on November 19: "Music is the handmaiden of all national ceremonies. Without it there can be neither pomp nor grandeur. . . . It is music we look to for uttering the grief of France on the day when the church of the Invalides . . . will receive the body of an illustrious general. On that occasion the students of the Conservatoire will perform music composed by a former student of the Conservatoire." [65]

On December 4, the day of the dress rehearsal, all of artistic Paris was present at the Invalides. The impression was overwhelming. Vigny wrote in his Journal: "The music was beautiful and strange, wild, convulsed, and dolorous. . . ." [66] The next day at noon the service took place before the royal family, the diplomatic corps, and all the fashion, power, and frivolity of Paris. Habeneck, who had been forced on Berlioz by the opposition, conducted more than three hundred musicians grouped left and right in the transept. During the first number, *Requiem and Kyrie,* things went well in spite of the usual mistakes by nervous performers. Hebeneck thereupon relaxed so fully that he nearly spoiled the effect of the fanfare in the ensuing *Tuba mirum* by failing to cue the small brass ensembles at the four corners of the orchestra. According to his habit, after setting the tempo, he laid down his baton preparatory to taking a

[64] Berlioz, who had not yet been paid for his previous outlay, was dunning the ministries on behalf of copyists and singers who were dunning him. On November 28, the official in charge of Public Monuments writes to the Director of Fine Arts that the appropriation has been otherwise spent. (*106*, 428.)

[65] *268*, 384.

[66] *1284*, 112. Vigny was a competent amateur musician. He attended Berlioz' concerts from interest as well as friendship, and on this occasion he had the additional reason of being a former Army officer who had known and esteemed General Damrémont. (*Ibid.*, 113.)

pinch of snuff — as Berlioz tells in his *Memoirs* — and the composer himself had to give the signal.[67] The rest proceeded without a hitch.

Whether the audience was moved or bored or bewildered by Berlioz' music it is impossible to say, since there could be no applause, but the critics were with few exceptions favorable. Nothing like the *Requiem* had ever been heard by human ears, and the impression of sustained power could not be gainsaid. It suggested to Heine the famous hyperbole to the effect that as a maker of music Berlioz was like "an antediluvian bird, a colossal nightingale or a lark the size of an eagle."[68] General Bernard sent Berlioz a well-turned note of congratulation which the

[67] *Mem.*, I, 312. The truth of this incident was first disputed by Hippeau, and later by Boschot, on the ground that Berlioz' letters after the event (to his mother and to Ferrand) do not mention it. Boschot also argues that Berlioz being a fighter and the holder of a critical post would have denounced Habeneck at once. These contentions rest on a negative, on the absence of evidence, and they overlook two facts:

1. In 1856 a short life of Berlioz appeared, by Eugène de Mirecourt, in which the incident is related (*292*). None of the friends of Habeneck, who was but recently dead, protested. No one in any case disputes the fact of Habeneck's old-fashioned habit of conducting. Mirecourt's book likewise disposes of Mr. Newman's suggestion that in old age Berlioz confused imaginings with reality (*62*, 210 *n.*) for the biography of 1856 is too full of small errors to have been written with Berlioz' help, and he himself cautioned a friend against its inaccuracies. (*93*, 242.) The inference is inescapable that others knew of the Habeneck incident before Berlioz wrote it down.

2. In a letter of April 28, 1859 to Ferrand, Berlioz refers to Habeneck's "crime . . . on the occasion of the first performance of the *Requiem*." (*L.I.*, 219.) Therefore Ferrand must have been told earlier, even though no letter remains to show when. One can imagine many reasons why immediately after the performance Berlioz did not want to include in his account a fact which might, by its nature, spoil the impression of complete success. George Osborne's report that Berlioz himself denied the story (*1016*, 69) is hardly credible, whereas the description of the incident by Charles Hallé (*Life and Letters Of*, L. 1896, 67), is that of an eyewitness: "To my amazement I suddenly saw Berlioz. . . ."

As for the audience on the day of the performance itself, its place in the dim-lit church would prevent it from noticing what was going on in the midst of so large a group of musicians. Lastly, the expectation of seeing Berlioz assail Habeneck in print after the concert goes against the composer's lifelong habit of not replying or attacking on his own behalf, but always in the name of general principles. The upshot is that the account in the *Memoirs* can be neither proved nor disproved, though the balance of probabilities favors its being true.

[68] *1261*, VI, 440. Despite his critical genius and his regard for Berlioz, Heine sometimes let his fancy bolt when he wrote of painters and musicians. His Paris news letters are filled with loose verbalism amounting often to error and always to exaggeration, witness the passage on Beethoven in *Lutezia*, Apr. 20, 1841.

papers reprinted, and Schlesinger, scenting a first paying success for one of his authors, opened a public subscription for the immediate engraving of the score. Unhappily, Berlioz' devoted sponsor, Lesueur, was not there to rejoice: he had died on October 6.

For Berlioz at thirty-four, it had taken only seven years from the Rome Prize to the nation's highest artistic trust — but what an obstacle race it had been!

Requiem, Realism, and Revolution

> It was a prey I had long stood in ambush for.
>
> — BERLIOZ on the subject of a *Requiem* Mass

In composing his *Requiem* or Grand Mass for the Dead, Berlioz had other things to take into account than his need to release the music within him. He faced a very definite practical problem. The Chapel of Saint Louis at the Invalides is a vast domed building which on the day of the funeral would be filled by many hundreds of people. The windows were blocked, the walls draped in black. Around the coffin flickered six hundred candles and incense boats. Four thousand other pinpoints of light dotted the gloomy shell. Major Lehoux headed the cortege with twenty-four muffled drums beating in the name of the twelve Paris legions, and Séjean played the organ for the service. When all this had been seen and felt and heard would come the *Requiem* music, not consecutively but with interruptions for intonings and responses.[1]

Now Berlioz had heard Mozart's *Requiem* at the Madeleine and one of Cherubini's at the Invalides. Comparing their effect in those large churches with that in the acoustic hall of the Conservatoire, he could see that the volume of sound must be brought into scale with the place, and that sharp contrasts must be established between successive numbers to sustain attention during the rites. For his purposes Berlioz found he needed 190 instruments and 210 voices, with additional timpani and brass choirs to be used in the *Tuba mirum.* This enumeration is striking, but it is not the chief point of interest in Berlioz' *Requiem.* Even the full deploy-

[1] *615.*

ment of these forces in the Vision – or rather audition – of Judgment is not characteristic of the work as a whole. In dealing with Berlioz it is always a mistake to remain under the spell of the immediately obvious facts and to suppose his mind moving on a single plane or aiming at a single effect. True, he wished to use again in perfected form his *Resurrexit* of 1825 with its admirable fanfare and timpani chords. But he also paid heed to the liturgy, the religious habits of his compatriots, and the special occasion. Through his teachers, Lesueur and Reicha, Berlioz was in touch with the revolutionary tradition of music for mass gatherings. He knew in detail how under the Empire Marshal Lannes had been buried, and as far back as 1825 he had asked the use of the Pantheon for his music.[2] Thus one national tradition made him take for granted the union of religion with daily life; another, more recent, used music to suit the needs of a people assembled. The original assembly, it will be recalled, was to celebrate the revolution of 1830, the prevailing mood being sad, solemn, and martial. Hence this *Requiem* must combine massiveness, dramatic intensity, and religious awe; it must be vivid and contemporary as well as lead the spirit to serenity – a work of Gothic art.

The Latin words before him gave Berlioz his dramatic impetus. They express terror, hope, resignation, gratitude, pity, joy, and faith. They speak of lakes of fire and gnashing of teeth, awful judgment and humble pleas. In the main prose or *Dies irae*, their staccato rhythm and overrich rimes, in a language no longer understood even by the educated, make them unsuitable for mere setting. Berlioz therefore extracted from each couplet or quatrain a mood or a contrast of moods, upon which he then built one of his ten movements. As he had done in his scenes from *Faust*, he freely joined distinct parts of his text when these answered to the same musical feeling. Music with Berlioz always takes precedence over words, and he carries into the sacred precincts his consistent view of music's function: to reproduce spiritual gestures.

The first gesture – *Requiem and Kyrie* – opens with a brief orchestral introduction, a repeated rising scale in the strings, which admirers of the prelude to *Parsifal* will recognize at once as having engendered the "Eucharist" theme with which that work begins. This is followed by the main six-bar theme for basses on the words *Requiem aeternam*, soon taken up by the other voices and varied through chromatic and modal effects derived from the initial scale. In the midst of the agonized, sweeping movement of despair, the episodes of the *Te decet hymnus* and *Lux*

[2] *106*, 428 and *235*, 160

perpetua contrast hopeful calm with an anxiety which returns in the awesome *Kyrie* on repeated notes. The voices end on a quiet dissonance and the graver strings close with a recall of the solemn opening.[3]

The second part is the renowned *Dies irae* employing the four brass choirs and timpani, which made Leopold Damrosch's musicians stand up and cheer when they first played it, and about which Edouard Colonne silenced a persistent audience by shouting "No encores of the Day of Judgment!"[4] The movement is built on three phrases of liturgical cast which cross and recross, surge and develop three times in three tonalities, each time with more fervor, thrice punctuated by rising tremolo scales on the strings. At the climax of the third scale, the fanfare bursts forth in melancholy grandeur, overlapping successively from the four corners of the orchestra, where the additional brass (trombone, cornet, tuba, and trumpet) have been placed.[5] Saint-Saëns, who heard the work under Berlioz in 1855, says: "I had read the score and was dying to hear the effect. The *Tuba Mirum* surpassed my expectations. . . . It seemed as if each separate slim column of each pillar in the church became an organ pipe and the whole edifice a vast organ. Yet even more I admired the poignant feeling of this marvelous work, the constant and incredible elevation of style — far more perceptible by ear than on reading, as is true of all the works of this composer."[6]

From a technical point of view, beyond the economy with which this mass of instruments is here used, great interest attaches to the role of the kettledrums, of which Berlioz wanted sixteen, played by eight per-

[3] Owing to his preconceived idea of what a "literary" composer is, Boschot takes a page to blame Berlioz for producing a "luminous clearing" when the words *lux perpetua* appear in his text. But who is it that sees luminosity when he hears major chords and phrases for upper strings and flutes? It so happens that Mozart, whom Boschot rightly idolizes, uses the *lux perpetua* in his *Requiem* to do precisely what Berlioz does — change the mood by taking advantage, as would any dramatic musician, of the two "programs" at hand. Boschot understands this well enough when he is not dealing with Berlioz: "Never did Mozart, that impeccable master, write music more closely linked to the meaning of the words [than in the *Magic Flute*] never did words or dramatic scenes receive from music a more faithful expression or an extension that goes deeper . . . Whatever belongs to man is here expressed. . . ." (*769*, 149.)

[4] *942*, 33 and *616*, 27.

[5] Admirers of Verdi's great *Requiem* will recognize the passage, for it occurs there in the same key — though Berlioz begins in the major — in the same rhythm, with the same triplets and the same dominant 7th chord. Verdi (like Félicien David) rightly felt that it must be taken, not adapted, though he used the considerably harsher sonority of trumpets alone.

[6] *441*, 627.

formers, so as to insure the correct intonation of the chords. Here was the realization of the musical effect (suggested by an attempt of Reicha's), which he had tried out in the *Francs-Juges* overture and the *Symphonie Fantastique*, and had now expanded: a sequence of timpani chords important enough to rank as a "line" under the ringing melancholy and doom of the fanfare.[7]

After such a climax which, musically speaking, is prepared from the beginning of the *first* movement and not merely from that of the second, the danger was to fall into bathos. Berlioz entrusted the actual words *Tuba mirum spargens sonum* to the basses in unison, seconded only later by the other voices in canonic imitation, and so preparing a soft close on *Mors stupebit et natura.* It is not alone the meaning of the prophecy, "Death and Nature will shrink in stupor" that determines the gentle ending, but fully as much the need of a fit musical transition to the *Quid sum miser*, a pre-impressionist tone poem which is also the first of those pages of the *Requiem* that Berlioz said were too often overlooked among the tremendous because "it requires a very fine musical sensibility to enjoy their style." [8] In this third portion, the plaintive melody is interwoven with the first phrase of the previous *Dies irae* in a short but moving confession of man's weakness and humility.

In the following number, the *Rex tremendae majestatis,* a solemn invocation interrupted by some unfortunate passages in quick tempo turns gradually into a renewal of anxious supplication. The full orchestra again gives intimations of destruction, after which calm reigns once more and leads to the touching six-part *a cappella* prayer *Quaerens me.*

The sixth and longest movement, the *Lacrymosa*, contrasts within itself the previous moods of a fated end and an unquenchable hope, and it does this in a manner which is not equally pleasing to every listener. The six-bar tenor melody, underlined by a strongly rhythmic figure in the orchestra, suggests awareness that "the day of weeping when man shall be judged" is an inescapable reality. (At a rehearsal of the work in 1941,

[7] One of the few good points of the 1947 movie depicting Berlioz' life was the demonstration of how solemn and almost sweet the drumming of 16 timpani sounds in this passage, scored for sponge-headed sticks throughout. "It was not until the time of Berlioz," says an authority, "that the modern timpani tone began to be realized and demanded. . . . He definitely asked for a musical tone . . . and it is safe to say that his suggestion revolutionized timpani-playing. . . . The whole section of the later *Treatise on Orchestration* . . . is full of deep insight as well as common sense, and a feeling for the player rarely found among composers." Kirby: *825*, 11 and 17.

[8] *M.C.*, 36.

the American composer Roger Sessions likened the atmosphere to that of the London blitz.) But the tenor phrase soon generates a variant in a more lulling rhythm that some critics find too reminiscent of an Italian aria in waltz time. There can be no doubt that Berlioz intended precisely that impression. In a letter to Ferrand written when he desired to have from him words for an oratorio on the Day of Judgment, he had said: "Avoid scenes of conflict as well as those which would call the brass into play. I want it to sound only at the end [no doubt his fanfare, which was all written]. But give me contrasts – *religious choruses mixed with dancing carols. . . .*" [Italics added.] [9] This is in effect the plan of the *Lacrymosa* of 1837; and if we go back to the Mass of 1825 we find in the *Resurrexit* a passage which resembles nothing so much as Rossini. We may, if we like, fancy that Berlioz was using God's artillery to vanquish his musical enemies, or we may make the Italianate melody stand for mankind's pathetic trifling in the face of extinction: either notion is a harmless irrelevance, provided we do not judge the music by imposing an unconscious "program" at variance with the simple contrast which Berlioz so persistently desired.

After the duple *Lacrymosa* comes the high point of the work in its meditative aspect. The Offertory, which Schumann said "surpassed everything" is one of Berlioz' great inspirations. On two notes, A and B flat, Berlioz fashioned a figure that the chorus of souls in Purgatory repeat unchanged throughout, while the orchestral accompaniment, treated in fugal style, weaves noble arabesques around the chiaroscuro plaint. At once a tour de force and a model of economy, this number must, like many of Berlioz' happiest productions, be quite familiar by ear before all its qualities emerge.

To balance the deliberate iteration of the Offertory, Berlioz then gives us a brief and sharply etched *Hostias*, which contains another musical "find" – the harmonic-orchestral idea of flute-and-trombone chords. Using the lowest (so-called 'pedal') notes on the trombone and continuing them with treble flute tones that seem like upper resonances of the original sound, Berlioz punctuates the short liturgical phrases for male voices in a manner at once striking and apt.[10] The sense of space derived from the range of pitch and the isolation, as it were, of the human voice

[9] *L.I.*, 104.

[10] Berlioz may have been meditating this musical idea for ten years or more, for we find at the end of the *Mort d'Orphée* "Bacchanale" a G for flute above a C on the cellos two octaves below. Verdi was struck by the *Requiem* version and adapted it twice – in *Otello*, Act IV and *Falstaff*, Act III.

seeking to placate God, are felt even if they do not come to mind through words.[11]

Again to avoid monotony, the *Sanctus* (No. 9) introduces a tenor solo, which is a good example of Berlioz' original melodic gift. Its soaring line over enharmonic modulations has a quality of "golden sweetness" unlike that of any other idiom in music.[12] The melody is interrupted by a vigorous *Hosanna* fugue of sizable dimensions, after which the *Sanctus* proper is resumed, to be followed by a reprise of the fugue in free form.

The final number, *Agnus Dei*, brings us material we have already heard in the first movement and in the *Hostias*. Having taken his usual pains to make the *Requiem* "one work" by smooth transitions and frequent thematic recalls, Berlioz evidently designed for the end a recapitulation that would further clinch unity. But hounded by the Ministry and by his copyists, he had no time to fashion this conclusion otherwise than adroitly. He did introduce interesting variants of the flute-trombone chords and of the orchestration in the *Te decet hymnus*, but one can imagine the richer and more complex finale in his own polyphonic style which he might have written, given time.[13] By a further chance, the score of the *Requiem* is the only one that Berlioz did not hold back for revision before engraving, since Schlesinger offered it for subscription immediately after the performance. When a second edition became possible, years later, Berlioz wisely did not touch the substance, cast in an irrecoverable style, but simply improved the Latin prosody.

"In that unknown land of boundless extent," says Mr. Cecil Gray, "which girds about the narrow beaten path of musical tradition . . . Berlioz has reared up gigantic pyramids of sound which will endure as long as music itself." [14] The *Requiem* is certainly one of these pyramids,

[11] This unusual combination must be heard in a hall without excessive echo. Like every delicate effect it can be muffed, especially by an unsure trombone. Some of the original players did not know that these notes were possible on their instruments. (*Tr.*, 202.)

[12] Paul Rosenfeld, *505*, 9. Kaikhosru Sorabji, the learned contrapuntist, dwells on the "melodic power" of "this glorious movement" comparing it with the *Agnus Dei* of the B Minor Mass, and using both to show that "atmospheric vocal noises are no substitute for line drawing in terms of tone." (*884*, 39.)

[13] The coda of the movement, using the sixteen kettledrums in a decrescendo from piano to pianissimo, is nevertheless a new and breath-taking inspiration.

[14] *719*, 214.

yet its size, which is one aspect of its greatness, is not quite what certain critics take it to be. Call the work "colossal" and visions of ungainly giantism are engendered which imply crudity of technique or intention. But if the *Requiem* proves anything about its author, it proves the opposite. Throughout we find premeditation, balance, unity, and minute care as to the smallest details of composition. The four brass choirs – not just trumpets, precisely in order that their sound may be smooth – must not hypnotize us. Out of possibly fourteen hundred measures in the whole score they play in about eighty. Out of ten numbers, only one whole and a half of two others bear any character that can be called violent. Criticism is nothing if it does not observe the proportions of the thing which it pretends, in the name of Proportion, to criticize. The *Requiem* possesses in fact what Baudelaire thought the supreme form of grace – energy. And this energy is not merely let loose; it speaks to us intelligibly: "Listening to the Mass, we find ourselves feeling as though some *vates* of a Mediterranean folk were come in a rapt and lofty mood to offer sacrifice, to pacify the living, to celebrate with fitting rites the unnumbered multitudes of the heroic dead." [15]

In speaking of the *Requiem* as colossal, we must also remember that music has several dimensions, and that the number of performers is not the sole measure of size. To begin with, the total number brought together do not by any means play throughout. In the second place, the work is relatively short – roughly one and a half hours' playing time. If we call it overgrown, what word shall we apply to Bach's *Saint Matthew Passion* (also scored for colossal forces relatively to its period) and to Wagner's five-hour stretches of music drama? Why is it, moreover, that mention of the sixteen kettledrums in the *Requiem* suggests "barbaric strength" whereas the eighteen anvils of *Rheingold* do not? [16] The fact is that, as Birrell said of Cardinal Newman, the hearers of Berlioz' *Requiem* "believe themselves to be revelling and rioting, whilst in reality they are being steadily driven along." [17]

Massiveness is of course aimed at and achieved in the *Requiem*, but it does not derive exclusively or even mainly from simple *piling up*. The

[15] *505*, 99.

[16] To object to the number of drums is really to object to the number of tones in the musical scale.

[17] Another student points out that "the level of dynamic intensity in eight of the movements is comparatively low throughout," and he suggests that this may cause an ordinary audience to feel that "they are not getting their money's worth." (*719*, 215.)

score does not in fact resemble a pyramid but rather a cathedral, whose grandeur comes from differences of size subtly contrasted.[18] After the hair-raising *Dies irae* comes the quiet *Quid sum miser,* to cause a different sort of shudder, in a style as noble and with contours as definite though small. One thinks again of the Gothic builders: "Chartres Cathedral is built of stones from Berchère, calcareous, hard and rough in appearance, but of a hardness to withstand any test. The blocks employed are of enormous size . . . ," [19] yet there is no disproportion between their bulk and the Virgin's head, nor conflict between the gray stone and the rose window, the thickness of the pillars and the flight of the *flèche.*

This comparison suggests another moot point: the presence or absence of religious feeling in Berlioz' mass. Romantic, even theatrical, significance is readily granted it, but not "true" religious faith. Apparently the *Dies irae* continues to ring in critics' ears and the mild prayers and contrite invocations do not. Or rather, the objectors have never really defined for themselves what they mean by religious. For some it is a uniform mood of pious submission which naturally excludes violent emotion. This should perhaps be called religious meditation, and Berlioz' *Quid sum miser* and *Quaerens me* reflect it.[20] In our day, Fauré built an entire *Requiem* in that mood, as he had every right to do, whereupon a critic blamed him for going counter to the intentions of the Church.

Now no one but the Pope can say what the intentions of the Church are, and in 1903, Pius X condemned as contrary to these intentions the often-used masses of Cherubini, Giorza, and Ohnewald, together with Rossini's *Stabat Mater,* all of which had been considered mainly or wholly religious in the sense denied to Berlioz. This seems to leave the religious spirit something distinct from the orthodoxy ascertainable only through official decisions, and everyone is thus free to interpret true religious expression to the best of his understanding. This is what Berlioz did, taking for granted – once more – the medieval tradition. If he thought of hell-fire and the Archangel Gabriel, so did the sculptors of Autun and so did the authors of the Latin words Berlioz was setting. If he put side by side terror and pomp, and humility and foolish hope,

[18] The true objectors to the style of the *Requiem* say more correctly that it is "chamber music suffering from elephantiasis" – that is, they perceive the fine work and would reduce its proportions, as one might want the Chartres "Queens of Juda" in statuette form.

[19] Viollet-le-Duc, *Dictionnaire des Beaux Arts,* II, 315 *n.* Compare Liszt on Berlioz: "Those masses of sounds are blocks of granite with which he builds his Pyramids." (*587,* 400.)

[20] At least one priest expressed a presumably religious appreciation of Berlioz' *Requiem* on its first appearance. (*L.I.,* 179.)

so did the designers of the north porch of Chartres and so did the religious John Donne, who also begins with a fanfare:

At the round earth's imagined corners, blow
Your trumpets, Angels, and arise, arise
From death, you numberless infinities
Of souls . . .

Of course, those who assume that the Muses curl their little fingers are bound to imagine that at the crack of doom the angels will lisp their summons into individual ear trumpets. Donne and Berlioz forecast the reality in stronger colors, with a result that is shocking indeed, "realistic" and on that account entitled to the epithets here employed: Shakespearean and Gothic.[21]

And these adjectives, like the work itself, also justify the description of "popular" and "democratic" in the Christian and modern sense. For in placing and using his vocal and instrumental groups so as to play virtually a dramatic role, Berlioz was simply extending the practice of the older antiphony which had influenced the French revolutionary composers. Coming only a generation after Gossec and Méhul, he assumed as they did that civic ceremonies must by their scale give an idea of the whole nation assembled; several times in referring to the performers of his three "monumental" works he spoke of them as "a people singing" [*ce peuple chantant*].[22] One can therefore liken his impatience with the few choristers of Saint Peter's,[23] or the single trombone and voice of Mozart's *Requiem*,[24] to the impatience of the French nation of 1789 with its unrepresentative court and sovereign.

[21] Henry Adams: "The Gothic artist saw his work as a whole, a mass, and its details were his amusement. . . . Chartres expressed, whatever else it meant, an emotion — the deepest man ever felt — the struggle of his own littleness to grasp the infinite." (*1041*, 141 and 106.)

[22] See also *Mem.*, II, 363; *L.I.*, 251. Méhul's *Chant National du 14 Juillet* was scored for soloists, three choruses and two orchestras, the six groups being kept distinct. Gossec, whose popular *Tuba mirum* was played thirteen times during the revolution, asked, for his second *Te Deum*, fifty serpents and "an army" of snare drums. In contrast with this, the moderation and economy that Berlioz displays while still fulfilling a kindred intent can be measured to a decimal. As for the linking of popular and religious forms with revolutionary celebrations, it is shown in the use of old folk songs fitted with new words and of religious services and scriptural phrases adapted so as to dramatize patriotism and liberty. (*129*.)

[23] See above, Chapter 8.

[24] Berlioz supposed that Mozart had merely sketched the instrumentation of his *Tuba mirum* after the "sublime phrase" with which it begins. (*1398*, Sept. 7, 1834 and *1386*, Aug. 9, 1835.)

Berlioz' connection with the past is unmistakable. Only, the connection is freer and the past broader than is convenient for easy classification. The tendency of critics is to make tradition a man-to-man relationship, an evolution of Russian dolls. Hence it breaks down at the appearance of the original mind, and critics swing to the opposite extreme: "A work like the *Requiem* has no antecedents." [25] This is true only in the sense that applies to every masterpiece. Berlioz was original against a background of aims and intentions half realized by his musical predecessors, fully realized by his remote ancestors, the artists of medieval France. He had over Gossec and Méhul the advantage of superior means and a sensibility shaped by a new epoch.

As a musician, his genius for finding appropriate ideas (Saint-Saëns's "incredible elevation of style") was joined to a capacity for organizing an infinity of details into a work whose size is not the result of formulas for note-spinning but of fused material and spiritual force. One result of such a fusion is that critics a century later can point to contemporaries who are still drawing on the original inspiration: Stravinsky and Sibelius can be, and have been, instanced.[26] Since any art can boast of but few works of this sort—at once seminal and traditional and original—it is then fair to say of Berlioz' *Requiem* that "it stands alone: there is nothing with which we can fitly compare it." [27]

[25] *505*, 88.

[26] See *Musical Opinion* for Apr. 1936, p. 358. The critic could have added William Walton (*Belshazzar's Feast*) and Gustav Holst (*The Planets*).

[27] *719*, 215.

11. The Hero as Artist: Benvenuto Cellini

January to September 1838

> Come, cheer me up with an account of the Roman Carnival!
> — SCOTT, on the news of his financial disaster

THE *Requiem* had been an artistic success. No one in Paris who was capable of exercising judgment could doubt that this new music was something to reckon with. The leaders of the Romantic generation never forgot it, and thirty-five years later, after Berlioz' death, Liszt was still pondering the powerful, inscrutable score.[1] No less important was the composer's own opinion of the work, for like the playwright, the musician can never be entirely certain that he has hit his mark. And Berlioz, who had canceled an edition of his Opus 1, and destroyed a good many other works, was hard to please. For the *Requiem* he always felt a special regard, in spite of the fact that he had never submitted it to painstaking revision. It enshrined some of his earliest musical *trouvailles*, and its subject had enabled him to express at once his humility and his pride. Two years before his death he declared that if all his works were ordered to be burned, he would ask a reprieve for the *Requiem.*[2]

But in February, 1838, he was thinking of the present, not of the past or future, and the present signified another large work, virtually finished. *Benvenuto Cellini* "existed" also, its orchestration all but complete. Yet unlike the *Requiem* it would have to be produced soon if the publicity it had already received were not to spoil its chances by becoming an old story. Now the Opera in March 1838 had on the boards a reasonably good commercial success, also on an Italian theme — Halévy's *Guido and Ginevra, or the Florentine Plague*. Nevertheless the agreement with Berlioz and the Bertins was fulfilled and *Benvenuto* went into

[1] "This prodigious and indeed sublime work." Letters of Jan. 26, 1868 and Apr. 21 and May 9, 1872. (*Briefe,* II, 115 and IV, 341, 345.) Compare other "discoveries" of it, by Bruckner (*926*, 371), Busoni (*944*, 41), Peter Warlock (*958*, 48–9), and Hans von Bülow (*174*, 512). [And again, *N. Y. Times*, Feb. 14, 1969.]

[2] *L.I.*, 302–3.

rehearsal, though not in a way to make the composer's life easier. All Berlioz knew of "the house" was from outside—the political intrigues and chicanery of its managers and its relations with press and public. He now entered its arcana and discovered how it functions as a curb market of artistic personalities: the lion will sooner lie down with the the lamb than the prima donna with the bass—though exceptions have been known; each singer believes that the other's bark is far worse than his bite, for they all know how to bite; and while every department acts as if the rest were a superfluous nuisance, all agree that the most needless and nettlesome is the author. Throughout the personnel, actor's vanity perpetuates a hundred treasured jealousies and teamwork is not a habit but a concession; as in politics, self-seeking cannot be distinguished from devotion to the cause; while beneath everything the hum of petty gossip plays a discordant counterpoint to the genuinely hard work done under pressure and fraught with risk.

Nor is the institution self-contained. The ballet draws into the wings a host of interfering gentry from the world of finance, politics, and letters; and in a state-run opera the bureaucracy, the trades, and the blackmailing press are grafted on to the main trunk, and live on it like parasites. How happy must a nation be which has no official theaters! Some maddening plant grows in the very heart of opera, and to this day history records no instance of an operatic house of peace and harmony.[3] A century ago in France, Berlioz could only keep his courage bright: "Intrigues have been weaving around me since the first two rehearsals, so that my head swims. But one must go on, keep an eye on everything and be afraid of nothing."[4]

What made his position worse was that he was at the same time embarked on a complex enterprise designed to make him Director of the Italian Theater. The building itself had recently been destroyed by fire, the manager had been killed while trying to escape the flames, and Berlioz was being put forward for the vacant post. The inducement was purely monetary, for according to the instructions drawn up by the Ministry only Italian works could be performed. We know Berlioz' feelings about that repertory, with a few exceptions. He himself would not be allowed to compose for his own theater and he would have no chance to run a choir school such as he wanted to develop in the tradition of Choron's.

[3] The late Giulio Gatti-Casazza, onetime manager of the Metropolitan Opera Company in New York, left instructions that no music should be heard at his funeral. *Requiescat* . . .

[4] *A.R.*, 370.

But the income would mean affluence; it would release time and remove journalistic pressure: he could compose. Perhaps too, if he became one of the potentates of the inner theatrical ring he could enforce an open-door policy in other musical establishments: in short, having favors to dispense, he would have power.

The ups and downs of this project, in which the Bertins and members of the cabinet were concerned, lasted three months. Part of the delay and difficulty was due to the fact that the concessionaires, whoever they might be, would be responsible for rebuilding the gutted theater. At last the bill naming Berlioz Director and enacting the conditions of tenure was reported unfavorably by the parliamentary committee, and the Chamber turned it down 196 to 32. Before and after this blessing in disguise – for it spared Berlioz endless worries of an alien kind [5] – the press argued the case with its usual knowingness and concluded that Berlioz had been turned down because the Bertins were behind him. They were theoretically "in power," but the opposition was just strong enough to beat them on secondary issues, and as an *avant-garde* artist, Berlioz constituted their vulnerable side. He was the buffer state which is the first to be overrun in the war of big powers.

Unfortunately this defeat in the national legislature and the press would probably encourage a cabal against *Benvenuto*, for its success would give too much comfort to its backers. The dilemma for a composer without private means was complete: no possibility of succeeding without pull, no possibility of succeeding with it. Berlioz was too far involved to withdraw, even had he been willing to condemn his family to penury, and he felt within him dramatic and organizing talents that should not be buried. Even when he was fully within his rights, the situation was still one of catch-as-catch can: he had had to make a scene in "the bureaus" in order to obtain full payment for his *Requiem*.[6] Now he was gambling his time, effort, and reputation on the most chancy of political platforms – the stage of the Paris Grand Opera.[7]

* * *

[5] He knew how foreign to him the enterprise was, and he was a party to it solely on the principle of leaving no stone unturned: "I am not made to juggle with finances and the task of building the theatre which [the government] stubbornly foists upon the director-to-be, is an extremely complicated business." (To Adèle, *A.R.*, 372.)

[6] The documents examined and reproduced by Tiersot (*308*, Jan. 17–Feb. 2, 1904) show that the account in the *Memoirs* is substantially correct, despite errors of date.

[7] Mozart in 1778: "When the opera is finished, it is rehearsed, and if these stupid Frenchmen do not like it, it is not performed – and the composer has

In his private life, Berlioz received equally mixed blessings during this first half of 1838. In January he experienced considerable alarm at reports of his mother's ill health, which made him hope to get away for a visit to La Côte. "I long for you tenderly." [8] She died the next month, aged fifty-three. A little earlier, the deaths of a good friend and of a near relative, both young, had already cast gloom over Berlioz' ceaseless activity. All his unhappy beginnings as a musician came back to him at the thought of his mother. More cheerful news came from Liszt, successful at Milan and joyfully sojourning on the Italian lakes with Marie d'Agoult. Reliving in his mind the pleasures of his own *Wanderjahr*, Berlioz sought to express his affection and sympathy with his fortunate friends by composing some trifle for Liszt's beloved. But nothing came to his pen. He had verses on hand that Brizeux had written at his request, and he sketched portions of a setting for the *Erigone* of Ballanche,[9] but neither composition seemed to take shape. "If I can find the time to work . . ." [10]

At least the fact of Adèle's engagement to Marc Suat, a solicitor from Vienne, near La Côte, was wholly good. Berlioz knew him well and esteemed him highly: "Your letter," Berlioz writes to his future brother-in-law, "made me very happy, and if I haven't answered sooner it's because my present work makes me lose both sleep and sense of reality. I snatch a moment to tell you how enchanted I am to hear of the lively affection you bear my sister. She is an excellent child, who will make you most happy, I know. As for you, I know the goodness of your disposition and my sister's future strikes me as secure — I may have misread your notes but are you thinking of coming with Adèle to Paris . . . can you? will you? It would be such happiness for me. . . ." [11]

His chief worry was now Doctor Berlioz' solitude and ill health. Hector wrote to his father: "Adèle tells me of testamentary dispositions which our dear mother made in her special favor, and she seems to fear

---

had all his trouble for nothing. If they think it good, it is produced and paid for in proportion to its success with the public. There is no certainty whatever." (To his father, Sept. 11, 1778; *219*, 910.)

[8] *A.R.*, 361.

[9] Pierre Ballanche (1776–1847) was a philosopher from Lyon, attached to the circle of Chateaubriand and Mme. Récamier. When Gounet first sent Berlioz one of Ballanche's works, its vaporous quality struck the composer as too mystical for him (*A.R.*, 257) but he was finally caught by the poet-philosopher's fervor for the antique and began work on a setting of the prose poem *Erigone*. The musical fragments for this are in existence (*8*). For a modern account of Ballanche see *1229*.

[10] *A.R.*, 365.

[11] *A.R.*, 366–7.

the effect of this on the mind of her brothers and sisters. And now it is you who tell me of your own intentions . . . which suggest the deep depression with which you face the future. . . . We'll talk later, much later, of all these money matters that you propose to me in such cold blood. In any case, as regards me, whatever you do will always be right. . . . Farewell, dear Father, don't worry about my future and think more about yourself. The best proof you can give of your affection for your children is to take care of your health and peace of mind . . ."[12]

In his own home, Harriet and the child continued to thrive (Louis, in his fourth year, is growing fast but cannot yet read) but the arduous repayment of debts kept the exchequer drained. At last the combination of business, intrigues, rehearsals, and journalism wore Berlioz down. He took to his bed with his ordinary symptoms – sore throat, fever, and headaches – getting up only to supervise the Opera rehearsals. He was later to describe this ordeal with humor, and sympathy for a fellow composer: "I could imagine the cruel slowness of these 'studies' in which everyone wastes time on trifles . . . , the witticisms of the tenor and prima donna, at which the unhappy author thinks he is obliged to laugh heartily. . . . I could hear the voice of the Director treating him with condescension mixed with blame in order to remind him of the great honor being done to his work by such sustained attention. . . . Then someone would come in to announce that the mezzo-soprano was going on vacation and the bass on sick-leave, whereupon it was proposed to replace the singer by an apprentice and give the leading part to a chorister. And so the composer felt himself being assassinated, yet took great care not to cry out."[13]

By the end of June, the voice parts had been pretty well learned, except that of Cellini – assigned to his old acquaintance Duprez who was vacationing. There remained the orchestra, some of whom were inclined to make trouble. The old-timers who took their cue from Habeneck declared they had never seen such difficult music. Yet at the same moment Habeneck himself was conducting five hundred musicians at Lille in the *Lacrymosa* of Berlioz' *Requiem*, and receiving great applause for it. In Paris, in the pit where *Benvenuto* was struggling to come to life, there were "millions of wrong notes, wrong tempi, and especially wrong rhythms. . . . This causes me so much irritation, so much torture of the nerves" (Berlioz confided to Legouvé) "that it is the sole cause of my present indisposition. I am not yet over it. But patience! We'll be ready for the first night by August 21st or 25th. . . . The overture, by the

[12] *A.R.*, 368–9. [13] *Soirées* (7th) *Eves.*, 85.

way, I think you'll be pleased with. I don't want to count my chickens before they're hatched, but if my score is published, you'll give me the pleasure of accepting the dedication, won't you? For after all it's you who gave the *metal* for casting the Perseus and it is to you that poor Benvenuto owes his work of art, such as it is." [14]

Though Duprez was inferior as an actor, he practised his role to Berlioz' moderate satisfaction and by mid-July everything was nearly ready. The censorship, it is true, "took away the Pope" from the cast and forced the substitution of a Cardinal, which somewhat spoiled the conflict of wills between the "bandit-genius" Cellini and Clement VII. The revolt in the orchestra had been more or less tamed, after which there was only "one more barrage, that of the newspapers and of one's intimate foes hidden in the four corners of the house." [15] What Berlioz was thinking of occurred even before the opening. An erstwhile friend, the German ex-priest and music critic, Joseph Mainzer, published a pamphlet elaborately seeking to discredit the composer, his writings, and his opera as yet unknown to the public.[16]

Benvenuto Cellini did not open on August twenty-first, nor on the twenty-fifth. There were unaccountable delays, conflicting announcements and denials, all matched by a steady cross fire of questions in newspapers friendly to Berlioz. The dress rehearsal took place on September 1, before a house of colleagues and critics, who kept distinctly cool. Two days later was the scheduled *première:* postponed again. Duprez had caught cold and none of the roles had been understudied. "Cellini" was given a week to cure his cold. This brought the opening to the tenth of September and everyone knew that on the fifteenth Mme. Dorus-Gras, the leading lady, was quitting the Opera. By accident or design, a *short* run had been assured.

The first public audience that heard the already maltreated score was most whimsical: it applauded the overture with great vigor, expressed its disapproval of the rather cheap scenery, then picked and chose, seemingly at random, from the rest of the offering. Mme. Dorus-Gras's roulades went well, but certain words of the libretto afforded great opportunities

[14] *A.R.*, 376–7. Berlioz here repeats his allusion to the final scene of the opera. But the score was never published during Berlioz' lifetime; nor ever in France; it is still unobtainable except on hire from theaters that own it, for actual performance only. To acknowledge his friend's help Berlioz was to inscribe first the *Benvenuto Cellini* overture, then a book of essays to Legouvé.

[15] *A.R.*, 375.

[16] *Chronique Musicale de Paris: 1ère livraison: M. Berlioz. Au Panorama de l'Allemagne,* Paris, 1838, 95 pp.

for ridicule. In an air of Cellini's it was said that "in early morn *the roosters crowed*." Laughter swept the stalls. What Parisian could lend credence to such crude romantic realism? The parterre hissed and the gallery's barnyard noises managed to disconcert the actors. No such fun had been had in the City of Light since the first English actors had put on Shakespeare. The cabal deliberately killed the opera. The music was hardly attended to.[17] Duprez-Cellini kept on singing as if he were in on the joke, though the two women in the roles of Teresa and Ascanio did their utmost and were warmly applauded by Berlioz' admirers.

The faithful cohort called for him at the end, but his name was drowned in the tumult. He barely escaped the humiliation inflicted on Henry James after *Guy Domville*, of coming forward to be jeered at. The press behaved in the usual way, strong on politics and on the faults of the libretto, weak or irrelevant about everything else.

The very next day Berlioz set to work altering words and making cuts. On the twelfth a second performance half filled the house. There was no more laughter, but not enough applause. On the fourteenth a fuller house witnessed a performance which, despite Duprez' cynical carelessness,[18] aroused the public to genuine enthusiasm. But the box office is inexorable: three thousand francs amounted only to one third of what Meyerbeer could "do."

At this point the press temporarily abandoned jokes and recrimination and suggested that an injustice was perhaps being committed. They urged Berlioz not to be discouraged, acknowledged the power of his music, the abundance of his ideas, and concluded that "such an opera is entitled to ten first performances." One critic roundly asserted that Berlioz "opens out to us a new continent."[19] Another, putting his finger on the difference between Berlioz and Meyerbeer, explained the conflict of tastes: "However useful and even glorious M. Meyerbeer's works may be, they are only transitional and . . . eclectic, which is a very different matter from creative . . . At certain times eclecticism is serviceable, for it sums up and prepares us for what is to come, but in order to last, a

[17] Except perhaps by Spontini, Meyerbeer, and Paganini, who were present.

[18] Duprez told the story himself at a much later date: his wife was momently expecting a child. In the midst of the opera, the tenor saw the doctor gesticulating his congratulations from the wings; the singer lost his head and virtually stopped the show. The doctor's words at the end of the act did nothing to restore Duprez' poise. In admitting his confusion, the singer excuses himself with allusions to Berlioz' "complicated music" which was "not exactly tuneful anyway." (*949*, 124.)

[19] Morel in the *Journal de Paris*, quoted in *85*, 445.

work of art must carry reality within its flanks. It must be a creation. *Benvenuto* is such a work. *Benvenuto* is a masterpiece."[20]

A private letter from a contemporary to Desmarest, the virtuoso violoncellist, shows how a witness who was free from party allegiance viewed the facts, and to what extent Berlioz could hope for understanding from the thoughtful minority:

> I thank heaven that an unforeseen obstacle put off the opening of *Benvenuto*. Its inexplicable failure would have caused me too much pain to look on directly, and I would rather take it in from a distance than be close to all the dirty business you tell me about. Whether as is said, poor Barbier's poem is no good, I hardly know; I paid no attention. But after all, what difference does the canvas make when a masterpiece has been embroidered on it? . . . One thing especially is beyond me and that is the reception given to the finale of the first act. I can hardly believe it. That the public should have failed to grasp at once all that is subtle, delicate, witty, and touching in this opera, I can perhaps understand. But this sublime finale, this magnificent conception which struck me like the fusion of a hundred thousand voices, distinct and single at first, then mingling and blending in a magnificent harmony, is fit to move the most vulgar clods, the most ungifted individuals. . . . I am no artist . . . but at the dress rehearsal, while listening to that finale I was sweating with excitement, I was shaking in my seat with wonder and enthusiasm. No one will persuade me that something which could move me so, ignorant as I am, is insignificant or dull music. Neither the public's opinions nor the hissing of a whole theatre will convince me that I was wrong. . . .
>
> But something which surprises even more, perhaps, and infuriates me, is the behavior of Duprez. . . . Duprez has forgotten that scarcely a year ago he too was making his debut, nervously trembling before the public, . . . he has forgotten that he would then have begged on his knees for the handsome support that Berlioz so generously accorded him. He forgot it, God help him. . . .[21]

The protracted dispute over the merits of the opera led to the challenging of a stubborn critic by an enthusiastic Vicomte. The duel did not take place, but it gave Berlioz an opportunity to defend Mme. Dorus-Gras, who had been accused of sabotaging her role. In an open letter defending the cast, he said: "She gave me her fullest support with a fervor I should be sorry to see misrepresented."[22] At the same time he stood by his librettists. The few words that had offended delicate tastes he felt were a trifle compared to the genuine dramatic interest of the whole.

[20] Chaudes-Aigues in *L'Artiste*, Oct. 1838.
[21] L. Jonnart: Sept. 24, 1838 (*502*, 412–3)
[22] *107*.

Later, with more experience of the theater, Berlioz further recast the scenes, making of the two acts an admirable text in three.[23]

Throughout this voluble post-mortem, after the first shock of disappointment, Berlioz seemed the calmest and most confident. He had heard his score and knew what it was worth. Besides, there was still a slim chance of dinning the music into the public's ears by additional performances. The composer knew that no amount of journalistic drum-beating was going to increase the size of his public. Art is a serious addiction which newspaper reports and common opinion mistake for a gastronomic exercise. In this instance, Berlioz had learned like the hero of his opera that the artist having lost his proper religious function in modern secular society, he is at the mercy of the casual passions of men. He can succeed only slowly, by building up, inch by inch, the canons of judgment appropriate to his unique creation.

Berlioz' Reform of Opera

> I am regarded as the subverter, the overthrower of the *national genre.*
>
> – Berlioz speaking of *Benvenuto* at its inception (1834)

A fair judgment of Berlioz' first opera may be deemed impossible because it failed under ambiguous circumstances and because nowadays no one knows the work. But this is inexact. Though during Berlioz' lifetime the opera failed again in London and had only a brief (though triumphant) revival in Weimar, it enjoyed a veritable run in Germany between 1880 and the first World War. Played to enthusiastic audiences in a dozen cities, its performances according to one calculation totaled

[23] A highly qualified judge, the American composer, conductor, and theorist Philip Greeley Clapp, witnessed a revival in Munich in 1910, and reports: "Berlioz' opera exhibited none of the shortcomings commonly alleged." (*155*, 4.) See also Weingartner's essay (*911*) and Gautier's statement after the *première* that the libretto was no worse and no better than that of other accepted works. (*434*, 146.) In fact, the history of opera criticism suggests that no good libretto has ever been written. That of *Carmen* itself has been damned, yet there is a vast difference between it and the farrago of *The Magic Flute*, which is none the less a sublime work. Critics too often speak like those mischief makers who say: "It's not that I mind myself, but others will certainly object." Has *Rigoletto* a good libretto – or *Traviata?* It doesn't matter!

more than six hundred. In the 1930's it elicited fresh and discriminating praise when Erik Chisholm included it in his Berlioz cycle at Glasgow, and a performance on the Paris radio by Inghelbrecht occasioned a critical study shortly to be quoted from.[1] What one critic or audience can admire, given the right conditions, others can; so one must conclude that despite its eventful history, *Benvenuto Cellini* was anything but stillborn. Rather, the work resembles the Emperor Barbarossa asleep in his cave but destined again for power.

Berlioz was thus quite right when, reviewing his score after fifteen years, he confided to his sister, "I like better than ever that dear old *Benvenuto,* which is more vivid, more fresh, more *new* – that is its greatest disadvantage – than any of my works."[2] This is no more than was to be said a hundred years later by the British critic who heard the radio version and studied the score: "Listening, it seemed strange that a work so rich in ideas and of such beauty, should have been for so long completely ignored. . . . This admittedly flawed masterpiece surely deserves as much popularity as, shall we say, *Boris Godunov,* which, incidentally, it resembles in form. One is no less a masterpiece – and no more flawed – than the other."[3]

It is invariably true of Berlioz' great works that the assimilation of their substance, the recognition of their form, and the enjoyment of their varied kinds of beauty is a much bigger task than seems required by the ordinary work of the same sort. Even a student who has gone to the trouble of searching and reporting his opinion may forget how much he has absorbed and how much calls for reflection. We may therefore sympathize with the Paris audiences of 1838 insofar as they were sincerely bewildered, and we need not be as surprised as modern critics at the unjust treatment of the score. It is no bagatelle which may be casually taken up, put on, or received.[4]

[1] By J. Bornoff (*546*). D. E. Inghelbrecht, it is worth noting, had been Weingartner's understudy as conductor of the Paris revival of 1913, when the opera "amazed" French critics brought up on the hearsay of its "failure." What failed again in 1913 was the whole repertoire (Weber, Gluck, Berlioz) which the energetic builder of the new Théâtre des Champs Elysées hoped to establish in competition with the subsidized houses. (See *258;* and, among the critics, Pierre Lalo, *549*.)

[2] *M.C.*, 91.

[3] *546*, 341. The piano score (French or German) is incidentally very poor.

[4] In *Akkorde* Felix Weingartner tells of his labors while producing the opera in Berlin. Among other obstacles was the stubbornness of the director of properties who had decided that in the last act the statue of Perseus was to be not cast but *broken* at every performance. Weingartner had to appeal to

When first produced even the overture was an offensive novelty, for the opera public was not accustomed to hearing ten minutes of instrumental music ahead of the real show – the scenery and the singers. As for the alarm of the habitués at the "fifth-column" attack which Berlioz was making on their pastime, it can readily be understood. Here was an opera on an Italian theme, with the usual melodramatic plot – father, daughter, lover, duel, abduction, predicament, denouement by papal authority: the work was obviously (and originally) meant for treatment as an *opéra comique*. Turned into an *opera semiseria*, the work was accepted as much on the strength of its colorful scenes as on account of Berlioz' reputation for serious music. He had thus found his way into "the house," where he was now blowing up the conventions from within. He had used an Italian opera to criticize Italian opera, as well as to revolutionize the French national genre. He had not yet dared to put his views into words, but he already meant what he said later: "A new opera? To begin with, *is* there such a thing as a new opera? Is not the form worn threadbare, played out, squeezed dry?" [5]

Berlioz knew the repertory as well as or better than any connoisseur, and he had the advantage of preferring the works that the connoisseur usually found heavy or dull – Mozart's and Gluck's, *Freischütz* and *Fidelio*. From them he could deduce principles which suggested to his inventive mind certain reforms that might revivify dramatic music. Though Berlioz introduces these gradually after the rise of the curtain, the form of *Benvenuto Cellini* is characteristic of Berlioz as dramatist. Hence the similarity with Moussorgsky's *Boris* noted by the modern critic.[6] The libretto, as we know, was written under Berlioz' direction; he had himself chosen from Benvenuto's *Memoirs* the scenes that he deemed dramatic-and-musical. Auguste Barbier and Léon de Wailly [7] had cobbled up a

the highest authorities to prevent this "attraction" from being featured. (*911*, 74.)

[5] *Soirées* (18th) *Eves.*, 197. One director of the Opera, whom Berlioz had dealings with at this later time, defended the common run of pieces by explaining that "*l'opéra est un art de joie.*" (*1005*, 32.)

[6] The principle is simply though inadequately put by a negative: "*Benvenuto Cellini* lacks a certain dramatic continuity and the various tableaux have little or no connecting links." (*546*, 343.)

[7] Wailly was a cousin of the well-known historian of the same name, a lifelong friend of Vigny, and one of the interpreters of English literature in France. He translated Swift, Sterne, Burns, and Thackeray, not to speak of *Uncle Tom's Cabin*. During the Bourbon restoration he had been secretary to Sosthènes de la Rochefoucauld – Berlioz' old bureaucrat acquaintance – and later had become an intimate of Berlioz' other friend and collaborator Auguste Barbier.

love-plot and written the verses. Vigny had gone over the finished product, and contributed one lyric — the fine Chorus of Apprentices.[8] Finally Berlioz speeded up the action in his revision for Liszt in 1852. The present text consequently represents his thought as both dramatist and composer, and the result justifies the categorical statement made earlier, that "Berlioz' opera exhibits none of the shortcomings commonly alleged." The critic significantly adds: " — although such singers and hearers as depend for their happiness on solos and set pieces might be disappointed." In short, Berlioz broke with the current routine and liberated opera once more, as must be done every fifty years.

What Berlioz gives us when "action, music and stage business are perfectly coordinated" is "an evening seemingly of Cellini himself — though one may suspect that when the mood was on him Berlioz was truer to Cellini's self-portrait than Cellini ever managed to be!" It follows that any future stagings of *Benvenuto* should be inspired by "the best practice in *Meistersinger*, *Don Giovanni* and *Falstaff*." [9] In some ways, *Benvenuto* is still beyond the latest of these scores, or to put it differently, is closest to *Don Giovanni;* for Berlioz' purposeful "discontinuity" is a principle of dramatic composition which has so far been adopted only by few. *Benvenuto* irresistibly suggests treatment by one of our enlightened motion picture directors. The decor, pace, drama, mass effects, and *youth* of the work call for a visual truth-to-nature that opera seldom has the energy to seek.

As much as from Mozart, Berlioz drew his method from Shakespeare and from his own dramatic symphonies, the *Fantastique* and *Harold*. He no more wanted music to "accompany" a verbalized tale on the stage than he wanted his symphonies to narrate events. The music was to contain the drama. Hence no arias as such, no set pieces, but a sequence of "occasions" in the shape of dramatic conflicts that could be musically rendered.[10] Explanatory recitatives must be kept to a minimum, for music must not be degraded by buzzing incessantly to every kind of chatter. The resulting music drama is thus a quintessence of imaginative and sensory perceptions. Just as Berlioz wished to rid the symphony of superfluous tissue and make it unremittingly expressive, so in his first so-called opera

[8] For the validity of this ascription, see *1190.*

[9] *155*, 5.

[10] The first act does indeed contain concessions to contemporary forms. A good idea of how novel the rest was as late as 1882 may be gathered from a detailed analysis written in view of a projected London performance. (*Musical Times*, Feb. 1882, pp. 61–6.)

he followed the equivalent rule of composing only what is composable — a *minimum vocabile.*[11]

Untrained to cross ditches without help, the French public found the "gaps" in Berlioz' dramas puzzling. Any audience equally unaccustomed to following intense and rapid musical thought would also think these dramatic scenes ineffective unless admirably duplicated upon the stage. That this would be duplication is shown by the fact that a trained critic who heard only the radio version readily understood *Benvenuto's* "drama by discontinuity." On this point, a writer not at all biased in the composer's favor has said that Berlioz' "attempt to escape the stereotyped opera forms" was "on the whole analogous to Wagner's." [12] This statement is important but it may mislead. Berlioz' reform of opera in *Benvenuto Cellini* rests on the same *grounds* as Wagner's — the failure of traditional opera to be genuine music drama because it is broken up by arias and dances and nonsensified by a uniform use of tricks. But Berlioz' whole effort was towards concentration and concision and radical skips; whereas Wagner's was towards elaborate development and continuity. Berlioz would let the audience supply — or forget — the unmusical, explanatory palaver. Wagner protracted and repeated both words and music so as to make action and detailed discourse match whole symphonic movements.[13]

The similarity and difference between Berlioz and Wagner are cut across by the fact that in *Benvenuto Cellini,* the composer again makes use of thematic alteration and recall "like veritable leitmotives." [14] There is a further kinship, as we shall see, in the plot and message of the play, but to put in a word the distinctive contribution that Berlioz made in *Cellini* (though in conformity with usage he called it an opera) it may simply be called a Shakespearean musical drama. This would distinguish it, on the one hand, from Wagner's Racine- or Hugo-like play patterns, and, on the other, from Meyerbeer's imposing but undramatic pageantry.

What then is the "flaw" to which the British critic justly refers? It consists in the two or three concessions that Berlioz made to contempo-

[11] He was so little dependent on words that in accounting for "The Fifth of May," composed in the same period, he says that he was moved by the musical sentiment which lay *behind* Béranger's "quasi-poem" (*L.I.*, 169.) See below (*passim*) the several subjects that he considered "anti-musical."

[12] Masson: *289*, 178.

[13] *901*, 156–8.

[14] *289*, 178. A comparison of the overture with the remainder of the score shows again Berlioz' power to develop and redevelop ideas seemingly fully exploited the first time.

rary taste – *fioriture*, repeats, and the like. They occur chiefly in the first act, to woo the audience, and they could, perhaps ought to, be cut with a light hand until a given public becomes familiar with the rest of the score. In the published piano edition, these few numbers are the easiest to read, whence the erroneous impression that the symphonic innovator yielded without a struggle to operatic convention.[15] The truth is that if *Boris Godunov* thirty-five years later, is said on account of its form to mark a date in the history of opera, that date should be moved back to 1838.

The action of *Benvenuto Cellini* takes place in Rome during the Carnival of 1532. The sculptor-hero is in love with Teresa, daughter of the Pope's treasurer Balducci, and he means to elope with her during the confusion of the merrymaking. A recitative followed by a grumbling *fugato* gives us Balducci in the act of lecturing his daughter. From outside come noises of revelry; the dangerous Cellini is mentioned just as a bouquet is thrown through the open window with a letter for Teresa in it. She sings a romance completely traditional in form, but melodically of extraordinary psychological finesse. Balducci leaves. Cellini enters, announced by a fragment of love tune in the cellos; he enlarges the melody, in which Teresa soon joins, the voices one beat apart being delightfully treated as a canon in octave. We are still in the operatic tradition, but handled with the *maestria* of a Mozart or Rossini.

Also traditional is the fact that Cellini has a rival, the old and academic artist, Fieramosca, who is even now concealed in the room.[16] The genius-lover continues his wooing and proposes the details of the elopement. Already in this ensemble, Teresa's part is entirely untraditional and "realistic." With the lover's pleading and the muttered comments of Fieramosca, the trio is as dramatically convincing as it is tuneful; it still sparkles after a century of other music fit to make us blasé.

Balducci returns and Cellini barely makes his escape, but Fieramosca, caught in an inner room, is now subjected to a stage lynching by servants, men and women, who come in from three sides to a marvellous allegro of comic confusion. The curtain falls on a choral *tutti* of dazzling polyphonic verve and clarity. The drama is launched.

[15] This may account for the summary verdict rendered by Mr. Grout, who farther on in his *History of Opera* accords Berlioz' *Troyens* a discriminating approval. (722, 318 ff.)

[16] The name may have occurred to Berlioz from reading d'Azeglio's *Ettore Fieramosca o la Disfida di Barletta*, published in Paris in 1833, or perhaps from seeing the subject acted out by marionettes in Italy

The second scene shows the Piazza Colonna with its antique monuments and, to one side, the booth of a traveling showman. Cellini awaits his mistress and sings in the expected way of tenors a "romance" full of genuine melancholy. As characterization, it shows the reverse side of the "hero," who is not always a great artist nor a great bandit, but a man also conscious of weakness – romantic self-knowledge. Benvenuto's fellow craftsmen, the master goldsmiths and their apprentices, enter and give forth in high spirits a melody of typical Berlioz rhythm, which is to recur with great significance: Cellini had urged them to sing the praise not of wine but of art. Perhaps they sing too long before they drink, and the reason may be that they lack the wherewithal, for at this point the Pope's messenger brings money for the casting of the statue commissioned from Cellini, and they fall to. As they drink they mock the ostler's usual remonstrance – "this bill unpaid – ten dozen bottles of good *lacryma Christi. . . .*" There is a needless reprise of the chorus, followed by the reappearance of Fieramosca plotting to thwart the elopement. He sings a mock-heroic air, lunging with his sword to an ingenious rhythmic sequence,[17] and chanting his bravura until we reach the great carnival scene.

On one side of the Piazza Colonna the strolling players begin their evening show entitled the Pantomime of King Midas. Balducci and Teresa enter, soon followed by Cellini and his apprentice Ascanio, disguised as monks in white and brown. The players harangue the crowd, the crowd talks back, against an orchestral background of infinite rhythmical variety and melodic power. The pantomime is a double satire – on the stage it satirizes Balducci, in the orchestra, Italian opera. There is an arietta for Harlequin (the enchanting love tune in D of the overture) which here puts Midas to sleep. There is Pasquinello's cavatina for *tuba coloratura*, which is a gem of parody (as well as the anticipation of a fine scene in *Petrouschka*). And there is the crowning of the tuba player by Midas – a direct hit at the nature of academic choice in musical competitions.[18] At this point Balducci angrily interrupts the stage show and leaves his daughter, who suddenly finds not one, but two pairs of "monks" designing to elope with her. Fieramosca and his accomplice struggle with Cellini, who stabs his rival's bodyguard. He is just being seized by the crowd

[17] Four bars adding up to twice seven beats, followed by two bars of six and (accelerating) two of five; the time signatures alternating 3/4 with 4/4 and 2/4.

[18] The tuba was originally an ophicleide, for in 1838 the tuba was still a novelty unknown in France. Patented by Wieprecht of Berlin in 1835, and accepted in the forties, it was not heard by Berlioz until his first German tour.

when the gun of Castle San Angelo signals the putting out of lights. Cellini escapes and Ascanio leads Teresa away.

For this incomparable scene "which ranks with the closing scene of the second act of *Meistersinger* in sustained musical inspiration and lucidity of polyphonic writing." [19] Berlioz drew upon some pages of his early mass which had there expressed his vision of the Last Judgment, and which had not suited the *Requiem*. In effect, the confusion of passion, death, cross purposes, and panic treated here would characterize equally well the conceivable end of the world in the Eternal City. He added the comedy, of course, and changed much besides, but we understand better in retrospect why he had in the meanwhile been composing witches' sabbaths and brigands' orgies. Here is the perfectly logical development of one side of his musical powers; in all these scenes he was perfecting the art of rendering simultaneous and conflicting passions with clarity.[20] In *Benvenuto* and the *Requiem* his technique fully matched his intention – as may be ascertained from a study of the successive versions of persistent ideas.

The finished style of orchestration, voice leading, rhythmic counterpoint, and melodic ornament in this *Benvenuto* finale is throughout of the first order, and it justifies Liszt's sober judgment twenty years later: "He has fashioned a most impressive scene in which a whole people is the main protagonist . . . a scene so full of movement, passion, excitement, and contrasts between light and dark, laughter and the throes of death . . . love and murder, cowardice and scorn . . . a scene in which for the first time the crowd speaks with its great raging voice . . . and which surpasses anything yet done in dramatic music." [21]

The third act takes us to Cellini's atelier, at dawn. The goldsmiths and foundrymen arrive, singing the guild chorus in minor, transformed into a dirge. From outside one hears a sad folk tune, which Berlioz had noted down in Italy and which he orchestrates here with the aid of a small goldsmith's anvil in lieu of triangle. Ascanio enters and tries to cheer Teresa with a barcarolle of irresistible lilt . . . "which would assuredly become very popular if it were at all known." [22]

Next, in accordance with Berlioz' ever-present sense of manifold life,

[19] *546*, 346.

[20] As late as 1906, music critics were discovering in a then new work entitled *The Clown* (by M. de Camondo) that it is possible to superimpose sonorities for dramatic effect without creating confusion or producing a mere blend. (*1385*, 1906, 351.) Later, Darius Milhaud played another variation on Berlioz' idea in the trio of *L'Ours et la Lune*

[21] *587*, 400.

[22] *546*, 346.

we hear a religious procession. It furnishes "a characteristic example of Berlioz' power of suggesting an immediate change of mood: in a very short number of bars he has created with complete naturalness an entirely different atmosphere. . . ." [23] Through beautiful modulations this *sancta mater, ora pro nobis* is intertwined with a prayer by Teresa and Ascanio for Cellini's safety. The artist returns and gives an account of his adventures which puts one in mind of Tannhäuser's Rome Narration. "Stranger still, however, is the coincidence of the musical phrase." [24] Cellini and Teresa thereupon sing a duet that does not forward the action, after which, in short order, Balducci strides in, followed by the Cardinal-legate (originally the Pope). Balducci demands Cellini's arrest; the legate demands the statue, threatening to have it cast by another craftsman. His theme, which some find too pompous,[25] works up to a dramatic climax in which Cellini's life, forfeit by murder, and his art – treasured by Clement VII – are balanced against each other: if he will cast the Perseus by nightfall, he will be pardoned.[26]

In the evening scene that follows, Cellini speaks with Berlioz' voice, the voice of the hero-artist pitted against his twofold destiny – the common fight against circumstance and the special struggle with his daemon and the materials of his art. The music reaches high moments of passion, despair, indignation and defiance, while moving "objectively" against the contrary background of the hostile forces – officialdom, fathers, and artistic Fieramoscas. Here we have not only Shakespearean roundness of character but also the intellectual and moral cargo of an Ibsen play. "Alone in my struggle, alone with my courage," sings Benvenuto as he prepares to cast his masterpiece. The thought of nature entices him: "Why not live, a shepherd on the mountains. . . ." But despite the blind urge to strike out against coercion, the artist grows absorbed in his task.[27]

The actual casting of the great statue is imagined as taking place behind

[23] *546*, 347.

[24] *546*, 347.

[25] This is the theme in G, first heard in the pizzicato strings after the first pause in the overture. Varied again and again it is united with the whirling allegro at the end of the overture, and sung by the Cardinal when granting absolution.

[26] The historic Pope had said: "Where am I to get another Benvenuto if you hang me this one?"

[27] Mr. Masson amusingly complains that this monologue "unrolls with exasperating calm when there is only one hour more in which to cast the statue." (*289*, 176–7.) Perhaps psychological time at this point supplants clock time, as in modern fiction. Casting the statue is just as impossible in point of time, as Berlioz well knew from reading Cellini's *Memoirs*, Ch. XLI–III.

the visible scene, presumably in the Coliseum, which is peopled with officials and onlookers. The furnace glows red and work begins, to a stirring trombone theme punctuated by a rhythm suggesting the bellows of the forge.[28] At the critical point, the metal grows short. To save his life and fame, Cellini pours into the furnace all the finished works in his atelier. Tragedy broods over the holocaust but victory is assured and the hesitant mob rallies to Benvenuto. As he undergoes the ordeal of congratulation, he ticks off in an aside the flatterers and trimmers. The jubilant goldsmiths take up their corporation hymn, the Cardinal absolves, and the people and principals rejoice in a finale of Dionysiac *élan*.

If the dominant musical conception of *Benvenuto Cellini* is the rendering of chaos clear through polyphony – the chaos of passions and purposes as they mingle in reality [29] – the abstract or intellectual conception which holds the scenes together is the Romanticist view of the artist as hero. Berlioz must have experienced a wonderful release for stored-up emotions as he penned love music, guild anthems, recitatives against bad artists and official busybodies,[30] parodies of false styles, mockeries of commercial minds and treacherous friends, litanies to nature and to the deity, as well as mass effects expressive of popular joy and simple throbbing life. When finished, the work was a visible-audible presentment of the conditions under which the "Perseus," serving as symbol of all works of art, is made. In his version, Berlioz repudiates equally the false-romantic and the false-realistic view of the process. The artist is in the midst of life, and art comes out of life. This implies that the artist must cope with his own passions as a man – risking his life for love no less than for fame – and struggle as well with the established rules and vested interests that simultaneously demand and thwart his work. He saves himself by an act

[28] Compare the six-note figure of this rhythm with the simpler beat of Siegfried's forging. It may possibly indicate a national difference between two kinds of blacksmiths' equipment, for the Dauphiné forges still extant use a clapper device which Berlioz' rhythm accurately suggests. We know, incidentally, that Hector as a boy was regularly awakened at dawn by the smith across the way. (*A.R.*, 158.)

[29] Chabrier: "My God! but Berlioz could put color, variety, and rhythm into [his works]. It spoils the unity, they say; and I say: Bunk! If in order to be One, music has to be dull, I prefer to look like Two . . . Ten . . . Twenty. . . ." (*176*, 171.)

[30] The score adroitly combines the traditional *recitativo secco* (as in *Don Giovanni*) with the measured kind, and with the Berliozian half-melodic *chant-récitatif*.

of virtuosity and conscious sacrifice.[31] Great art is thus shown to be neither a product of routine devoid of inspiration and energy, nor an improvisation open to dilettantes. It is not even a wholly individual thing but the fruit of well-led co-operation. Cellini and his mates are craftsmen in a guild and the full subtitle of the opera is significant: *Benvenuto Cellini, or the Master-Goldsmiths of Florence.*[32]

Operagoers will scarcely have failed to notice that between Cellini and his *maîtres-ciseleurs* and Walther and the *Meistersinger* there is that same "strange coincidence" which critics have noted between part of the music and Tannhäuser's Rome Narration. A German student of music-drama has summed up the relation between the two works: "Not musically but in contents, *Benvenuto Cellini* reminds one constantly of *Die Meistersinger.* Fieramosca is an evil and narrow-souled character like Beckmesser; like him he is the unwanted lover of the heroine. . . . In both works the lovers plan an elopement by night during a street tumult . . . and there are still other resemblances in incident which space forbids listing." [33]

The elopement at night is not of Berlioz' invention. He doubtless read it in Hoffmann's tale of *Salvator Rosa* where Wagner may have found it too. But the intent of the whole work, taken with such minor ideas as the listing of foods in the innkeeper scene, shows beyond a doubt that the dramatic substance of *Die Meistersinger* is a *bürgerlich* transposition of Berlioz' original. The same dramatic use of the "folk" as protagonist, the same twofold struggle of the artist, the same vindication by means of the finished work, the same treatment of the message as tragicomedy — these elements which have made *Die Meistersinger* a great statement of the nineteenth-century religion of art [34] cannot have taken such similar shapes independently in two minds otherwise as closely in touch as Wag-

[31] Hans von Bülow, who as a young man worked at the *Benvenuto* revival of 1852, devoted some six articles to the score which had made him so enthusiastic. Besides the music, he discussed the moral question whether the artist stood outside the laws, and the esthetic problem of the artist's relation to tradition and to his public. (*548*, 70–3.) The thoroughness with which Bülow mastered the work enabled him to give it a notable production at Hanover in 1879 and at the end of his life, despite his neo-classic conservatism, he was still "in love with Berlioz' *Cellini.*" (*172*, 373–4.)

[32] Cellini was a Florentine who presumably took his workmen with him to Rome at the Pope's behest.

[33] *683*, 343.

[34] Edmund Crispin: "*Meistersinger* — apart from *Henry IV* — is the only thing I know which convinces one of the essential nobility of *man.*" (*1245*, 128.)

ner's and Berlioz'.[35] When the *Memoirs* of Benvenuto first aroused Berlioz' interest, Wagner was twenty years old and when the opera was first put on, he had not yet reached Paris, where the "revelation of a new world of music" – through Berlioz – awaited him. This was still twelve months away; the year was still 1838.

[35] The plan of Berlioz' work is so to speak classic in its appeal: Franz Lachner, Kapellmeister at Munich, took it over bodily for music of his own in 1849. In 1845, Rossi had composed a Cellini in Turin, and so had Berlioz' classmate Schloesser in Darmstadt. Later attempts are: Leo Kern's in Budapest (1854), Orsini's in Naples (1875), Bozzano's in Genoa (1877), and Saint-Saëns and Diaz, both in 1890 in Paris. Still later, a post-Wagnerian brew of the same materials was given by Pfitzner in his *Palestrina*. There the Council of Trent is the Beckmesser: it broods over a Mass of the hero's which (with the aid of the Pope) is finally triumphant but happily not given in full to the audience. Curiously enough, a more "exact" dramatization of Cellini in Spain, eight years after Berlioz', failed because "it sought to embrace too large and complicated a subject within the limits of drama." (*1122*, 205.)

12. The Dramatic Symphony: Romeo and Juliet

October 1838
to September 1839

. . . Let music's rich tongue
Unfold the imagined happiness. . . .
— SHAKESPEARE, *Romeo and Juliet*

A "FALLEN AUTHOR" at thirty-five, Berlioz could look back on seventeen years of unremitting struggle. Though he had not had to murder anyone in the process, his Teresas had been won and his Perseuses fashioned by sheer Cellinesque energy. As he tried to keep his opera afloat through the autumn of 1838, the score of the *Requiem* was published — the first work for which he had not had to pay. But the engraved notes had value only for other musicians, and only for the most gifted at that. Knowing that for his music to create a public, "it must be heard and heard frequently,"[1] Berlioz managed to obtain no fewer than eleven announcements on the official billboard that *Benvenuto* was to be played "any day soon."

By mid-October the words regularly put beneath the mention of other works were: "This is being played while awaiting the fourth performance of *Benvenuto Cellini.*" Owing to the departure of Duprez and Mme. Dorus-Gras, two new singers had to be rehearsed, and the beginning of November found Berlioz exhausted. Once again he took to his bed, despite other pressing cares: his brother Prosper had been sent to boarding school in Paris and depended on Hector's attentions.

On the uncommon mind of the boy of eighteen, the capital had the same effect as it had exerted on his elder brother in the now remote 1820's. A new world was opening out to the sensitive, nervous young provincial; his faculties were intensely aroused, and by a singular recurrence these were also musical faculties. Prosper went to the performances of *Benvenuto* and was later able to reproduce from memory at the piano large portions of this complex score. Sainte-Beuve, who made a point of searching biographies for indications of talent in the brothers and sisters of great men, would have found here a Mendelian proof that the Berlioz males of the seventh recorded generation were born musicians.

[1] *A.R.*, 381.

Prosper was even something more. Matching Hector's literary facility, Prosper began to develop a supernormal mathematical gift which astonished his new teachers. Though the school building was far from Berlioz' house, Hector went there often and tried to lessen the boy's homesickness, to dull the pangs of their mother's recent death, to give and to receive the affection which their upbringing had made either scant or stormy. There is something heartrending about Berlioz in this brief period – sick, fighting, harassed, and showering a fruitless maternal care on Prosper.[2] For the boy died suddenly, three months after his arrival, on January 15, 1839.

The fourth performance of *Cellini* had not yet been given when the New Year began, though everything had been in readiness by November 21. Berlioz was then in bed, feverish yet satisfied, when just a few moments ahead of curtain time, notice of one of the singers' illness postponed the work. The same thing happened on December 2, despite a formal listing, and without any illness to account for the new delay. Three days before, a concert of his works at which Berlioz could not be present was extremely well received. Public indignation at the treatment of the opera added to the warmth of the notices. A second concert was scheduled for December 16, but Berlioz did not know whether he could rouse himself to direct it.

He was played out by a series of events comparable to the most intricate plot of Dumas, and in which he was almost the only one aware of all ramifications: "My sisters," he told his father, "wrote to Prosper asking him for details of the . . . multiple machinations that surround the production of my opera. The poor boy is far from being in a position to answer, and even I can hardly do it by letter. But d'Ortigue has just published a book in which everything is quite clearly set forth. When I say 'everything,' I mean 'almost everything' because there is many a detail which I asked him to suppress. I haven't yet broken with the administra-

[2] Here is what Berlioz reports to his father after a few weeks: "Prosper works hard, the headmaster has told me several times how well satisfied he was. You know that we have always been on very good terms, my brother and I, and I can assure you I have his full confidence. The best way to have it is to show confidence in him. He complains of being in a school for little boys: I do not know whether it was on purpose that you chose this particular school. He needs blankets; he is freezing cold in bed. He would also like to be able to work in his own room, like some of the others. I find him more advanced than I had expected: his mind is fairly well stocked and it seems to me my sisters have judged him pretty severely. His mind may be slow in developing but sooner or later it will turn out remarkable. He is wild with joy when I can go out with him and it does as much for me." (*A.R.*, 386.)

tion at the Opera . . . [which] is a world of intrigue as complex as any that goes on at court." [3]

As for the causes of the present imbroglio, Berlioz had sketched them two months before: "To tell you all the goings and comings, cabals, disputes, and insults to which my work has given rise is impossible. It is a miracle to have stayed in the saddle. The fury of certain newspapers against what they call *my system* gives you only a dim notion of their fighting madness. Pamphlets are being written. It is a mêlée in which my defenders utter almost as much nonsense as my detractors. It must all be borne; it will all dissipate in time. The French have a mania for arguing about music without possessing either the rudiments of the art or any feeling for it. It was so in the last century; it is so, and will be so. . . . I count on my music . . . far more than on anything that can be said in its favor. But there have been so many changes to make because of the alteration of the text that I am stupid with fatigue." [4]

D'Ortigue's three hundred and fifty-page book [5] was a full vindication as well as a very sound critique, for d'Ortigue not only knew music but had "the feeling for it" and he could assess Berlioz' "musical revolution" in every department of the art even when he himself disliked some of the results. D'Ortigue's thesis was simple: Gluck had fought the Italian school of his day in order to reform opera in the direction of dramatic force and extended musical means. In fighting the modern Italian opera, still ridden by convention, routine, and misplaced virtuosity, Berlioz was carrying on Gluck's work. Had Berlioz not been ill, as well as worried by illness in his family near and far, he could have felt that his achievement in *Benvenuto* was very precisely measured by official opposition and admirably consecrated by d'Ortigue's essay.

On December 16, he was able to get up and conduct. The program included selections from Gluck and Berlioz' symphonies 1 and 2. In the hall of the Conservatoire which was filled to capacity, Berlioz had a roof-raising success. In 1838 in Paris, one concludes, there was a phalanx of some twelve hundred people who understood and admired Berlioz' music. They were not numerous enough to uphold an opera, but they justified the existence of an orchestral composer even though his financial reward was inadequate. Certainly the moral support was immeasurably greater than anything our own century has been able to do for comparable

[3] *A.R.*, 385.
[4] *A.R.*, 380–1.
[5] *De l'école musicale italienne et de l'Académie royale de musique* [the Opera] *à l'occasion de l'opéra de M. H. Berlioz*, Paris, 1839.

innovators, for a Varèse or a Van Dieren. Nor has our collective practical faith in the arts been able to match the individual largesse of a Paganini. For it was at this very concert that the thin cadaverous figure of the virtuoso came to the front of the stage and declaring in his hoarse whisper that "Beethoven had at last a successor" knelt at Berlioz' feet in full view of the circle of friends and handshakers.

Two days later, Berlioz – who had caught more cold on coming out into the damp fog – received the often quoted message:

> Beethoven being dead, only a Berlioz could reincarnate him. I who have fed on your divine compositions, worthy of a genius such as yours, feel it my duty to ask you to accept in homage the sum of 20,000 francs, which the Baron Rothschild will remit on sight of the accompanying note.
>
> Believe me always your affectionate friend
>
> NICOLO PAGANINI

Berlioz replied:

> How can I express my gratitude? Though I am anything but rich, I feel bound to say that the approval of a man of genius touches me more nearly than the kingly generosity of your gift. Words fail me. I will go and embrace you as soon as I can leave my bed.[6]

The newspapers having reproduced the letter and told of the act of homage on bended knee, Paris was as excited as if a new revolution had broken out. The scene was re-enacted on the stage by impersonators of the principals;[7] and Paris naturally had to "explain" what it could scarcely grasp – *giving* away twenty thousand francs, and to a composer! Paganini moreover had the reputation of being a miser, which in reality was but the desire not to be fleeced by plausible beggars, and not to be swamped by requests for charity concerts.[8] Stories were soon made up to accommodate old rumors and new facts. The first inspiration of the crowd was that with twenty thousand francs Berlioz would surely buy a house. Then it sought to incriminate Paganini's motives: by his gift to Berlioz, he was purchasing public esteem; or else Paganini had not given the money, but only lent his name to cover a present from the Bertins to their protégé and newspaper critic.

When these tales reappeared in books in the fifties, Paganini's son

[6] *A.R.*, 387–9.

[7] *235*, II, 184.

[8] When Paganini refused to play for another artist's benefit, he was "a miser," but when he played in the cholera-infested city for the benefit of the plague victims, no one bothered to call him a hero.

utterly denied them, and modern students of the violinist's career sustain the good faith of the man and the deed.[9] Human motives are mixed, no doubt, and Paganini may have enjoyed the histrionic side of the adventure, but he chose in accordance with his instinct and reason: there were dozens of others to be a patron to – more popular than Berlioz or less popular, richer or poorer. Paganini could buy himself whatever magnanimous role he wished, and he chose unerringly an artist who would use the gift to create music, not to set up housekeeping. In Paganini's own words, "I saw a young man full of genius whose strength and courage might have ultimately broken down under the strain. . . . I said to myself, 'It is my duty to help him.' . . . When my claims to musical renown are reckoned up, it will not be the least that I was the first to recognize a genius and draw public attention to him. . . ."[10] The whole incident may strike us today as ostentatious, overemphatic, but it speaks of its time as well as any deed of Roman virtue or Greek courage speaks of theirs, and the overemphasis of twenty thousand francs was one that Berlioz found himself able to bear with equanimity.

Besides this "metal" which spelled for him the leisure to compose, Berlioz had two other pieces of good fortune by way of Christmas gifts: d'Ortigue's book appeared and caused considerable stir, and he was named curator of the Conservatoire library at an annual salary of fifteen hundred francs. Though there were delays, the appointment was ratified in February and made retroactive to January 1. Berlioz' immediate superior, the librarian, was Bottée de Toulmon, a scholar who was also an admirer and who had written excellent critiques – especially of the *Requiem* – in the *Gazette Musicale*.[11] Under him, short of earthquake or revolution, Berlioz would have a lifelong post whose duties were extremely light.

Berlioz paid his visit of gratitude to Paganini and in telling all his good news to Adèle gives us a glimpse of the virtuoso as he was and as he was thought to be: "You know he has lost the use of his voice [from tubercu-

[9] But see Jeffrey Pulver, *Paganini*, London, 1939, pp. 297–8. A moment's thought is enough to dismiss the malicious imputations: how could Paganini both be a miser and act the bountiful for a pair of newspaper owners – themselves assumed too delicate to make the handsome gesture outright? What could induce the stubborn violinist to write a faked message, to kneel in public, and to protract the deception until his death? See Mr. Pulver's own estimate of Paganini's proud character, *ibid.*, 306–9. Mr. Richard Franko Goldman, who has examined the Paganini papers in the Library of Congress, was kind enough to tell me that no new document on the gift to Berlioz is to be found in this voluminous collection.

[10] *Journal de Paris*, Jan. 18, 1839, quoted in *300*, 127.

[11] *1398* (1837) 331 ff.

losis of the throat.] . . . When he saw me, tears came into his eyes. I confess my own were not far behind my lids. He wept, this man-eater, this murderer of women, this ex-convict — as he has so often been called. . . . Then, wiping his eyes and striking the table in a loud burst of laughter, he started to address me volubly; but as I could not clearly follow his words, he went to fetch his little son to serve as interpreter . . . I gathered that he was 'very happy . . . because the insects who write and speak against me would be rather abashed. . . .' What a rumpus the news [of his gift] will make in Germany and England. Such a gesture — and from an Italian . . . but one must add that he does not compose Italian music." [12]

Then, unaware of the significant and touching jump in his thought: "I hope my father will be satisfied. . . . Now I shall be able to make my trip to Germany. It so happens that many German artists are in Paris this winter, and they exhibit towards my music a most encouraging fanaticism." [13]

A few days later, on January 11, 1839, the fourth and last performance of the original version of *Cellini* took place. It was precisely at this time that Prosper took sick, recovered momentarily, then died. Berlioz wrote on the same day to Jules Janin, "I am very sad today. I have just lost my brother, a poor boy of nineteen whom I loved." [14] Hector could only do what he had always done with grief: repress and bury it. But the effort brought on the usual nervous reaction, visible in his next letter to Liszt; to be affectionate and talk of music and recall Italian days was like passing from a place of torture to a perfect world:

I am ruminating a new symphony, which I'd love to go and finish near you, at Sorrento or Amalfi — (Go to Amalfi!) — but it's impossible. I'm in the breach and must hold it. I have never led such an agitated life. . . . My followers send me a mass of prose and verse, and my detractors anonymous threats. One of them . . . advised me to shoot myself — isn't it delightful? . . . This is a sort of life I like about as much as you do, but by dint of tumbling among the breakers we should manage to tame them and keep them from rolling over our heads.

And so you're in Rome. M. Ingres will surely welcome you, especially if you will play him our Adagio in C-sharp minor of Beethoven and the A-flat sonata of Weber. I greatly admire the fanaticism of this great painter's musical passions, and you will heartily forgive him for loathing me when you remember that he adores Gluck and Beethoven.

How I enjoy chatting with you tonight! I love you so, Liszt. When shall you come back to us? . . . I've had a severe bronchitis, which for

[12] *A.R.*, 391. [13] *A.R.*, 391–2. [14] *A.R.*, 394.

a while made me think of Gluck's ode "Charon calls you" . . . Why am I so gay? Our friends are for the most part sad. Legouvé has a painful gastritis. Schoelcher has just lost his mother. Heine *is not happy*. Chopin is ill in the Balearic islands. Dumas drags his chain, which feels heavier day by day. Mme. Sand has a sick child. Hugo alone stands calm and strong. . . .

Please remember me to Mme. d'Agoult. I sincerely thank her for her interest in the success of my doings. She does it from affection for you, but I am not the less grateful. Farewell. Farewell. I embrace you with my whole soul and wish you a north wind – since you are in Rome. Your friend.[15]

The life of "tumbling in the breakers" was more tedious than the image suggested. The regular turning out of copy for the newspapers, the business calls, the correcting of proofs (the *Benvenuto* overture was coming out in full score), and the pelting succession of operas, virtuosi, and ballets – they had to be seen to be reviewed – all broke up the inner stream of thought indispensable for creation, not to say necessary to a humane existence. Berlioz' constant subacute irritation from these causes did not contribute to peace at home. Though the certain signs of a domestic rift cannot be pointed to for another eighteen months, it is likely that already at this time Hector and Harriet were in disharmony. She, wounded in her professional pride by repeated failures, knowing that her debts were a drag on her husband's career, and feeling that this lessened her right to demand more of his time, became restless, jealous, and in the end more demanding than she herself wished to be. True, there were visitors, friends, plenty of activity and no lack of intellectual excitement in the home. And there was Louis to love and the household to take care of, but Harriet's difficulty with French interfered with all these pleasures, just at the time when her physical charms were waning and her late-awakened love for Hector was reaching a peak of possessiveness.[16]

He, on his side, harassed, nervous, impatient, always rushing into his workroom to dash off a *feuilleton* or seize a musical idea in its flight, must have been equally unsatisfactory as a married partner. He was extremely fond of his little boy and played with him in whirlwind snatches of gaiety, but even this may have seemed to Harriet a further exclusion.

[15] *A.R.*, 395–9.

[16] From all we know of her early life and character – that is, her exemplary virtue – it may be plausibly inferred that her emotional development corresponds to that described as a generality by Freud: "When later the retarded development of the wife becomes rectified, and . . . the full power of love awakens in her, her relation to her husband has been long undermined [by psychical as well as physical unresponsiveness]." (*1167*, 180.)

Hector was lavishing his affection, his energy, his zest on everyone but her; she had no means left to center them again on herself – or so it seemed.

Despite later insinuations and the odd reasoning that because Berlioz met singers and ballerinas, and his wife was jealous, he must have given her cause for jealousy, no rumor at the time even hinted of infidelity on his part. Considering the degree to which the lives of all Berlioz' contemporaries, and his own, were reflected in the daily press, it is unlikely that his enemies would have left us ignorant on this score. And again, it is not likely that Berlioz, if in love with another woman, would have yielded to such *épanchements de coeur* as we saw him addressing to Liszt. Given the "mechanism" of Berlioz' genius, the musical love scene he was beginning to compose argues rather the absence of love than its possession: only once did he find himself able to write under the actual impact of a feeling.[17] When we add that the love music being written made use of still another boyhood melody associated with Estelle, we may infer that Berlioz was only longing or ready to love, and we shall not be surprised at the later breakup of his marriage. At the moment he was too busy, too exhilarated by Paganini's gift of freedom, too full of musical strength – exuberant in his previous score, latent in the *grandissime symphonie* now in progress – to engage either in flirtations or in a passionate affair. In the last resort, Harriet could, for a time, rely on Berlioz' strong family feeling and thoroughly bourgeois sense of dignity.

In April 1839, his beloved Adèle was married to Marc Suat. It would have been a great satisfaction to go to the wedding, but how could he, with or without Harriet? If she went, she might be snubbed; if he went alone, it would be a victory for provincial prejudices. He pleaded the perfectly real pressure of duties, but he would have been less than human had he not felt regret; and inevitably associated with this feeling were Harriet's inadequacies. With her loving tact, Adèle proposed that she should come to Paris after her marriage and take back with her little Louis, who would thus have a vacation in the country and be his parents' advocate in the hearts of his Dauphiné relatives. Hector was touched, though he could not help noticing that no one but her had written to him since the wedding. Harriet first consented to send the boy away, then wept, then agreed again. The father felt he must warn his sister: "He is the most charming and badly brought-up child you ever saw. He threatens

[17] The *Elégie* included in the *Irish Melodies* of 1829. See *Mem.*, I, 99, and compare his dreaming of Estelle's garden during the time he composed the *Requiem*. (*Mem.*, I, 308.)

everybody with his sword and utters all sorts of insults when crossed. He swears like – like his father . . . withal he is charming, and enchanted at the idea of picking peaches and strawberries with his grandfather, but I don't know how he will take his parents' absence: he can't be away from them for one evening without tears. Well, you'll see when you come to Paris." [18]

Despite more illness, due to nerves and bad weather (it was a freezing cold spring) the writing of the new symphony was proceeding. At the same time, a certain thawing out of officialdom was noticeable – as if after all *Benvenuto Cellini* had been a success. On May 10, the Comte de Gasparin awarded Berlioz the Legion of Honor, and the next month, on the death of Paer, the press urged the Institute to elect Berlioz. Paganini's words, "the successor of Beethoven," had become a catch phrase embodying another consecration. Berlioz, not yet thirty-six, seemed the master of instrumental music in France. Nor does it look different in retrospect: between 1830 and 1860, no one in Europe was writing music of comparable power.

Berlioz was not to enter the Institute so soon. He learned that the aged and embittered master whom he so deeply admired, Gasparo Spontini, was a candidate for the vacant seat and he withdrew. He also spurred on his friend, the poet Emile Deschamps, to write a pamphlet on behalf of Spontini's election. To this, the tactless Spontini returned "an incredibly ridiculous letter" which he made public, but he was elected just the same.[19] Berlioz was wise enough to overlook the older man's blunder, knowing that musical genius does not preclude wordly ineptitude.[20] He continued to admire and to soothe in his last unhappy years the master whose career in some ways resembled his own.[21]

When the new symphony was near completion, Berlioz undertook a new project looking to his vindication at the Opera. Since nearly everyone but himself had blamed the libretto for his failure, he would secure one from the best manufacturer, Meyerbeer's own appointed tradesman, Eugène Scribe. On August 31, 1839, after approaches and interviews,

[18] *A.R.*, 402.
[19] *L.I.*, 187.
[20] "He has been virtually hounded out of Prussia, and so I felt it my duty to write to him. In such a case one must miss no opportunity to put in a word that might restore a little calm to the lacerated heart of the man of genius, regardless of his faults or even of his egotism: the temple may be unworthy of the indwelling deity, but the god is a god." (To Ferrand, *L.I.*, 194.)
[21] *Soirées* (13th).

Berlioz wrote to him: "I shall not take the liberty of telling you the kind of dramatic ideas that would suit me best: you know perfectly well what they are. However, in seeking a subject which would afford occasions for broad musical developments, and passionate and unexpected effects, it may be useful for me to tell you that certain individuals and groups are deeply uncongenial to me – Luther, for example, the Christians of the Lower Empire, and those brutish Druids." [22]

Berlioz goes on to say that he wants a *simple* love plot, however passionate, combined with scenes of terror "in which mass action would have a place." The Middle Ages, he says, or the last century (that is, the eighteenth) would suit him equally well. "I should greatly love an antique subject, but I apprehend the costumes and the prosy positivism of our audiences. Naturally, this does not mean that one must keep always in the heroic or dithyrambic style. On the contrary, I am fond of contrasts." [23] "The antique" stood here for Berlioz' cherished Virgil, just as the rejected eras and persons stood for the cruelty which he abhorred. A Virgilian libretto by Scribe would no doubt have engaged Berlioz' fullest attachment and robbed us of the epic *Trojans*, fashioned altogether by Berlioz twenty years later; but the popular playwright knew better than to make such an attempt.

By an odd coincidence, as Berlioz was writing of scenes of terror, a woman living in his apartment house went mad and threw the other tenants into a panic.[24] Berlioz had to remove his wife and child for a few days, just as he was about to write to Kastner concerning the new symphony: "I have finished, quite finished, what might be called altogether finished: not another note to write, Amen, amen, amenissimen." [25]

The full title of the work was *Romeo and Juliet, dramatic symphony for chorus, solo voices and orchestra*, and Berlioz at once set about getting a hearing for it. For three whole months he had been practically a free man, a composer working on unmortgaged time. Now the business of copying parts, rehearsing, and reviewing others' works claimed him again. In addition, he found himself appointed Special Master by an equity court, and charged with arbitrating a suit pending between the violinist

[22] *86*, 580. It seems probable that Berlioz had not read Luther's *Life and Table Talk* by Michelet, in which he would have found that Luther loved music next to theology and like Berlioz himself played the flute and guitar. From other references it is clear that in Berlioz' mind, Luther stood for Puritanism and the wars of religion.

[23] *Ibid.*

[24] *A.R.*, 406.

[25] *A.R.*, 406.

Charles de Bériot and three different publishers, French, English, and German. Berlioz had to work up the facts and render justice without letting his equal involvements with colleague and publisher affect his judgment.

While he was accomplishing this feat, his friend Dietsch was rehearsing the choruses in *Romeo*. Berlioz was himself gathering his orchestra, sending out requests and notices by hand, procuring special instruments,[26] or scouring the town for two good harpists. Because of the shortness of time, Berlioz devised the method of rehearsing his instrumentalists by groups – strings, woodwinds, and brass and timpani in separate places. Thus the two days for each section plus two for all together became the equivalent of six or eight rehearsals. As soloists he had Dupont (who had ably succeeded Duprez in *Benvenuto*), Mme. Stoltz (the Ascanio of the same opera), and Alizard.[27] In his favorite Salle du Conservatoire, "resonant like a good violin," Berlioz would have two hundred performers. The date of the *première* was November 24, 1839.

A week before, advance publicity began to appear. Janin in the *Débats* summoned the faithful, promising (in Berlioz' very words to him) that "the symphony by itself and without the accessories of Shakespeare's play, will make known to you the sum of passion contained in the original." This was the essence of the dramatic symphony as a genre, the literal "music drama." The same day, a society columnist, the poetess Delphine (Gay) de Girardin, reported that the seats were sold out and that the fashionable world was busy haggling and trading for them. "Come, dears: you will hear wonderful things. Just see the libretto . . ." and the writer filled up her column with verses quoted from an advance copy of the Prologue.

[26] Such as the little "antique cymbals" akin to those which the Bible calls "tinkling" – no misnomer as is sometimes believed.

[27] Louis Alizard (1814–50) was a violin pupil of Urhan, who discovered his voice. A fine bass, he made himself into a barytone in order to be taken on at the Opera. Tuberculosis set in in his larynx and carried him off at the peak of his success.

The Third, Model of the Dramatic Symphony

> No one, I suppose, will misunderstand the genre to which this work belongs.
> — BERLIOZ' Preface to *Romeo and Juliet*

On reading the first notices of Berlioz' new work the Paris public may well have wondered, "What sort of symphony is it that has a libretto and verses to quote?" Beethoven's choral Ninth was scarcely known; Berlioz' note on the *Fantastique* was ten years past, and though all his intervening scores had been at once dramatic and symphonic, this was the first to exhibit in one form all the resources of the genre. November 1839 is therefore a milestone in the composer's history and in that of nineteenth-century music: in his own history, because here was the logical outcome of the *genre instrumental expressif* which he had taken up as Beethoven's successor; in the history of music, because paralleling the great fact of Liszt's presence at the *première* of the *Fantastique*, the *première* of *Romeo and Juliet* numbered among its hearers a youth of twenty-six named Richard Wagner. From the "revelation" which Wagner admitted experiencing[1] comes not only an important part of his own musical development, but his confusing attempts to theorize against Berlioz. When that confusion began to threaten in the late forties, Berlioz wrote for his *Romeo and Juliet* the short explanatory Preface which opens with the ironic sentence quoted at the head of this section.

The Dramatic Symphony, as its name seeks to show, is a symphony and a drama; it follows — to use the terminology used in Chapter 7 of this book — "two programs, both formal." The first and most important is the musical-symphonic pattern. In *Romeo and Juliet* the outline of the regular symphony, though enlarged and supplemented, is easily recognized. If we begin with the familiar orchestral excerpts we find that the first (actually Part Two of the symphony as a whole) is a double allegro — Romeo before, and at, the Capulets' ball. Its form combines certain features of the rondo and the sonata form. The next part, the love scene, is an adagio; and the next is the famous Queen Mab scherzo, after which comes a complex Finale.

This Finale is a choral ensemble, as in Beethoven's next-to-last sym-

[1] *245*, 234–5.

phonic plan. But just as in the sketches of the projected Tenth, Beethoven felt the need to introduce the voices at some point well before the end – perhaps in the adagio – so Berlioz, without knowing these intentions, felt that the "too sudden appearance" of the chorus in a final movement was "harmful to the unity of the composition." [2] On musical grounds, therefore, a choral symphony presented a problem whose solution called for a new structure. Berlioz decided to introduce the voices gradually, and in so doing to exercise the care of an architect whose edifice must seem balanced and proportioned from all sides.

Since the work is symphonic, it was logical to begin with an orchestral (fugued) Introduction, near the middle of which occurs a "solo" for tenor trombones and ophicleide which is marked "with the character of a recitative." We are thus insensibly prepared for vocal utterance in the next number, called Prologue. In this, a contralto solo and a small chorus of sixteen voices sing the subject of the drama – the feud of the two families and the star-crossed love of their offspring. This very brief quasi-recitative leads to the instrumental statement of several of the later themes – sadness, revelry, and finally the love theme which leaps out exultantly.

The solo voice next sings of young love in strophe and antistrophe. The small chorus then resumes with a few words on Romeo, Mercutio, and Queen Mab, whose airy being forms here the subject of a *scherzetto:* she lends the comic-fantastic element to the tragedy, as a scherzo may in any symphony. The remaining seventeen bars of the Prologue dwell on the tragic death of the lovers and the reconciling of the families, the close itself being on a vocal figure drawn from the later funeral march. A pause, and Part Two, the previously mentioned instrumental rondo-allegro begins, ushered in by a slow introduction.

The function of the Prologue has accordingly been threefold: it has prepared the ear by subtly combining vocal and instrumental music; it has prepared the mind by stating in brief form the main musical themes to be later developed; and it has prepared the imagination by summarizing the subject of the drama. Berlioz naturally drew the idea of a Prologue from Shakespeare's play, as Shakespeare had drawn it – in the person of a chorus – from the ancient music drama of the Greeks: throughout the ages drama and music combine their forms whenever congruent. Berlioz' musical handling was so logical that Wagner adopted it a quarter century later when he made *Rheingold* the theme-stating prologue of his *Ring* trilogy.

[2] Preface to *Romeo and Juliet, Min. Sc.*, vii.

From this point we can go on to speak of music and drama as one, in keeping with Berlioz' interweaving of their formal requirements. The symphonic Part Two takes Romeo through the contrasting moods of lonely sadness and of indifference to the gaiety of the concert and ball. In order not to let us forget the voices, Berlioz next provides a brief choral interlude[3] which introduces the adagio: the Capulets sing as they leave the festive dance which has just resounded in the orchestra. There is even a touch of satire in this vocal nocturne, for what the lightheaded guests sing as they depart is the theme of the ball music in the wrong meter, 6/8 instead of 2/2.

The adagio unfolds its tragic passion instrumentally "because first of all, this is a symphony and not an opera . . . and also because . . . the sublimity of the love itself made its expression so full of danger for the composer that he preferred to give a wider latitude to his imagination than would have been possible with words. He had recourse to the instrumental idiom, a richer, more varied, less limited language, and by its very unliteralness infinitely more powerful."[4]

Likewise the ensuing scherzo which stands for Queen Mab suggests lightness and free fancy without in the least following Mercutio's long speech full of concrete images. The form of the scherzo is regular, with slight variations dictated by the nature of the musical material. We have now heard some fifteen minutes of instrumental music and it is time to recall the voices. A funeral march provides the occasion by means of an ingenious and original device: it is scored for orchestra with a psalmody (single repeated note) in the voices, and continues thus as far as the midpoint, when the disposition of parts is reversed: the orchestra holds the monotone and the chorus of Capulets sings the dirge. The mood and material of this combination have insensibly shifted for us the vocal and instrumental balance. In the first half (psychologically measured) of the drama, the orchestra predominates, but the voices are never very far away; in the second half the voices predominate and allow the climax that has been planned from the first to employ all the resources of modern music without upsetting the symphonic form by a top-heavy conclusion.

But this fullness even in the Finale is not reached at once. After the funeral march comes a short instrumental *scena* which recalls earlier motives, and marks, with the end of purely instrumental music, the end of the tragedy itself. Berlioz' sense of symmetry makes him introduce here the songlike invocation for woodwinds which balances the trombone

[3] Omitted in Toscanini's Victor recording. (*1456.*)
[4] Preface, *Min. Sc.*, vii.

recitative in the very first section of the score. The *scena* ends pianissimo on the disintegrated fragments of the love theme.

The vocal Finale thus stands outside the main action, again in balance with the Introduction and Prologue. Its design is that of a gradual crescendo, which incidentally served as the model for Wagner's practice in *Tannhäuser* and elsewhere.[5] First we hear a recall of the feud theme: the outraged families wrangle vocally over the corpses. But soon the voice of Friar Laurence recites what has happened and entreats the warring clans to make peace.[6] He proposes the oath of reconciliation in the "air" which follows the recitative, and as he pleads first one chorus *sotto voce*, then the other, joins in majestic phrases that slowly cause the vengeful hearts to expand; a threatening figure in the lower strings keeps taunting them with tragedy until their voices overwhelm it in a song expressive of the gladdened will at peace with men. The music drama is concluded.

A Wagnerite critic who did not approve of the Dramatic Symphony could truly write that "Berlioz has pursued his double goal with a rare tenacity and displayed extraordinary skill in the ungrateful task. . . . The score shows . . . a complex plan . . . which must have been long pondered and painstakingly followed."[7] As we know, Berlioz had been thinking of *Romeo and Juliet* for about ten years. From the first he had said of the play that "everything in it is designed for music," by which he meant his quintessential kind of musical résumé.[8] He never had any intention of taking the play or any reduced version and "setting it" from beginning to end. This is what he meant when he remarked of his own work that it did not *resemble* Shakespeare's masterpiece.[9] He chose or invented strictly musical situations, which it would be easy (as before) to reduce to a series of familiar musical terms.[10]

[5] *1290*, 83.

[6] His solo matches the contralto's stanzas about young love in the Prologue.

[7] *489*, 65. Compare Otto Lüning (of Chur), "The structure of this tremendous work is completely thought out, symmetrical, and grounded upon inner necessity." (*363*, I, 25.)

[8] *V.M.*, II, 90. He did not know that Beethoven had considered this same play of Shakespeare's before choosing *Fidelio*, nor that he associated the Juliet tomb scene with the adagio of his quartet Op. 18, no. 1.

[9] *Mem.*, II, 261.

[10] For example:

Music	*Drama*
1. Thematic Catalogue	PROLOGUE
2. Reverie and Bacchanal 3. Nocturne: Adagio amoroso	ACTION
4. Scherzo	INTERLUDE
5. Marcia funebre 6. Scena: Invocation and Love-death	DENOUEMENT
7. Choral finale: recitative, air, and ensemble	EPILOGUE

Berlioz' belief that the music-dramatist must follow a different road from the playwright's, even though inspired by him, is shown by the fact that in the first version of the *Romeo* symphony there were two prologues, as in the play. Berlioz soon cut the second – musically rich as it was, according to Heller's account – because Berlioz saw that it spoiled the form of the symphony. At the same time, it was truly Shakespearean to unite in one work lyric and dramatic expression and prose besides. When the score is well known it shows in a multitude of ways the art with which Berlioz avoids jarring us as we move from one mood and type of sound to another; how constantly and yet naturally he keeps echoing in one movement the theme or atmosphere of another. As in *Benvenuto Cellini,* the leitmotif plays its role – Wagner heard it there – but so free and flexible that it needs no labels to mark its uses. Not a device for the theater, it is rather an illustration of the rule that ornament must flow from main subjects. The drama is thus not external to the music, nor added by the poet's contributing something which music lacks: the drama is in the music. It is only the *story* around the drama that justifies the verses and the libretto, for those who want to know the names of the dramatis personae and be reminded of Shakespeare's plot.

When Toscanini gave *Romeo and Juliet* entire for the first time in New York this century,[11] one critic declared that, for him, the work

[11] Oct. 7, 9, and 11, 1942. A technical note: If one collates the two French editions of the symphony, one finds in the Adagio a difficulty with regard to the placing of the mutes. The German Edition is obviously wrong, but the second French Edition, which the Eulenburg miniature score follows, also presents a puzzle. It may be corrected by keeping the first and second violins unmuted until p. 151 b. 2 (*Min. Sc.*), and muting only the second violins at that point.

To this correction, Mr. Toscanini objects and substitutes another, as he kindly explained to me during a conversation sought by him before his first New York performance of the work. He contends that Berlioz cannot have intended to put mutes on the second violins and violas playing *pp.*, while keeping them off the first violins and cellos. Toscanini accordingly takes them off all the strings throughout the passage. The first French Edition, reproduced in the *Treatise,* furnishes some warrant for this reading, but if one goes back to the Chorus of Shades in *Lélio* (p. 9 b. 1), one finds part of the strings muted, part unmuted. It is very likely that Berlioz tried out the effect over a broader range in *Romeo*. The retention of the marking *pp.* would then be the proofreader's error, and not the direction to use mutes. Berlioz' autograph corrections on the engraved score at the Bibliothèque Nationale tend to bear out this view. It is worth adding that a similar combination of muted strings with unmuted is found in Brahms' chamber works, as well as in a modern *Adagio for String Quartet* by Mr. George Perle (1938).

"had come to stay." [12] Others expressed reservations, saying that the familiar orchestral excerpts were great music, but that the other, unfamiliar parts were not. It is no reflection on their musicianship that the chief enthusiast after this performance was the writer of the concert notes, who had attended the rehearsals and analyzed the score. After a second performance, five years later, many of the other critics' reservations disappeared.[13] The music no longer sounded new and strange, the sequence of the parts seemed more logical, and the mind could master the profusion of art which a contemporary of Berlioz' had found in the score: "Heavens, it's beautiful! But it keeps on until one is dazzled." [14] That it is not any programmatic literalism which makes the work difficult is shown by the complaints of operagoers familiar with Gounod or concerned about Berlioz' neglect of Shakespeare's plot.[15] The formalists of course object to the dramatic symphony that it is a hybrid, neither symphony, oratorio, nor opera.[16]

The work is no hybrid but a new species. Berlioz' "long-pondered plan" is simple and logical: given his notion of modern music, instrumental and vocal, his ideal of "one work," and his dramatic faculty, fertilized by Shakespeare's poem, the real problem of form was to achieve unity, variety, and balance in a series of movements displaying all the newest technical resources – vocal, choral, and instrumental. Tradition supplied the framework of the symphonic sequence, here enlarged to accommodate other elements in close concatenation. If the alternation of air, trio, and chorus in Haydn's *Creation* is intelligible, then soloists and double chorus can surely mingle their voices in *Romeo and Juliet* as they do in secular oratorio, opera, or sacred works like the *Saint Matthew Passion.* For Bach, too, was deeply influenced by opera and deeply repelled by its conventions. Yet the *Saint Matthew Passion* contains some of the most magnificent recitatives ever written. Do they *belong* to opera like a patented device, or would saying so be to import into a musical question the irrelevant question of where, in what house, or linked to what subjects, certain forms of sound are usually heard? [17]

[12] Mr. Robert Bagar in the *N. Y. World Telegram,* Oct. 8, 1942.

[13] Precisely what happened in Paris in 1890. See *406,* 140 and 147–9.

[14] Quoted in *300,* 133.

[15] *E.g.,* Mr. Richard Stebbins: *518, passim.*

[16] Miss Dika Newlin (*842,* 157–8). On the other side, Romain Rolland, Saint-Saëns, Alfred Ernst, Charles Koechlin unhesitatingly call *Romeo and Juliet* a masterpiece as well as a model for later composers.

[17] The oratorio itself is only "sacred" by association. Akin to the masque, it is a secular, "storytelling," dramatic form. When Handel began to write dramatic oratorios instead of operas the outcry, the ridicule, the jokes and the

This hardening of random associations has gone regrettably farther now than in Berlioz' day. His contemporaries could readily accept the form of *Romeo and Juliet* and appreciate its symmetry because nearly every concert included vocal and choral pieces side by side with symphonic. There could be no reasonable objection to making a meaningful oneness out of sensory experiences that were found acceptable separately. Less than a year after Berlioz' dramatic symphony, Mendelssohn fashioned a kindred work, which his friend Klingemann christened a "symphony cantata." [18] This was not so tightly knit an affair as *Romeo and Juliet* but it shows the feasibility of building up larger forms out of lesser. Fifty years after *Romeo and Juliet,* César Franck constructed his *Psyche* upon the same plan. Actually, what we hear today when Bruno Walter gives us Gluck's *Orpheus* on the concert stage, or when we play it on discs is close to a symphony cantata. Vocal solos and choral movements follow upon instrumental pieces, the effect being enhanced, not diminished, by the absence of ragged scenery and bad costuming.[19]

In his dramatic symphony, then, Berlioz was fashioning a synthesis based on his masters, Beethoven, Weber, and Gluck. Considering the Ninth Symphony the starting point for all modern music, he built his new form on the expanded but recognizable skeleton of the four-movement symphony. From Gluck's later works (which he called "vast dramatic poems") [20] and Weber's use of little instrumental *scenas* before or after vocal movements, Berlioz likewise drew elements of form visible in the grand design for which he had been steadily striving since his prize cantatas. A dramatic, choral symphony on a Shakespearean subject was thus the logical outcome of a tradition and an internal development as well. In short, the new form was evolved like any other historic [21] genre.

---

imputations of artistic folly were as violent as the later ones against Berlioz – and almost identical in wording.

[18] *The Hymn of Praise*, op. 52. In Mendelssohn's letter acknowledging "the admirable title you have hit on so cleverly," he says he has added four new pieces and much improved "the three sets of symphonies." Moreover, he is seriously thinking of "resuming the first *Walpurgisnacht* under the same cognomen." (*1366*, 214–5.)

[19] Toscanini's broadcasts have brought us concert operas in parts, just as Berlioz used to do with Gluck and Spontini. The American composer Mark Brunswick has done the same at the College of the City of New York, and Mr. Stokowski has reduced Wagner operas to concert form on discs. These alterations are by no means equally justified: the point is rather that they are feasible.

[20] *Grot.*, 197.

[21] The so-called *genres* arrive at their moment of fixity only after successive mixtures; there is no more pure race in art forms than in human life.

Whether we look back to Berlioz' early scores, or ahead to the *Damnation of Faust, Les Troyens,* and *Beatrice and Benedict,* we see the same conception of *dramma per musica.* Given such consistency, it cannot be said that the shape of these works was the result of accidental circumstances – the prospect or the impossibility of operatic staging – for the works designated as operas suggest the Dramatic Symphony; the oratorios and other sacred works (*Te Deum* and *Infant Christ*) suggest the Dramatic Symphony; and the work which the German editors class with *Lélio* as a "secular cantata," namely the *Damnation of Faust,* equally suggests the Dramatic Symphony.[22]

The *Faust* subject is conclusive. Berlioz' *Eight Scenes* composed in 1828 were arranged as an embryonic drama, with poetic tags acting as transitional stage directions.[23] After the vocal *Faust,* Berlioz devoted himself to the instrumental genre, though suggesting by the pattern and the program notes of the *Fantastique* that the words might be considered as the sung portions of an antique drama. *Lélio,* especially in the *Tempest* fantasia, was a further essay in fusion, after which *Harold in Italy,* with its instrumental cantos, had for a time been planned to include voices. In *Romeo and Juliet* the chorus sings, antique fashion, the themes are enunciated and the fusion is achieved. The conclusion is irresistible that Berlioz, far from being swayed by diverse influences and opportunities, preserved throughout his career the fixity of mind of a monomaniac. Only, he had all the flexibility of a sane and intelligent man who, for each purpose and with each new subject, alters and adapts his preferred procedure.

The body of his work thus constitutes, not a system, but a complete series of variants on one form. Though he liked for public convenience to keep close to the conventional designation for each score,[24] he actually freed composers from enslavement to the mold and its label, and led them to respect the subtler demands of their dramatic subjects. It was after him, and not before, that the orchestral repertory came to be enriched by "Poems," "Meditations," "Portraits," and "Orations," with or without voices. His own nomenclature, modest in itself, expressed his concern

[22] Landormy gives it that title in his Introduction. (575, 7.)

[23] See above, Subchapter 4. The manuscript fragments of the unfinished opera *Les Francs-Juges,* which antedates the *Faust* scenes by four years, shows the same construction by alternation of sizable orchestral movements and vocal and choral scenes.

[24] *Grot.,* 227. He used "symphony," "dramatic symphony," and "opera," side by side with "dramatic legend," "sacred trilogy," etc. The *Damnation of Faust* he referred to, at first, as a "concert opera" to make its character quickly intelligible, but after its performances throughout Europe, he always called it a "dramatic legend." *Grot.,* 31.

with design. Though his own deviations from the Dramatic Symphony may seem remote at the extremes, the intermediate ones touch, each specimen leading to the next through kinship of substance or subject.[25] To classify his contributions to music the proper term therefore is the one he chose for *Romeo and Juliet;*[26] to classify him as an inventor of forms, we need only keep in mind the fact that he explored the resources of the Dramatic Symphony — "a form," says an excellent German work of reference, "whose first model, given in *Romeo and Juliet,* is not yet near the end of its influence."[27]

In its day this third symphony by Berlioz was more than a seminal work and its title more than a symbol of freedom; work and title marked a synthesis. Music had long been subjected to institutional uses — the church, the stage, the tavern, the village green — and a good part of its hardening into sacrosanct genres was simply mutual ignorance by each group and its caterers of what the others did. Being afraid that the public would mistake his intention, the venturesome composer would only timidly adopt the forms or devices of another style. The Romanticist nineteenth century's intelligent realism and historical sense perceived the possibilities that lay in forgetting these arbitrary boundaries which were social rather than musical. The result was that henceforth in serious music — and especially in that of Berlioz — the folk song, the church modes, the instrumental and vocal soloist, the orchestral and choral masses, were given roles in accordance with a careful plan adapted to the special occasion. That is the lesson of *Romeo and Juliet* and its historic significance.[28]

* * *

[25] Thus the *Requiem* is closer to the *Te Deum* than the *Harold* symphony, but the *Funeral and Triumphal* symphony would easily link the two last-named.

[26] It should have struck previous biographers of Berlioz as absurd to write separate chapters (as they do) entitled successively "Dramatic Symphonies" and "Dramatic Works."

[27] Dr. Alfred Einstein in *1343,* 51. It may seem *outré* to call some of Berlioz' orchestral songs "dramatic symphonies," yet that is the import of what is actually said about them: Mr. Wotton points out that *La Captive* is "a miniature symphonic poem," and another critic describes *Le Spectre de la Rose* as "a fully developed scena." (*310,* 82; *596.*) As for the ambiguity of the term symphony, it is not of Berlioz' making. Well into the nineteenth century, "symphony" could mean any concerted piece — overture or intermezzo — using symphonic devices. The "symphonic poem" is not a symphony in form, though it is *symphonic* just as are Wagner's operas. Berlioz himself uses "symphony" to describe the "Royal Hunt and Storm" which is an orchestral interlude in *Les Troyens.*

[28] In her provocative book on the modern symphony entitled *Mahler, Bruckner, Schoenberg* (N. Y., 1947), Miss Dika Newlin seems to recognize and yet to misconceive this historic role. She refers to Berlioz' "apology" for the

But as he shaped his new work in the state of freedom conferred by Paganini's gift, Berlioz was not thinking of posterity, nor even in any marked degree of his audience. The musical tide inside him was at the flood and he was addressing himself to the task of channeling it into an ideal correspondence with the Shakespearean drama he knew so well.[29] The English critics who, looking at the music, have said that Berlioz' symphony *is* "Romeo," and those who have denied it, are equally right and they can be reconciled by a *distinguo*. True, the brief recital of facts does not follow Shakespeare; the funeral march is wholly a creation of Berlioz', and so is the protracted oath of reconcilement in the Finale. As for the tomb scene, its four brief sections are inspired by the so-called "Garrick ending" of the play which was current in the early nineteenth century.[30] But what Berlioz has done – to use Van Dieren's words – is to "suck all the music" from the poem,[31] just as Shakespeare sucked all the poetry from the old play and set it to a music of his own. In Berlioz' version of the legend and in Shakespeare's, the fusion of lyric and dramatic elements was a bold innovation on the part of two young geniuses.[32]

---

choral element in *Romeo and Juliet,* as if the composer had been uneasy about it. She makes this error in part because she accepts uncritically the old notions about Berlioz' sense of form – as her remarks about the first movement of the *Fantastique* prove. Then she argues against the idea of Berlioz' Dramatic Symphony by maintaining that it sacrifices the inner coherence of structure which Beethoven respected in the Ninth – except (says Miss Newlin) for the dramatic recitative in the last movement. This exception is of course fatal – not to Beethoven's sense of form, but to the critic's thesis.

Her reasoning further involves the absurd contention that it was out of formal considerations that Beethoven wrote the vocal parts of the last movement so awkwardly. The truth is that Beethoven's treatment of the voice elsewhere shows the same disregard of performers, and that his recorded words express nothing but scorn for their convenience. Finally, his sketches for the Tenth and his practice in the last quartets show clearly that he was ready to jettison "form" in the sense of conventional symmetry whenever it suited his dramatic sense or his notion of superior art. That is why his late works were long held to be riddles. All attempts to hold him to a "so far and no farther" is in effect a denial of the very argument for which he is invoked.

[29] "*. . . je nageai sur cette grande mer de poésie . . . sous les chauds rayons de ce soleil d'amour qu'alluma Shakespeare. . . .*" *Mem.*, I, 341.

[30] This "ending" shows – in Hazlitt's words – the "double revival of hope when the lovers meet at the tomb and the double agony of despair." Knowingly or not, Garrick was returning to the Italian original which Shakespeare adapted, and Hazlitt's feeling was that "Garrick has altered 'Romeo and Juliet' not spoiled it," although the emotions produced by the new ending caused him "deep distress of mind." (*1257*, IX, 81–2.)

[31] *526*, 26–7.

[32] *1270*, 256 ff. Shakespeare was presumably 31, Berlioz 35.

Shakespeare himself dwells on the musical quality of his work and virtually tells Berlioz to compose his adagio in pure sound:

> How silver sweet sound lovers' tongues by night,
> Like softest music to attending ears! [33]

In both the play and the symphony, passion is lifted beyond sensuality and as it were vaporized by the pressure of tragedy and the high intellect of the poet-protagonist Romeo; in both, the touches of vulgar realism are sudden, the pace is swift, and the subtleties so numerous that a single performance no more reveals them in the articulate language than in the musical.[34]

If we seek proof that Berlioz understood what he was trying to translate, we need do no more than follow any good interpretation of the play by a critic who does not know the symphony, such, for instance, as John Jay Chapman. Berlioz' decisive inspiration, we remember, lay in grasping the musical function of the Prologue. "The prologue," says Chapman, "is a riddle to which the play is the answer. . . . Shakespeare's choruses are not finger posts for dull minds: they play variations on the theme. They instruct only the instructed." [35] As for the instrumental Introduction: "The street fight with which this play opens is a carefully worked-up scene, which comes to a climax in the entry of the prince." [36] Berlioz had no effort to make in order to match this Shakespearean "passion for realism." [37] But the listener must watch for "the subtler truths of Shakespeare which have always been lost upon the stage." [38] Just so in Berlioz' Prologue the statement of themes is swift and allusive; it can "instruct only the instructed." The relation between the *scherzetto* and the later scherzo does not disclose itself at once – it is "a riddle"; even the stanzas for contralto may when first heard convey inadequately that "passionate warmth and penetrating languor" which another critic, examining the music alone, has noted.[39]

The symphony's Introduction and Prologue set the ideal, invisible stage.[40] Part Two introduces us to Romeo – "a lyric poet in the intensity

[33] Act II, Sc. ii, lines 167–8

[34] "Our blood is stirred . . . but our constitution could never stand the reality," as John Jay Chapman says of the play. (*1064*, 149.)

[35] *1064*, 148.

[36] *1064*, 147.

[37] *1064*, 136.

[38] *1064*, 147.

[39] *406*, 193.

[40] Chapman: "The truth to nature is of a kind that the stage is almost powerless to render." (*1064*, 139.)

of his sensations, a child in his helplessness beneath the ever-varying currents and whirlpools of his feeling. He lives in a walking and frenzied dream." [41] Berlioz' double allegro corresponding to this conception somewhat resembles the rondo form, that is, it brings back a characteristic theme after interludes, some of which are themselves repeated in whole or in part. It opens with the reverie entitled *Roméo Seul*, and goes on to *Tristesse*, *Concert et Bal*, *Grande Fête Chez Capulet*, the effect being to subject the initial motif to the "ever-varying currents" of sadness, gaiety and crowd exuberance. Romeo is as it were taken dreaming through a bacchanal, like his later alter ego, Tannhäuser. The opening "call," twice repeated in its halting incompleteness, is shortly developed with a passionate counterpoint which ends in a rhythmic anticipation of the ball theme. But the festivities are still distant. A second theme (larghetto for oboe), also beginning with an upward "call" and accompanied by a figure of which the germ was in the previous section (as well as in the stanzas of the Prologue) leads to an elaborate cadence preparing us for the fête. The music for this breaks out in all its glitter and agitation, soon to be joined and topped by the theme of the larghetto in the winds.[42] Thereafter the rhythms of revelry mix, clash, go to pieces and resurge, ceasing only near the end to permit a fragment of the oboe theme to be heard at the throbbing close.

Romeo's bacchanal has taken him from lyric soliloquy to naturalistic merrymaking. Now a sequence of sustained chords for strings, flutes, and horns restores the contemplative mood. It is broken very briefly by the distant nostalgic chanting of the Capulets leaving the fiesta. Then the adagio, nocturne, or love scene begins. A repeated violin flutter heard during the calm mysterious opening furnishes the material for the later allegro *agitato*, while the passionate love theme develops in its first or lyric form which runs through the movement like a refrain. Next it generates a contrasting "prose" version or *chant récitatif*.[43] From then on, although the material is familiar, the repetitions are varied until a *sforzando* scale passage ushers in darkness and tragedy.[44] There is a return of the earlier *animato*, which increases in urgency but dies away before the last sounding of the love theme and the quiet close on a changed rhythm.[45]

[41] *1064*, 136.

[42] It is scored for *one* trombone and woodwinds, all marked *forte;* not "the trombones bellowing *fortissimo*" as certain analysts keep repeating.

[43] It begins in the flute soon after the return to tempo I. (*Min. Sc.*, p. 152, bar 4.)

[44] *Min. Sc.*, pp. 159 ff.

[45] *Min. Sc.*, pp. 174–5.

At no point is there any reason to suppose that Berlioz was illustrating Shakespeare's words or depicting the song of larks or the nurse's knock on Juliet's door.[46] But there is every reason to think that he was at one with his author in his views on love. In all that Berlioz wrote about operatic Romeos, and in a special invective against "Capulets" who seek to destroy "such rare epic passions," [47] we recognize the characteristics which make the figure of Romeo more lifelike than popular.[48] Most commentators agree in ascribing to Berlioz' adagio the purity that comes not from reticence but from incandescence, from the tragic, not sultry, acceptance of fate. The music also conveys a sensation of limpid depths which may be associated with nature in stillness, young love, or night-time – the quintessence of the mood *ad-agio*.[49]

The ensuing Queen Mab scherzo resembles the familiar type with double trio. Its opening with false starts and frequent reprises vaguely suggests flight without unbalancing the form, just as later on a somewhat martial section reminds us of a corresponding passage in the *scherzetto* of the Prologue. Berlioz' idea that the Queen Mab speech could be transmuted into a scherzo had occurred to him at Rome and he had at once imparted it to Mendelssohn – only to regret his words lest his friend forestall him,[50] the musical atmosphere of fairyland being already implicit in the mood of certain Beethovenian scherzos. Mendelssohn duly adopted the suggestion for his own use when he came to write his suite for *Midsummer Night's Dream*, but as Saint-Saëns pointed out, what gives to Berlioz' Queen Mab its incomparable lightness and grace is not solely its delicate orchestration, but its style.[51] The technical imagination at work

[46] The lark was Wagner's programmatic interpretation though the bird does not even occur in this scene of the play. The other suggestion was Tovey's. Where will critics find the nurse's husband's bawdy joke?

[47] *Grot.*, 76–7.

[48] Chapman: "Such pure passion . . . is not easily forgiven in a man . . . He is not Romeo unless he cries like a baby or a Greek hero." (*1064*, 139 and 140.)

[49] Berlioz' caption for the movement is simply "The Capulets' garden, silent and deserted," which is of course a "stage direction" to precede the music. In all the references he makes to having performed the piece, there is no allusion to "events" in the music. Only once does he speak of anything not directly musical, namely the "moonlit scene" in a letter to Lecourt. (*M.C.*, 10.) When the Odeon wanted to stage Deschamps's translation of Shakespeare's play and to "illustrate it" by excerpts from the symphony, Berlioz thought it foolish. (*Corresp.*, 248.)

[50] *Mem.*, I, 212 *n.*

[51] *386*, 6. "As I went into [Queen's] Hall," writes Busoni to his wife in 1919, "I heard sounds of Berlioz' *Queen Mab*. This piece is a little miracle." (*175*, 285.)

— as in the play of harmonics which seem flung off the tip of the phrase — makes the airiness intrinsic.

So far, then, musical form within each movement is self-contained and intelligible. Deviations from standard patterns are due in each case to the nature of the material, nothing else. That these structures are also dramatic in feeling is due to the choice of themes as well as to the intense rhythmical life which Berlioz has imparted to the whole score. Romeo the "man of moods — in quarrel, a man of action" [52] had the same electrical temperament as his musical interpreter, and this communicates itself through the great metrical variety of the music. Notice how in the Introduction, Berlioz treats in a fresh way the agitated *fugato* of the quarrel after the quasi-recitative in the brass: he is playing with a rhythmical figure, that is, fashioning pure music, and yet how expressive! Again, the adagio could easily end in the quiet swing of the last fragmented phrase, but four measures before the end Berlioz alters the rhythm, and together with unexpected pleasure gives us a sense of having passed beyond anxiety and passion.

The funeral march which follows the scherzo is a vocal and instrumental movement, but it follows no verbal scheme. The words reiterate the single idea of "strew on her roses" and could easily be replaced by a vocalized "ah," as in the funeral march Berlioz was later to write for *Hamlet.* Here development is partly by fugal imitation and partly by contrast of the elegiac theme with the rhythm of the "monotony." After lamentation we come upon a passage which in another context might seem almost gay: its appearance in this place is like a hint of the extreme youth and sweetness of the dead Juliet.[53] But the close of the march brings us back to somber thoughts, and the short instrumental coda sketches a rhythm of menacing aspect. The tragedy within the tragedy is about to begin.

It is this next section, the tomb scene, which has lent color to the charge that Berlioz, overstepping the bounds of music, turns the symphony to illustrative uses. Weingartner calls this particular scene the only fragment of program music that Berlioz ever wrote.[54] In all the rest, he

[52] *1064,* 140.

[53] Critics have wondered why Berlioz inserts a funeral march at this point, when Juliet has not yet died. To follow the objectors on this literal plane, one might say that Juliet is drugged and *believed* to be dead; but it is even more important to remember that a symphony is not a play and therefore not subject to the same requirements of time and consecutiveness. In Berlioz' music-tragedy this movement has a place and — as the sequel shows — it occupies its proper place.

[54] *394,* 201; *754,* 71–2.

feels, one can discern the outlines of classic form; here not. And moreover here one can follow actual events, the effect being ludicrous.[55] What "events" Weingartner saw, it would be difficult to say on his behalf. The music consists simply of four very brief contrasting sections — an anxious allegro reminiscent of the "quarrel" theme of the Introduction (later remembered by Tchaikovsky in his *Romeo and Juliet* overture); an invocation, which transforms the love theme into the love-death and which Weingartner excepts from his strictures; a second allegro — after a wonderful rhythmic bridge passage — expressive of joy that is *un*refined; and a single page ending pianississimo with the faint echo, in whole notes, of both Romeo's reverie and the love theme.[56] The drama is done; all the rest is Postlude.

These twenty or thirty pages of the entombment are extraordinarily vivid and may induce visions in some listeners, but one can safely defy anyone to say what they imitate. When Toscanini rehearses this section, it is clear that the most it suggests is a variety of bodily gestures — impatient, tender, exuberant, defeated — like any music that is dramatic. It is as music that the scene is most interesting, for it chiefly employs material that we have heard before. Only, it is distorted, disguised, broken up. The invocation is a magnificent orchestral song without words. As for the brusque transitions, they convey nothing but the abruptness of pace suitable at that point. The true listener (as against the imagist) will, if he forbears to programmatize, readily discover that here is no substance foreign to the rest of the score. Far from being a weak spot in the Dramatic Symphony, this scene is perhaps the high point of its effort to be concise, free of the stereotypes, conventional "joints," and punctuation marks: the section is an equivalent to modern nonsyntactical poetry.[57]

Half a century ago, Koechlin protested vigorously against the omission of the passage, saying that "simply from the technical point of view, let alone the dramatic," it deserved to be restored.[58] It is barely possible that the expurgators had followed Berlioz' wish, expressed in a sarcastic

[55] *754*, 72.

[56] A signal example of thematic plasticity in Berlioz: compare *Min. Sc.*, 276 bb. 14–24 with 55 bb. 8–10 and 156 bb. 1–3.

[57] I owe this analogy to Robert Pitney, the musician and critic already cited. In a later review of various *Romeo and Juliet* operas, Berlioz makes clear what he wanted to avoid. He is speaking of the tomb scene in Bellini: "Juliet comes down with measured steps toward her motionless lover and they begin to talk over their little concerns — 'Whom do I see?' — 'Romeo' — 'Juliet alive?' — 'From a seeming death my waking on this day restores me to your love?' — 'True: there are no stone walls in heaven.' " (*A Trav.*, 342.)

[58] *1386*, quoted in *406*, 195.

note to a late edition of the score: "The public being devoid of imagination, this scene should be omitted whenever the symphony is not performed before a chosen audience familiar with Shakespeare's play, that is to say, it should be omitted in nine cases out of ten." More likely, it was felt that by "imagination" Berlioz meant visualization, the music being deemed by an overwhelmingly Wagnerian population as inadequate to stimulate vision. We thus have the familiar paradox of a passage of dramatic music being impugned (a) because it makes us see, and (b) because it does not.

In the Finale, at any rate, there is no difficulty. The opera-trained listener can both see and hear Friar Laurence and the two choruses representing the warring families. Occasionally he can even hear the words, which recount what has happened, invite the enemies to forget their feud, and intone the oath of reconciliation. The architectonic reason for this Epilogue was shown earlier. The dramatic purport, once again, lies not in the words but in the contrast between the Friar and the two hostile groups. One need not understand their words in order to feel creeping over one the magic of lofty persuasion, which little by little wins over the hesitant choral mass. As one musician has put it, "the spirit of a Biblical tale hovers over this final scene." [59]

This analogy suggests very forcibly what Berlioz had in mind when he desired his symphonic drama to be played before an audience familiar with Shakespeare. He did not ask the "chosen listeners" to supply mentally what he, the composer, had either omitted or translated; he wanted them to grasp quickly and easily the occasions for the musical sequence, and to be at home among the meanings of the tragedy so that they would not have to invent one of their own in response to the musical expression.

For Berlioz, Shakespeare's *Romeo and Juliet* belonged to the body of secular scriptures which every educated man should know by heart.[60] How would Renaissance painting, medieval sculpture and stained glass, and sacred oratorios affect us if we did not instantly know the names, relations, and motives of the dramatis personae? What would a musical Buddhist make of the repeated cry of "Barabbas!" in the *Saint Matthew Passion?* The previous explanatory words are seldom heard and they

[59] *289*, 154. Critics who find this finale "coarse" in comparison with the exquisiteness of earlier movements should reflect that collective emotions ought not to be rendered with the same elegance, finesse or lyric fire as individual feelings: the Capulet and Montague families are not a pair of lovers nor a volatile fairy queen.

[60] Note his disgust when an educated Englishman or Frenchman confessed ignorance of Shakespeare or Goethe. (*L.I.*, 286; *M.M.*, 285.)

scarcely count when compared with the violent musical expression. This in turn takes full effect when the general intent of the whole work lies deep in our minds, stilling idle curiosity. In the same way, we can look pictorially at the Madonna and Child the moment we have ceased wondering what this obsession with motherhood can possibly mean. In no other way does Berlioz' Dramatic Symphony function, once we possess the traditional tale that inspired it. Far from bringing forward the literary or visual or narrative aspect of drama, Berlioz wished us to know it so well that we would forget it and let the music speak the ineffable.[61]

This relaxed attitude, which was certainly natural to Berlioz and is apparently less natural to others, was the source of the lifelong misunderstanding between him and one of the first hearers of *Romeo and Juliet* – young Wagner. Aged twenty-six, fresh from his German province, and living as yet obscurely in the French capital, Wagner experienced, on hearing Berlioz' symphony, what he himself called "the revelation of a new world of music." [62] This was due partly to the power and precision of the orchestra, partly to the music itself. As the composer of two very slight operatic scores and a few overtures and songs, Wagner could reasonably "feel like a child" in comparison with his elder by ten years.[63] But even then, if we are to credit the recollections of forty years later, Wagner was critical of the Dramatic Symphony. He could not accept it for what it was but attempted in vain either to reduce it to the traditional pattern of the symphony or to programmatize it into the semblance of an opera.

When Wagner had heard three more Berlioz symphonies, had returned to Germany, and had begun to grope towards his own dramatic synthesis, he disparaged *Romeo and Juliet* with little regard for his own debt to it and none for consistency. He had learned from Berlioz what the musico-dramatic problem of the century was, and from the substance of *Romeo* he had absorbed enough to serve him in a number of his own later works. Mr. Gerald Abraham was not the first to notice the exact coincidence between Romeo's reverie and Tristan's motif for a similar situation, but

[61] In Shakespeare's *Henry V*, when the chorus says: "On your imaginary forces work . . ." and again "eke out our performance with your mind," the appeal is surely not to our power of *seeing* what isn't there, but of *understanding* what is not shown. There is, moreover, a large and impressive body of opinion, beginning with Dr. Johnson, in favor of reading Shakespeare rather than seeing him acted.

[62] *245*, 235.

[63] *Ibid.*

he was the first to trace in detail the intimate connection between the two dramas. He concludes: "*Romeo and Juliet* was written when Berlioz was at the zenith of his power; *Tristan* when Wagner was at his, but *20 years later.*" (Italics in the text.)[64]

The important fact is, of course, not the lifting of a few themes from a colleague's score – that is an established practice among musicians[65] – but the discovery by Wagner in Berlioz' *Romeo* of a musical idiom allowing the expression of certain moods for which no earlier music supplied precedents. The abandonment of repetition except when dramatically motivated, the treatment of melody as a sinuous line which need not turn a corner every four bars, and the art of subtle psychological variation in themes once established – all this new armory of musical devices was in *Romeo and Juliet* and it constituted a new art for him who had ears to hear.[66]

Wagner, it is true, came to reject what he took to be the "system" behind *Romeo and Juliet*, and his revolution was to carry Berlioz' conception of the symphony-with-voice back into the precincts of the opera.[67] He asked that music there should be as rich, as symphonic, as continuous, as exact in performance, and as solemn as it might be in church and concert hall combined. The old distinctions fell away as to what was an operatic and what a non-operatic instrument, what was sacred and what was profane. In other words, Berlioz' secular scriptures, composed and sung in the symphonic style, became the Wagnerian opera as soon as

[64] *407*, 242. For more detail, see Subchapter 24.

[65] Through Wagner and Gounod (who attended the rehearsals), that "Romeo" theme of Berlioz' has been worked over by dozens of musicians, including César Franck, Massenet, Mahler, Strauss, and Tchaikovsky. Pizzetti's overture to *Fedra* (1912) is a good example of its longevity.

[66] Melodically, the old master of thirty-six was even more daring than his pupil was to be twenty years later, *e.g.*, in the *Tristan* version of the theme Wagner feels compelled to add to the Romeo phrase a little conventional tail of three rising notes, and then repeats it so, whereas Berlioz stops on a single pizzicato note (twice) before giving it a really ample development of twenty bars.

[67] In Wagner's *Opera and Drama* (1851) which represents a return to eighteenth-century ideas over the heads of the Romanticists. This is characteristic of the mid-nineteenth century reaction to Romanticism in all the arts and even in science. Here is what Marmontel, the protégé of Voltaire and librettist of Piccinni, wrote in 1795 of his intentions in opera: "I wanted action to be full, close, tightly knit, and its component situations linked each to each so that they might become the motive of the singing. This would then be nothing but the more lively expression of the feelings informing the scene, and the airs, duets and choruses should accordingly be blended with the recitatives." (*Memoirs*, Bk. IX.)

music was reattached to acting and scenery: the Dramatic Symphony germinated the Music Drama.

Between the two men who in November 1839 heard the same momentous concert there remained other differences of style, temperament, and philosophy. But we cannot understand why these were so stubborn until we see how closely the two musicians agreed on the problem and on the means of dramatic music in their century.[68] It was a just but incomplete critique which described Berlioz and Wagner as "the two enemy brothers descended from Beethoven." [69] Wagner later proved to his own satisfaction that music cannot yield drama without being linked with words, nor be associated with an action unless the action is staged. Berlioz as we saw was not averse to writing dramatic music for the theater, but he made every effort to preserve music formally and dramatically independent from its associates. He preferred to compose discontinuous "scenes" and indicate in printed words their locale, rather than to link musical ideas to unmusical discourse or behavior. To make up for this self-imposed limitation, he strove to extend the inherent expressiveness of melody, harmony, rhythm, and tone color. That it was inherent and only "associated" with a subject he showed in the free way he assigned and reassigned some of his most poignant melodies. The second Romeo theme (larghetto for oboe solo) was originally used, not for the *Tristesse* of Romeo, but for the gloomy introspection of Sardanapalus on his death-bed. Similarly, the Capulets' concert music in an earlier form accompanied the dancing bayaderes in that same prize cantata of 1830. For Berlioz there was in short no such thing musically as a Romeo leitmotif, but only a connotative relation between phrase and personage.

The esthetic question then is whether we can be asked to bear in mind this unemphatic parallelism, or whether we must be shown a flesh-and-blood Romeo in red tights and slashed sleeves. The second way, Wagner's way, is the more assured, for as Dryden says "our eyes are our best witnesses." Berlioz' way is the way of imagination; "rich music's tongue," as Shakespeare instructs him, is to tell "the imagined happiness" – or death. This avoids literalism and keeps open the possibility of multiple interpretations; it is suggestive and symbolic instead of "realistic," though the reality it suggests is no less solid for being unconfined.

* * *

[68] In his last days, according to Mottl, Wagner would brook no criticism of the *Romeo and Juliet* score. (*307*, 370.)

[69] Scudo: quoted in *667*, 590.

But this discussion of music drama must not make us think that with his *Romeo and Juliet* of 1839 Berlioz had said his last word, nor suppose that Wagner had uttered his first. One had created a masterpiece; the other had been awakened by it. But both were still young, so was the century; and the slight difference of age between the acknowledged and the incubating genius might reasonably suggest that they were to run on parallel courses. Yet Berlioz at thirty-six had accomplished half his work, and by the year 1840 just beginning, his specifically "French" period was virtually over.

13. *Vox Populi:* Funeral and Triumphal Symphony

November 1839 to August 1840

. . . some day a grateful France will raise a proud monument on his tomb. . . .
— WAGNER on Berlioz

THE FIRST TIME that the Paris audience — now more than ever enriched by the presence of foreign artists [1] — heard the *Romeo and Juliet* symphony was a critical moment in Berlioz' career. The work was new in every way, hence difficult to grasp. It might be hissed like *Benvenuto* by those who wanted to confirm their own adverse judgment or carry on the war against the Bertin family; or worse, the symphony might be chillingly received, politeness emphasizing disappointment. But Berlioz had not even finished conducting Part Two when loud, sustained, and spontaneous applause broke out. The "Ball Scene," or rather Bacchanale, broke the ice; the scherzo and Finale completed the victory. At a second concert a week later, the performance was technically far superior and the public acclaim spread more widely over the work. At the end the performers rose and kept up their bravos so enthusiastically that the composer-conductor almost lost his poise.

For his father's pleasure, Berlioz went into details about both occasions. At the *première* the Queen had failed to come, but the two young Princes were there. Balzac, looking over the assembly, had described it as "the brain of Paris." As regards receipts, it appeared that nearly 1500 francs' worth of tickets had been bid for in vain. The hall was full, and in spite

[1] Besides Liszt, Wagner, Chopin, and Heine, those likely to follow Berlioz' concerts included J. P. Pixis of Mannheim; Karl Halle (later Sir Charles Hallé, the founder of the Manchester Symphony); Sigismund Thalberg (Liszt's onetime rival on the piano); George Osborne from Ireland; the Alsatian Georges Kastner; Stephen Heller from Budapest; old Kreutzer's nephew Léon; François Seghers, the Brussels violinist who played in the Conservatoire orchestra; César Franck, another Belgian who was completing his last year in that institution; finally, musicians from the French provinces such as Auguste Morel of Marseille and Lambert Massart, newly appointed violin master at the Conservatoire.

of numerous press seats, the gross was 4559 francs. These details Dr. Berlioz conveyed in his turn, with a tub of butter, to his daughter, adding that the news gave him a fresh lease on life.[2] In proving himself, Hector had proved his alarming boyish predictions of sixteen years before.

The third concert on December 15 was still more satisfactory for the artist: both performance and appreciation were more exact; comments and criticisms by trusted friends gave Berlioz the pleasant feeling of good work done, which might be further polished and perfected for years to come. The press was almost uniformly favorable and the younger men were wholeheartedly for the young master. Stephen Heller, the pianist and symphonic composer, wrote to his older friend Robert Schumann how gratifying it was to see the progress that public opinion was making about a genius who refused to commercialize his art.[3] Gautier attested the triumphant result of Berlioz' "unshakable will" which he declared indispensable to an artist in polemical times like theirs, for "originality acts on the French public like a red rag on a bull." [4]

It was the first time in the history of French music that anyone had dared to give the same symphony three times in close succession. Knowing that he must be played often to be understood once, Berlioz undoubtedly helped to establish the practice which many concertgoers now follow, of deliberately subjecting themselves two or three times to a work that is new and strange.[5] For this privilege, the Parisians paid a total of 13,200 francs. Deducting expenses, Berlioz earned for a year's composition and two months' conducting, exactly 1100 francs. "Once and for all, serious music does not keep its man. . . . Paganini is in Nice . . . enchanted with *his* score: it certainly is his score, for it owes its existence solely to him." [6]

* * *

[2] *A.R.*, 407–9.

[3] *268*, 509–10. Heller should not be confused with Berlioz' intimate, also a pianist, Ferdinand Hiller.

[4] *La Presse*, Dec. 11, 1839 (*434*, 147).

[5] The practice was resumed and extended by Stravinsky for the *première* of the *Sacre du Printemps* which was played twice at the same concert; more recently Mr. Stravinsky did the same thing with his Mass for voices and wind. (1949.)

[6] *A.R.*, 414. When the score appeared, it bore a dedication to Paganini, just as the score of the *Benvenuto Cellini* overture – the only part of the opera to be published – was dedicated to Legouvé, who had advanced Berlioz money for completing the work. All of Berlioz' dedications were expressions of gratitude, and when this happened to coincide with affectionate personal relations, he habitually referred to the work as "your" or "our" score, *e.g.*, *Harold in Italy*, dedicated to Humbert Ferrand. *L.I.*, *passim.*

January 1840 saw Berlioz undergoing the inevitable depression. Exhausted and irritable, he was also worried about Harriet's health. She had tonsillitis and respiratory trouble which made him fear a recurrence of pleurisy. Young Louis, who had attended one of the concerts with his mother, was now down with measles. Being closeted, sick, with a sick family, after the excitement of victory, brought on the old spleen. "Everything bores me, disgusts, offends, and revolts me." [7] This mood made him oversensitive to the malicious inanities of a critic like Alphonse Karr,[8] and overhardened to the touching gesture of an English admirer of Beethoven's who bought from Berlioz' publisher the baton with which *Romeo* had been conducted. The collector had insisted on the article's genuineness being guaranteed. "I guarantee it," wrote Berlioz, "and may God grant that the merit of the work will justify, at least in part, the admiration expressed in this novel way." [9]

It was clear that Berlioz at thirty-six should have been exclusively concerned with music – its composition, conducting, and criticism – not with publicity, management, Bertin politics, and the turning out of *feuilletons* about nothing: the fresh call to renewed musical activity for a first concert in 1840 (on February 6) pulled him out of the dumps as nothing else could. Carrying out an original idea sponsored by the *Gazette Musicale* and very probably due to Berlioz himself, this concert was free to the subscribers of the magazine. The Schlesinger publishing house supported both enterprises; that is to say, substituted a musical premium for the usual kitchenware or set of classical authors with which subscribers have been immemorially enticed. At this first symphonic dividend, Berlioz' *Cellini* overture and *Harold* symphony were played with admirable finish. The rest consisted of arias and virtuoso pieces by other hands.

The effort and pleasure once over, Berlioz relapsed into gloom. It was not all weariness or temperamental failing. Berlioz had reached the high point of his possible career in Paris and saw what it was worth. He could subsist only by exceptional means – such as the gift from Paganini, which had prepared and publicized *Romeo* as a gala occasion. Only then would the fashionable world reinforce his 1200 followers. The net gain even under the best conditions was meager, and galas could recur only at wide

[7] *L.I.*, 190.

[8] Balzac, who had many serious quarrels with his journalistic critics, wrote in 1843 a satirical "anatomy" of their ways, winding up with a parody of Voltaire's epigram: "If the Paris press did not exist, it would be imperative not to invent it." (*1235*, *Oeuv. Div.*, I, 226.)

[9] *L.I.*, 188. The London newspapers had given Berlioz' new work extended notice; the head of the Philharmonic had attended the *première*.

intervals. As for the subscription concerts of the *Gazette Musicale*, they afforded merely a modest conductor's fee and a chance to repeat certain works. It was plain that the times were not favorable to the establishment of regular symphonic concerts, affording a decent living to all those concerned. On the contrary, the "railroad decade" was under way and the spectacle of its greedy folly was beginning to discourage all sensitive minds.[10] Berlioz, for all his estrangement from state politics, noticed and reported it: "These are unlucky times, when artists ought not to be alive . . . when people, beholding them, only think: 'We are bored and it is you who are boring us.' "[11]

The Romanticist generation, just in proportion as it had shed its undergraduate pose and gained mature solidity, ceased to interest a public that wanted chiefly to gape and to scorn what it gaped at. The bourgeois monarchy having given up all risk and all appeal to the imagination, whether through the drama of domestic politics or through a clear-cut foreign policy, was relying on the most selfish of self-interest to keep the nation occupied and untroublesome. The new prime minister of 1840, Guizot, despite his stern and noble view of constitutional liberties, was soon reduced to corrupt means of ruling and answered all demands for a wider franchise with the phrase "*Enrichissez-vous.*" *Things* were in the saddle, as Emerson said, riding mankind. And the curious result was that despite men's concentration on clear, tangible, personal interests, everyone was bored: wild speculation expressed the desire for excitement at any cost — an excitement which the variety of civilized intellectual products no longer gave. Beethoven, observed Berlioz, had lost his snob appeal: "The dilettantes in the boxes no longer feel they have to keep up the pose which they had been assuming for ten years past. They are frankly bored."[12]

But so far Berlioz and his fellows of 1830 were disgusted and bored only by the outward shape of things. Their inner life was just as fresh and exciting as it had ever been, even though they no longer put on a show to amuse and enrage the bourgeois. Their task was now to accom-

[10] The year 1839 saw the opening of four important railroads, including the Paris-Versailles line. This evident mechanical progress was not discounted or disliked by artists and philosophers, but it widened the breach between "those who own and those who earn" — to use Vigny's words. (*1284*, 236.) Others such as Louis Blanc, Ximenes Doudan, Lamennais, Liszt, George Sand began to see that the fight over social reform would drive art still further out of the world's consideration. (See, under the appropriate decade: *188; 1188; 210.*)

[11] *1398* (1840) 177.

[12] *1398* (1840) 215.

plish what they could in the teeth of passive resistance. By mid-March 1840, the new ministry being in power, Berlioz approached M. de Rémusat with regard to a possible commission. The plan of a *fête funèbre* had been in the composer's mind since his return from Italy, and it would seem fitting to carry it out for the tenth commemoration of the July Days. On the spot where the Bastille had stood until 1789 a column was being erected which would be dedicated on the anniversary day. The ashes of those who had died fighting for liberty in 1830 would be transferred to a cenotaph at the foot of the column. Hence the procession would require a funeral march of military character – a "funeral triumph."

This proposal, which was soon accepted, represented Berlioz' only chance of avoiding still another costly sacrifice to the muse: if he composed and played a new work uncommissioned, he would be out of pocket to his family's detriment. The Opera maintained toward him the attitude of a hibernating bear; Scribe was in no hurry to provide the libretto he had promised; nor was Duponchel, as may be imagined, eager for a second *Benvenuto* which in all probability would be still newer in form and contents.[13]

Duponchel was really troubled. Meyerbeer had refused permission to have his new opera (*L'Africaine*) put on. He could afford to wait, for, as his mother-in-law boasted, he did not have to earn a living, and he wanted the public to work up an appetite for his fare by being disappointed at other hands. This left Duponchel with only Donizetti's *Martyrs*, which would probably not carry the overhead. The director might have to resign. In these straits, managers or their entourage are likely to have a fit of memory and bethink themselves of masterpieces: there was talk of reviving *Freischütz*. But the idea was soon dismissed, after debating how the work could be "arranged." An unsigned note in the *Gazette Musicale*, very likely written by Berlioz, concluded: "The plan is given up, fortunately for poor Weber. The danger is past."[14]

On May 27, while Berlioz was hopefully at work on his Funeral Symphony, Paganini died. In the *Débats* a week later, Berlioz expressed his sorrow and admiration.[15] Although he had never heard his benefactor play in public, he was familiar with the virtuoso's innovations in technique

[13] Berlioz, it is true, had promised to make the Scribe score "simpler and easier to play" (*86*, 580) but about the upshot the unintelligent suspicion of an opera director is possibly more reliable: he knows nothing about music but he can smell out his natural enemy.

[14] *1398*, May 17, 1840.

[15] Reprinted in *Soirées* (16th).

and style of composition, both for violin and for orchestra. Berlioz was also impressed by the accounts of the improvised duets which Paganini playing the guitar had engaged in with his friend the violinist Sina, and which no one had ever been admitted to hear. The article on Paganini turned into one of those excellent biographical sketches which Berlioz has left us about Beethoven, Spontini, Chopin, Lesueur, and others. More than any of his contemporaries, Liszt excepted, Berlioz understood and sympathized with Paganini's strangeness. He could feel the reserve and *contemptus mundi* behind the affectation of eccentricity, and he easily responded to the Shakespearean juxtaposing of deep feeling and boisterous humor such as Paganini had indulged in at their meeting after the gift. Berlioz himself would later develop something of the same forbidding exterior, quickly melting at the touch of genuine emotion or artistic intelligence. Meantime he had shown his gratitude and reverence for the old man dying in Nice by serving as his go-between in a pending lawsuit.[16]

During the completion of the July Symphony (as Berlioz usually called it then) his artistic nourishment from without was meager. The Conservatoire did give Beethoven's Pastoral again, together with fragments of Bach and Handel, but Berlioz was pleased neither by the performance nor by the music of the two older masters. He was downright academic about Bach's harmony, not knowing enough of the work to grasp its idiom. A later concert brought a psalm of Handel's which Berlioz found magnificent, but these two composers, with whom Berlioz had certain esthetic affinities despite divergent traditions, remained alien to him until almost the end of his life.[17] The narrowness of the concert repertory in any epoch, as well as the rigidity of style with which works outside the common choice are played, is responsible for anomalies of the kind, which exist to a far lesser degree in arts other than music.[18] To this day, though

[16] In a letter of March 1840 to his lawyer and friend Germi, Paganini says: "You may freely write to this same friend Berlioz, whom you must not confuse with the common scum of [musicians] but should look on as a transcendent genius such as rises but once in every third or fourth century; a man of perfect probity and worthy of our confidence. (*225*.)

[17] On the kinship between Bach's art and that of Berlioz, see Albert Schweitzer's *Bach*, and below Subchapter 24. On the relation to Handel, see Romain Rolland's *Handel*, 109. The young Saint-Saëns used to play Bach to Berlioz in his later years. (*386*, 8.)

[18] A judicious student of Handel writes: "Throughout the first half of the 19th century fragments of *Messiah* were feebly executed by amateur choral societies. . . . The *Messiah* remained unfamiliar to most Frenchmen till after 1900. . . . Like Berlioz and Wagner, Liszt found the 'Hallelujah-perruque of a Handel' tedious and old-fashioned." (*841*, 265, 266, and 278 *n.*)

Bach is moderately "available," who can say that he has a good knowledge of Handel's dramatic music?

Berlioz consoled himself for the "desperate sameness" of operas and concerts by rereading Virgil, Molière, Shakespeare, La Fontaine, Cervantes, Bernardin de St. Pierre, and a few moderns: Balzac, Vigny, George Sand, Victor Hugo. The last-named had in fact just published a new volume of verse, *Les Rayons et les Ombres*, which chimed in with Berlioz' somber thoughts and his musical activity as well: the last poem in the collection was on "The Return of the Emperor" and the Preface was postdated so as to make its appearance fall on the anniversary of Napoleon's death. That very day, Berlioz wrote to Hugo: "If to feel is to live, I have lived much today. I read your lines this morning. At noon . . . I followed the people to the foot of the column [Place Vendôme], that immortal poem of the other emperor's. . . . Now I bow to you in tears and worshipful admiration." [19]

Like the *Requiem*, Berlioz' new symphony had to be finished one month before the date of its performance, which was July 28. This had the same effect of cramping the working out of the last movement in each composition, and it took the same toll on the body and nerves of the composer. July was a month of harassing work done against time. The work being scored for military band, Berlioz had to keep in mind the desire of all the participating groups to have a share in the performance. Large forces were available, though not distributed ideally among the instruments. Moreover, the piece had been commissioned for the procession through the boulevards to the Place de la Bastille, and outdoor music is unsatisfactory except under specially arranged acoustical conditions.[20] To increase the number of players does not help — they must play together, they must be led by a visible leader, and the proportions of various kinds of timbre must be kept sounding coherent. This is difficult if the performers have to march and reverberators are lacking. Berlioz gathered 207 musicians, some of them professionals who would help lead the less competent sections of National Guardsmen. Among the trained instrumentalists were the visiting band of Bavarian cornets who had recently given concerts in Paris.[21]

Berlioz again followed his system of rehearsing by groups which saved

[19] *A.R.*, 418.

[20] Berlioz had learned in 1833 that — as he maintained ever after — "music is not made for the street." (*L.I.*, 131.)

[21] For the distribution of instruments, see Supplement 5.

both money and energy.[22] And these preparations exposed him again to the usual malicious rumors that make the Paris *boulevardiers* feel they control the destinies of art. Berlioz' symphony, it was said, was unfinished; complete rehearsals could not begin; the partial ones were going badly. The fact is that by July 19 the rehearsals were going quite well and Berlioz was arranging for a public dress rehearsal, indoors. To this performance, which would at least be audible, he invited friends, critics, and notables. Chopin's ticket, signed by Berlioz, is still extant. Put into English it reads:

Sunday July 26 at 11.30 A.M.
Concert Hall rue Vivienne
Dress Rehearsal of the Military Symphony
Composed by M. Berlioz
For the Funeral Ceremony of July 28
H. Berlioz
This card will admit two.
Funeral March, Hymn of Farewell, Apotheosis.[23]

For a government as frail and composite as that of the July Monarchy, the "Twenty-eighth" was necessarily a political occasion – it was not yet a patriotic day for the whole nation. The fête had accordingly been planned in order to give the bellicose Parisians the impression of still being the heroes they were during the first revolution and Napoleon's Empire, and by means of this external pomp to reconcile them to a very cautious and unmilitary foreign policy. The people's demand for glory had something in it of the artist's attack against Philistinism: populace and artist both aspired to make life serve nobler ends than trade. But just as an artist must live – even a Berlioz sacrificing fame and comfort to his ideal – so the people grumbled at social and political conditions which they felt restricted life without the compensation of glory. Hence the cry of Reform. On the morning of the twenty-eighth the comic weekly *Charivari* came out printed in white on a black cover, with a cartoon showing mortuary remains and bearing the caption: "Funeral Procession of Liberties Dead for the Citizen, in step with the Procession of Citizens Dead for Liberty." Further on, with a pun on his name, there was a dig at Berlioz, "who will perform his defunct funeral march. A few unlubricated carriage wheels will add to the effect of his composition."

[22] The first written statement of this practice is in his letter to Lecourt of Apr. 19, 1840: "it is the only way to obtain a good performance of modern music." (*86*, 581.)

[23] Facsimile in Karlovicz, *Souvenirs Inédits de Chopin; A.R.*, 419.

Thus Berlioz appeared to the agitators as a minion of princes, a favorite of the government, even though his feeling about that government and his convictions about national ceremonies were precisely those of the opposition. By a paradox easy to understand, it was soon clear that the reformers did not care to commission symphonies either; when oppositions came into power they acted towards art like all other governments – at once neglectful and oppressive. The people and the artist could apparently not enter into the natural relation of expressing and responding to a fundamental feeling which they sincerely shared.

The *Charivari*, which employed another great artist neglected by public and government alike – Honoré Daumier – was blind to this social and cultural contradiction. And being ignorant of music, it needlessly feared the "noise" of Berlioz' Fourth Symphony. In spite of its two hundred performers, Berlioz tells us, the work "resounded very little or very imperfectly."[24] Once for all, serious outdoor music was unpractical. Wearing his uniform of the National Guard and conducting with his sword, Berlioz could lead only the few front ranks of his marching orchestra. Down the open boulevards, amid the shouts of the people, the political altercations within the crowd, and the panic caused at one point by the near upset of the fifty coffins piled on a flag-studded dray (twenty-four horses could scarcely set it in motion) Berlioz' majestic sonorities scarcely carried. Only when the parade stopped at a point where the sound was reflected by houses and trees did the music have a chance. By then, the performers, having repeated the March several times, were blown and miserably broiling under the noonday sun.

Finally, an hour or more after noon, the procession reached the Place de la Bastille. The burial service was elaborately performed and silence at last secured for the symphony. Berlioz' band occupied bleachers from which all could see his decisive beat, and he was on the point of raising his sabre to signal that arresting rhythm on muffled drums which begins the Funeral March, when the legion of the National Guard which had been on duty at this spot since 8 A.M. (it was now 3 P.M.) could no longer contain itself: it wanted to parade and go home. Their own drums beat and 60,000 men tramped across the Place for two hours, to an accompaniment of shouts from the crowd. Of Berlioz' symphony, as he himself reports, "not a note survived."[25]

This was but a temporary extinction. Owing to the simple presence of his name on the program, more people heard of Berlioz in one day than

[24] *Mem.*, I, 346.
[25] *Mem.*, I, 347.

if he had given concerts or written operas for twenty years.[26] The very fact that his composition had not been heard kept it fresh, and a concert featuring the work would be sure to draw. He quickly mustered his men again, adding string parts to relieve the monotony of the brass bass,[27] and sought to carry out his frustrated intentions for the last movement by setting as a choral climax a few lines by Emile's brother, Antony Deschamps.

On August 7, an audience of standing-room size jammed the Hall rue Vivienne, and the unfilled demand was such that three more performances were planned amid general enthusiasm. Only one took place, on August 14, 1840, because a piece of unsettling news diverted public attention from art to politics: while Berlioz was re-creating in sound the Revolutionary-Napoleonic legend, its heir-apparent (in both senses of apparent) had attempted his second coup: Louis-Napoleon had landed at Boulogne. He too had been arrested, like the symphony, but not extinguished. For in these days everyone outside the government was a Bonapartist, even the Republicans, who could stress the liberal side of Napoleon's career.[28] Indeed, the government itself was Bonapartist to the extent that it wanted to be national and that it did not want to be more liberal. In May the Chambers had voted to bring back the ashes of the Emperor to Paris, to rest "among the people that he loved so well." It was a cheap substitute for war or administrative efficiency.

Still the nephew's attempted *coup d'état* put a different complexion on the uncle's return, and a new sense of caution at once affected Berlioz' availability as a musician for official occasions. His *Ode on the Death of Napoleon*, composed five years before to Béranger's verses, was about to be published and he had asked permission to dedicate it to Louis Philippe. Berlioz' old friend and protector in Roman days, Horace Vernet, who steadily painted Napoleonic scenes for the government at the rate of one hundred thousand francs each, had offered to obtain for Berlioz an audience with the King. But after Louis Bonaparte's raid on Boulogne the opportunity was gone, the King never replied, and it became compromising to associate one's work or person with Napoleonic sentiments.

Yet that association remained in the mind of one observer, who may himself have been under the spell of the Emperor. Writing years later about Berlioz, Wagner declared that he always visualized him "at the

[26] One notes this at once in the letters of contemporaries, *e.g.*, *188*, I, 426.

[27] As did Stravinsky, for the same reason, in his Concerto for piano and band.

[28] The chief locomotive of the Eastern railway had been publicly christened the "Napoleon" the year before.

head of his troops, leading the orchestra like a Napoleon." [29] Very likely Wagner had been in the crowd on July 28 as he had been at the *Romeo and Juliet* and subsequent concerts. He knew Berlioz by sight, for he had submitted articles to Schlesinger, the owner of the *Gazette Musicale*, who had published them on Berlioz' advice. This was Wagner's first emergence from obscurity since he had come to the capital. Desperately poor and doing hack work, he was passing judgment on native and foreign music and also acting as correspondent for the Dresden *Abendzeitung*. To that paper he was soon to contribute a sizable essay on Berlioz, in which after describing his character at second hand he paid respect to the man's determined will to create without a thought of money or ignorant opinion. Finally, Wagner gave his views on the *Funeral and Triumphal* symphony: "I am inclined to rank this composition above all Berlioz' other ones: it is noble and great from the first note to the last. Free from sickly excitement, it sustains a noble patriotic emotion which rises from lament to the topmost heights of apotheosis. When I further take into account the service rendered by Berlioz in his altogether noble treatment of the military wind band – the only instruments at his disposal here, . . . I must say with delight that I am convinced this Symphony will last and exalt the hearts of men as long as there lives a nation called France." [30]

Fourth Symphony: A People's Music

> Let no one think that the number of performers is of small moment. Music on the grand scale requires a grand performance and what is false in other circumstances is true here, namely that in a vast enclosure quantity must prevail over quality.
> – BERLIOZ on religious ceremonies (1829)

One hundred and seven years after Berlioz had produced his *Funeral* symphony for military band, native New Yorkers and summer visitors to the city were given the first opportunity of hearing it on this side of the Atlantic. Richard Franko Goldman, in writing a survey of band music

[29] Quoted in *307*, 261.
[30] Dresden *Abendzeitung*, May 5, 1841 (*243*, VIII, 131–7).

some years before, had rediscovered the work. Until then the accepted generality was: "There are no great compositions for the band." [1] Of course, the habit of superficial judgment being all too common in musical matters, some persons need only to be told that a composition is scored for two hundred wind instruments in order to act like the critics of *Tom Jones* who (as Fielding says) "called it low and fell agroaning." But what Berlioz designed and Wagner admired was something else than brass and blaring. It was, in Wagner's words, "a composition altogether popular in the most ideal sense. . . . I should indeed call it national rather than popular . . ." [2] in short, a piece of democratic art.

The revolutionary ideal of art for the masses, which Berlioz inherited in purified form precisely because he was not contemporary with its beginnings, has often been invoked and talked about; it is another thing to put it into practice. For in spite of the broad human feeling required, the artist must tread a very narrow path if he is not to fall into alternative dangers – on the one side, queasy condescension to his untutored audience; on the other, vulgar platitude. Nor must he simply *depict* common emotions for the pleasure of the sophisticates; he must find original ways of being at once elevated and simple.[3] Wagner felt sure that "every urchin in a blue blouse . . . would thoroughly understand the July Symphony." By what magic did the difficult, strongly intellectual art of Berlioz mold itself to the proper shape? [4]

The symphony is in three clearly "characteristic" movements: a funeral march, a farewell hymn, and an apotheosis. Berlioz has again dramatized his subject in the most direct and fitting way. To any one who might ask, "What are we doing here?" his three "acts" reply: we are marching to the tomb; we are saying farewell; we are dispersing to the tune of a glorifying hymn – an apotheosis.[5]

[1] John Redfield in *Music, a Science and an Art*, N.Y., 1930, p. 301. While still a student in 1927, Mr. Goldman himself had uttered this conclusion in an article for academic readers. (*807*, 30.)

[2] *243*, VIII, 134.

[3] Chesterton: "Ordinary people dislike the delicate modern work not because it is good or because it is bad, but because it is not the thing that they asked for. When they walk behind the brass of the Salvation Army band instead of listening to harmonies at Queen's Hall, it is always assumed that they prefer bad music. But it may be merely that they prefer military music." (*1155*, 77.)

[4] Seventy-five years later, Debussy concurred, to his own surprise, in Wagner's judgment that Berlioz' music had power to move the plain people. (*789*, 187.)

[5] It is interesting to compare this simplified and strictly musical expression of the nation's ritual with the elaborate plan drawn up by David (the painter)

Muffled drums open, solo, in a menacing rhythm which recurs throughout the first movement with the brutality of bare fact interrupting the numbness of grief. Then comes the march theme proper, solemnly intoned by the brass – unmistakable Berlioz in its breadth, but so scanned here that it is in no way elusive. After being declaimed twice, a derived theme of purer, more intimate grief follows, set forth by clarinets and flutes. The contrast may typify anything one chooses – masculine and feminine utterance; public and inner sorrow; brass and wood; solemnity and humbleness. Out of these two plaints and the drumming rhythm, the long processional is developed. Its symbolism is purposely obvious – war, a people on the march and grieving – at the same time as its development is symphonic. Doubtless because the cortege was to traverse a long distance, Berlioz planned the movement so that the first section, which works up to a great crescendo on the pedal held by the trombones and ophicleides, is heard entire a second time, but with each phrase amplified, elaborated, commented on by a profusion of countersubjects drawn from the main ones. The effect is that of an infinite lament, which reflection deepens without foreseeing how it may end.

The second climax reached, the march returns to the woodwind theme, now purged and almost reconciled. The cadence brings back the rhythm in a context which anticipates the third movement's apotheosis. Though of close workmanship, this funeral opening fulfills the requirements of simplicity and elevation. The hearer needs no explanation, and even the tone deaf must be aware that something solemn and grand is assailing their eardrums.

The second movement, which is very short and lightly scored, introduces a new mood. The march rhythm is replaced by a metric resembling that of speech, while the instrumentation suggests a dialogue between the trombone solo declaiming a kind of recitative and the orchestra acting as "chorus." In character, this "recital" belongs to the genre of the several similar passages for trombone found in the *Francs-Juges* overture, and the *Harold* and *Romeo* symphonies.[6] Here the utterance is at first incomplete,

---

for the ceremony of the Supreme Being, June 8, 1794. This employed not only all the musicians of Paris but representative groups of singing citizens, classed by age and sex. There were several "stations" traversed by the procession, which performed rites at each of the elaborate altars, and scenic backgrounds designed for the purpose. This was a popular music drama in the Wagnerian sense: that of Berlioz is its condensation into sound alone. A full description of the revolutionists' plan is given in *1303*, 1584.

[6] There are excellent musical reasons why the trombone should be used as a reciting instrument. Not only is its tone rich and penetrating without harsh-

like the cello voice which opens the choral section of Beethoven's Ninth; then it gathers momentum and unfolds in a touching melodic statement which justifies the alternative titles Berlioz gave to the movement—"Farewell Hymn" and "Funeral Oration." [7]

This simple melody, which the American composer and critic Carter Harman called "one of Berlioz' triumphs," [8] leads directly into the Apotheosis which concludes the symphony and as it were resolves our anguish. This last part begins with a pianissimo drum roll that rises sharply into a trumpet call. We suddenly hear again the muffled side drums, but the fanfare continues and lifts us out of woe and fear to the point where we will sing and march in tune with a new melody, marked *allegro non troppo e pomposo*. It is so phrased that its shape and notes must soon become familiar to any crowd. This theme alone, developed very simply, indeed conventionally, in the manner of a good brass-band march, supplies all the substance of the movement; it makes one think at once of Mendelssohn's "War March of the Priests" and Wagner's "Kaisermarsch," both subsequent. Here and there in Berlioz' finale, his special touch can be seen in the way we have come to expect (*i.e.*, in unexpectedness) but generally the Apotheosis remains musically primitive and solidly unpretentious.

The fact that the composer had to finish the work quickly meant that he did not give this movement its obviously intended form—that of a rousing piece which an audience can hear for the first time and yet sing with the chrous at the last reprise. When after July 28 Berlioz asked Deschamps for words and set them for voices in unison, he was only adding the kind of tone color which he wanted to hear, and which in other days he might have heard from the throats of the people.[9]

As it was, the Apotheosis march as Berlioz left it became, in France

---

ness, but upon it, unlike other brass instruments, notes of different pitch must be played slightly detached, or else a portamento (slide) is the result. The effect of this limitation is to give a trombone phrase a kind of resemblance to a phrase made up of distinct words.

[7] Berlioz uses the title *Hymne*, throughout his works in the sense of "Praise" and not at all in the English, churchly sense of hymn.

[8] *N. Y. Times*, June 24, 1947. "Distinguished . . . elegiac, and poetic," said Mr. Francis Perkins in the *Herald-Tribune* on the same day.

[9] Still later, Berlioz arranged the melody proper for separate choral performance. To combine this with the symphonic movement would, owing to the change of key, have required reorchestrating the whole movement, and by that time band instruments had themselves changed so much that the entire work would have needed revision. See another arrangement and its history in *308*, Sept. 3, 1905, 284.

at least, his most popular work. It certainly passed the private test that certain professed musicians apply: it can be whistled. We have moreover the testimony of Berlioz' rather envious colleague Adolphe Adam, who gives us at the same time a sample of current musical thought: "I like neither the man [Berlioz] nor his work, but fairness compels me to say that the peroration of the second movement is very effective and superior to all he has done hitherto. The first movement and the beginning of the second form an inexplicable mess. But the last movement is really very good: there is no melodic invention but the rhythm is clear, the harmony original, and the entrances well managed. It's really a great advance, for the phrases are squarely cut every four bars and thus can be readily understood." [10]

Despite the catchy simplicity of the last movement, the symphony forms a stylistic whole. When Sir Hamilton Harty revealed the work to London audiences in 1934, most British critics expressed the usual pained astonishment that such an interesting work should have been so long neglected. "I have found," said one of them, "all the supreme qualities of Berlioz' genius in [this] . . . extraordinary canvas employing an enormous wind band, every piece of which justifies its inclusion." [11] The scale of the canvas is of course one reason for its absence from the usual repertory. For performance by the Goldman Band in 1947, the symphony had to be reduced and rescored: some of the original instruments are obsolete and the band was perforce one quarter the size of the original group. To the task of reduction the composer-conductor, Richard Franko Goldman brought his great artistic integrity and musicianship, yet the result did not fully communicate or satisfy the original intention.[12] It was

[10] *499*, 479–80. Among other things, Adam could not forgive Berlioz his low estimate of Auber – "Auber," said Adam, "whom I consider the first musician of the century after Rossini." (*Ibid.*) At the very same time, Wagner was writing in his German papers: "There is really a vast distance between [Berlioz] and the author of *Le postillon de Longjumeau*," precisely this same Adam, who only came round to Berlioz in the fifties. (*Ibid.*, 482.)

[11] Havergal Brian: *Musical Opinion* (1936) 591. According to modern students such as Redfield and Goldman, the modern symphony band would use a clarinet choir of about fifty to correspond to the orchestra's string section, a woodwind section of twenty-four, and brass totaling twenty to thirty more, with timpani besides. The difference between this and Berlioz' balance is largely due to the increased range and power of the bass instruments since 1840.

[12] A technical note: in recent times, owing to the absence of a "Berlioz tradition" handed down from conductor to conductor, the tempo of the Apotheosis has been a subject of debate. It is marked in the score *Allegro non troppo e pomposo*. In his modern edition Mr. Goldman adds: quarter note equals 120, though the original carries no metronome mark – probably because Berlioz felt that the movement could be taken at various speeds. Neverthe-

good music with great moments but it fell short of the "popular sublime" that Wagner experienced.

This raises the important artistic question, so often mooted about Berlioz — and indeed first stated by him — whether massiveness of effect through volume of sound is or is not an integral part of certain musical conceptions. He said it was, and hostile critics have concluded that this implies something damaging about these particular works. In this view

---

less, the modern tendency to make it a quick march should be deprecated. The considerations to bear in mind are these: Berlioz' description of the fanfare and song of apotheosis shows that he designed the piece as a solemn kind of jubilation: *allegro* refers to the mood and *non troppo* restrains the pace. If the movement is taken at 120, it is denatured into a sort of polka.

Now the reasons which made Mr. Goldman, and Sir Hamilton Harty before him, take this piece as a quick march are that we have previously heard two slow movements and need a change, and that the development of the Apotheosis theme is not sufficiently rich to sustain a slow unfolding. The second argument is better than the first, for the allegro quality of the theme with its repeated triplets is surely enough to give a sense of variety after the second movement. As for the development, we must remember that the function of the whole work is popular, and that when we reach the finale the people are participants, emotionally if not actually. The simplicity and repetitiousness, which made Adolphe Adam rejoice and which struck Wagner as fitting, are part of the whole design, and it is a sophisticated mistake to hurry over them as if to palliate a weakness.

Lastly, the conductor seeking the right tempo may bring to bear additional sidelights: when the pianist Thalberg, who had heard the symphony under Berlioz, wrote his *Grand Caprice pour piano sur la Marche de l'Apothéose de H. Berlioz*, he marked the opening *maestoso* and indicated no fast movements until the obviously caprice-like variations at the end. Before this we have andante, lento, cantabile, and other indications of the singing character of the theme. This character is borne out by the tempo at which it was taken by the Conservatoire orchestra when they made the film *Symphonie Fantastique* in 1946–1947. In his biography, M. Boschot refers throughout to the *grande idée* of this finale: he would hardly call it so if he considered it a rapid rout after too much funereal contemplation.

Again, Bernard Van Dieren, who heard the broadcast conducted by Sir Hamilton Harty in 1934, complained of the fast tempo, as did T. S. Wotton in an article published shortly thereafter. (*154*, 162 and *586a*.) Berlioz himself reports a serious misapprehension of the tempo by musicians who rehearsed the work ahead of his arrival in Lille (*Grot.*, 298–9) and in the *Treatise* (p. 300) there seems to be an allusion to the same kind of misconception. Going through his later works one finds two passages also marked *Allegro non troppo* and differing widely in character. In *Les Troyens* Part I, Act II, Finale, the quarter note equals 138; in the *Emperor* cantata, it equals 100. The question obviously is not one which can be finally settled unless the missing edition of the *Apothéose*, announced by Wieprecht in 1843 should turn up bearing a metronome mark. Meanwhile conductors should give a try to the tempo range 80–100 before embarking on the 120 of the New York revised edition.

there is such a thing as "intrinsic music" which is independent of volume, timbre, or dynamics.[13] With this belief goes the assumption that it is easy to be impressive if one uses large means, which in turn fosters the illogical conviction that the presence of many players means noise.[14]

The question is not one of taste but of musical fact – assuming that music is the art of sound and not an abstract game. Berlioz' primary interest in composing some of his works for large groups of performers is made clear in the words quoted at the head of this section. He was among the first to note the relation between quantity and quality in performance, and he goes on to illustrate his observation: "Let a great work be performed at Notre Dame by sixty chosen singers, and let the same score be sung later by 500 choristers unselected yet competent: in the first performance the effect will be meagre, out of scale or downright poor; in the second, the effect will be majestic, imposing, sublime; the impression received will be profound; the composer's intention will be understood, and art will manifest itself in all its grandeur." [15]

These words concluded an essay upon religious music written in 1829, before Berlioz went to Rome. There, as we remember, he complained of the inadequacy of music as performed in Saint Peter's and he computed its requirements on the basis of the architectural scale. Berlioz' pragmatic premise that music exists as produced is of course that which allows a listener to complain of a bad performance; but Berlioz was more thoroughgoing than the ordinary listener and he included under bad performance any discrepancy of scale in *both* directions – that of insufficient volume, giving the audience the strained feeling that the music is being overheard from a great way off; and that of excessive volume, which either deafens the hearer or blurs the style of the piece.[16]

[13] This was Chopin's feeling about Berlioz' music, and particularly about the *Funeral* symphony, which was perhaps the last work by his friend that Chopin went to hear. They hardly saw one another thereafter, and Chopin soon indoctrinated Delacroix and George Sand with the notion that Berlioz' instrumental requirements were somehow a denial of art. The all-sufficiency of the piano is still a familiar dogma, though one would like to ask Chopin and his fellow dogmatists why – if timbre and volume do not matter – they require the best available piano, one with a good tone, with dampers and pedals and a proper sounding board.

[14] These beliefs seem so self-evident that the reporter from one of the news magazines which gave an account of the New York *première* wanted to know how the Berlioz symphony compared with Tchaikovsky's 1812 Overture "for sheer din."

[15] *1377*, Apr. 11, 1829, 55.

[16] When Berlioz played Mozart – or his own Queen Mab scherzo – he was careful to reduce the orchestra to the dimensions he thought suitable. See his discussion in *Mem.*, I, 355.

Only three of Berlioz' major works require a specially large body of players, and they are naturally the ones commissioned and designed for festival occasions, religious and national: the *Requiem*, the *Te Deum*, and the *Funeral and Triumphal* symphony.[17] Yet even in these works, the dosage of sound is carefully arranged so as to avoid the monotony of an unremitting display of power: in the *Requiem*, as we saw, the extra forces are used only twice, in movements totaling less than ten per cent of the playing time. In the *Te Deum*, the nave-filling organ is used most sparingly and its full force reserved for the very end. The *Emperor* piece and *Hymne* are no less discreet in their use of strong effects, and the *Funeral* symphony, it will be remembered, includes a gentle second movement, largely given over to the solo trombone. One is bound to conclude that Berlioz, far from wallowing in "tremendous" effects, is very prudent about unleashing them.

He further insisted on the acoustical fact that soft passages depend for perfection on the presence of large numbers. The roughnesses and unevenness of attack cancel out, producing a solid round tone. As Mr. Patrick Hughes wrote a few years ago, "How can one keep [from enthusiasm] on noticing at the end of a *pp* passage [in the Funeral March of the symphony] eight trombones quietly put their instruments down, having been playing all the time. There is a book to be written about these two Berlioz works [the *Requiem* and the symphony]." [18]

In what Berlioz says about quantity, therefore, the stress is upon musical results; he calls for masses either when individual quality (*e.g.*, trained voices) is lacking or when the output would be dwarfed by large spaces.[19] There is evidence, moreover, that Berlioz frequently performed his "monumental" works with fewer players than he asks for in the score.[20] Either the hall or the distribution of available instruments motivated these reductions, which the first twenty years of his career had made him adept at improvising. It is therefore another groundless superstition that he inaugurated the evil of asking for exorbitant means and could not compose

[17] The *Emperor* cantata and the *Hymne à la France* are much shorter and lesser works of the same type.

[18] *586.*

[19] In writing casually to Liszt about his own just completed "Fifth of May," Berlioz says: "I had to have it sung by 20 basses for lack of one good one." *A.R.*, 304. In our day, for the same reason, the Bethlehem Choir in an emergency assigns a solo part to six soprani in works like the B Minor Mass.

[20] The Apotheosis, notably during his first German tours (*M.E.*, 15, 29, etc.) and even the *Requiem* (*A Trav.*, 288) and *Te Deum* (*207*, II, 37); but the adaptation calls for uncommon judgment.

unless he had them.[21] The numbers stipulated in Berlioz' scores signify simply the optimum conditions for the playing of a given work and indicate the correct balance among parts. In the "colossal" works, Berlioz' ideas of number were the fruit of experience verified time and again by his own supersensitive ears. Experience has confirmed it after him, for every time that a conductor follows Berlioz' suggestions precisely, the critics exclaim at the unsuspected rightness of the result – especially in works that they knew from less exact performance.[22] Berlioz had no a priori prejudice in favor of volume; it is we who have a priori ideas in favor of a standard orchestra. Berlioz hated noise and loved music – so much so that he was not content to hear it spottily rendered.[23]

These were the considerations Berlioz took into account when he faced the task of composing in the symphonic idiom for military band, and which made him ask for a total of two hundred and seven wind instruments.[24] He had to employ elements which could compare in range and flexibility with the string sections of the concert orchestra and which could provide the bass without monotony.[25] Unfortunately, the great revolution in the manufacture of the brass came after Berlioz had scored this work and it must now be rearranged. In his modern version, Mr. Goldman was quite right to introduce five saxophone parts: Berlioz was the earliest user of the instrument, not only out of friendship and admiration for Adolphe Sax, but because he liked the "mellow, half-veiled" tone of this newcomer to the family of reeds.[26] Similarly, the tubas (baritone or euphonium) cor-

[21] The first charge was carelessly uttered by Saint-Saëns and has since been repeated on his authority. For the second, Berlioz himself is the "careless" authority: he wrote to Schumann that he needed large means (*Corresp.*, 119). He should perhaps have said, "larger than I can usually obtain," though even this would be an overstatement in the light of a good many scores of his that use the simplest orchestra. Compare Delacroix's exaggeration that he can paint only large pictures (*182*, I, 90).

[22] *E.g.*, the addition of choirboys for the last chorus of the *Damnation of Faust* (*582*, 32) or the presence of four harps in the *Symphonie Fantastique*. (*632*.)

[23] All his reviews, from his twenty-second year onward, attacked current practices that made for noise, whether it was the voice production of singers who shout and shriek, or the scoring of composers who with bass drum and cymbals "bring the county fair into the orchestra pit," or the rearranging of old scores by adding trombones which destroy all balance.

[24] For the distribution see Supplement 5. It is worth adding that early critics of Beethoven's first and second symphonies (1800 and 1802) were disposed to call them symphonies for military band because they were so heavily scored for winds. (*853*, 16.)

[25] The bassoons accordingly have virtuoso parts throughout their range.

[26] *Grot.*, 68 and see below, Subchapter 16.

rectly replace the ophicleides as Berlioz would have wished; yet Mr. Goldman's "convenient" reduction expressed in, say, three bassoons instead of sixteen, and two snare drums instead of twelve, demonstrates upon hearing that Berlioz knew what he was about when he called for absolutely larger forces. Even with the Central Park shell to reflect the sound, and even on the records taken at the near-by microphone, the music is not that which Berlioz and Wagner heard.[27] For the opening salvo the pair of muffled drums is too thin; throughout, the lack of bassoon tone robs the ensemble of a desirable reedy quality; the wonderful dialogue in the first movement between brass and wood does not stand out in sharp contrast; and the total dynamic range being reduced, the intermediary nuances tend to pass unnoticed, so that we arrive at the seeming paradox that it is primarily for delicacy and subtlety of effect that Berlioz required large ensembles.

We come to his other purpose. In that same early essay on religious music he wrote: "The ancients graced their ceremonies with a musical pomp [*appareil*] of which we no longer have any conception. What must we think of our orchestras of 50 players and our choirs of 40 voices when we read in the Scriptures that more than 4000 Levites were used in the temple of Solomon to sing the praises of God?" [28]

The example of Greek drama and its associated festivals was also in Berlioz' mind – as it was later in Wagner's – and with the same intent of arousing a collective emotion through a work of art of broad popular appeal. Such a work must be on a large scale not only because massiveness calls for a special style – which in turn creates the genre that Berlioz called "monumental" [29] – but also because festivals imply participation rather than spectacle, and the many performers assembled serve to represent the people for whom they sing. Ten thousand persons may gather to hear a coloratura soprano and will enjoy her performance, but on certain occasions such a ratio results in a spiritual as well as a numerical discrepancy. When that triumph of suspension engineering, the Brooklyn

[27] The mere volume registered on the discs can of course be amplified at will but to no avail – which shows again that it is not noise but quality and scale that justify Berlioz' numerical demands.

[28] *1377* (1829) 55.

[29] Whether or not the famous analogy between architecture and music holds good, the parallelism as to scale is exact, that is, size is an absolute as well as a relative factor: a building four times as big as another, if rightly proportioned, acquires a new quality, which is not merely an increase in the qualities already present in the smaller edifice.

Bridge, was formally opened in 1883 in the presence of Governor Cleveland and President Arthur, the bells tolled and the whistles on the river tugs blew amid a general uproar of human tongues, but music – well, music was not forgotten: there was a cornet solo by the virtuoso Jules Levy.

This kind of disproportion, worse than omission, was the sort of public absurdity Berlioz vainly protested against long before Brooklyn Bridge was thought of. As an artist with a very lively social sense, he conceived how the elite of a great country must musically celebrate their power, however crass. But the cultural forms and the cultural means were lacking, as they still are now.[30] Today we have so standardized tastes and musical resources that one must scour the capitals of the world to find three E-flat clarinets who can play in tune. In Berlioz' time – as he said looking back after 1848 – "it is not the voices alone that would be wanting . . . to reveal to Paris . . . the sublimities of monumental music. What would be equally wanting is the cathedral of vast proportions (the chapel of Notre Dame not being suited to music) and also, alas!, faith in art, a direct and impassioned impulse towards art, the calm, the patience, and the discipline of pupils and artists, together with the strong will – if not of the government, at least of the wealthy classes – to attain the goal after perceiving its beauty and worth. Lastly, money would fail us, and the undertaking would come to grief from want of support. We have only to remember, as a small instance of a mighty truth, the sad end that Choron came to after he had with slender resources obtained such important results in the field of choral music: he died of grief because *for economy's sake* the July Monarchy abolished his school." [31]

When Berlioz wrote this, he had just heard in London the Anniversary Meeting of the Charity Children in Saint Paul's, and he had been shaken to the depths of his being by the six thousand five hundred voices singing "All people that on earth do dwell," and other hymns. Sixty years earlier, Haydn had been moved to tears in the same place by the same cause, which Berlioz analyzes: "The prodigious effect of this unison is due, as I believe, to two conditions – the enormous number and good quality of the voices, first; and next, the disposition of the singers on rising tiers of benches. The reflectors and the makers of sound being in good relative positions, the whole atmosphere of the church is assailed from so many points at once,

[30] So much so that when Schoenberg's *Gurrelieder* was heard in New York, a critic could speak of its massive musical requirements as a piece of "colossal impudence," suggestive of a "psychological quirk." (*826*, 196.)

[31] *Soirées* (21st).

in depth as well as surface, that it begins to vibrate in its entirety; hence its resounding power acquires a majesty and a capacity to affect the human frame such as the most artful devices of music played under ordinary conditions have not hitherto produced." [32]

Berlioz goes on to wonder whether the quality of these children's voices may not be due to good nutrition, evidenced by their visible good health. "These English children . . . in no way show the sickly and underdeveloped aspect of our youngsters from the Paris working class, worn out as it is by bad food, overwork and privations." [33]

Then, reverting to the cultural problems, Berlioz sketches the possibility of paralleling in France this annual London festival and even improving upon it. He recurs to the scheme he had broached in 1837 for his *Requiem*, of using the unused Pantheon, which is not so large as Saint Paul's but is of the right shape acoustically.[34] It would hold a "small orchestra" of three or four hundred instruments and in place of untaught orphans a well-trained choir of four thousand mixed voices. They could then perform "a work written in a style suitable to such means, on a subject in which grandeur should be blended with nobility, and which should express all the elevated thoughts that can move the heart of man. I believe that such a use of the most powerful of the arts, seconded by the spell of poetry and architecture, would be truly worthy of a nation like ours and would leave far behind the vaunted festivals of antiquity." [35]

This lifelong concern of Berlioz' was at once a projection into the mid-century of the French revolutionary ideal and an extension of Beethoven's dream for the social function of the Ninth. In both men, individualists though they were, the impulse was to balance private by public emotion in a deep artistic protest against excessive concentration on the self. The triumph of mercantile individualism and the decline of religious faith in the nineteenth century spurred the desire of certain creators to recapture for art the privilege of expressing collective feelings. The "fraternity" of Schiller's *Ode* and the "elevated thoughts" that Berlioz wished to embody

[32] *Ibid.*, 225. The tradition of monumental music in England dated back to the Handel Commemorations in the 1780's (see Burney's *General History of Music, passim*), and something like it seems to have begun in Germany in Weber's time; see *1017*, 96.

[33] *Ibid.*, 225. The first factory act prohibiting the employment of *children under eight* had been passed half a dozen years before but it was not enforced.

[34] *L.I.*, 103–4. Berlioz had desiderated the Pantheon for music of this sort as early as his Mass of 1825 (*235*, II, 160). He asked for it again in 1840, hoping to play the *Funeral* symphony there. Its use was never granted (*1385*, Aug. 4 and 11, 1912).

[35] *Ibid.*, 225–6.

were alike rebukes to the prosperous bourgeois who thought he thrived by his own singlehanded efforts.[36] Bourgeois complacency, as embodied later in Dickens's Podsnap, went with conventionality and a fear of stirring the depths. The Podsnaps wanted an individual virtuoso to patronize while he played for them in the drawing room, and an individual painter to do them a landscape that would fit over the fireplace. Art stood in danger of being completely domesticated. Music in particular, by falling back into the place of entertainment, would lose the expressive powers it had won and content itself with teasing the mind by a species of stunt. Current taste reminded Berlioz of Molière's marquis who was engaged in putting all of Roman history into madrigals.[37] For in spite of all that has been said about the nineteenth century's love of size, it had no taste for grandeur. Prince Albert's plan for a Crystal Palace in which to show modern industry as a cultural undertaking only made him scoffing enemies; and like the Duke of Orleans he was rebuked by his nearest advisers for wishing to associate with men of genius. For genius too is outsize and oversteps conventions both in refinement and in simplicity.

In France, all that the government would provide for national holidays was military parades, and the account of July 28, 1840 tells us how poorly organized they were. In truth, despite a superficial and show-off patriotism, "the nation" scarcely existed. The government was unrepresentative and it rightly feared that public assemblies would lead to public disorder. A secular collective art was therefore impossible. The nearest approach to it was the opera, and Wagner himself – for all his advantage in coming after Berlioz – only led Europe back to a somewhat magnified opera. In his revivified form of it the desire for communing through music and drama was present, but what was its social significance? After [three-quarters] of a century no one seems to know.[38]

Berlioz' conception of a national art transcended the contemporary views of nation, class, and culture, and he created bigger works than France could, until recently, assimilate.[39] But it may be asked in the light

[36] It was in this same decade that Louis Blanc first used the term *bourgeoisie* to mark off a class distinct from the people. (*Histoire de Dix Ans, passim.*) In 1837, Jean Reynaud had defined the term as "those who were above want" (*Encyclopédie Nouvelle*, art. Bourgeoisie) which sufficiently shows the split in the formerly homogeneous Third Estate: the bourgeoisie was now regarded as an aristocracy but without taste or tradition.

[37] *A Trav.*, 343.

[38] How reconcile, for example, Shaw's *Perfect Wagnerite*, Dickinson's *Musical Design of the Ring* and Paul H. Lang's essays on Richard Wagner. (*790*, 1–3 and *832*.) [Add the remarkable biography by Robert W. Gutman, N. Y. 1968.]

[39] See below Supplement 1.

of his contempt for politics whether he was a true democrat or – as his birth and ability might well make him – an aristocrat. At times he seemed like many others deluded by the mirage of the Napoleonic legend. Does this imply a hankering after absolutism? The *Funeral and Triumphal* symphony itself had its genesis in recollections of Bonaparte's Italian campaign, and later the *Emperor* cantata expressed something of Berlioz' faith in the nephew of the great man. Two thoughtful artists, the painter Odilon Redon and the novelist Romain Rolland, have expressed regret at Berlioz's failure to side with the rising forces of democracy.[40] While recognizing Berlioz' greatness of character, Redon deplores that the musician should have been scornful and skeptical about the future of republics. And yet, as even Berlioz' harshest detractor is compelled to admit, there is in all of Berlioz' music a strong element of popular feeling.[41] In every drama that Berlioz conceived the role of the people is fully and admirably represented.[42]

These two sets of facts appear contradictory only if put in political terms. Berlioz sincerely despised politics for the very reason that partisanship divided persons and ideas that he wanted to keep joined, while it took no cognizance of the ideas that mattered to him as a craftsman and creator. The ordinary contrast of democratic and aristocratic breaks down in describing the artist, for art means discrimination, judgment, selectness, superiority – which count as aristocratic virtues; and art means also recognizing and expressing the common feelings of mankind and cutting through the crust of convention to the simplest realities. Hence the artist, and especially the dramatic genius, is often a "democrat" in his choice of subject matter and an "aristocrat" in dealing with it. Poetry, as Hazlitt showed, is always aristocratic because "its language naturally falls in with the language of power."[43] He is speaking of Shakespeare's *Coriolanus* and he means that we side instinctively with the hero and against the crowd because of his greater nobility, courage, and breadth of mind. The observation suggests its counterpart, which is that in order to represent a crowd as hero, the artist must choose its highest, most selfless emotions. If these are fine but simple, their mere multiplication will raise their esthetic merit. One rogue weeping – to use Hazlitt's language – does not move us, but a mourning nation, regardless of the cause, is a mighty spectacle. Berlioz describes music in similar terms, insisting that it is "like great poetry,

[40] *1275*, 214–5 and *504*, 51–5.
[41] Jean Marnold (*460*, 370).
[42] See below the *Damnation of Faust, L'Enfance du Christ*, and especially *Les Troyens*, in which the working classes are aptly celebrated.
[43] *1255*, 50.

essentially aristocratic,"[44] yet he recognizes, as we saw a little earlier, the validity of common emotions raised to a high significance by the sheer extent of their sway. The obvious conclusion about his "nature" in this regard is that Berlioz is both aristocrat and democrat, depending on what element of his work one chooses to abstract from the rest.[45]

His behavior conformed to this inclusive range of sensibility. He could listen with unaffected joy to a peasant air or follow a fife-and-drum corps "like a child"[46]; and he could also be entranced by the late works of Beethoven when they were, not caviar, but poison to the general.[47] What he could not endure (it was this source of his anger and contempt that gave him the reputation of being arrogant) was the tawdry operas of "the first musician of the century," Auber, and even the more skilful synthetic products that Meyerbeer provided for the strong heads among the bourgeoisie. Such works were "popular" in the box-office sense and they did entertain large numbers of people throughout Europe – one has only to think of all the detachable airs and ballets which amateur singers and pianists played at home. This was a popularity Berlioz never did and never will attain, but in three of the works for communal use that he managed to impose on his compatriots and their pear-shaped king, he fully achieved his goal of blending grandeur with nobility and simplicity with elevation, which is to say the democratic and aristocratic elements within him.

Of these three works, the *Funeral and Triumphal* symphony comes nearest to being entirely popular. Yet so little are we accustomed, even in a century of populism, to the intent of social art when it is divorced from current propaganda, that hearers of this symphony may still find the last movement vulgar, regretting to the end the varied "elegance" of the first two.[48] The mixed public that attends "pop" or band concerts is no surer of itself; it has had on the whole a poor education of the heart as well as of the mind, and it is likely to feel that a rousing march can be enjoyed only if not taken seriously. "Real" music, acceptable on a "higher level," must speak of "finer things." Hence it is that in nearly every one of Berlioz'

[44] *Mem.*, II, 139; see also I, 216.

[45] Two critics, one French and one German, have explicitly asserted this. (*584*, 323 and *376*, 333.) The drama of one against many is a genuine conflict only when a composer feels this double sympathy – as in the conflict between Friar Laurence and the warring families toward the end of the *Romeo and Juliet* symphony. But this is also the reason why the themes of this Finale cannot be of the same musical order as those of the love scene.

[46] *A.R.*, 202 and 123–98 *passim.*

[47] *A Trav.*, 303.

[48] *154*, 147.

twelve great works, some fragment offends this high-brow taste by the revelation it affords of some aspect of feeling which is "common," "banal," "vulgar." [49] What this rejection overlooks, actually, is art — the art with which the composer has rendered and even commented upon his crude or coarse subject matter. Where, in the vast repertory of unknowingly vulgar music will one find anything as expressively and exquisitely vulgar as Berlioz' two dozen marching and drinking tunes? [50]

This critical error occurs most often in persons who classify by externals and heed no further. A fanfare is enough for them to make them act as Fielding says his critics did about his realism. To the artist, on the contrary, the banality of a device only incites to original uses. Thus do Hardy and Shakespeare disinfect words whose associations are low or cheap, and thus did Berlioz work upon a threadbare form: "When I had finished the March and the Funeral Oration, and found the theme for the Apotheosis, I was held up a good while by the fanfare, which I wanted to have rise up from the depths of the orchestra to the high note on which the song of glorification bursts forth. I composed I do not know how many, all of which failed to satisfy me: they were either vulgar or too narrow in form, not sufficiently solemn or lacking in sonority, or badly graduated. What I dreamt of was the call of the archangel's trump, simple yet noble, bedight as in armor, soaring radiant and triumphant and overpowering in its fullness as it announced to heaven and earth the opening of the Empyrean gates. I stopped at last, not without misgivings, with the one now in the score, and the rest was soon finished." [51]

[49] The considerable yet secret party of anti-Beethovenians, or half-Beethovenians, make the same charge against such works as the *Egmont* overture and the finales of the Fifth and Ninth. An excellent musician who has often sung the work once said to me: "The 'Agnus Dei' of the *Missa Solemnis* is incredibly vulgar — it is pure Hollywood."

[50] As an example of his powers of discrimination, compare the "joy" expressed in the Hosanna from the *Requiem*, the Finale of *Harold in Italy* and the Auerbach's Cellar scene from the *Damnation of Faust*

[51] *Mem.*, I, 345–6.

INTERCHAPTER

14. *The Century of Romanticism*

All I read about Romanticism is wrong.
—Pushkin to Bestuzhev, 1825

According to the books, the flowering of art and action known as Romanticism came to an end in France in the early eighteen forties. To say this is to posit that between Berlioz' *Romeo and Juliet* symphony and his next comparable work, the dramatic legend entitled *Damnation of Faust*, something occurred in European culture to outmode his cast of thought and that of his contemporaries. In poetic drama, the failure of Hugo's *Les Burgraves* in 1843 has often been used to mark the end of literary Romanticism. It is a corresponding fact that Berlioz' *Faust*, when produced in 1846, aroused little public response and lay unregarded in France for thirty years.

In support of the theory of failure it can be shown that the *Funeral and Triumphal* symphony of 1840, built on feelings and ideas dating back to the Italian journey, marks a noticeable halt in Berlioz' career and in the times, for the work looks back in a period of diminishing freedom to the glorious dead of 1830, and in the life of the composer it closes an era of intense production, matched by ten years of hard-fought battles on native ground. Though beaten at the Opera, Berlioz had established himself as the unquestioned leader of French Romanticism in music; yet thereafter conditions at home compelled him to carry his revolution abroad, which resulted in a slowing down of his output. Finally, the style of these later works being different in certain respects from the earlier, they have been taken as signs of recantation and Berlioz has been described as a Romantic-by-accident, a young rebel who sobered down, an essential classicist who temporarily strayed.

If we considered just these facts, historic Romanticism would remain as a flashing series of productions occupying little more than a decade of French history. But this way of approaching the movement is bound to mislead. For if Romanticism had so narrow a base it does not deserve to be the name of an epoch; and if on the contrary, the term properly designates one age of man in Europe, then the fate of a single work by a Hugo or a Berlioz cannot be a sufficient test of decline. There must be certain more general truths as yet unformulated.

In seeking out these truths, it is important to avoid the extremes of literalism and of vagueness. Bearing in mind the character and scale of European culture in epochs preceding the Romantic, we should be prepared to find, in the period under review, neither complete uniformity nor radical confusion. True precision, as scientists know better than critics, is relative to the magnitude of the thing measured: you must not push the decimals beyond the limit of significance. If historians have failed to find unity in Romanticism, it is because they either were expecting too much or magnifying what was little. In the hands of biographers this amounted to tailoring a separate Romanticism for every artist.

Now Berlioz' deeds and those of his fellow artists in the years 1827 to 1840 sufficiently show that an implicit unity of purpose and desire existed among the French Romanticists. They recognized, moreover, in the works and writings of other Europeans – Scott, Goethe, Beethoven, Hoffmann, Byron, Goya, Pushkin – intentions akin to their own. Lastly, the revival in nearly every cultural center of figures previously obscured or misunderstood – Shakespeare, Dante, Spinoza, Vico, Montaigne, Ronsard, Villon, Cellini, Rabelais – testifies to the presence of a common outlook such as is implied whenever a single name is given to an age. For all the differences due to individual sensibility, the conscious and articulate men of the first half of the nineteenth century shared a common attitude toward life and art, and that attitude is definable. Romanticism may or may not be the name we would choose for it, but this name being historic, traditional, it must be kept – and if possible filled with the right historical contents.

It is not enough to say that Romanticism was a revolt from the Reason of the preceding age, as idealizers of that age pretend; nor that the movement originated in Germany and spread by contagion, as the political enemies of Romanticism would have us believe; nor again, that this characteristic culture of the nineteenth century was a hodgepodge of earlier tendencies, as our neoclassicists confidently assert. Like every large manifestation of the human mind, Romanticism has deep roots – roots in the past and in the eternal potentialities of human beings: the roots in the past being simply previous expressions of those same potentialities. Scholars who find Romanticist germs in seventeenth-century Pietism, or in eighteenth-century sentimentality and nature worship, are perfectly correct. For the neoclassicism of those centuries had its dissenters, who grew more numerous as time went on, and from them the Romanticists properly so-called drew important elements. Berlioz, it is clear, derived an explicit part of his musical conceptions from the Encyclopedists. He was familiar with Rousseau's *Dictionnaire* and "Letter on French Music," and although he combated Rousseau's demand for a simple musical texture, which ruled out counterpoint and expressive harmony, he respected other elements of Rousseau's theory and at many points fulfilled the ideal that Rousseau proposed to the French for creating a music distinctively theirs.[1]

Even more directly, Berlioz carried out, enlarged, and developed the musical suggestions of his immediate predecessors, bred on the Encyclopedia — Lesueur, Gossec, Méhul, Grétry, Reicha, Monsigny, down to Rouget de Lisle. This relation supplies one clue to the significance of nineteenth-century Romanticism as a whole. In any art or country, Romantic work begins when form, substance, and conception are all of a piece. Thus in Germany, Lessing attacks French neoclassicism in the 1760's, but continues to write classicist dramas: form and intention are at odds. It is only in Goethe and Schiller that we find the new product, previously called for, but not previously embodied. In England, Walpole's "Gothic" novel or Percy's *Reliques of Ancient English Poetry* indicate a new desire — for the supernatural and the folk ballad — but we must wait

[1] The points on which Berlioz cannot but have agreed with Rousseau may be found in such articles of the Dictionary as *Contre-sens* ("the lack of expression is perhaps the greatest enormity of all. I should prefer music to say something other than it should, rather than that it should say nothing at all.") In the "Letter on French Music" (1830 edition of the *Works*, vol. X) one finds innumerable points of concurrence between the two theorists: on strict tempo (284), distinct melody (285), expressive nuances (286 and *n.*), vigor and pace in modulation (293), inexpressive fugues and musical pedantry (298–9), sparing use of dissonance (300), precision and sobriety in harmonic effects (303), lively recitatives (305), plastic melody (308), "one work" by means of recitatives (309), orchestral comment (311 and 315), ridiculous illustration of words (317), independence of musical expression (318).

The "Letter of an Orchestral Player" which follows the first letter resembles the fictional tone of Berlioz' *Soirées de l'Orchestre* and anticipates several of Berlioz' principles: on accurate and energetic performance (320–24) etc. As for the essays discussing Rameau's system, the whole tenor of Rousseau's argument is pragmatic in the manner that Berlioz was later to make his own. See pp. 333–5, 337, 339, 341, 343, 347, and 348: "Harmony does not consist in the relations among vibrations but in the concourse of sounds resulting therefrom."

Rousseau's review of Gluck's *Alceste* is again full of observations that Berlioz would endorse, side by side with others he would repudiate. What is truly amazing is the similarity of tone and the power of logical deduction in the two men. In a fragment on bells, Rousseau writes: "If one were to compose airs for jew's harp, it would be imperative to make their character suit the jew's harp. But in France, musicians take pleasure in denaturing the quality of each instrument." (383.) Finally, Rousseau's lyric scene entitled "*Pygmalion*" reads like a shorter version of *Lélio*. (479–85.)

until Scott's romances and the *Lyrical Ballads* of Wordsworth and Coleridge before the desire is satisfied. The odes of Collins and Gray and the forgeries of Chatterton still have the transitional look. In French poetry, the midway mood is absolutely explicit: young Chénier, over whom Berlioz brooded, had written the famous line:

Let us upon new thoughts write antique verses.[2]

He himself did as much as he could to enlarge neoclassical diction but the unmistakable break comes only thirty years later, when Lamartine published his *Méditations Poétiques*. The signs of "crossing over" are so uniformly repeated throughout Europe between 1750 and 1830 that they can be taken as diagnostic.[3]

This holds for Poland, Russia, Italy, and Spain, where corresponding evolutions took place: everywhere in the eighteenth century a spontaneous demand brings about a return to native traditions accompanied by sentimental affectation of various sorts: simplicity, medievalism, and tearful emotion. More solid works and ideas gradually emerge until by 1800 Europe was ready for an artistic renascence. In any cultural center, foreign examples and translations had currency precisely because the indigenous mood was receptive. In France we see Berlioz, Hugo, Michelet, Delacroix, Sainte-Beuve, and others strongly moved by foreign writers. But the reason they read Goethe two decades late (and Shakespeare two centuries) is that the work of the imagination in France had been retarded by twenty-five years of war and censorship. No influence could enter until the artistic sensibility was ready for it.

This gradual reformation of the western mind is something rather more awesome and worthier of attention than the supposed revolt of a number of young men against the conventions of their elders. Romanticism did

[2] *Sur des pensers nouveaux, faisons des vers antiques.*

[3] They help moreover to disprove the idea of "Romanticism by contagion." Certain critics maintain that France turned to Romanticism because Mme. de Staël wrote a book *On Germany* in 1810: how was it, then, that Chateaubriand who knew nothing of German literature was writing Romanticist esthetics in 1800? Conversely, if Germany is the common source, how is it that Kant, Goethe, Herder, and others acknowledge in their characteristic new works a great debt to Rousseau and Shakespeare? Or again, if Rousseau is alone credited with this onerous paternity, how does it happen that James Thompson was writing *The Seasons* in 1725, and French novelists of the mid-eighteenth century were hailing Richardson as the rediscoverer of human emotion? The crisscrossing of influences in so cosmopolitan a culture as the European was infinite and cannot be sorted out along national lines.

not in fact devour its parent, rationalism or classicism. The eighteenth century lingered on, and paradoxically it is often the eighteenth-century survivals into the nineteenth that are most frequently attacked as the distinctive traits of Romanticism.[4] By the time that Romanticism had purged itself of sentimentality, self-pity, and grandiloquence, and had thus found its unique character, it appears to some observers unrecognizable or "chastened," which is equivalent to saying that the ungainliness of adolescence is the true figure of the man.

The three blemishes just named are but different symptoms of one state, which is that of anticipation. Sentimentality takes its rise in the eighteenth century (in Sterne, Richardson, Rousseau, and the "tearful" playwrights) because passion is still believed to be antisocial, and the adequate forms of expression for it are lacking although its worth is beginning to be known. For to act sentimentally is not, as commonly thought, to revel in emotion, but to show and indulge feelings while shying away from their consequences. The Sentimental Journeyman sheds tears over the donkey because true compassion for man would really mean changing the social order. Tears become the sign of right feeling, which so far means only right opinion *about* right feeling.[5] In truth, before we can understand social evolution from Rousseau to Freud we need a Natural History of Tears. The Romanticists' references to weeping at any rate require a double interpretation. When Berlioz describes the physical effect of music upon him and weeps at the finest, gayest parts of the *Barber of Seville*,[6] those tears are the unaffected result of intense participation, the resolution of a total strain — as in the frequently reported instances of athletes at a

[4] As a measure of the cultural overlap, it is useful to remember that it was not until 1835 that the French Academy authorized the spelling *-ait* in many words so pronounced — a reform demanded by Voltaire — nor the naturalization of *opéras* with final *s* and accent. In Berlioz' handwriting and usage many traces of the eighteenth century are still to be found. Technologically, moreover, in the 1830's the use of envelopes was a novelty, lead pencils were a new invention and so were friction matches.

[5] Thus in the late eighteenth century Mme. Dufrenoy was forced to explain to her friends that she had a good heart although she was physically incapable of shedding tears when convention required it. (*1212*, IX, 149.) In the next generation, Hazlitt offers a more balanced view, which most Romanticists shared: "Tears may be considered as the natural and involuntary resource of the mind overcome by some sudden and violent emotion before it has had time to reconcile its feelings to the change of circumstances." (*The English Comic Writers*, 2.)

[6] Compare Tolstoy's account of Prince Andrey's weeping as he listens to a song in *War and Peace*, Part VI, Ch. 19.

race, sailors after a rescue, or statesmen in a crisis.[7] Social convention alone decides whether such manifestations are yielded to or confessed. Verbal convention thereafter makes of tears an expressive reference – witness Mozart's account of financial distress: "Tears prevent me from completing the picture! – "[8] Conversely, when Berlioz reports or predicts that audiences will weep or did weep on hearing a piece of music, it is a shorthand term which means no more and no less than our emphatic modernisms: "went into ecstasies" or, colloquially, "turned handsprings."

The same social rules control grandiloquence. The unlucky words which Berlioz used in exchanging batons with Mendelssohn strike us as pompous and absurd.[9] They are of a kind with Victor Hugo's sententiousness and Balzac's melodrama; all of them hark back to Bonaparte's mode of addressing the Grand Army, and this in turn comes out of the eighteenth-century feeling for antique and primitive grandeur.[10] In Voltaire, eastern sages and prophets speak as Berlioz did to Mendelssohn, though Berlioz' source was undoubtedly James Fenimore Cooper, himself reared on the neoclassics. The debates of the French revolutionary assemblies breathe the same epic diction. Through the power of the *Zeitgeist* to assimilate a rich diet, the flavor of Ossian, of the American Indian chief, and of the Roman heroes merged in one heady anticipation of greatness. Still in the eighteenth century, Bonaparte's hand thrust in the coat unmistakably conveyed to his compatriots the austerity of the Republican consul; it was a promise of constitutional rule like the grin on a modern president of the United States. The true Romanticist rhetoric, which comes later, is more vibrant than solemn, and rhetoric disappears from conduct in proportion as it informs great art. We know that Berlioz' foreign hosts found him almost too reserved and self-controlled. They had expected manners at once fiery and grandiose, but he had achieved a vivid grandeur in music and did not need to exhibit the same in life – whether as Mohican, Bonaparte, Gracchus, or Roi Soleil.

Real accomplishment similarly dissipated youthful melancholy and self-pity. It is inaction and unfledged power that make gifted youth mope, or deceive them into thinking that to be miserable is to be great. The belief

[7] See *Life*, July 12, 1948; Ciano's *Diaries* (*passim*) and *N. Y. Times*, Aug. 27, 1948: "General Hodges in Tears on Leaving Korea"; Sir Walter Scott weeping at a discussion of politics (Lockhart, II, 328); Wellington after Waterloo (*1230*, 178); Dr. Johnson (in Boswell, *passim*).

[8] *219*, 1394 (March–April 1790).

[9] See Chapter 16, *n.* 12.

[10] Look at David's painting of the brothers Horatius swearing revenge or death.

that great sensibility betokens genius is valid only when the sensibility is of a kind that brings forth fruits, that is, the power to feel must make a man act. He continues to suffer as Berlioz did, and he may be unreconciled to the terms on which he holds life and genius, but he no longer fears his weakness, knowing its worth. He no longer seeks to cover it up as the eighteenth century tended to do, with an affected strength, for he knows that the contradiction of weakness and strength is the polar axis on which Romanticism revolves.[11] From that moment of full recognition as we see it in Berlioz after the Italian journey, Romantic melancholy is replaced by stoical pessimism, and the man himself embodies the ideal of the Indian chief which the conventional phrases of a bygone age failed to evoke.

Despite conceded limitations and an eighteenth-century aspect, Napoleon was of course the living example of heroism who remained an object of wonder to the most remarkable men of his time. Beethoven, Byron, Stendhal, Carlyle, Hazlitt, Manzoni, Goethe, Hegel, Berlioz, and many others, were in that sense Bonapartists. Berlioz' Military Symphony was planned while traversing the theater of Bonaparte's first great campaign, and the same cluster of feelings also inspired his *Cinq Mai*, *Te Deum*, and *Impériale*.[12] This does not mean that Berlioz' contempt for politics dissolved in the rays of Napoleonic glory. His scorn of conquerors' ethics as well as his hatred of violence persisted; but like most artists who lived close to the event he extracted from Bonaparte's career a quality meriting itself the name of art. Stendhal, who wrote two books on Napoleon, tells us precisely what this was: "His superiority lay entirely in the faculty of finding new ideas with incredible speed, of passing judgment upon them with perfect reason, and of carrying them out with a strength of will as yet unequaled."[13] Elsewhere, Stendhal declared: "I experience a kind of religious feeling in daring to write the first sentence of Napoleon's story,

[11] The expressions of this insight during the Romantic period are legion. One may cite at random De Quincey's remark about Oliver Goldsmith: "Our revolutionary age would have unsettled his brain. The colossal movements of nations, from within and from without, the sorrow of the times, which searches so deeply; the grandeur of the times which aspires so loftily—these forces, acting for the last fifty years by secret sympathy upon all fountains of thinking and impassioned speculation, have raised them from depths never visited by our fathers, into altitudes too dizzy for *their* contemplating. . . ." (*1204*, II, 285.)

[12] Only a quarantine kept the young musician from going on a pilgrimage to Elba and Corsica in 1832. (*A.R.*, 194; *Corresp.*, 96, 98.)

[13] *1240*, 47.

for it is the story of the greatest man who has come into the world since Caesar." [14]

This emotion, so foreign to our hearts and so complicated for us by later irrelevancies, holds within it many of the elements that Romanticism chose to stress from among the permanent tendencies of man. But we fail to understand this complex attitude if we simply repeat the phrase "romantic hero" and think merely of egotism and tyranny. Stendhal and Berlioz were as prompt as Beethoven to criticize Napoleon's selfish and narrow personal ambition and to reject perpetual war. What Stendhal admired was a quality — the heroic — which was not limited to warriors, as Carlyle was to show, and therefore deserved to be admired wherever found.[15] We must remember that if Bonaparte came to stand for all Europe as a heroic type, he earned that title in competition with thousands of extraordinary talents who had been heaved up by revolution and who had become not solely generals but orators or statesmen, administrators or codifiers of law.

The era believed in genius because it had seen it at work: Pitt, wartime Prime Minister in his thirties; Hoche, a great general among many, dead at twenty-three; the sons of peasants and cobblers risen to fame before middle age — this was the striking new social fact. It entirely changed the meaning of Greatness, which was now regarded as a faculty, not a rank. From Danton and Carnot to Nelson and Wellington leadership went to men whose strength all lay in genius, not position, who "formed new ideas, judged them, and carried them out" in the teeth of convention and routine. They were indefatigable workers, "tireless athletes," as Berlioz and Delacroix were to be called, and ever ready to prove their worth. Measured by that exacting standard, Napoleon outtopped them all. Hence he could stand as their prototype. He was the Individual that the new social order proposed to liberate, and he himself for half a dozen years acted as revolutionary liberator. It was no illusion to suppose that when careers were open to talents, these would manifest themselves early: the familiar instances of youthful maturity in Keats and Shelley, Leopardi and Byron, Bonington and Evariste Galois, Schubert and Berlioz, are a handful among a host.

Since the phenomenon was new, men studied it, and the most thoughtful arrived at the conclusions we must share if we are to understand their outlook: originality and energy are virtues because they supply the ideas needed in a period of reconstruction. But judgment, reason, self-detach-

[14] *1240*, 19.

[15] Carlyle's *Heroes,* it is too often forgotten, comprise the god, the prophet, the poet, the priest, the man of letters, and the king (or leader).

ment — features of the Faustian "double man" — are equally necessary for choosing among the inspirations that the "inexplicable mechanism" of genius throws up. Finally, will power is required to make the idea — the imagined reality — a reality in fact.

This defines the character of the romantic creator in any field, and it only remains to ask why admiration and even religious feeling are involved in a sequence that seems psychologically so natural. The answer is that the Romanticist had a sense of the world's resistance to change, to originality, and to genius. Against his thousands he found millions in whom art, glory, will, and the conquest of reality evoked no response. There seemed to be two varieties of the human species, the heroic and the conventional; Faust and Wagner; or again: the Philistine and the artist; the dedicated and *l'homme moyen sensuel.* Whence the war depicted by Stendhal in *Le Rouge et le Noir*, by Balzac throughout the *Comédie Humaine*, by Berlioz and others in their memoirs.[16] Inevitably, those who did more or wished to do more arrogated the superiority to themselves. The new aristocracy, they argued, must rest its claims on the kind of power that Stendhal found in Napoleon. Self-appointed at the beginning, this natural aristocracy was either sustained or denied by the heterogeneous world, which is why Balzac's Rastignac, looking down on Paris, says: "It's between you and me." [17]

Viewed against the mass of mankind, the hero is Hegel's "world-historical character," the man who is both the embodiment and the creator of novelty.[18] For it is a mistake to regard the struggle between the genius and the Philistine as one of pure antagonism: there is love as well. For one thing, the genius is in most instances sprung from the undistinguished mass; for another, the mass — now to be called "people" or "nation" — also possesses genius. Its traditions, which are the source of all true history, are a collective repository of art, wisdom, and heroism. The French revolution simply laid bare this reality by making the people for the first time a self-aware agent in history. Soon after, Romanticist art for the first time dramatized the people's existence. The historians gave the anonymous

[16] It is impossible to read Goethe's *Autobiography* without recognizing the importance to him of Frederick the Great's contemporary achievements as warrior-king. One might surmise that the early appearance of the new Romanticist literature in Germany owed as much to this proto-Napoleonic symbol as to the inadequacy of the imported French style.

[17] *Père Goriot*, last chapter.

[18] Hegel's notion was obviously inspired by Napoleon's career. (*Philosophy of History*, Introd., and Part IV.) It is a striking coincidence that as Hegel was finishing his first great work, the *Phenomenology*, he looked up and saw Napoleon's troops entering Jena.

crowd a genuine role in their narratives; the mob scenes in Scott, Carlyle, Hugo, Prescott, or Michelet added a new dimension to literature, and a Delacroix or a Berlioz could without affectation compose works like "The Twenty-eighth of July" or the carnival scene of *Benvenuto Cellini.* And from time to time, the mass responded, as we shall see when we find Berlioz conducting an incendiary March in Buda-Pesth.[19]

The conflict between leader and led was thus ambivalent, but the inevitable difference between their activities, together with the fact that power is always indivisible, led to the growth of two standards within one culture: creator and consumer valued the same things in opposite ways — life, art, pleasure, money, success. The works of the creators consequently show the characteristic Romantic tension: they express the time, place, people, and tradition, but without the consent of these inarticulate elements, and they project "*ins Blaue hinein*" the next step in that tradition.

It is consequently an error to say that for the first time in history the Romantic artist is "divorced" from society: his whole art is a social mirror reflecting a social struggle. His own complaint is, on the contrary, that he wants to speak for his speechless fellows, instead of ignoring them as under the monarchy, and the populace objects, saying: "We do not feel, think, or act as you represent us." [20] Worst of all, this reluctant populace is not the real populace, but a limited group of well-to-do burghers with set ideas on the fine arts. Far from wanting to find their true life, full of conflicts and deficiencies, depicted in the works of contemporary artists, the bourgeois want these works to beguile, flatter, and soothe their bruised egos. Their mode of life and their prejudices must be as deeply respected by the artist who wants to succeed as the preferences of the princely patron ever were by his household entertainers. To the Philistine, art must remain entertainment through illusion while pretending to give the joys of self-knowledge.

It is clear why the artist's war has to go on. It goes on *against* the Philistines because their full dense mass can be lighted and lightened by art, and it goes on *amid* the Philistines because they are part of life and because Romanticism is committed to inclusiveness. Indeed, from one point of view the unheeding *are* life in the sense that they define its social conditions: they are Polonius and Gretchen's neighbors, Fieramosca and

[19] See Chapter 16.

[20] On the cultural split between nation and elite during the so-called classic centuries, see *1210*, 428 ff

Beckmesser. To be "realistic," Romantic art stays close to the data of the workaday world; to bring novelty, it depicts the endless drama of the individual and the group. The conflict ranges from hell to heaven, and the drama is cast with personages drawn from all mankind. In representing this reality through art the Romanticist necessarily traverses a comparable range, from the wretched to the great, and from the dullard to the genius whom the natural conspiracy of dullards forces to become a hero.

To sum up, all the relevant disciplines – history, psychology, social analysis, and the criticism of art – lend weight to the proposition that Romanticism is related to the previous age not in the way of revolt but in the way of revolution. Romanticism did not merely oppose or overthrow the neoclassic "Reason" of the Age of Enlightenment but sought to enlarge its vision and fill out its lacks by a return to a wider tradition – national, popular, medieval, and primitive as well as modern, civilized, and rational. At its fullest, Romanticism cherishes both experience and tradition, both emotion and reason, both the Graeco-Roman and the medieval heritage, both religion and science, both folk art and its cultivated offshoots, both formal strictness and the claims of substance, both the real and the ideal, both the individual and the group, both order and freedom, both man and nature. Its aim is inclusiveness, the recognition and placement of all experience as *pro tanto* valid, and the creation of a livable cosmology for man at the high point of his complexity and self-consciousness.

Actuality of course denies the complete fulfillment of this program – or to put it differently, Romanticism encounters what looks like irreducible contradictions, because it starts from man and accepts the contradiction which exists in him. Man is both great and puny, destined for glory and for wretchedness, superior to his fate and crushed by his fate, but he may achieve individual salvation through some unpredictable and unprescribed reconcilement of opposites which in retrospect we call his career. He must run the risk of failure because, as Pascal long before had said, "He is embarked." The outcome of the voyage depends on his individual energy, daring, openness to experience, stoutness of heart, greatness of intellect and imagination.

It follows that Romantic accomplishment appears more incomplete, less equipoised than work done in the spirit of exclusion, of elimination of opposites, of social or other guarantees against risk, of refusal to accept as real the second branch of each dilemma. Romantic work is the work of self-reliance, tension, and perpetual innovation. It leads to the creation of the unique form for each conception, and hence to the regard for individual tone, nuance, local color, and what modernism calls "experiment." It leads also to the mixing of genres, because Romantic analysis undercuts verbal logic and asks why a man should not laugh and weep during the same evening's entertainment. The Romantic mingles comedy and tragedy and clears Shakespeare of imputed bad taste.[21]

Romantic criticism revivifies the arts by questioning the current – and historically recent – formulas in the light of experience: is it a fact that because the media of the several arts differ the realities which they evoke are distinct? – words rendering only actions, painting only images, and music only emotions? This has often been asserted but has it been ascertained? Experience shows that these various means of striking our senses do but *suggest* what neoclassical rule says they *give;* hence it is possible to extend communication across the arbitrary bounds: De Quincey can write in words an introspective "Dream Fugue" whose form justifies its musical title, and Berlioz can reclaim that same title and form for the last movement of his first symphony. It is a further fact that the Greeks and Romans who are presumed to have set the fixed boundaries of each genre did nothing of the kind. Aristotle, Longinus, and Horace are closer to Romantic precept – and the works they examine are closer to Romantic practice – than the works and precepts of their neoclassical eighteenth-century interpreters. "Hence," said the Romanticist, "let us build in the open country, in the light of reason and experience: the zoning laws belong to an absolute monarchy that is dead." [22]

The metaphor is a summary in itself: Romanticism is part of that great revolution which drew the intellect of Europe from a monarchical into a popular state, fom the court and the fashionable capitals into the open country and the five continents, from the expectation and the desire of fixity into the desire and expectation of change. No such enlargement of mental and physical horizons had been felt since the previous "Romantic" era, that of the expansion of Europe in the sixteenth century – whence

[21] Paraphrasing Hugo's Preface to *Cromwell*, 1827. (*1262*, 19–50.) See also Berlioz' comments on Shakespeare (*Mem.*, I, 97–8), or almost any of De Quincey's essays, especially his "Rhetoric" and "Theory of Literature."

[22] The "laws" of music did not claim descent from Greek legislation, but from Rameau's rationalization of harmony: "When I think," said Berlioz, "of the realm of chords which scholastic prejudice has declared forbidden ground, and which since my emancipation I regard as my own domain, I rush forward in a kind of frenzy to explore it." (*A.R.*, 88.) And again: "Lesueur's system was borrowed from Rameau and his speculations on the vibrating string which he terms 'the sounding body' – as if strings were the only vibrating bodies in the universe; or rather, as if the theory of string vibrations were applicable to all other sounding bodies." (*Mem.*, I, 30.)

the sympathy of the later for the earlier period. Both were ages of exuberance and exploration, and both yielded comparable fruits: men of "universal" scope and works of art whose conception likens them to complete worlds.

Nineteenth-century Romanticism would accept nothing less than the universe as a naked fact because it witnessed – or foresaw – the wreck of a society. But Romanticism faced the cultural task of primitive men without the relaxed responsibilities of primitives. It had to reabsorb the realities which the preceding two centuries had quite literally put out of court – wild nature, passion, superstition, myth, history, and "foreign parts." It was consequently not "exoticism" but discovery when Chateaubriand or Byron sought out the Near East or the Far West, when De Quincey or Nerval explored the world of dreams, when Goethe or Berlioz recaptured the supernatural, when Delacroix or Scott depicted the Middle Ages, when Rousseau or Wordsworth looked within themselves for sentiments hitherto concealed, when Pushkin and Balzac imported the commonplace and the extraordinary into fiction: Romanticism was a comprehensive Realism.

There is no doubt that Romanticism accepted an enormous challenge and made an enormous claim. But to begin with, it inherited an enormous fortune, which had been accumulating since the fall of Rome. The Middle Ages, the Renaissance, and the Enlightenment were an open treasure house, in which lay half hidden still older deposits, Pagan and Christian. When the twenty-five years of revolution had cleared the ground for a new start, the Romantics could build like first settlers who had not only brought with them perfected tools but who could also boast of abundant technical talent. In sheer amount of intellectual gifts, few epochs can match that which stretches from the birth of Goethe in 1749 to the death of Berlioz one hundred and twenty years later. This span, which brings it to within the birth years of eminent men now living, makes Romanticism the parent century of our own times. This is the major difficulty in seeing it steadily and whole. We have grown up within our father's house and our striving for independence makes us abhor the language spoken there. Until very recently our best critics have used every means to dissociate us from the Romantic era. It is they who keep repeating that the movement failed over a hundred years ago and that the monuments of Romanticist art are all "flawed masterpieces." The flattering inference is that after 1850 a new cultural start was made from whose finer strain we are sprung.

Correctly interpreted, this double protection against the original Romanticism might be acceptable, but it is not likely that the anti-Romanticists would accept the necessary clauses of interpretation. Romanticism "failed" as a movement because, like all movements, it was the work of men. Cultural history is a succession of failures in which are embedded great achievements or, alternatively, a succession of achievements which end in failure. The work of an age is like a glacier, which strews the ground with debris, but also marks its passage with great terminal moraines. Greece, Rome, the Middle Ages, the Renaissance, the Reformation, the Enlightenment, all failed to usher in the millennium or to exhaust the possibilities of the human spirit. Death, fatigue, accidents of all sorts, put an end to whatever is "working" or has worked. Berlioz' vision of music festivals commensurate with the needs of a great modern nation failed, as we shall see, because the elements he sought in the social order were antagonistic among themselves, and no doubt also because he had not at his command the political power of a Louis XIV or Napoleon – who in their sphere also failed.

Hence those works of Berlioz' which were conceived for the nation's use lack the adventitious yet necessary merit of having been assimilated by his living compatriots. And this is true of innumerable other works sprung from kindred conceptions in the other arts.[23] Does this mean that the great sketches of the Romantic cultural edifice are on that account worthless? They are accurately termed "flawed masterpieces," for no earthly work is flawless, and sketches are all we have of any period. In time, our love and desire fill them in, which creates the pleasing illusion of perfection in the distance: the Mozart symphony seems lucid and perfect because it no longer strives to speak, as it once did, of a life at hand, and so no longer provokes outraged comparisons. Habit, moreover, has given us an indulgent taste for the style's characteristic weakness or the form's inevitable padding.[24] But to good contemporary judges the work seemed rough and full of flaws.[25] Horace may tell us that sometimes Homer nods, but we palliate the dullness under jargon or sentimental

[23] *E.g.*, François Rude's high-relief panels for the Arc de Triomphe. Though he is the great sculptor of the Romantic movement, Rude is scarcely known as such or in any other guise. Of his complete project for decorating the Arc only the "Call to Arms of 1792" was commissioned and executed. One modern critic, Miss Rebecca West, has written of her visit to the Rude museum at Dijon, but with uncomprehending eyes (*Ending in Earnest*, 148); the 14th *Britannica* has no article about him.

[24] Compare Racine's *galanterie*, Pope's commonplace, Shakespeare's bombast.

[25] See above eighteenth-century objections to Gluck, Mozart, and Beethoven, Chapters 3 and 4.

attitudes that are entirely of our own making.[26] It is proper that we should do so, but it follows that what we rightly value and call perfect is enjoyed at the cost of a wise and magnanimous overlooking of flaws. After a time — as Shakespeare's reputation proves — this becomes automatic and unconscious. The pressure of a relentless modernism which keeps offending us helps develop this receptivity for the work of thirty or fifty or a hundred years ago, all *its* modernism spent. Thus did a twentieth-century critic discover that the music of Berlioz' *Damnation of Faust* was "cleanly classical." [27]

After making allowance for a changing perspective, there remains the broad distinction established earlier between Gothic and classic principles of art. The perfection of Romanticism is to bring into a tense equilibrium many radical diversities. It consequently produces work that shows rough texture, discontinuities, distortions — antitheses of structure as well as of substance. From the classical point of view these are flaws; but they are consented to by the Romanticist — indeed sought after — for the sake of drama; they are not oversights on the artist's part but planned concessions to the medium and the aim it subserves — as in engineering one finds gaps, vents, or holes to balance the effects of expansion by heat or stress of vibration. So, far from lacking a sense of form or neglecting its claims, the Romanticist abandons the ready-made formula because its excessive generality gives it too loose a fit. He constantly alters or invents formal devices — as Berlioz did in the *Symphonie Fantastique* — so that the work of art may satisfy the several requirements of subject, substance, and meaning, rather than simply fulfill a routine expectation.[28] The result is a characteristic distortion or asymmetry, which may be observed equally in Gothic and Romantic work, in Shakespeare, Goethe, Berlioz, Hugo, Delacroix, or Stendhal. Hence, the folly of applying a classic or symmetrical "stencil" over a Romanticist conception: the parts that come through to the observer are bound to seem incoherent and to violate "the" form.

A comparison of such attempts in the several arts yields historical proof of unity in Romantic principles, and serves to exonerate any great artist from the usual charges he is made to endure singly. Here is Delacroix

[26] *E.g.*, Zeus's bragging and bullying at the beginning of the Eighth Book of the *Iliad*, and the innumerable lines or half-lines of rhythmical filler.

[27] See above, Introduction, and *562*

[28] Delacroix: "Do not run after a vain perfection. There are certain faults — or deemed such by the vulgar — which often are what gives life." And again: "To make a wholly new kind of painting — by the extreme variety in the foreshortened parts." (*182*, I, 96 and 52.)

being taken to task: "By the aid of brilliant color he partly conceals his uncertain draughtsmanship; but the drawing is ragged, and the segments composing his pictures are broken by gaps and fissures. He obtains vividness by his sketchy technique, but the agonized faces, the swirling naked bodies, the faked ramping chargers, the theatrical Medea, . . . are too unsubstantial, too obviously put together by dextrous invention to convey the dramatic truth which Delacroix imagined he brushed into them. . . ." [29]

This might be called the standard accusation, at large and in detail. Change only the technical terms and titles of subjects and you have the usual denunciation of Berlioz the colorist who lacked "draftsmanship"; of Balzac, the melodramatic contriver of empty effects; of Stendhal, the injudicious artist who was led astray by love of the picturesque and who neglected motive to the detriment of clear design.[30] But the constructive power of the great Romanticists – as the world is beginning to see in Berlioz – cannot be measured by casual or hostile inspection. Study is needed in order to find the deep premeditation of structure within a work which seems at first all improvisation and surface effects. Thus did Van Gogh and Emile Bernard study Delacroix, of whom Bernard asserts: "No one more than Delacroix took greater care to establish his shadows with earths, ochres and blacks in order to weld together all the parts of his compositions . . ." [31] More interested in color, Van Gogh finds that Delacroix's composition also owes something to that supposedly adventitious element: "He proceeds by color as Rembrandt by values, but one is as good as the other." [32] We shall find that Berlioz, whose form can be vindi-

[29] (*1071*, 446.) This is but one of a host of disparagements of Delacroix, from R. de Croy (*1072*, 161 ff.) to A. Clutton-Brock, who accuses him all at once of literariness, superficiality, formlessness, and impatient workmanship. (*1068*, 100–1.)

[30] On Berlioz, see for example, *1362* and *718;* on Balzac, Faguet's biography; the objections to Stendhal may be inferred from this spirited defense: "Stendhal knew what he was about. . . . They have told [us] time and again that he was obscure (what a legend!) that his aridity and minuteness of style, his passion for paradox, his *difficulty*, in a word, kept him from being an author of the first rank . . . What they have always seemed loath to do is to present him on his own merits." (*1239*, Preface.)

[31] *236*, 33.

[32] *236*, 96–7. Washington Allston, the American Romantic painter, wrote of his visit to Paris in 1817: "It was the poetry of color which I felt . . . [the] great colorists addressed themselves, not to the senses merely, as some have supposed, but rather through them to that region . . . of the imagination, which is supposed to be under the exclusive dominion of music." (*1117*, 41.)

A Session at Liszt's House, by Kriehuber (Vienna, 1846)

LEFT TO RIGHT: Kriehuber, Berlioz, Czerny, Liszt, and Ernst

"Farewell, dear friend, until Vienna: Yours everywhere . . ."

— LISZT (*Open Letter to Berlioz*, 1839)

cated on traditional grounds, similarly made of tone color an element of structure and likewise incurred the charge of using it as a cloak.[33]

Beyond technique and justifying technique is the provocative question of subject matter. Although critics often pretend to disregard the subject of a work of art, they respond to it; and if repelled, attempt to rationalize the impression by impugning the form. It was very justly said by one of Stendhal's first admirers in the 1880's that recognition had been denied the novelist because "he had taken the dangerous privilege of inventing for himself unique feelings and writing of them in an unexampled style." [34] The objections to Berlioz' subjects are familiar: violent, fantastic, extravagantly emotional. The modern critic cited earlier against Delacroix speaks of the painter's state of mind as "Byronism," which is "an extinct malady"; he takes it for granted that because "Greece [is] of less significance than Persian oil fields," the "Massacre at Scio" depicts unreal "hollow forms." [35] This was written before the last World War, during which it was curious to observe the quick resuscitation of these various "Romantic" and "Byronic" subjects under the stern teaching of European events.

The lesson of course is not merely that we must refrain from asking Romanticist work to show a classical surface, it is also that we cannot appreciate the art of any age without first acquiring an equivalent of the experience it depicts. Since we cannot turn the clock back, we must immerse ourselves in the literature, the history, and the speech of the period and observe its recurrent features, just as we might try to decode a cipher without a key: the longer the text in the unknown tongue, the sooner we unriddle it. But just as in ciphers or in kindred tongues resemblances lead to serious misconceptions, so between the speech of Romanticism and ours, confusions are bound to occur unless this overlapping is recognized and the separate meanings finely distinguished. Earlier chapters of this book tried to show in the person of Berlioz the effect of having been born at a certain time with an impressionable temperament. In him and other creators this temperament produced the works by which we still judge the times. Now by 1840 the point has been reached where the revolution of

[33] For the rationale of Berlioz' forms: Tovey (*590*, 76), Newman, *passim*, and Supplement 6. On color as a part of structure, Van Dieren (*526*, 24 and 27).

[34] Paul Bourget in *1058*, 278. Championing Stendhal was at that time an unpopular and even a discrediting occupation – a further parallel to the situation of Delacroix and Berlioz. (*1241*, v; *1107*, 33.)

[35] *1071*, 443. But three pages farther, he adds: "I have no fault to find with his subject matter."

Romanticism may be considered over, though its makers live on. They continue to produce and exert influence, but European culture is caught between their action and the strong reaction of a second generation of men who know Romanticism though not its grounds.

What happened from first to last may be likened to a symphony in four movements. The initial Romanticism or first phase (stretching from 1790 to 1850) put forth all the themes used in western culture until our own times. The next three phases, commonly called Realism, Impressionism (or Symbolism), and Naturalism developed single themes previously stated, worked separate veins of the original deposit: they were periods of specialization. None of these four phases neatly stops in order to let the next begin. They orchestrate their tendencies as best they may and project themselves into the present age.

After 1840 one discerns moreover a movement steadily diverging from the main evolution of Romanticism and its various offshoots. This once again calls itself Classicism. The neoclassic impulse is the same whether it moves Puvis de Chavannes, Brahms in mid-career, or Stravinsky in his postwar restlessness seeking "authority, order, and discipline."[36]

The crisscrossing of styles, movements, and opinions then becomes wonderfully complicated, but not beyond analysis. The first transformation is that of the hospitable realism (with a small *r*) of the Romantic period into the specialized, restricted, and embittered Realism of the Realists with a large R. The change came from a desire to simplify in order to grasp the Real more surely and closely. The Realists carved themselves a path down the center of experience, taking as real what mankind share in common, what is ordinary, tangible, recurrent. Realism corresponded to the materialistic science of the fifties, which displaced Romantic vitalism. Soon Realism came to mean not simply the common but the sordid; it began not alone to "correct" Romanticism by reduction but to reproach it for failing to make its extraordinary visions an every-day occurrence.

Whereupon in the eighties a new generation of artists, also seeking the real but dissatisfied with the Realists' limited definition of it, discovered that the true haunts of the Real were no longer in the factual and the commonplace but in the subjective and the mysterious, in "impressions" and "symbols." This was phase three, clearly related to Romanticism and sometimes called "neoromantic."[37] In the same decades (eighties and

[36] *889*, 31.

[37] All art records impressions and uses symbols, but when new symbols designed to reconvey fresh impressions are called for, it is likely that artists will adopt names and slogans suggesting the total absence of symbols and im-

nineties), still other men dealt with the decay of Realism by reacting against the reaction, and strengthened the dose of concreteness in their art by borrowings from science and sociology which they called Naturalism.[38]

This schema is necessarily abstract, but what it states as a generality is what everyone admits in detail: studying Balzac, the Impressionist Henry James says "every road comes back to him." [39] Delacroix, says the historian, is the fountainhead of modern painting: Corot, Courbet, Daumier, Signac, Van Gogh, Odilon Redon, and Renoir looked back to him and proceed from him.[40] Yet not everyone whose eye can spot an Impressionist canvas would see its "descent with modification" from any given Delacroix. The reasons for this are two: according to the "schema" here given, there is bound to be *more* impressionism in an Impressionist than in a Delacroix; for the impressionist element is but one of Delacroix's many perceptions whereas it is the whole stock-in-trade of the Impressionist. The Romanticist is inclusive, his descendants exclusive. It cannot be too often repeated: technically and philosophically the Romantic is encyclopedic, his successors are specialists. They refine, extend, sort out, then multiply what he has found and made.[41]

The second reason is corollary to the first: you must know where to go in Delacroix to find the clearest foreshadowing of later methods; you must, for example, turn to his canvas "Jesus on Lake Genesareth," and find in it what Signac and Van Gogh found.[42] If you seek instead Delacroix's meaning for the Realists, study "The Algerian Women"; for his Naturalism, the "Noce Juive" or "Massacre at Scio" – his Romanticism being the sum total of these styles, made into *his* style, by fusion with the less definable elements of an individual sensibility.

This hypothesis may easily be tested upon Berlioz, and even by using evidence from an opponent: "There is not one Berlioz," says Mr. Elliot, "there are half a dozen; and they are as different from one another as

---

pressions in the work of their predecessors. Thus the Romanticists' clamor about truth and drama meant new truth and more vivid drama; and oddly enough they were called "Naturalistic" and "Symbolic" as well as accused of cultivating "art for art's sake." (*1114*, 304 ff.)

[38] Huysmans, the Goncourt brothers, George Moore, and others show how Symbolism and Naturalism can coexist in one man or one work.

[39] *The Lesson of Balzac* (1905), p. 116.

[40] *1115;* and – among other notices – the "remarkable relationships" observed at a recent Delacroix-Renoir show (*N.Y. Times*, Feb. 17, 1948).

[41] This holds true in other disciplines than art, in science, historiography, philosophy, economics, etc.

[42] Van Gogh: "Ah, the beautiful painting of Delacroix – 'The bark of Christ on Lake Genesareth' . . . oh what a piece of genius!" (*236*, 112.)

they are different from all other composers. The Berlioz of the *Requiem* and the *Te Deum* is poles apart from the Berlioz of *Benvenuto Cellini*. What have either of these in common . . . with the composer of *Romeo et Juliette* . . . ? What of him who penned *Les Troyens* – or that unique middle section of *L'Enfance du Christ?*" [43] Berlioz answered ahead of time: "A change of subject requires a change of style," [44] and the explanation is endorsed by those who have made it their business to trace the development of nineteenth-century music. Students of "Realism in Music" [45] can point to the ways in which Berlioz translated nature symphonically without imitation yet with a vividness which makes him seem to some listeners *only* a Realist. Other scholars point out that one of the founders of the Impressionist School, Debussy, grew up as an admirer of Berlioz and continued to be his debtor in technique and conceptions.[46] Of their own accord, the German Naturalist Richard Strauss, and the Russians with Moussorgsky at their head, acknowledged their indebtedness to the aspects of Berlioz' art which were akin to theirs.[47] One has but to hear *A Night on Bald Mountain* after the last movement of the *Symphonie Fantastique* or *Don Quixote* after *Harold in Italy* to perceive the connections – connections, it goes without saying, which leave the merit and originality of the later composers absolutely intact.

The only reason – apart from its interest – for investigating this kinship is that it spells Open Sesame to dozens of historical riddles, while preventing the confusion of individual sensibility with *Zeitgeist*. Sensibility is the artist's personal touch – the tone or temper which no one is bound to like. *Zeitgeist* is the predominant outlook, the tone of time. Use for comparison Debussy's nocturne *Fêtes*, which discloses almost like a manifesto the Impressionist point of view. In this short atmospheric piece the melodic material is presented as if broken up; it is almost satirically distorted. The merrymaking begins afar off and we receive merely an *impression*, which so to speak interposes the sophisticated self between the vulgar noises of the fete and the delicate ears of the listener. But Debussy is only able to avoid what he might call rhetoric by relying on our knowledge of the real thing. If we had never overheard a parade nor listened to Berlioz' *Roman Carnival* overture, Debussy's fragments would fail to be

[43] *278*, 203.

[44] Attentive criticism says of Turner: "In a sense his 'manners' were almost as many as his pictures, or at any rate as his *subjects* . . . The styles are not successive but concomitant." (*1093*, i-ii.)

[45] See *464*; *685*; and 779. Also Mr. Elliot (*278*, 147–9).

[46] *975*, 10 and 17; *453*, 113.

[47] *685* and *220*.

evocative. Indeed, Debussy repeatedly alludes to Berlioz' *Carnival* in his own *Fêtes* by touches of rhythm, melody, and timbre. But on purpose Debussy's pace stays unarousing and the melody never achieves breadth. Unlike the Berlioz saltarello, the nocturne does not make anything happen before us, much less involve us in its swing. For Debussy's conception is that of an observer who tells, Berlioz' that of a dramatist who recreates. Yet just as Debussy's allusiveness marks his reliance on previous art, so we find on the Romantic work anticipations of the Impressionist technique. Berlioz' *Carnival* contains at least one passage of Impressionist "comment" through distortion, when theme and rhythm "go to pieces" in a way comparable to the kaleidoscope of *Fêtes*.[48]

The Impressionist may of course abandon his spectator's post and yield to the lure of energy: in the Prelude to *The Afternoon of a Faun*, the broken melody on which the opening section is based leads to a highly rhetorical passage of so romantic a strain that it reminds one of the *Benvenuto Cellini* overture. It is the proportion of these two elements that determines the difference in style and in generations. To sum up: as in Delacroix, so in Berlioz one finds the constituent elements of subsequent styles down to the present,[49] and in these styles a residue of the pure Romanticism; only its amount is minimal because of the imperative necessity to do something other and neater than their great and Gothic predecessors.[50]

In accounting for Debussy and his stylistic departure, it is usual to pit him against Wagner, whose historical role is deemed to be Romanticism at its culmination. In the present reading of the facts, Wagner already represents the anti-Romantic mood of the neoclassic and Realist. This view is shared by almost all his early apologists except Baudelaire. In *L'art romantique*, Baudelaire treated Wagner as Delacroix's counterpart, but allowance must be made for the critic's propagandistic motive and imperfect knowledge of music. The common opinion of the refined zealots of the *Revue Wagnérienne*, ranging from Mallarmé to Houston Stewart

[48] *Min. Sc.*, pp. 40–42. Dr. Alfred Einstein, in his *Musik Lexikon* of 1926, based on Eaglefield Hull, calls Berlioz outright the "father of Impressionism in music." (*1343*, 51.) An historian of harmony, E. Kurth, has explained the basis of the kinship. (*831*.)

[49] For another example at random, see the harmonic structure of Berlioz' song *Sur les lagunes* and compare it with the technique characteristic of the modern French song writers, beginning with Duparc.

[50] Paul Valéry (*1134*, 145) once defined Baudelaire's problem as "how to be a great poet without being either Lamartine or Hugo or Musset" – and so had Baudelaire himself expressed it in a preface to *Les Fleurs du Mal*. (*1237*, 11–2.)

Chamberlain, bears out the interpretation here proposed.[51] Their editor-in-chief, Edouard Dujardin (the same whose novel supplied a hint for Joyce's *Ulysses*), was explicit on the point: "Wagner is no Romanticist; Berlioz is; Wagner reproduces all of life, not a given emotion." The writer adds, to be sure, that Wagner's art offers a double synthesis which embraces everything from Bach to Berlioz in music, and from Racine to Hugo in drama.[52] But Mallarmé in a neighboring essay makes the distinction – although on national grounds – between the poetic or imaginative Romanticist art, and the more earthy Realistic.[53]

All the evidence points to the fact that Wagner considered himself a Realist. His belief in the need for words, action, and scenery to fulfill the aim of musical discourse was strengthened by his study of Feuerbach, the materialist, and Vischer, the advocate of a new realism in opera.[54] To Wagner, history was not real because remote and "romantic." The "naked man," as he told Liszt, could only be shown through the common fund of legend and its vivid embodiment on the stage. By these means he taught the younger generation music and philosophy at once. He was solid, continuous, and literal. The Wagnerian Revelation (as it was freely termed) was described as "positivist and mystic" – again no paradox when one remembers how naturally the father of Positivism, Auguste Comte, came to top off his philosophy with a mystical authoritarianism. By 1845 Comte's active disciple Littré was beginning to preach and proclaim the Positivist era. In every field Romanticist variety and freedom were being tightened up into rigid systems. Without changing its nature, Romanticism came to seem more than ever loose, unpredictable, and lawless. "As against the antithetical ways of Hugo and Berlioz," says one critic, "Wagner gives us Racinian Realism." [55] Another, who writes on "Wagnerian Painting," says: "Wagner does what Puvis de Chavannes did in opposition to Delacroix, whose romanticism was frequently crude." [56] And a third: "Berlioz occasionally makes us marvel, touches us often, but his preoccupations

[51] The contributors included in addition: J. K. Huysmans, Emile Hennequin, Paul Verlaine, Villiers de l'Isle Adam, Catulle Mendès, René Ghil, Stuart Merrill, Hans von Wolzogen, and Alfred Ernst – this last being the son of Berlioz' friend, the violinist Heinrich Ernst.

[52] *1403*, 76 and 130–1.

[53] *1403*, 198.

[54] "*Vorschlag zu einer Oper*" (1844). The opera, says Vischer, must turn from the subjective to the objective by a fusion of all the arts and a reliance on the truth of myth. For this purpose he suggested and sketched a Nibelungen libretto. (*Kritische Gänge*, II, 399 ff.)

[55] *1404*, 98.

[56] *1404*, 107.

are no longer ours. . . . But Wagner, Wagner is enamored of intimate truth and unity." [57]

The claim is revealing: all schools of art strive toward reality and unity, but they dispute about the hiding place where reality lies and about the devices for rendering it. The Realist with a capital R contends that the sensations which recur, which are common and fixed in Everyman's experience, best convey reality. This fixity and material truth Wagner achieves with his gigantic system of leitmotives, involving the tireless recurrence of short, denotative themes linked to persons and objects; while his continuous and as it were explanatory developments effectively persuade the senses that they touch the Real. This the Romanticist does not dispute, but he holds the effect and the means to be but one kind among many. The direct blow which he too aims at the senses he prefers to deliver through infinitely varied appeals to the imagination.[58]

It is in fact the common complaint that Romanticist work "appeals to the imagination rather than the heart." [59] The distinction occurs spontaneously to dozens of writers dealing with the Romantics, and what it implies is that the observer recognizes the artist's intent but is not immediately moved by its expression. He is not moved because the means chosen are not sufficiently massive, direct, usual – the "heart" is the place where familiar symbols strike, where, so to speak, melodrama comes home. It is no attack on Realism to point this out, for ultimately all art worth discussing must somehow move the patient. The argument is whether all the roads that lead to Rome must be equally short and straight.

[57] *1405*, 124–5.

[58] Both in England and in France, critics complained of their own untouched hearts and overworked imagination as soon as genuinely Romantic work began to appear (*e.g.*, in 1818 the *Edinburgh Review* on Hazlitt's *Lectures on the English Poets*, and in 1830 the *Moniteur* on Martinez' *Revolt of the Moors*). Since then, the cleavage among critics has remained distinct, as may be seen in the footnote following.

[59] Any sampling will show, in the uncertainty of diverse phrasing, what it is the critics are trying to unriddle – the relation of intellect to imagination, and of "heart" to what they call the Real:

On Stendhal: "The qualities of his style, like those of his mind, go more directly to the intelligence than to the heart . . . and this is the greatest cause of his unpopularity." Charles Simon, 1926, *1128*, 15.

On Hugo: "His poetry is the work of the imagination rather than the heart." R. Fernandat, 1928, *1105*, 179.

On Berlioz: "*The Damnation of Faust* lends itself rather to the play of imagination than to a real representation." Paul Landormy, 1931, *575*, 7.

On Goethe: "*Faust* is a play designed rather for the ideal stage seen in the imagination than for actual production on the boards." Albert Schweitzer, 1932, *1123*, 140.

To the ordinary and the doctrinaire Realist alike, our representative Romanticist Berlioz does not, for all his imputed volcanism, move the heart.[60] "Flawless dramatist though he is, he does not touch us." So said the Wagnerian Teodor de Wyzewa, who rejected Mozart and Shakespeare for the same reason.[61] And the reason is that Berlioz and Mozart and Shakespeare require us to be something more than sensitive, namely imaginative, which is to say that we must both feel and act upon our feeling; imagination, like all romantic faculties, is a fusion of opposites: it blends feeling and reason, apprehension and action, sense and idea.[62] Readers of poetry who prefer Shelley to Keats will understand how the distinction applies to these poets: Keats is directly sensual and moves even those who never infer his ideas. Shelley moves no one who is not capable

[60] See comments above on Berlioz' melody, Subchapter 4 and also *1033*, 44.

[61] *1404*, 158, 193 and 267. In Shakespeare, the short scenes, the frequent breaks, and the allusive or mixed styles of dialogue must inevitably strike the classicist and the Realist as less than adequate. It is noteworthy that within ten years of Shakespeare's great popularity in Paris – a popularity created by the enthusiasm of the Romantic professionals (so to speak) – he was neglected until Gémier and the Théâtre Antoine in the Symbolist (neo-Romantic) period. It was this eclipse which contributed to the ending of the career of Harriet Smithson Berlioz.

[62] Baudelaire: "The imagination [is] the supreme and absolute faculty, which replaces the heart – or what is called the heart – from which reason is ordinarily excluded. . . . Imagination is that sudden, active energy, that quickness of decision, and mystical fusion of reason and passion, which characterizes those born to act." (*1049*, 416.)

Wordsworth defines the same faculty: "Reason in her most exalted mood." (*Prelude*, XIV, 188.) It was known to the Romantic sixteenth century, for Vasari speaking of the great Venetian painters, tells of *certo fiammegiare* – a kind of flaming passion.

Thoreau finds it natural to say: "Comparatively, we can excuse any offence against the heart, but not again the imagination. . . . The Imagination knows – and it controls the breast. It is not foundationless but most reasonable, and it alone uses all the knowledge of the intellect." (*1280*, 140.)

Shaw has one of his most autobiographical characters say: "Never mind my heart: an Irishman's heart is nothing but his imagination." (*John Bull's Other Island*, 17.)

Delacroix terms it "a delicacy in the organs of sense which makes one see when others do not see, or makes one see differently." (*182*, I, 87.) And Ruskin, defending Turner's Romantic esthetics, declares that "no art is noble which in any wise depends upon direct imitation for its effects upon the minds. . . ." It should depend on "that mode of symbolical expression which . . . in no wise trusts to realisation." (*1120*, III, 164–5.)

Berlioz' statement on imagination is to be found in Lélio's monologue before the Chorus of Shades: it amounts to an identification of the music-making power with the ability to conceive reality – something like Coleridge's *esemplastic* faculty. (See *Biographia Literaria*, Ch. 10.)

of feeling thoughts — whence his false reputation as "an ineffectual angel." [63]

In short, the triad of artistic ways runs as follows: neoclassic art appeals chiefly to the common, central perceptions of the mind: it is general and abstract; Realism, to the common, central perceptions of sense: it is of the heart and the senses; Romanticism assumes the active co-ordination of mind and heart (or sense) and plays an endlessly modulating tune upon the great distributor of impulses and re-creator of experience — the imagination.

We can now unriddle the critical paradox which says — as above — "Berlioz touches us often" and again, "his music is cold, lacks eloquence — it moves us not." One listener has, or uses, his imagination while the other is waiting for his heart to be engaged. The felt contrast between Wagner's *Tristan* and Berlioz' *Romeo and Juliet* is an audible demonstration of the esthetic difference. It is not merely that at Wagner's opera one sees, whereas at Berlioz' concert one merely hears; it is that Berlioz' sounds are not designed to sweep us off our feet and impose their tale of love and death, but rather to start and guide an imaginative act — what for want of better words we have called a "gesture of the spirit" — which remains as invisible and intangible as the music.[64] This is not to draw invidious comparisons, for it is perfectly clear that hitherto public judgment has always been rendered in favor of the direct hit — genius being equal. The preponderently imaginative artist, be he Berlioz, Goethe, Shelley, Delacroix, or Stendhal, is at a disadvantage when pitted against Wagner, Schiller, Keats, Corot, or Flaubert. Even the neoclassic is better off, for *his* rarefaction occurs where rarefaction is accepted, in the intellect.

Accordingly, Wagner knew what he was about when he loaded his

[63] Joseph Warren Beach has aptly said of Keats and Shelley: "In voluptuousness . . . it is hard to choose and fairly easy to distinguish between them. The sensuous effects of Keats seem more earthy, since in him the color is more often attached to solid substances, while in Shelley, it is so much more likely to be the tenuous attribute . . . of elements in motion and spiritual essences." (*1050*, 12–13.)

[64] For example, in Berlioz the unleashed spring of the great love theme when first sounded in the Prologue is a pulse that may speak to the imagination of fond meeting, eager recognition, transports of joy, embrace, or any other mental and physical concomitants of exuberant energy. It is unattached to the story, or even to the idea of love. Compare in *Tristan,* Isolde's waving scarf and the realistic figure that accompanies it in the orchestra, or still better, in the love scene, the rhythm and dynamics paralleling a physical act that the laws of the land will not permit Wagner to incorporate into the *Gesamtkunstwerk.* [This legal restriction seems to be disappearing: 1969.]

music drama with an intricate allegory and at the same time repudiated the imaginative use of music in the very words of Heart-versus-Imagination: "So-called 'tone-painting' has been the manifest last stage of an absolute-instrumental music's evolution, no longer addressing itself to the Feeling, but the Phantasy, an experience which anyone may make for himself by hearing a Mendelssohnian or still more a Berliozian composition on top of a tone-piece of Beethoven." [65]

It was no desire for meaningless "purity" which led Berlioz to prefer idealization and equivalence to direct Realism; apart from the *Zeitgeist*, it was a temperament essentially sober and aristocratic, which did not need thick sensations to move it. The contrast between Berlioz' wiry orchestration and Wagner's rich impasto is as the difference between Delacroix's glow and Courbet's opaque solidity – all four admirable in their place. Had Berlioz been a mid-century Realist, he would have put bells in the Easter chorus of his *Faust* (as Wagner was to do in *Parsifal*). He contented himself with plucked notes in the basses. He could have scored his Ride to Hell so as to sound no less physically exciting than the ride of the Valkyries; instead, he simply outlined the forward motion in a persistent but light design for the violins – we infer, with Marlowe's *Faustus*, that "hell is in the mind, nor am I out of it." Most conclusive, perhaps, is the forging song in *Benvenuto Cellini*, for here and in *Rheingold* each composer espouses a species of realism; but Wagner makes sure of his effect by an excellent combination of stage noises, orchestra, and eighteen anvils behind the scenes. Berlioz transmutes the bustle into a theme (trombones and basses) and by rhythm and dynamics alone evokes the forge as an accompaniment which rises and dies with the hope, fear, and distress of his hero: the reality is shown through the motions of the spirit; ideal connotations arise out of the transfigured sounds of nature.

From this conception which – it must be said again – was itself natural and unpremeditated in Berlioz, it is easy to derive the Symbolism of the later French school. We have thus looped the loop, joining Romanticism to its grandchild, neoromantic Impressionism, while showing the relations of Realism and neoclassicism to each other and to their pair of opposites. In musical Symbolism or Impressionism, Romantic imagination becomes even more remote from things and their direct rendering – precisely as in Monet's canvases touches of shimmering light replace solid objects and in Seurat the world is all dots.

* * *

[65] *243*, II, 332.

There would be no need of any schema, distinction, or terminology if our impressions of art were as pure and accurate as we tend to think they are. Everyone believes himself blessed with immaculate perception, though the most casual view of printed or spoken opinion proves the reverse. Buried assumptions waylay and trip us up without so much as apprising us of our stumbling. That is why like mariners we must correct our course by taking frequent bearings and making allowance for every kind of tide and drift. Unless we have charted the main currents of an age we mistake the usual for the unique and our judgment fails. So far we have placed Berlioz in his times by defining his forebears and successors, but in order to complete the topography of his age, there remains one element to describe. This is the secular religion of art with its corollary, the mission of the artist in society.

Romanticism did not invent either the creed or its main commandment. They were implicit in the Deism of the Enlightenment, which made science (and the works of reason generally) the justification of man's existence. In music, Mozart gave this idea expression in *The Magic Flute* (1791), whose freemasonic allegory teaches a moral not very remote from Beethoven's setting of Schiller's Ode in the Ninth: the brotherhood of man and the fulfillment of the divine in him.[66] But until the next century, the doctrine was only a catchword or a precarious policy. As Stendhal said, good intentions had been strenuously voiced for a hundred and fifty years and the task of the nineteenth century was to carry a few of them out. The practical Romantics supplemented the cult of science and pure reason with the cult of art precisely because they felt that art was closer to action. In the beginning, sang Goethe, was – not the Word – but the Deed; and Napoleon, as Goethe and others saw him, represented creativeness in fact.

In the same social sphere the artist had a mission, which was to lead mankind to self-fulfillment by exalting heroism and the tragedy of effort. This raised art to the status of a religion, in the same degree that man had once more accepted his kinship with the gods. "All deities reside in the

[66] Although Mozart's idiom was, in its outward manifestation, that of the "classic" century, his temperament and opinions were strongly marked by the period of cultural ferment through which he lived: he was in his twenties when *Werther* was sweeping Europe, and though Mozart's sensibility was tempered by irony, his letters show him to have been as nervous and tempestuous a character as Beethoven or Berlioz. Those who deny his connection with the age of Rousseau must rely on a conventional view of the times and the men. See rather W. J. Turner (*1026*, 227).

human breast," said Blake more in humility than in pride;[70] this conviction marked off certain men as dedicated without preventing them from worshipping in the traditional way. A Chateaubriand, a Coleridge, a Newman, a Schleiermacher could even lead a renascence in their several churches, though other men were kept from orthodoxy either by the churches themselves or by their own inherited "enlightenment." Such were Goethe, Blake, Lamennais, and Berlioz. The result of this exclusion was to transfer their faith to Nature and Spirit under various guises,[71] the most important of which was the experience of a supreme revelation through art.

Thus the so-called *mélange des genres,* of which the Romantics are accused as if they were little boys who had scrambled their elders' precious belongings, is actually the statement of a vision and the expression of a religious belief. There is no compounding of elements originally separate; as in Plato, tragic and comic commingle; only the words are two; which is to say that no *mélange* takes place. The Romantic perceives experience afresh, and the lines of demarcation necessarily fall in new places. Goya, writing home from Paris about David's atelier says that drawing and painting are two different things, meaning by this that "painting is the expression of life through color." And he asks, "Where do you find life in what [David's] pupils do?"[72] Goya's distinction between artisanship and art replaces the old academic categories and posits that a continuity exists between life and art comparable to transubstantiation in a sacrament.

This Romantic insight often had its basis in a superabundance of natural gifts, for we find a more than common doubling of talents in many of the Romantics; they took in the universe through more than one specialized sense – Goethe as poet, scientist, and painter; Hoffmann as musician and novelist; Hugo as poet and draftsman; Delacroix as painter and musician; Blake as poet and engraver and painter; Gautier as poet, painter, and balletomane; Berlioz as musician, critic, and poet.[73]

The analogical power is ever religious, and since it existed among many Romanticists in the form of a native endowment, it bred the faculty which

[70] *Marriage of Heaven and Hell.*

[71] Blake was presumably an enemy of "Nature," but only in its eighteenth-century sense of a dead nature, since his vision of spirit embraced the physical and the created as well as the creative.

[72] *1104,* 13.

[73] See also Tieck's protégé, the painter Philip Runge (1777–1810) whose advice to artists in *Feuerkugel* and *Ueber die Analogie der Farben und der Tone* contains admirable precepts.

enabled them to span the extremes from the vulgar to the sublime and to find divinity in the whole range of phenomena. When Géricault painted the "Raft of the Medusa" from a sordid report in contemporary newspapers, he shocked those who allowed art no kinship except with other art, but he was actually in the great tradition of Dante who created Paolo and Francesca out of recent scandal and swooned before his own creation.[74] Similarly, Hugo's vindication of the ugly, Goethe's of the fantastic, Nerval's of the subconscious – forerunners of Realism, Naturalism and Surrealism – implied the transcendental faith which Margaret Fuller put so quaintly when she said "I accept the universe." It is the essential religious acceptance, in contrast with that moral haggling over kinds which draws chalked circles, and which will no more tolerate its genres mixed in art than its genders in church.

One result of this truly orthodox love for the products of nature and art was to raise great literature to the rank of scripture. We know how Berlioz worshipped his favorite authors, how he read and reread them with a sense of their daily application to his life and to all life. It is easy to consider this a sort of mild megalomania, and to smile in his *Lélio* at the reincarnations of Hamlet and Horatio. But if Shakespeare's *Hamlet* is not about such men as Berlioz, whom is it about? "Such men as Berlioz," according to the very doctrine of godlike man which Shakespeare echoes in *Hamlet*, would in some measure be every man; so that far from being megalomaniacal, the Romanticist's absorbing of all great poetry as his proper food is a sign of true simplicity and right reason. Secular scripture is destined for the laity in proportion to their strength of stomach: it is the democratic, Protestant assumption. If it is fitting for every Lutheran cobbler and barmaid to read Job as a personal homily, it cannot be unfitting for Berlioz to take *King Lear* as an exegesis on his own life.[75]

Berlioz was so candid in this identification that he acted as if everybody conned the same good books and knew them well enough to understand the occasions which had prompted his music – just what Bach assumed when he set the Passion or the Gothic glazier when he fashioned the tree of Jesse.[76] It was a shock for the Romanticist to find that his religion was not shared and that his sacred books remained little known, or known by title only, as solemn entertainment which is best avoided. For it was one of the misfortunes of Western culture at the beginning of the Romantic

[74] *Inferno*, V, 73–142.

[75] Goethe and Shakespeare, he wrote in his twenty-fifth year, were "*les muets confidents de mes tourments, les explicateurs de ma vie.*" (*L.I.*, 24.)

[76] In this light one may read the "Prologue on the Stage" in Goethe's *Faust*.

century that although it had inherited the wisdom of three thousand years, distilled in numberless masterpieces, it had failed to incorporate its emotions about them in a common worship of the spirit so revealed. Since the Reformation certain historical causes – chiefly political – had shackled the oecumenical movement of the intellect, and free individualism no less than the previous dogmatic rule meant strife instead of Community.

In consequence the self-appointed teachers of mankind – for who else could appoint them? – must accomplish their mission in ever deeper bitterness. Throughout the great century, artists, philosophers, theologians, and men of science toil in despair, hardly ever finding one another in the melee of irrelevant slogans and untranslated creeds. They remain, in Shelley's phrase, "unacknowledged legislators," not so much because of the world's envy as because of its ignorance – ignorance of the fact that spirit exists and has laws.

Though in seeing this the Romantics were often dismayed – and some turned to instituted religions as more likely to preserve and foster what they held dear – most of them accepted the terms of their mission and fought out their battle singlehanded like the Hebrew prophets. Blake, Carlyle, Coleridge, Hugo, or Berlioz thundered anathemas or chanted hymns of praise with the same kind of self-renewing faith, and regardless of the increasing hebetude of their listeners. Under industrial conditions direct speech became more and more difficult. The extension of controls, commercial or other, led to such attempts as we have seen and shall see Berlioz making, to "seize power" and gain a rostrum from which to harangue the unbelievers. But the disadvantages were great, inasmuch as power must always express some tacit majority. To arouse and win over such a majority would inevitably have meant reducing the scope and subtlety of the message: this is what Realism undertook, and in various places, notably in England under the aegis of the Victorian Compromise, it brilliantly succeeded – by self-limitation. In France the results of hugging the commonplace may be gauged by reflecting on Flaubert's invective or Renan's contempt. The dark nibbling disk of the eclipse was already in sight by the early forties, which is why Romanticism is held to have ended then. But any eclipse must have an end, and neo-Romanticism, throwing into relief the somber monuments of the middle period, came into view at last: it was an afterglow, to be sure, a reflection of Romanticism, but with an iridescence of its own, and in facing the light in order to reflect it, it told us where shone the sun.

15. *Music for Europe:* A Travers Chants

September 1840 to September 1842

> Whoever lived and cheered (as I did) at the time of Berlioz' concerts in Germany can bear witness that never was any dazzling musical phenomenon ever greeted with such excitement and enthusiasm. . . . His music came as a fiery meteor above our heads.
>
> – HANSLICK forty years later

A *Funeral* symphony that Berlioz also called "Military" was by no means out of place in the summer of 1840. Threats of war were in the air. France's exclusion from the European conference about Egypt had aroused patriotic anger in Paris, and Thiers gave orders to increase the army and navy. The flare-up of Bonapartism led to cries of "Avenge Waterloo!" and "Reconquer the Rhine!": Europe's most incorrigible aggressor nation since the fall of Spain seemed once again on the warpath. But the time was the nineteenth century and the Germany that France threatened was but a cultural entity. Desire for retaliation existed as yet only in the minds of a few, such as the patriotic poet Becker, who bandied rimes with Musset in a pair of silly poems about the intrinsic nationality of the river Rhine.[1]

Nonetheless Louis Philippe pushed forward the completion of the Paris fortifications. But the populace was suspicious: they were sure these ramparts were meant to be used against them rather than a foreign enemy; so they grumbled loudly, not yet aroused to revolution, like their comrades in London, who a few months before had presented to the Queen the first People's Charter bearing 1,280,000 names and had risen up at Newport in "Jack Frost's Revolt." The class struggle was being given doctrinal form

[1] *Sie sollen ihn nicht haben, den freien, deutschen Rhein* and *Le Rhin allemand*. The quarrel inspired many other poems, and the pathos of the situation is that quite a few of these utterances sprang from genuine liberal feeling. Such was the misused *Deutschland über alles* of 1841 by Hoffmann von Fallersleben, whom we shall meet again.

in Louis Blanc's *History of Ten Years,* in which the bourgeoisie was named and charged as the enemy of the people. A change of ministry purged these warlike feelings of the French. Guizot came to power and a decade of grim devotion to pocket-filling began.

Almost the last event capable of arousing the historical or poetic imagination was the entombment, at the close of the year, of Napoleon's remains in the chapel of the Invalides, where Berlioz' *Requiem* had resounded two and a half years before. The entire Orleans family was present to do homage to Napoleon's memory, and 150,000 soldiers were on parade, but all the guest of honor's living relatives were either in prison or exile. The government – curious to relate – had asked Berlioz for a new triumphal march to grace the occasion, but he had wisely refused, saying that a suitable work could not be improvised in two weeks. He did not want to dim the effect of his *Funeral and Triumphal* symphony by a hasty variation on the same theme, and he took a malicious pleasure – so he told Adèle – in seeing what Auber, Halévy, and Adam would do when faced with the task. At the dress rehearsal of their pieces, some of the musicians came and congratulated Berlioz instead, one of them saying: "Today puts you on top of the Colonne Vendome."[2]

In reporting the ceremony to his sister, Berlioz made a remark about Mozart's *Requiem* which was used for the service: "*Despite the fact that it is a masterpiece*, it made a poor showing . . . under the dome of the Invalides; it is not fashioned in scale with such a celebration."[3] Berlioz' feeling for appropriate *mise en scène* – a feeling he expressed just as readily to his detriment when he admitted the total blotting out of his own symphony – also made him criticize other parts of the Napoleonic ceremony: "I had only a few moments of partial satisfaction with what the gunners did; they fired just as though it were the baptism of the Count of Paris or some other embryo Prince. I should have liked, instead of those five little cannon afflicted with a head cold, some five hundred mortars bursting with flames as the cortege entered. Nothing of the kind. Everything missed, muffed, even the artillery."[4]

This is a good instance of the grounds upon which the sophisticated Parisian public considered Berlioz a madman and a corrupter of the national tradition: he was never content with the half-baked conception and slipshod execution of an idea; he wanted the complete and concrete

[2] *A.R.*, 423. The column on which Napoleon's statue stands.

[3] *A.R.*, 423. [Italics added.]

[4] *A.R.*, 423. Thackeray, another eyewitness, agreed with Berlioz, and gave a satirical account of nearly every aspect of the affair. (*1221.*)

fulfillment of it, especially when the occasion concerned an eminent performer such as Napoleon. It is one thing to hate tyranny and violence. It was another to forget that the Emperor had fought with huge armies and had covered Europe from Spain to Russia carrying liberalism and death. There was a difference of scale between this and the paper war through which the hotheads of 1840 were venting their bellicose emotions, and the difference exactly matched that between Adolphe Adam's genteel chorus and the military *Te Deum* that Berlioz was already planning in his mind.[5]

Meantime, although the comic papers of the day had pictured him carried to heaven in a broken bass drum,[6] Berlioz sought once more to show the would-be musical, would-be national, would-be Napoleonic operagoers what a grand celebration should be, and to underline his purpose he coined the term Music Festival, which has remained attached to the genre. This concert, scheduled for November 1, 1840, called for the usual diplomacy in order to circumvent the jealous opposition of colleagues. The Opera's new director, Léon Pillet, was favorable to Berlioz, but the conductor was still Habeneck, then sixty years old, whose outlook upon the younger musician constantly shifted according to circumstance. The question now was, would Habeneck give up the podium to Berlioz? The press took a hand and sarcasm did not sheathe its fangs: " 'Wouldn't you like to hear something new and strange?' asks M. Berlioz. 'Well, I bring you marine trumpets, wet drums, broken timpani and cracked saucepans . . . I want an orchestra, two orchestras, ten orchestras. I have composed humanitarian symphonies, lethal masses, and an opera which will never be popular.' "[7]

This was one way to announce the double bill planned by Berlioz and consisting of four numbers from the *Requiem*, fragments of the *Romeo and Juliet* and *Funeral and Triumphal* symphonies, the first act of Gluck's *Iphigeneia in Tauris*, some Handel and a madrigal of Palestrina's. Worse than the Parisian jokes was the rumor that, with Habeneck's encouragement or consent, the players were going to sabotage the performance. If Habeneck did not lead them, said one paper, they would

[5] Berlioz could equally well imagine massive effects for the celebration of peace. See below *Les Troyens*, Subchapter 23.

[6] *Charivari*, Nov. 1, 1840.

[7] *Charivari*, Oct. 25 and Nov. 1, 1840. The satirist doubtless thought that a marine trumpet belonged to the brass family and made a loud noise. It is in fact a gentle *stringed* instrument, the so-called nuns' violin, which M. Jourdain in Molière quite sensibly likes to listen to, though the groundlings laugh at him on the principle of Berlioz' lampooner

rather go and build the fortifications. Yet the rehearsals were in progress. Berlioz again used his new method of rehearsing the players in separate groups meeting in separate places – three choral sections and three instrumental. This produced rapid and easy mastery of the parts, though Berlioz, going from one to another and beating time for entire days, lost his voice from fatigue and grew more and more nervous as November first approached.

Habeneck had decided to yield his place and Berlioz was conducting. To insure perfect ensemble, he had placed three subconductors among the mass of four hundred and fifty performers. They took their beat from him and prevented the voices from dragging as so often happens in large choral groups. The act from Gluck went well and so did the numbers from the *Requiem*. Between the two works, Berlioz went to inspect the trumpet crooks to make sure that no joker or foe had tampered with them. His good friends among the players reassured him, and even reproached him for doubting their loyalty. At the end of the *Lacrymosa*, the practically full house broke out in thunderous applause.

In the ensuing intermission a distressing incident occurred. A journalist named Bergeron sought out Emile de Girardin, editor of *La Presse* and a pioneer of popular journalism, and slapped his face.[8] Mme. de Girardin, in the box with her husband, had hysterics. The slap in the face obviously had political intent and the garbled report of the incident spread panic in the house. The Bonapartist coup was still in everyone's mind, as well as the attempt that summer to assassinate Victoria and the Prince Consort. People both feared and looked for significant violence. The cautious part of the audience went home, which left only a few to hear the second half of the program. After the Handel and Palestrina and before the *Funeral* symphony, political feeling boiled up even in that small knot of people. Someone called for the "Marseillaise." The police commissioner, who was present, thought fit to defend his King and Master and shouted, "No Marseillaise!" The evening ended with a handful of somewhat frightened and very inattentive listeners; which enabled the comic papers to print the taunt that Berlioz had organized his festival in order to receive an ovation from his close friends and relatives.

Ridicule was the one comfort left to the lesser men of a deeply disappointed generation. The final split had come between the creators and the naggers living on in envious dejection. This meant that by and large

[8] Girardin's chief innovation was the short editorial written in bulletlike sentences – the style of the late Arthur Brisbane.

the burden of the artist's life changed from a struggle against academicism to a struggle against the journalistic spokesmen of Philistinism. From this moment on the careers of Hugo, Vigny, Delacroix, and Berlioz became a ceaseless guerrilla. Within three years of this Berliozian fiasco, the failure of Hugo's drama *Les Burgraves* would be interpreted as marking the end of Romanticist art in France, but what is marked rather is the end of its being tolerated — the Revocation of the Edict of Nantes for serious art. Thereafter, not simply the still productive Romanticists, but every school was treated as heretical and subjected in life and death to abuse and ridicule.

Typical of the new state of mind, in the same year as the *Burgraves*, was the anonymous publication of a satirical novel which directly involved Romanticism and Berlioz. *Jérôme Paturot in Search of a Social Position* begins by showing its hero, who makes cotton nightcaps, aspiring to be a poet; then winning wealth by a fluke, and before entering politics seeking to be a patron of the arts.[9] Accordingly he, or rather his wife, hires a long-haired composer-conductor to give a festival for a charitable purpose. The account of the fete unmistakably alludes to Berlioz and his works. "The walls of the concert-room," we are told, "were solid and withstood the noise. Lives were safe, but not one's ears."[10] Louis Reybaud, the author, who was an economist, devotes half a dozen pages to a musical description, of which only one or two phrases are telling: "Princess," says the composer to a patron, "I shall find again for you the Hymn of Creation, lost since the Deluge." The novelist spoils this fair thrust by adding: "More than once I had heard it said that the inventor of festivals had devised a process by which he put public and private life into music."[11] And soon the satire — despite Thackeray's approval of its gentility[12] — turns to slander: "The hero of the evening, worn out by the emotions of childbirth . . . escaped and hastened away to compose the review article

[9] *1274*, Part II, Ch. 5. The author was Louis Reybaud.

[10] *1274*, 186. [11] *Ibid.*

[12] Thackeray reviewed the novel for *Fraser's Magazine* and after quoting several portions identified the musician in so many words as Berlioz. "Whether," he added, "this little picture [of him] is a likeness or not, who shall say, but it is a good caricature of a race in France where geniuses *poussent* [grow] as they do nowhere else." (*1222*, 287.) Thackeray having said of the work as a whole that it is "three volumes of satire in which there is not a particle of bad blood," and compared it favorably with Balzac, "who is not fit for the drawing room," he was later taken to task by Henley, who pointed out that the charge against Berlioz of reviewing his own works could hardly be considered in "good blood." (*679*, 19.)

with that same hand which had written the score and wielded the baton. Modern geniuses are like that: they multiply their claims to fame and are equal to every task." [13]

This last quip was in keeping with the author's debunking of Napoleon and was well-fitted to earn the approval of Thackeray, who, seemingly doomed to failure, was inclined to meanly admire mean things: " 'Give me a mutton chop and a thousand a year.' In the fortunes of honest Paturot this moral is indicated with much philosophical acumen . . . there is perhaps a great deal of sound thinking and reflection hidden under [his] cotton nightcap." [14]

The intellectual eclipse that Renan ascribed to the second Empire beginning in 1852 had in reality begun a decade before. Berlioz noted it in his reviews of symphonic concerts: "One sees there pale women raising their eyes heavenward in a studied manner, and red-faced men trying hard not to fall asleep. . . . Clearly the audience cannot understand anything but martial sounds, crude contrasts, or flirtatious melodies. . . . If [Beethoven] had been alive, they would say he had failed, for the first movement of the *Eroica* was applauded by almost eight people, the Funeral March by ten or twelve, the Scherzo by fourteen or fifteen, and the Finale by four or five. It has cost me a handkerchief, which I somewhat damaged with my teeth." [15]

There comes moreover a time in the life of every artist when the attitude of the public towards him is set. He is a hero or a wit or a saint or a devil once for all. He seems all of a piece and he must die, or at least become a senile Grand Old Man, before his reputation changes. Berlioz having become known early, his treatment by the Parisians hardly changed, though he himself was still developing in both character and technique. He was the "fiery romantic," the man whose opera had failed, the excessively mental composer who was not tuneful. He stayed, in short, at the stage of "notoriety" rather than fame, and this largely because he continued to be his own producer instead of winning the one sign of musical fame understood by his century, success at the Opera.

It was not for want of trying. As far as he could Berlioz campaigned on all fronts. While forwarding his festival plans, he was composing small works to balance the monumental with the *intime:* "I want you," he wrote to Legouvé, "to hear what I composed last week on your charming verses about the Death of Ophelia . . . If you like the music, I shall instrument

[13] 1322, 189.
[14] 1323, 291–2.
[15] *1398*, Jan. 14, 1841.

the piano accompaniment for a pretty little orchestra and will have it played at one of my concerts."[16] For his other good friend Théophile Gautier, and upon his verses, Berlioz likewise composed the six great songs, *Nuits d'Eté*, which he published in June 1841.[17] And within the same months he was still scheming to obtain the vaguely promised libretto from Scribe. For this purpose he even endured the agony of going fishing with him, at the cost of missing an afternoon with Delacroix.[18] But Scribe's name was such an open sesame at the Opera that its bearer would not readily commit himself; he pleaded that he was extremely busy. Berlioz then tried to induce him to collaborate with Frederic Soulié in the making of a half-ghostwritten libretto. Failing this there was the possibility of reviving Weber's *Freischütz* and being put in charge of the enterprise.

This did succeed, but not without incredible complications which show that it was neither Berlioz' personality nor his musical technique that created confusion around his undertakings, but an absolutely vicious tradition of musical management. In March 1841, the Opera announced that Berlioz would direct the rehearsals of *Freischütz.* This meant that he would also compose the necessary recitatives and perhaps a ballet, since the operagoers could tolerate neither spoken dialogue nor a masterpiece unrelieved by dancing. The proposed title – *Robin des Bois* – was that of the absurd but successful arrangement of Castil-Blaze, whom Berlioz had denounced sixteen years before. One result of trying to capitalize this past publicity was that, in spite of repeated protests from Germany, the rights in the opera remained the property of Castil-Blaze and Sons. Since they had despoiled Weber, the Blaze family now felt – on the principle of "set a thief" – that Berlioz was robbing them.[19] So the press campaigns against Berlioz began anew. An anonymous article in the *Revue des Deux Mondes*, doubtless written by Henri Blaze, sought to discredit Berlioz as a conductor of works other than his own. He, who had never replied to a single criticism, felt obliged to refute the accusation of adding parts to the old masters. The reference was to his recent festival concert:

"*Iphigeneia* was performed exactly as written; therefore no one can have

[16] *A.R.*, 435.

[17] The choice and the titles are by Berlioz, with Gautier's consent. The actual dates of composition are not known.

[18] Possibly a sitting for his portrait, a project which was never resumed. This was unfortunate, for otherwise we should have had Berlioz' portrait in three styles, those of Delacroix, Courbet, and Daumier. See below Iconography.

[19] What is more, the opera "belonged," in a performing sense, to the Opéra-Comique, whose singers, managers, stage hands, and ushers rose as one man and swelled the opposition to the revival.

heard any ophicleides in it. As for Palestrina 'a few sopranos' cannot have been 'sufficient for him' since his madrigal . . . is in four parts. The critic must moreover have been oddly absent-minded if he found the work 'crushed under instrumental pomp,' since I performed it, as written, without accompaniment. These are the misstatements I wish to have corrected, for they libel me in my capacity as interpreter of the great masters." [20]

The periodical did not print Berlioz' letter but alluded to it jokingly. Jokes took care of everything, including unspent aggressiveness. "Our musical world," wrote Berlioz early in 1841, "has been rent of late by a thousand rival ambitions, which go beyond the bounds of patience and reason and attain the pitch of envy and hatred." [21]

By April, Berlioz was at work supplying *Freischütz* with recitatives written in the style of Weber himself, as well as arranging the *Invitation to the Dance* and other fragments for the ballet. Just then Liszt came back from Italy indignant at the pitiable sum that had been raised throughout Europe for the projected monument to Beethoven. To raise more money he and Berlioz gave an all-Beethoven concert on April 25. It consisted of the E-flat piano concerto and the Pastoral: the public expressed its satisfaction by clamoring for Liszt's "Fantasia on Themes from Meyerbeer's *Robert le Diable*." [22]

The next month the Opera was rehearsing Weber, and quite appropriately the *Gazette Musicale* asked the young German musician Richard Wagner to write one or more articles for it on the subject of the opera. Berlioz had especially liked one of Wagner's previous essays — an imaginary visit to Beethoven — and had drawn attention to it in his own column in the *Débats*. Wagner now wrote two which, had Berlioz been like his French colleagues or like Wagner himself, he would certainly have "edited" or suppressed. For without having heard or seen a note of Berlioz' recitatives, Wagner condemned them — politely enough, but in a way to prejudice the public against the entire revival. Besides setting himself the precedent of passing judgment on Berlioz without knowledge, Wagner assumed that Berlioz' recitatives would be fiery, dramatic, "personal," and would therefore kill the airs and choruses that they introduced.

Berlioz let the articles appear, with only a heading to the effect that Wagner was judging the work from the point of view of German tradi-

[20] *Corresp.*, 132.

[21] *1386*, Feb. 14, 1841.

[22] The proceeds were less than might have been hoped, for all the musicians, except Liszt and Berlioz, demanded, then and afterwards, the regular pay for their services. (*235*, II, 360.)

tion.[23] This, of course, Wagner had every right to do, condemning in so many words any change from Weber's originally spoken text. But he also and illogically concluded that if *Freischütz* must be made into a grand opera, no one could do it better than Berlioz, "a man of genius whose poetic verve is of irresistible energy." [24]

As so often in their relations, it is Wagner who is hasty, impetuous, and incoherent, and Berlioz who knows what he is about. Berlioz' aim was to rescue and restore Weber's masterpiece. This he did with a solicitous care to which his manuscript testifies. He copied out the translated words under the parts himself so as to make sure that neither rhythm nor melody should be destroyed for prosody. The recitatives might seem overlong – that was unfortunately determined by the number of words – but they were written as tightly as possible and not at all to show off Berlioz' "energy." [25] The ballet music came from Weber himself, directly from *Oberon* and *Preciosa*, indirectly through Berlioz' orchestration of the *Invitation to the Dance*. In that task, Berlioz could truly say, "not a note has been changed." Berlioz knew his Weber and respected his work.

At first the cabal led by Blaze dimmed the success of the opera, but it overcame their efforts and even made money – almost as much as the Meyerbeer repertoire and a great deal more than *Don Giovanni*.[26] Wagner fulfilled his prediction of not liking it. He uttered his distaste in a serial for his Dresden paper, largely devoted to congratulating himself on being a German and hating everything French.[27] Of Berlioz' obvious feeling for Weber or the faithful musicianship of the revival, there is hardly any mention.

Although Berlioz had not come to the end of his tribulations with the

[23] "We deemed it proper to publish this essay because on all questions it is right to hear both sides and our readers will find pleasure in seeing *Freischütz* treated exclusively as a German work." (*1398*, May 23, 1841.)

[24] *1398*, reprinted in *243*, VII, 178–82. Eight years later Wagner set his hand to revising the dialogue and recitatives of *Don Giovanni* for a performance in Zurich (1850), and lived to re-instrument the Ninth for the dedication of Bayreuth (1872).

[25] The historian of opera, W. Apthorp, remarks that: "These recitatives of Berlioz', by the way, were probably the first attempt at doing anything colloquial in that line in French." (*695*, 147 *n.*) For the score, see *18*. Their mode of delivery was beyond Berlioz' power to change: the slow "broad" style was too deeply ingrained; we find Saint-Saëns still complaining of it forty years later.

[26] *268*, 583.

[27] Dresden *Abendzeitung*, July 16, 17, 19, 20, and 21, 1841. When a few months later Wagner wrote to Berlioz asking him to use his influence so that a benefit might be given for Weber's widow, Berlioz replied cordially, saying he would try again to persuade the authorities. (*235*, II, 185.)

Freischütz, it was dropped from the repertory within six months. Nevertheless it served him while it lasted by helping the sale of his *Nuits d' Eté*, which appeared towards the end of June 1841, and of which more will be said on a later page.[28] Their success at this time only shows again the advertising power of the Opera. Two months later that establishment performed large parts of Spontini's *Cortez,* which Berlioz was able to enjoy as an uninvolved spectator. Like the *Freischütz,* the work of Spontini enabled him to relive the enthusiasms of his youth. "I feel a hundred and ten years old." [29] He felt bound to express his admiration direct to the old master, sketching in the course of his letter the idea of a musical center for Europe. There the great masterpieces would be given with the utmost care, at wide intervals, before a prepared public. These performances would correspond to the great religious ceremonies of ancient Greece. Music would be sought out in a receptive spirit "instead of finding the art relegated to public charity . . . like a waif that the world is trying to turn into a prostitute." [30]

By this metaphor, Berlioz passed judgment on the Opera – he thought it "music's house of ill fame" [31] – as well as on the social pressures that dictated its taste and forced composers like him to submit or starve. One form of the pressure could be shown by the fact that his minor share in the *Freischütz* brought him automatically more than two hundred francs at every performance, tax free, whereas the gigantic efforts of his symphonic concerts rarely netted over one thousand francs once and for all. At his last "Festival" he had had to forego the five hundred francs agreed upon as his conductor's fee and even to pay three hundred and sixty francs out of his own pocket; for upon every "amusement" the Ministry of Public Charity levied for the poor one eighth of the receipts. The music of Berlioz and Beethoven thus helped square with God the accounts of a grasping bourgeoisie.

In September 1841 Scribe at last delivered the first act of the new libretto. The subject, under the ghoulish title of *La Nonne Sanglante,* was drawn from a recent translation of Lewis's *Monk*. Scribe thought the midnight mood of the *Huguenots* and *Robert* still strong with the public, but Berlioz set to work with only superficial alacrity.

Even if this operatic theme had been more congenial, Berlioz had grave preoccupations which might in any case have lamed his inspira-

[28] See Subchapter 27.
[29] *L.I.,* 191.
[30] *A.R.,* 427.
[31] *Soirées* (10th and Epilogue).

tion: a break in his domestic relations seemed inevitable. For many months now life with Harriet – and life for the child – had become increasingly difficult. Ever more jealous, she greeted her husband's daily return with scenes so violent as to terrify young Louis. She suspected Hector of love affairs with every woman he mentioned in conversation or in reviews; she scrutinized his mail. From an unhappy woman she had become a scold, and finally she took to drink.

On his side, no doubt, he had little strength left for conciliation. He came home with frayed nerves from a weary struggle kept up by constant self-repression, only to face the grind of writing articles which too often required the same kind of diplomacy.[32] He would have needed still more to deal with Harriet in whom he found, instead of affection, reproaches. Even had his temperament been more easygoing, less electric, it would have been difficult for him to maintain his love illusions about her. She was getting stout; reclusion and drink made her slovenly.[33] Although she had in the past courageously shared Berlioz' views of artistic integrity, she had no direct interest in music and she now strenuously opposed his ancient purpose to give concerts in Germany. In all their discussions, moreover, his flashing mind and superior command of language must have given him an advantage that only aggravated her misery. Their marriage was doomed.

Given this state of things, there was after a time cause for Harriet's jealousy.[34] On his first trip out of France since the Italian journey, Berlioz

[32] He termed reviewing "a dog's life – either biting or licking," and told his friends how to interpret some of his tactful reviews: "I said what I thought about Halévy's *Le Val d'Andorre* but the opposite is true of Clapisson's *Jeanne la Folle*." (*M.E.*, 258.) Again, he vents his impatience in a note to his editor: "The need is universally felt that I should express myself in writing upon *La Seraphina*. I shall therefore get to work and try to speak of everything except that emetic. . . ." (*127*.)

[33] Though as late as August 1841 a journalist writing in the hostile *France Musicale* calls Mme. Berlioz "a charming woman indeed – none other than the famous Miss Smithson, the illustrious English *tragédienne*." (*1383*, 1841, 285.)

[34] This order of events is that given by the latest writer who has reviewed the facts, M. Etienne Rey, in a book for a series on the loves of great men. Previous to his summing up, it had been believed that Berlioz at this time had innumerable affairs. His friend Legouvé had said so in his Recollections, and M. Boschot had accepted the testimony uncritically. M. Rey questions it, doubting first that in a troubled time, Berlioz should "abandon himself to a series of fugitive amours" of the theatrical sort. "No other witness save [Legouvé], no allusion, no letters, not a word of Berlioz, usually so expansive and outspoken, supports or confirms the assertion." (*302*, 146.) He might have added, "Not a whisper in the press." But there is one word more to say. As T. S. Wotton has pointed out, Legouvé, though well-meaning, is by no means

was accompanied by a young singer, Marie Recio,[35] who thirteen years later became his second wife. The first marriage was not wholly destroyed. It died hard, the agony lasting from 1841 to the final separation in the autumn of 1844. In a more enlightened time and place, an uncontested divorce might have regularized this painful situation. As it was, Berlioz' position, and even more that of his son, was left ambiguous yet unchangeable – a perpetual moral burden. He naturally continued to support wife and child, though some of his contemporaries found this quixotic, and it is amply evident that after the separation Berlioz continued to bestow much thought and affection on Harriet. He had said, "I will never leave her." He came to feel that he must leave her, but not completely, never finally. He was so constituted that his "tenacity" would not let him yield anything on which he had once set his heart, even if it were a dream like the love-image that he had fastened on the unfortunate Harriet Smithson.

His feeling for Marie Recio was very different. She was a half-French, half-Spanish singer of mediocre talent, but of pleasing exterior and lively disposition, who succeeded in catching Berlioz' attention when perhaps others in the Parisian theaters had failed. She doubtless saw in him an aid to her career, but must also have found him attractive and lovable since she clung to him even after the end of his willingness to help her succeed. For him, the love affair seems to have been a weaker repetition of the Camille attachment. Marie, too, was a musician, had a watchful mother (though a far better woman than Mme. Moke), and knew how to cast a spell. For a long time, now, Hector had been starved of womanly sympathy. Harriet's late-awakened passion was too aggressive to be endearing, and we may read in Hector's virtual love letters to Liszt and to Adèle, as well as in the tenderness of the great music written in this period (the songs especially) how balked his outgoing affections were. Just then, too, he was at the critical turn from mature to middle age. Ever conscious, he

---

accurate. Like every reminiscer, he confuses times and places, and as his contemporaries remarked, he showed towards women a mixture of gallantry and chivalrousness that perhaps made him take Harriet's complaints at face value. He also liked to make "good stories" and in the passage where he innocently incriminates Berlioz he gives no sign that he had received his friend's confidences. As for Berlioz, he said not only in his *Memoirs* but also to his confidant Adèle that he had given his wife no cause to be jealous. When he did give such a cause, the fact was kept neither from Adèle nor from Harriet.

[35] Her real name was Marie-Geneviève Martin. She was born in 1814 near Paris. Her father, a captain, had married a Spanish woman, Sotera Vilas; both had taken part in the Russian campaign, after which he had died, leaving the family in straits. Marie had studied singing with Banderali and was, when Berlioz met her, under contract at the Opera.

dropped a word of his feelings to the faithful Ferrand: "I feel that I am going downhill very fast . . . The idea that life has an end, I notice, occurs to me frequently. So I find myself snatching rather than culling the flowers on the stony way . . ." [36]

It meant a shift in bearing and manner, half organic, half conditioned by the changing times. He writes to the same trusted friend: "Believe it or not, there has come over me, in place of my former artistic fury, a kind of cold-blooded poise, a resignation, or contempt, if you like, in the face of whatever offends me in current musical practices. I am far from being alarmed at this change in myself. On the contrary, the older I get the more I see that this outward indifference saves my strength for a struggle where passion would cripple me. It's like love again: if you seem to flee, you will be run after." [37]

This simile contains a prophetic hint of his affair with Marie Recio. He left with her for two concerts in Belgium on September 18, 1842, but on his return a month later went back to his own home. By mid-December, which was to open his carefully planned tour of Germany, he intended to go alone, but Marie persuaded him to let her go with him. When she insisted on taking part in his programs, making scenes at the very thought of any other prima donna, he tried again to shake her off. Since infancy he had had enough of scenes, which may be why he was plagued with them in all his loves. Marie at any rate caught up with him at his next stopping place and he resigned himself. He sanctioned their relations by designating her, during an awkward social moment, as his second wife, and she soon gave up her pretentions to a singing career and loyally devoted herself to helping him. She kept his accounts, and, when he was in Paris, provided him with a quiet and well-kept home. He bore the expenses and included her mother in the arrangement; the two women were good managers and their *intérieur* must have been a relief after the disorder of Harriet's house and the spectacle of a badly reared child in violent and intemperate hands.

The first phase in the dissolution of Hector's marriage to Harriet occupies the period from the fall of 1841 to the September following, when Berlioz and Marie Recio left for Brussels. This twelvemonth had not been without important musical activity on Berlioz' part, nor without further signs of the gradual decay of the Orleanist regime.

In November 1841, possibly under the stimulus of the work he had done on Weber's piano waltz, Berlioz began to publish in the *Gazette Musicale*

[36] *L.I.*, 195. [37] *L.I.*, 193–4.

a series of articles on instrumentation — the first draft of the later epoch-making *Treatise*.[38] He had given two more concerts, at one of which Artot had played a new composition of Berlioz' for violin and orchestra, *Rêverie et Caprice*.[39] The work is unimportant save as an indication that Berlioz could with a little practice have turned his hand to "slick" money making stuff. Written as a favor to his violinist friend, the short composition has no program or significance beyond the contrast indicated in the title.[40] It suggests Wieniawski without being as successful as he in his genre, and here and there it also suggests the real Berlioz without sustaining that impression.

During the summer, Berlioz received permission to dedicate his *Funeral and Triumphal* symphony to the Duke of Orléans, who now and then bestowed his genuine regard upon artists and intellectuals. In October the work was played again at the Opera; the last movement, *Apothéose*, was becoming Berlioz' indestructible war horse. Meantime the Prince had been killed in a carriage accident and many hopes for the future of the regime died with him. The grief of the seventy-year-old King at his son's death was both personal and dynastic. A regency was spoken of, but popular unrest made the prospects of any orderly succession very doubtful. The July ninth elections had gone against the government, even though the franchise was limited to two-hundred thousand wealthy men, each casting his ballot on behalf of approximately fifty unrepresented adult males in the nation. If this voting aristocracy was turning more liberal, the monarchy was in danger. News from England confirmed the feeling that further reform was making headway. Feargus O'Connor agitated and produced a second People's Petition, so large that it had to be cut into portions and carried into Parliament by sixteen men. On its being refused, he called a general strike. "The sacred month" succeeded in the midlands, though it only led to his arrest in London. Two more attempts were made to assassinate Victoria. Both in England and in France, moreover, the industrial revolution was achieving social and cultural, as well as political expression. When Guizot undertook, as a sincere doctrinaire liberal, to "fight tenaciously against anarchy," he saw the middle class as "the rational mean between two absurdities, divine right and popular sovereignty," which he also called "the threat from below." He feared the proletarian agitation stirred up by Louis Blanc's widely circulated *Organi-*

[38] *1398*, 1841, Nos. 60 to 64; 1842, Nos. 1 to 29.

[39] Based on a fragment first sketched for *Benvenuto Cellini*.

[40] On another occasion Berlioz listed it in a program as *Tendresse et Caprice*. (*285*, 226 *n.*)

sation du Travail, Proudhon's "Property is Theft," and the less economically conscious views of hosts of republicans.

In this atmosphere, the decline of Romanticism, which is to say the settling down of artistic effervescence, was no individual phenomenon within each creative mind. Rather, it resulted from a redirection of public energy – toward railroad building, speculation, and agitation for reform, no less than toward the repression of democracy. The demand of the well-to-do for entertainment at any cost was the counterpart of volcano-sitting and stock-market nerves. The steam engine was in fact transforming the sensibility of mankind by changing its responsiveness and its pace. Berlioz, who took his first train trip in these years, reports how backbreaking the new convenience proved.[41] But it was astonishing to cover sixty-five leagues in a few hours, which enabled one to leave Leipzig, rehearse in Dresden, and return to Leipzig in time to hear Mendelssohn the same day. Whereas the Prince's runaway horses had killed one man by a relatively clean death, the dreadful Versailles railroad accident had mangled, charred, and suffocated sixty persons as undramatically as our rudimentary airplanes do today.[42]

Berlioz's compatriot and fellow-romantic Stendhal was therefore well advised to die, of natural causes, that same year – within a week of Cherubini, Berlioz' earliest official enemy. Only three people attended Beyle-Stendhal on the way to his grave, and forty years were to pass before anyone in France dreamed of taking his books seriously. In 1842, he was merely a salon wit who had died of apoplexy like the *bon vivant* that he was. Berlioz' slight contact with him in Italy had probably slipped his memory, or if present, had only reminded him of a Rossini fanatic who was too much of a littérateur to be a judge of music.

Cherubini's death was another thing. It left a vacant seat at the Institute, to which Berlioz had reasonable claim.[43] His competitors were Adam, Auber, Onslow, and a younger man, Ambroise Thomas, who had been Lesueur's last pupil. Berlioz' name was carefully omitted from the first list presented by the musicians of the Institute to the full body, thus con-

[41] *M.E.*, 40.

[42] In 1844, Vigny wrote one of his great poems, *La Maison du Berger*, in which he sings the passing of the Open Road and the mechanization of our individual destinies.

[43] It is difficult for citizens of a federal union to appreciate how much power and financial advantage result from membership in the national Institute of a centralized state. A professorship in a great university only begins to approximate this degree of leverage while creating the same ambiguity as to actual merit.

firming Swift's dictum that "when a true genius appears in the world, you may know him by this sign, that the dunces are all in confederacy against him." [44] Berlioz withdrew his name and Onslow was elected.

Berlioz had meantime written an obituary review of Cherubini's career, in which he did his former oppressor full justice.[45] He knew what qualities to look for in the limited art of the Franco-Italian master, and he pointed them out to the public. This act of impartiality was by no means due to the hope of flattering Cherubini's colleagues at the Institute; Berlioz knew better than to think justice to the dead would flatter the survivors. He acted simply on critical principle, as he did whenever he wrote about Rossini's *Barber*, *William Tell* or *Comte Ory:* he hated Italian music and disliked in Rossini as a man the cynical affectation of commercialism, but he could not refrain from praising genius. Anecdotes and bon mots were something else again, reserved for lesser occasions.

This disinterestedness carried Berlioz still farther. Cherubini had been Director of the Conservatoire and it was likely that the leader of its orchestra, Habeneck, would succeed him. This would leave the conductorship of the Opera orchestra vacant and Berlioz sought to obtain it, even though its acceptance would disbar him from having any work performed at the official theater. As early as October 1841, he had written to Ferrand, "I was and still am in line for Habeneck's post at the Opera. It would be a musical dictatorship of which I should hope to make the most in the interest of art." [46] In other words, he would use his influence to raise the level of musical performance through respect for the written note, since as mere conductor he could neither choose what to perform nor submit works of his own composition. The advantages to him would be the salary and the good will of the players. We can again infer from this voluntary choice of Berlioz' that the Scribe opera did not tempt his musical daemon to manifest itself. The fragments that he composed make us glad that the libretto did not blossom. How could it? It was neither Virgil nor Goethe nor Shakespeare, and Berlioz had not included it among those flashing intentions of his thirtieth year.

The orchestra post was not reassigned. Auber was chosen head of the Conservatoire and Habeneck stayed where he was. Berlioz therefore pursued his plan to visit Germany and give concerts. It was an ideal time for him to leave Paris where journalism, domestic life, and public apathy were alike inimical to art. On this first trip Berlioz visited Brussels twice, Frank-

[44] "Thoughts on Various Subjects."
[45] Reprinted in *M.M.*, 25 ff.
[46] *L.I.*, 195.

fort-on-Main, Hechingen, Carlsruhe, Stuttgart, Weimar, Leipzig, Dresden, Brunswick, Hamburg, Berlin, Hanover, and Darmstadt. In eight months he gave nineteen concerts. He was not able to arrange performances at all the places he visited, but everywhere he established friendly relations and studied the local resources of musical talent. Long before, Weber had thought of writing a guidebook for orchestra conductors who had to travel in Germany, but the work was never finished and Berlioz had to develop from scratch the technique of the musical conquistador. With stretches of residence in Paris and London, this was to be his life for twenty-five years: he did not cease from his mission until within two years of his death. If in the twelve years since the *Symphonie Fantastique* he had, as d'Ortigue wrote, accomplished a musical revolution in France, he was now, like a second Napoleon, carrying it to the four corners of Europe.[47]

Philosophy of a Musical Mission

> It is indeed dreadful to have to tell oneself, and with pitiless certainty: "What I find beautiful is beautiful for me, but it may not be so for my best friend. . . ." Such truths are palpable, evident, and only a stubborn adherence to a system prevents their recognition.
>
> — Berlioz in *A Travers Chants*

A mission implies a set purpose, just as a revolution implies a doctrine. One may well ask, therefore, what purpose and doctrine lay behind the revolutionary mission that Berlioz was undertaking in the most theoretical and academic of countries — Germany.[1] Although he repeatedly declined to make a system out of his convictions, he had thought and written about his art for twenty years. His scores and published views had simply

[47] This was soon to be said by a German in Germany itself. See below Chapter 23. For d'Ortigue's statement, see *185*, 319.

[1] They even called a concert an "academy" after the old Italian habit. As to "musical mission," note in Berlioz' *Memoirs* (I, 86) the reference to Weber's in those very words. Again, in 1836 Berlioz had written about finding Barbier congenial because "no one understands better than he the worth and seriousness of the artist's mission." (*L.I.*, 173.)

broadened the channel he had first cut in his initial essay of 1823. Most recently, he had contributed a formal definition of music to an encyclopedia and he had written three papers on Gluck's lyric dramas for the *Gazette Musicale*. These essays, together with an analysis of Beethoven's symphonies and the earliest account of his Italian journey, Berlioz would shortly issue in two volumes entitled *Voyage Musical en Allemagne et en Italie.*[2] The critical parts of this work he recast and republished two decades later as *A Travers Chants*. In both titles, the idea of voyaging through the worlds of music stands out, but the poetic wit of the second title [3] so aptly describes Berlioz' deeds that it suggests itself, ahead of its actual appearance, for the title of this chapter.

The mission Berlioz assumed as composer was to develop dramatic music on Shakespearean lines, and as theorist to defend the German or symphonic conception of the genre against the Italian; in other words, Gluck, Mozart, Beethoven, and Weber as against Pacini, Vaccai, Donizetti, Bellini, and the lesser works of Rossini. This was no sentimental partisanship. Berlioz' conviction rested on three postulates about the nature of his art: 1. That modern music was a new and independent art. 2. That music possessed intrinsic significance, which he called "expressiveness." 3. That music could not be judged by pre-established scholastic rules, but only a posteriori, through experience, by ear – in a word, pragmatically.

The belief that the *genre instrumental expressif* was the youngest birth of the human spirit, just come to maturity,[4] Berlioz derived from direct observation, for his pragmatic temper went with an ability to make exact discriminations. He was therefore a pluralist in his judgment of art forms, and what he saw was not simply that the convention known as equal temperament dated back only a century and a half, before which harmony and tonal structure were unknown or radically different, but also that within the life span of a single man – Beethoven – music had sloughed off the bonds of its primitive attachment to dance and words: its forms and its utterances could now develop at will. Moreover, in the multiplication

[2] See *V.M.; 53; 54.*

[3] The title substitutes *chants* (songs) for *champs* (fields) in the French idiom meaning "across country." It faithfully renders Berlioz' sense of freedom in the two realms for which he had predilection. In a kindred mood, Cyril Connolly made the same pun on word and idea when speaking of *la clé des chants* (*1069*, 86). See also *1394*, May 13, 1905, 365.

[4] "Music today has the strength of youth; it is emancipated, free, and can achieve whatever it purposes." (*A Trav.*, 312.)

and perfection of instruments, music was finding new ways to be expressive *überhaupt.* The modern "revolution" could then be easily defined: any composer who followed Gluck in "dramatizing the orchestra" and who followed Beethoven in making form organic was a soldier in the war of independence. Trial and error, innovation and pragmatic testing were the signs of the disciple on mission. The guilt of the Italians, and to a large extent of the French operatic composers, lay in toying with the new gains and, by dilution with old routine, reducing them to insignificance: they were reactionaries, or to use Berlioz' words, "infidels in regard to expression." [5]

Among the old ways were such things as the virtuoso's supremacy over the composer – the singer who changes his part, interrupts with encores, draws attention to himself as more important than his role; or again, the belief that music is for "pleasure" in the narrow sense of "pastime." [6] At the same time, Berlioz wanted music to keep its connection with life, through its adaptation to the needs of drama, psychological delineation, mass expression, the rendering of nature, and expressiveness *tout court.* But in so doing it must be jealous of its rights and keep as free as possible from accessories and empty conventions – the accessories for the dramatic musician being words and stage effects; the conventions being the clichés, padding, repeats, or anything else done "because the public expects it." [7] The self-sufficiency of music also excludes the fusion of the arts preached in the eighteenth century and practiced in the nineteenth by Meyerbeer and Wagner. On this cardinal point, Berlioz takes issue with Gluck, whose famous preface to *Alceste* [8] he otherwise approves: "When Gluck says that music in a lyric drama has no other end but to add to poetry what color adds to drawing, I think he is guilty of a fundamental error. The musician's work . . . already contains both drawing and color; and to carry on Gluck's simile, the words are the *subject* of the painting, hardly anything more." [9]

[5] *Grot.,* 229–36.

[6] This is what Berlioz meant when he said, "Do you think I am listening for my pleasure? I want music to set my nerves in vibration [*me fasse vibrer les nerfs*]." (*185,* 311.) Shakespeare's Jaques had previously said: "I do not desire you to please me. I desire you to sing."

[7] *E.g.,* Berlioz' analysis of the public's failure to applaud a beautiful aria in *Fidelio* because it does not end with a rousing allegro. (*A Trav.,* 76 and below, Chapter 26.)

[8] *Epitre dédicatoire,* Vienna, 1769.

[9] *A Trav.,* 154. In this respect Berlioz is at one with Mozart; like him he wanted – on occasion – the poet to fit his words to the pre-existing music.

Berlioz goes on to reassert the rights of music as sound: "Expression is by no means the sole aim of dramatic music; it would be foolish and pedantic to disdain the purely sensual pleasure of melody, harmony, rhythm, or instrumentation, independently of their power to depict the passions . . . And even if one should want to deprive the hearer of these pleasures and not let him turn his attention away from the main object, there would still be numerous occasions when the composer must alone sustain the interest of the lyric drama. In dances, for example, in pantomimes and marches, in all the pieces where instrumental music is the only fare . . . what becomes of the poet's sway? There, surely, music must contain both drawing and color." [10]

Berlioz then shows the consequence of these principles applied to particular works: they must possess *musical* form: "It was still true thirty years ago that most of the instrumental compilations which the Italians honored with the name of Overtures were grotesque absurdities. Gluck himself, under the influence of bad example, and being moreover . . . not so great a musician as he was a composer of scene music, allowed himself to put forth that incredible inanity, the *Orpheus* Overture. He did better for *Alceste* and still better for *Iphigeneia in Aulis.* His theory of expressive overtures gave the momentum which later produced symphonic masterpieces, . . . though here again, in overdoing a sound idea, Gluck fell into error, not this time by limiting the power of music, but by ascribing to music a power it will never possess. For he says that the overture must indicate the *subject* of the drama. Musical expressiveness cannot go that far. It may render joy, sadness, gravity, playfulness; it will show a striking difference between the joy of a pastoral people and that of a warlike nation, between the grief of a queen and the sorrow of a village girl, between calm, serious meditation and the ardent reveries which precede the bursting forth of passions. Or again, by using the characteristic musical styles of different peoples, it will be able to distinguish the serenade of an Abruzzi brigand from that of a Tyrolese or Scottish hunter, the evening march of religious pilgrims from that of cattlemen coming home from the fair . . . But if it wishes to go beyond this immense circle, music will have to have recourse to speech, whether sung, recited, or read. Thus the overture to *Alceste* will foretell scenes of desolation and tenderness but it will never impart either the object of this tenderness or the cause of this desolation." [11]

The allusions in this passage to movements in his own cantatas and

[10] *A Trav.*, 155–6.
[11] *A Trav.*, 157.

symphonies[12] show the way in which Berlioz found in Gluck's work the true precepts while signalizing their distortion in Gluck's theorizing. On a last important point, Berlioz quietly condemns his revered master who had made light of innovation: "Composers had already blackened a good deal of score paper by the time Gluck wrote, and any musical discovery whatever, though it were but indirectly connected with dramatic expression, was not to be despised."[13]

These extracts are enough to show that Berlioz' doctrine was double-edged. Against the upholders of routine and convention he preached expressiveness and psychological or dramatic truth; and against the theorists who wanted to subordinate music to stage effects or poetry he preached the formal unity of musical structures and the sensuous pleasure they can give apart from expressiveness. This is a position which critics apparently find it hard to grasp, or rather to classify – hence easy to misrepresent. In the history of ideas, all Third Positions incur this fate, the two-party system being intellectually simpler as well as more appealing to the instincts of partisanship.

What is more, the comfort to be derived from a rigid verbalized system – which can engender rules and provide the means of sectarian inquisition – makes the flexible pragmatist suspect to all. Berlioz knew this but did not yield to the temptation of cobbling up some absolute theory to furnish his followers with a creed. Gluck was an intelligent man and yet had misconceived the character of his own work; this suggested that perhaps artistic theory is a task apart, which most creators may be ill-fitted to take on. The principles that count must be looked for in a man's works rather than in his pronouncements; so when Berlioz' great admirer, Johann Christian Lobe, asked him for an esthetic creed, he replied, "My esthetic is in my works, in what I have done and what I have not done."[14]

Berlioz did not of course undervalue the critical warfare he was even then waging in new territory, but he recognized the danger of taking a description for a rule. Unlike Wagner, he did not utter manifestos and then compose. His significant choices came out of experience, in both

[12] Namely to *Cleopatra* and *Faust* (Gretchen), the Religious Meditation, the first movement of the *Symphonie Fantastique*, and the third and second of *Harold in Italy*.

[13] *A Trav.*, 158.

[14] *M.C.*, 132 and below. Lobe (1797–1881) was a composer, critic, and theorist predisposed by nature to understand Berlioz: as a youth of twenty-three he had called on Goethe and tried to show him how antiquated were the ideas of Goethe's musical oracle, Zelter!

senses of that word – the things he felt within and the works he heard and studied. And his studies, as we know, took place equally in the library, the opera house, and the concert hall. The current repertory was a hodge-podge of styles and genres, and if we except the works of Beethoven and a few others we have only a very imperfect notion of what Berlioz' musical experiences were. We know little at first hand of the Italian and French operas that he reviewed, and we know only a fraction of the works of Weber, Gluck, and Spontini – the tradition of which is virtually lost – to say nothing of the eclipsed Meyerbeer, then a dazzling sun.[15] As for the symphonies, concertos, airs, and fantasias that kept virtuosos alive in that half century, most of their names have died with those who heard them.[16] It thus takes an effort of the imagination to recapture the state of mind which it was Berlioz' mission to work upon and reform. He addressed, on the one hand, a public of exclusive opera-goers who became deaf the moment they could not also see; on the other, a fashionable and academic circle of amateurs, reared on the eighteenth-century classics and contemporary "little pieces," to whom Bach meant C. P. E. or J. C. but never J. S. All but a few felt that the uncouth Beethoven went too far. On this basis, if we eliminate what Berlioz preached and played, go on to reconstruct the features of what was then "music," and then jump ahead to the conceptions and the substance of modern works such as those of Debussy, Mahler, Strauss, Moussorgsky or Schoenberg, we can gauge the impact of Berlioz' mission and judge the merit of his Third Position, which repudiated alike the purveyors of airs and operas and the feeble imitators of classical masterpieces.

In setting out for his German tour, Berlioz was under no illusion about its inherent difficulties. Although a few years before Liszt had written him an open letter, saying, "Germany is the country of Symphonies; it is therefore yours," [17] Berlioz knew better than to take music for a universal language. His very devotion to certain masters implied that there was not one Music but many music*s*. And he knew from Liszt and others that in

[15] We may gauge this difference in part by what Rimsky-Korsakov says of the Gluck tradition being extinct in the early 1900's (*885*, I, 4) and by what Shaw had to tell the innocent Wagnerians about the genuine music contained in the Italian and French operas of the first half of the nineteenth century, particularly Meyerbeer's. (*880*, 30.) See also *901*, 142 ff.

[16] All but a few of Berlioz' friends, co-workers and critics were "well-known composers": Heller, Reber, Hiller, Pixis, Kittl, Bourges, Méreaux, Morel, Thalberg, Schloesser, Kastner, Moscheles, and so on.

[17] *210*, 264. Earlier still, Schumann had also publicly urged Berlioz to visit Leipzig.

Germany almost as much as in France, the taste for the Italian kind prevailed. Its inroads had helped darken Beethoven's latter days, and the resistance to it had only stiffened the upholders of the native tradition into academicism. At Leipzig, for instance, even Mendelssohn seemed musically modern and venturesome. Hence Berlioz would have to overcome the host of dilettanti, virtuosi, soprani, true or false *castrati*, and eternal *scholastici*.

Like most creators he would also have to fight the stiffer battle arising out of the originality of his own personal idiom. For music is not only *not* an international language cutting across political and cultural boundaries, it is also a form of individual utterance of which every hearer has to learn the vocabulary and syntax.[18] At the very least, each composer's work is a dialect of the main speech current at the time and place, but more often — and this was and remains true of Berlioz — the "new music" communicates new modes of musical thought which only deceptively employ the same technical means as previous music: they are of course "the same" in the abstract and in retrospect, but their first concrete presentation immediately puts the hearer on the defensive; he invokes earlier standards of beauty or meaning and the ancient debate begins afresh.

Berlioz was very much alive to this permanent state of artistic affairs, which he often analyzed in print, but which to this day is imperfectly recognized. Ernest Newman suggests that on this account a history of music is perhaps impossible to write — no one masters sympathetically all the musics, and in practice "love of music" reduces itself to the worship of one composer.[19] The late M. D. Calvocoressi was similarly dismayed to find that the critical Babel could not be explained away by greater or lesser degrees of competence in the critics.[20] The *dis*sensus is irreducible. But to Berlioz, who was among the first to explore it, this realm of cultural truth had far-reaching implications, affecting his critical and compositional techniques, his social conception of art, and his ultimate philosophy of life.

Not once but again and again throughout his writings he discusses this primary dilemma, the cause of immeasurable anguish: how is it possible

[18] All his interpreters in France before 1842 — d'Ortigue, Liszt, Bottée de Toulmon, Bourges — dwell on this point and try to show that Berlioz' melody, structure, and orchestration are unfamiliar but logical, unlike tradition but rationally related to it. Berlioz knew that all these attacks and arguments would have to be gone through again in Germany.

[19] *483*.

[20] *775*, 25. He went even further and collected instances to show that in musical criticism an appeal to fact was frequently unavailing or impossible: the intent of the observer creates the "fact" which another, equally honest and competent, finds imaginary or different. (*1391*, 1934, 229 and *n.*)

to reconcile artistic convictions with the plain fact of the dissensus? Berlioz is at a concert with a friend whose judgment he respects; a Beethoven adagio is being played. Berlioz is transported while his companion remains cold, and is even angered by the music.[21] This paradox is not simply an external phenomenon, to be recorded with amused interest by a third party: it involves the whole reality of art, especially for the creator. The critic cannot believe in Absolute Beauty; the artist must believe in it. Unless he is a mere contriver, an artificer, a charlatan, he must work in the conviction that there is such a goal for him to reach.

Nor is this the end of uncertainty, for experience confuses us still further by seeming to offer a partial verification of the creator's pragmatic hope: "At the first hearing [of Beethoven's Second Symphony] Kreutzer fled the hall with his hands on his ears. . . . Let us not forget that Mr. Kreutzer's opinion of Beethoven was that of 99 musicians out of 100. . . , nor that without the repeated efforts of an imperceptible contrary-minded fraction of the public, the greatest composer of modern times might still be scarcely known to us." [22] History, in short, gives evidence of the possibility of change. What at any time was modern and ugly *becomes* beautiful.

There is, too, a mysterious affinity between new art and the younger generation, so that it seems as if recognition of the absolutely beautiful was constantly being reached. But this recognition is neither steady nor complete. "Understanding" follows fashion, comes in waves, depends on the persistency of a conductor or a group. At any one time, the repertory of music resembles, not a body of literature, nor even a well-stocked library, but a one-volume anthology, a capricious *Oxford Book of English Verse*. We see this in the relentless repetition of the piece that "represents" a given composer to the exclusion of his other work. At any one time also, it requires a kind of fanaticism — like Berlioz' and Liszt's for Beethoven — to maintain public faith in an artist or a school, and this faith, no more than any other kind, never achieves universality.[23] There are still anti-Beethovenians and anti-Mozartians. At best what we see is a number of overlapping sects which ignore or condone one another's existence (or

[21] *V.M.*, I, 287.

[22] *V.M.*, I, 264.

[23] "Invariably," wrote Berlioz in 1842, "one comes back to intolerance and fanaticism when art is at stake, or religion, or love. Those artists who tolerate all things and manage to be constantly calm have probably never believed in anything nor loved anything." (*1398*, 1842, 149.) As a youth he had written: "That which transports one individual remains unintelligible to others and may even seem to them ridiculous." (*A.R.*, 71: 1829.)

else join forces against a common infidel) in the smug belief that each worships the true God.

Less apparent but no less real is the subdivision of musical faith by *genres.* It is rare to find any devotee for whom music means all or even several of the forms which it has historically assumed. Many concert-goers scorn opera; the zealots of chamber music will not enter a symphony hall; the piano brigade detest choral music; the passionate followers of song recitals are unmoved by violin soloists; the "classicals" in a body loathe jazz; the jazz fans look upon traditional pieces as a junk heap from which to pick up tunes. Among performers and pundits the provincialism is even worse. The violinist who for twelve years has trained his fingers to play the Wienawski concerto faster than any man alive is absolutely deaf to a slow "easy" tune in a Bach sonata; while the scholar or teacher who knows all that the Vatican manuscripts tell us about counterpoint is convinced that no real music has been composed since 1700.[24] As for educated instrument makers, don't talk to them about anything but the harpsichord or the old organ. Historical knowledge misapplied has completed the atomizing of art, so that nearly every time the word music is used it really stands for an accidental fraction of its total meaning.[25]

Berlioz' own historical sense brought him a different message. Although he made no pretense at being a scholar or musicologist, he grasped the essential point that among the Western arts music had developed late, often in isolation from intellectual enlightenment, and that consequently it had almost always been shackled by prejudice. In the Foreword to his *Treatise on Orchestration*, he reminds his readers that: "When Monteverdi tried to add the chord of the unprepared dominant seventh, criticism and denunciation of every kind were heaped upon him. . . . When melody came to prevail, the cry was that art was degraded and ruined, and the sanctity of rules abolished – it was clear that all was lost. Next in turn came modulation. . . . The first who tried to modulate into an unrelated

[24] A great modern architect has said that in his radically new art museum music should be broadcast for the delectation of visitors – but no music later than that of Mozart and Haydn.

[25] In a recent work on teaching, edited by the U. S. Commissioner of Education, one finds music defined as "a field [which] represents [*sic*] aesthetic sensitivity in relatively pure form, uncomplicated by subject appeal, functional purpose, dense historical, sociological and philosophical relationships, or close correlation with other fine arts." (*1106,* 205.) This statement which obviously excludes from the "field" of music songs, operas, cantatas, military and sacred music, and much of the dramatic instrumental music of five centuries, comes from a symposium entitled *Toward General Education:* what are we to expect from writers dealing with *special* education?

key was inveighed against. He should have foreseen it. . . . The innovator could keep saying 'Do but listen; see how gently the modulation is brought about, how well motivated and ingeniously linked to what precedes and what follows, how delightful it sounds.' 'That is not the point,' he was told. 'This modulation is prohibited; it must not be done.' But since on the contrary it *is* the point, *the only point*, here and everywhere else, non-relative modulations were finally accepted." [26]

Berlioz' training at the Conservatoire had largely consisted in observing prohibitions and he knew how these avoidances form our taste: the boy drilled against the split infinitive grows into a man who sincerely shudders at its presence. It takes a Schumann or a Scarlatti to calmly say "Count the fifths and leave us in peace." Expounding Beethoven to his readers, Berlioz accordingly defended those violations of academic rules that seemed to him self-justifying. For instance in discussing the Sixth Symphony, he takes up the forbidden resolution of the 6–5 chord on the subdominant: "This harmonic effect is most severely reproved by scholastic doctrine . . . [though] it is most felicitous . . . and the sudden passing from *piano* to *forte* on this singular change of harmony . . . doubles its charm." [27] He points out likewise that if Beethoven defied the "principle of unity" by bringing together the two unlike themes in the instrumental part of the last movement of the Ninth Symphony, it is too bad for the principle.[28]

More than that, Berlioz discovered that change and improvement themselves create prejudices in reverse. Living in an age of rapid orchestral innovation, he had to remind the public that chamber music was a high form of art and to show how senseless and inartistic it was to demand at all times a large ensemble displaying the latest brass. "It is even possible," he adds ironically, "to compose exceedingly beautiful music for the keyboard, since Beethoven has written for the piano some sonatas that are perhaps superior to his admirable symphonies." [29]

The task of the artist who is at once original and comprehensive is therefore double. First, in composing he must remain entirely pragmatic,

[26] *Tr.*, I.

[27] *A Trav.*, 45–6.

[28] *A Trav.*, 57. Berlioz' early admirers independently made the same kind of remark about him. Zani de Ferranti praised him for making violations of the rule seem more attractive than its observance and Ehlert declared that the errors of giants were more interesting than the correctness of ordinary mortals. (*Mem.*, I, 351 and *425*, 182–96.) Both these comments were elicited in the course of Berlioz' first German tour.

[29] *1398* (1842) 442.

that is, follow his musical instinct and test the results in context and by ear, regardless of the rule and also regardless of any systematic wish to break the rule. He must dare and see what happens, not in order to shock the bourgeois (that is only an incidental reward) but in order to find out how his mature judgment and that of others respond after the passage of time. This is why Berlioz kept all but one of his scores for years before publishing, why he destroyed several early ones, and why he heeded the remarks of d'Ortigue, Liszt, Heller, and other critics, as well as the advice of humble performers in the many orchestras which he led.[30] There was thus a thoroughly empirical control through fresh experience, through pre-existing knowledge, and through divers sensibilities, which gave innovation its sole warrant of worth. No one knew better than Berlioz how much the art of music depends on the inspiration and powers of others and no one acknowledged his debts more fully and frequently.

Still, it was not enough to insure the integrity of the product, letting it take its chance in a culture ruled by competitive passions and incomplete dogmas. The art of music is especially vulnerable to both, because its existence is by nature transitory. Accordingly, the creator with a mission and without protectors must — and this is his second task — serve as midwife to the work of art by teaching the public what to hear and how to think. For his part, Berlioz felt that he should not do so upon the body of his own work. He chose Gluck, Weber, and Beethoven as the masters whose interpretation would best acclimate his contemporaries to modern dramatic music, including his own. We have already seen how, in discussing Gluck's theories, Berlioz alluded to elements discoverable in his own symphonies. His discussion of the last movement of Beethoven's Ninth says not a word of the *Romeo and Juliet* symphony, but none the less throws a great light upon its conception.[31] He seized topical occasions to make clear what he considered important as well as strictly speaking undefinable. For instance, when polytonal effects became a fad in the sixties, he who had ventured upon their use in 1830 wrote (apropos of Offenbach): "All this may be done, no doubt, but only with art, and here the effect is put forth with a carelessness and an ignoring of danger that are unprecedented." [32] It was a question, he felt, of preserving the

[30] Sometimes, as in the orchestral "Prelude" of the *Te Deum*, he acquiesced too readily in the objections and pure chance has preserved a small masterpiece. (See below, Subchapter 19.) As to the tradition of Berlioz' respect for the performing musicians whom he trusted, see *588*.

[31] *A Trav.*, 53–4.

[32] *M.M.*, 326.

"very substance of music," which could indeed be molded to the creator's will, but "the way must first be found" (*il faut la manière*).[33]

Again, whenever performances of his chosen masters afforded the chance, he drew attention to facets of music that are usually overlooked. He had observed that "an audience which would be instantly critical of poor intonation can listen without displeasure to a piece whose expression is entirely false"; [34] and he knew that to increase the general awareness of "expression" was not gratuitous: it protects the masterpiece from absurd objections: "I have often heard people make fun of this first theme [in Beethoven's Seventh Symphony]. Perhaps the charge that it lacked nobility would not have been made had the composer written in large letters at the top of his allegro, 'Peasant Dance.' For although some listeners do not want to be told that any subject has presumably been treated by the musician, there are others ready to condemn an idea which appears strange unless they are given some reason for this strangeness beforehand." [35]

Berlioz had good reason to know that dramatic music without commentary stood at the mercy of the uncultivated imagination. To the audiences of the 1840's – and possibly of the 1940's – the *inherent* expressiveness of music was a closed book. If a given theme or movement was vaguely titillating and allowed their individual daydreams to go on undisturbed, they found the music "beautiful." [36] If not, the tune or piece was held to be ugly, affected, "unmusical." Like children, who often mistake sweetness for flavor, they wanted candy all the time, and composers stood ready to furnish such music, however dangerous to diabetics.

Even for connoisseurs of stronger stomach, Berlioz' dramatic range seemed excessive. What a modern writer said about the emotional accuracy of Berlioz' melodies must be said about his contrasts and conjunctions: they proceed from a moral realism that alienates many sincere listeners.[37] The majority of those who are said to enjoy any art demand quite literally a diversion; they want not so much an ordering of life-stuff as a softening of the contours of experience; and it is no exaggeration to say that it takes them from six hundred to two thousand years to grow accustomed to the sterner methods of a Homer or a Dante. Even had he wished to, Berlioz could not have complied with the Tired Business

[33] *M.M.*, 328.

[34] *A Trav.*, 10.

[35] *A Trav.*, 44.

[36] Santayana: "What most people relish is hardly music; it is rather a drowsy revery relieved by nervous thrills." (*Reason in Art*, 51.)

[37] See below (Subchapter 17) Jacques Rivière's opinion of a scene in the *Damnation of Faust*.

Man's requirement. Beethoven's "Peasant Dance" in the first movement of the Seventh struck him as of equal beauty with the Allegretto which follows it, "that high sublime in symphonic music." It was not the contrast as such, not the shock of surprise that moved him; it was the ideal correspondence with a full and varied reality.[38] When he was reading Lamartine in Rome, he found him "delicate, celestial" but regretted that the poet was "so incomplete: he never leaves the skies." [39] When Berlioz was discussing librettos with Scribe, he urged the dramatist to provide scenes which would not "keep steadily to a heroic or dithyrambic style; on the contrary . . ." [40]

For the artist as evangelist, music presents yet another difficulty: it is such a powerful tonic that most people's nerves do not easily recover their poise under its impact, and so cannot report truthfully what displeases them. Thus one man will object to the harsh modulations in a piece that does not modulate; another hates the accompaniment of a theme which is in fact unaccompanied.[41] Sound, in short, acts like a drug that causes hallucinations; its devotees respond allergically, fantastically, to the slightest deviation from blandness. If one adds to these impediments the lack of stylistic sense in composers, performers, and concertgoers alike, one can measure the strength of the resistance which a Berlioz encounters in his path. His mission seems self-centered until one perceives how few elements of understanding he can count on; the broader his scope the more he must teach, explain, and rationalize by means of analogies.

Because of this, perhaps, Berlioz has been called a "greater artist than musician" by some who did not quite see the trap their distinction led to. For the either/or would imply that musical sound is not so much material for an art as substance for a trade ruled by routine.[42] If one translates the comment as "more artist than practiced hack" or "more artist than confectioner" the fallacy gives itself away. Nine times out of ten, what is meant by "truly musical" is the cliché, the *inevitable* association of ideas, the tastefully bromidic.[43] It is consequently no paradox to say that when

[38] The marvel of *Fidelio* was that all its parts were differently superb. (*A Trav.*, 75.)

[39] *A.R.*, 173. Compare Byron to Thomas Moore: "Tom, don't be so damned poetical."

[40] In 1839: *86*, 580.

[41] *Grot.*, 167–8.

[42] To rebut this view is, once more, the point of *Benvenuto Cellini* and *Die Meistersinger*.

[43] This is shown by the quick and flashing fame achieved by a certain order of talent which after twenty years subsides into the third or fourth rank of worthies.

Berlioz seems "unmusical," he is likely to be not remote from, but close to, the original sources of all music. He is recapturing and using the inherent plasticity of his material and disregarding only the turn or shape which the hearer of settled musical habits expects.[44] This is not to say that whatever Berlioz does in the way of free handling must be accepted without question; it is to say rather that any criticism of his work must make sure that disapproval or displeasure does not spring merely from expectation denied – something like the feeling one has when a traditional misquotation is replaced by the poet's original words.

An additional sign of Berlioz' direct contact with the intrinsic and historic sources of his art is the number of elements which he feels impelled to treat simultaneously or in quick succession. In his encyclopedia article he had enumerated and defined them: Melody, Harmony, Rhythm, Expression, Modulation, Instrumentation, the Point of Origin of Sound, Dynamics, and the Multiplicity of Sounds.[45] A tenth element which needed no definition but to which he attached importance was the negative one of silence.[46] If one compares a Berlioz score with that of any contemporary down to Moussorgsky and the Impressionists, one is struck by the integral role Berlioz assigns to silence.[47] Not only does he frequently give the first sketch of a melody the barest accompaniment or none at all, but his harmony is never thick, any more than his orchestration or polyphony. There is air, as it were, around the structural members (as in medieval or modern architecture) and the prevailing transparency in every section is designed to heighten the moments of pressure, complexity, or artful disorder.

The net effect is a unique sort of aliveness, a breathing quality. Berlioz may have learned this lesson from Gluck – who condemned opera scores that "stank of music" – or from Nature, whose steadiness hides behind intermittence. In either case, the result is capable of disconcerting tastes formed on other models. The sense of forward motion is more easily conveyed by steady singleness of thought and continuity of sound as, say, in a Bach chorale or a Brahms symphony. But the lighter texture can be

[44] Newman's studies of Berlioz' form and melody, or Koechlin's of his harmony and counterpoint, demonstrate this beyond doubt (*484* and *453*). But see further Supplement 6.

[45] *A Trav.*, 1 ff.

[46] The Roman Muses included *Camena tacita*, or Silence. Among the Greeks – which may be considered symbolic at this point – the Muse of history, Clio, was credited with the invention of the guitar

[47] In *L'Enfance du Christ* even the pauses between sections are measured.

no less solid at the same time as it affords a special pleasure of its own — what Emmanuel in speaking of the *Harold* symphony called "particles of pure sound . . . music weighed and doled out as a precious substance." [48]

This precious substance Berlioz worked at with an untiring hand until it was so molded in all its aspects as to afford sensuous, structural, and expressive interest simultaneously. No detail was too minute to consider in the total effect *as heard* — hence difficult choices had to be made between rival virtues. This is what leads to the two divergent interpretations of his technique which Berlioz was to encounter in Germany as elsewhere. On the one hand he can seem heedless or crude because he goes against the refinements of common practice: squareness, the pairing in cut or shape of elements that are usually made to match, well-filled harmony or smooth modulation. On the other hand sensitive musicians can come to see with Schumann what a "fine engraver's hand," what "stylistic elegance," what concision, economy, and care to make everything "tell," Berlioz exhibits in his work.[49]

To become aware of this, however, takes time and thought. The usual analysis only ascertains the harmonic and formal structure of a movement and takes the other elements as bonuses which it is pleasant to have. In Berlioz we cannot make this distinction between superstructure and base. To him neither orchestration nor dynamics nor any other detail was a priori of secondary importance, for nothing was absolute. All elements were constitutive and modified each other. Thus the quality of a melody could determine an alteration in the form (say a shortening of one of its parts) if the theme, otherwise appropriate, did not deserve extensive development. This curtailing might in turn call for a heightening of rhythmical force and a richer orchestration to restore equilibrium by equivalence instead of symmetry.[50]

Berlioz' pragmatism goes deeper, therefore, than a desire to achieve the right auditory effect at the moment of performance. It poses the problem of relative values and so impels him to search for the highest harmony possible among the greatest number of elements. This is par excellence the technique of the dramatist, to whom rendering the object in the round

[48] *427*, 255. Compare Proust: "Perhaps the most beautiful passage in Flaubert's *Education Sentimentale* is . . . a white space. Flaubert . . . [composes] like a musician." (*1112*, 205–6.)

[49] After Schumann the critics I quote or paraphrase are, in order, Otto Luening (of New York), Saint-Saëns, and Pierné.

[50] This is a rough account of what occurs in the second section of the *Roman Carnival* overture.

matters more than any other quality. Yet it does not prevent temporary concentration on one purpose: the dominant feature of a movement may, for dramatic or other reasons, be rhythm rather than melody (*e.g.*, Introduction to *Romeo and Juliet*), counterpoint rather than orchestration (third movement of Symphony No. 1), harmony rather than thematic development ("Herod's Dream"). Moreover, musicians are attracted like other men by "problems" that stimulate their technical imagination. Berlioz was constantly incited in this way, though he never felt that triumphs of technique were the goal of art, or exempted one from supplying other sources of interest. He would have strongly discountenanced Wagner's rationalization – in answer to an inquiry about his lack of rhythm – that after all one cannot have everything.[51]

Berlioz' esthetic principles are easy to sum up: music was an art related to life through the recently magnified expressiveness of sounds; all the elements of music were capable of receiving or contributing to Form; the highest music must be as complete and independent an art as possible, even though there are many mansions on Parnassus – many genres and musical idioms. Absolute beauty was therefore a chimaera, however much one's "fanaticism" desired it – especially as creator. As critic, one must be a pluralist. For the dramatic composer, the primacy of music meant the shaping of forms suited to words or action but never subordinated to them, and more often wholly autonomous. The occasion of a drama might be civic, social, or simply imagined; it should in any event need but a few signs to recall the mood or the myth to the hearer's latent responsiveness. Where this was lacking, the public must be taught by word and performance.

Such was the art which Berlioz in 1843 had been cultivating for two decades. He had produced some fifteen sizable works, of which about half deserved to be taken as models in contemporary music, and which actually were beginning to be regarded as such: just four years before, Schumann had written as editor of a leading music review, "Honestly, I grudge the paper for [a hostile essay], for as far as I am concerned, Berlioz is as clear to me as the blue sky; but of course in other respects the affair is sufficiently important. I think there is really a new era dawning in music; in fact, it must."[52] A new era could only mean new works in abundance, and the only convincing demonstration of the new principles must con-

[51] *732*, 220.

[52] *232*, I, 139. It appears from an earlier letter that the objector was judging without having heard any of the works he condemned (*Ibid.*, 122).

sist in artistic successes. Berlioz had little hope of seeing his *Benvenuto* revived on any German stage – opera managers being seldom venturesome – but he had four symphonies, four overtures, a dozen songs and one *Requiem* mass with which he could by himself indoctrinate the rising generation of musicians in Central Europe.

16. The Art of Composition: The Treatise

January 1843
to July 1845

As far as I know, all writers repeat his observations on orchestral technique. They do not always acknowledge the author . . . But . . . Berlioz' subtlety of construction is beyond the cerebral powers of authors of pedagogical treatises.

— Van Dieren in 1935

Berlioz' first trip to Germany was also an opportunity for renewing many old friendships. Companions of youthful days were now established men nearing middle life. Ferdinand Hiller — Camille Moke's former admirer — was musical director in Frankfort. Schloesser, Berlioz' classmate at the Conservatoire, held a post at Darmstadt. At Leipzig, besides Robert Schumann whom he had never met but who had publicly invited him six years before, there was Mendelssohn occupying a well-entrenched position. Berlioz' discreet letter of inquiry from Weimar drew from his friend of Roman days a cordial invitation. Berlioz replied in January 1843:

You are wonderfully good and kind, as I was sure you would be. Luck is on my side these days: the concert went well and this morning I received your letter. . . . Yes, indeed, I should very much like to give concerts in Leipzig. If it does not depend on someone's special permission, granted as a favor, I should like to give two, since I see that expenses are moderate. . . . Though it irks me, I shall have to begin with my old stuff, my latest scores being still in Frankfort, whence they are being forwarded. So please thank the directors [of the *Gewandhaus*] and tell them I shall be happy to present on the 22nd the Finale for three choruses from my *Romeo and Juliet* symphony. But they must be warned that the part of Friar Laurence requires a first-rate bass.[1]

This letter illustrates Berlioz' problems and procedure. From one center he prepared the concert for the next by arranging for a personal invitation and, if possible, securing the co-operation of a friend. From Stuttgart he had written to Meyerbeer at Berlin, and to an old Conservatoire man, Chélard, who directed the Weimar "chapel";[2] and from Weimar to Karl

[1] *M.E.*, 26–7.

[2] Hyppolite Chélard (1789–1861), Rome Prize winner in 1811, was a productive opera composer whose success came to him in Germany. He had volun-

Lipinski, concertmaster at Dresden, where Wagner, just turned thirty, had become court conductor. At Stuttgart, where he had no acquaintance and where no one spoke French, he (who knew no German) managed pretty well by speaking with Dr. Schilling in Latin.[3] Everywhere he was known through his *feuilletons* which for three years had been reproduced in German, chiefly in Schumann's *Neue Zeitschrift für Musik*.[4]

The financial arrangements varied. Berlioz bore the cost of transporting himself and his music, as well as of any extras on the spot — he usually had to import at his expense one or two instrumentists such as the harp and English horn. He supervised the rehearsals and, if the local rules allowed it, conducted. In return he received half, or sometimes less, of the net profits. This was no lavish compensation, for the halls were generally small, the price of admission was low,[5] and his own outlay considerable. He had with him "500 pounds of music," which the railroads in their infant weakness were unwilling to carry with any guarantee of delivery. So the parts and full scores had to go by mail coach at exorbitant rates. Traveling and living in hotels was also costly, especially for a man of reputation who could not scrimp too obviously. As keeper of the purse, Marie was of great help, for she had habits of economy which she could exercise on Berlioz' behalf with complete propriety. He was thus able to send a good part of his earnings to his wife and child, which supplemented the royalties from the *Freischütz* that he had made over to them.

From the start of his tour, Berlioz' art and person made him many new friends. At Brussels, the guitar virtuoso and music critic Zani de Ferranti became an enthusiastic advocate; at Hechingen, the Prince took part in a performance specially arranged by Berlioz for a very small ensemble; the King of Württemberg also proved very gracious; at Dresden, Baron von Lüttichau, superintendent of theaters for the Saxon King, seconded Berlioz' efforts with great courtesy; at Brunswick, he made a lifelong friend of the composer Robert Griepenkerl; in Berlin, Alexander von Humboldt introduced him to the King of Prussia. In turn, Berlioz introduced the harpist Parish-Alvars to Chélard, and many other instrumentists and singers to officials who needed their services or might help them.

---

tarily removed there when his *Macbeth*, on a libretto by Rouget de Lisle, had failed in Paris in 1827.

[3] *V.M.*, I, 30. Gustav Schilling (1803–1881) was a prolific musicologist and critic until about 1857. He then emigrated to the United States, for no known reasons, and died obscure in Nebraska.

[4] For a fairly complete list, see the appendix of *286*.

[5] A top rate of 48 kreutzers (about 25 cents) was not uncommon.

It was a musical round, and Berlioz had to charge his memory with the names, capacities, and concerns of dozens of artists in order to act efficiently in his new role of impresario for himself and musical missionary at large.

The most rewarding moments of this first trip were the concert and visit at Weimar; the meetings with Mendelssohn and Schumann at Leipzig; the lively discussions with Lipinski and Wagner at Dresden; the enthusiastic ovation at Brunswick. Elsewhere the response to Berlioz' music varied from respect to hatred, just as the performances varied from poor to perfect. Marie's desire to sing did not make for success, but her pretensions were soon reduced to one song, "Absence," which Berlioz orchestrated for her. It was at Weimar that he shook her off for a time, before this compromise arrangement had been reached; [6] and it was there that he enjoyed the pleasure of a successful concert and the free run of a town whose artistic associations were particularly inspiring.

The memories of Goethe and Schiller and Mme. de Stael, the smiling aspect of the countryside, the neat walks in town and outside, and at night the mild moonlit sky, enchanted him. The fever and sore throat that had plagued him at Frankfort disappeared.[7] Invariably the atmosphere of intellect and art proved a cure for ailments of nervous origin. The one flaw in his enjoyment of the ducal city was his discovery of Schiller's narrow dwelling: "Can it be that these two small windows light the garret where . . . the great singer of every noble feeling wrote *Don Carlos*, *Mary Stuart*, *The Robbers*, and *Wallenstein?* Is it here that he lived like a poor scholar! Ah! Goethe ought never to have allowed it. He, a rich man and minister of state, might surely have softened the lot of his poet friend — or was this illustrious friendship not genuine? I fear it was genuine chiefly on Schiller's side . . . Ah, Schiller, you deserved a less human friend." [8]

At Leipzig, Mendelssohn and Berlioz greeted each other like old companions, long separated, who both shy away at first, expecting a rebuff. But nothing of the sort ensued; on the contrary their earlier friendship was cemented for life. Mendelssohn still sincerely disliked Berlioz' music

[6] Pourtalès compares Berlioz' eluding of his mistress with the incident of Liszt's shaking off Lola Montez. Liszt had a double reward: the adventuress whom he liberated for higher things showed her gratitude by sending him a decoration from her new protector, the King of Saxony.

[7] The winter of 1842–1843 was unusually clement, and proportionally rife in respiratory infections.

[8] *Mem.*, II, 43. Berlioz was quite misinformed in this matter and his remarks have value only as an indication of his feelings.

and Berlioz knew it. Yet Mendelssohn helped to rehearse and produce it, and Berlioz no less sincerely admired and praised his friend's works till his death and after. Curiously, it was Berlioz' orchestration that Mendelssohn could not stomach: "It is so entirely slovenly – scrubbed up anyhow – that one has to wash one's hands after reading one of his scores." [9] The melodies he rather liked, and most of all he liked Berlioz as a man, knowing after renewed contact what qualities of mind and heart lay behind the distant or ironic exterior: "It grieves me [that Berlioz should compose as he does] because Berlioz is intelligent, cool, and sensible in his judgment, and always thoughtful." [10] Mendelssohn helped him, says Berlioz, "like a brother . . . His patience was indefatigable." [11] They exchanged batons, and it was on that occasion that Berlioz, remembering his boyhood admiration of James Fenimore Cooper, wrote as a gift card the *jeu d'esprit* which when published caused a flurry of censure.[12]

Close to Mendelssohn was Schumann – who had praised and played Berlioz' earliest works – and with him Clara, his pianist-wife, whom Berlioz had met at the Bertins' house in Paris. Schumann was already plagued by the depression which marked his latter years and hence exceedingly taciturn, but he let drop a word which deeply touched his visitor: "The Offertory [of the *Requiem*] surpasses everything." [13] At the concert, the *Symphonie Fantastique* was applauded, together with *Rêverie et Caprice*, played by the virtuoso concertmaster Ferdinand David; but the public as a whole was rather of Mendelssohn's opinion. Despite Schumann's discreet but single-minded propaganda, *die Tante* (as musical Leipzig was familiarly called) found Berlioz a dangerous revolutionary.[14]

[9] *217*, 97. This opinion was probably due in part to ingrained habits of *reading*. Schumann had replied to a similar objection: "Pardon me, but you are judging without having *heard* the overture. *You have no idea* of his way of treating the orchestra." (*1226*, I, 122.)

[10] *217*, 133.

[11] *Mem.*, II, 54.

[12] These are the remarks: "Great chief! We have promised to exchange tomahawks. Here is mine, which is rough; yours too is plain. Only squaws and pale faces are fond of ornate weapons. Be my brother! And when the Great Spirit shall have sent us to hunt in the land of souls, may our warriors hang up our tomahawks together at the entrance to the council." (*Mem.*, II, 54.)

[13] *Corresp.*, 134.

[14] Between the long review of the *Fantastique* in 1835 and this meeting with Berlioz, Schumann had written notices of two other works and countered a number of violent attacks. His clear intuition is shown by the final words on Berlioz' sincerity being equal to Haydn's (*508*, 192 and *n.*) and although he

Why, asked the critics, did he not write harmonies like everybody else? Why did he use instruments not generally found in the classical masters — harp, ophicleide, English horn? The summing up, though adverse, was perceptive — which usually means the beginning of the end for any conservatism whatever; it protests but sees the point: "Berlioz refuses to please us; he wants to be 'characteristic' . . . he seeks to liberate music, tolerating neither shackles nor boundaries. His fancy alone he regards as law. . . . After the Witches' Sabbath of the *Symphonie Fantastique*, Weber's 'Den of Wolves' is a lullaby." [15] Mendelssohn's friend Moscheles was similarly stung: "His barbarous and wicked counterpoint seems to want to show that ours is pedantic." [16]

At Dresden, hallowed for him by the memories of Weber's conductorship, Berlioz heard Wagner direct *The Flying Dutchman.* Although the score did not move him deeply, and he is said to have found the instrumentation excessive, Berlioz saw as soon as anyone else that Wagner was an artist worthy of special attention. He admired the "uncommon energy and precision" with which Wagner conducted. But the two men seem to have had few opportunities to converse. Baron von Lüttichau — "a tall thin man with a hard, dry face" (Wagner's description) — monopolized whatever time was not taken up with rehearsing. In the brief intervals of relaxation Berlioz chatted with Karl Lipinski who, like Lobe at Leipzig, was already a stout disciple. Lipinski suspected Wagner of obstructing Berlioz' efforts, but the two concerts were none the less successful, well attended, and financially profitable.[17] The players were so enthusiastic that on the day of departure they serenaded the composer under his windows.[18]

After a second turn in Leipzig, a little more satisfactory than the first, a racking ten-hour trip in an open coupé brought Berlioz by March 1 to Brunswick. There he was greeted by his old friends, the four brothers of the Müller quartet, and the orchestra proved to be "*excellentissime.*" At the

---

later lost touch with Berlioz' artistic development, he made good his boast to posterity of having been the first German to proclaim the Frenchman's genius.

[15] *Allgemeine Musikzeitung*, quoted in *300*, 164.

[16] *597a*. But Moscheles lived to revise his judgment. Writing to his daughter in 1859, he says: "All that you tell me about Berlioz interests me especially, because he is certainly among the fighting artists one of those who have the most inventive power and one who does not distort art of set purpose. His *Benvenuto Cellini*, which I heard in Weimar, gives me the highest expectations for the forthcoming *Troyens*." (*978*, II, 297.)

[17] *M.E.*, 54 and *n*.

[18] "Windows"! The word reminds one with a shock that Dresden's charming streets and monuments — the Zwinger among them — are a pile of ruins: saturation bombing in the Second World War. We progress!

first trial of the Queen Mab scherzo, however, the players broke down in confusion. This gives us a good idea of the average technical ability in an unusually good orchestra, or rather, it confirms Wagner's estimate of four years before when he first heard Berlioz conduct in Paris: the new music was composed for, and had to be played by, virtuosos. The conception of the orchestra was being transformed, and the thing itself reshaped into a new instrument.

After fatiguing rehearsals, the conductor-composer had his reward. The audience stood up and cheered and the players invited their leader to a banquet of one hundred and fifty covers. There were speeches, toasts, reiterated invitations, and what is more, the critic Griepenkerl wrote a pamphlet expounding Berlioz. "I confess," wrote the composer to Heine, "that these demonstrations made me very happy." [19] Hamburg gave him equal satisfaction. As Berlioz wrote to his father after the first of these triumphs, "I have been wanting to write to you for quite a long time. I do not know what instinct made me wait until I had a really great success – greater than the rest – before telling you anything. I do not think I shall ever have another like this recent one. The performance, first of all, was marvelous. . . . Then they put crowns of laurel on my score, on the stage. . . ." [20]

In Berlin, the composer had his first experience of the disagreement-in-reverse which may occur between public opinion and the critics' judgment: the audience cheered and the papers damned. Meyerbeer – Spontini's successor in the post of royal music director – was officiously present helping Berlioz and keeping up the instructive relations he had initiated in 1829. Frederick William IV, King of Prussia, came to the concert, heard *Romeo and Juliet*, and was charmed. He came a second time, all the way from Potsdam, and finally gave a small party in Berlioz' honor – only a dozen guests or so; but after a space the curtains at one end of the apartment flew open and three hundred musicians under Wieprecht, the bandmaster, played the *Francs-Juges* overture.[21]

It was now late May. After two more concerts, Berlioz' first care was to see Harriet and his son. The meeting must have been painful, and to live

[19] *Mem.*, II, 86. Wolfgang Robert Griepenkerl (1810–1868) was the son of the editor of Bach's instrumental works, a teacher also, a composer, and a writer on musical and literary subjects. (*440.*)

[20] *M.E.*, 39. Berlioz' eagerness to please his father never changed, as if he could never sufficiently prove his affection and obedience.

[21] It was probably during this visit that Wieprecht expressed the wish to bring out an edition of the *Apothéose* of the *Funeral and Triumphal* symphony. It was announced but has so far not been found.

with them again disheartening, for he wrote to Adèle: "Your children are, I hope, in good health. Harriet often speaks to me of your quiet and happy household. She envies you. Louis has grown up . . . and will write you a letter. Harriet is beginning to grieve again because I have had another offer from the London Philharmonic to conduct a concert . . . But the trip is not yet decided upon; they have not replied to the musical and financial stipulations I made. We both send your husband greetings, and kisses for your little daughters, and we kiss you *into the bargain* . . ." [22]

While London was pending, Berlioz wrote to Ricordi, the music publisher at Milan, where he remembered hearing the fine orchestra of La Scala. The possibility of a concert there was tempting, but nothing came of the suggestion.[23] Meantime there was enough to do in Paris. The score of the *Funeral and Triumphal* symphony was being published and Thalberg wanted to make a free piano transcription of the Apotheosis, which required complicated adjustments between two publishers.[24] As for operatic plans, the libretto of the *Nonne Sanglante* still hung fire. Berlioz had made but little progress with the first act. If his voyaging in new lands had stirred him up spiritually, as was probable, the result was not immediately apparent, nor was it likely that the impressions gathered from new aspects of nature and fresh musical emotions would suit Scribe's banalities. Rather, the German countryside had awakened recollections of his early fondness for Goethe's *Faust*.

Of more immediate importance was the forthcoming publication of Berlioz' *Treatise upon Modern Instrumentation and Orchestration*, which was a revision and expansion of the series of articles published since 1842 in the *Gazette Musicale*. For the version in book form, Berlioz had illustrated his chapters with musical quotations from the masters and himself. As the best and most objective proof of his "science," the volume must now be launched throughout Europe. To this end, he secured permission to dedicate the work to the King of Prussia. It was a kind of authentication from Berlin, from Germany, which the interlocking arrangements of publishers and the drift of musical opinion made desirable. Already the previous year, an unauthorized German translator had hailed the technical essays, and with his slim collection had prepared an audience for the complete *Treatise*.

[22] *M.E.*, 50.

[23] He was, however, made a member of the Saint-Cecilia Academy of Rome. (*392*, 693.)

[24] Schlesinger in Paris and Breitkopf und Härtel in Leipzig (*17*).

Finally, Berlioz had his journalistic duties to take up again – his "semi-critiques," as he called them; for residing as he did in Paris he could scarcely say all he felt about his colleagues. Yet in the course of supplying the market these colleagues could not prevent their scores from undergoing Berlioz' judgment, just as if the works had not been mere commercial products – semi-works of art. Berlioz' first *feuilletons* on returning from abroad consisted of letters from Germany – reports and anecdotes on his recent trip, which enabled him to thank his recent hosts, and which formed the core of a volume of musical travels to be published the following spring. Destined for the *Débats,* these letters detailed the conditions under which the art of music was carried on in the middle of the ninteenth century, and their substance was preserved for inclusion in the later *Memoirs.*[25]

For the *Gazette,* Berlioz combined not fact but fiction with musical ideas long pondered and produced a notable document: the serialized novelette called *Euphonia,* in which he set forth the ideal conditions for producing the great works since Gluck and Beethoven. The imagined Euphonia was a city organized for music the way Paris or London were not even organized for making boots. Besides anticipations of Dalcroze eurhythmics and modern conservatory teaching, Berlioz' plan is the blueprint of Bayreuth.[26]

Pressing practical affairs also occupied him. Through his influence, Marie Recio had been engaged at the *Opéra-Comique.* She again failed to attract notice, which marked the end of her musical career. Berlioz henceforth supported her and her mother, relying on the care and affection she gave him as well as the quiet which he could no longer expect at home. Nevertheless he was frequently to be found at that home, with his old unhappy love and their son.

During his absence in Germany, moreover, a project he had discussed with his friend Baron Taylor had taken shape. Under the title of Association of Musical Artists, a group of Paris musicians had agreed to band together for mutual aid and the furtherance of modern music.[27] Berlioz

[25] *Mem.,* opening chapters of volume II; chapters 52 to 61 in the Newman edition.

[26] The fictional essay, with the significant subtitle "A Novel of the Future," is reprinted in *Soirées de l'Orchestre* (25th) *Eves.,* 249–87. In the original, the anagrammed names of the dramatis personae hark back to the Camille Moke episode and the tale depicts a melodramatic "revenge." In the reissue the names were changed, and the serious portion set off under the heading "Description of Euphonia." For the text and its relation to Wagner's plan, see Supplement 4.

[27] Isidore-Justin Sevérin, Baron Taylor, was born in Brussels of English parents and died in Paris in 1879. During his busy life he was a man of letters, an engraver, a soldier, a sociologist, a public official, and a patron of the arts.

was a charter member. Shortly the Association decided to sponsor symphonic concerts, with a view to relieving the individual composer of just those risks that Berlioz had so long shouldered alone. By September 1843 a festival was planned which Berlioz was to direct in December. In between, a concert of his own at the Conservatoire earned him a rousing ovation and a few hundred francs. The program included — among more familiar pieces — a trio from *Benvenuto Cellini*, the *Rêverie and Caprice* for violin (played by Alard), and the great song "Absence." The Apotheosis from the fourth symphony brought the audience to its feet. The press for once was short of jokes. Berlioz' singlehanded efforts were termed "a prodigy of human will power," and it was noted that the audience listened ". . . with religious silence" between its salvos of applause. "Woe to anyone hereafter who shall dare deny M. Berlioz' genius." [28]

Habeneck of the Opera did not deny it, he feared it — principally as a rival orchestra leader. He therefore managed to prevent the concert of the Association from taking place. Despite all his hard-won success, Berlioz' position was as precarious as ever. As a free lance he was a menace to others and hence to himself; for if one of his enterprises failed, he must redouble his efforts in the face of lost prestige; and if it succeeded, it only closed the ranks of the placemen against him. He was to official music what Swift was to the Church of England: alarmingly strong as an underling, therefore never to be made a bishop. No institutional group could assimilate so much genius, neither side could quit the struggle. It must go on. Aptly reflecting on "our culture and our form of government, which victimize the artist in proportion as he remains an artist," [29] Berlioz drew out his score of *Benvenuto* and, reliving its vigorous inspiration, was impelled to compose on two of its themes a new overture, the now well-known *Roman Carnival.*

In the Spanish campaign of 1823 he was aide-de-camp to General d'Orsay; a few years later, as director of the Comédie Française, he helped the Romanticists secure a foothold, and it was then that he and Berlioz met and developed feelings of mutual esteem which lasted through life. After the July Revolution, Taylor made several trips to Egypt for the purpose of securing the Luxor obelisk which now stands in the Place de la Concorde. In 1838 he was appointed Inspector of Fine Arts and shortly thereafter he organized the first mutual aid society for men of letters. Its success led him to found four others, all of which have survived. He wrote several plays as well as lively accounts of his travels in Switzerland, Italy, France, England, Germany, and Greece.

[28] *269*, 47.

[29] *269*, 49. It was after his concert of Nov. 19, 1843, that his enemies at the Conservatoire managed to deny him the use of the hall forever after by securing a ministerial ruling against its being rented.

Worked up symphonically, this felicitous by-product occupies in the complete *Benvenuto* the place that Beethoven's *Leonore* overture does in *Fidelio.* Each sufficiently anticipates elements of the music drama so that it seems a pity to play it ahead of the second act. Yet the music so clearly belongs to the larger work that its separate performance is a tantalizing hors d'oeuvre. Berlioz played his *Roman Carnival*, separately of course,[30] at his first concert of February, 1844, and the new work was encored. The overture soon became a general favorite and finally a concert "war horse." Being simple in its contrast of love song and dance, it was found "melodic," it was compared to Schubert, and it even caused a few of Berlioz' fanatical enemies some embarrassment. "What is the fascinating overture you have been playing?" the conductor Seghers was once asked. "That was the *Roman Carnival* by Berlioz." "Well! I must say – " "You're right," broke in one of Berlioz' friends, "I agree with you that he ought to be ashamed to go against an honest man's prejudices in that way." [31]

On the same program Berlioz, still fresh from Goethe's Weimar, had announced the hitherto unperformed Gretchen song from his *Eight Scenes* of 1828. It again remained unperformed because the singer was ill, but his revived interest in the score was to last and to bear fruit. At the moment, the chief novelties on the program – aside from his conducting the saltarello of the Carnival *alla romana* instead of at the chugging pace Habeneck gave it when *Benvenuto* was staged [32] – were two songs from the *Irish Melodies* of his youth. He had revised them, and one, the *Chant Sacré*, which dated back still further to his second prize cantata, was to go through yet another transformation which happens to mark a date in the history of instrumentation.

Three years before, Adolphe Sax, a young Belgian musician with a scientific turn of mind had come to Paris from Brussels with thirty francs in his pocket. His plan was to develop systematically the wind choir of the orchestra, and he needed the support of eminent performers and

[30] The least desirable practice is that occasionally followed, of using it as an overture before the *Romeo and Juliet* symphony, *The Infant Christ*, or *Harold in Italy:* this mixing of works and styles is a serious dramatic mistake.

[31] *Mem.*, II, 365. The comparison with Schubert is curiously exact as to a passage near the close of the *Rosamunde* overture; yet Schubert's score was not discovered until some 20 years after Berlioz had written his *Carnival.*

[32] A recent work of reference states: "Its introduction is slow and lyrical, and is followed by a wild *tarantella* as danced by the participants in a carnival. . . ." (*1287*, 63.) On the proper tempo of the saltarello, which should by no means be a wild tarantella, see Cauchie, "Respect for Rhythm," *1391*, Oct. 1, 1929, 890.

composers to obtain the necessary financial backing. One interview sufficed to convince Berlioz, who gave him a public endorsement in the *Débats*. Meyerbeer, Rossini, and Kastner followed suit with testimonials such that all other instrument makers leagued themselves against Sax. When he developed an entirely new instrument, later named saxophone, his rivals took steps to oppose the patent on the ground that it was not new. He defied them to produce its like and once again enlisted Berlioz' support. The composer could write stingingly and from experience about such innocent conspiracies. Would he also score a work for the new reed instrument and the other wind improved by Sax? Berlioz fell in with the idea of a "propaganda concert." [33] His old "Prayer" from *Herminie* which had become a six-part chorus, he now arranged for two clarinets (soprano and bass), two bugles (large and small), a small trumpet, and a saxophone.[34] The new version was only a qualified success, largely because Sax's new instrument was still imperfect – the saxophone "leaked" – and the inventor-performer forgot the fingering. Berlioz' little work was not repeated, though Sax and his friends gratefully serenaded the composer at home with the same instruments, much improved, later in the year.

Between the spring and summer of 1844 five more concerts either featured Berlioz' music or consisted entirely of his works. The *Roman Carnival* and the Weber-Berlioz *Invitation to the Dance* had, together with the Sax venture, renewed the public's interest in the composer. A helpful catchword began to pass current: Berlioz was the foremost *instrumental* composer of the day (*i.e.*, don't, my dear, expect coloratura effects or wonders at the keyboard). Still, the tyranny of the piano was now unshakable and at one of these concerts the *Roman Carnival*, whose structure and atmosphere are wholly orchestral, was rendered to thunderous applause by eight hands on two pianos – the forty fingers being those of Pixis (the arranger), Heller, Hallé, and Liszt.

Stephen Heller, who also composed, could well wonder "why do we not hear Berlioz played by the Conservatoire [that is, by the Concert Society, not merely in their hall at Berlioz' expense]. He is the greatest

[33] *939*, 13, 51–2, 213–4. See also *861*. It can readily be guessed that Habeneck and his troopers of the Opera opposed Sax.

[34] *1398*, Feb. 11, 1844, 43. Modern reference works keep repeating that the saxophone "made its first appearance in a symphonic orchestra in 1844." This is ambiguous: the first concert appearance was in Berlioz' piece. Toward the end of the same year, Berlioz' friend Georges Kastner scored a part for saxophone in his oratorio *The Last King of Judah*, which was played at the Conservatoire.

French composer. Must he first make up his mind to sleep the long sleep? Once dead, he will live for a long time. The cry of 'Berlioz is dead' will make thousands shout: 'Long live Berlioz!' " [35]

In May the *Voyage Musical* – part autobiography, part music criticism – went to press with a dedication to his royal highness the Duc de Montpensier. The two handsome volumes, priced at fifteen francs, appeared in August and sold very well. In four years they were out of print, and whether he knew it or not, Berlioz had given status to a new literary genre – that which his great forerunner Weber had not lived to establish firmly and which his great follower Wagner would amplify still further. Opposite the title page of the *Voyage Musical* was a lithograph of the author as conductor – his first portrait, excluding caricatures, since Signol had painted him at the Villa Medici. A little later at Vienna, Prinzhofer drew a finer portrait in a similar pose.[36] We see Berlioz in the full strength of maturity and at the height of his second period of fighting success. This is the way he looked and remained to the thousands of European musicians who played or spoke with him during the first campaign of 1843–1855, and who did not see him in the later one, as an old man.

Holding his public position as orchestral virtuoso by main strength of composing, conducting, and organizing, Berlioz cast about, in the spring of 1844, for his next occasion. That summer the first great exhibition of industrial products was to be held in Paris. Always interested in science and technology, Berlioz saw no reason why the show should not close to the accompaniment of music. He and the violinist Strauss (the master of the dance in Paris as his unrelated namesake was in Vienna) petitioned the Ministry for the right to present a double program – a serious celebration in the afternoon, a program of dance music in the evening.

The idea being new and perhaps profitable, it raised enormous opposition. Everyone expressed a different fear. The police commissioner thought that the mob might storm the Tuileries. Why the mob, if so minded, could not do it without music was not explained. Again, though Berlioz did not intend to fill the afternoon concert with his own works, he could not play every living composer's hymn or march. Hence the omitted musicians formed a cabal, under the natural leadership of Habeneck.

Berlioz was busy unknotting every intrigue when Strauss fell ill and the whole burden of organization dropped on his partner's shoulders – from overseeing the printing of handbills and filling out requests for constables

[35] *269*, 55.
[36] See page 480.

and firemen, to gathering from all over France and rehearsing in Paris the twelve hundred singers and players who would participate. In spite of the careful drilling of this small army, the dress rehearsal on July 31 was a near-fiasco: in the vast hall of machines, the carpentering of stands and the dismantling of steam engines made music virtually inaudible.[37] At last, leading seven subconductors, each with his battalion, Berlioz created order and music out of noise and disarray. That night the stands had to be altered under his direction because the chorus blocked the orchestra.[38] A preliminary survey of ticket sales was wholly disheartening.

But the next day the people rushed in a whole hour before the concert, and from beginning to end applauded the music. Berlioz himself had composed a short *Hymne à la France* which, as he said on another occasion, "not having been done with the aid of time would not be preserved by it." [39] Still, his magic has touched the work at more than one point, in the rhythm especially, and in the breath-taking economy of the orchestration.

The hall being lined with curtains, flags, and other decorations, the volume of sound pouring down on the audience was by no means a Niagara, on the contrary. The preceptor to the King's sons, Cuvillier-Fleury, who was also a colleague of Berlioz at the *Débats*, gave a first-hand account to the Duc d'Aumale immediately after the event: "No spot could have been more badly adapted to the purpose, for the hall is entirely lacking in the resonance necessary to favor Berlioz' attempt, which was patterned after that of the German musical societies. But where else could he put his 1200 performers? He would not give up a single contrabass – so everyone rushed to his aid when he called. The crowd was a brilliant one. Your young brother, the Duc de Montpensier, was in a box to which I had the honor of being invited, and he was seen – to everyone's satisfaction – applauding with all his might the refrain of the chrous from [Halévy's] *Charles VI*, 'Never will the English rule!' The execution was truly formidable because the entire audience joined in." [40] This enthusiasm caused a governmental tremor. Louis Philippe was at the moment on good

[37] An accidental demonstration of the fact that those who think large-scale music is noisy do not know what they are talking about. Those same sensitive ears tolerate without protest the deafening racket not only of their industrial and commercial pursuits, but also of their dance halls and cocktail parties.

[38] In Central Park a hundred years later, for the American *première* of the *Funeral and Triumphal* symphony, the same occlusion took place: music is always at the mercy of the man with a hammer.

[39] *Grot.*, 294. It none the less served in 1948 to celebrate in France the centenary of the 1848 Revolution.

[40] *1158*, I, 328–9.

terms with England, which was of course sufficient reason for the public's singing defiance. Berlioz was haled before the Prefect of Police, who charged him with having provoked the demonstration. This was easily refuted, since the program had been posted and approved in advance. In spite of the incident, the Duc de Montpensier sent Berlioz a congratulatory letter and a handsome piece of china.

As might have been expected, Berlioz was nearly dead. During the intermission he was wet to the skin, his teeth were chattering, and his face was unrecognizable. For a moment his alarmed friends among the orchestra did not think it safe to let him go on. They sent for fresh clothing and set up an improvised screen of harps with their slip covers, behind which Berlioz mopped himself, changed, and caught his breath. Marie, who was singing in the chorus, saw him safely home. The reaction came less than three weeks later, in the form of a fever diagnosed as possibly typhoid. His old teacher, friend, and physician Amussat bled him and ordered him out of Paris for a complete rest. Berlioz went to Nice.

It was at Nice that nearly fifteen years before he had spent the twenty happiest days of his life, after Camille's treachery and the mad attempt to commit suicide. He found again the "sublime sea" and serene skies of his "return to life." He found the old martello tower up in the rocks, and soon, under the spell of nature and memory, he began to compose the overture which he had sketched at the same time as the *King Lear* and *Rob Roy*.[41] But though the mood was propitious and the will and musical daemon in working order, the tired body put obstacles in the way. The overture was finished and christened, for association's sake, *Tour de Nice*, but at a first hearing in Paris the next year, Berlioz put it aside for recasting.[42] A new melody came to him, *La belle Isabeau*, and found more favor in his eyes, since he published it at the first opportunity.

He came back to Paris restored and found that an entertainment king by the name of Franconi wanted him to direct a festival at his establishment, the *Cirque Olympique*. This time, at least, Berlioz would not have to do his own managerial chores. Just then the mind of musical Paris was being stirred by the revelation of a new musician, Félicien David,[43] who for ten years had been composing unplayed and unknown. Now at a concert in the Conservatoire, for which David had had to borrow

[41] A century after that first visit a memorial plaque was affixed on the tower. (*Illustration*, Nov. 26, 1932.)

[42] It emerged brilliantly as the *Corsair* overture. See below, Chapter 21.

[43] Not to be confused with the North German violinist Ferdinand David, who had played for Berlioz as concertmaster in Leipzig.

twelve hundred francs like Berlioz in 1825, he displayed a talent for atmospheric pieces of oriental coloring which infatuated the public. As a disciple of Saint-Simon, the doctrinaire socialist who advocated a Christian technocracy, David wore clothes of a utopian light blue, and with hair falling to the shoulders paraded on the boulevard with a gay band of fellow-believers who sang his party hymns. They came to the concert, and celebrated on the streets afterwards to such effect that the citizens who had stayed at home were sure it was a new revolution.

It was not even a revolution in music. David's most famous piece was a "Caravan Procession" from an oriental suite, *Le Désert*, which suggests rather too much the Pilgrims' March from *Harold in Italy*. The form of David's *Symphonic Ode* was likewise derived from Berlioz' early essays at a dramatic symphony. But this did not keep Berlioz from seeking out David, asking him for works to put on his programs, and giving him a cordial and detailed boost in the *Débats*.[44]

Meanwhile rehearsals for the Franconi festival were begun, but not satisfactorily from a musical point of view because the oval bowl made sound reverberate unpleasantly. The four scheduled concerts took place once a month from January to April 1845. At the first, despite bad acoustics and a ragged performance, the *Tuba mirum* of the *Requiem* and the *Hymne à la France* came through. This was music, said one critic, "fitted to electrify the masses." [45] It was then that Berlioz heard his *Tour de Nice* overture and decided to lay it aside.

The second concert was given over to David and the pianist Leopold von Mayer, who performed a new "Moroccan March" of his own composition.[46] At the third concert, in March, Berlioz introduced Glinka to the Paris public by playing excerpts from *A Life for the Czar* and *Russlan and Ludmilla*. The two composers had met when both were still students in Italy and had found their views of music highly congenial. Both were more or less consciously founding new schools of dramatic music upon a solid background of national traditions, and it was no accident that their paths should cross again in 1844, nor that later their musical tendencies should merge in a common influence upon the Russian Five. In a long article in the *Débats*, Berlioz followed up his presentation of the music with criticism and biography, and Glinka, whose main object in coming to Paris had been to study Berlioz at close range, declared himself more than rewarded. He heard the music, read Berlioz' new

[44] Reprinted in *M.M.*, pp. 219–37.
[45] *269*, 77.
[46] Later orchestrated (with a new coda) by Berlioz (*Ger. ed.*, vol. XVIII).

works in manuscript, and felt that his own talents had been at once consecrated and fertilized during the encounter.[47]

The fourth and last concert in April was chiefly devoted to Berlioz' own works – those that he felt were least known and undeservedly overlooked because of their mild and subtle coloring – his Impressionist movements, so to speak, such as the Offertory of the *Requiem* and the Queen Mab scherzo. His performers were now playing at the top of their form, and he was musically well satisfied, but public support was dwindling as other novelties drew the crowd away from Franconi's *Cirque*. The impresario lost money and the decline unfortunately coincided with the finest rendering of Berlioz' finest work.

With hardly time to catch his breath, but only to be bled again, Berlioz left for Marseille where his friend the cellist Lecourt was eager to have him conduct. The local talent, especially the singers, were worse than inadequate, yet Berlioz managed to inspire them with some rudiments of musicianship by June 19. Like many a Berlioz *première* before an unprepared audience, the concert left everyone cold. A second performance on the twenty-fifth went better, musically and financially.

On the way back to Paris, Berlioz stopped at Lyon where George Hainl – soon to be a devoted friend – directed the Grand Theatre. To the regular orchestra, Berlioz added amateur singers and other instrumentists bringing the total to two hundred. Among these, he had included his old teacher Dorant, met by chance on the streets of Lyon. He was the versatile player of several instruments who had taught Hector the guitar at La Côte and helped him with his first harmonizations. In presenting him to the orchestra as a first violin, Berlioz took occasion to express his affectionate old memories in a characteristic little speech: "Gentlemen, I have the honor of presenting to you a very able teacher from Vienne, M. Dorant. He has in our midst a grateful pupil – myself. You may shortly be thinking that his pupil is no great credit to him, but I beg you to welcome him as if you thought otherwise, for this is in any case what he himself deserves." [48]

The public of Lyon was as slow as that of Marseille to like anything but the sure-fire pieces. It responded not at all to the Pilgrims' March, but rose to the March of the *Fantastique*. The *Apothéose* of the *Funeral*

[47] Letter to Nestor Koukolnik (Paris, April 15, 1845), *192a*, 83–5. Berlioz' essay, reprinted in *M.M.*, 205–15, was republished as a separate work in Milan for a Glinka revival in 1874.

[48] *Grot.*, 279. Berlioz adds: "It was to me a singular emotion to be conducting the 'Pilgrims' March' and the 'Scenes in the Country' with my old master playing, whom I had not seen in 20 years." *Ibid.*

Symphony — to us the least interesting of movements when detached — was found "sublime, thrice sublime." [49] A second concert, after the orchestra had learned a little more and had serenaded their trainer, caused greater pleasure and even stirred the local gentry to entertain their fellow countryman.

By July 25, Berlioz had just one week to turn around in: back to Paris to write a few columns overdue by reason of his absence, to thank by letter all his friends, hosts, and helpers in the provinces; then off again for the great musical event he had been dreaming of: the inauguration of Beethoven's statue at Bonn.

Structure and Harmony Through Timbre

> Beethoven did not write music for the eye.
> — BERLIOZ on several occasions

The *Treatise on Modern Instrumentation and Orchestration* which Berlioz published by subscription early in 1844 may be considered the portable lexicon of his artistic doctrine. At this virtual mid-point of his career, Berlioz' direct action upon the musical centers of France, Belgium, and Germany had established him as one who was making musical history. His works might charm or repel, they left no one indifferent. Meanwhile his conducting proved him a master of the practical side of his craft, an artist of unimpeachable integrity; his *Treatise* would show the many-sided knowledge upon which both his practice and his art were grounded. The success of the work was immediate, far-reaching, and permanent. Had modern copyright rules been in force, Berlioz could have lived comfortably on the proceeds of this work alone.[1]

Though the orchestra has changed in the intervening hundred years, the essence of Berlioz' teachings has not grown obsolete and the detail has been easily amended to conform with the new designs and possibilities of instruments. In our century, eminent technicians, such as Richard

[49] *269*, 87.

[1] Within his lifetime it went through several German and English editions, and after his death it was translated into Italian and Spanish. The latest re-issue is an English translation of the Richard Strauss edition, New York, 1948 (*51*).

Strauss and Felix Weingartner, have been content to edit Berlioz' text; nor have new works on the subject, like Gevaert's or Rimsky-Korsakov's, superseded it. The survival of this textbook – usually the most perishable of literary goods – can only be compared (aside from Euclid) to that of William James's *Psychology;* and in both the modern instances the cause of longevity in spite of the progress of the science is the same: the philosophic personality of the writer.

It is this quality which makes the *Treatise* good reading even for those who have only a remote interest in orchestration, and which has given to Berlioz' ideas influence even in quarters where these ideas are consciously resisted. There is hardly a composer since 1844 who has not at some time or other looked into the book.[2] Many have taught themselves from it, and we know from freely offered testimony that it has served as the inspiring guide of many a distinguished beginner – Mahler, Delius, Elgar, Moussorgsky, Busoni, Vincent d'Indy, and Debussy are among those who have told us so.

A book designed ostensibly to inform the student about which shakes are difficult on the B-flat clarinet and how far down the tenor trombone can play may seem at first sight ill-adapted to spurring others to musical creation. Still less would it seem to explain the characteristics of Berlioz' individual style. The *Treatise* does not, it is true, expound the technique of composition nor didactically enunciate artistic principles.[3] It sticks to its business of teaching Instrumentation; but it constitutes none the less a course on musicianship from which it is possible to deduce the workings of Berlioz' mind and from which any reader can learn much about Art in general.[4] As William Wallace says, the work "came as an awakening and a message which no one in the world of music could afford to disregard." [5]

Berlioz achieved this result quite simply by means of historical and critical comments upon current practice; by pointed precepts regarding harmony, rhythm, melody, and counterpoint; by expressions of admira-

[2] Sir Charles Stanford gives a typical indication of the contemporary response: "The organist Robert Prescott Stewart [active in both London and Dublin] knew well how to orchestrate and one of his favorite books was 'our Hector's' (as he called Berlioz) *Treatise on Instrumentation.*" (*1016*, 50.) Compare the way in which Wilhelm Mayer, Ignaz Dorn, Alexander Ritter, and other influential teachers used the *Treatise* to arouse their pupils – Busoni, Bruckner, Richard Strauss. (*926*, 174; *944*, 41.)

[3] *901*, 232.

[4] Saint-Saëns: "My whole generation was brought up on the *Treatise* and, I may say, well brought up." (*386*, 5.)

[5] *1315*, III, 730.

tion or disgust, by analyses of musical passages; and not least by redefining and reclassifying the technical matters that form his subject. But like everything that Berlioz set his hand to, this compact essay is also a work of art, its artfulness carefully concealed; the contents of the book are deceptively simple and light.[6] Every philosophic insight being unobtrusively in its place, the great subjects that Berlioz settles in passing would have to be extracted and grouped by kinds, and then recast in academic language, if one wished to bring out the weight and completeness of the teachings: this is the way in which a textbook of human anatomy seems fuller and weightier than a living man.[7]

The winged, transparent prose suggestive of Voltaire is matched by a corresponding rationality. Berlioz' standards are: Order, Precision, Economy, Practicality, and Elevation of Style. His knowledge of the past puts him ever on guard against absurd extremes: in the very brief introduction he shows that historically all the constituent elements of modern music have been first resisted, then misused, or overused. The art of Instrumentation, "which was virtually unknown at the beginning of the last century," is still in an unsettled state, characterized by exaggeration. Berlioz concludes: "It takes much time to discover the musical Mediterraneans and still more to master their navigation." [8]

After self-control, Order – albeit an original order derived from a revolutionary definition: "Any sounding body put to use by the composer is a musical instrument. From this follows the division of the means at present at his disposal." [9] This starting point in natural objects rather than in the practice of one instrument chosen as prototype has important consequences for harmony which will occupy us later.[10] As for the division of instruments into kinds, Berlioz' logic bases it on the mode in which the "sounding bodies" set the air in motion. This discloses eleven

[6] Saint-Saëns noted this about Berlioz' teaching in general: "He would give illustrations apparently off the point, but they started one thinking and opened up undreamed vistas." (*386*, 5.)

[7] Stendhal: "If the Academicians had received the manuscript of my *Life of Rossini*, they would have regarded it as written in a foreign tongue and would have *translated* it into beautiful academic language . . . but if I had tried so to write it myself, I should have been bored and doing fool's work besides . . . who among us can write like Montesquieu so that seven lines can furnish four pages of very reasonable amplification?" (*1054*, Part II, Reply to Letter I.)

[8] *Tr.*, 1.

[9] *Tr.*, 2.

[10] Note the contrary outlook down to the end of the century: "Berlioz seems to ignore what he missed in being unable to play the piano, an instrument which holds the key to the science of harmony . . . the true, the practical kind of harmony." (*283*, 197–8.)

families of instruments (the human voice taking its place among the wind instruments) and forecasts the overarching conception of the modern orchestra with which Berlioz concludes the *Treatise;* for the reunion of these eleven choirs constitutes "a great instrument capable of making heard, simultaneously or in succession, a multitude of sounds of diverse character, and whose power is mild or colossal depending both on whether it unites all or a part of the means now available . . . and on the skill (or lack of it) in the choice and placing of these means under favorable acoustical conditions. The performers of every kind who make up an orchestra might be said to be its strings, tubes, boxes, and plates – wooden or metallic – and to resemble machines that have become intelligent, though still subject to the action of a huge keyboard touched by the conductor under guidance from the composer." [11]

In such a view, orchestration is a constituent element of music,[12] not a polish or coloring matter applied from outside to a pre-existing, quasi-finished work. The idea of "coloring" has its place, but it is secondary in the same way that other musical elements may at times supply modest ornaments, or again may contribute to dramatic expression. Otherwise timbre is to be considered a thing in itself, capable of producing "impressions *sui generis* (whether motivated or not by an expressive intention) which are independent of the concurrence of the other three great musical means." [13] Berlioz then distinguishes – he was the first to do so – between instrumentation strictly so-called, which is a discipline, and orchestration which is an art. The former, dealing with the range and power of instruments, may be acquired by study; the latter, which he calls "poetry" or the "poetic aspect of instrumentation" is "as little teachable as the art of inventing beautiful melodies, beautiful chord successions, or rhythmic figures that are original and potent." [14]

Orchestration being a relatively new element, it not only enters as a constituent of form, but must itself possess form. Hence the need to study the combinations of instruments "in groups, in smaller orchestras, and in great masses; how they should be united, or mixed so as to modify the sound of some by the sound of others, and thus produce a sound that

[11] *Tr.*, 297.

[12] Rimsky-Korsakov: "It is a profound error to say, 'such and such a composer is a good orchestrator, such and such a piece is well instrumented.' For instrumentation is one of the facets of the very soul of the work." (*855*, I, 2.)

[13] *Tr.*, 2. Compare Matisse in 1948: "I came to understand how one could work with expressive colors which are not necessarily descriptive colors." From "The Way of Color" (*Propos de Henri Matisse*), *Art Présent*, No. 2, 23.

[14] *Tr.*, 2 and 293.

none could individually or generically produce . . ." [15] At the same time, the properties of these sounds must be adapted to the ways of harmony, counterpoint, rhythm, expression, and vice versa. To compose for orchestra is thus a perpetual adjustment of diverse and sometimes irreconcilable claims, just like the art of the landscape painter or poetic playwright. It is this perpetual striving for the highest possible yield of varied artistic satisfactions which conditions technique as Berlioz understands it, and which explains how a treatise on the function of the instruments can at the same time reveal its author's philosophy of art.

Believing that in his day orchestration was both backward and excessive, Berlioz began his work of sanity by pointing out every instance of confused purpose, slovenly habit, and terminological error. He advocated a new nomenclature so that the division into transposing and non-transposing instruments should be clear at a glance; [16] he rescued a number of instruments such as the viola from neglect and misuse by pointing out their unique qualities; [17] he inveighed against indiscriminate writing for horns and trumpets as "fillers" of the harmony; [18] he protested against the barbaric practices that had followed the Italians' introduction of the bass-drum and cymbals into the opera,[19] and showed how necessary it was to find new figures for fanfares on the cornet, whose tone quality was unpleasantly associated with banal ideas; [20] he pointed out how unsatisfactory it was to join the trombone with the lower strings;[21] and how impossible it was to supply an instrumental bass for vocal parts which did not include their own.[22]

Finally, he upheld as the chief condition of good order the maintenance of Proportion. Thus, he deplored the practice current in his day of adding horns, trombones, trumpets, and percussion to the old opera orchestra without proportionately increasing the number of strings: "Equilibrium has been destroyed, the violins are scarcely heard, and the result is a detestable ensemble." [23] Nor are order and proportion related to quantity

[15] *Tr.*, 2.

[16] *I.e.*, by dropping the names based on the instrument's fundamental note and using only the name of the key in which it actually plays.

[17] *Tr.*, 34 ff. The viola is apparently still in need of rescuing. See the spirited essay by the distinguished American violist, Louise Rood. (*860.*)

[18] *Tr.*, 180 and 191.

[19] *Tr.*, 275.

[20] *Tr.*, 191 and 198.

[21] *Tr.*, 205 and 233.

[22] *Tr.*, 249.

[23] *Tr.*, 294. Compare Lalo: "When I hear at the concert the excessive sonorities of Wagner, I am charmed because the great mass of strings balances the

merely, but to quality — as when contemporary French and Italian composers "write for horns . . . without taking into account the enormous difference between open and closed notes, between some closed notes and others . . . [thus] throwing sounds haphazard into the orchestra. The poorer texture of the old masters is obviously preferable to this ignorant and odious waste." [24] This wish for economy naturally leads to precision and practicality. Throughout, Berlioz preaches and illustrates the need of the orchestral composer to leave nothing to chance, to use no instrument without knowing exactly what notes it can furnish, in what strength and with what effort; and to study the many ways by which to maintain the musical virtues of just intonation, tone quality, and audibility.

For he continues to regard music as "an art based above all on the study of the impressions produced by sounds on the human ear." [25] Any effort made by the player, or any intention prescribed by the composer, which cannot affect the ear is at once futile and outside the domain of music — hence the insistence on not scoring for the eye. This does not of course mean that unknown effects may not be tried, but they must be tried and tested in the only conclusive way, by ear. Berlioz welcomes new instruments, describes the saxophones, and other Sax instruments, the Melodium (organ) of Alexandre, the Octobass of Vuillaume (reaching a third below the double bass); and at the same time he urges the retention of instruments falling into desuetude through caprice or indolence, such as the viola d'amore and Basset horn. For his ultimate aim was double: to include in his great orchestra-instrument every distinctive timbre, and of each timbre to possess a complete family covering the widest range of notes. These might then be used as melodically and harmonically independent choirs, sounding as many different "lines" whose reunion would form the characteristic polyphony that has aptly been called "polychromy." [26]

Zest for any new artistic medium can lead in two directions — towards virtuosity and towards expressiveness. The developing power may be shown off as remarkable in itself or as rich in undreamt-of suggestions.

---

brass, but those same passages which I have heard in all the German theatres — excepting Bayreuth where, I am told, the balance is perfect — cause me a most disagreeable surprise — the brutality of the brass overwhelming the insufficient number of strings." (Letter of May, 1888, *200*, 117.)

[24] *Tr.*, 180; see also the chapter on trumpets p. 191. Horn writing has been altered by the substitution of the valve instrument but the principle remains.

[25] *Tr.*, 288.

[26] *552* and *526*, 24. [The RCA Victor sound synthesizer used by composers of electronic music is a near-realization of Berlioz' dream.]

The definition of instrumentation given by Berlioz includes both possibilities; and having told us earlier that Expression was one of the nine facets of music, he was very likely to stress it in discussing the nature of instruments. Indeed, the hasty reader of the *Treatise* may be so struck by what might be called its psychological insights – often so detailed as to distinguish among the several registers of one instrument – that he may regard Berlioz' interest in orchestration as being insistently poetical.[27] This impression is not in itself false; it is false only if one forgets the rest, including the historical place of Berlioz' *Treatise*. Throughout the eighteenth century musicians had sensed the poetic powers of the orchestra and had in fact theorized on the subject ahead of their full realization. As far back as 1713 Johann Mattheson had sought in his *Neu-Eröffnete Orchestre* to open to music the ways of poetry and dramatic realism and to unify under one conception – called by him *orchestre* – the separate disciplines of vocal, instrumental, and operatic music.[28]

Half a century later, as Berlioz never ceased proclaiming, Gluck began to explore the sensitive and emotional character of the instruments. By the turn of the century Gluck's followers, serious and light, had at least an interest in orchestral innovation; and Mozart's instrumentation, though limited in resources, was – as Berlioz said – "perfect." [29] The Encyclopedists meanwhile dreamed of music drama, and found it natural that one of their number should, like Stravinsky in our day, publish his views under the title *Poétique de la Musique*.[30]

Using the same vocabulary, the Alsatian theorist Georges Kastner brought out in 1836 a *Cours d'Instrumentation* "considered in its poetical aspects." [31] Like Berlioz, though half a dozen years younger, Kastner had studied under Reicha and was in touch with advanced musical circles. But a comparison of his work with Berlioz' *Treatise* shows what a stride forward the latter represents. It is not merely that Kastner, even in his

[27] *E.g.*, "We saw that the clarinet has four registers: each of these has a distinct timbre. That of the treble has something piercing which must be employed only in the fortissimo of the whole orchestra . . . those of the medium and of the *chalumeau* suit melodies, arpeggios, and short figures; and the bass is fitted especially for those held notes of a coldly menacing effect, those black accents of motionless rage, of which Weber was the ingenious inventor. . . . The characteristic of the medium range is that of a proud, noble tenderness which makes it available for the expression of the most poetic ideas and feelings." *Tr.*, 137–8.

[28] See the admirable monograph on Mattheson by B. C. Cannon, New Haven, 1947 (*937*).

[29] *Grot.*, 225.

[30] Lacépède; see above, Chapter 7

[31] See *822*, *823*, and *824*.

revised editions of 1837 and 1844, is incomplete, unclear, and unsystematic, but that his conception of the "poetic" side remains primitive, literal, and unanalytic, as in most of his eighteenth-century predecessors. He finds interesting, for instance, the effects obtained by Adam's use of whips and carriage bells in *Le Postillon de Longjumeau*, or Halévy's use of anvils in *La Juive*. Though he cites Berlioz' *Fantastique* and *Requiem* with a respect approaching awe, what really attracts him is the imitation of barking dogs in Méhul's *Chasse du Jeune Henri*, while his notion of chiaroscuro goes no farther than the nuances piano and forte.[32]

Contrast Berlioz dealing with this same "poetic" purpose as he finds it in Gluck, the topic being the flute:

> The sonority of this instrument is soft in the medium, rather piercing in the upper register, and strongly characterized in the low notes. The timbres of the medium and high notes have no very marked expression of their own. They can be used for melodies and accents of various kinds, but without their being able to rival the naive gaiety of the oboe or the noble tenderness of the clarinet. It therefore seems as if the flute were an instrument almost devoid of expressiveness, which one may therefore introduce any- and everywhere, owing to the ease with which it can perform quick passages and sustain the high notes of the orchestra in completing high-register chords.
>
> All this is in general quite true, yet if one studies the flute closely, one discovers that it possesses an expressiveness of its own, and an aptitude for rendering certain moods that no other instrument can compete with. If it is a matter of imparting to a sad melody an accent of desolation, though humble and resigned at the same time, the weak sounds of the medium range, in the keys of C minor and D minor especially, will unquestionably produce the necessary nuance. Only one master seems to me to have fully availed himself of this pale coloring: I mean Gluck. In listening to the air-pantomime in D minor which he wrote for the scene of the Elysian Fields in *Orpheus*, one perceives at a glance that only a flute should play the melody. An oboe would have sounded too childlike, and its voice would not have seemed sufficiently pure; the English horn is too grave; a clarinet would have been better, no doubt, but some of the notes would have been too loud, and none of the softer notes could have been kept to the mild, veiled, self-effacing sonority of the F natural in the medium and the first B flat above the staff, which give so much melancholy to the flute in this D minor key where they recur.
>
> Finally, neither the violin, nor the viola, nor the cello, whether solo or in groups, was proper for the plaint, sublime to the highest degree, of a desperate and suffering shade. It required the very instrument that Gluck chose. And his melody is so conceived that the flute lends itself to all the anxious moments of this unending pain, still marked as it is by the pas-

[32] *822*, 35; *823*, 56.

sionate accents of earthly life. At first it is a scarcely audible voice, which seems afraid to be heard; then it moans quietly, rises to the pitch of reproach, then to that of deep sorrow, as of a heart torn by incurable wounds, and falls back gradually into plaintiveness, the sweet moaning and murmuring of a soul resigned to grief – what a poet! [33]

This, the longest "poetic" interpretation in the *Treatise*, takes us beyond refined discrimination based on technical knowledge: it shows how Berlioz studied the masters and how he understood expressive instrumentation – in a word, how he composed and how he was able to write the *Treatise*.[34]

So much for Berlioz' sense of the poetic, which is only a part of what he understood by "musical." His orchestral research was not spurred by the wish to combine whips and piccolos in a rendering of postillions, but by the desire to invent and discover the uses of novel sounds. While still in Rome he had written prophetically to Ferrand about some fairyland verse: "It is enchantingly full of grace, freshness, and light, but I shall put it aside until later. Now is not the time to compose music to it; the art of instrumentation is not sufficiently advanced: *we must wait until I have dematerialized it a little. . . .*[35] [Italics added.] This "dematerialization" Berlioz had achieved in the intervening decade, and doubtless some of the poet's grace had gone into Queen Mab. But as one must not dwell exclusively on the poetic, so one must not stress the atmospheric side of Berlioz' orchestra. A glance at the passage on the flute shows that the use of the instrument for harmonic purposes is mentioned early, and throughout the *Treatise* Berlioz' solicitude for a complete, concise, and clearly audible harmony is paramount.[36]

Unlike most of his contemporaries, Berlioz felt that true harmony should be a resultant of all the musical forces at work – not melody or structure alone, but rhythm, expression, dynamics, and most significantly

[33] *Tr.*, 153.

[34] His frequent references to "the ancient composers" with regard to usage prove how thorough was his search in the eighteenth-century repertory in addition to Gluck, Mozart, and Beethoven. The German and the Italian instrumental composers he did not, of course, know, both because they were in many cases not published and because their style was not in Berlioz' sense orchestral. His contemporaries, whether he liked their works or not and regardless of his personal relations with them, received credit wherever due. Thus he cites Rossini, Auber, Habeneck, Helévy, and Meyerbeer for innovations he considered valuable

[35] *L.I.*, 108.

[36] See the chapters on the viola, p. 34; cello, pp. 43 and 46; double basses, pp. 53, 61 and 74; piano, p. 100; organ, p. 168; trombone, pp. 205 and 223; voices, pp. 249 and 252; timpani, p. 254; concertina, pp. 288–289; melodium (organ), p. 290.

timbre. This explains why critics or theorists brought up on keyboard practice find Berlioz' harmonic writing puzzling or disagreeable, and why some have tried to find in the composer's early virtuosity on the guitar a reason for such things as his "awkward bass." [37] The question cuts deeper than idiosyncrasy; it reaches, through the mass of superstition about harmony, down to Berlioz' fundamental sense of music as heard and as multilinear – his pragmatism and his pluralism. To make this relation clear, the essence of his practice and the objections to it must first be indicated.

For this purpose the *locus classicus* is the third bar of the very song "Absence" which Berlioz orchestrated in Dresden during the period reviewed in our present chapter. In that measure, the resolution of the tritone B–E sharp is wrong according to the textbooks, and to keyboard ears hearing or imagining the piano version it may perhaps sound odd. For them the bass of the next chord should be A sharp instead of F sharp. But to orchestral ears hearing the "same" notes, the resolution is not only acceptable but it actually takes place correctly according to rule: the lower note on the oboe and second clarinet goes down to A sharp while the upper, on the voice, goes to F sharp. The other instruments break in (giving the "false" note) but without obscuring the resolution, and the composer has thus achieved a number of musical purposes: he has "avoided the unbearably banal affectation" – to quote Koechlin on this passage [38] – of mutilating his opening phrase for the sake of the eye; he has resolved his chord correctly for the ear; and he has followed his method of considering instrumental groups as independent voices. In short, his harmony is at once polyphonic and orchestral, as against the conception, engendered by keyboard habits, of chords as monolithic pillars "supporting" the melody.

Similarly, Berlioz displays a fondness for unisons and octaves, which in the pianistic idiom are felt as showing a weak harmonic instinct. But in the orchestra the different timbres result from the unequal prominence of different upper partials; hence an adroit combination which seems a unison *on paper* produces for subtler ears the audible equivalent of a chord.[39] The fineness of Berlioz' "analytical ear, surely the most sensitive to sound," [40] is only matched by the care with which he avoids repeating

[37] See the article by W. Denis Browne (*418*, 141 ff.).

[38] *453*, 87. A critic who can be very choosy has called this song "the most perfect thing Berlioz ever wrote." (E. Walker: *604*, 104.)

[39] *465*, 132.

[40] *1315*, III, 730. In the *Treatise*, Berlioz unwittingly illustrates how analytic his ear was. In speaking of untuned instruments, he draws attention to the

his effects.[41] If Berlioz in 1838 had obtained the professorship of harmony which he applied for at the Conservatoire,[42] he would undoubtedly have put his ideas on the subject into a second treatise, which would have saved critics much trouble. As it is, it would take a fluent harmonist who was at the same time an expert in acoustics to deduce the principles implicit in Berlioz' scores.[43]

Such a student's analysis would not merely reconcile the rules of harmony current in 1840 with the actual chords that Berlioz heard and wrote in combined timbres. It would once for all drive misplaced abstraction out of musical criticism. In the phrase "the same notes," used earlier in this chapter, "same" was put between quotation marks to suggest how clumsy our nomenclature is when seeking to define the elements of an art. We call *C* every sound at recurring intervals from a deep boom to a shrill whistle; we speak of the "same chord" whether strings or woodwinds play it and regardless of register; we also say the "same chord" if it is insistently repeated a dozen times, as Beethoven likes to do, even though the twelfth repetition *feels* no more like the first than the twelfth lash on your back feels like the first. Our words are patently false, which helps to explain why "identical" devices in two artists yield such different effects, mean different things.[44] And it is precisely because the character

---

"singular and real charm for the ear of a multiplicity of unisons, that is, the simultaneous production by a very large number of instruments of the same nature of whatever noise they emit. Thus in watching infantrymen at drill, one notices . . . that the small crackling noise of shifting arms and the dull sound of the butt striking the ground give . . . when produced by a thousand men, a brilliant ensemble which forces attention, which is pleasing, and in which I detect a certain vague and secret harmony." (P. 281.)

[41] As a single example of Berlioz' unobtrusive variety, notice how in the apparent repetition of the flute-and-trombone chords in the last movement of the *Requiem*, the flutes are written in four parts, as against the three indicated in the earlier movement.

[42] The reason Cherubini gave for not nominating Berlioz was that he did not play the piano.

[43] It may be well to remind the reader that the science of musical acoustics bore its first fruits in the work of Helmholtz some 20 years after Berlioz' *Treatise on Orchestration.* A modern student would point out, for instance, that the expressive qualities of the flute as described by Berlioz come from the fact that in the middle and upper register its tones give forth virtually no harmonics. What Berlioz heard as the "strongly characterized" lower register is due to the richer harmonic contents of those notes, in which the octave and the fourth stand out.

[44] Schoenberg points out in his *Theory of Harmony* how a sequence may be construed out of four identical diminished sevenths rooted upon different bass notes by imagining between each pair a pause for "reinterpretation." (*870*, 306–7.)

of the basic units named in any art defies ultimate classification that in a great work the substance carries a unique meaning.

Berlioz' harmony has always satisfied the most fastidious judges, from Schumann who admired its force and concision to Koechlin who says that "from the expressive point of view Berlioz is a greater harmonist than Handel, Beethoven, and even Wagner up to *Tristan*." [45] Masson adds: "He proceeds by successive touches on the essential points, and one must admit that these touches are of a sureness, originality, and daring that deserve admiration. He does not hesitate to write the expressive harmony even if it lies outside accepted usages." [46] The concision owes much to Berlioz' long practice as a student and a critic of "the rules"; his proceeding by touches results from his direct scoring for, and testing by, the orchestra. He discovered that effects of undoubted subtlety on the keyboard disappear when transferred to the instrumental choir, and he found new subtleties avoiding the harmonic overload which often results from this transfer – the new art must fit the new medium: anything else would be writing for the eye.[47]

Considering this problem and Berlioz' solution it is remarkable that in him the chords or progressions which lie outside current usage are very sparingly used. This is also true of dissonance.[48] In many instances where Berlioz gives an impression of harshness or singularity in progression, it will be found on a closer look that it is the expectation he raises, the context he suggests, by the chord or progression, and not the notes themselves that are uncommon and cause surprise.[49] For the rest, Ernest Newman showed as long ago as 1905 that Berlioz' harmonic style was part and parcel of his idiom, and that so far from indicating lack of thought

[45] *452*, 131.

[46] *465*, 131. "Just try," says Koechlin, "under a given bar in one of his melodies, to write what you think is the 'true bass' – a sixth, for example, in place of the tonic which you find 'awkward'; and you will see what a platitude you have produced! Don't you suppose that he could have thought of your sixth, had he wanted to? . . . If he did not, it is because he knew what he was about." (*453*, 176.)

[47] *719*, 213. Mr. Newman likewise has pointed out how in a score of Richard Strauss's "a good third of the notes" are "perfectly superfluous. . . . It looks far more impressive on paper than it actually sounds." (*374*, 302.)

[48] It would take us too far afield to consider dissonance in Berlioz. But see in the next chapter the discussion of the "Invocation to Nature" in his *Faust*.

[49] One might instance the treatment, both harmonic and rhythmical, of the "Caliban" episode in the *Tempest*, or the conclusion of the trombone solo in the *Funeral and Triumphal* symphony, as samples of the logical though uncommon touch. This has been noted by independent students such as Saint-Saëns (*385*, 406), Koechlin (*453*, 177), Hippeau (*283*, 197–8), and Hadow (*443*, 285).

or knowledge, it grew more and more individual as time went on.[50] Having reflected on the subject for thirty years more, Mr. Newman could only laugh at the academic minds who "rail at Berlioz' harmony . . . merely because his harmonic sense was different from, and subtler than, their own."[51] Saint-Saëns went one step further and made a prophecy. Because Berlioz' writing was not based on enharmony (that is, on the piano's tempered scale) Saint-Saëns felt that his alone might survive of all the music which for two centuries had exploited equal temperament, that is to say, keyboard harmony.[52]

Berlioz himself had dealt with this subject in a chapter of the *Treatise*, but without dogmatism. Although he preferred just intonation, he was reconciled to the practical adjustment which occasionally transforms the orchestra into a great tempered instrument. With the theorists – whether of physics or of music – who found insuperable difficulties in uniting discrepant values of the "same" note, he had little patience.[53] In short, Berlioz unwittingly agreed with his predecessor Mattheson: "Numbers in music," Mattheson wrote, "do not govern but merely instruct; the Hearing is the only channel through which their force is communicated to the inner soul of the attentive listener . . . the true aim of music is not its appeal to the eye nor yet altogether to the so-called 'reason' but only to the Hearing. . . ."[54]

It would take more than a subchapter to draw out of Berlioz' *Treatise* its many lessons and relate them to his musical practice. In a limited space one can only draw attention to the remaining topics that Berlioz treats and try to characterize his orchestral style as one finds it in his works. But first it is necessary to banish one old legend. Combating as he did all vulgar abuses, Berlioz could not have been more displeased by anything than by praise for his supposedly "glorious disproportion."[55] It is critical nonsense to begin with, and the extravagance it imputes is contrary to

[50] *374*, 50–2.

[51] *486*, Jan. 21, 1934.

[52] *386*, 21–2: "From this heresy [enharmonic writing for other than keyboard instruments] has sprung almost all modern music; it has been too fertile to give us the right to deplore it, but it is none the less a heresy destined to disappear in the distant but inevitable future . . . What then will survive of present-day work? Perhaps only the music of Berlioz who, never having learnt the piano, had an instinctive objection to enharmony."

[53] *Tr.*, 288.

[54] *937*, 124.

[55] *887*, 12.

fact.[56] Like anyone who thoroughly understands his medium, he knew that economy does not mean smallness of expenditure but nice calculation of means and ends. Whether in art or in hospitality economy is never skimping, nor can there be a predetermined measure of what is enough.[57] The concluding chapter in Berlioz' *Treatise* must therefore be read with care, and not used — as is often done — for facile expostulation. It is in those pages, of course, that Berlioz describes in a sort of Blake-like vision the orchestra, large and small. He speaks of an ideal ensemble of 465 instrumentists, to whom a chorus of 360 may be joined. These totals have been quoted as if the very digits betrayed the madman. But as with any balance sheet one must read and grasp the point of the appropriation. This large array Berlioz terms a Festival Orchestra; the ordinary orchestra he sets at 119 performers, which is only a few more than the accepted twentieth-century total of 110.[58] Berlioz moreover explains that he wants his large masses, not for din but for smoothness, not for double *f's* but for quadruple *p's*. A final tutti of eight hundred winds and strings would certainly yield volume, but more smoothly, hence more musically, than a scratch orchestra of thirty. "Vulgar prejudice," as Berlioz points out, "calls large orchestras *noisy*, but if they are well balanced, well trained and well led, and if they perform true music, they should rather be called *powerful* — and nothing can be more dissimilar than those two designations." [59]

In the Berlioz orchestra, which harnesses the several species of controllable sound, the orchestrator's power was indeed enlarged but the

[56] Sir Charles Stanford, who disliked Berlioz' music, acknowledged this in a vigorous image: "Berlioz knew too well the glories and beauties of individual instruments to encourage his successors to throw them all into a cauldron and boil them together." (*1362*, 172–3.)

[57] "Why two flutes should be right and three flutes shameful extravagance; why the double clarinet should be looked upon as an interloper; why the tubas should be thought the inferiors of the trombones merely because they came in later — these and a hundred other things pass the comprehension of everyone who gives ten minutes' serious thought to the orchestra." (*405*, 114.)

[58] Incidentally, the foreign editions of the *Treatise* are often at fault in reproducing the distribution of these instruments as well as in adding them up.

[59] *Tr.*, 297. W. G. Whittaker has drawn attention to the fact that Berlioz had a sort of precursor in vocal orchestration, Thomas Tallis (*c.* 1505–1585), whose "motet *Spem in alium* is in forty parts . . . The portion where all voices move independently suggests the throbbing cries of many nations prostrate before their Maker and is a curious anticipation . . . of the extravagant dream of Berlioz . . . in the final chapter of his work on orchestration." (*914*, 89.)

traditional structure was by no means destroyed. With Berlioz as with Beethoven the proportion of strings to the remainder is three fourths. It was after Berlioz that by the increase of the winds, and especially the brass, the ratio fell to two thirds.[60] Nothing can be more erroneous than to ascribe to Berlioz the brazening of the band. Though he drew attention to the melodic use of several neglected woodwinds, and had like Gluck a fondness for trombone recitatives, he gave the great majority of his melodic ideas to the strings, usually the violins.

He has still another reason for requiring a large body of players – a reason derived from his contrapuntal sense. From his earliest performed work of 1825 he wanted to subdivide the main sections of the orchestra into lesser groups and entrust each with a real part. By this means he obtained that steel-mesh texture which some find objectionably thin; though by using numerous strings in octaves or unisons (often without the double basses) he could attain a rounded softness unapproached by any other master.[61]

His scoring, if truly read, is consistent: he usually states the lowest number of strings to be used in any one movement and almost invariably reserves the brass. The three trombones, two cornets, two trumpets and one or two ophicleides (later supplanted by tubas) [62] are a regular part of his orchestra, but they seldom play in more than a few portions of the work. The horns – still hand horns in the early works and therefore not available for extended melodic use [63] – lie between the trumpets and trombones, forming with them a family. Their union in a movement comes only at the point of theme reunion characteristic of his form.

In his handling of the woodwinds, besides their constantly expressive or melodic use, one notable feature is the employment of the English horn as the middle voice of the group.[64] Another is the retention of four bassoons. This was the usual number available in French orchestras, a

[60] This was due in part to the heedlessness with which the Wagnerian *Ring* orchestra, scored for playing virtually *under* the stage, was brought out *upon* the stage of the concert hall and imitated in its original form. (See *921*, 117.)

[61] It is for such a pianissimo that he wants the second small band of strings in his orchestral song *La Captive.*

[62] It was during his German tour that Berlioz first came to know the tuba and the *Treatise* at once recommended its use (p. 229). Though Berlioz continued to write ophicleide parts because tubas were introduced late into France, his annotated scores at the Bibliothèque Nationale bear the indication "change to tubas"; but see below Supplement 5.

[63] *753*, 456 ff. Berlioz recommends the valve instruments in *Mem.*, II, 94–5.

[64] Wagner first used it so in *Lohengrin* doubtless remembering the Adagio of *Romeo and Juliet.*

remnant of the glut of bassoon tone frequent in the eighteenth century. Berlioz ordinarily writes for bassoon in two parts and in a work like the *Funeral and Triumphal* symphony entrusts a good deal of the bass to the instrument.

As regards percussion, Berlioz was so inventive that after him the group must be regarded as the Fourth Estate of the orchestra.[65] Beethoven had been the first to give these instruments motives and solos. Berlioz used them in addition for protracted harmonies and what he called "the coloring of rhythm." At the end of the third movement of the *Fantastique*, for example, a wonderful effect is achieved by letting the English horn sing its solo over three kettledrums tuned in seconds. In the *Requiem*, the sixteen kettledrums form a choir that provides three- and five-part double chords to stand against the brass. But Berlioz did not prescribe noise: even at the *ff* all sixteen are played with sponge heads, and the four tam-tams and cymbals are used with equal moderation. As for the bass drum, it either comes in as the last step in a bacchanalian climax (*Romeo* ball scene) or else it is struck piano, in menacing counter-rhythm, as in the *Francs-Juges* and *Benvenuto Cellini* overtures. Berlioz' percussion pianissimos are in truth an anticipation of modern music for drums, both classical and jazz. One thinks of the soft bass drum passage in his *Ode on Napoleon's Death*, and of the cymbals (also *pp*) that yield a magical effect during the *Sanctus* of the *Requiem*. In *Lélio*, again, the chorus of shades haunt the living to a *pp* stroking of the big gong (tam-tam).

At every point, Berlioz is true to his aim of extracting the quality of a sound without violence, and ridding it of the crude associations it may have acquired by misuse. He is still fighting his French and Italian contemporaries when he wants a cloth spread on the drumhead, or when he mutes the clarinet by putting its bell in a pouch; when he forbids the cymbal to be fastened to the drum, when he invariably requires sponge-headed sticks, and when he orders a suspended cymbal to be struck lightly with such a stick.[66]

It would take a book even larger than the *Treatise* to list all the novel, charming, majestic, or tender instrumental ideas that Berlioz found for himself and put into his scores.[67] An excellent sketch of such a book was

[65] He pointed out, incidentally, that the kettledrum notes are in unison with the cellos, and not an octave below as some musicians kept repeating. (*Tr.*, 267.)

[66] *Tr.*, 267, 144, 262, 275, 279. In the *Benvenuto* carnival scene, the din of many cymbals is dramatically in order, as in Mozart's *Entführung*.

[67] "All his works are studded with original effects ranging from picturesqueness to splendor." (*1305*, 2544.)

in fact written not long ago, a product – as one might have expected – of German scholarship.[68] In the author's learned pages, one finds technical and esthetic discussions of the main innovations in Berlioz' scoring, from the use of harp harmonics to the pizzicato arpeggio done with the thumb which is explained and called for in the *Damnation of Faust*. The writer also treats of the historical and artistic relations of Berlioz' orchestra, both to his predecessors and to his followers, and concludes that its lasting influence may be traced most distinctly in Germany, Russia, and France. Through Saint-Saëns, Gounod, and Reyer, Berlioz acted upon the French Impressionists from Fauré to Debussy, "who owed more to Berlioz than he was conscious of." In Germany, by way of Liszt, Wagner, and Cornelius, it was the Naturalists (Strauss, Pfitzner, and Reznicek) who profited; while in Russia, the entire modern school learned from Berlioz, as did Tchaikovsky and Stravinsky, "on which point much could be demonstrated." [69]

Mr. Bartenstein notices the parodoxical fact that the individuality of Berlioz' methods is such that the best students of the orchestra cannot, on reading his unfamiliar scores, represent to themselves how they must sound. The master's influence was thus exerted through the ear and through the scoring of later composers who first studied him in performance.[70] Often, as Saint-Saëns remarked, the arrangement seems to go counter to common sense. Yet as he added, "It *sounds;* it sounds marvellously!" [71] Weingartner said as much to Bartenstein, and Pierné writes to the same effect. Bartenstein explains this difficulty of judging a Berlioz score by the fact that the reader usually looks for expressive intentions whereas Berlioz is creating "pure sound relations."

This is of course what the composer himself maintained. Theorists and conductors had previously shown how in Berlioz' disposition of forces

[68] Hans Bartenstein, *Berlioz' Instrumentationkunst*, vol. 28 of Karl Nef's series on the musical sciences, Leipzig, 1939. (*673*.)

[69] *673*, 148.

[70] This corroborates the necessity Berlioz lay under of touring Europe to play his music. Left in book form it might have remained a riddle. But this same fact also shows up the folly of those who apply the "piano test" to such works, or any other test than correct performance. It passes understanding why critics who usually define perfection in art by saying that "nothing can be added or taken away" love to "test" music by reduction – Runciman's "piano test" or Brahms's habit of hiding melody and bass in order to judge a song. Others "test" poetry by removing the adjectives, and painting by consulting a black and white reproduction. Do they subject their women to mutilation to test their beauty?

[71] *386*, 3.

"all the work has been done ahead of time,"[72] but the modern scholar is the first to demonstrate that "Berlioz appreciated at all times that orchestration is a means of formal organization; he therefore utilizes timbre as a value in the structure, as may be seen unequivocally in a movement built on the classical sonata scheme such as the first of the *Symphonie Fantastique*."[73] That Berlioz was conscious of how new this was, we know from the distinction he drew between instrumentation and orchestration. If the orchestrator assigns to each instrument its uniquely playable part, he obtains timbre as an independent quality; and to handle this he must devise ways that will give it shape, variety, recurrence – all the attributes of structure. Failing this he would be neglecting certain ideas aroused by the sensations, he would be shutting out one aspect of musical experience. For example, in the treatment of instruments as families, we do not hear simply the English horn, but the middle voice of the woodwinds. This does not suggest space, as does the physical distance or closeness Berlioz occasionally calls for, but it establishes the instrument's position along an ideal dimension.[74] Such is the point of the flute-trombone chords or of the voice-and-woodwind orchestration of the opening bars of "Absence": we are not given an effect but a relation. Similarly, we measure the components in Berlioz' use of contrary nuances – forte in strings against piano

[72] *1305*, 2547. With respect to practicability, Berlioz differs from both Beethoven and Wagner, whose hopes occasionally outran possible performance. In the *Ring*, Wagner wrote for "five instruments that existed only in imagination . . . and he did not get what he expected." (*921*, 225.)

[73] *673*, 142–3.

[74] The common definition of music which distinguishes it as a "time art" from such "space arts" as painting, is after all a very rough notion. It is true that music unrolls as time passes, and vanishes with the instant; this is what makes it hard to discuss. But it would be equally true to say that a piece of music must be perceived, just like a painting, instantaneously in all its parts. Short of this the significant relations of beginning, middle, and end are lost. Such godlike comprehension is doubtless impossible, although Mozart said that he mentally heard his compositions in one act of thought.

On the other hand, no painting other than a very small one can be taken in at one glance. Yet unless we strive in both arts for that comparative, simultaneous, single perception, we run the risk of misunderstanding the work. This, which rather damages the description of music as a "time art," is true of almost all new music and of Berlioz' music in particular, since everything in it, from his transformation of themes to his arrangement of sounds in space, acts as a constituent of the total form. It might be added that although he paid great attention to "the point of origin of sound," he reprobated the metaphor by which we speak of "high" and "low" notes, especially when used by composers for illustrative effects. (*A Trav.*, 225–7.) The metaphor, probably drawn from bodily sensations in singing, loses its point when applied to other instruments than the voice.

in winds. Here the interest lies in the contrast *plus* the relation of each voice to its potential strength. Throughout we may say that in the care he lavishes upon instrumentation, Berlioz is not simply handling "colors" but composing "values."

Being "composed" in the strictest sense, the Berliozian orchestra is in all ways an adjusted instrument – intimate in the songs, in *The Infant Christ*, or in certain movements of the dramatic works; powerful and monumental at other times. Always highly articulated, it need never sound the same, no uniform "style" need reduce a variety of moods and intentions to one generalized blend of scraping and blowing. In Berlioz there is in fact no "blend" at all. Each of his works has an atmosphere and plasticity of its own, the few unconscious reminiscences of texture only emphasizing the remarkable diversity. In effect, the scores and the *Treatise* taken together correspond in the nineteenth century to Bach's earlier example of teaching and creation in the *Well-Tempered Clavichord*, *Art of Fugue*, and other "textbooks" – precept and example from the hand of a master.

Berlioz' seeming specialization – in reality his role as pioneer and settler of a new realm – cannot any longer be suspected of serving as the refuge of a composer who sought to cover up bad draftsmanship by the use of iridescent tints. This charge has also been used to discredit the work of colorists in the history of painting, but in reality it is never applicable: "color" does not conceal faults, it emphasizes them.[75] But if we try to elicit "the latent truth which all superstitions may be charitably supposed to contain," we can see in Berlioz' orchestral style certain features which at first create confusion and lead the unwary to fall back on the formula of "mere effects." Weingartner, it will be remembered, made this mistake when he originally came to the pizzicato basses in the *Cellini* overture.[76]

[75] This can be demonstrated from the very definition of the terms: if an "effect" generates a form, a continuous line whose purpose and modifications are rational, it ceases to be a trick; if, on the contrary, no such thing follows, the trick reveals itself as such. It is therefore self-contradiction to say that an artist *builds up* his art out of tricks or effects. To build means to compose. This truth is only obscured by the fact that effects, when described or when very new, seem to be "mere" effects; whereas old effects, such as tremolo, types of bowing, pizzicato, double stops or muted strings, seem to be "music itself" – which indeed they are. The very name *pianoforte* denotes nothing but a pair of effects, and the first devotee of instrumental color was the man who blew through a tube instead of remaining "classical" by using only his vocal cords.

[76] See above, Subchapter 4.

The paradoxical cause of the error is that from the point of view of the unaccustomed ear, most of Berlioz' music is *in*effective. Berlioz noticed this himself from the time of his earliest *premières* and his German experience confirmed it. To this day, unfamiliar listeners of his unfamiliar music must be prepared for disappointment, and even an incomplete disappointment. Just as Sherlock Holmes said to the man who was unable to see that he was being followed, "That is what you must expect when I am following you"; so one must expect that the finest of Berlioz' works will at first appear like partial confusion. One misses the rich, steady-streaming sound to which more recent masters have accustomed us; one's attention flags because of the very delicacy of the "solo" parts. Until we become attuned to the new scale of nuances and the sinewiness of the scoring, the texture seems at times thin, at other times capriciously rough. Berlioz does not give us what our perhaps narrow habits make us desire.

Surprising as it may seem, the best preparation for Berlioz' orchestral texture is that of Mozart's operas. Setting aside the moods and melodic ideas which belong to different centuries, the dramatic sharpness and clarity in both men is much the same [77] – at the opposite end of the scale from the style of Strauss and Wagner, despite their debt to Berlioz. He disliked the thick impasto which comes from mixing timbres and which we now tend to accept as the sound of *the* orchestra. To stress the difference one might say that hundreds of Berlioz' pages are really a unique kind of chamber music, with concerto-like sections framed within more massive yet always aerated ensembles. This is consonant with his personality and amounts to self-expression in the best sense. For Berlioz must be called an imaginative spirit rather than a throbbing heart; he was – if the distinction may be made – not emotional but passionate: white heat, not red. He loathed wallowing, and his love of sound was sensuous, not sensual. This is the best reason why he will never satisfy the greater number, who necessarily come under Flaubert's definition of *l'homme moyen sensuel.*[78] And it is this too which distinguishes Berlioz from Wagner – each an irresistible artist for one type of human organism and psyche. One might express the difference architectually by contrasting the George Washington bridge in New York – wiredrawn, suspended, vibrating like an aeolian harp – with the no less admirable Egyptian colonnade at Luxor – massive and overwhelming by its immediately felt solidity.

[77] It is a mere detail but Mozart and Berlioz are almost alone in using the first violins and violas in octaves instead of violins I and II.

[78] In Berlioz' words: "Music is understood only by a very limited number of cultivated minds; it acts on the uncultivated solely by its sensual side. Hence . . ." (*M.E.*, 147.)

It is relevant to this comparison between the two artists to contrast their opposite valuations of Rhythm. The *Treatise* says of the untuned percussion instruments that one of their functions is "to give color to rhythm." Elsewhere Berlioz deplores the fact that this department of music was in his day "the least advanced of all." [79] In his ideal Musical City he wanted "twenty classes in rhythm," and what he would have taught in them is the esthetics of an element which he himself carried to the highest point of complexity and expressiveness. He would have shown how rhythmical balance may be achieved without the symmetrical subdivision of phrases, how accents may be made stronger by *not* falling on the strong beat, and how a rhythmic pulse may unify a whole movement in a quite different way from the obsessive tom-tomming in certain modern scores. Lastly, he would have exemplified from his own works what he called "harmonies of rhythm," that is to say the counterpointing of several rhythmic lines – Mozart had shown the way in *Don Giovanni* – to create what Richard Pohl later called "polyrhythm." [80]

As against this physical and intellectual preference for giving sound a marked and varied contour in time, the German school, led by Wagner and ending with Mahler and Schoenberg, showed a relatively weak interest in rhythm. Owing to this neglect it has become a part of tradition that true "romantic" feeling swims about on an unbounded musical flow. The pacing of emotion is then achieved by frequent climaxes, as in Wagner, which again contrasts with Berlioz' preference for long slow progressions of which the listener does not immediately perceive the goal. Caught between this dynamic delay and the unexpected metrical forms, Berlioz' German-trained listener feels like the landlubber on the deck of a ship. The resulting discomfort is serious, for rhythm lies deep in our bodies and is least subject to argument, whence it so often happens that our musical tastes manifest little more than our rhythmic sympathies and antipathies.

True, when we once become aware of these unsuspected factors in our enjoyment, we are better able to hear Berlioz' music as it actually is. This experience reproduces what happened during Berlioz' tour in Germany: performers and conductors who worked over the music found their enthusiasm increasing in proportion to their knowledge. "How it all sounds!" exclaims a conductor in our own century. "Nothing in the score

[79] *Tr.*, 253; *A Trav.*, 10.

[80] *552* and *708*, 134. See in *Lélio* (Chant de Bonheur) the five-beat figure which accompanies the 6–4 chorus without coinciding with the bass. Berlioz would have welcomed the instruments developed by Theremin and Cowell which produce up to seventeen simultaneous rhythms.

is unnecessary, everything is in its proper place. Details that seem at first sight most insignificant have their hidden purpose which is revealed on performance . . . In his moments of greatest simplicity he is always full, rounded, and of the utmost perfection. . . . It is well-nigh miraculous." [81]

To Berlioz it was easy – easy in the sense of the Shavian formula that great art is either easy or impossible. Hear how simply he states his own aims and methods as he reviews Liszt's first orchestral score. Liszt's instrumentation, says Berlioz, "is remarkable by its power and variety. One never hears in his orchestra the succession of similar sonorities that make certain works, otherwise worthy of respect, so tiring for the listener. He knows how to make appropriate use of small and large means, and he does not ask of either instruments or voices more than they can give. In a word, he has shown at one stroke what one might have feared not to find in him all at once, namely *style* in orchestration, such as he already possesses in the other departments of music." [82]

The work that elicited this self-revealing comment was the cantata Liszt had composed for the Beethoven celebration at Bonn in 1845: it might well be called the first fruit of the French master's teaching of his art upon German soil.

[81] Gabriel Pierné (*1305*, 2548 and 2543).

[82] *Soirées* (2nd Epilogue) *Eves.*, 329. Liszt had written one orchestral score earlier, the Fantasia for piano and orchestra on two themes from Berlioz' *Lélio*, which Busoni found unpublished in 1907. (*175*, 116.) The work had been played in Paris in 1835 (*995*, II, 38–9), but apparently Berlioz did not account it an original work. Liszt's first symphonic poem was not orchestrated till 1849.

17. *Form and Philosophy:* The Damnation of Faust

August 1, 1845
to October 19, 1846

This word "damnation" terrifies not him.
– MARLOWE's Dr. Faustus,
about himself

WHEN BERLIOZ called himself, or allowed others to call him, "a musician three quarters German," [1] he had in mind no musical nationalism, either of spirit or of technique, but only a grateful feeling for the artistic sympathies he found in contemporary Germany, a feeling heightened by his admiration for his musical models, all of whom were German. In the course of his dozen visits to this region which was still a land of artistic internationalists, Berlioz made many more friends than enemies, but still more important, he soon drew from the cultural contact the inspiration that produced one of his most resplendent scores, the *Damnation of Faust* of 1846.

The fourteen months that saw its completion began most appropriately with Berlioz' departure for Bonn, on August 1, 1845. Beethoven's statue was to be dedicated in this, his native town, after incredible (but usual) obstacles had been overcome by Liszt,[2] and the unveiling on the fourteenth was to be preceded by numerous musical events: we have just read Berlioz' comment on Liszt's commemorative cantata.

The rest of Berlioz' account of the proceedings gives us an excellent insight into the musical manners of the period, while showing at the same time his grasp of organization and his sense of humility in the presence of Beethoven. Not that Berlioz had had anything to do with the arrangements of the fete, beyond contributing twenty francs toward the statue and conducting without fee Liszt's money-raising concerts. Liszt and Liszt alone was "the soul of the festivities" and the "delegate from the wide

[1] *A Trav.*, 317.

[2] These are related in part in Liszt's articles in the *Gazette Musicale* for 1839 (*210, passim*). By the end of that year, the total sum collected among French musicians was 424 francs 90 centimes (= 85 dollars of the period; *ibid.*, 265).

world."[3] But even Liszt's money and zeal had not been enough to galvanize Europe or the Bonn Committee. Though Frederick William of Prussia attended, with Queen Victoria and her Consort as his guests, and though musical celebrities from England, France, Russia, and Central Europe came to demonstrate their faith, Beethoven's eminence was far from an established fact. Italy sent no representatives, neither did the Paris Conservatoire. In fact, all the French musicians present were there unofficially. The Conservatoire had refused to give a concert for the benefit of the celebration when Liszt petitioned for it. And there were other notable absentees: Wagner, Glinka, Mendelssohn, Schumann, Marschner, to say nothing of the entire crowd of French and Italian opera makers.

The local Committee, it is only fair to add, had issued its invitations somewhat casually and had made no provision whatever for the reception of any but titled guests. To get to hear the Mass in C in the cathedral and avoid being crushed to death by the Bonn citizenry, Berlioz had to slip in through the artists' entrance; and later, for the unveiling of the statue, to vault a fence. "Taking one thing with another, the invitation I received from the Committee in charge of the festivities did not actually prevent me from witnessing them."[4] Still worse, the Committee had neglected to call on the best available performers, and the orchestra purposing to honor Beethoven with his own music was needlessly inadequate.[5] "To do the right thing would have been not only possible but very easy, merely by asking our leading instrumentalists everywhere six months in advance . . . But this would also have meant overcoming narrow nationalistic ideas, which in circumstances of this kind can only have disastrous results, and which are besides infinitely ridiculous to all sensible people."[6]

Nor did prejudice affect only nations. "It will be asked how and why there could be any ill-will against Liszt . . . to whom the credit must go for initiating and carrying out whatever has been successful at Bonn . . . It is chiefly this deserved credit . . . which gave offense. Some had a grudge against him because of his extraordinary talent and success; others because he is witty, and yet others because he is generous, because he has written too fine a cantata, because the others' compositions . . .

[3] *Soirées* (Second Epilogue).

[4] *Soirées* (Second Epilogue).

[5] For example, there were "eight or nine cellists trying to compete with a dozen double basses." *Ibid.*, 320.

[6] *Ibid.*, 320. Berlioz is hinting at the fact that there was some anti-French feeling among the Bonn patrons, which led to a few unpleasant incidents during the Beethoven week itself.

were unsuccessful, . . . because he speaks French too well and knows German too thoroughly, because he has too many friends, and doubtless because he has not enough enemies. . . ." [7]

As is usual in celebrations, some unfamiliar works of Beethoven were played, and some well-known works played for the first time as written. *Ad hoc* songs and hymns by venturesome living composers filled the subsequent programs. From lack of foresight, one of these outdoor cantatas remained inaudible. "A similar fate was reserved for the German song, chosen by competition and crowned by a jury which had probably heard it." [8] The last program, reorganized by royal order, joined to an overture and songs by Beethoven the Weber piano concerto. This was played by Madame Pleyel, Berlioz' onetime fiancée, whom he praised in his review. Then came virtuoso pieces – mostly variations on operatic airs – finally a small musicale was given at Bruhl by the King of Prussia, to which Berlioz was invited. There he heard Jenny Lind for the first time. "Her voice, of an incisive metallic timbre, great power, and incredible flexibility lends itself equally to mezzo-voce effects, to impassioned expressiveness, and to the most delicate embellishments." [9] At the same concert, Berlioz' lifelong favorite, Garcia's daughter Pauline, who was in private life Mme. Viardot, sang three pieces "exquisitely," and Liszt and Meyerbeer played. Midnight struck and Berlioz returned to Bonn by railway "dead drunk with harmony, wearied with admiring, feeling an irresistible need of silence and calm." [10] He found lodgings in a cottage at nearby Königswinter, where he collected his thoughts and wrote his article. In the course of its skillful combination of reportage, anecdote, philosophizing, and music criticism, he found a place for drawing the artist's moral, obvious and self-interested, but eternally right and needful:

"It is very fine to glorify in this fashion the demigods who are no more. . . . Today, all these intelligent and sensitive beings on whom [Beethoven's] genius has shed its radiance, turn to him as to a benefactor and a friend . . . But it is too late. This Beethoven in bronze is unaware of all this homage, and it is sad to think that the living Beethoven, whose memory is thus honored, might not have obtained from his native town in the days of suffering and destitution which were so numerous during his

[7] *Soirées* (Second Epilogue).
[8] *Soirées* (Second Epilogue).
[9] *Soirées* (Second Epilogue).
[10] *Soirées* (Second Epilogue).

troubled life the ten-thousandth part of the sum lavished upon him after his death." [11]

Back in Paris after this spiritual bath, Berlioz found nothing to keep him on that exalted plane but his own thoughts. The Opera "is in a state of madness, beastliness, and feeble-mindedness to the very tip of its long ears."[12] Scribe's verses and plot for *La Nonne Sanglante* reminded him of their destination. Berlioz dropped them where he had left them and took up instead a double project – to revise and enlarge his "Eight Scenes" into a complete dramatic work based on Goethe's *Faust* and to pursue his musical mission by "invading" Austria. Early October found his plans laid for leaving later that month. Before setting out he had tedious business to attend to: suing a delinquent vicomte who owed him five hundred francs on a bill of exchange, and turning out some pieces for harmonium which had been commissioned by his friend, the organ manufacturer Alexandre. The three pieces add nothing to Berlioz' stature, though one of them again exemplifies a characteristic mood and technique in the solemn religious fugato of the "Hymn for the Elevation of the Host." [13]

On the way to Vienna, Berlioz had to stop at Nancy, being ill. He soon recovered, though he and Marie missed the steamer at Regensburg and had to go by post chaise. They arrived in Beethoven's second home town on November 2, 1845. Cordially received on the strength of his earlier German reputation, Berlioz was immediately in the musical swim. A concert with which he had nothing to do, but to which he was urged to go, showed him what a thousand Viennese amateurs (four hundred instrumentists) could do. To his surprise they played with extraordinary "verve and precision" the *Magic Flute* overture – "that wonderful work, of which the motion is so fleet and the texture so tightly and delicately woven." [14]

His own rehearsals were a delight, only topped by the knowledge that he was in the Theater an der Wien whose boards Beethoven once trod. Moreover, musical Vienna was agog at the recent discovery of Gluck's place of burial. Discovery implied forgetfulness and Berlioz could not refrain from exclaiming, "Viennese! you are almost worthy of inhabiting

[11] *Soirées* (Second Epilogue).

[12] *M.E.*, 111.

[13] *Ger. ed.*, vol. VI, p. 36 ff

[14] *Mem.*, II, 183. The remainder of the comment explains why Berlioz would not employ a large orchestra in playing the classical masters.

Paris!" [15] But they had not forgotten how to be lively at concerts. At Berlioz' first they encored the *Roman Carnival* overture, and divided on the rest of the program. The press and the green rooms were buzzing with discussions of the "new esthetic." Two more concerts in November brought the composer's local fame to a high pitch and secured him a new batch of affectionate devotees. The audiences, as he wrote to a friend in America, "are most gracious to me; they applaud fit to shatter their knuckles and make me encore as many as four numbers in one concert." [16] One of these was a charming bolero, *Zaïde*, which Berlioz had just taken from his unpublished melodies and orchestrated.

On the eve of Berlioz' birthday, that is on December 10, a hundred and fifty musicians gave a banquet in his honor and presented him with a baton of silver gilt, bearing the titles of his works, as well as the names of the first forty subscribers to the presentation. Baron de Lannoy, the Austro-Belgian composer, former director of the Vienna Conservatorium, in speaking for the musical home of Gluck, Mozart, Haydn, and Beethoven, expressed the hope that the stick would remind Berlioz of the music lovers who now joined in the cry of "Long live Berlioz!" [17] In his reply, the composer immediately associated the other French musicians then in Vienna (naming Félicien David) as sharers in this token of fraternal feeling.[18]

Berlioz had to extend his stay. In the course of it, he visited the famous hall where Johann Strauss and his choice band produced the waltzes which had added a new glory to Vienna's musical renown. Greatly impressed by the quality of both the music and the dancing, Berlioz did not hesitate to call Strauss a genuine artist and to commend his orchestra as superior to many more pretentious bands. He also noted with pleasure the rhythmical interest of Strauss's compositions which "made use of every beat in the bar" for syncopation or secondary rhythmical lines, in a manner that Berlioz himself had advocated earlier against the proponents of squareness and the strong beat.[19]

For the additional concert Berlioz had proposed to give the Dramatic Symphony, *Romeo and Juliet*, and the suggestion had been eagerly taken up. "And all this," as Berlioz wrote to Desmarest in Paris, "is due to our dear old *Symphonie Fantastique*. The Scenes in the Country and the

[15] *Mem.*, II, 199.

[16] *M.E.*, 118.

[17] *1398*, Dec. 21, 1845.

[18] A more than verbal flourish of amity, for it seems that on Berlioz' arrival David had behaved with ill-concealed jealousy, despite the welcoming hand Berlioz had given him in Paris the year before. (*502*, 417.)

[19] *Mem.*, II, 195 and *1398* (1834–40) *passim.*

March to Execution have turned their hearts inside out. As for the *Roman Carnival* and the 'Pilgrims' March,' they are now popular pieces. (Things have gone so far that pies are named after me.) The musicians are first-rate, and the orchestra is young — half Czech, half Viennese — and trained by me, since it was only made up two months ago. It is now as strong as a lion. This morning, I rehearsed in addition the Kärntnertor orchestra (the leading orchestra in the Germanies) for . . . my concert tomorrow. . . . On the 30th I shall have the chorus and orchestra of the theatre, doubled in numbers, for *Romeo and Juliet* complete. For Friar Laurence I have Staudigl, who is a fine strong bass. And what a musician! . . ." [20] Other details follow of a more intimate nature: "Marie is radiant with pleasure at all this success. . . . What is the exact amount of the tailor's bill outstanding . . . ? Will Latte [the publisher] pay his usual price of 200 francs for *Zaïde?* I am going to bed a little weary from rehearsing." [21]

Romeo and Juliet, given on January 2, 1846, proved too difficult a dose for the audience, but the performers having grown familiar with it felt, like the later New York critic, that the work "had come to stay." As the double chorus ended, they raised a great shout for the composer, as well as a banner bearing commendatory verses. Berlioz had not conducted and thus had heard his score for the first time with relative detachment, jotting down numerous alterations for a future edition.

Despite the hurly-burly he was in a composing vein. His new sketches for *Faust* were taking shape; notably the Enchantment scene, which had grown into three variations upon the original theme of 1828. It was encouraging — and so different from the Parisian battle — to have one's musical output understood, even if sometimes rejected; for partisanship here seemed to be about his work, not about his affiliation with the Bertin family or his relations with the minister of the day. Though no one was calm enough — as the critic of the *Theaterzeitung* wrote — "to assess his extraordinary talent, . . . wherever he goes with his music love springs up and hate also. Berlioz acts like spiritual yeast and causes a general ferment of the mind." [22] A fifth concert, spontaneously organized to honor him as he left, and an audience with Metternich completed Berlioz' round of pleasures.[23]

[20] *M.E.*, 124.
[21] *M.E.*, 125.
[22] *269*, 105.
[23] It was during this interview that he was asked whether he always composed for 500 instruments and replied "No, sometimes I use only 450." Considering how often this has been quoted to prove Berlioz' lavishness by his

He felt happy and grateful. On the eve of his departure (as originally set) he had sent to the Friends of Music — the thousand whose performance he had enjoyed — a letter of compliments: "The magnificence of your ensemble, the power of your resources in the superb rendering of the three great German masters [Mozart, Haydn, and Beethoven] never kept one from perceiving the vivid harmonic sense animating each orchestral or choral section, nor the musicianship that guided them through the notable difficulties of the scores . . . This marvelous performance, largely the work of amateurs, would be enough to assure Vienna's musical pre-eminence over all other European cities." [24]

Now for Prague, whence there were signs of Berliozian "ferment" even before the trip was thought of. Young Dr. Ambros, the critic and musicologist, urged the visit and took upon himself all the preparations for it. Schumann's review of the *Fantastique* was familiar to the younger crowd of composers and a new conductor-composer-professor, Johann Friedrich Kittl, had just begun to impose Beethoven on the conservative townsmen's taste. This undoubtedly fortified them for the advent of Berlioz. Three concerts in mid-January 1846 insured him a reception as enthusiastic as Vienna's. The musicians especially took fire. Classes from the Conservatoire came to learn his ways of rehearsing. Tomaschek, the dean of Czech composers, then over seventy, declared himself "one-third won over." The intellect and aristocracy of Prague were similarly split, but with the larger fraction favorable.

A more regrettable division was that of the gate receipts, much diminished by complimentary seats, and by the theater manager's levy of twelve per cent. "The only thing to do is to render unto Caesar, as usual, what does not belong to Caesar." [25] Berlioz promised to return soon if *Romeo and Juliet* could be rehearsed in his absence. It is clear that he was deliberately working, not for public applause, but for the approval of the next generation of composers, determined to give them his richest and most advanced thought as exemplified in the Dramatic Symphony. The audiences at large were obviously better able to appreciate his first works first.[26]

Meanwhile Vienna wanted still another concert, scheduled for February 2, which Berlioz returned to direct; and by that time Buda-Pesth was

---

own words, it may be said here that the retort to the Prince was a piece of irony.

[24] *M.E.*, 119.

[25] *M.E.*, 131.

[26] The *Roman Carnival* is an exception to be explained by its thematic simplicity.

feeling the "musical earthquake" (so said the *Wiener Theaterzeitung*) and was clamoring for his presence. A friend advised Berlioz to bring the Hungarians an orchestral version of one of their national airs. Berlioz chose the so-called Rákóczy theme, and spent the night preceding his departure fashioning the now famous March.[27] He was still in the flood tide of his creative urge and what he made of the military tune was a short symphonic poem of irresistible effect.

The story of its first performance is told in full in the *Memoirs*, its most interesting points being the various signs of the Hungarians' nationalistic fever, which was to burst forth two years later. M. de Horvath, to whom Berlioz showed his new score tried to warn him: "Your exposition of the [Rákóczy] theme is marked *piano* and we are in the habit of hearing it start *fortissimo*. . . ." Berlioz would be affronting national honor, but he kept calm. "Yes," he said, "your Zigeuner play it *ff*, but never fear, you will have a *forte* such as you have never heard. . . . In all things one must look to the end." [28]

The effect was what he foresaw. The gentle woodwinds and strings which state the theme after the rhythm-setting fanfare, lead it very gradually into the battlelike climax with dull pulses of the deep drum on the off beat. Dismayed at first, the hall was electrified at the end. In the green room, Berlioz was embraced and wept over. An unprepossessing, haggard veteran, seizing his hand, told him in halting French, " 'Monsieur, monsieur . . . me poor devil Hungarian . . . Forgive excitement . . . the French they revolutionary . . . know how to make music for revolutions.' It was almost frightening," adds Berlioz, "it was sublime." [29]

The Hungarians, as well as Berlioz' Viennese and Czechish friends,

[27] *Mem.*, II, 210. M. Boschot, who on principle always believes the opposite of what Berlioz says, doubts that the March was written so quickly. The point would be of slight importance if it did not by implication raise the questions of boastfulness and lying. Berlioz mentions only three pieces and one whole work — the *Requiem* — as having been composed with unusual speed. This is one of the pieces. At other times, he mentions movements which took laborious working over before they satisfied him. Therefore in the present instance he was not trying to prove himself cleverer than he was. In Berlioz' original version the Hungarian March lacked the present coda, consequently it could have been written in a ten-hour night at the rate of a dozen bars an hour, which is no unbelievable feat. But M. Boschot is so filled with "the spirit that denies" that he could not even read Berlioz' statement to the end: " — the parts," exclaims Boschot — "being, I suppose miraculously copied on the instant!" The parts, as Berlioz indicates, were copied in the usual way at his next stopping place. On the genesis of Berlioz' March, see E. Haraszti (*572*).

[28] *Mem.*, II, 211.

[29] *Mem.*, II, 213. Confirmed by contemporary accounts. (*572*, 217.)

were going to be plunged in revolution sooner than they thought, and the composer might have told them that the art thereof can only be made after the fact, when the feelings can be recalled in tranquillity and given form. It is no less genuine art for being retrospective, as is shown by the fact that Berlioz' *post*revolutionary march could look forward and inspire an anonymous hero of '48.[30]

Berlioz' muse continued active. His plan for *Faust* was clear in his mind, and its music, like the march he had just written and could use for the work in hand, came into being of its own accord. Having lost his way one night in Budapest, he wrote the refrain of the Peasants' Dance on a street corner, under the lamppost. At Breslau, his next stop, more numbers came, including the students' song. Everywhere he is "furiously at work." But suddenly he misses his old Paris comrades and "the whirlwind of ideas in which one moves." [31] So he told his affectionate brother-in-arms Joseph d'Ortigue, in all sincerity, for Vienna had just offered Berlioz the post of Imperial Kapellmeister. He declined without hesitation, which with him argues previous thought: Paris tugged at his heart, of course, but he also must have considered that his critical post at the *Débats* was a necessary and induplicable weapon of defense, while at the same time its obligations left him free to carry on his European mission. The Imperial Chapel would fetter him. In the foreign-speaking city, once his musical honeymoon with the Viennese was over, he would be merely another working musician in a small provincial colony of outsiders. No. The mission was paramount—and besides, there were Harriet and Louis for whom he felt responsible in more than a material way.

Once more in Prague at the end of March 1846, Berlioz made new converts with his *Romeo and Juliet* and two other concerts. The supper following the dress rehearsal was graced by toasts; Liszt drank to Berlioz' "erupting crater of genius"—drank so efficiently that he was with difficulty prevented from fighting a pistol duel "at two paces" with a Bohemian nationalist.

Pleased with his latest corrections in the score of the Dramatic Symphony, Berlioz was still, as Lesueur had said long ago, "streaming music from all his pores." One night he was awakened by the thought of a melody which made him "tremble lest he forget it." He used it for the angels' greeting to Margaret which closes the *Damnation of Faust.*

[30] The exception of Rouget de Lisle's "Marseillaise" occurs at once, but its being the work of a very ordinary mind, raised by emotion and drink to an unusual pitch of excitement, may well reinforce the rule while seeming to disprove it.

[31] *M.E.*, 135.

Before returning to Paris Berlioz had taken on a collection of errands and messages to and from musicians. It was an admirable artistic freemasonry: he was to buy two violins in Paris for the Prague Conservatoire; another Czech musician, the young Hanslick, who in those days was still favorable to modern music, wanted a recommendation to Liszt; the Vienna clarinetist Tropianski wished to transfer to Paris – these were but a few of the occasions for letters and visits. To Mendelssohn, Berlioz sent greetings and congratulations on his *Midsummer Night's Dream*, which he had heard for the first time at Breslau: [32] "I have never heard anything more deeply Shakespearean than your music. . . . I would have given three years of my life to embrace you. Farewell, farewell. Please believe that I love you as much as I admire you, which is to say a great deal." [33] Finally on April 19 a "very brilliant and very profitable" concert at Brunswick – where he had so many close friends – marked the close of the second campaign.

The "whirlwind of ideas" in Paris turned out, when near at hand, to be mostly wind. This did not include Berlioz' circle of intimates, all of whom were as weary as he, though with rather less to show for it. Gathering his impressions of musical life, he could see that when compared with Central Europe Paris was stagnant. It was no longer the hub which it had been three decades before when the Conservatoire, with its faculty of over one hundred, rivaled the numerous theaters and private societies in attracting quantities of foreign musicians, many of whom came to stay. Although no other center replaced Paris, that subtle but perceivable fluid which accompanies the motions of the spirit was flowing in the contrary direction. Prague now had a great Conservatory, Vienna the best orchestra, and the separate German states an enormous urge to produce and perform. Though this activity owed much to decentralization, to the diversity that comes of pluralism, it seemed also to go with the desire for national unification. The goal of statehood and constitutional liberty aroused strong feelings bent on something greater than self; whereas in France the *status quo*, moderately good but monolithic, aroused only hatred and self-despising. In politics, disgust was held in check by despair, and in the arts a kind of torpor overcame even the best minds. "Here," wrote Berlioz to a German friend, "we have nothing

[32] The overture Mendelssohn had composed at seventeen, in 1826, but the remaining numbers of the suite, including the delightful scherzo, were new since he had met Berlioz again and rehearsed *Romeo and Juliet* with him.
[33] *M.E.*, 137.

but shabby scores, sprinkled with shabby melodies, accompanied by shabby orchestras, sung by shabby singers, and listened to by a shabby public, which fortunately never listens to them twice and forgets them at once."[34] The exceptions to this oblivion meant less than nothing – as Berlioz later showed in a little anecdote of his own invention. A sea captain, whose distant cruises bring him to the capital at wide intervals, notices that every time he leaves Paris he sees Donizetti's *La Favorita* on the bill, and every time he returns he sees Donizetti's *Lucia.* "No," says a fellow mariner, "that's an exaggeration . . . when *I* leave for India, it is true I also see *La Favorita,* but when I return they do not always give *Lucia:* they often give *La Favorita* again." [35]

The Opera had in fact died in its tracks and the public had begun to notice it; the press was up in arms against Pillet's directorship. As for Berlioz, strengthened in his own faith by his trip abroad, he had dropped all operatic schemes. Though for brevity he spoke of the *Damnation of Faust* as a "concert opera," it is no such thing. The form had grown out of the Eight Scenes and was a further extension of the dramatic symphony. Its completion and instrumentation were going satisfactorily throughout the summer, with but one interruption. Jules Janin, amiable and ever-ready, had written a cantata for the opening of the Northern Railway at Lille on June 14. He naturally applied to "friend Berlioz" for the music, which was put together in a few nights.

This *pièce de circonstance,* like half a dozen others in Berlioz' output, does not greatly signify. As the composer ironically put it, "If I had had three *full* days, it would have been fit to live 40 centuries more." [36] Yet in addition to further proof of the composer's speed, one finds one or two passages of real beauty in this song celebrating Peace, the Nation, and the Workers. Berlioz went to Lille – "the most musical town of the French provinces" – in order to conduct the work. Three military bands would also play, beforehand, the *Apothéose* of the *Funeral* symphony. At the end of this the local National Guard wanted to discharge its artillery. "The cannon are on the program," they told Berlioz, "the public expect them, and we cannot back out." Berlioz consented, conferred about the signal for the explosion, and proceeded to conduct. But on the final chord, no cannon: the fuses had burnt out to no purpose. The rest was silence and Ber-

[34] *M.E.,* 145. Compare Tocqueville: "I lose my mind trying to recall that maze of petty incidents, petty ideas, and petty passions; of private self-seeking and incoherent projects in which the public men of that time exhausted their lives." (*1223,* 2.)

[35] *1386,* May 14, 1863.

[36] *Grot.,* 294.

Berlioz in 1845, by Prinzhofer

"His masterly conducting . . . was one of the decisive influences in my musical life."

— HANS VON BÜLOW (*Autobiography*)

lioz dashed to his other chorus and orchestra, indoors, to conduct the cantata.[37]

The social aspect of music continued to occupy him. In order to celebrate — and to feed — the musicians of Paris, their Association planned a festival like the one projected three years before. The *Apothéose* of the *Funeral and Triumphal* symphony was to be played, and this time the concert took place with the aid of forty regimental bands. Berlioz being in sympathy with the object but having had no share in the arrangements, could judge them with some detachment. He concluded once more that open-air music was a delusion and that the organizing powers of his compatriots were not equal to their tradition and opportunities: "The French, who fought the campaigns of the Revolution and Empire, and who made good the July uprising, cannot manage to build a concert hall." Behind this lay moral defects. "What we lack is seriousness, gravity, calmness . . ., the qualities that make the adolescent superior to the child and the mature man superior to the youth. . . . We lack the ability to rise above petty passions, petty ideas, petty objects. We lack the ability to examine instead of half seeing, to listen instead of overhearing, to think before speaking. We lack the ability to scorn maliciousness and the wretched popularity that we gain by it; we lack the ability to believe — and to believe steadfastly — that the spirit that creates is superior to the spirit that destroys."[38]

Suiting the action to the word, Berlioz set on foot a celebration for the anniversary of Gluck's death. Baron Taylor and the Musical Association were for it; the indestructible opposition was against it. Part of the objections may have been due to the fact that the work chosen by Berlioz and the Association was the former's *Requiem;* but the other, greater barriers were raised from sheer hatred of seeing something succeed. Berlioz circumvented the willful obstructionists, collected his musicians, trained them by sections, and gave at the Church of St. Eustache on July 29 a performance of his *Requiem* which the participants long remembered.

Berlioz was by now a seasoned commander-in-chief. He could make up programs, cope with officialdom, draft publicity notices, watch the accounting, see that notables were sent tickets, and kindle the zeal of janitors; he could rehearse, conduct, train the amateurs, cajole the professionals, disarm the grumblers, and impart passion to the mass. He knew how to word reminders and sugarcoat admonitions; he could induce the

[37] *Grot.*, 300–4.
[38] *269*, 118–9.

press to write, the printers to print, and the public to come.[39] His mind was an electric distributor which gave the well-timed spark to each cylinder of his vast machine. He did this without the aid of secretaries, telephones, dictographs, typewriters, automobiles, or benzedrine. It was a princely expenditure of nerves, and Berlioz loathed the impression of coercive pushing which it could not help generating like ozone in the air around a dynamo: "Thanks to the ill-will provoked by my criticism in the *Débats*, and to the raging anger of envious natures, I can make my way in Paris only like a red-hot cannon ball that hisses, burns, and shatters. I have noticed that this hostility increased during my absence in Germany." [40]

Meanwhile the invisible inner mechanism, the demon inside the cannon ball, was still functioning in the frictionless world of thought. On a trip to Enghien, Berlioz found the rhythmic finale for Part II of the *Damnation;* at Rouen, where he went to see his son at school, and to rest from practical affairs, he wrote the love duet of Part III and began the polishing and fusing of all the scenes and parts. "I am working strenuously," he wrote to his father, "on a large work which is nearly done and which I want to put on in Paris by the end of November." [41] And a new faculty, long latent, was developing: "I have had to be poet and musician both, because my score, begun and pursued across country, in Bavaria, Austria, Hungary, Bohemia, and Silesia, was going faster than my versifiers in Paris and I was thus compelled to do without them. It quite surprised me to be able to." [42]

For another six weeks he worked with "all the care and patience of which I am capable," and on October 19 he dated the last page of the completed score.

[39] For this typical activity as reflected in notes and letters, see *M.E.*, 155–66, and almost any collection of his autographs, from the Paris Conservatoire to Harvard University. Here is a sample: "My dear Monnais — Enclosed the program. Could you prefix a few lines about the hall which will be magnificently decorated, lighted, and heated; whose acoustics will be excellent; and where the ladies will be visible almost from head to toe [low-edged boxes] and hence will dazzle by their gowns? I rely on you for the musical froth. Greetings : Yours, H. B." (*90*, 213–4.)

[40] *M.E.*, 152.

[41] *Ibid.*

[42] *M.E.*, 152. Notice the phrase "begun and pursued across country" which records an experience that may well be the source of the title *A Travers Chants*. As for earlier and later instances of Berlioz' being his own poet-librettist, see the summary below, Subchapter 23.

Depth and Design of the Damnation

> The composer would have led Faust to any spot whatever, had he found the slightest musical reason for doing so.
>
> – From Berlioz' Foreword to *The Damnation of Faust*

Most American listeners know of the *Damnation of Faust* three orchestral excerpts – the Hungarian (Rákóczy) March, The Dance of the Sylphs, and the Minuet of the Will o' the Wisp. To know these is to know rather less than nothing about the work from which they are taken, since their extrusion gives them a false prominence together with a misleading context. When they are played in succession, as they once were on a world-wide network for a war celebration,[1] their effect is like that which might be obtained by reciting Hamlet's three soliloquies in a row.

For the *Damnation of Faust* is a highly organized entity whose parts cast mutual reflections one on another, and whose philosophical purport deserves as much meditation, after full and repeated hearings, as that of *Don Giovanni* or *Tristan*. Not that its aim is to preach. The work may be penetrated on several planes, defined at one level by Sir Thomas Beecham's dictum that it is "a bunch of the loveliest tunes in existence"[2] and at the other by Jean d'Udine's opinion that the work is "a plastic expression of Nature" which "suggests its philosophy indirectly by the lucid and vivid rendering of a symbolic drama."[3]

In France, where it has become the best known of Berlioz' large works, where it is indeed "popular" and a money-making score, it is undoubtedly taken as a "concert opera" whose central situation has been learned from Gounod's *Faust*, and whose music has come to be known by ear from Edouard Colonne's unrelenting repetition of the score beginning in 1877.[4] Two of Berlioz' conditions were thus fulfilled: the "secular scripture" which occasions the music could be taken for granted, and the music was made familiar by frequent hearing.

[1] March 9, 1944 in honor of the U. S. Army Air Force.

[2] *1380*, May 27, 1933.

[3] *568*, 13 and 11. Jean d'Udine is the pseudonym of Albert Cozanet (b. 1870), a theorist and composer who founded an important choral school in Paris in 1909 and has written extensively upon music and musicians.

[4] Between 1877 and 1903 the Colonne orchestra played the work an average of half a dozen times yearly. See Supplement 1.

But the *Damnation* is not an opera, neither a concert opera nor any other kind. It is, as it subtitle shows, a Dramatic Legend adapted to music in keeping with Berlioz' fixed principle.[5] He recast his *Eight Scenes* of 1828 and added to them a dozen more, the twenty scenes being grouped into four main parts, each made continuous by recitatives. The whole aim is compactness: "Berlioz' concision in the *Damnation of Faust* is almost unbelievable, if one considers that in two and a quarter hours so many high-colored tableaux, so many entanglements, are displayed before us. As for their variety, it is naturally very great in an artist who eschews sentimental monotony and is inspired instead by the eternal diversity of the phenomenal world." [6] It is this diversity which nullifies, and ought to prevent, the attempt so often made of carrying the *Damnation* to the stage. Such transfers always involve mutilation, interpolations, utterly needless visual effects — and moreover leave the spectator disappointed.[7] For the drama of the *Damnation* is symbolic, invisible, evocative. Had Berlioz intended an opera, his design would have been notably different; he would not have limited himself to three principals, chorus, and orchestra, and other scenes would have been chosen: we know this on his own authority, in letters relating to the requirements of a true *Faust* opera.[8]

What Berlioz drew for his Legend from Goethe's presentment of the phenomenal world (to use the words of the critic quoted above) falls in with his usual dramatic method. He chose objective situations capable of being translated into music. Thus in the first scene Faust sings of returning spring; in the second he hears peasants singing and dancing under the lindens; in the third he hears an army on the march — through hearing the Rákóczy March itself, which quite naturally forms a rousing finale for this first part. The three scenes are joined by forward-moving recitatives, as well as by a symphonic working up of the three themes

[5] [Twenty] years ago, Mr. Arthur Honegger used the same subtitle for his very similarly constructed score, *Nicolas de Flue*. (American *première*, New York, May 8, 1941.)

[6] *568*, 12.

[7] So said Mr. Richard Capell on seeing Sir Thomas Beecham's adaptation in Covent Garden (*1380*, May 27, 1933). The Paris Opera version, in the repertory since 1921, is a deplorable affair, but at least it does not introduce pieces from *The Infant Christ* into the markedly different music to which Faust is damned. This cobbling up, however, has gone on at Brussels, Monte Carlo, New York, and elsewhere ever since Clarence Gunsbourg started the staging mania in 1893, and produced a forged autograph to prove that he was fulfilling the author's intentions. (*M.E.*, 164.) On his patchwork, see Debussy, *789*, 175–81 and the definitive objections of an English critic in *558*.

[8] From London to Scribe in 1847–8 (*235*, II, 188–93).

(or rather, two themes and one rhythm) the whole constituting our introduction to the character of Faust. In short, the hero-philosopher considers Nature, the joys of the people and the lure of military glory; the "action" is at once particular (psychological) general (dramatic) and musical, for what we hear is the conjunction of a pastoral song, a carol, and a march.

Part II follows Goethe's initial scene in Faust's study. The hero muses on life and death in a *chant récitatif* treated fugally, and is about to take poison [9] when the Easter chorus breaks in and makes him abandon his resolve. He joins in the magnificent six-part chorus which is one of the small masterpieces within the greater. It ends on a heart-rending lament which forecasts both the melodic soliloquy of Faust alone in Gretchen's room and the later Invocation to Nature. The philosophic limits of the drama within which Faust moves have been set: the search for surcease through contemplation, the possession of earthly and divine love, and the pleasures and contingencies of the world.

To implement these last, Mephisto appears without ado, announced by the three sizzling trombone chords which form his spiritual signature.[10] Faust scorns the magic that "the poor demon" can show, but follows him to Auerbach's Cellar. The ensuing succession of musical moods is dazzling by its pace and brilliance. The chorus of drinkers, Brander's song of the rat, the parody "Amen" fugue for the dead rat, Mephisto's political satire on the flea, and the terse recitatives that link them, prove that the young melodic genius of 1828 had ripened into a consummate music-dramatist. As August Halm says: "Berlioz' ability to make the drama come out of the parts and not out of the story – this I call Berlioz' claim to fame as a dramatist. . . . The ideal direction of the whole drama issues from the power of music. . . . This is genuine music drama, as against the plays that are merely 'composed,' the verbal dramas that are 'set to music.' " [11]

[9] Berlioz' words, "Verse-moi le poison qui doit illuminer ou tuer ma raison" bring irresistibly to mind Baudelaire's equally "romantic" lines in *Le Voyage:*

Verse nous ton poison pour qu'il nous réconforte.
  Nous voulons, tant ce feu nous brûle le cerveau
Plonger au fond du gouffre, Enfer ou ciel, qu'importe!
  Au fond de l'Inconnu pour trouver du nouveau.

[10] The cornets and bassoons fill out these syncopated chords. Saint-Saëns, as a professional musician for the stage, could not get over the "stroke of genius" by which Berlioz transfixes Mephisto with three notes. (*1006*, 207.)

[11] *570*, 100. August Halm was a theorist, music critic and conductor in Munich (1869–1929).

The scene shifts magically, invisibly, while the violins alone and four woodwinds trace a brief whirling figure that brings us to the enchantment scene. Mephisto sings the lulling *Voici des roses* to a quiet but threatening accompaniment, entrusted chiefly to the trombones. The effect is a fresh sample of what Beethoven had done in *Fidelio* and Spontini in *La Vestale*. Mephisto's lullaby is now taken up as a variation by the chorus of sylphs and gnomes, who cast their spell on the sleeping Faust. He sees Margaret in a dream and thrice calls her name. This variation ends *ppp*, after which a third one begins, instrumental only – our familiar excerpt, Dance of the Sylphs, which is as it were the echo of the preceding.[12]

In a short recitative the awakened Faust demands a sight of the living Margaret. Mephisto bids him join the passing throng. A march rhythm in pizzicato is heard, briefly traversed by a chromatic bassoon phrase that ushers in the soldiers' chorus, soon followed by the student song in Latin which Berlioz wrote (both words and music) in Breslau. Then, by a device Berlioz especially liked, the two choruses are heard together, the students accompanied by the brass, the soldiers by the woodwinds, brief pauses having been artfully left for this overlapping. Each song keeps its own tonality during the ensemble and each its rhythm, respectively 6/8 and 2/4, while the strings scan the two common beats.[13] "The whole reaches an intensity of life, a tumultuousness of action, and a musical dynamism absolutely unheard of before Berlioz."[14] This musical slice of life dies away to a return of the bassoon theme over the throbbing beat of the strings: it is the end of the second part.

Part III begins *ex abrupto* with Faust in Margaret's chamber. He sings (as in Goethe) a hymn of thanks to twilight, the friend of lovers; after which comes a purely Berliozian invention – the long undulating melody for strings with a linear modulation, whose mood prepares us for Margaret's entrance. But the meeting is not yet. She appears and remains alone, her recitative telling of her premonition of evil and of the lover she has seen in a dream. The music hints phrases of the later love song. Gretchen now sings of faithful lovers in the ballad of the King of Thule.

[12] This musical idea is a favorite one of Berlioz'. In *Lélio* the "Aeolian Harp," in the *Requiem* the *Quid sum miser* are variation-echoes of the number they follow. Hence the relative futility of playing these pages by themselves.

[13] The instrumental distribution recalls the *Francs-Juges* overture, and the melodic combining had occurred in several of his previous scores, but the dramatic idea may have been suggested by a performance of Monsigny's *Le Déserteur* which Berlioz saw and highly praised in 1843.

[14] *561*, 40.

This is the haunting, quasi-modal tune that Berlioz wrote in Dauphiné just after his discovery of *Faust* in 1827.[15]

At this point Mephisto takes charge of the innocent girl: he calls up the spirits of evil in a stern Evocation, and sets them to dance the Minuet of the Will o' the Wisp. This, as d'Udine pointed out is "the first instance of absolute impassiveness known in music." It is the original *ballet mécanique* – "music fit to frighten, made of sharp, cutting rhythms, of mysterious gusts which swell and collapse suddenly, of brief strident cries, and of total insensibility. . . . These melodic flare-ups and intermittent bursts seem to obey the command of a diabolical master and take on I know not what aspect of fascinating and cruel hardness."[16] Certainly, coming as it does after Mephisto's directions to the malignant Kobolds, the piece can stand the critic's reading-in of demonic intent. It makes one think of the different but equally infernal music that Mozart wrote for the Commandatore – and one thinks no further: the common (or Covent Garden) variety of operatic devil has no kinship with these two.

Not content with spectral manifestations, Mephisto sings Gretchen "a moral song, to mislead her more certainly." This serenade Berlioz had also written for his earlier score, to a guitar accompaniment. He rescored it, replacing the guitar by a small orchestra which concertizes with the large.

After this ditty has ended on a sardonic "Ha!" from the chorus, a very short recitative between Faust and Gretchen leads to their love duet, which acts as both a recognition and a seduction scene.[17] The twenty bars of this last phase of the human drama drop without warning into an extremely vigorous trio and finale representing the neighbors' discovery of the lovers. Faust repeats (and spoils by a trite coda) his beautiful love lament, but he is overborne by the voices of the crowd, in which

[15] The subtitle is "Chanson Gothique," which has excited some critics' risibilities because it is not, of course, a restoration or imitation of the Goths' presumable love tunes. Berlioz never thought it was. The adjective *gothique* was used till late in nineteenth-century France to mean "popular," "of folk origin." (See Delacroix's *Journal* and Sainte-Beuve, *passim.*) Berlioz' ballad has the "breathings" exactly where an untaught country girl would put them – hence his first note to the score asked that it be sung "without expression," *i.e.*, without expression *laid on* – and it ends, like so many French and Italian country tunes, with an "Ah!"

[16] *568*, 13.

[17] This duet is not at first especially winning, partly because it contains echoes-in-reverse from the later *Carmen*, partly because its psychological compression is possibly too great. But like much else in Berlioz, it improves on further acquaintance.

Margaret's pleas and Mephisto's sarcastic advice only increase the ordered confusion. It is needless to point out that the swiftness of this combined climax and denouement in three hundred and fifty bars, very lightly scored until near the end, is, except for the repeat, utterly unoperatic: the action is in the mind's ear.

The forsaken Gretchen opens the fourth and last part with her "romance" based on *Meine Ruh' ist hin* but not treated as a spinning song. In form and dramatic power, the song compares with any great lied of Schubert's, Schumann's or Wolf's.[18] The close "*O caresse de flamme*" reaches the sublime effortlessly and justifies the description of the whole as "music of touching simplicity and ardor."[19] With no break, the last repetition of the refrain on the English horn joins a muffled rhythm on the timpani with which we are already familiar: it is the soldiers roaming the streets. In the distance they sing fragments of their wenching song. Bugles (really horns and trumpets) blow taps as Margaret laments the end of another day when her lover has failed to come. Bits of the students' chorus mingle with her despair as the English horn melody twice tries to reach completion and falls both times into the marching rhythm.[20]

There is a pause and we are with Faust among the "rocks and woods" which Goethe makes the setting for his scene. Faust addresses to Nature, majestic and indifferent, the spiritual longings that no experience has yet satisfied. The lines in French are by Berlioz himself and worthily express the pantheistic faith which he poured out in the music.[21] A new height

[18] Early recordings of this song helped break the monopoly of the "three excerpts" and served as "a reminder of the magnificent music there is to be found in the Berlioz opera." *N. Y. Times*, Feb. 15, 1948.

[19] *Ibid.*

[20] Here one may note the parting of the ways for those whose idea of art is of something uniformly sweet and remote from life. Thus the excellent critic Jacques Rivière, writing to his friend Alain Fournier in 1905 when both were at college and saturated with the symbolist spirit—". . . Berlioz is absolutely devoid of taste. For example, after the admirable plaint of Margaret, *d'amour l'ardente flamme*, he has gone and thought up the idea of sticking in bugles playing taps! That, I tell you, beats everything. It's impossible to destroy more brutally the impression one has just created. It's such an enormous absence of tact that it puts you in a bad humor." (*193*, I, 200.)

[21] Nature immense, impénétrable et fière,
Toi seule donnes trêve à mon ennui sans fin;
Sur ton sein tout-puissant, je sens moins ma misère,
Je retrouve ma force et je crois vivre enfin.
Oui, soufflez ouragans, torrents, précipitez vos ondes,
Croulez rochers, criez forêts profondes,
A vos bruits souverains, ma voix aime à s'unir.
Forêts, rochers, torrents, je vous adore; mondes

is reached here at a bound and sustained through ten pages of unequalled power. This cry of a soul as desolate as Pascal's in the face of the infinite spaces ends on a hypodorian cadence which superbly renders the feeling of unsatiated aspiring. Suddenly we startle to the chilling sound of Mephisto's voice telling Faust that Gretchen has poisoned her mother. As the rapid dialogue flashes between the two, remorse on one side, cynical amusement on the other, one hears hunting horns in the distance: they accompany the tragedy without being part of it.[22]

Under the weight of this new horror – for Gretchen, says Mephisto, used the drug as a sleeping potion in hopes her lover would visit her – Faust consents to make a pact with the demon if he will save her. "What matters tomorrow, if I am racked in the present hour." But we never rejoin Gretchen. We plunge with Faust and Mephisto toward the abyss, in a hurtling but wholly symbolic "ride." As it proceeds, with the strings that give the rhythm but not the pounding of horses' hoofs, Faust's monotone is embroidered by a lament on the oboe, the voices of praying women and children are drowned out, and weird dissonances in the brass prepare us for the supernatural. It is the sole movement in the entire work which belongs to the category of the fantastic. With a single resonant chord given out by the whole orchestra but held by the winds,

> On a sudden open fly
> With impetuous recoil and jarring sound
> The infernal doors, and on their hinges grate
> Harsh thunder, that the lowest bottom shook
> Of Erebus.[23]

The scene is Pandemonium and the Princes of Darkness sing in the unknown tongue to which Swedenborg refers, and which Berlioz reinvented for his purposes.[24] Yet the atmosphere is not what one would

---

> Qui scintillez, vers vous s'élance le désir
> D'un coeur trop vaste et d'une âme altérée
> D'un bonheur qui la fuit.

[22] "This indifference on the part of nearby humanity . . . forms a musical commentary sufficient to freeze us with horror." (*568*, 12.)

[23] *Paradise Lost*, Bk. II, l. 879 ff.

[24] Berlioz did not say, as his commentators have supposed, that he had found this speech in Swedenborg, but only the idea of it. Berlioz' first essay with mysterious syllables goes back to the Italian journey, when he composed lines for his Chorus of Shades in *Lélio* which the border police took for a revolutionary code. In 1846 he returned to the idea of such vocables for his *Faust* and supplied French words for the Shades. (See *690*.) The work of Swedenborg's that Berlioz read must have been the Spiritual Diary, also called *Memorabilia*, *1224*, 262–7.

expect. Faust's reception has at first a certain grandeur and it conveys a certain macabre excitement, but what follows lacks the fiery-festive *élan* we associate with the keepers of brimstone. For Berlioz conceived the infernal regions as a sort of awkward middle-class party trying to romp and be gay. As Halm wittily remarks, "The rhythm is willing, but the harmony is weak." [25] Then the rhythm itself breaks down in despair and the music whines. Gradually, the lost souls pick up courage and attempt a fanatic religious dance, Scythian style, in 3/4 time, to which they sing a lifeless chorus which ends in the hush of fear before their master. The whole is a hymn to odious desolation; or in other words, sixty years before Shaw's *Man and Superman*, Berlioz shows us that Hell is dullness, stupidity, and weakness of will.

The dramatic legend does not end on this note. In an Epilogue on earth, a reciter tells us very tersely that the mystery of Faust's perdition took place and that quiet was restored below. This affords a transition of sixteen bars to the final Scene in Heaven, where Gretchen is received in forgiveness for having loved so well. The divine melody of her translation is the one which woke Berlioz in the middle of the night at Prague, and we may well share his anxiety at the thought that he might forget it.[26]

How faithful, one must ask, is this kaleidoscope of musical forms composed to Goethe's drama? Is it a whole, or is it a haphazard exploitation of whatever is picturesque in the philosophical poem? In the first place, Berlioz made it clear that he was no more setting Goethe's drama than he had set Shakespeare's *Romeo*. As he explained in his one-page foreword to the score, no dramatic work can be made into music-drama without extensive alterations. Moreover, although he acknowledged the profound effect that reading Goethe had had upon him, he reserved the right to modify the legend precisely as Goethe had done before him.[27] Berlioz has Faust damned (since the expiatory second part of *Faust* is outside his purview) he omits Valentin, the duel and the infanticide, and he places the compact with the Devil nearly at the end, under the pressure of Gretchen's reported suffering.

[25] *570*, 91.

[26] He did not forget it, but the Paris public usually does, clapping loud and long before the end. Mr. Ernest Newman also forgot it when he wrote that "the work ends with a macabre ride to the abyss." (*845*, III, 164.)

[27] Berlioz cited Marlowe's *Faustus* as a previous treatment which did not stay Goethe's hand. Later the composer regretted having explained himself to "people who need to have it proved that one had no intention of draining the Caspian Sea or blowing up Mont Blanc." (*Min. Sc.*, Avant-Propos; *M.C.*, 202; and *Mem.*, II, 261.)

Despite these liberties which Berlioz took for translating an action into music, he adhered very faithfully to the form and spirit of his model. Goethe's form is the Shakespearean "open construction" pushed to its ideal limit. Lacking the aid of the spectator's imagination there is no more "continuity" in the two poets than there is in Berlioz without the hearer's. But Berlioz has condensed the drama still further to three characters (the role of Brander in the Auerbach Scene is a mere vocal contrast by means of the bass register) and a sequence of "moments" in which music and action can be wedded in a single form.

The true continuity of the work is twofold: by the art of the musical psychologist each character has his own "speech," *e.g.*, Faust's recitatives and melodies are Faustlike throughout. In the second place, by the art of the symphonic composer, the score is unified through thematic recall, repeat, and echo. From beginning to end, numberless ornaments, rhythms, and timbres act as unobtruded leitmotives to make the music one texture. This naturally does not appear on a first or second hearing.[28] At first everything seems episodic, undirected, discrete. But this is a superficial impression due to the pace, the variety, and the force of invention unremittingly displayed.

With Goethe's poem before us, we can learn from the *Damnation of Faust* what those situations were that Berlioz thought implicitly musical. The nine songs, first, then eight or nine more occasions which clearly suggested music – pastoral scenes: the opening reverie and the hymns to twilight and to nature;[29] then charms and spells,[30] love dialogue and its sequels,[31] moody introspection,[32] and lastly the ride to the abyss.[33] For two further scenes, Berlioz had only the barest hint, in one line each: the compact in the open heath with hunters' horns nearby was doubtless suggested by the scene where Faust pities Gretchen "in misery . . . despair . . . delivered up to . . . condemning, unfeeling Man."[34] Musical vividness required that Faust's sense of "unfeeling" be rendered palpable by indifferent activity, the hunt. Finally, Berlioz felt like Mozart in *Don Giovanni* that the action must not end on the clanging gates of

[28] Rivière, for instance, wrote: ". . . The only link, I believe, that one can discover, is a recall of the first theme in the second and last parts." (*193*, I, 199.) There are in fact dozens of reminiscent links.

[29] Scenes I, VIII, and XIV of Goethe's text, which is full of musical hints.

[30] Scenes III and XXI.

[31] XII and XIX.

[32] I and VIII.

[33] XXIV.

[34] XXIII: "A Field."

hell, but should be framed off by a reflective Epilogue, on earth and in heaven. Gretchen's cry, "Ye angels, holy cohorts, guard me," and the reply "She is saved!" were enough to occasion the final chorus of angels.[35]

The two dramas, poetic and musical, are thus proportional though not congruent; and their spiritual import is equivalent, not identical. That the *Damnation* has been charged with lack of philosophic depth is due to a very literary idea of musical meaning. Had Berlioz set philosophic *words* to almost any music whatever, most persons would call the result deep. It would have struck him as shallow. Any given scene illustrates Berlioz' entirely different conception of philosophic depth in music – as the critic saw who thus describes Mephisto's serenade: "A musician could write for it a melody more or less sarcastic, having in itself no specific virtue and attaining no farther than the usual opera piece. That is what Gounod did. Or again, one could have tried to indicate by means of an orchestral paraphrase, by a contrapuntal complexity, and by a mosaic of leitmotives the work of perversion and the black machinations of Hell. A German composer would have done just that. Berlioz did otherwise. He kept to the form of the traditional serenade – but what a guitar he fashioned for it! The whole quartet of strings, scraping furiously, seems to say 'this is a serenade, only a serenade,' but the dry pizzicati, dismally brutish, add a flavor of death: sensation here does all the cruel work."[36]

There was of course the formal possibility of summing up in a number of instrumental or choral movements the composer's idea of the several characters, each typified by a single theme. That is what Liszt did, and Schumann; it is also Wagner's later system. But instead of this subjective or discursive "concentration on the feelings . . . Berlioz moves our hearts and minds by first striking our senses with a whole world of sharp, concrete objects. The advantage of such a system is twofold: it permits concision and it insures variety."[37]

The difficulty of this simple method is that it requires the hearer to reflect, and to reflect upon accurate perceptions. Take an example from the close of Part II: the soldiers sing of girls and glory; the students sing of girls and gaiety; the two songs once established, they mingle. But when we hear them the second time, the recurrent dying fall on the brass which accompanies the students' song, coming between the shouts of the soldiers,

[35] Goethe's Scene XXV. This desire for a frame around the tragic picture being evident in artists such as Mozart and Berlioz, those portions of their respective works are frequently cut in performance by people who obviously know more than the masters.

[36] *568*, 11–12.

[37] *568*, 10.

imparts to the ensemble a desolate, forlorn, almost suicidal character which is as profound a moral comment as the sorrow of Ecclesiastes. Each of Berlioz' songs or movements is thus double: it is an object and an embodied criticism upon it. The ballad of the King of Thule is a folk song, but listen to the double basses and the countersubject for viola, both musically appropriate, yet full of foreboding. Or again in Gretchen's lonely plaint, love, memory, and the innocent vulgarity of the girl herself — expressed in the *gruppetti* — work up to the climacteric utterance, ennobled by passion, on the words " — and in his arms to die."

The merit of the method is that the idea resides in the music, and the success of the artist is that he was both purposeful and nonsystematic about what he was doing. He did not, in penning the students' song, say to himself, "Here is where I preach the vanity of sensual delights by means of cornets." Rather, he felt at once the lure and the futility of roistering, as Goethe did, and in seeking to reproduce them objectively he found the timbre and cadence that answered.[38] The degree of this self-knowledge obviously varied. The pantheistic Invocation was the core of Berlioz' philosophy but he struggled long before he extracted from the simple means that he chose to use the tremendous result we now hear.[39] An artist's technical imagination, so to speak, grows with the years. In the first version of Mephisto's serenade, as we saw, the blithe malicious tune had a guitar accompaniment. In the *Damnation*, the guitar consists of the sixty strings of the orchestra and the chorus of devils chimes in on the second refrain. But Berlioz goes further, and it is here that the listener must keep pace with the composer: in this refrain, Berlioz scores a false start on the flute which stops the chorus while Mephisto goes on: for a reason that defies analysis this is devilry incarnate. Rhythm and form carry the connotation with not a single imitative detail.

The entire score deserves study from this point of view.[40] For although our knowing the story of Faust and our hearing some of the words help to still our whys and wherefores, they do not provide the clue to the inherently, musically, "characteristic" elements. Just as in an unnamed symphony we say "the last movement is based on a chorale treated thus

[38] For confirmation, note the vocal expression of the same feeling in Faust's recitative "*Assez, fuyons ces lieux où la parole est vile . . .*" (*Min. Sc.*, 132, bb. 2 ff.) One thinks of the "vulgar tavern musick which," says Sir Thomas Browne, "makes one man merry and another mad, but struck him with a deep devotion."

[39] Available separately on records *1424, 1425, 1426*.

[40] See the admirable analysis of the opening movement by Jules Combarieu: *779*, 285–305.

and so," here as analysts we should say "lullaby, love song, lament, serenade, invocation, headlong ride, march, choir of angels," and so forth.[41] The upshot would be a reconstruction of the dramatic purport of the *Damnation*, which in turn would suggest its "philosophy," as follows:

Part I — Man in Nature: the simple life and the path of glory and power. Faust rejects the last, but

Part II — he is tempted by doubts, bewitched by sensuality and dreams of love.

Part III — Gretchen, who feels and represents the love that Faust only dreams, is transfigured and destroyed by it under worldly law. Meanwhile

Part IV — Faust has reverted to self-torturing in the face of nature, and is justly damned for his failure to rescue Gretchen; whereas she is saved.

This "philosophy" is the more persuasive in that Berlioz did not consciously force it into plot or words but let it express *him*, through his choice of musical scenes and their treatment. One is incidentally struck by the similarity of meaning between this sequence of scenes and that of the *Symphonie Fantastique*, also inspired by a reading of *Faust*. The Berlioz version of Goethe's drama is interpreted by d'Udine as the working out of "psychological justice" in contradistinction to Providential justice and Fatalism alike,[42] and the consistency of Berlioz' outlook is all the more evident that even in dealing with the specific Faust theme he deviates somewhat from Goethe. In both poems, Faust's odyssey exemplifies the romanticist creed of experience and action; it vindicates love above prudence and pleasure while asserting moral responsibility and recognizing evil as a positive force to be fought.[43] Berlioz likewise shares Goethe's esthetic respect for the forms of the Catholic Christian religion and feels humble before its human wisdom, though lacking the faculty for accepting its dogma. He adds his private discovery that Hell is dullness. But the core of the two dramatists' *Weltanschauung* is their pantheistic worship of nature, and here their expressions diverge. Berlioz interprets the cosmos as being more indifferent than Faust felt it to be. From the very opening, Berlioz' Invocation reminds us of the baffled Faust who cries, "*Wo fass*

[41] Who can hear or remember the words of ensembles — whether *Viva la libertà* in Mozart or the Easter chorus and Concert of Sylphs in Berlioz?

[42] *568*, 13.

[43] It seems likely that Goethe was purging his remorse at the abandonment of his youthful love, Frederike. Was Berlioz thinking of Harriet?

ich dich, unendliche Natur"; rather than of the later "*Erhabener Geist.*" It is not fanciful to find in the twenty-seventh bar of the piece [44] an intimation that the musician felt his adoration of the impassive world to be a presumptuous fallacy. The invoker resembles Shakespeare's Timon of Athens, who says:

> Common mother, thou
> Whose womb unmeasurable, and infinite breast,
> Teems, and feeds all; whose self-same mettle,
> Whereof thy proud child, arrogant man, is puffed. . . .[45]

Indeed, the inspiration of Shakespeare is everpresent behind the work of both the nineteenth-century artists. It is from him they both learned that verse, prose, catches, rhetoric, dialogue, and fanfares could combine into a coherent unified work of art, provided that psychology, inherent expressiveness, and imaginative truth were sustained.[46]

Similarly, Berlioz had learned from Beethoven the art of enhancing the value of successive musical numbers by making them "diversely beautiful," [47] by using all the resources of the orchestra and all the forms of musical discourse. The result entitles us to conclude with an English critic that "the more one studies . . . '*cette magnifique Damnation de Faust*' as M. Gounod calls it, the more one marvels and likes, the more one discovers to admire. There is lovelier music in the *Romeo and Juliet;* there are greater aims and larger effects in the *Requiem;* there is nobler drama in the *Troyens*, with a loftier style and a simpler perfection of technical inspiration and achievement. But in variety and completeness, in movement and romance, in life and color and charm, the *Damnation* is unrivalled, not only among the works of Berlioz himself, but as it seems to us, by anything produced by the masters of symphony since Beethoven." [48]

Mention of Beethoven and the symphony appropriately introduces the question of form. The *Damnation of Faust* has marked affinities with the Dramatic Symphony. But in *Romeo and Juliet* the orchestral and the vocal elements were balanced in a recurrent interweaving. Here the human voice predominates throughout, for which reason the work has no over-

[44] The bass rises to G under a persistent B flat while the D comes down to C, forming a cavernous fourth though only a few strings and the bassoons accompany the voice. (*Min. Sc.*, 339 b. 1.)

[45] Act IV, Sc. iii.

[46] The reader will remember that the *Eight Scenes* of 1828 were sandwiched between successive pairs of quotations from Shakespeare.

[47] *A Trav.*, 75.

[48] *556.*

ture: it opens with seven bars of Faust's pastoral theme, given to the violas in unison before he himself sings it in somewhat altered form, richly accompanied. Yet within the score the purely orchestral moments are numerous, though brief; the three concert excerpts are merely the detachable ones among many. Of these three, one occurs in each of the first three parts; the fourth part being preponderantly vocal as is fitting for a finale. To mark the close of each part, Berlioz has adroitly chosen numbers of some massiveness: the first ends with the March (another reason why an orchestral overture would have been redundant), the second ends with the joint choruses of soldiers and students; the third ends with the three solo voices in conflict with the mob that breaks off the love scene – the only scene that shows a touch of the operatic.

For the fourth and last close (Gretchen's Apotheosis in Heaven) Berlioz wished an additional chorus of two or three hundred children, which would give that power-in-softness he desired, as well as sustain the burden of concluding. This choral close balances the Easter Chorus in Part II, just as the orchestral March and Minuet balance each other in I and III. The first three parts open with Faust, the last – in which Faust sinks to perdition – with Gretchen; each opening is individual and characteristic and marks a leap forward in the drama, just as each closing is collective, anonymous, and, except the last one, tragically soulless. In short the whole arrangement betrays a masterly plan.

Within each part also, one can see the effect of "all the patience and care" Berlioz mustered. The alternation of vocal registers and of solos, with ensembles, recitatives, and purely orchestral interludes, shows the same skill in providing rest through contrast, the same love of subtle preparation and resolution, the same urge to construct "one work," which we have seen gaining strength ever since his Opus 1.[49] When one knows the *Damnation*, it is inconceivable that any other fragment by Berlioz could be inserted into it. In the Dramatic Legend, to be sure, the outline of the four-movement symphony which was still perceptible in *Romeo* is no longer present. Part I of *Faust* does contain a symphonically developed section, just as Part II contains a set of variations, but their intent, like that of all the other parts and sections, is dictated by drama on the one hand, and on the other by these considerations of balance, preparation, and conclusion, which have just been enumerated.

These are of course the original, primitive, and eternal considerations

[49] Marnold concedes Berlioz real merit in this branch of artistry, but for reasons of his own does not consider this to have much to do with the art of music. (*460*, 362.)

that have governed the elaboration of all forms from the most rigid, the fugue, to the most nearly improvisatory, the toccata. But the conservative always asks whether music will not cease to be music if it abandons the set patterns. When Berlioz was fashioning his dramatic works under the guidance of musical instinct and the fundamental conditions of structure, Adolphe Adam was still arguing that Rossini was a greater artist than Beethoven because Beethoven had no regard for forms.[50] The assumption seems to be that musical substance is so fluid that if the arbitrary frontiers and signposts are removed art will perish. A distinguished lecturer once said, analyzing at sight the Mozart piano trio in B flat: "We now come to the contrasting second theme." But there was no second theme. In its place Mozart had given the violin the first theme in a different key. This lessened the contrast while introducing a new artistic element: the unexpected. It did not spoil the form — it varied it; but it upset the lecturer, and this is as dangerous as the offense Samuel Butler calls "a wound in the solicitor."

The issue of form is indeed so disturbing that one seldom finds it clearly put. That four-letter word acts like the bite of the tarantula, and those who remain calm are only displaying the serenity of souls armored against reason. To make matters worse, nearly everyone seems to have interested motives for saying that form is a mystery inaccessible to simple mortals; it even appears that great artists were deficient in it, while scholars, especially the heaven-born tribe of academic musicians, possess it by nature.[51] Finally, since Pater's unfortunate and ignorant hypothesis, music is widely held to represent "pure form" — whatever that may mean — and success in it to betoken marked powers of construction.[52] The truth is that most musical forms have been imposed from outside upon a material which is very malleable, and that the instinct for what is inherently musical remains, as Koechlin says, elusive and diverse.[53]

[50] "Beethoven . . . composed admirable symphonies . . . but he composed only symphonies. His sonatas and quartets are more or less developed symphonies scored for more or fewer players. It is useless to cite his Mass and his *Fidelio*. *Fidelio* is not an opera but an admirable symphony, in which the voices play a subordinated role . . . The Mass is no more a vocal work than is the Choral Symphony." (*1383*, 1841, 386.)

[51] In academic halls one hears it said of Meredith's sixteen-line sonnets in *Modern Love*, "of course they are not sonnets," though an earlier lesson states that the *original* sonnet form varied from twelve to twenty-five lines. Nor is the academic point made simply on behalf of nomenclature, but against Meredith's "sense of form."

[52] For an attempt to make matters clearer, see Supplement 6.

[53] *729*, 632 and *452*, 120.

These are some of the reasons for the confusion and the acrimony of the debate which a Berlioz was bound to find raging about him. As a dramatic musician coming after Beethoven's expansion of the symphony into a vocal-instrumental genre, Berlioz could only further and complete the fusion of expressive elements. The very social structure of the nineteenth century impelled him to it. After the bourgeois revolutions, Haydn's resident orchestra at Esterhazy castle could no longer be the prevailing medium of musical production, nor was the new, public orchestra any longer a thing remote from the cathedral choir and the resources of the metropolitan opera. Rapid transport and the secularization of belief had combined with the presence of a paying public to abolish this earlier segregation: all conceivable musical elements could now meet under Berlioz' baton. In his work, accordingly, all known forms and devices coexist and cross-fertilize: the folk song with refrain, the *durchcomponirtes lied,* the six- or eight-part chorus (accompanied or *a cappella*); the march, waltz, or minuet; the recitative and *chant récitatif;* the major-minor system and the modes; the sonata-allegro, the fugue, the free variation and the unifying leitmotif; the virtuoso voice, the choir, the organ, and the orchestra. Music, in short, had established its great lexicon and declared its right to free speech.

It is not likely that a man who dealt constantly in his writings with the questions of form presented in Beethoven, and who composed the massive portions of his own works with the care for unity and coherence that we have seen, should on the smaller scale of a single movement have lacked the qualities he displayed elsewhere. Yet it has been assumed that he did lack them, an assumption due to the fact that he was carrying forward Beethoven's musical re-formation even before Beethoven was fully understood. In the very first movement of his first symphony, Berlioz reinforces unity by welding a phrase of the Introduction into the theme of the ensuing allegro, by combining a single motif with the material of five contrasted movements and by superimposing (in the last) two widely divergent themes in the course of a double fugue.[54] Berlioz was certainly setting himself as many problems as any theorist could desire, and apart from one or two stumbles which we noted, he solved them for the greater good of the guild.

He likewise met the demand for coherence, but here complications arise which cannot be unraveled by reference to Beethoven; for Berlioz

[54] *Min. Sc.*, 214 ff. Compare the similar combination of two melodic fragments in the Ninth Symphony, last movement.

was a different temperament, working on different materials, namely, his own distinctive melody. The development formulas he learned at school or studied in Beethoven were thereby rendered useless for his purpose, for they imply short figures or themes, which grow by addition, by being twisted and turned one bit at a time, in order to arrive at an unfolding, a large-sized melodic (or harmonic) culmination.

Berlioz works on the contrary with a completed statement from the beginning. Perceiving the true nature of his material he saw that the regular German way would not do for him, and that he must abandon even the idea of a "development section." Better than some of his successors, who were also lyricists,[55] he knew how tedious it would be to hack away at his long phrases like a sailor picking oakum, and go mechanically through the motions revealed in the German phrase "*thematische Arbeit.*" The admirable side of the German classical technique might be called synthesis: it builds up from a germ the full-blown flower. Berlioz' way is analytic: he develops his themes by total or partial transformation, by reduction, by parthenogenesis, and he does this throughout an overture or movement, rather than in a designated spot. If sought for at the usual point the expected *Arbeit* will not be found, and the hasty reader will conclude that Berlioz was incapable of development. The truth is that Berlioz uses all the devices of development and more, and by the time he has finished with a musical idea it has both yielded all it contained and struck out new shoots. In the opening scene of the *Damnation* for instance, the seventeen variations or returns of the theme constitute a completely adequate analysis of it. It is a full "development" even though arrived at by an inversion of the usual method; and the interruption of its treatment after forty bars, only to recall it after another thirty – which happens again more briefly – satisfies our wish for symmetry. Despite an apparent confusion adapted to the dramatic purpose, the handling gives us statement, episode, and return: it is perfect form.[56]

This is a relatively simple instance. Elsewhere, as in the Minuet (to which, by the way, Berlioz restores the grave pace of pre-Haydn days), the interderivations of the several motives and their modification by

[55] *E.g.*, Brahms and Tchaikovsky. Liszt occupies a middle place in this regard; Wagner is of course in the short-theme tradition.

[56] Mr. Newman came to the same conclusion about the allegedly programmatic "Royal Hunt and Storm," finding it formally more satisfactory than a Brahms symphonic movement. Obviously there are two (or more) criteria of perfect form, depending on one's view of the materials and the purposes of art.

timbre and rhythm are more difficult to grasp, especially if the name Minuet arouses very definite expectations. Yet "form," and regular form at that, is not hard to find: Berlioz keeps the traditional alternation of motifs, and using the repeats for sinister emphasis (the dynamics aiding) goes on to a lyrical section which corresponds to the old trio, after which he returns to the first motif. This he allows to "fall apart" so that – and in this Beethoven was first – he finds occasion for a sort of coda, presto, in 4/4 time, heralding the serenade which we are about to hear from Mephisto, on a theme introduced earlier.[57]

Throughout, the principle of the "thematic catalogue," first used in the Dramatic Symphony, *Romeo*, is adapted to the needs of the Dramatic Legend of Faust, where it replaces the routine transitions and standard couplings that Berlioz scorned. Hence the charge of fragmentariness or patchwork ceases to be plausible when the whole work lies well in the ear. It is fair enough that Berlioz should not eat his cake and have it too – be an innovator and succeed like Mendelssohn – but it is temperament as much as reflection that impelled him to seek compression without loss of clarity. Aristocratic in gait, Berlioz' muse prefers to skip intermediaries when they can be "understood." Being thus elliptical, he runs the risk of being obscure, but it is the obscurity of wit, not of unawareness.[58]

As Schumann observed, it is usually in his harmony that Berlioz allows himself the most startling discontinuity – as in quantum mechanics or the divided palette of a Delacroix. For example in the Pandemonium of the *Damnation*, he leaps from a B major chord held by the whole orchestra and chorus to a lightning figure for string basses written in F.[59] That the effect is dramatically successful does not make it any more a violation of coherence than Shakespeare's hurtling sequence of images in "To be or not to be." To condemn the latter as "mixed metaphor" or the former as technical ignorance of the rules of modulation would be to argue against evidence of the same artists' power to sustain metaphor and to modulate.[60] Worse, to object would be to overlook in the incriminated

[57] *Min. Sc.*, 219 bb. 1–10.

[58] He sometimes seems afraid of his own tendency and puts in links to lessen the shock – as Schoenberg finds he has to do: "There was at hand from the start a sufficient amount of motival forms and their derivatives, rather too much than too little. The task, therefore, was to retard the progress of the development in order to enable the average listener to keep in mind what preceded, so as to understand the consequences." (*868*, 74–6.)

[59] *Min. Sc.*, 389 bb. 4–5.

[60] It is true that in our day, as in the eighteenth century, Shakespeare has been deemed an incompetent artist who did not know how to develop an

passages the preparation by means of the previous hectic pace — in Berlioz, namely, by the harsh progressions that scan Mephisto's dialogue with the princes of Hell. In other words, coherence is relative to the character and intensity of the context.

Coherence is likewise a function of the length of line, which in Berlioz as we know is more akin to blank verse than to the couplet or ballad meter. His melodic wing span consequently often stretches beyond the usual limits of tonality and necessarily affects his harmony. As commentators remark, although Mozart's harmony flows more gracefully than that of Berlioz, "Mozart himself could not have dealt with Berlioz' [phrases] as he dealt with his own . . . The curve has altered."[61] Hence the modal or neomodal character of many Berliozian passages and his development of these subtler means of achieving harmonic coherence which were discussed in the last chapter. Whereas the main concern of the classical composer was to bind and brace his piece by key relationships, Berlioz often relied on other elements — timbre, rhythm, and melodic recall. He thus ushers in the last step in freeing form from the single criterion of tonality enharmonically defined; it is the step just preceding twentieth-century pantonality.[62]

All this augments rather than diminishes Berlioz' preoccupation with form.[63] It was no mere lip service to an ideal when he condemned shoddy construction even in Gluck and Weber, or when, during the composition of *Les Troyens*, he wrote to a friend "I am now seeking for the form, without which music does not exist. . . ."[64] In this lifelong search

---

image and create logical structures — a regular Berlioz, in fact. See below, Subchapter 25.

[61] Hadow (*350*, II, 285). See also Constant Lambert: "With Berlioz the harmonic thought is never allowed to cramp or dominate the thematic outline, and that is what his admirers mean when they claim that he is first and foremost a melodist . . . When Berlioz uses a descending chromatic phrase in one of his themes he is not, like Delius, allowing the melodic line to follow meekly a harmonic sequence, nor like Strauss is he merely sliding from one position of a chord to another. He is actually using each degree of the scale for its expressive significance." (*1391*, June 1929, 505.)

[62] This evolution was predicted, if not preached, by Fétis in Paris as early as 1832, possibly as a result of the vistas opened out to him by Berlioz' first works. (*995*, I, 324 ff.)

[63] That he was very critical of his own structure is shown by the changes he made in passages of which we have various versions (*e.g.*, *Herminie* and the *Fantastique*, 1st movement; Rákóczy manuscript and final text; as well as by his discarding the *Rob Roy* and *Tour de Nice* overtures, from which he fashioned the *Harold* allegro and the *Corsair*.

[64] *S.W.*, 30. He addresses the young Gounod on the same subject: "No, my dear Gounod, the faithful expression of feeling does not exclude musical form.

Berlioz was bound to invent new forms – among others, the symphonic poem, which is found not in the *Symphonie Fantastique* as is sometimes said, but in the orchestral song *La Captive*. Berlioz moreover used three structural principles that later came to be recognized as founding new forms: the one designated < >, which Wagner adopted for several of his Preludes and which is originally found in the second movement of *Harold in Italy;* the device I have termed "thematic catalogue" first used in *Romeo* and again, as it were distributed, throughout the *Damnation;* and the allegro-juxtaposition form, frequently found in the overtures and dramatic symphonies.[65]

But Berlioz neither named nor systematized these devices. If he had composed ten symphonies on the *idée fixe* plan of his first two, he would certainly be known as an inventor, but it is noteworthy that he stopped when he had given two different models of the scheme. He retained only the free use of the leitmotif. Again, the Prologue of the Dramatic Symphony is a first sketch, both for Wagner's Prologue to the *Ring*, and for Berlioz' own practice in the *Damnation of Faust*, but in the last-named work the principle is preserved without re-employing a Prologue. It would seem as if this dislike of exact repetition marked the inventor, whereas frequent identical reproduction marks rather the exploiter – whence a possible inference as to misplaced credit. But credit is less important than results, and a glance at Berlioz' successors shows that his teachings in form were not lost. Strauss's *Heldenleben* and *Don Quixote* are closer in conception to Berlioz' first two symphonies than to Liszt's works. Liszt's own *Christus* and *St. Elizabeth* are closer to the Dramatic Symphony and the Dramatic Legend than to the symphonic poem. And we have seen that in the domain of staged opera Wagner and Mous-

---

The shape of the dialogue given your characters was perhaps detrimental to the development of your melody . . . but surely your versifier would have been willing to give his thought another form, which it was your duty to sketch for him. The business of the musician is before all things to make music. . . . In certain cases it may happen that the subject forces the composer to present in a kind of prelude ideas only half exposed, which he intends to develop; but then he must willy-nilly get round to developing them, for what must not be is that the hope of seeing a piece of music begin and end should be continually disappointed." (*M.M.*, 268–9.)

[65] Weingartner: "When the older masters combined two or more themes simultaneously, it was usually in fugal form . . . It is in an entirely free form that Berlioz contrasts two themes with each other . . . a compositional technique that has become very frequent since his day. What fine use Liszt made of his predecessor's device in . . . *Tasso* . . . and how magnificently do the three main themes ring out at the end of the Prelude to *Meistersinger!*" (*394*, 200–1.)

sorgsky owe a good deal to Berlioz' form, without their own genius for modification being in the least impaired.

Berlioz would have been the first to say that he had created nothing *ex nihilo* but had taken tradition at its farthest point and added to it in the immemorial way of "descent with modification." He was in this respect a traditionalist like Beethoven; like him he preferred form to be "a hidden presence," and he could have shown if need be that the *Damnation of Faust* was an offshoot of the Choral Ninth and *Fidelio* via the dramatic symphony.

18. Song in Time of Revolution

October 1846
to June 29, 1848

That singular Republic of 1848, which managed to shoot down, imprison, or deport all the real republicans, leaving at the head of affairs only royalists.

— SAINTE-BEUVE in 1869

THE *Damnation of Faust* was ready to be heard by the end of November 1846. To a journalist, possibly one of the Escudier brothers, who published music as well as the weekly *France Musicale*, and who had turned suddenly favorable to Berlioz, the composer dashed off a typical preconcert note:

DEAR FRIEND,

Here are three notices just as they come. I am groggy with making arrangements. We rehearse all day today, but I shall try to go and see you about four o'clock. Yours . . .[1]

To d'Ortigue Berlioz also wrote, saying that if he were to quote anything it should be the verses: *Nature immense, impénétrable et fière.* The article moreover should not stress the daring of his enterprise, but should on the contrary say that this concert form ought to have been tried long since. The "daring" lay in the gigantic risk Berlioz was taking in the production at his own expense of a work which though not an opera was of comparable dimensions, and which was to provide the sole entertainment of the afternoon.

He had hired the Opéra-comique — the only available place — for two Sundays a fortnight apart. The rehearsals were very satisfactory. The tenor Roger sang Faust in excellent style and the other soloists were adequate. Berlioz had a bad turn when it was announced that on the same day as his *première* the students of the Conservatoire were giving a concert for the benefit of flood victims. But the Comte de Montalivet, who was Minister of the Interior and who respected Berlioz, postponed the students' concert. For over a month the "Berlioz press" prepared the public. The Duc de Montpensier and his new duchess notified the composer that

[1] *308*, Aug. 7, 1904, 252–3.

they would attend, and the composer mustered his faithful: Gautier, Janin and the rest.

But the public was not to be wooed. If anything was to take its mind off political agitation and resentment against every established thing, it must be novelties like the English troupe who, in flesh-colored tights, posed in protracted tableaux that the eager viewers agreed to call artistic.[2] In the summer just past, two more attempts had been made on the life of Louis Philippe, bringing the total to seven; while the guerrilla in North Africa which was to be an outlet for restless nationalism remained inconclusive. Revolt was in fact brewing in various parts of Europe, much of it engineered by refugees in Paris. Prussian and Austrian Poland rose; Portugal was rent by civil war; and the Franco-British entente was broken, precisely by the success of the Duc de Montpensier in winning the Spanish princess.

In Paris, business was in depression. "Money was hiding," as the animistic phrase has it. The flood victims were only a few of those suffering from want. High prices and layoffs had provoked a riot in that weathervane district, the Faubourg St. Antoine. No masterpiece, were it ten times as irresistible as the *Damnation* [3] could overcome the fever of uncertainty, the self-centered fear now gripping the Paris bourgeois. Even if the citizen with money in his pocket had wanted to break the current of his gloomy thoughts, he would have turned away from Goethe, Berlioz, and Romanticism, and toward the cozier side of art – toward Scribe or Ponsard for drama, Auber or Clapisson for music.[4] In all the arts, an instinctive regrouping had come about, vaguely known as the School of Common Sense. That the days of Shakespeare and *Faust* were far in the past, Berlioz could feel when he climbed the podium and bowed to a half empty hall.

The performance naturally suffered, though two of the numbers were encored. Berlioz did not despair – yet, for he had a second chance on December 20. But the reviews were more sharply divided than before. Gautier after the dress rehearsal had set the seal on Berlioz' position as the one musician in the vanguard of French art: "With Hugo and Delacroix, he completes the trinity of Romanticism." [5] But the irritable Scudo at the

[2] *1180*, 345.

[3] "The emotion . . . and the drama . . . are eminently human; and both are so brilliantly, so perfectly presented as to be absolutely irresistible." (1885: *556*.)

[4] *Les diamants de la couronne* and *Gibby-la-Cornemuse* by these respective masters were among the successes of the year

[5] *434*, 144 and again 153 and 168.

Revue des Deux Mondes frothed at the mouth. In the lobby, Adam gloated over Berlioz' apparent defeat. Janin ended a truthful report of divided opinion with a superb: "I pity Berlioz and I envy him." [6]

In the face of the disaster, the convinced admirers among professional musicians felt that they must mediate between Berlioz and the public. D'Ortigue, always precise, went into details: "Being wholly absorbed in his innovations, . . . M. Berlioz loses sight of his audience and goes beyond the bounds where their perceptions stop. M. Berlioz is of the stature of the great masters, and has gone farther than Mozart, Beethoven, and Weber, not because he is superior to them, but because in his hands art has taken a step forward . . . He will continue to fight the good fight, but there will always be a gulf between the way in which the mass of the public conceives of art – owing to the theories commonly taught – and the way M. Berlioz conceives it." [7]

Before the next performance it started to snow, so that on December 20 the hall was only a quarter full. Those present formed such a select group that they were enchanted with the music, even though Roger declined to sing the Invocation to Nature.[8] To solace the composer, his admirers organized a banquet presided over by Baron Taylor, and had a gold medal struck in honor of the work. Offenbach made a speech in the name of German music, Osborne in the name of English. The romantic contrast between glory and wretchedness, greatness and misery, could not have been better contrived by fiction. Homage and failure greeted this work which was to be resurrected thirty years later as the productive mainstay of the Colonne repertory, and to be accepted without effort as "the masterpiece which is the *summa* of nineteenth-century French music." [9]

Meantime Berlioz was financially ruined.[10] In a letter to his sister Nanci he could but thinly cover up his profound depression, of which he later said that this indifference of the Parisian public had wounded him more deeply than any previous blow.[11] To insult and misrepresentation he had grown hardened; neglect was more galling. Nor could the investment of

[6] *1386*, quoted in *269*, 137.

[7] *269*, 140.

[8] Thirty-five years later, Roger candidly admitted that "in those days" Berlioz' melody did not seem melodic; now it was "a revelation . . . I used to sing under him, *but I did not understand him.*" (*345*, 190.)

[9] *581*, 117.

[10] The Opéra-comique being small and yielding only 6000 francs when full, Berlioz had doubled the price of tickets, for the cost of copying and performing would together exceed the first day's returns.

[11] *Mem.*, II, 264.

time and energy be recouped by later concerts as he had done for earlier compositions: "There is no concert hall in Paris." This was now true, for the Opera was dead set against Berlioz and controlled the Italian theater, while the Conservatoire, as we know, had made a rule that no "outsider" could use its hall during the season.[12] "Moreover the government is becoming economical in a fashion that was unthinkable five years ago. The Minister in whose jurisdiction the arts are placed cares about them rather less than he does about the grocery business. There is nothing to be done in this ruthless country and I can only hope to leave it as fast as possible . . . I am like a beast of prey, forced to seek my food afar: only barnyard fowl thrive on the manure heap. I have made up my mind. Despite the cold weather, I am going by land next month to St. Petersburg."[13]

A feeling of resentment verging on sour grapes was not Berlioz' sole motive. St. Petersburg had been in his mind for two years past, and even before that time he had been attracted by what was reported of the success of his *Requiem* there.[14] Vernet had visited Russia in 1840 and been well received, and more recently, Balzac had returned from his courting of his future wife, Mme. Hanska, and was extravagant in praise of the country's welcome to artists. "You will not be able," he told Berlioz, "to come back with *less* than 150,000 francs."[15] And as a sort of pledge for his prediction he offered Berlioz the loan of his fur coat.

Before Berlioz could leave he must settle his new debts. Friends helped out: Bertin of the *Débats* advanced five thousand francs; Hetzel, the kind and intelligent publisher of Victor Hugo, a thousand; Adolphe Sax, twelve hundred. On the point of leaving, Berlioz had another gleam of hope that he might after all entrench himself in Paris. Pillet's management of the Opera was doomed, and a public scene by the power behind the throne, the singer Rosine Stoltz, hastened its end.[16] The winning team for the new directorship was Duponchel, former director in the days of *Benvenuto Cellini*, and a mediocre writer named Nestor Roqueplan. This partnership, not as yet appointed, had backing from the Rothschilds as well as from the *Débats*. It could be inferred that Berlioz would be made conductor. This was in fact promised by the eager candidates but soon

[12] *M.E.*, 167.

[13] *M.E.*, 168.

[14] *L.I.*, 193. Produced in 1839, by Romberg, it had earned 5000 francs for the impresario. A few years later the Imperial Chapel had commissioned Berlioz to prepare harmonizations for certain liturgical chants.

[15] *Mem.*, II, 268.

[16] On being hissed she tore her handkerchief with her teeth, shouted defiance to the public, and stalked off. Returning, she met the applause given to a colleague by threatening her with upraised hand.

written off as a pre-election promise. Berlioz must leave France. In February 1847 he wrote to Balzac, taking him up on his offer of the coat, which was duly delivered.[17] It must have been made of *peau de chagrin* if it fitted the thin musician after housing the rotund novelist. At any rate on St. Valentine's day Berlioz set off alone by way of Belgium and Germany. The comic papers signalized the departure of M. Berliozkoff in a bass drum drawn by four horses.[18]

The composer had no expectations on the scale that Balzac forecast and he meant to take every precaution against further loss. Accordingly, he stopped off at Berlin and obtained from the King a letter of introduction to his sister, the Tsarina.[19] The trip thence was extremely uncomfortable and more than usually cold, especially from the Russian frontier onward, four days and nights by sleigh.

A first concert was planned, prepared, and carried off with lightning speed within two weeks of Berlioz' arrival, that is to say on March 15. The Tsarina was present as well as the nobility and the representatives of the arts — a gala occasion which was also a memorable success: "Encores enough to make one dizzy. The program included the *Roman Carnival* Overture, Parts I and II of the *Damnation*, and the *Funeral and Triumphal* Symphony." [20] After shaking the hands of many new friends and drinking a bottle of beer, Berlioz inquired about the receipts: eighteen thousand francs — a clear profit of twelve thousand. "I unconsciously turned my face southwest . . . and murmured, 'Ah, my dear Parisians!' My life was saved." A second concert met with equal success. The Tsarina and her sons (of whom the elder became Alexander II) showed the visitor marked attentions, gave him valuable gifts, and went wherever he performed. "If the Parisians chose to punish me for having composed my latest work, the Russians have amply made it up to me." [21]

Four more days in a sleigh ("which shakes one up like shot in a bottle being scoured") brought Berlioz to Moscow, where the orchestra and

[17] *M.E.*, 170–1.

[18] This insistence on the bass drum as a symbol shows to perfection how myths express subjective feeling through false objects. The users of the bass drum *à outrance* in nineteenth-century music are the French and Italian opera composers and its sole enemy in Paris was Berlioz. See *Treatise* and above, Subchapter 17.

[19] Humboldt, who liked Berlioz, was apparently the go-between for this request, with which Frederick William complied in a facetious tone. (*235*, II, 209.)

[20] *M.E.*, 174–5.

[21] *M.E.*, 175. In a note of sardonic ambiguity, destined for the newspapers, he had announced his *Faust* as having just earned in Paris a unique reception. (*98*.)

choruses were by no means so good as the picked German group in St. Petersburg. But the applause on April 10 and the profits that went with it were equally gratifying. "The Russian aristocracy has grown delirious over *Faust*. . . . While I am giving these concerts in Moscow . . . the Grand Theatre [in St. Petersburg] is rehearsing *Romeo*." [22]

The return to the capital was slowed up by the spring thaw, but this delay only heightened the pleasure of finding on his return the large well-trained ensembles playing and singing *Romeo*. "It is imperially organized." He rehearsed them in sections as usual, and gave himself wholly to "the divine Shakespearean poem." The excitement of the performance and the warmth of the public response were too much for him. After many curtain calls, he retired to the green room where Ernst the violinist (who had played in the *Harold* symphony) found him dissolved in tears. " 'Nerves,' " said Ernst, " 'I know all about it.' And he let me weep like an hysterical girl for another 15 minutes." [23]

Another strain on the thirtieth for a repeat performance was followed by a depressive reaction. He experienced one of his fits of loneliness in the midst of friends. He thought of Liszt, newly in love with the Princess Carolyne Sayn-Wittgenstein, who was temporarily in Russia, and wrote him a long letter for her to deliver by hand. "I think a great deal about you, and the opportunities of speaking of you here are many, for people love and admire you as much as I do. Don't you think you and I go around a good deal? Just now, I am sad, sad enough to die of it. I am having one of my bouts of *isolation;* and it is the playing of *Romeo* that brought it on. In the middle of the adagio I felt my heart contract, and here I am, caught by the evil for Lord knows how long. My wretched temperament!

"But enough of this. I have played a deal of music here. . . . Now the King of Prussia has had me notified by Count Roeden that the Berlin Opera is at my disposal to put on *Faust* entire. So I'm going to Prussia, but my heart is not in it. Will I recover it? There I go lamenting again. What misery to be an electrical machine that can be electrified. The Princess tells me that you compose a great deal. When is your *Sardanapalus* due in Vienna? . . .[24]

"Farewell. I embrace you. I should like to see you. The sun shines as in Italy – 34 degrees of heat [93.2° F.] – a torture. Come hither ice, fog,

[22] *M.E.*, 177.
[23] *Mem.*, II, 292.
[24] Apparently an Italian opera of Liszt's which was never produced. See *235*, II, 368.

insensibility! Farewell again, don't laugh at me: if you do I shall know it wherever you are." [25]

Berlioz' sense of isolation, brought on by overwork or the aftermath of battle, was his old trouble, rooted farther back than adolescence; it was the passion for Estelle, for solitude in the fields, mingled with yearning for a love he never knew and was never to know. The absent Marie was not the one to make him feel that his real experiences were being shared. Worldly in a small-minded way – as her P.S.'s to some of Berlioz' letters attest [26] – she had ceased being either spirited or naïve. Alone and brooding, Berlioz easily deluded himself into thinking that he loved one of his choristers, a modest young woman who lived by her needle and was betrothed by her family's will to a man on his way to Sweden. She took pity on the great artist in his distress. It was an innocent affair: they walked arm in arm along the Neva and talked – for she knew French fairly well – or Berlioz would sing to her. He knew she did not love him, but she spoke like Faust's Gretchen as she wondered what he could see in so ordinary a creature as herself, and the poetic and musical associations redoubled his grief masked as love.

However much the mind might stand off and judge it, this was no trumped-up feeling on Berlioz' part: it was the imagination of love, out of which, for gifted and erotic but unsensual natures, all art springs. "There are so many sorts of love," Berlioz confided months later to a friend. "The kind I feel is the true, grand, poetic love. I have known it since the first time and nothing is more beautiful. With the love of art, there is no other divinising of the human heart. With it the world grows bright, horizons enlarge, all nature takes on color and vibrates in endless harmonies, and – one loves, that's all, one loves!" [27]

From this first visit in 1847, Russia felt that Berlioz' music was pregnant and prophetic of the future and wanted to keep his scores at the Imperial Library.[28] But Berlioz had no copies and could not leave them. He did leave warm supporters, notably Vladimir Stassov, Alexis Lvov,

[25] *M.E.*, 178–80.

[26] *E.g.*, *135*. Certain biographers state that Marie did accompany Berlioz to Russia. There is no direct evidence for this and from the letters of this period it seems more likely that she met him in Berlin on his return.

[27] *M.E.*, 211. One need not go back to Dante's *Vita Nuova* for ascertaining the bond between love and art. W. J. Turner opens his *Orpheus, or The Music of the Future* with the statement: "Music is the imagination of love *in sound*. It is what man imagines of his life, and his life is love." (*899*, 9.) Stendhal repeatedly expresses the same view. (*1242*, Ch. 16 and *931*, *passim.*)

[28] *Moscow Gazette* quoted in *345*, 208.

and Count Michael Wielhorsky, whose appreciation of his work had considerable effects on the national art. Berlioz on his side had received an unforgettable impression from the liturgical music of Bortniansky.[29]

On his way to answer the Prussian King's invitation, Berlioz stopped at Riga, where he gave a concert by arranging some of his scores for fifty musicians, playing even the Chorus of Sylphs for orchestra alone. The audience was sparse, for the population was at the docks along the river, watching and trading as eleven hundred ships unloaded grain. But in return for his pains he had "the great good fortune" of seeing *Hamlet* well performed. "I was again, as always, all stirred up over this marvel by the greatest genius who ever lived. The English are right to say that next to God it is Shakespeare who has created most. One ought not to allow his masterpieces to be shown before a haphazard gathering of dolts, half dolts, semi-literates, grammarians, schoolteachers, baby nurses, ladies of fashion, *demi-mondaines*, old crones, dandies, wheat brokers, horse traders and traveling salesmen . . . [even if] God has put them on earth in order to keep artists humble and clip the wings of their ambition." [30]

Four days later Berlioz was in Berlin assembling his forces for the *Damnation*. In two weeks all was ready, but it was June 19, the season was far advanced. The horse races had just begun, and the King used his privilege to request that the concert start at six. Half the audience therefore came an hour late. Still, despite this handicap and that of two inferior singers, several encores were called for.[31] Frederick William asked him to Sans Souci; they talked where Voltaire had lived and Bach had played; walked in the gardens and parted pleased with each other. The King awarded Berlioz the Red Eagle, but the Berlin returns were slight. A truer compensation in artistic form roused Berlioz from his growing fatigue — "*La Vestale* entire, that is, as scored, without cuts. In spite of the [singers'] inadequacy it made — especially at the rehearsal — a profound impression. The last air, which is never sung in Paris, is sublime." [32]

In Paris, as Berlioz could see from the newspapers, the Opera after five months was still being tussled for. "In three days we overturn a dynasty, but it takes all this time to pass from Pillet to Coignard or some other. . . . In truth, it is everywhere the same. The King of Prussia has an Intendant

[29] He wrote an article upon it in the *Débats* for Oct. 19, 1850, reviewed Lvov's history of the Russian chapel, added a biographical sketch (*Soirées* [21] *Eves.*, 231), and edited as well as performed a number of his works. See *M.E.*, 308–9.

[30] *M.E.*, 184.

[31] But not given, because Berlioz did not distinguish the words *da capo* (instead of *bis*) above the applause.

[32] *M.E.*, 189.

who in all matters goes against the public, the artists, the court, and the King himself. Yet the King keeps him, though Meyerbeer is giving up from discouragement." [33]

When Berlioz reached the French capital on July 7, the new directors had been in office one week. Within a month, the pair with the Flaubertian names, Duponchel and Roqueplan, had forgotten all their pre-nuptial courting of the powers, including Berlioz and the *Débats*. But with the composer once more in residence the comic papers had really fresh material for their wit tinged with envy: "M. Berliozineff has been made a prince. . . . He has had his armorial bearings engraved on his guitar." [34] Berlioz quickly gauged the Opera situation and by mid-August sent a note to the new heads giving them back their latest word.[35] He had released to Scribe full rights to the libretto on Lewis's *Monk*.[36] He had also accepted a complex but apparently attractive offer to go to London. The musical businessmen, Marie and Léon Escudier, had acted as intermediaries between Antoine Jullien, a French impresario married to an English wife, and Berlioz. Jullien was to open a new opera company at Drury Lane, of which Berlioz was to be conductor. Out of his salary of forty thousand francs a year, Berlioz would pay four thousand to Escudier, plus ten per cent on any contracts for special concerts that Berlioz might give under Jullien's management. The high rates were due in part to the computation in pounds sterling (London was expensive) and in part to Jullien's views of big business in art, which he had hitherto made profitable. Berlioz wrote up his Russian and German trips for the *Débats* and looked forward to England.

On the strength of his new engagement and in order to be in physical shape for it, Berlioz took a vacation; and since tangible success always put him in mind of his father, he went home to La Côte, taking with him his pale, blond little boy of thirteen. Berlioz did not manage to see Humbert Ferrand who despite his real affection could never bestir himself in time to meet his old friend. But Berlioz kept him informed of his doings and read with appreciation the ex-poet's gentle brochures on politics.[37]

[33] *M.E.*, 186. Meyerbeer had replaced Spontini as music director.

[34] *269*, 163.

[35] In their reply, which has been preserved (*Corresp.*, 47) they express appreciation for the "affectionate terms" of his disengagement notice. Though Berlioz wrote scornfully about the Paris situation to his intimates, he never abandoned diplomatic courtesy in the actual scrimmage.

[36] It was later given to Gounod who produced *La Nonne Sanglante* without success in 1854.

[37] *Compte-rendu sur le Voyage en Sardaigne . . . par M. le Comte . . . de la Marmora*, Paris. (See *L.I.*, 196.)

La Côte had hardly changed in fifteen years, except that Dr. Berlioz was of a spectral thinness and near his end. His gastritis reduced him to an insufficient diet and to a steady course of opium. Partly deaf and very much alone, he was a pitiable old man of seventy-one. The sight of him shocked Hector, who nonetheless succeeded in enlivening him with anecdotes of his journeys, and even made him laugh. For young Louis, life in the open air with his father was a gleam of unimagined happiness. They romped together as if they had been brothers, and Hector himself was rejuvenated. But in the evening, he and the Doctor could only talk of the approaching end, or of the death, earlier, of those whom neither had seen at the last: Hector, his mother; Dr. Berlioz, his son Prosper. The old man was also likely to dwell on questions of inheritance and could not be turned from the subject. Berlioz left at the end of his fortnight knowing he would never see his beloved father again.

The month of October was devoted to preparations for the London trip. Berlioz now had a faithful copyist and guardian of his mounting pile of music, Roquemont,[38] from whom he could reliably order parts to be made, counted over, or dispatched. This aid lessened the necessity of carrying everything with him and it would be indispensable in Berlioz' new post abroad, where he would need the music of others. Before leaving, Berlioz had singers and instrumentists to engage, endless errands to run, and masses of proof to read. He found time to notice and encourage a young contralto, Mlle. Charton, whom he did not know but in whose future he believed as soon as he heard her. She repaid him sixteen years later by creating the role of Dido in his *Troyens*. But for the moment art in France seemed to him "dead, putrefying . . . The more I see of foreign nations, the less I love my native land. Forgive the blasphemy." [39]

Sensing as he did the decay of an epoch and feeling inwardly chilled at the thought of his father, he preferred to make the journey to London in solitude. It required "a series of *coups d'état*" to obtain from Marie the right to go alone. Not that he had any intention of abandoning her or of taking up other attachments. He continued to support four people in two separate households, giving time to Harriet (whose apoplectic condition had become alarming) and to Marie and her mother. But he did not want to mar his first meetings with his English colleagues by letting Marie's heavy-handed ways overshadow his tact and *savoir-faire*. On his way to England, he accompanied Louis to his boarding school at Rouen, where

[38] Berlioz thanks him feelingly in the *Memoirs* but spells his name indifferently Roquemont and Rocquemont, as do the other writers who speak of him.

[39] *L.I.*, 197.

two good friends, Méreaux[40] and Baron de Montville, made his unhappy youth a little less solitary.

On November 5, 1847, after an easy crossing, Berlioz arrived in London. He lodged with Jullien at 76 Harley Street and was aghast to discover the size of megalopolis. It took three quarters of an hour to go from the house to Drury Lane where his orchestra (for the first time *his*) greeted him most cordially. He knew a good many of the French and German players, and he found that his English was adequate to his needs. He spoke with a relatively slight accent, but took a little time to catch all that was said to him.

Rehearsals began for the first scheduled opera, Donizetti's inevitable *Lucia*. This was to break in the public gently. What Berlioz looked forward to was the staging of Gluck's *Iphigeneia in Tauris*, Mozart, and possibly Spontini. Jullien also had the notion that Berlioz should flatter the British by composing on "God Save the Queen" something like his Hungarian March. This absurd suggestion forecasts Jullien's approaching insanity.[41] Naturally, nothing came of this proposal, though Jullien's natural extravagance grew alarmingly. He wanted a two-act ballet from Gautier at a thousand francs an act, and Berlioz had to arrange for it as well as for the choreographer and the music by local talent. He had to corral Mmes. Dorus-Gras and Barth-Hasselt who had been vaguely engaged. Despite the artist's businesslike catching up of the irresponsible businessman's errors, things went quickly downhill. It came out that Jullien had lost

[40] Jean-Amédée Lefroid de Méreaux (1803–1874), son and grandson of musicians, was a pupil of Reicha and a well-known teacher of piano and theory. He had settled in Rouen after a brief but brilliant career on the concert stage. He published articles and piano etudes, edited the older masters of the keyboard, and made a piano arrangement of Berlioz' *Enfance du Christ*, about which see *96*, 148–9 and *M.C.*, 237.

[41] Louis Antoine Jullien (originally Julien) was born in 1812, the son of a Swiss bandmaster. He studied three years at the Conservatoire, then became conductor-manager of dance concerts for which he composed quadrilles on popular tunes of the day. Insolvent by 1838, he left Paris for London, where he soon established popular promenade concerts at one shilling. His orchestra of nearly a hundred pieces was excellent, and from 1842 on he gave annual series, winter and summer, as well as toured the country, presenting a mixture of popular and classical music. To draw the crowd he advertised "monster" shows on topical subjects and costumed himself gorgeously. His black hair and black moustache (a novelty), his velvet chair and jeweled baton, handed to him on a salver, were frequently caricatured, but they made him a national institution. *Punch* (just founded) dubbed him "The Mons." and Dickens and Thackeray wrote of him. When Melville arrived in England in 1849 he went to Jullien's concert the day after landing and greatly enjoyed himself. (*Journal: 1265*, 23.)

fortune and credit *before* taking Drury Lane, so that he now cut all salaries by one third, which was a trifle since he did not pay them. *Lucia*, though excellently done, was only a moderate box-office success, and Balfe's new piece which followed was no hit.[42]

Linda di Chamounix was the next choice and by January 1848 Berlioz was "working like a dray horse," rehearsing all afternoon, conducting all night – a twelve-hour day. London, like Paris, was suffering an epidemic of midwinter grippe, which Berlioz caught. He "took as medicine the chores and the drafts of Drury Lane,"[43] since the situation could be saved only by energy. Meantime, Jullien's advisers gathered and took counsel of Berlioz. He proposed to enlist public support by means of a striking *artistic* novelty, such as Gluck's *Iphigenia in Tauris*, and he explained its requirements. Jullien's response was: "There are helmets, we are saved!"[44] Berlioz finally gave up by the end of January 1848, taking to his bed with a serious bronchitis. "They are playing *Linda*. . . . I have the good luck to be ill."[45] He recovered in time to put on the *Marriage of Figaro* in a manner to impress Wilhelm Ganz, but it did not draw.[46] Berlioz had received altogether one month's salary; Jullien was bankrupt and planning to start again in New York.[47]

Berlioz' spirit was a prey to many dark thoughts. Mendelssohn had died the day before Berlioz landed, and his posthumous oratorio, *Elijah*, was being performed in his memory. "How wonderfully great and beautiful it is," wrote Berlioz. "We have all been deeply moved by the loss of this superior artist, whose death is a stout blow inflicted on our art."[48] And to Lvov in Russia: "I have just heard poor Mendelssohn's last oratorio. It is magnificently great and of an indescribable harmonic richness."[49] But the *Antigone* of Sophocles, given with Mendelssohn's incidental music, had failed. The perpetual need to overcome resistance, to persuade by will and convince by material gain, was depressing. In his fever and lassitude the musician thought of the superb concerts "imperially run" by the order of the Tsar, and he longed to be at last somewhere put in charge of what

[42] For these facts see *333*, 287. Balfe's *Maid of Honor* was a resetting of Flotow's *Martha*.

[43] *Corresp.*, 157.

[44] *Mem.*, II, 316.

[45] *Corresp.*, 164.

[46] *955*, 4. The young musician, later conductor of the New Philharmonic, had just come from Germany to join his father, the last of this distinguished musical family from Mainz.

[47] He stayed in the United States from 1851 to 1854.

[48] *M.E.*, 205.

[49] *Corresp.*, 163.

he could do best – produce music. From France the news was disquieting. The republican banquets of December 1847 presaged trouble – or less likely, reform – which the concluding of peace in North Africa only postponed for a time.

Other thoughts of Russia assailed Berlioz. He had written to his friend the cellist Tajan-Rogé at St. Petersburg enclosing a note for the little singer Berlioz had loved, feeling himself to be "a young fool of over forty," and he had received a reply – a last reply, full of good sense, honesty, and affection. "I am grateful to her," he wrote in thanking Rogé, "for reviving in me the pain I was trying to forget." [50] But brooding in bed was useless and was in fact a forbidden luxury, for Drury Lane being on the rocks, Berlioz had scheduled a concert of his own works for February 7. His new friend J. W. Davison, music critic of *The Times* and founder of *The Musical World*, was helping him to get on his feet and make his music known. The mission was in its third phase.

To help the concert, Berlioz asked Vigny for a letter of introduction to Count d'Orsay, with whom Vigny was on terms of close affection, and who could give Berlioz entree to the artistic circle of Lady Blessington. Berlioz was already in touch with Macready, who gave a dinner in his honor, and with theatrical writers and critics, thanks to whom Berlioz saw a good many plays.[51] Sir Henry Taylor's *Philip van Artevelde* was the novelty of the season but Berlioz preferred *Othello* and the to him suggestively entitled *New Way to Pay Old Debts.* In answer to Berlioz' request Vigny wrote a very warm letter to d'Orsay who soon replied that Berlioz had quickly become one of theirs: "He is a friend of . . . all the shepherds of our time, society being composed only of those and of the numberless sheep." This *esprit de corps* had the useful result of making the critic of the *Athenaeum*, Chorley, change his mind about Berlioz' music and write of it pleasantly for the first time.

London concertgoers had for five years past heard a few of Berlioz' overtures but this February concert was to be a full-dress presentation. The volatile Jullien, however, had tried a last stroke to recoup his fortunes. Taking with him Berlioz' best players he was touring the United Kingdom in a series of promenade concerts. The orchestral rump that was left had to be rehearsed five times and the chorus eighteen. In the end things went well enough, the public cheered, and the press was almost

[50] *M.E.*, 211.

[51] Macready had acted with Harriet Smithson in Paris twenty years earlier and Berlioz probably knew, as he stepped upon the stage of Drury Lane, that it was the spot where Harriet had made her London début at eighteen.

entirely favorable. One of the converts was Edward Holmes, the friend of Keats and biographer of Mozart, who had come strongly prejudiced. *The Times* and the *Illustrated London News* led the chorus of enthusiastic and discerning praise. "Jullien," said the latter journal "may be forgiven much for giving the London public a chance to hear Berlioz. . . . Had he been named Musical Director at Drury Lane and not merely chef d'orchestre, it would have been better for himself and better for the interests of Lyric Drama." [52]

Once again honor was safe and intrinsic success achieved in the face of material loss: Berlioz began to plan a second concert; but Jullien had just wits enough left to appropriate the money of the first without paying anyone anything. The orchestra that Berlioz had trained was therefore disbanding. The music publisher Beale, it is true, was willing to issue a good many fragments and piano arrangements of Berlioz' work, but royalties would be distant and probably not large.[53] The ancient Society of British Musicians, under the patronage of the Duke of Cambridge, gave Berlioz a testimonial dinner at which – against the usages of the society – a toast was drunk to the guest of honor. Berlioz replied in a manner which he says was contrary to his custom too, for "I was cool and self-possessed and was thus able to properly thank the public, the musicians, and the critics." [54]

When Berlioz wrote this to Brandus, the French publisher who had taken over the *Gazette Musicale*, still another "Reform Banquet" had been planned and prohibited in Paris. The prohibition had been a declaration of war between the people and the government. The February Days (twenty-second to twenty-fourth) had begun to the cry of "Long Live Reform," Guizot was down, barricades were up, and the insurgents marched, with the troops, to the Tuileries. While the Chamber discussed a Regency of Louis-Philippe's grandsons under the Duchess of Orleans, a mob which included the Swiss painter Arnold Böcklin interrupted the proceedings. A provisional government headed by the poet Lamartine, the scientist Arago, and the political theorist Louis Blanc, was appointed by acclamation. The Republic of 1848 was born.

[52] *311*, 88 and 90.

[53] Such arrangements, by travestying Berlioz' whole conception of music, undoubtedly did much harm to his reputation in a century so pianistic as the nineteenth. He himself always disliked these reductions, which neither Chopin's help nor Liszt's genius could render faithful. His embarrassed comments deserve to be read as a final demonstration of the essential difference between music conceived for orchestra and that for the piano. See *M.E.*, 105; *M.C.*, 73; *207*, I, 230 and 237.

[54] *M.E.*, 218.

For each section of society, reform means the reform of the abuses it feels most, and Berlioz naturally hoped for the end of monarchical interference in the arts: no more tax levies on concerts, no more censorship of songs, no more arbitrary disposal of the means of production. "I hope, in short, that we shall at last be free to be free – unless we are in for a new mystification." The silence of his French friends was alarming. "What's happened to M. Bertin?" Being an Orleanist, the Director of the *Débats* was rumored to be in hiding. But what could make Desmarest the cellist and Brandus the publisher keep mum? Berlioz begged Morel to tell him what had happened "to all our precious villains, as Shakespeare calls them." [55]

By the middle of March the answer was self-evident. Cultural activity had utterly ceased in France; it was "dead, rotted away, and buried." Berlioz must face the task of building himself a new position in England. Revolution was now aflame in Prussia, Austria, and the Rhineland; in Rome, Naples, Ireland and Bohemia. Short of Russia, there was no dwelling place for music on the Continent. Jullien had converted Drury Lane into an equestrian circus, and having no liquid assets feared no lawsuits. He had blithely defaulted on all his contracts. But Berlioz could not default on his four dependents in France and must use his pen to earn his living. He proposed critical and travel articles to Davison, but as one can tell at a glance, *The Times* is not a French newspaper, which can accept casual copy from outsiders. Berlioz inquired of the new Minister of the Interior whether his one hundred and eighteen francs a month as curator of the Conservatoire Library would still be paid. He had no reply.

Yet he found time to hear and comment enthusiastically on Mendelssohn's *Italian* symphony, which he much preferred to the *Scotch* – "fresh, lively, noble, and masterly . . . a superb piece." [56] This was given at a concert of the Philharmonic Society, which Berlioz' well-wishers would have liked to see extend a welcome to the French composer. But the board was conservative and cautious. The directors of Covent Garden, on the other hand, were interested in a Musical Shakespeare Night in which Berlioz' *Tempest*, *Death of Ophelia*, *King Lear*, and parts of *Romeo* would figure. But opposition developed: Berlioz was caught again between the equivalents of the Conservatoire and the Opera.[57] He worked at his piano arrangements for Beale and at a vocal version of the *Apothéose* from the

[55] *Corresp.*, 165–6.
[56] *M.E.*, 222; *Corresp.*, 168.
[57] He was told by Prince Albert's music director that everyone in London was delighted with Berlioz' presence except the native composers. (*85*, 647.)

Funeral symphony, for the movement had aroused cheers at his concert and he was told that amateur singers throughout England would snap up a choral version.

Beyond this, his only capital was himself, his past, and his achievements. Pondering them, he took out the two volumes of his *Voyage Musical* and set to work telling his life, filling in the gaps, beginning at the beginning – his birth forty-four years before, in another era of European massacre. His career might be over, but the artist's memoirs of his experiences might survive the flood and be of use.

As he sketched in his Preface the circumstances under which these memoirs were being written, during the last week of March 1848, the tide of revolt touched London. The Chartists assembled to cries of "Down with the Ministry. . . . The Charter and No Surrender!" They planned another mass meeting, a petition and a march to Parliament. To fend off revolution, 170,000 special constables were sworn in, one of whom was Louis-Napoleon Bonaparte, nephew of the late Emperor. Troops were quartered in the houses and the Tower guns mounted. The Duke of Wellington was put in charge of all the government forces and a proclamation was issued against "assembly for disorderly purposes." "Time presses," wrote Berlioz. "Republicanism sweeps with its steamroller over all Europe. The art of music which for so long was everywhere dragging out its life is good and dead today. . . . England, where I now live, has shown me a noble and cordial hospitality, but at these first quakings of the continental thrones, swarms of bewildered artists seek asylum here. . . . Will the British capital provide subsistence for so many exiles? Will it lend an ear to their songs of sorrow amid the proud clamors of neighboring peoples which are crowning themselves kings? Will it resist such an example? *Jam proximus ardet Ucalegon.* Who knows what will have become of me in a few months – I have no assured means for myself and my family. Let us therefore make use of the flying minutes. . . ." [58]

The moment was doubly bitter, for the financial needs of Harriet and Marie had brought the two women into a cruel tangle, after which Marie had decided to rejoin Berlioz in London. He could obtain money due him neither from Jullien (who was at last in debtor's prison) nor from the French vicomte who owed him five hundred francs. Worst of all, the Escudiers had been made bankrupt by the revolution and although "they cannot be compelled to pay me what they owe, I shall be compelled by the original contract to pay what I do not owe them." [59] He had to borrow

[58] *Mem.*, I, ii-iii.
[59] *M.E.*, 226.

at revolutionary rates to provide for Harriet and Louis, while he and Marie moved to modest lodgings in Regent's Park. "I am convinced that I am *de trop* in this world." [60]

By sheer will he busied himself about another concert. French musicians were arriving in droves and they lent him their services. On June 29, at the Hanover Square Rooms, after eight months of virtually continuous overwork, he gave a brilliant concert which was worthily received and brought little. It was evident that musical London, like Paris, was intellectually ready to appreciate what was new, vigorous, and unconventional, but was not in any way organized to support it. Berlioz was like a poet producing a "little magazine," who prints what is later the great literature of the period, but cannot at the time sell it. The paying institutions in London were the two Italian theaters, which ran a handful of favorites by Bellini, Rossini, and Donizetti – and not their best works at that – and the orchestra and oratorio societies, monopolized by Handel, Mendelssohn, and their living imitators.

As for Paris, it was swimming in blood. Three days before Berlioz' concert, from the twenty-third to the twenty-sixth of June, the unemployed in the national workshops – the original WPA – had risen in protest against the threatened cessation of their dole. Entrenched in the eastern part of the city, they faced the government like a foreign army and were treated as such. General Cavaignac brought reserves and battered down the barricades with field guns. It was civil war. The Archbishop of Paris was killed trying to stop it. The rebels finally surrendered, and with a savagery to which both sides had been led by equal fear, the government deported wholesale and without trial all the prisoners taken. Public feeling turned sharply in favor of strong rule and against all popular social aspirations. All parties, all citizens, were now legitimately afraid. Had Cavaignac not loyally believed in republican government, he could have made himself dictator; the situation was in the pre-Napoleonic stage of 1795, the pre-Cromwellian of 1651. Paris was a stricken field.

This was the City of Light that Berlioz had loved, had made his name in, and was now compelled to return to. He entertained no illusions. In May, even before the second outbreak had attested France's social and political alienation from art, he had written to the architect Louis Duc, his old companion of the Villa Medici, a letter which summed up the facts and reflected the many lights thrown upon them by Berlioz' mind:

[60] *Corresp.*, 172.

London 26 May 1848

MY DEAR DUC:

Our piece (the *Apothéose*) has at last come out. It was thought necessary to tamper with my sub-title. I had written: "Composed for the inauguration of the Bastille Column," and farther down: "Dedicated to M. Duc, architect of the *Bastille* Column." This made it clear why the column came into it at all and wherefore the dedication was appropriate. But since the last Chartist agitation, the London bourgeois has a deep dread of whatever is related from far or near to revolutions, and in consequence my publisher refused to consider any mention on the title page either of your monument or of those to whom it was put up.

I have sought in vain an opportunity to send you the score, together with the Scotch airs you asked for. Instead, I send you the *Apothéose* by itself, for a package of the kind you request would cost a great deal. The Hungarian March for four hands has also been published by Beale, and the Chorus of Sylphs will appear shortly. Our piece would I think be quite impressive if sung by a large chorus and instrumented. I may have it performed in Paris if it becomes possible to give music there. Meanwhile you'll have to be content with the piano score.

Speaking of Paris, the reproaches that my friends make me about my absence are scarcely founded if they think that my staying away is doing me harm. A man must have a tricolor flag over his eyes to fail to see that music in France is now dead, and that it is the last of the arts to which our rulers will pay attention. They tell me I am sulking at my country. I certainly do not sulk at it: that is putting it too mildly; I flee from it as one flees a barbaric shore when one is looking for civilization, and this I have done not merely since the Revolution. For a good while I have stifled in myself the love of France and uprooted from my heart the foolish habit of centering all my thoughts upon her. During the last seven years I have lived solely from what my works and concerts have earned me in foreign lands. Without Germany, Bohemia, Hungary, and especially Russia, I should have starved in France over and over again. Friends write to me of "positions" to take, of "posts to apply for." What position, what posts? There aren't any. Isn't Auber at the Conservatoire, Carafa at the Gymnase, Girard at the Opera? What else is there? Nothing. And the love of mediocrity — has that been swept out of French minds by the Revolution? Possibly, but in that case it will have been replaced by the love of worse men and things (if there is indeed anything worse than mediocrity).

No, I have nothing to do in France, except cultivate the friendships that are dear to me. For my career I have attempted enough, suffered enough, waited enough. I shall not fulfill it there. In France I have undergone nothing but vexations more or less disguised; I have found only a stupid opposition because the national mind is stupid about the higher reaches of art and literature. I have an invincible and ever-growing contempt for those "French ideas" which other peoples do not even suspect. Under the previous government I found nothing but scorn and indifference; I shall now find nothing but grave preoccupations added to scorn and indifference. I wrote three times to Louis Philippe when he was King requesting an audience. I did not even receive *a reply*. I wrote to Ledru-Rollin recently and he was of the same politeness as the King. There is only one lyric theatre in Paris – the Opera, which is managed by a nitwit and closed to me. Don't you suppose that if Duponchel is dismissed, they will not find twenty others like him? Some day, perhaps, I shall be approached, when I shall be very old, very tired, and no longer good for anything. But at that time I may not have lost my memory, and this belated confidence in me – *if it comes*, will only be the more painful.

I have therefore nothing better to do than what I am doing now. If I am a savage, I hold on to my freedom, I keep going as long as the earth will have me, as long as the woods have wild life and deer; and if I often feel weary, and sleepless, suffer from cold, hunger and the insults of the pale-faces, at least I can dream alone above the waterfall and in the silent forest, worshipping nature and thanking God that he has left me the sense of her beauty.

I saw *Hamlet* recently. . . . What a world is that masterpiece! And what ravages *that fellow* makes in one's heart and soul! Shakespeare meant to depict the nothingness of life, the vanity of human designs, the despotism of chance, and the indifference of Fate or God toward what we call virtue, crime, beauty, ugliness, love, hate, genius and folly. And he has cruelly succeeded. In the performance, this time, they had deigned to give us *Hamlet* as written, and almost uncut – an unusual thing in this country where one finds so many people who are superior to Shakespeare. . . . For that matter, they do the same to music: Costa has instrumented and corrected for Covent Garden Rossini's *Barber of Seville* and Mozart's *Figaro* and *Don Giovanni*.[61]

Here ends the message of explanation, expostulation, and resignation. But the writer must have been conscious of excessive and self-centered seriousness in addressing a friend to whom he says *tu* and whom he wished first of all to please by a dedication and a gift. So Berlioz adds a paragraph or two in a lighter vein:

Let me tell you, by way of stopping this verbiage, that I am preparing a concert . . . for June 29. That is all my news. . . . I may say, I miss our delightful, easy, unpretentious conversations at Mme. Vanderkelle's, and the fine wit and cultivated opinions with which M. de Montville flavors them, and your own enthusiastic shouts and leaps at whatever is beautiful, and your admiring words shot through puffs of tobacco (I mean smoke), and the reclining position of the ladies while we discuss.

Only one thing has always shocked me in those gatherings – a dull and indecent thing which Mme. Vanderkelle does her best to conceal and yet fails to, a thing unworthy of a house like hers, and one that offends all good company. I mean her upright piano. No, madam, in a house ap-

[61] *M.E.*, 227–31.

pointed like yours, it is not permissible to sport such a cupboard; it is not permissible, in a choice circle such as your salon, to let an instrument like that be heard. It is indeed a crime of *lèse-art*. On this pun,[62] I shake you all by the hand, and beg you – what was I going to beg you? Ah, yes, beg you not to let Duc sing the *Apothéose*. A thousand heartfelt greetings. – H. Berlioz.[63]

The Artist in Society

> Shot down in Vienna by Windischgrätz in December 1848 . . . Poor Becher!
>
> – Berlioz' note on his friend's photograph[1]

The man who had orchestrated the Rákóczy March and, previously, the "Marseillaise," meanwhile composing a Napoleonic Ode, a *Funeral* symphony, and a national *Requiem*, was certainly a man possessed of the common touch, as well as an artist sensitive to popular feeling. Berlioz had sought to take direct part in the July days of 1830, he had dedicated a song to Emmet, expressed sympathy with Menotti, and been caught by the ideas of Saint-Simon. In all his dealings with the sizable mobs who heard or performed him, moreover, he had quickly shown himself a leader. After his appearance in Hungary, the youth of Gyor sent him an engraved loving cup as to one who had helped to quicken their national aspirations, and a movement was subsequently set on foot in Hungary to cast Berlioz in the role of a champion of the national liberties. It was hoped he might use his renown to win concessions from Austria.[2]

All this would lead one to suppose that when the Revolution of 1848 broke out in France, Berlioz would favor it, and that his dislike of politics,

[62] *Lèse-art* = les arts = lézard (it is the crime of a reptile).

[63] *M.E.*, 231–2.

---

[1] Alfred Julius Becher (1803–1848) was a composer and music critic of widely catholic taste, who wrote a biography of Jenny Lind and also edited the democratic journal *Der Radikale* during the stormy days of Vienna's revolution. Caught bearing arms when the city fell, he was court-martialed and shot on November 23, 1848 (not December, as Berlioz thought). On the photograph he had written "Remember from time to time, my dear Berlioz, one of your sincerest admirers. February 27, 1846."

[2] The Hungarian newspapers of the time, as reported by E. Haraszti. (572, 230.)

born of experience with variously oppressive regimes, would vanish in the fresh breeze of liberty. For a brief moment he had a glimmer of hope; [3] but to imagine that this could last is to take a sentimental view of revolutions and to misunderstand the "extensive" considerations which, as early as 1832, kept Berlioz from partisanship.[4]

The first impact of the revolution was hardly calculated to reassure an artist. Although the provisional government included a poet and a man of science, all cultural activity in Paris immediately ceased, and men of all shades of opinion who lived by their art had to seek their living abroad.[5] In the second place, even for those who had the means to stay, the atmosphere was well-nigh unbearable. A day or two before Berlioz wrote his friend Louis Duc a long letter from London, an observer who was an intimate of the new government men such as Arago, Tocqueville, and De Broglie, was writing from the country to one of them: "What do you do when you are not camping on the open squares of Paris? Everybody seems like a patient who can reasonably count only on two or three months more of life." [6]

The truth is that even before the second outbreak in June, the spirit of 1848 had already impressed its disruptive character upon qualified observers, regardless of party. The initial success of the revolution had in fact been made possible by the general decline of authority and intellectual power which had been going on for about half a dozen years.[7] So that Berlioz was neither mistaken nor purely self-centered when he saw in the revolution not merely the end of a regime but the end of an epoch. Like many others – ranging from Renan and Gobineau to Leconte de Lisle and Baudelaire, he was ready to support a republic that could both proclaim

[3] *M.E.*, 219 and 223.

[4] To his mother, from Rome, March 20, 1832: "As for my radical indifference to politics, it comes from a more extended sequence of ideas than you suppose, and so we won't refer to it again." *A.R.*, 194. He gives glimpses of these ideas on pp. 150, 172–188, 250, 262 and 347; *L.I.*, 78, 90, 107–8 and 116; *Corresp.*, 70, 89, 94.

[5] Besides Berlioz' enforced exile in London, where Chopin, Roger, Hallé, and other French musicians soon joined him, Sainte-Beuve and others had to find literary work in Belgium or Switzerland, or else be destitute. The poetess Desbordes-Valmore subsisted on charity; Musset's librarianship was abolished; Gautier's and Vernet's livelihood was curtailed and Adolphe Adam went bankrupt. The rest of Europe was soon affected. Verdi, who had just bought a house, saw his new opera fail at Trieste; the cessation of music in Germany killed off a fifty-year-old journal such as the *Leipziger Allgemeine Zeitung*, and from all parts exiles began to stream into England.

[6] *188*, III, 208.

[7] Sismondi placed the beginning of the decline around 1842.

and defend new freedoms,[8] and as we shall see he gave it a try. But his skepticism as to the outcome was soon verified by events. The explanation is not simply that Berlioz had reached mid-career and made a reputation with the aid of kings and princes, but that 1848 in France represents a new mode in revolutions, and one inevitably inimical to culture as Berlioz understood it. If 1830 was a sixth and last attempt to entrench the liberal claims of 1789, the republicanism of 1848 was the first bid for the establishment of the populist, collectivist society which our century is still struggling about. We may therefore generalize and say that 1848 in France split the century in half, and by creating new conditions of life for artists wrecked the careers of all those who remained true to what Lionel Trilling aptly calls "the high and exigent culture" of the prepopulist era.[9]

Fairly soon after the establishment of the July Monarchy, it is true, Hugo, Gautier, Vigny, Berlioz, Delacroix and others began to complain of the government's indifference to art, and to groan at the public's neglect of their best efforts. Tracing the vicissitudes of Berlioz' career supplies the representative details of this uneasy relation. But it is important to remember that by and large the relation was one of indifference and not hostility, neglect and not persecution. Louis Philippe snubbed the Romantics and frowned on his son's patroning artists not because he feared their political opinions but because he knew that their innovations, daring, and love of glory went against the cautious moralism of the epoch – the moralism later named after Queen Victoria – which was simply revolution insurance bought by repressing the generous energies.

The July Monarchy could accordingly commission a *Requiem* mass to celebrate a dead general, and a *Funeral* symphony to bury those who had put it into power, but at the sight of the works themselves it rightly felt – through that mysterious balance of conscious and unconscious forces we call a culture – that Berlioz and his peers spelled danger. Louis Philippe did not know as we do that the *Requiem* and the Symphony were born of Napoleonic visions; he probably did not read Balzac or the *Charterhouse of Parma;* but his instinct was sound in not vouchsafing an

[8] *Corresp.*, 166 and 170. As late as May 1848, he expressed himself as ready to undertake any task of musical reorganization in Paris if "by some impossible chance" he were considered the fit person. (*90*, 215.) The literary counterpart of Berlioz' feeling may be found in the pages of *La Liberté de Penser*, edited by Jules Simon, Renan, Baudelaire, Michelet, Quinet and others. Their hopes collapsed by the end of 1849.

[9] *Partisan Review*, Aug. 1948, 888. In his admirable biography (1949), Mr. Herbert Weinstock ascribes to the revolution and consequent financial worries an effective part in hastening Chopin's death.

answer to Berlioz, just as his Philippestine bourgeoisie was right to neglect Stendhal's novels.

If then the Orleanist reign lives in history by the greatness of the men it overlooked, why did not its passing lead to their vindication? [10] Why did Berlioz at once fear the evil of a worse mediocrity, and why instead of a paean of geniuses rejoicing, was there for nearly two years a Babylonian exile of artists? The answer lies in a number of inescapable truths which must be recognized before one can grasp the problem of the artist's relation to society.

A revolution is – to use current cant – a society in crisis; but modern society since 1789 is in a state of perpetual crisis, of almost continuous revolution. We saw how Berlioz' productive years were punctuated with riots, attempted assassinations, and repressive measures – all of which conditioned the development of his career and of his artistic output. What art can spring from or represent this chaos? And at the same time, how is it that Romanticism is the true culture of the French Revolution? Obviously the true culture of a revolution comes after the event, the culture makers being either opponents of, or, if indifferent, opposed by the revolutionary forces. In any case, the conditions of a going revolution are especially inimical to art: there is no wish, there is no preparation, and there is no money for art because, strictly speaking, there is no need for it. When art is consciously used by revolutionists as a means to prestige or propaganda, the result in the artist is even worse than when, as in 1848, it is treated with contempt. In a word, there can be no song in time of revolution.[11]

This generality may be tested by reference to art and artists during the French Revolution, during the Napoleonic Wars – which outside France bore the character of revolution – and during the twentieth century, provided that one studies art with reference to an artistic and not a political criterion.[12] The question is not one of doctrine but of essence. The

[10] Balzac: "I trust, for the sake of Louis Philippe the First, that posterity will say 'under Victor Hugo's reign, under Lamartine, under Béranger, there was a king who took the name of Louis Philippe.'" (*1169*, 286.) Adolphe Boschot neglected the hint and entitled his second volume on Berlioz: "A Romantic Under Louis Philippe."

[11] One may take the seeming exception of the "Marseillaise" as indicative. Its maker, Rouget, was soon politically suspect and he had to wait thirty-eight years to be saved, accidentally, from destitution. What political revolutionists want from art is more neutral work like Cherubini's *Salpêtre Républicain.* (See *1303*, 1584.)

[12] See a sketch of such a study in my essays *Of Human Freedom*, N. Y. 1939/1965.

principle is not that reactionaries love art more than radicals or vice versa, the principle is that art and politics, which concur in several important respects, differ in others that are decisive. The opening paragraph of Berlioz' letter to Duc supplies a trivial but clear example. The composer had given his *Apothéose* a subtitle and dedication that bore a meaning only if taken together and that expressed his unaltered liberalism; but the publisher, acting wisely on political and commercial grounds, censored the words. One may say that a politically minded artist ought not to have mentioned revolutionary monuments *in England* in 1848. Quite so, but in that view the artist's desired political character becomes mere timeserving. Again, the composer had in this instance fashioned his statements *as an artist,* that is, he had made his words carry meaning. But politics and commerce care nothing about coherence, looking only to what they term practical results.

Other, more momentous occasions are equally ruled by the highly inartistic element of chance. An opera of 1829 makes the fortune of a composer and a singer because its plot seems an allusion to current affairs.[13] Fifteen years later, Berlioz had to justify himself to his backers in government circles and explain that the chorus by Halévy which he had conducted at a festival meant no anti-British feeling on his part. As far as he was concerned it was a good piece of music which happened to be about a king dead four hundred years before, but the politicians were thinking of the current Entente. From the point of view of politics, art is always irresponsible; from the point of view of art, politics is always irrelevant. Art is in fact self-contained relevance – not absolute, but carried to the highest degree. Every artistic element in a finished work has to fit though the heavens fall. If the work is also to fit a public occasion, it must do so fully and frankly, and not in the skittish fashion of a political person or platform. The history of politics is the history of inessentials raised to temporary significance. A Roman legion refused to fight under an excellent general because his name, Atrius Umber, was forbidding; and among us national leaders can keep their place only if they smile (in the democracies) or frown (in the dictatorships). All this is *political* fitness, that is fitness of the moment, and fitness of the unconsidered.

Commercial fitness is one degree above, but still subject to irrelevance. When Berlioz' *Les Troyens* was first produced, the Virgilian characters were at a disadvantage because a distributor of pencils had adopted a Roman-helmeted hero as his trade-mark. The bromidic part of the public was capable of only one association: "It's like seeing Mangin and his

[13] Auber's *Masaniello;* see above Chapter 4.

pencils on the stage!" What a Roman helmet has to do with lead pencils can never be explained, whereas the composer's connection with the *Aeneid* is intimate and clear; yet it is commercial fact that prevails and Berlioz who is, commercially speaking, in the wrong. Had he really wanted to succeed, he should at every point have taken care to ascertain public taste and prejudice as they affected the market of 1863, instead of starting blindly eight years before and writing a masterpiece. The artist's grievance naturally takes for granted the desirability of a certain kind of art and artist – the high art produced by the individual, self-aware, principled artist who is to the entertainer what the Hippocratic physician is to the quack. Both may have genuine gifts but they exercise them according to different ethics. And there lingers in the very civilization that prefers the quack a tradition of seeking the true healer.

Now it is obvious that in its attitude to art a popular revolution combines the actual demands of both politics and commerce. The revolutionary doctrine is a shifting, uncertain, arbitrary thing,[14] and the fact that the people are sovereign means also the enforcement of their legitimate tastes and prejudices. Even when these chance to be spontaneously fine and straightforward there is a natural tendency on the part of the people's leaders to show their worth by preferring and enforcing a conservative choice. The political liberal in art is usually unable to see above his own fences, and inclined to think that to see above them is to tear them down. It follows as the night the day that in times of liberal revolution high art suffers or ceases to be.

Nor is this all. While the revolutionary situation confronts the artist with all the obstacles of politics and trade, it adds to these the impediments of war. We can be as perceptive as we like later on about the merits of the glorious revolution of this or that date, but while it is going on, revolution is war. When the days of some unforgettable month are "over," they are not over but followed by a state of martial law, or by a sense of insecurity which generally leads to dictatorship. Life is precarious and thought at a standstill. The single law of politics at such times is: "Are you for or against?" and the single law of trade: "Only necessities are marketable." While the shots ring out the artist can hardly be said to be in his element. Beethoven had to take refuge in his brother's cellar when the French were "liberating" Vienna with bullets, but no one would say this was the ideal retreat for a symphonic composer. And for some time to come the new rulers have other things to think about than the living con-

[14] Berlioz at twenty-eight characterized politics as "That tall skinny wench with shifty eyes, a pale face and a hard heart . . ." (*A.R.*, 150.)

ditions of that minority interest, Beethoven. There is in fact no such person, but only Herr Beethoven, that fellow John Milton, a certain Hector Berlioz. Government cannot see with the eyes of posterity and discern whom it should protect, nor does it care. Victor Hugo was a powerful advocate of the principles of 1848, but this did not keep Sobrier's mob from threatening his house. Sainte-Beuve was no menace to the Republic but he was saved from armed assault within the walls of the Institute only by the accidental intervention of Horace Vernet who commanded a company of National Guards and lifted the "siege." [15]

It is necessary to dwell on particulars such as these because our usual reading of history as the interplay of forces or ideas casts a pall of abstraction over events and blurs their shape. We must see, as far as possible, *both* what the contemporaries vividly felt and what slowly emerges after study under the perspective of time. Thus the principles of 1789, revived and extended in 1848, may form the subject of our admiration without making us forget that on the spot much of what happened was meaningless chaos. We may greatly value the historic effort without being committed to approving the deeds of a casual gang, heated with action and driven by inward fears to threaten a poet or destroy a work of art. Even in a Baudelaire the first impulse was to do a private job of killing his stepfather. Lesser minds are not thinking of great principles nor of the verdict of posterity; rather, they seem inclined to bayonet those who are.

For quite apart from the political passion of the moment, there is in most men during revolution a strong urge to destroy, from "an envious kind of wrath" against intellect and its products. This explains the recurrence throughout history of iconoclastic movements – to loot the English monasteries because Henry VIII has made a religious revolution, or to smash the stained glass made by their own artisan ancestors because the Third Estate is in power. This might be called the Alaric Complex after the self-aware conqueror who said, "I feel something within that compels me to burn Rome." In the twentieth century the burning of books is doubtless one manifestation of the same desire, for in this and in the hunting down of intellectuals everywhere, the pretext of danger is obviously false. One has only to compare the armed power of the modern state with that of an individual writer or musician to see that the extermination of thinkers is for pleasure only – the addition of torture proves it. And the fact that nowadays not merely political thought but thought that abstains from politics is grounds for suspicion shows that the link between popular movements and iconoclasm is not accidental.

[15] *1212*, XIII, 19 *n.*

Of course, to say that the quiet thinker or the artist in his studio is no danger to the state is not to deny that a single man's intent – even his unconscious intent expressed in art – may prove a social force, and hence a cause of ultimate disturbance. Jesus, preaching love, brings a sword; and in the rhythm of a Beethoven scherzo there is as much aggression as in an armed assault. It was not simply association of ideas which made the Hungarian nationalists find Berlioz' music revolutionary. Romanticist art at large is implicit criticism of routine and convention – hence it is revolutionary. The response of first audiences whether to Beethoven or Berlioz or Delacroix or Blake shows how true this is: the work is rightly felt to be deliberately violent and new, and it rouses to anger. Yet this very fact defines the difference between revolution through art and simple iconoclasm: the one is loose and chaotic; the other ordered and in the highest degree civilizing. And civilization in this sense is just as objectionable to the mass of men as throwing up barricades, for it spells change; which is why no man can give birth to a new idea or form of art without incurring penalties. Genius is a crime.[16] For society has true interests to maintain – ease, stability, and the avoidance of risk – all of which are threatened by innovation.

The creative artist thus belongs to a class apart, equidistant from the solid citizen and from the political rebel, because his outlook is opposed to the first and his method is opposed to the second. What happens to a Berlioz in a culture like Louis Philippe's we have seen: artist and society feel each other's aggression and fight it out. Inertia and insults, challenges and artistic shocks – these are what lie behind the threadbare terms Philistinism and *épater le bourgeois*. The swearing and cursing against the burgher-at-hand by Beethoven, Berlioz, Liszt, Flaubert, or Shaw are simply peacetime bombs and bayonets. But the artist, unlike the political rebel, inevitably fights single scout. He cannot in his own domain follow a social doctrine. This is not from lack of discipline but from a recognition that doctrines are least common denominators, vaguely expressed, whereas his task is to supply highest common multiples, the fullest, most precise expression of new thought in the medium which he commands. Hence the apparent lack of cohesion and mutual understanding among the artists of any generation.[17]

Since in civil peace and civil war alike, victory lies with the crowd, the

[16] The sociologist Durkheim defines crime as "any act followed by a penalty, whether inflicted by law or by social forces." (*Méthode sociologique*, 80.) This is obviously interchangeable with the biographer's description of genius at work and what he incurs by it.

[17] *E.g.*, Delacroix, Stendhal, and Berlioz.

artist can only expect defeat. In seemingly fortunate exceptions – Wagner's or Tennyson's – the defeat still takes place, by the crowd's perverting the thing said. Thus the creator is compelled from within to fulfill his destiny and from without to suffer for his loyalty to fate. This is known as tragedy, and the prototype of the artistic creator is Prometheus. But in periods of social chaos, the chances of a five-act fulfillment are lessened. Milton was left unmolested by the "captain or knight-at-arms" whom he invoked, but Georg Büchner was hounded to death and Garcia Lorca causelessly murdered: it was pure luck that in 1848 Hugo and Wagner were spared instead of speared. As for the expectation of life under our improved totalitarian control, it is unnecessary to dwell on its precariousness or on the childish justification of rules of darkness: their only effect is to make the nineteenth century begin to glow like a Golden Age.

In the light of the facts it is therefore visibly absurd to keep prattling about the divorce of the artist from society as if they had ever been married: they are and must remain at war. But a body politic that knows its best interests will allow the virus of art to circulate freely within its veins, as an inoculant.

It may be objected that Hugo and Vigny and Sainte-Beuve and Berlioz were men and citizens as well as artists, and that as such they must bear the common responsibilities of men in society, especially since they were eager for a share in governmental patronage, social approval, and commercial success. If the regime was not to their liking, why did they not reform it? On what grounds could they claim both the right to criticize and the repose of a lofty isolation? Two of the Romanticist poets at least, Hugo and Lamartine, sought to act as the conscience of the nation: why not Berlioz and Vigny?

The question leads us deeper into the role and the nature of art by developing another aspect of its divergence from politics. When Berlioz expressed his disgust while himself maneuvering "politically" on behalf of some artistic project, it was neither innocence nor incapacity that prompted his abstention from politics. He knew the game and had a knack for the diplomacy required, but he scorned the objects for which the majority of men were striving and the motives that actuated them. In fact, he described politics very much in the terms used by one of his most politic contemporaries, soon to be Minister of Foreign Affairs under the Second Republic.[18] The artist's dislike of hypocrisy, of the boredom of

[18] Tocqueville: "When I think that [the men of the July Monarchy] are growing indignant at seeing the people violate the Constitution by doing for

business, and of makeshifts that end in futility, unfits him for what is falsely called "practical politics." [19] It is art, on the contrary, which seeks the permanently practical by disregarding the vanity and self-interest of the customer, the constituent, or the powers that be. For an artist to be also a political man, therefore, would require him to have two natures, two talents – which is not inconceivable – but which would no more establish a rule or a duty for artists than Byron's being a boxer and swimmer requires other poets to be athletic.

It would also require him to have two lives, since both art and politics, when taken seriously, are bound to be full-time occupations. There is certainly no evidence that the attempt to straddle both has ever contributed to success in either: Hugo and Lamartine were not conspicuous successes as statesmen, and their verse, even in its popular aspects, did not depend for its quality upon an inside knowledge of public affairs. Was Böcklin a better painter or Wagner a more consummate musician for having taken part in riots? [20] Rioting only earned Courbet exile, that is, it cost him the means and peace of mind for making his last years productive. As for Berlioz' friend Becher, who took up the profession of revolutionist and died of it within a few months, he was a sheer loss which we can virtually measure in cultural terms. In short, the instinct which drives the artist to stick to his last and keep out of the highly technical make-believe of politics is a very useful protection, which incidentally gives him the right to keep ignorant politicians out of *his* technical concerns. The clinching argument is that this aloofness and even this contempt for governance does not in any way preclude sympathy with the general will nor response to the national temper. Berlioz is the best proof one could desire: his works for popular and national occasions have the ring of the genuine metal and transcend in their broad social sense all the party loyalties or doctrines that one might naïvely suppose prerequisite to composing the right notes. This is so true that in celebrating the centenary of 1848, France did not go back to the Saint-Simonian hymns of Félicien David, but performed the *Funeral and Triumphal* symphony and the *Hymne à la France*.

Louis Napoleon precisely what they themselves . . . proposed to him, I find it difficult to imagine a more noteworthy example of the variability of men and of the vanity of the great words Patriotism and Right under which petty passions are apt to cloak themselves." (*1223*, 251.)

[19] As Gide says of another artist: "He was apolitical because there is no politics without fraud." (*1249*, III, 338.)

[20] Wagner's attempt at interfering with the conduct of foreign affairs when he finally became the favorite of a king only endangered his position and made him ridiculous.

At the time, it took another artist to perceive this. Then as now, "advanced" political thinkers were suspicious of intellectuals and wanted to expel them from the party of reform and deny them the future rewards. The issue was joined when George Sand refuted the arguments of Michel de Bourges, using Berlioz among others as a test case, and saying: "Maybe he is wicked enough to think in secret that mankind is not worth a chromatic scale . . . but you may be sure that one can think such things and still not be the enemy of man. . . . When we shall have to build the New City of Mind, rest assured that everyone of us will aid in proportion to his strength – Berlioz, who is very brave and proud, will come with a spade, I with a toothpick, the rest with their arms and will-power."[21]

Now one reason, apart from genius, that Berlioz and his peers were able to achieve such a just expression of their times, even while fighting their times, is that they still lived and worked within the accepted order. In this regard as in others, 1848 marks the turning point, the watershed of the century. Before 1848 the majority of European artists belonged by birth or desire to the ruling class and remained part of it. They were born not only to property but to a social tradition; their families, as we saw, half supported them in the strange profession of art, and they themselves retained in their work and behavior the bourgeois virtues of sobriety, industry, orderliness, and self-respect. To this they added aristocratic aspirations to honors and riches for serving the nation through uncommon talents. Believing in genius and self-dedication, they had the consciousness of superiority and the tastes that go with it. And precisely because they lived in a world run by the bourgeoisie for gain and public plunder, they rejected that part of their own tradition and ideally took the side of the people: they were Tory Democrats besides being bourgeois and *grands seigneurs*.[22]

After 1848 this peculiar threefold position became untenable. The class war that split France and spread to Central Europe showed that the people were moved by envy and hatred which, however understandable, were even poorer qualifications for ruling than bourgeois greed. What alienated men like Berlioz from the Republic that had promised liberty was that its doctrines remained dead letters while its performance showed lack

[21] *Revue des Deux Mondes,* June 1835, 723.

[22] For Berlioz' understanding of the poor, see *L.I.*, 91; *Soirées* (18th) *Eves.*, 201 as well as *Grot.*, 10–12, 90–1, and his special sympathy with the humble, underpaid performers in his own art, *passim.* Nor had he any scorn for the underlying instincts of the crowd in matters of art: he merely thought those instincts perverted by commercial cynicism and vulgar fare. See *Soirées* (10th) and *Mem.*, II, 226.

of skill, absence of thought and want of self-discipline – the exact reverse of the artistic virtues.[23] Meanwhile fear of anarchy drove the worse elements of the former ruling classes to adopt dictatorship, chauvinism, and *Realpolitik* as stopgaps – brute force and vulgar expedients in place of law.

Between anarchy and cynical demagogy, both hostile to intellect, the artists of Europe began their great retreat. They no longer hoped for the high places under state patronage nor even the middling bourgeois positions created by publishers and audience. The younger ones gradually withdrew into a state within a state: bohemia; [24] they lived, dressed, acted differently from the world, rejecting the symbols of respectability and taking up alcoholism, homosexuality, and physical abjection almost more in protest than from inclination. Ultimately they fled to places untouched by hard money and dress suits – whether tropic isles or the haunts of hoboes. It became the new sign of self-dedication to die in the asylum or the paupers' hospital.

No matter what their individual fate might hold in store, these new generations of artists were bound to be antisocial, if only because they linked all that they saw triumphing – industry, nationalism, and democracy – with everything that was ugly, corrupt and brutish. Some turned accordingly against their immediate masters, confusing the original hopes of the Romantics with the reality that had to come to pass. Hence, paradoxically, the very success of a Berlioz with his *Requiem* or Festival works made him look as if he had pandered to democracy and mediocrity: within half a century after the *Funeral* symphony, the artistic eye had turned inward and was exclusively projecting on the screen of the imagination, not the mourning of France over the dead of 1830, but the woes of Pelléas and Mélisande.[25]

[23] "At the coming of liberty, equality, and fraternity I believed for a moment in my emancipation" – the speaker is Music, personified as a petitioner to the Minister – "but I was mistaken. When the hour of liberation from slavery struck for the Negroes, I indulged in fresh hopes; I was again mistaken." (*Soirées* (10th) *Eves.*, 119.) Just above this passage, he compares the inadequate plan for giving working-class children a free musical education (favored by Berlioz) with the futility of the National Workshops.

[24] The earlier form of the differentiation was Dandyism, whose connotations give a fair index of the social descent between 1830 and 1890, between Byron and Verlaine.

[25] Huysmans's hero Des Esseintes, in 1883: "Then . . . secular music is a promiscuous art which one ought to enjoy at home and alone, as one reads a book; [but] to taste it, he must needs have mixed with that inevitable public that crowds to theatres and besieges the *Cirque d'Hiver* where, under a broiling sun, in an atmosphere as muggy as a wash-house, you see a man with the look of a carpenter bawling . . . to the huge delight of the crowd. . . . He

In between, that is to say during the decades from 1850 to 1870 or from one civil war to another,[26] was the arid period which the surviving Romantics, too far committed to change their outlook or mode of life, had to endure. It was the Era of Positivism (as Littré called it), of Materialism (as English science and German philosophy deemed it), of Realism (as literature recorded it). Realism was simply the concrete side of Romanticism – the substratum without the ideal, without the faith, and sometimes without the meaning. It produced an admirable literature of depiction and of implied criticism, and an equally admirable school of painting, from which Pre-Raphaelitism sprang in the very year 1848. Ultimately, it yielded in music – with an admixture of Romantic and symbolist elements – the operas of Wagner and the later Verdi. But in the workaday world, the change of temper only augmented the crassness that had in fact defeated the Romanticist hopes. The spirit (if it may be so called) of incredulous materialism, of pride in pettiness, of almost mindless self-indulgence, is enshrined in the pages of Flaubert's *Education of the Feelings*, which deals with this Great Divide even more thoroughly than *Bovary*.[27] Baudelaire sums up the new order of things in a sentence: "The artist . . . found himself facing a society . . . absolutely fagged out and brutified, yet gluttonous, hating only imagination and loving only possession." [28]

In short, before 1848 hope and struggle seemed still possible. A fine arc of energy had been described with its base in the last decade of the eighteenth century and its highest reach in the years 1827–1840. It sank into the ground in 1848. To say this is not to make a handful of artists and thinkers the only men who justified their existence during that half century, but

---

had never had the courage to plunge into that bath of promiscuity in order to hear Berlioz, some fragments of whom had nevertheless won his admiration by their high-wrought passion and abundant fire. . . ." (*1263*, 317–8.)

[26] In 1870, young Bizet writes in words echoing those of Berlioz: "Between the excesses of the reds and the whites, there will be no place for decent people. Music will have no future here. I shall have to go abroad – Italy, England, or America." (*940*, 76.)

[27] Doudan calls 1848–1849, "the great winter of our century" (*188*, III, 234). For the revolutionary background of this disillusioned epoch see in *L'Education Sentimentale* Part III, Chapter I, which dramatizes all the conceivable plans propounded during the Republic's lifetime, and depicts popular agitation: "No more Academies and Institutes; no more missions, no more Bachelors of Arts, down with University titles!" – "No! Let us keep them, but let them be conferred by universal suffrage, by the people, the only true judge!" The scene modulates to an attack on the rich, and closes, after passages of personal dialogue, with the account of a riot.

[28] *1049*, 412–3.

merely to show the permissive character of those years. The artist's role as an upsetter, a ferment, a maker of revolutions without bloodshed, is clear; but this is only a phase in the life span of a masterpiece. There must come a time when the world says: "Yes, this poetry, this music, embodies a moment of the human spirit. Thus did our fathers live and feel; in this work we can see their humanity together with their uniqueness, and for us the spectacle is beauty." But with the break of 1848, this time of recognition was delayed, those who should have been willing disciples and grateful descendants turned blind and bitter, and we are only now beginning to see that the masters who wrought into shape the imaginings of that first half century — and did it more lastingly than the statesmen or financiers — had to have the courage of Titans to pursue their struggle into the darker time of their declining days; while those who followed under coercion of circumstances no longer permissive, could only save their small freedom by reducing their aims and foregoing part of their mission. The exclusive cultivation of the inner world is the refuge of the oppressed — so is the growing sense of the past — and we shall see that Berlioz himself after 1849 undergoes that subtle influence of time: his three great works of the last twenty years despite their continuing power, originality, and strength, deal perforce with no present occasion but with history or the comic spirit.

The task of the artist, then, is to arrest life in its flow and cast it into forms resistant to time, for accomplishing which he must have security of life and limb, sustenance and public response. The last pair of requirements takes us from the politics to the economics of art. If artistic power is incompatible with political life, it may be said to be not so much in contradiction as at cross purposes with business. One need not bring up Scott's or Mark Twain's great bankruptcies to show the wasted energy of the artist in business. Berlioz' compulsory efforts as an impresario are ample proof of the fact. Nor has this generality much to do with the old confusion of ideas which implies that the artistic temperament is unbusinesslike: Berlioz and many other artists have been models of order and practicality. Their ill success came from not thinking day and night about what was salable and how to sell it.[29]

Society cannot do without Trade or Politics; hence these two interests are in the right just as much as Art. It is because everybody is in the right

[29] A brilliant short statement on the contrast between artist and tradesman has been given by the distinguished American designer, W. A. Dwiggins, in "The Technique for Dealing with Artists." (*1075*, 83–100.)

that we witness a real drama. When narrating Berlioz's life one must take his point of view in order to show the spirit of the man and his work, but it would be possible and equally true to write a parallel account from the point of view of the publishers who wanted to sell his scores, the opera managers who went gray trying to part the public from its money, and the Ministers of State who dreamed of oubliettes when they saw Berlioz coming to ask for the sums due him – which they had already spent. For – it must be said again – it is of the essence of trade to make profits and of politics to balance budgets by cutting corners.

In this triangular duel Art can claim only one slight superiority – it makes no false pretenses while the other two interests do. Opera houses and publishers pose as patrons of art; governments and nations want to claim the fruits of individual genius. Whole peoples have the audacity to say, "*We* have produced Shakespeare," (or Bach) and critics conclude, "The English are not musical, the Germans are;" – utterances so crude as to be downright indecent. Not even a Medici Pope or a Louis XIV can lay claim to have done much more for art than supply the materials and tolerate the workman. When Poussin was brought back from Rome to work at the Louvre against his will, all that absolute power could do was to see him safely home after he had suffered insults and frustration. The facts of Michelangelo's or Cellini's commissions are to the same effect, which is why Berlioz paraphrased them in his *Benvenuto* and his satirical novelettes. The historical truth is that there is not and there has never been a workable system of art patronage in European civilization, ancient or modern.[30]

Art exists on sufferance until it conquers through militant admiration,[31] after which it lingers on by a coalition between its true lovers and the parroting approval of the crowd. And this usually comes posthumously, for connoisseurs are grave robbers, esthetic necrophiles. In order to reach anything resembling the first stage, the living artist has to compromise

[30] We may think the Middle Ages an exception. Unfortunately not enough facts are available, but those at hand seem to show that pious bishops and fearsome barons were no better patrons than Renaissance cardinals and railroad magnates. The influence of a common religion no doubt helped to make "the public" accept original designs in art – though El Greco in a pious milieu did not find it so. In any case, the religious motive obscures the issue since it suggests that criticism may be silenced by consecrated use, not by quickened apprehension or respect for handiwork. One might as well instance secular occasions when patriotism gave popularity to an otherwise neglected artist – Beethoven after the *Battle* Symphony and Whitman after "O Captain! My Captain!"

[31] *E.g.*, the English, German, and French Romantics' "plugging" of Shakespeare, the Berlioz-Liszt-Wagner crusade for Beethoven.

with Trade, occasionally with Politics, and almost always with fashion, the really paying patron of art in our society being the passionate snob — C. Snobius Maecenas.

This will continue until artists find an acceptable system of support enabling them to say "a plague on both your houses." Then, possibly, respect for the conditions and processes of artistic creation might grow, as all respect grows, in the face of independence, which is to say, of power. So far, none of these conditions, neither psychological nor practical, have even been studied. There exist, it is true, practical associations of artists, which from Berlioz' time to the present have seemed the only alternative to state patronage and commercial self-help. When he founded, with other musicians and with the aid of that most intelligent of men, Baron Taylor, the first Association of Musicians in France, Berlioz had in mind the co-operative idea, marketing in common without going through the ruinous middleman, and securing a public by a group appeal more impressive (and on the face of it less self-seeking) than that of the individual composer. We shall see in the next chapter what obstacles such an association had to encounter. By the end of the century it was still powerless to oppose officialdom.[32]

In time despair led to a second type of self-defense, on the trade-union principle. As Berlioz pointed out, no help being likely to come from on high, nor from the scattered and uninformed public, musicians must help themselves.[33] By propaganda in the press such as he could provide,[34] and pressure upon the legislators, the ordinary orchestra player's miserable lot might at last be remedied. This has in fact happened, as a part of the general emancipation of labor through trade-union tactics. But success has been bought at a price. As in every contact of art with trade and with politics, contamination, not of morals but of art, has ensued; for in our unyielding social order the only way to fight exploitation and monopoly is to exploit and monopolize in return. By acting restrictively and co-ercively, musicians' unions have established their right to good wages and warded off wholesale liquidation in the face of a technology Berlioz could

[32] See Alfred Bruneau's dealings with opera managers in the nineties, at which time he was put off with the disingenuous excuse that they were thinking of putting on Berlioz, now happily dead. (*936.*)

[33] *Soirées* (10th) *Eves.*, 121–2.

[34] See the preface to the *Grotesques de la Musique*, in which to show the performer's plight he develops a sardonic account of the violin player's ruinous upkeep of his white tie. The preface is addressed to the personnel of the opera, who had so often played or sung for him gratis, and is signed, "your devoted comrade." He always felt solidarity with his fellows in both music and journalism, and belonged to their respective associations.

only dream of.[35] But in so doing they have necessarily trampled on the artistic principles of fitness and flexibility, to such an extent that a Berlioz or a Liszt, for all their devotion to the underpaid, might find it hard to choose the lesser evil. They would discover that the amateur musicians on whom they depended were now hampered at every turn by unions as well as by special combinations of professionals, and that in the scramble for "rights" the very thriving of one musical enterprise is now officially and unblushingly "viewed with alarm" by another group: a full circle to the days when Pillet, as manager of the Opera, could obtain a ministerial decree to close the Italian Theatre on *his* nights.[36]

Every step in the process is intelligible and worthy of approval, yet the results for art are no less damnable – as when one union of musicians threatens retaliatory measures against broadcasting by their transatlantic fellows; when the well-being of its members forbids them to cross the threshold of certain studios, or when they give up their essential character altogether by accepting payment for standing in the place of a conceivable musician who is not hired because he is not needed.[37] It would be news if a musical union refused to play because the work of a master was being distorted or disarranged for commercial reasons.

Union practices are of course no worse than the so-called understandings among radio and recording companies, which are rather misunderstandings of every cultural aim. When a conductor who "belongs" to Station RFD conducts by permission an orchestra that has a contract with

[35] Berlioz' scientific imagination was at all times very lively. He called for the electric metronome and remote time-beater ten years before it was built; and he recurrently forecast the fact of directed aerial navigation, wireless telegraph, and other practical devices for travel and communication. (See *Soirées*, *Grot.*, and *Mem.*, *passim.*)

[36] That was in the 1840's; here is the 1940's: "The . . . ban on foreign broadcasts . . . is a necessary measure due to present-day conditions in order to protect the employment of our musicians. . . . An announcement by the State Department that the following programs were to be arranged (quote) opera from Italy, Russian Symphonies from Moscow, and French, British and Latin-American composers and orchestras (unquote) certainly gives us cause for alarm. Such a long-range program presents a definite threat to the American musicians' employment opportunities and would eventually lead to a general breakdown of social and economic standards." (*The International Musician*, vol. xliv, No. 9, March 1946.)

[37] "The theatrical committee reported on its review of the show *Winter's Tale.* Motion made and carried to classify same as a drama with music, stipulating the musical production scale and that a minimum of eight members and a conductor must be employed therefor." (*Allegro*, Feb. 1946.) Unavoidably, modern organizations in the interests of teachers and performers of music outnumber three to one those that protect composers. (*1329*, 1935.)

the PDQ network, the powerful intellects in charge cannot find a way to allow the orchestra's regular broadcast to take place. The art of music in all its branches must remain silent while announcers burble about the resumption next week of the great public service that "brings you Mozart through the courtesy" of a cheese or cosmetic.

The fierce fight for property rights paradoxically leads to nonproduction. This same barrier, bottomed on indifference, has virtually stopped in this country the extension of the repertoire of music on discs, while the international exchange is so impeded by customs rules that it is a diplomatic tour de force to import sets of records made in such distant lands as France and England. When one adds to all this the increased costs of copying, printing, and distributing music, the taxes and licenses and fees which frequently make symphonic composers *decline* to be played – each performance being a luxury-offering to his pride – one is more than ever persuaded that Berlioz still belonged to the ages of faith in art.[38] For although he lived in a country ruled first by a king and later by a dictator, he only had to endure insults, relative poverty, and misrepresentation. He was never instructed under pain of death how to make the melodic follow the party line. He enjoyed not only the friendship and respect of the truly great, who still formed a noble company throughout Europe, but also a free access to every part of that continent for the fulfillment of his mission.

We can measure from the utopian aspect of these historical facts the degree to which our supercivilized forms of trade and politics have throttled art. Music is an excellent yardstick, involving as it does so many wills and interests, though other forms of artistic life today are likewise threatened with the same extinction. The substitute uses for talent, as in the motion-picture industry, all show the mark of the new "populist" culture, which is thin and sentimental rather than simple and massive, rigidly conventional rather than inventive and revolutionary. Were Berlioz alive now he would not find the means, and not a tithe of the understanding, which enabled him in spite of all odds to succeed. For financial reasons alone he could not afford to write for full orchestra, he therefore could not have tried out and codified the resources of that instrument. He would be reduced, like so many musicians today who want occasionally to hear what they compose, to the chamber ensemble or string quartet

[38] "When on April 21st, Dr. Vaughan Williams's new Sixth Symphony was performed at the Albert Hall, the composer himself received only £68. £8 of this came from the Albert Hall, £60 from the B.B.C. for the broadcast – yet the critics agree that the Sixth Symphony is probably his greatest work." (*News-Letter from London*, Apr. 30, 1948, p. 6.) As Dickens said: "Poetry costs money, cut it how you will."

– media certainly capable of producing the sublimest works, but whose use under compulsion or as a *pis aller* is equally certainly opposed to the spirit of art. It would be but another compulsion added to the rest.

In 1848, on the threshold of the hundred years that have brought about these world-wide paradoxes in the very name of freedom, popular government, and the extension of culture, Berlioz was returning to a blood-soaked Paris with little hope but with the same Socratic determination to heed the daemon within.

19. *Vision of a Virtuoso:* Te Deum

July 14, 1848
to May 9, 1851

I am a composer and was born to be a kapellmeister . . . [the rest] is with me a side line.

— Mozart in 1778

The city to which Berlioz returned on the doubly revolutionary date of July 14, 1848 was an intellectual desert and a visible shambles. The narrow crooked streets, which had made the raising of barricades easy, showed scars of the fighting, looting and arson. Violence had not quite ceased. "The people kill the poor young constables whenever they catch them alone." [1] The angel of liberty on Duc's column, Place de la Bastille, had a bullet through its gilt body, and the Tuileries were a mass of litter.[2]

Of Berlioz' friends, many were abroad, others stayed with relatives in the country, still others were out of circulation as they made shift with menial jobs. Berlioz saw a pianist playing on the streets for pennies; painters served as crossing sweepers. "I am again living as when I was a medical student in the Latin Quarter, on 80 or 100 francs a month," wrote Berlioz to his brother-in-law. His only source of income was the *Débats*, for "nothing is left of what used to exist in the way of art . . . No one even thinks of it or talks about it." [3] "We attended the opening of the Opera," said Berlioz in his first *feuilleton*, "and some malicious wit suggested that the word should be taken in the sense of 'autopsy.' " [4]

The Chamber did vote "aid" for the dispossessed and unemployed artists, but it was far short of adequate. "Besides, in order to economize, they take back with one hand what they give with the other. Thus, the committee

[1] *M.E.*, 241.

[2] Delacroix: "Disgusting devastation . . . everywhere the signs of degradation, and an evil smell . . . everywhere the portraits have been hacked to pieces." (*182*, II, 254, 269; see also *188*, III, 214.)

[3] *M.E.*, 240. Among other disturbing changes, the publishing house of Schlesinger had passed into the hands of Brandus, who at first ignored Berlioz completely. (*M.E.*, 219.) Maurice Schlesinger, incidentally, was the original of Arnoux in Flaubert's *Education Sentimentale*, and the publisher's wife actually the object of Flaubert's distant adoration — as transcribed in the novel.

[4] *1386*, July 26, 1848.

on the Conservatoire proposed yesterday to abolish my post in the library and to divide my salary among the other employees." [5] It is true that Berlioz' office was a sinecure, but he himself was just proposing to the authorities that his status be changed. "It was not my doing if the Conservatoire failed to use my services more actively: the musical views of the previous Director [Cherubini] always kept me at arm's length . . . Yet I could, for instance, hold a chair of Instrumentation. This modern branch of the composer's studies is not taught anywhere, and general opinion has it that I possess the requisite knowledge and that I have even made contributions to it. I have moreover written a treatise on the subject which has been translated into the chief European languages." [6]

The "Citizen Minister" of the Interior did not establish such a chair, but through the influence of Louis Blanc's brother Charles – an engraver and art critic who was the new Director of Fine Arts – Berlioz' post and salary were maintained. It was fortunate, for the newspapers had cut their rate of pay to half, and his expenses were increasing by reason of Harriet's worsened health. She was half paralyzed and must have constant attendance. Adèle's husband, the faithful and intelligent Marc Suat, lent Berlioz some money. At the same time, Adèle told her brother of her apprehension at their father's condition: he died a few days later, on the twenty-eighth. "The agony of the last days," she wrote again, "was dreadful. He looked like a galvanized corpse, shaking continually . . . and asking us for impossible things . . . Our caresses would calm him down . . . I held him in my arms with frenzy when he was at his worst. Nanci would run away in terror . . . He was shown your portrait and called you by name, and immediately asked for pen and paper . . . One day, seeing his eyes in search of something, I asked if he wanted anything. 'Nothing, daughter,' he said in the tenderest voice, 'I am looking for your eyes.' This fatherly word reduced us all to tears." [7]

Berlioz could not go to La Côte until the following month. He did not see the long train of sincere mourners – patients and poor people – who followed the country doctor to his grave. Berlioz, still at work on the Death March for *Hamlet* which he had begun in London, could not help associating it with the death of his father, and consequently would never trust himself to play it. In these months an angry kind of worry over the ways and means to keep alive was his normal state. It would have been

[5] *M.E.*, 240.

[6] *M.E.*, 239. This statement exaggerated, or rather, anticipated, the actual translations of the work.

[7] *Mem.*, II, 320–1.

infuriating to go under (as did his friend and early benefactor De Pons who took poison) when so many idle and useless functionaries were managing to survive. "These people are our enemies – a thousand times more so than the wretches who kill on a barricade. . . . The only problem is for us to avoid dying and to take our time about it." [8] This abstract fury masked affectionate apprehension about his friends in Vienna and the Germanies, and especially about Liszt. As soon as Berlioz heard from Belloni, his friend's secretary, who was in Paris, he could write: "Everyone asked me about you in London, but I had absolutely no idea on what European barricade you stood. . . . So many bankers have failed that I very much fear you have suffered losses. Farewell. I hope to see Belloni tomorrow and to make him talk about you. . . . Your forever devoted: H. Berlioz." [9]

Berlioz left for his birthplace on August 18 and stayed in Dauphiné until September 10. The empty house and familiar horizons, the reunion with his dearly loved Adèle and her kind husband opened up his heart. Nanci came too and he melted to her also despite their mutually uncongenial ways. The subject of inheritance likewise had to be discussed. Each of their shares was worth about 130,000 francs, but since the whole consisted of real property it would be unwise to try to liquidate it at once when the market was stagnant. The three nevertheless had to go to Les Jacques near Grenoble, to sort out personal effects, and it was there that looking across the river valley Berlioz thought again of his Estelle and decided to go on a pilgrimage to the site of his ideal childhood love. The account of this visit, given in one of the best pages of the *Memoirs*, was doubtless written soon after the event. From his relatives Berlioz found out what was known of Estelle, now Mme. Fornier, a widow of fifty with four children, one of whom was finishing law school in the same class with a young cousin of Berlioz'. Hector took what he termed "the strange liberty" of writing to her, excusing her in advance if she chose to "laugh at the grown man's recollections as she had done at the child's worshiping." [10] He received no reply.

In Paris, grimmer feelings were to be his lot. About the middle of October, Harriet suffered a fifth stroke – while Berlioz and her son were with her, fortunately – but when her doctor was out on call. "For two hours, Louis and I scoured the neighboring streets of Montmartre without

[8] *M.E.*, 244. Delacroix, the following year: "After luncheon, I heard of the death of poor Chopin . . . What despicable rogues fill the market-place while that beautiful soul burns out!" (*182*, I, 325.)

[9] *M.E.*, 245. The word "forever" is in English.

[10] *Mem.*, II, 330.

SCHUMANN — SIDNEY LANIER — NIETZSCHE

LALO — FLAUBERT — BRUCKNER

L. DAMROSCH — MOUSSORGSKY — HUGO WOLF

Eminent Berliozians: 1835–1890

"Berlioz . . . the veritable savior of our world of absolute music . . ."

— WAGNER (1850)

finding any physician in. The poor woman was all this time unconscious and more like the dead than the living. Finally her own doctor arrived and bleeding brought her round. . . . One result, however, is that her speech is more impaired than before and it is almost impossible to understand her." [11]

Berlioz accompanied his son back to Rouen and kept him informed of his mother's condition: "She is still in bed and under orders not to talk. The least emotion, too, would be fatal to her. So please do not write her a letter like your last one to me. It is distressful to see you giving yourself up to moping and idleness; you will be eighteen [in four years] without having any career to go into . . . You keep telling me that you want to be a sailor; you must want pretty badly to leave me behind, because once you are at sea God knows when I shall see you. If I were free and independent I should leave with you and we would seek our fortunes in India or elsewhere, but even to travel takes means. . . . And my career as a composer keeps me in France. I would have to give it up if I left the Old World for the New. I write to you as to a grown boy. You will think all this over and you will understand. For no matter what happens, I shall always be your best friend, *the only one* entirely devoted to you and full of unchangeable affection for you. I know you love me and that will make up to me for everything. . . . Tell me again about your teeth: have they been thoroughly cleaned? Farewell, dear child, I kiss you with all my soul." [12]

The heartfelt attachment expressed in this letter – the first that remains of Berlioz' correspondence with his son – does not conceal a certain remorse which Berlioz doubtless felt at having left Louis for six or seven years alone with his mother, or still more alone in boarding school. The causes of the boy's melancholy indolence were perfectly evident to the father, who also sensed the child's desire to retaliate and "leave him behind." Not that Berlioz had abandoned his son; but in those years of travel to Moscow and back, and when Berlioz had come within sight of solid material success, he had been too preoccupied to be anything but deficient as a father. And those same years had transformed the winsome, "badly brought up" baby into a shy despairing adolescent. His "qualities of heart," said his aunt Nanci, were "of a rare sort and most endearing." And she lectured her brother trying to prove that a good heart was much better than a brilliant mind.[13]

* * *

[11] *M.E.*, 250. [12] *M.E.*, 251–2. [13] *M.E.*, 253.

Toward the end of October 1848 Berlioz, aided by Baron Taylor, prepared and led a concert for the benefit of the Musicians' Association. Organized under extreme difficulties, it was intended in part as an inducement to the new Republican leaders to think better of the arts. Four hundred and fifty performers were gathered in the theater of Louis XIV at Versailles, which the public had been admitted to only twice since its construction. The prices were moderate and the program was to suit all tastes without any condescension: Rossini, Meyerbeer, Gluck, Mozart, Beethoven, and three small works by Berlioz. Both orchestra and audience shunned elegance of dress and made up for this populist pride by showing pleasure a little rowdily. The event turned out badly for Berlioz, by reason – as always – of political interpretations.

His willingness to make music "for the people" was felt to be ill-timed because everyone now predicted the coming of "an Emperor." Louis Napoleon had been elected to the Assembly by four districts, had had his election returns disputed, then validated, had shrewdly declined to take a seat that "might embarrass the government," but declared himself ready to follow the people's will. Whereupon he had been re-elected by five districts. The glorious associations of his name and the disgust felt at the Republic's squabbling incompetence made Bonaparte a likely winner of the presidency. At this date the Empire was not inevitable, yet it was widely spoken of as the next step,[14] its presumed style and dignity contrasting with the bad manners that had, among other things, given offense at the Berlioz concert. On that occasion, it seems, "little old Marrast" the president of the Constituent Assembly, had slouched in the armchair of Louis XIV and had appeared, in his lemon-colored gloves, to be enjoying himself altogether too much.

The Republic, though slow, was not ungrateful. It kept Berlioz in his Librarianship, paid the arrears of his salary, and added five hundred francs "to encourage him as a composer." Cavaignac, the republican soldier, was doing all he could to restore the popularity of the regime which the sabotage of the National Workshops and the bloodshed in June had nearly destroyed. The campaign for the presidency in December had been the last chance for staunch republicans and socialists to prove that the country deserved self-government. When that chance failed by producing instead a demagogue, all but a few felt that their hopes had been illu-

[14] Doudan: "To exchange King Louis Philippe for the Emperor Louis Napoleon is really too ridiculous a notion. To wreck France during eight months in order to achieve this magnificent result is a deed fit to make us immortal in the eyes of History." (*188*, III, 230.)

sions, and that a true republic could only be the work of a later generation. In the interim between his Republican concert and Bonaparte's success, Berlioz summed up the situation for one of his Russian friends: "What changes since then [1847] in our unhappy Europe! What cries and crimes, what follies and blunders, and what cruel mystifications . . . Paris is still in a fever and has attacks of delirium tremens. To think of the peaceful works of the mind or to seek the beautiful in art and letters under such conditions is like trying to play billiards on a storm-tossed ship. . . ." [15]

Berlioz worked nonetheless. In his reconquered Library at the Conservatoire, he went on with his *Memoirs*, parts of which might make salable articles. He had finished the Death March for *Hamlet* in late September and joined it to the "Death of Ophelia" and the "Religious Meditation" to form a volume which he entitled *Tristia* (after Ovid's "Sad Pieces"). It appropriately signalized for Berlioz a year of exile, defeat, and mourning. He had also revised *La Captive*, the melody that had charmed Rome seventeen years before, making it now into a miniature symphonic poem for voice and orchestra.[16] These small but beautifully finished works once behind him, he could begin the new year with a fresh enterprise: a companion piece to his monumental *Requiem* in the form of an equally large-scale *Te Deum*.

The germinal idea dated from the Italian notebooks of 1832, but only part of that inspiration had gone into the *Funeral* symphony. Berlioz' plan, it will be recalled, was to celebrate the nation's great dead with a vast symphony in seven movements. The idea did not recur to him now because of any similarity between the heroic first Napoleon and his nephew the President, elected in December 1848. Citizen Bonaparte had stumped the country like a vulgar politician, promising peace and plenty, and pretending attachment to republican institutions. The Berlioz *Te Deum* on the contrary was to be a religious and military fresco more closely related to the revolutionary era of which 1848 had revived certain aspects – war, grief, and the terror of divine justice. As for the political fact, Berlioz did desire an Emperor such as Napoleon to put an end to the "grotesque and disgusting farce" and "pretentious stupidities" of the Republic, yet he abstained from voting "so that I shall be sure not to have contributed to any catastrophe." [17]

[15] *M.E.*, 257.

[16] It was first sung in this form by Pauline Viardot in London, at Berlioz' concert of June 29, 1848, and only subsequently published.

[17] *M.E.*, 255, 256.

Composing had to go on to an accompaniment of brain squeezing for the "relentless" newspapers. The *Débats* was publishing less and paying little – only eight francs a column, but the *Gazette* kept appearing weekly and paid by the line. Berlioz' printed remarks on the new operas were thus not so concisely witty as the comments in his letters: he could not afford it. "Meyerbeer," he informed Count Wielhorsky, "has begun rehearsing his *Prophète;* he is a very courageous man to risk launching a work of those dimensions at a time when riots or a change of government . . . can cut him short, however great his eloquence. Halévy has just won a tremendous success with his *Val d'Andorre* at the Opéra-Comique. It is really good. There are in his score some charming melodies and things of a high and just style. *I said what I thought* when I wrote of it. It is quite the other way with [Clapisson's] *Jeanne la Folle:* no ideas, no style; it's simply gross, dull, and flat. You will wonder how grossness can combine with flatness. I do not know how the composer did it; it is one of his trade secrets." [18]

A few months later, to Berlioz' delight, the second act of *La Vestale* was put on by the Conservatoire, whose public was properly overwhelmed.[19] By that time (February 1849) Liszt was again in touch with Berlioz, exchanging confidences and even offering financial help which Berlioz did not have to accept. The pianist was himself going through a bad time as regards both money and personal relations.[20]

"I was much upset," Berlioz writes back, "as you can well imagine. But I know how energetic and decided you can be in crucial moments . . . Still, your project [to go to the United States] seems to me *violent* – to cross the Atlantic to make music for Yankees who just now think only of California gold! You are the best judge of the advisability of such a trip. As for what can be done here, I really don't know: it changes with the riot-meter.

"The Italian Theatre flaps only one wing; the Opera never had any, but they say *Le Prophète* will supply the want of them. . . . When the crowds who are coming to the Industrial Exhibition have gone, when the new Chamber is elected and seated, when the emotion caused by the premières of *Le Prophète* has calmed down, maybe you can try something. We are all impatient to see you." [21]

The reference to the several "first nights" of the new opera alludes to

[18] *M.E.*, 258.

[19] *Corresp.*, 176.

[20] These difficulties were connected with his establishment in Weimar, where he lived with the Princess Carolyne Sayn-Wittgenstein – of whom more later.

[21] *M.E.*, 260–1.

the special effort Meyerbeer made just then to win over Berlioz by inviting him to a private rehearsal. At the same time, possibly at Meyerbeer's instigation, the Conservatoire asked that Berlioz allow something of his to be played at their concerts. The German composer whose mastery of the operatic world was unchallenged seemed eager to have the approval of a less variable judge than the public, and perhaps to share with Berlioz the artistic ground which Meyerbeer in his own mind knew that Berlioz occupied. At any rate, he addressed him as "Dear and Illustrious Master," and expressing his "love" and "fear" of him, invited him in successive messages to several of the rehearsals, signing the last note: "Your devoted and trembling Meyerbeer." [22]

The day before the occasion of this curious testimonial, two excerpts from the *Damnation of Faust* were given by the Conservatoire. This sudden reopening of a symphony society which had been closed to him since the early days of the *Rob Roy* overture (sixteen years) made Berlioz feel nervous about the outcome. The gracious invitation might prove another blow, especially since his erstwhile admirer Narcisse Girard, who had been eclipsed by Berlioz as conductor, would lead the orchestra. The players anyhow were very friendly, and as it turned out the audience also. The composer could feel that his success was like "the overturning of a barrier . . . If the other Great Walls of China that still hem me in . . . should likewise collapse, perhaps the music I have composed might receive the same welcome here as in the rest of Europe and I might be forgiven for being alive and French. Perhaps I might also produce new works, more important than those I have been engaged on . . ." [23]

Right or wrong, Berlioz felt that recognition on home ground was necessary to his career. "You cannot imagine," he wrote to Janin, "with what heartbreak I sit down to my task when I am convinced that my work will be well received only abroad." [24] Though he kept counseling himself to be patient, he doubtless seemed to his friends impatient and certainly unresigned. Yet he had gauged the French temper accurately for a century to come, and he knew better than his friends the difference between working for a well-disposed steady audience and working in

[22] *235*, II, 139–40. The conclusion of this note is as good as a self-portrait. It reads: "I love you enormously, as you know; but tonight I fear you even more than I love you, because of my wish that my score should make a good impression on you. A thousand greetings and a thousand thanks for having come to the rehearsal night before last." (*Ibid.*, 140.)

[23] *M.E.*, 266.

[24] *M.E.*, 267.

the void. It was not long after this artistic interregnum in Paris that for poignant practical reasons Berlioz denied himself the right to compose a symphony of which the ideas came to him in sleep on two successive nights.[25] His phalanx of twelve hundred in the best days of the 1830's had not disappeared but they were discouraged too, and even more distraught. The continuity of mind and will which he could maintain through all vicissitudes could not be expected of them – it could not even be found among his enemies. Thus Fétis, who was present at the concert of April 15, 1849, begged permission to produce Berlioz' symphonies in Brussels. "The man," wrote Berlioz to his sister, "who has written so much to prove that they are anything but music – what puppets!"[26]

The *Te Deum* was growing slowly amid the usual interruptions. Liszt had given up the trip to America and was planning to come to Paris instead, and join with Berlioz in a concert which could be linked with the much-touted Industrial Exhibition. Meanwhile Meyerbeer's advances constituted a diplomatic problem. Berlioz could not help seeing in him an ambiguous sort of well-wisher who exploited others' musical dramatic inventions without saying so,[27] yet was not wholly ungrateful: in Berlin Meyerbeer had assisted him and later had been a prime mover in the presentation dinner after the *Damnation of Faust*. He was moreover a genuine musician whose artistic conscience was real as far as giving the operatic public full value for its support. But Meyerbeer was also an intriguer who

[25] *Mem.*, II, 349–50: "On waking the next day I could recall almost the whole first movement . . . in A minor. I was going to start writing it down when I suddenly reflected: if I set down this movement, I shall be led to compose the rest. The expanding of my thought which is now usual with me may give this symphony a very large scope. I shall perhaps devote three or four months exclusively to the work, during which I shall more or less give up my feuilletons. My income will suffer, and once the symphony is done I shall be weak enough to let it be copied . . . and performed . . . I shall lose money that I do not possess. . . ." After a second night's dreaming of the themes and forms, the project was set aside forever. " 'Coward!' some young fanatic will say . . . 'You should have taken the risk, you should have written it and ruined yourself. One has no right to drive away a thought and annihilate a work of art which begs to be born.' My dear young man, you would be less severe if you had seen the spectacle then before my eyes [of Harriet's decline]. I did not flinch earlier, in the days when one could still hope from the consequences of a bold attempt. There was in the Paris of those days a select public . . . And my wife, besides, was all alive and the readiest to encourage my efforts."

[26] *M.E.*, 270.

[27] The opinion of those competent to judge, from César Cui to Arthur Hervey, supports the view that Meyerbeer drew heavily on Berlioz' melody, instrumentation, and dramatic conceptions. *712*, 251; *723*, 48; *673*, 81.

had "captured" the Opera and posted his henchmen – such as Girard and Alexandre – in key positions. According to an expressive exaggeration circulated by Heine, the musical boss had "bought his way for the next hundred years." [28]

Berlioz' review of *Le Prophète* was therefore hard to write. On the surface a work of praise, with its few objections tactfully hedged about, it really expressed a very qualified approval of the opera. One has only to compare this cool judicial report with Berlioz' no less critical but thoroughly life-breathing studies of Gluck to assess the difference and to conclude – as against certain critics – that the art of Meyerbeer did not enthrall him.[29] A letter to his sister shows the extent to which Berlioz felt constrained: "I am also free of my article on *Le Prophète*. . . . Meyerbeer has the good sense not to take amiss the four or five reservations I put into my ten columns of praise.[30] I should have liked to spare him the pain . . . but there are certain things that must absolutely be said out loud. I cannot let anyone think that I approve or even condone the compromises which such a master makes in favor of the bad taste of a part of the public. . . . The score contains some very fine things side by side with feeble and detestable ones. But the splendor of the show will make everything pass muster." [31]

Sincere even in his diplomacy, Meyerbeer chose to head the delegation which in July presented the medal struck in honor of the *Damnation:* it had been impossible during the two years since the banquet to find the gold with which to make it – a fortunate delay, for it brought the token to the composer after the success of the two excerpts at the Conservatoire instead of after the failure at the Opéra-Comique.

But family concerns for the moment outweighed all else. Harriet had caught the cholera during the spring epidemic – Berlioz suffered only a bout of grippe – and he had nursed her during nights of continuous

[28] *1261*, VI, 308; *Mem.*, II, 347. Singers and others have since told how Meyerbeer's handsome gratuities would induce them to prolong the run of his works. The press was similarly taken care of. (*770*, III, 115.) This musical politics continued even after his death, one of his numerous secretaries, Johannès Weber, keeping up an insidious campaign against the works of rivals.

[29] *Mem.*, II, 346. The general view is reflected in young Bizet's enthusiasm: "Meyerbeer is the Michelangelo of music." (*973a*, 9.) Delacroix admired Couture in just the way Berlioz admired Meyerbeer. (*182*, I, 225.)

[30] Ten columns was a trifle compared with Fétis's five successive articles in the *Gazette*. Some critics disliked the opera as being "theology set to music" but felt that it represented such a large investment that it could not be allowed to fail.

[31] *M.E.*, 269.

vomiting. Now Nanci developed an undiagnosed ailment which despite Hector's less than complete affection for her caused him deep uneasiness. It turned out to be cancer of the breast, which carried her off a year later and made of Berlioz a convinced advocate of euthanasia.[32]

Harriet at last recovered and seemed even in better health than before, though still paralyzed and incoherent of speech. As for Louis's plans, Berlioz furthered them with the help of the Bertins who put him in touch with a Captain Page, recently reduced to half pay by the Republic but still enthusiastic about the sea. So much so that Berlioz' own wanderlust revived: to hear the sea! to travel! He yearned to leave Paris and smell again the poplar woods along the Arno, which a friend in the diplomatic service alluded to in a letter; he wanted to forget the *feuilletons* ("they will kill me in the end") and settle down in solitude at Les Jacques, which was to be his share of the family estate. He planned a reunion in Grenoble so that he might see Nanci in her illness, take stock of the property, and renew acquaintance with old friends of his mother's – "if any are left" [33]: in short he was alive with outgoing emotion that was virtually objectless.

In Paris, the "hair-raising comedy" was going on: near-riots, provincial delegations dressed in the garb of 1793, and endless debate and gossip as to the fidelity or the deep designs of the new Prince-President. The no less new American President, General Taylor, was giving the deriders of republics cause to jeer when the report of his inaugural quoted him as saying: "We are at peace with all the world and the rest of mankind." Elsewhere reaction was seeping back into power. By treachery and savage force Austria, Italy, Hungary, Bohemia, Prussia and Denmark were won anew to kings. Constitutions were torn up and rebels indiscriminately shot. Richard Wagner, who had rioted and made speeches in Dresden, fled before the enemy and took refuge in Paris. He arrived just in time to see another insurrection fomented by the news that French troops under Oudinot were helping to overthrow Mazzini's republic in Rome. President Bonaparte quelled the Paris republicans while his general chose July 14 to announce the reconquered sovereignty of Pius IX.

Wagner's loss of place and livelihood was somewhat compensated for

[32] "No physician dared to have the humanity of putting an end to her agony by letting her breathe a phial of chloroform. It can be done to spare a patient the pain of a surgical operation lasting a quarter of a minute, but it is forbidden to deliver one from six months of torture. . . . The most horrible thing in this world for us sentient and conscious beings is inexorable pain without possible compensation and carried to the highest degree of intensity; and one must be barbarous or stupid or both to refrain from using the sure and gentle way available nowadays to put an end to this." (*Mem.*, II, 333–4.)

[33] *M.E.*, 275.

by a fine gesture of Liszt's, supported by Berlioz: Liszt was putting on *Tannhäuser* in Weimar and sent a long eulogy of the opera to Berlioz, who reproduced it in full in the *Débats* with a cordial introduction.[34]

Berlioz' trip to Dauphiné had to be given up: Harriet was too ill. And Nanci had gone to take the waters at La Mothe.

When doctors send a patient to a watering place, it is generally because they are at their wits' end. . . . I cannot tell you, dear sister [this was to Adèle] what sad and deep thoughts bind us three to whatever is a reminder of our wonderful and excellent father. The memory of him will never leave me. The approaching anniversary of his death gave it fresh and painful force. I have his book,[35] as you know, annotated by him, and I have just read it. His pencillings showed him pondering and correcting with great care, and I was struck afresh by the fine integrity with which he practiced medicine, as well as by his sagacious mind, which should have shone in a wider circle. But his ineffable goodness and the attentions he lavished on us children are far deeper motives for our regret. . . . I should like to see you both; give me at once some wholly truthful news of Nanci. I shall write to her soon.

I have got back to my work (music, I mean). I am finishing, polishing, completing my new score. A sort of feverish impatience grips me because with regard to music I am still revolving a *number of projects.* And I want to set them down as soon as possible. This ardent occupation is the only one that can help me to repress a growing love of travel. I dream only of ships, seas, distant isles, adventurous explorations. My musical voyagings through Europe have only developed this half-buried instinct of old. I can see its futility, its childishness, but can do nothing about it. Were it not for my obligations here, I would again take a chance on productive tours in [Scandinavia] and in Russia, where I was so well received. Perhaps I may be able to go to Holland this winter: it's three steps away, thanks to the railroads. Travel on land is so easy and so cheap these days. . . .[36]

No single document, perhaps, conveys so naturally the interlinked emotions, sensations, and intellectual interests to which Berlioz responded and

[34] *1386,* May 18, 1849. Berlioz wrote fifty lines of warm and graceful eulogy, recalling Wagner's stay in Paris, his musical articles in French, and his subsequent removal to Dresden where his talents as poet and composer had met the success they deserved. One can measure the later Wagnerite frenzy by noting that the English translator of Wagner's Prose Works finds this encomium inadequate and too clearly due to Berlioz' friendship for Liszt. (*243,* III, 470–1.)

[35] *167.* Since its award of a prize by the Montpellier Academy of Medicine, the work had been favorably mentioned in the leading textbook on therapy. (*307,* 325.)

[36] *M.E.,* 279–80.

out of which he achieved in his art a balance of contrary tensions. From the child's loving remembrance of one parent to the mountaineer's love of space and distance; from the concert-leader and organizer to the composer whose music wells up in him regardless of outward circumstance, we have here the compass of his tendencies accurately self-surveyed. Nor is it farfetched to see in the longing for ocean voyages and Pacific isles a first sign of the European artist's repudiation of industrial urban life, later acted out by Rimbaud, Gauguin and others. For Berlioz, of course, the ethical motive, which dated back to readings of Diderot and Bougainville, was just then reinforced by the sight of young Louis's curiously similar longings.

During the first week of October 1849, the *Te Deum* for three choruses, organ, and orchestra was finished, and Berlioz had to begin devising an occasion for the usual testing by audition. He obtained an audience from the President of the Republic, but was preceded by a deputation of sixty long-winded provincials. He waited an hour and a half and got only excuses for his pains. Not seeking a second chance, he determined to try emancipating himself and the art of music in France from dependence upon the state. The means was to be a Philharmonic Society, which he at once set about organizing.

Dietsch, of the Opera, would conduct the chorus, many devoted friends would play for modest shares of the early profits, and the choice of pieces would be made by a representative committee. But the idea of a private person starting any such enterprise was too new in France: it lasted only eighteen months. Its cash reserves were inadequate, and Berlioz' connection with it was enough to consolidate a resourceful opposition. But it gave a dozen concerts, it publicized the idea that was too new, and it established the foundations upon which the later organizations of Pasdeloup, Colonne and Lamoureux were reared. By a just return, it was these orchestras that made known to the French the more accessible parts of Berlioz' concert works. Meantime an independent, unofficial society, neither limited in repertory like Seghers's "Saint Cecilia," nor politically doctrinaire like David's "Union," would satisfy the composer's undeviating musical ambition. What he called his "life sentence at hard labor," namely journalism, he knew to be the merest sideline. "Give me orchestras to lead," he promised, "give me rehearsals to go through, let me stay eight or even ten hours on my feet, practicing with the chorus, singing their parts when they miss, while I beat time for the rest until my arm gets cramped and I spit blood; let me carry music desks, double basses, and harps; compel me to correct proofs during the night time, and I will do it. . . . I have done it and can do it again." [37]

The Philharmonic Society received from the outset more spiritual than practical encouragement. There was a distinguished list of sponsors from the worlds of music and fashion. The press favored the plan without grasping its difficulties: "The society comes into being just at the right moment, in a musical twilight, when among artists and audiences alike the desire to act was succumbing to paralysis." [38] But the "action" came from Berlioz' will power and stayed there. For a year and a half he assumed the gigantic task of corralling and rehearsing the players, handling the publicity, watching the finances, soliciting aid, and arranging or composing music for the programs. In the flush of initial success he was a whirlwind of versatility and good humor; at its decline a year later he was sick to death. In between, the problem was threefold: finances, authority, and musical fare.

The first concert on February 19, 1850 brought in four thousand francs and was hailed as a triumph. The net profit amounted to twenty-seven hundred francs, which had to be divided in equal shares among ninety instrumentists and one hundred and ten singers, plus three shares for the chorus master, Pierre Dietsch, and four shares for Berlioz as conductor and General Director. This meant that for three rehearsals and one concert, each performer received thirteen francs and the two leaders about fifty francs apiece.

For such poor sums, the Society could not command prompt and faithful attendance at rehearsals, nor did its outlay secure anything but a very poor hall. What was even worse, the group was divided in allegiance: the singers — Opera people — "belonged" to Dietsch; the orchestra was devoted to Berlioz. This might have gradually been forgotten had not Dietsch fancied himself as a composer, and had an accident not brought the division to the surface.[39] At Angers, in mid-April 1850, a corps of troops marched in rhythm across a bridge and broke it. Hundreds of officers and men were drowned and the whole country was in mourning. The Philharmonic Society proposed to give a benefit for the victims'

[37] *Mem.*, II, 160; but note that the passage begins: "Let me be given *scores to compose*. . . ." [Italics added.]

[38] *269*, 230.

[39] Pierre Dietsch (1808–1865) will be remembered as choral conductor under Berlioz at the first performance of the *Requiem* in 1837, but much later he acquired a kind of *ex post facto* renown for having composed a *Flying Dutchman* opera on the text which he bought from Wagner. (1842.)

families at the Church of St. Eustache, and the question came up whether a mass by Dietsch (he had four on hand) or Berlioz' *Requiem* should be played. After some wrangling within the Committee, after Berlioz' offer to resign so as to let the benefit proceed, and after a protracted dispute between the singing and the playing members, the *Requiem* was given, under Berlioz' sole direction. It was an impressive performance which netted a large sum.

Henceforth, Berlioz made every effort to find other modern music than his own to put on the program. Remembering his difficult beginnings he had provided in the statutes that each year the Society would play the work of a young Rome Prize composer after his return from Italy. None had yet been submitted. Berlioz' friend Morel, a founding member of the Society who had left to take up duties at Marseille, had an overture which was played. Then a rich amateur named Cohn proposed a work which he would pay to have performed. The Committee reserved the right to consider it, and ultimately had it played to a house full of M. Cohn's friends. Works by Weber, Halévy, Spohr, Léon Kreutzer, Mendelssohn, Gluck and Beethoven were passed on and put in rehearsal. An Italian prima donna named Frezzolini and loaded with jewels was exhibited as well as allowed to sing.[40] But it was only too plain that apart from the great classics, the only music that drew the public and elicited important notice was Berlioz' own. During its short life, the Society accordingly played (besides the *Requiem*) two of the symphonies, parts of the *Damnation* and several of the small choral works, to which Berlioz had now added two: *La Menace des Francs* (March and Chorus) and the "Shepherds' Farewell," the first completed movement of the later *Infant Christ.*[41]

Yet it was impossible for external and internal reasons to have the Philharmonic Society feature Berlioz alone. The fact was that in France certainly, and in Europe almost to the same extent, there was in 1850 no one else on whom to draw. It was indeed a twilight, and far from rejoicing at being *facile princeps*, Berlioz felt it with acute wretchedness.

[40] Working by democratic committee meant that Berlioz' experienced judgment was often overruled, while at the same time outside pressure was centered on him in the belief that he was in sole charge. For example, the patron of Mlle. Catinka Heinefetter had to be put off with tact and wit: "We shall see if there is some way to use her talents on a later program and we thank her meanwhile for her gracious offer. I was unable to attend her début but you were there and that is enough for me — but *were* you there? Best greetings." (*M.E.*, 287 and *n.*)

[41] See below, Chapter 22.

"I am utterly sad — Spontini is dead." [42] Lesueur, Chopin, Mendelssohn, and now Spontini. Schumann was entering his last decade in ill-health and mental darkness; Liszt was given over to conducting and virtuoso work and was so far only planning his symphonic poems; [43] while Wagner as far as anyone knew was still far from his true path. In the *Débats*, Berlioz wrote Spontini's obituary, and to his friend Morel he dropped a word about him that reveals the sense of void in which he felt himself working: "I had come to love him by dint of admiration." [44]

One result of this situation was to help create the legend of Berlioz' egotistical scorn of his contemporaries and complacency about his own merits. He gave offense by his admiration of the great dead, for he seemed to claim kinship with them and so to reproach the living mediocrities who — to the onlooker — seemed just as good. No public can understand why an artist who is conscious of great powers would enjoy feeling humble in the company of the mighty, nor has criticism yet taught the world to differentiate between an artist's impersonal egotism and the common brand of self-love. The world thinks that a Beethoven or a Berlioz, a Wagner or a Delacroix, should be ashamed to feel the reality of his genius, or should have at least the decency to say nothing about it.[45] And yet we know that the Lord looked upon his handiwork and found it good, but we fail to draw the inference: the power to create implies the power to judge, and occasional failures of judgment in mortal creators prove nothing against the rule. Berlioz could see how the modern world was corrupting, or at least confusing the artist's proper self-regard: "The vanity of actors and authors," he wrote on New Year's Day 1851, "is no longer caused by love of fame, but by the crass love of money, by avarice and the passion for luxury, by insatiable material greed. They want hyperbolic praise because this alone stirs the crowd and leads it to this one or that. And they want the crowd because it alone brings money.

"Hence today one no longer finds artists able to limit themselves to

[42] *M.E.*, 311. Wagner's report of what Berlioz said to Spontini on his deathbed is apocryphal since Spontini died in Italy.

[43] With the exception of *Prometheus*, though even this did not reach final form until nine years later

[44] *M.E.*, 311. As Stendhal did for the musicians of 1820 one may list the composers who (besides those mentioned in the text) might reasonably claim attention in 1850: Auber, Adam, Carafa, Czerny, Draeseke, Flotow, Gade, Heller, Hiller, Kastner, Kittl, Lachner, Marschner, Moscheles, Nicolai, Pixis, Reber, Ries, Suppe, Verdi, Vesque de Puttlingen.

[45] Delacroix in 1847: "I have been making some bitter reflections on the profession of artist; the isolation, the sacrifice of almost all the feelings that move the majority of men. . . ." (*182*, I, 178.)

the making of a few polished, unlucrative works, preferring a moderate and painstaking output to the constant exploitation of their overworked minds. . . . They are forced . . . to draw upon everything and assimilate whatever is assimilable, like those infusoria called *vortex*, which create a whirlpool in front of their ever-open mouths so as to engulf every animalcule that comes near them. . . . Let us save time, for time is money, and money is everything." [46]

He could have added that the same barometer of public opinion was more and more decisive in the supposedly higher spheres. Spontini's death had left a vacancy at the Institute, and to fill it Berlioz was the logical candidate. He paid the necessary calls. At the first ballot a younger man of the theater, Ambroise Thomas, was elected by a majority of thirty. The remaining eight votes were split among Niedermeyer and Batton. Not a single vote was cast for Berlioz.[47]

While certain persons were trying to "dephilharmonize our society," that is, bring disunity into its ranks; and while "the rascally Italian press" (Scudo and Azevedo) were trying to chill the enthusiasm of the instrumentists, Berlioz learned the truth about Nanci's desperate condition. He tried, in the teeth of hopelessness, to give her courage by chatty letters of Parisian doings: Hugo's salon was full of ugly old ladies, but at least there was no bad music served. Dumas had a daughter of nineteen, "too much like her father to be pretty, but whose somewhat gracile quadroon appearance . . . heightened by a sequin headdress, made her look like an odalisque from Madagascar. Farewell, poor dear sister. God grant that you may have read this letter to the end, and that it may have helped you forget your pain for two minutes. I shake your good Camille by the hand. Farewell again; I kiss you." [48]

Then a month later, to Adèle: "Give me at least some news of yourself. Your silence is disturbing. I am afraid of your grief, though you must have suffered a thousand times more than I while watching the torture and agony of our poor dear just delivered. . . . Are you ill? In that case, let

[46] *1386*, Jan. 1, 1851. Compare Delacroix again: "What I saw yesterday augurs badly for the future of the French School. . . . The pygmies of today, I should say the insects, have neither true feeling nor the least real learning. . . . A stupid skill in handling is their highest goal." (*182*, I, 223.)

[47] Those unfamiliar with French traditions may think this was a natural retort to the satirical shafts Berlioz had shot into the august body, but such was not the reason for his exclusion at this time. Most of the great men who have found their way into the Academy began by attacking it and felt no inconsistency in seeking admission to it — on the principle that the opposition may occupy the place it has first bombarded.

[48] *M.E.*, 295–6.

Suat write to me. Farewell, I kiss you. Poor sister! We are now only two."

In June 1850, news came that Balzac was back from his second Russian journey and married to his long-courted love, Mme. Hanska. Berlioz wrote to him immediately: "Since the eve of my trip to Russia, I have not seen you once, which makes three enormous years. Have you ever thought of the anguish that would be felt by certain passionate beings at seeing the features of their idol only in mirrors thrice removed? That is the way I feel not having seen you. . . . In less roundabout fashion, let me ask you when I can go and shake your hand and beg you to introduce to Mme. Balzac one of her most devoted servants."[49] The simile of the mirrors betokened, among other things, Berlioz' physical weariness. He had constant stomach cramps, headaches, and the need of sleep. The pace he had set himself was, *mutatis mutandis,* the pace that Balzac had followed too, and that carried him off two months after Berlioz had greeted him – another void among the ranks of his peers.

That winter of 1850, filled with the business of the Philharmonic, Berlioz' son set out on his apprentice voyage to the West Indies. The father was on tenterhooks until he received his first letter, from Haiti. It had taken fifty-three days, and thus began for Berlioz' overapprehensive nature a fresh source of torment. The letter reported good health, good spirits, and also the death of a friend in the new world, to whom Berlioz had recommended his son. This led Berlioz to review the losses by death which he had suffered for three years past, besides his father and sister: Balzac and Chopin, Mendelssohn and Spontini, Frédéric Soulié and numerous foreign musicians or patrons of music for whom Berlioz felt regard and gratitude – Alfred Becher and Count Batthiany, both shot, in Austria and in Hungary respectively; Prince Lichnowski, mobbed by peasants; and the oldest friend and patron of all, Augustin de Pons (he had lent the money for Berlioz' Mass of 1825) who being destitute had taken poison.[50]

Louis's return to France in the spring of 1851 dissipated some of Berlioz' gloom. The boy looked grown up and well, and both were pleased, for Louis had made the flattering discovery at Haiti and other ports of call that he was the son of a famous man on whose account he himself was readily invited. On his side the father found in his boy signs of maturing intelligence and responsibility. The second apprentice cruise would still have to be paid for, but after that the young sailor could support himself.

49 *M.E.*, 298–9.

50 *M.E.*, 305. Berlioz had tried to help the once wealthy De Pons by inserting notices of his musical qualifications in the *Débats.*

Together they went to see Harriet who still lived in the house at Montmartre where Louis had been born. She could sit in the garden, see her boy during his shore leave and her husband when he had a free hour between rehearsals. The climb up the hill to her house was easier now that steps had been built and Berlioz came often, for she needed attentions that only he could interpret to her nurses: she spoke even less French than before, virtually none at all, and enunciated very imperfectly.

During this period also Berlioz succeeded his good friend Bottée de Toulmon as Chief Librarian of the Conservatoire. This brought a slight increase in salary and an opportunity to add to the teaching resources of the library by creating a collection of instruments. A few weeks later, the Minister of Commerce appointed Berlioz to the jury which was to judge musical instruments at the forthcoming London Exhibition of 1851. Though this was everywhere hailed as a great honor, Berlioz foresaw the delicacy of the task ahead: "I am very much afraid . . . that there will be . . . a stormy contest between the instrument makers of Paris and those of Berlin. All are friends of mine and I shall be caught between hammer and anvil. But I am resolved to be a Minos worthy of such assizes and not to render Injustice. The Lord knows (or rather I wager that He does not yet know) where I shall find lodgings. . . . The Minister . . . cannot say whether the English management has kept a kennel for us in the Crystal Palace or elsewhere . . . But then the Minister is very young – only four days old." [51]

A trip to England at this juncture of the Philharmonic's affairs was most opportune. Berlioz could leave the Society with honor instead of sinking with it, dragged down in part by the desire of some to make it pay at all costs.[52] Berlioz' English friends expressed delight at the news of his mission and at the prospect of seeing him again, for as the *Illustrated London News* had said, he was "an excellent classical scholar, a choice wit, and full of fine enthusiasm." [53] There were, in addition more than casual

[51] *M.E.*, 319–20.

[52] There is extant the draft of a note to Brandus, the music publisher, which shows to what unpleasantness the Society and its Director were exposed. After saying that the mere thought of Brandus's proposal (whatever it was) gave him nausea, Berlioz writes: "I will never consent to accept for the artists whom I direct what I would not accept for myself if the business regarded me alone. There is far less evil in material loss than in the confusion brought into the musical world and the public mind by turning a serious undertaking into a fashionable vulgarity; and it would be a libel on our players to imagine their feelings different from mine. If the thing comes up again, say that you *did not dare* to propose it to me. Ever yours . . ." (*M.E.*, 323–4 and *n.*)

[53] *311*, 90.

hints that a great musical project might be set on foot if he were in London to lead it: the score of the *Te Deum* was ready for performance if some great occasion, musical and national, should call for an original work.

Te Deum, Space and Counterpoint

> I write three lines to tell you that the *Te Deum* was performed today with magnificent precision. It was colossal, Babylonian, Ninivite . . . yes, the *Requiem* has a twin . . . What a pity I am the author of it all. I could write a curious article about it. . . . This time it isn't a matter of *piccoli paesi*, but of a scene from the Apocalypse.
>
> – BERLIOZ to Liszt on first hearing the work (1855)

Conceiving music for occasions set in the midst of life, the young Berlioz had, on his return from Italy, imagined Bonaparte's victorious army poised on the crest of the divide, looking back downward upon the Italian plain in a farewell to its dead, and again downward as it crossed home soil to reach the capital and the celebration of its triumphs.[1]

Such was the "stage" imagined in 1832. As the traveler's impressions receded, the scheme changed to the more general celebration of all France's great men, and out of this came the *Funeral and Triumphal* symphony of 1840.[2] This left unused a number of ideas which in the ensuing nine years gathered to themselves fresh associations. We glimpse this fact through coincidences that Berlioz himself was probably unaware of, though their purport is confirmed by the score. The *Te Deum* is religious and military in a mood predominantly sober and meditative. It consists of seven choral numbers arranged as follows: an opening song of praise, the *Te Deum* properly so called, whose theme recurs as a leitmotif; the Hymn *Tibi omnes;* a Prayer (*Dignare*) which is introduced by a brief orchestral

[1] Musical Notebook quoted in *308*, 1906, 362. Berlioz had written a free verse stanza for one of the movements.

[2] Written for the heroes of July, it will be remembered, but in the year of Napoleon's translation from St. Helena.

prelude of military character; the *Christe, rex gloriae;* a second, individual prayer (*Te ergo quaesumus*); then the *Judex crederis* — another vision of Judgment Day. For military occasions only (and for orchestra alone) there is a concluding March for the Presentation of the Colors.

This plan shows a significance beyond the Napoleonic; it links the *Te Deum* with the *Requiem* of 1837 and we shall find that certain of the musical ideas go back as far as the Mass of 1825. Meantime, Berlioz had composed the Dead March for *Hamlet* — another military scene[3] — and had been led by the revision of his *Death of Ophelia* and *Méditation religieuse* to the kindred atmospheres of death and prayer. Contemporary events, as we saw, reinforced this complex of warlike, funereal, and doomsday feelings. If we turn to the music we discover a veritable network of associations worthy of a study in the manner of John Livingston Lowes's *Road to Xanadu* or Newman's *Unconscious Beethoven.* To point out the most obvious, the *Hamlet* March has a clear affinity with the first movement of the *Funeral* symphony, seeming a condensed and more intimate rendering of the same conception; and the military march which concludes the *Te Deum* bears a resemblance to the Apotheosis of the same earlier symphony, again more concise and more subtle. It is as if the years 1848–1849, during which Berlioz' affections were so often and so violently wrenched by death, had reduced to quintessence ideas long held latent on these eternal woes.[4] The two pairs of parallels thus appear as first and second studies of familiar subjects.[5]

As for the continuity of Berlioz' religious thought, it is attested in the *Te Deum* by the scale and dramatic form of the work, which is clearly designed to make it a companion piece to the *Requiem.* There are other links: the repetition of the same chant on the words *Pleni sunt coeli* in each score is undoubtedly purposeful; again in the *Christe, rex* of the later work occurs a melody from the early *Resurrexit* which supplied

[3] Berlioz prefixed to the score the words from Shakespeare which had first suggested a musical situation: " 'Let four captains bear Hamlet, like a soldier to the stage; . . . and, for his passage, The soldiers' music and the rites of war . . .' "; concluding with: " 'Go, bid the soldiers shoot.' *A dead march* . . ."

[4] In the *Hamlet* March the instrumental use of the voices, labeled simply "Women and Men," and vocalizing a series of "Ah's" at intervals, is as original as it is moving. At the end of the March, "after a terrific triple forte effect, there is a dead silence; then a long, deep, sustained note; then occur about twenty bars of the most hopelessly despairing music I have ever heard, and then the drums take up their dreadful figure, and so the whole march winds to a close." (Christopher Wilson in *Shakespeare and Music,* quoted in *310,* 140.) Mr. Wilson can hear the despairing passage again, somewhat weakened, in the close Grieg gave to "Asa's Death" in his *Peer Gynt* suite.

[5] Cf. Delacroix's *Medea* in 1838 and 1850.

parts of the *Requiem.* Finally, both *Requiem* and *Te Deum,* though relatively short, are "monumental" music designed to fill a cathedral vault; their conception is spatial as well as auditory,[6] which accounts for their uncommon requirements. For the *Te Deum,* Berlioz wants some hundred strings with the usual winds in proportion, two choruses of one hundred singers each, plus a third of six hundred choir boys.[7] But instead of the additional brass groups found in the *Requiem,* Berlioz here uses the organ as an antiphonal voice, never adjoining it to the orchestra but letting "Pope and Emperor" (as he said) dialogue from opposite ends of the nave.[8]

In each of these twin religious works, our sense of scale is skillfully awakened and kept on the stretch by varying the distribution of forces (one number in each – the *Sanctus* and *Te ergo* respectively – is scored for tenor solo) as well as by contrasting the dynamics of successive sections, sometimes within a movement, at other times between a consecutive pair. Finally, in the *Judex crederis,* one of Berlioz' most powerful "monotonies," relieved by marvelous and hair-raising modulations, he combined the insistent effect he had obtained in the *Requiem's* limpid Offertory and the strenuous effect of the *Lacrymosa.* Throughout the later score, repeats or echoes of the solemn opening theme makes its solemnity prevail and give it a more pervasive unity than that of the *Requiem.*[9] As for

[6] It will be remembered that in the *Requiem* the brass choirs are placed at the four corners *of the orchestra* (not the hall) to make the point of origin of sound act as a musical element. An interesting parallel, one century later, is provided by Egon Wellesz's definition of what he called the New Instrumentation in the 1920's: "The monumental style is like the new architecture – a projection out of space into Time, with a clear and distinct treatment of lines (*Linienführung*)." He goes on to find this "new classicism" in Busoni, upon whom, as we know, Berlioz' influence was great. (*913,* 13.)

[7] Yet as Berlioz points out in a letter to Liszt, the composition of the orchestra is quite normal, only the voices are numerous, whence by reductions proportioned to a minimum of one hundred and thirty good voices, the work can be readily and adequately performed. (*207,* II, 37.)

[8] In the *Treatise,* Berlioz had argued the inadvisability of ever uniting the sonorities of orchestra and organ. Other theorists and practitioners, such as Saint-Saëns and Vincent d'Indy, agree with him; though the remark has roused the ire of certain organists who display more heat than light in discussing the question. The distinguished performer, Mr. E. Power Biggs, for instance, curiously suggests that "it is just as well Berlioz was of this opinion, for any organ composition of his would have been pretty frightful." (*765,* 221.)

[9] The affinity of this theme both with plain song and with the contour of popular melodies such as those of the fifteenth-century masters (*e.g.,* Dufay) has been remarked upon. The handling of the polyphony and plagal harmony in the Prelude again suggests Jannequin and the old French masters, whose revival came only twenty years after Berlioz wrote. The rhythmic subtleties, to be sure, are modern, but the archaism just noted is intentionally carried out

coherence, it is achieved in the *Te Deum,* as always in Berlioz, through fine adjustments between the close and the beginning of successive numbers. The whole work could be played with only two breaks.

The "emotional schedule" is likewise fashioned for balance. The first hymn (*Te Deum*) is a double fugue expressing the religious (and Romantic) contrast between man's wretchedness and God's infinite mercy. Joy and trembling alternate in many shades, until uncertainty is swept away in a resolving modulation which brings us to the second hymn, introduced by the organ. The children sing a *Sanctus* to the Lord in which the other voices soon join to proclaim the majesty and goodness of the Almighty. The orchestra closes on a return to the organ melody and prepares us for the "military" Prelude – a march in the ancient style, based on the *Te Deum* theme. "A miracle of genius" – says M. Boschot, whom it is a pleasure to quote in a moment of admiration – "this orchestral episode is not sixty measures long; it does not take three minutes to play; yet it suggests multiple visions, it evokes a throng of sentiments. One is tempted, in speaking of it, to compare it to some of those brief scenes in Shakespeare whose work so profoundly affected Berlioz." [10]

The *Dignare* is a gentle prayer composed of long interlacing melodic lines, with the organ weaving in its quietest tones. Indeed throughout the work the organ is used with extreme moderation, both in amount of time and in the pulling of stops: flutes, trumpets, and *Grand jeu* are its usual limits, the *Bombardes* being reserved for the climax. The *Christe, rex gloriae* corresponds to the *Rex tremendae majestatis* of the *Requiem* and is the only movement which may be said greatly to surpass its prototype. In both, Berlioz was attempting the very perilous expression of "pomp and circumstance." If awe in the presence of the Almighty and his hosts is reserved for another moment, and the present feeling is only wonder and amaze, there must be in the music a mingling of spontaneous rejoicing with loud huzzas, and no striking of the deeper strains of adoration, since the praise is exclusively of surface and of show. In the *Requiem,*

---

in the orchestration of both the "military" sections. It is as if we heard Berlioz' childhood memories of the First Empire, when the old bands still kept to their *ancien régime* repertory.

[10] *269,* 219. We are indebted for the preservation of this Prelude to the reverent spirit of the Russian Five, and particularly to Balakirev, who completed the German edition from the manuscript that Berlioz had presented to the St. Petersburg Library in 1862. In the French edition, Berlioz had discarded the Prelude because of modulations which his musical intimates found "suspect." (See letter to Liszt, *207,* II, 17.) To our modern ears they sound unexceptionably fresh.

though the movement ends superbly, it stumbles along the way. Here it proceeds from an apparent *aria di bravura* to an overwhelming close. "The frank breadth of style and its epic simplicity, the vast proportions of the developments, the conscious mastery of an impressive technique, as well as the calm power of hundreds of voices, choral and instrumental – voices of thunder like the numberless voices of nature – transfigure a piece which seemed at first ordinary and which becomes colossal, formidable. The pyramids of Egypt are only a geometrical shape, but their superhuman mass moves the spectator, and . . . mysteriously hints to him that they are alive." [11]

This pragmatic verification of Berlioz' belief in the true musicalness of mass when properly handled, and his knowledge of its handling, suggest a necessary digression. In distinguishing the monumental style from the subtly or the exquisitely sublime (having himself no partiality for one over the other) Berlioz did not use the analogy of the Pyramids, Napoleonic though they were. He used the adjectives "Babylonian" and "Ninivite," which has misled certain critics first into thinking that exaggeration was Berlioz' normal attitude, and second that he went out of his way here to color the musical reality by farfetched similes. We must accordingly consider words for a moment. The music being monumental, Berlioz' comparison with the constructions of antiquity is exact. But whence the image "Babylonian, Ninivite"? Probably from Sir Henry Layard, who in 1848–1849 published two volumes on *Nineveh and its Remains*, accompanied by *Illustrations of the Monuments of Nineveh*. If despite his interest in distant climes, Berlioz missed seeing this first work, published while he was in London, he very likely saw the second series, *Discoveries in the Ruins of Nineveh and Babylon*, with *Illustrations* also, published in 1855, when Berlioz was again in London, and moreover in the very year in which the *Te Deum* was finally performed and Berlioz used the epithets for the first time.[12]

The pyramid of sound raised in the *Rex gloriae* is a summit from which we ascend still higher into the exquisite, ethereal, Mozart-like prayer of the *Te ergo* ("we beseech thee") scored for tenor solo, sopranos, a few

[11] *269*, 220.

[12] Letters to Liszt, April 30 and to Morel, June 2, 1855. Heine had used the terms earlier about the *Requiem*, but Berlioz did not read the passage until (again) 1855, when Heine's *Lutezia* appeared in French. Mr. Ernest Newman, prefacing some writings of Schubert, bases a dubious theory of intellectual temperament upon these and other adjectives used by artists; and like M. Masson who calls Berlioz' terms "romantic," he ascribes them to the *early* Berlioz. The actual chronology suggests greater caution. (*1008*, v; *289*, 202.)

strings and woodwinds. The melody speaks of the divine for all those to whom Berlioz speaks at all. Others find the line wandering, elusive. It is indeed marked by what was earlier termed "delay"; the unfolding waits upon the exploration of several side branches, each a delicate arabesque of sound and an adumbration of the heart in prayer. In this and in the intermediate episode for sopranos, one finds moreover Berlioz' deep masculine tenderness – a quality of passion free from uncertainty or fear, which was always in him like a calm underground lake beneath his convulsed outer self.

The climacteric *Judex crederis* which follows is the peak of Berlioz' power in the monumental style. Hearers who are drawn to the vigorous achievements of youth, for all their angularity, prefer the *Tuba mirum* or the *Lacrymosa* of the *Requiem.* Those who look for long-sustained inspiration which fully conceals the marks of craft and seems effortless in the overcoming of inherent difficulties, choose the *Judex crederis.* "It surpasses in fullness and power all his other productions . . . it must be placed amongst the greatest movements in music."[13] The plenitude suggests that the *Te Deum* marks a plateau in the Romanticist's work, a steadfast power ushering in the final serenity and simplicity. Yet the later style argues no repudiation of the first. One of Berlioz' most indisputable claims to greatness is precisely this faculty of presenting so many facets of himself to admirers and detractors that there is no consensus as to which is "the" masterpiece nor "the" quality which he stands for. A dramatist of boundless resource, he does many things with equal felicity, suits his technique to subject and defies encompassment.[14]

This, for him, second dramatization of the last judgment is built on an obstinate phrase for the basses, punctuated no less insistently by the shrill cries of the E-strings and flutes until a prayer for forgiveness sung by the sopranos interrupts the mingled anguish and menace. But it is only for a moment. The basses start anew, gathering to them the other voices and all the six hundred children in a vast crescendo of despair. At its culmination comes a flash of silence, then a brief return to the prayer, which is cut short by the archangels' trumpets.

Placing this bright gleam of sonority near the end of what is strictly the last movement of the work permits the military epilogue to link itself to the rest. Its function being to accompany the procession of flags to the altar, it is a march, sinewy in rhythm and scoring. When the theme is entrusted to the oboes, bassoons and violas alone, twelve harps in unison

[13] *310,* 166.

[14] See below, Subchapter 25, the diversity of feelings about the work or works to be ranked as his best. Each of his twelve major scores has its devotees.

add their radiance in an effect of magnificent lightness and force. The organ joins in with imitations of the opening *Te Deum* theme, after which the orchestra restates the theme of the Prelude and the March ends, together with the work, in triumph.

One cannot close the discussion of the *Te Deum*, so rich in vocal and orchestral counterpoint, without taking up the question foreshadowed here and there in previous chapters: is Berlioz to be regarded mainly as a monodist – a homophonic composer – or as a polyphonist? This would seem to be easily settled by reference to fact, but faulty terminology and hasty generalization keep postponing an answer, even among so-called experts. A deficient contrapuntist, say some, echoing Mendelssohn. "There is as fine contrapuntal writing in parts of the *Te Deum*," retorts Cecil Gray, "as in any music of the post-Beethoven period." [15] A rooted objection to contrapuntal treatment, wrote the late Calvocoressi.[16] But a captious contemporary of the *Requiem* objected to Berlioz' excessive use, precisely, of counterpoint.[17] The reader who has followed the present account of the intervening works must have noted that in nearly every one of them Berlioz wrote one or more *fugatos*. These free fugues, short or long, occur in the *Symphonie Fantastique* (last movement), *Harold in Italy* (first), *Romeo and Juliet* (Introduction and Funeral March), the *Damnation of Faust* (twice in Part II) and *Benvenuto Cellini* (once in each act). We shall find three more instances in *The Infant Christ* and *Beatrice and Benedict*, which taken with the *Requiem's* three and the pair in the *Te Deum*, brings to sixteen the number of fugues in free style introduced by Berlioz in nine out of his dozen major works.

This bald emuneration clinches once for all the question of Berlioz' attitude towards counterpoint. Besides, in his other works and in movements not analyzed here, he constantly employs other contrapuntal devices, particularly canonic imitation. No one with ears to hear can miss the delicate counterpoint in the pastoral movement of the *Fantastique* nor the somber one at the beginning of the March.[18] Lastly, Berlioz had a strong penchant for the juxtaposition of melodies – whether in the course of development,

[15] *719*, 213.

[16] That this remark should come from the sincerest of "fact-finding" critics is not without irony and should inspire humility in all his colleagues. (*776*, 38.)

[17] "He has put three fugues into his *Requiem*. It is odious and grotesque." (The critic of the *Constitutionnel* quoted in *300*, 112.)

[18] *Min. Sc.*, pp. 103–12; 123–9 and pp. 133–40. Note at the beginning of this last passage the "contrary motion" as to dynamics, the bassoon melody being marked *cresc.* and the theme in the strings *dim.* (P. 133 b. 11.)

as in the *Harold* allegretto or at the conclusion of a movement: nearly all his overtures use this device, which Weingartner goes so far as to call an independent invention and a personal hallmark.[19]

This being so, Berlioz may be said to have extended the polyphonic ideal melodically as he extended it through the counterpointing of rhythms, dynamics and timbres.[20] It has been said, of course, that strict classical counterpoint is the "ethics" of music, which casts upon other elements of the art the odium of immorality or fraud. The grain of sense in this doctrine is that the co-ordinating of many voices is, so to speak, *la spécialité de la musique*. That Berlioz understood this very clearly is shown by his fondness for subdividing his orchestra into autonomous groups for each of which he sought to write real melodic parts; it is shown further in his unceasing desire to achieve among nonmelodic elements the fullest disjunction compatible with clarity: rhythm, timbre, harmony, melody, and dynamics are to him so many "lines" in a total polyphony.

A fair test of his success is that a certain type of academic mind detects the practice and impugns it as unheard of;[21] but modern scores from Strauss to Varèse – not to speak of jazz – testify as plainly to the fruitfulness of Berlioz' technical imagination. At the same time, it is perfectly fair to consult the experts upon Berlioz' use of traditional vocal counterpoint, especially as found in his *Te Deum* and *Requiem*.[22] We have already seen Mr. Gray's approbation of Berlioz' writing in that form. Another theorist, who taught so many distinguished American composers, Dr. Percy Goetschius, calls the double fugue of the *Fantastique* "a masterpiece of contrapuntal skill."[23] A third professor of the art, August

[19] *394*, 200–1. Melodic juxtaposition commended itself to Wagner, who employed it in his revision of *Tannhäuser* and most brilliantly in *Meistersinger*.

[20] On these elements see above, *passim*, as well as Richard Pohl, *552*. Also *526*, 24 and *427*, 248: "Before Berlioz the nuances in each group seemed obliged to move all in the same direction. He makes them independent whenever this appears necessary."

[21] "Berlioz in the *Lacrymosa* of the *Requiem* has attempted the impossible: he has used his instrumental forces in small groups. This is self-contradictory." (*85*, 368.) In his own day, Berlioz' musical friend Legouvé had similarly deplored that the composer should seek to achieve at once magnitude of scale and refinement of detail. "This," said Legouvé, "is self-contradictory." (*362*, 139.)

[22] It may be noted in passing that Berlioz usually adheres to the six-part writing favored by the French tradition in which he was taught (three women's voices, two tenors, and a bass) rather than the more common division into four or eight parts. He shows in the *Treatise* (pp. 231–2) that six-part writing allows the use of more kinds of natural *tessituras*, at least as these occur in the climate of France.

[23] *436*, 297.

Halm, says of the "Amen" fugue in the *Damnation of Faust:* "Thanks to the art and skill of the composer, it belongs among the finest of short vocal fugues." [24] And Koechlin, casting his eye over the whole of Berlioz' output, feels justified in calling the composer's genius "contrapuntal by nature." [25] The second question, then, of the *merit* of Berlioz' frequent use of counterpoint, must be settled in his favor; he can bring as many pundits to testify for him as there may be objectors in the name of scholastic rules.[26]

The controversy of course exemplifies the failure of criticism while showing once again the elusiveness of "fact" in art.[27] But it also accounts for one of the needlessly dark corners in the Berlioz literature. Those who speak of his music as homophonic seem to consider exclusively his expressive harmony and to be influenced less by the evidence of their ears than by what they believe Berlioz wrote about fugal treatment. The legend goes that he "hated fugues." Cherubini, who had passed him four times in that subject, made bons mots against Lesueur's pupil, and these are idly repeated to support the dogma of Berlioz' "aversion" to counterpoint.

What did Berlioz actually say? On several occasions he attacked the use in religious works of rapid vocal fugues on the word "Amen." This is in fact the point of his brief parody fugue in the *Damnation.* It is given to the crew of revelers in Auerbach's cellar precisely because, as Berlioz said: "All the fugues on the word 'amen' are fast, violent, noisy; they resemble nothing so much as a chorus of drinkers interspersed with bursts of laughter, for each part is vocalised on the first syllable of the word: A---a-a-a-a-men, which produces an effect at once grotesque and indecent. These traditional fugues are nothing but senseless blasphemy." [28] That is the negative side. On the positive he says: "No doubt one could write a beautiful fugue of a truly religious character to express the pious wish, *Amen.* But it would have to be a slow fugue, full of humility and quite

[24] *570,* 82.

[25] *453,* 193.

[26] Pursuing his discussion of the point, Koechlin considers that although Berlioz in 1830 knew nothing of Bach and never attained that type of mastery, he nevertheless stood alone as a contrapuntist, his critic Mendelssohn being "rather harmonic than fugal . . . timid and scholastic despite his facility and undeniable gifts." (*453,* 193–4.)

[27] Calvocoressi in his later years collected examples of the critical deadlock by which, for instance, a theorist like Vincent d'Indy, who agrees in principle with Brahms's views of tonal unity, can find that composer deficient and wrongheaded throughout. (*1391,* 1934, 229 and *n.*)

[28] To the Abbé Girod, *Corresp.,* 238–9. These words are almost identical with those Berlioz had used a quarter of a century before. (*1377,* 1829, 55.)

short. For however well one renders it musically, the repetition of a word cannot be protracted without becoming ridiculous." [29]

Berlioz is here solely concerned with the correct expression of religious feeling. On fugue or counterpoint as musical subjects, this is his opinion, set forth in his twenty-fifth year: "Is it a mistake, then, . . . to teach fugue in the schools? Certainly not. It is a most useful exercise which accustoms the students to solving many harmonic difficulties, and it teaches them to extract all the possibilities from a melodic idea. It is even true to say that the fugal style, when modified, can sometimes be used felicitously in a slow movement, although the use made of it so far in Masses is to my mind . . . an aberration. . . ." [30]

His own practice, then and thereafter, exhibits this "modification" of the fugal style. He handles the fugue form freely, as well as deviates from the so-called laws of counterpoint. This he did neither ignorantly nor impatiently, but in keeping with a conception of art which differs from that of the original polyphony for voices alone. If Berlioz interrupts his fugues or does not finish them, just as Handel does, it is because he and Handel, as dramatic composers, know that a strict and full-blown fugue is rarely appropriate except as a work by itself.[31] As for the relaxation of the rules, or rather their extension in the light of fresh considerations, all great composers have set a precedent for it, from Bach to Mozart [32] whose counterpoint – like that of Berlioz – struck his musical colleagues as too rough and too free.[33]

We are told, it is true, that Vogler or Raff or one of a dozen other secondary figures knew more counterpoint than Mozart or Beethoven. So much the worse for them: theirs must by definition have been a non-

[29] *Corresp.*, 238.

[30] *1377* (1829) 54. Mozart in 1782: "For if a fugue is not played slowly, the ear cannot clearly distinguish the theme when it comes in and consequently the effect is entirely missed." (*219*, III, 1194.)

[31] Berlioz' passages in unisons or octaves have the dramatic purpose of concentrating attention by simplicity and power, at moments where continuing the polyphony would divide interest. The authority on the technique of choral composition, Mr. Archibald Davison, illustrates this principle by quoting from Berlioz' *Requiem* (end of *Rex tremendae*). (*1301*, 64 and Ex. 78.)

[32] It is a recent affectation to consider Bach a strict or scholastic contrapuntist, or even a cool, classic perfectionist. See *The Organ Works of Bach* by Harvey Grace, and some objections down to the present day about Bach's "incorrectness." (*452*, 122.)

[33] "Distasteful to his contemporaries," says Jahn. (*968*, II, 457.) Sarti found as many as nineteen "errors" in thirty-six bars of one quartet. (*621*, 32 *n.*) The "scene of the three orchestras" in *Don Giovanni* was accounted pure barbarism. (*931*, II, 182 and 185.)

functioning, Pickwickian counterpoint, since it contributed so little to giving their works the breath of life. Beethoven at least could use what he knew, and he knew something about music which apparently cannot be communicated or codified. Similarly, Berlioz' counterpoint seemed to Moscheles inexcusably free, whereas to us that of Moscheles is quite excusably dead. Art may have its laws but it is a curious code which seems infallibly to put the great creators among the wrongdoers while those it clears are freed – for oblivion.[34]

The fact is that there is and can be no written law. "There is no such thing as bad harmony, counterpoint, form or melody judged apart from the living body of the music. . . . Berlioz' technique does fulfill its purpose within the living body of his music."[35] Which does not prevent the academic judge from pursing his lips at a visual "error" and from itching to correct it, as in a student exercise, without even suspecting the absurdities that "correctness" might entail. The Battle of the Rules in music is fortunately beginning to turn in favor of the empiricists as against the upholders of an abstract virtue which has never existed outside the textbooks and whose enforcement is in fact antimusical.[36] The same substitution of facility and fidelity for truth and invention distorts judgment in all the arts. Weak critics need signposts, touchstones, fetishes – and their dogmatism soon spreads. In painting, the rules and the need to forget them has produced two well recognized forms of the art, one of which is known as "academic" and presents the ridiculous spectacle of being "correct" according to an outmoded but ever-shifting set of rules: to be an Impressionist nowadays is the acme of academic correctness; it gets you hung as it once nearly got you hanged.

The one eternal verity in the whole matter is that there are born to

[34] The same "code" is found in literature: "The ability to write English correctly," says Lounsbury ironically, "does not belong to the great masters of our speech. It is limited to the obscure men who have devoted themselves to the task of showing how far these vaunted writers have fallen short of the ideas of linguistic propriety entertained by their unrecognized betters." (*The Standard of Usage*, pp. 135–6.)

[35] Laurence Powell: *377*, 156.

[36] "Most of the textbooks," said W. R. Spalding in discussing tonal counterpoint forty years ago, "make a great mistake in laying so much stress on what may not be done . . . A large part of the student's energy is taken up in obeying long lists of rules, more or less arbitrary, and his natural instinct is thereby deadened." (*1361*, vii.) The pragmatic method which this criticism implies has been admirably embodied in our day by Mr. Walter Piston in *Counterpoint*, which treats of the contrapuntal essence as something more than manipulation, and is not ashamed to cite an example from Berlioz' *Harold in Italy*. (*1347*, 80.)

every art persons with a remarkable facility for learning who are not and never will be artists, and whose only hope therefore is to produce the simulacra of art by observing the rules.[37] Old or new, these are transmitted narrowed down from some past practice, whose attested success is thought to be still paying dividends. In nature one finds plants which resemble other plants and bear the same name with a qualifying adjective – "False Solomon's Seal." In art, the same nomenclature might well obtain and with better reason, since the poor plants designated as false cannot help themselves. Men presumably can, which is why Berlioz in his writings so often made the distinction between true music and its imitation.

To profit from this lesson, the criticism of music must catch up with that of the other arts and permanently rid itself of the clichés and superstitions which darken its teachings. It must for example cease its unconscious punning on the word "bass" as if it signified the *base* of the musical edifice; it must stop pretending to be "as strict as mathematics" – which makes the innocent suppose that hidden octaves are like an error in addition – and it must really begin to believe what it has been mumbling about the importance of form, sound, and logic; only, in the concrete masterpiece, the discovery of these elements will tax the re-creative imagination a good deal more than the usual procedure of applying a ready-made stencil over the fresh design.

Carrying out this injunction as regards Berlioz, and judging his technical powers by the time he had composed the *Te Deum* tells us much about his stature as an artist and the nature of creation. Mastery seems to depend on a variable balance between ease and difficulty, the difficulty being of course self-imposed and arising as a material result of a worthy conception. In writing a *Te Deum,* Berlioz wished as usual to develop certain musical ideas that came unsought – this being the element of congenital ease, of genius – and to achieve as well the common desiderata of unity, coherence, and local finish, for ease in which he had been maturing a technique.

Had he been content, like many an artist, with this double goal, he would assuredly have produced a fine work, readily intelligible in the light of his previous and ensuing scores. But his invariable aim was higher. Each new work with him was to represent at once the sum of his knowledge, the treatment of original themes, and the fresh solution of a unique set of problems, all creating together the appropriate atmosphere, the style of that work and no other. The *Te Deum* differs from the *Damnation of*

[37] Constant Lambert: "Skill in the manipulation of purely academic counterpoint can be acquired in a few months by almost any person of average intelligence, whether musically gifted or not." (732, 254.)

Faust which precedes it, from *The Infant Christ* which follows it, and from the *Requiem*, which has roots in the same musical material. This uniqueness springs from the technical challenges that Berlioz set himself: the antiphonal use of organ and orchestra and the further exploitation of space as a musical element; an original sequence of pedals and again, in the Prelude, of modulations starting from B major to end in D major which make the piece tonally discursive without disunity; the building of the last choral movement on a *basso ostinato;* and throughout, the wide use of neomodal melody, harmony, and polyphony. Whatever one may say about the detail of these ventures, the net effect is not merely fineness but greatness; and perhaps greatness is not attainable apart from this double goal which smaller minds find contradictory – size and subtlety. As M. Boschot points out: "It is easy by means of repeats and artifices of instrumentation and polyphonic writing to compose a musical work of large dimensions. But in order to keep it from seeming empty and rhetorical, the ideas must be themselves great. Now in no part of the *Te Deum* do the developments exceed the power of the idea; the work is really great because throughout the conception is great. And one can only admire the simplicity of the means . . . The voices and instruments are soberly employed, and each, whenever used, produces to perfection what is expected of it. The style has that classic mastery . . . which betokens a masterpiece." [38]

[38] *269*, 225.